Merchandising

Theory, Principles, and Practice

Merchandising
Theory, Principles, and Practice
SECOND EDITION

Grace I. Kunz
Iowa State University

Fairchild Publications, Inc.
New York

Executive Editor: Olga T. Kontzias

Acquisitions Editor: Joseph Miranda

Assistant Acquisitions Editor: Jason Moring

Associate Production Editor: Elizabeth Marotta

Art Director: Adam B. Bohannon

Director of Production: Priscilla Taguer

Assistant Editor: Suzette Lam

Publishing Assistant: Jaclyn Bergeron

Copy Editor: Jenn Plum, Words & Numbers

Cover Design: Adam B. Bohannon

Library of Congress Catalog Card Number: 2004101105

ISBN: 1-56367-353-3

GST R 133004424

Printed in the United States of America

BRIEF CONTENTS

EXTENDED CONTENTS

PREFACE

Merchandising is planning, developing, and presenting product line(s) for identified target market(s) with regard to pricing, assorting, styling, and timing. Throughout the business sector, product lines and services must be planned, developed, and presented. Merchandising is most distinct as a business function among firms that deal with products that have demand for frequent change. Consequently, the foundations of merchandising principles are rooted in the apparel business. The textiles and apparel business is fascinating to study and, compared to other industries, has many unique characteristics.

1. Textiles and apparel is a globalized industry that constitutes nearly one tenth of world commerce (Cline, 1990).

2. In the United States, textiles and apparel are ranked second only to steel in terms of essential commodities for national defense (A Look at the Facts, 1992).

3. Apparel has long been recognized as having more demand for product change than other consumer goods.

4. Globalization and increasing vertical and horizontal integration have resulted in greater complexity of merchandising processes and dependence on technology.

5. Quick response business systems have revolutionized textile and apparel business operations.

6. Most apparel production systems remain labor intensive in spite of many innovations in technology.

Most consumer goods manufacturers and retailers are facing some of the same kinds of conditions now being addressed by the textiles and apparel sector. These firms are realizing more frequent product changes, shorter lead times, and attempts to maintain lower levels of inventory without sacrificing customer service. With current business trends, merchandising principles, particularly related to merchandise planning, are widely applied throughout the consumer goods sectors. Although merchandising is often regarded primarily as a retailing function, these principles are being applied in global manufacturing and retailing of all kinds of products throughout manufacturing and retailing sectors. This textbook addresses these merchandising challenges.

Beyond being updated throughout, the primary innovation in the second edition is the integration of Sourcing Simulator, Student Version from Textiles and Clothing Technology Corporation [TC]² into the Integrated Learning Activities at the end of each chapter. Sourcing Simulator assists in shifting the focus of a merchandising course from calculating numbers associated with merchandising decisions to interpreting the mathematical outcomes of those decisions. Although students still need to understand how outcomes are derived, it is equally important, and perhaps more important, to be able to evaluate merchandise planning options related to achieving sales, gross margin, and operating profit goals. Sourcing Simulator can test financial effectiveness of optional pricing, budget, assortment, delivery plans, and many associated decisions. Sourcing Simulator's output of over 30 measures of inputs and financial outputs may be intimidating at first. However, the Integrated Learning Activites are set up to help both faculty and students gain confidence and understanding of both inputs and outputs of the simulation.

This text is targeted to the junior/senior collegiate level. Prerequisites are assumed to include a basic textiles and apparel industries class and/or basic business classes. Some understanding of product development processes is useful but not essential. A merchandising math class could either be a prerequisite or follow-up to a course based on this text. Also, a merchandising course based on this text is an excellent prerequisite to a merchandising internship. This text can provide the foundation for a graduate-level merchandising course if the Recommended Resources at the end of each chapter are incorporated into the reading assignments.

Throughout the text, Mike's Bikes, a single unit retailer, is used as a continuous case study with application of theory and principles to the Mike's Bikes scenario presented in each chapter. The result is an integrated look at the application of merchandising principles to business decisions. In addition, Learning Activities and Cases are integrated into each chapter to provide an interactive, active learning environment. Most of the cases are drawn from the trade press to provide a "flavor" of the style and emphases of trade-related literature.

Merchandising Analysis Portfolio (MAP)

This textbook is designed with an active learning format. This means students are not just "fed" information, but rather are expected to participate in the learning process. Educational research shows that students who are engaged in active learning learn more, understand it better, and retain it longer than in passive learning environments. Sometimes, students work individually, with a partner, or in teams. In any case, it is helpful to discuss decisions related to merchandise plans with other people. How you are organized to proceed is up to your instructor.

Integrated Learning Activities (ILAs) at the end of each chapter throughout this text provide an opportunity to develop a Merchandising Analysis Portfolio (MAP). For successful merchandising related interviews in today's job markets, a portfolio displaying your understanding of merchandising processes is as essential for merchandisers as it is for designers. ILAs presented at the end of Chapters 1 through 9 provide an opportunity to apply concepts presented in each chapter to create an ongoing integrated merchandise plan, first. You will have the opportunity to create "pencil" merchandise plans for the retailer of your choice. Then, you can test the potential financial productivity of your plans using Sourcing Simulator, the software package accompanying this textbook. You can test the financial productivity of your "pencil" plans as originally conceived, then make modifications and repeatedly test and interpret the outcomes. The combination of the development of your "pencil" plans and the Sourcing Simulator analysis provides a comprehensive experience in understanding the relationships among components of a line plan. You will have the opportunity to gain confidence in your merchandising abilities and present the results in portfolio form (MAP) to impress any recruiter.

To set up your MAP, a system that works well is a three-ring binder (about an inch thick) with a dozen dividers, a highlighter, a paper punch, and a calculator. A simple calculator with square root and percent keys works fine. If you have a more complex calculator, be sure to practice with it so that you are comfortable operating it. Also, a few pocket folders can also be helpful for keeping track of your hard work.

It is essential to keep your merchandise plans, based on ILAs at the end of each chapter, together. Planning decisions based on each chapter provide a foundation for the next chapter. Keeping your plans organized, complete, and up-to-date will make the whole process much easier for you.

Helping you understand what merchandise plans are, how components of merchandise plans related to each other, how to formulate plans, and how to interpret them are primary objectives of this textbook. Your MAP will help you find your way through the merchandise planning process. Get your materials for your MAP together so you will be ready to start at the end of Chapter 2.

Background of Sourcing Simulator—Student Version (SS)

During the late 1980s and early 1990s, the primary focus of the U.S. textiles and apparel industry was developing quick response (QR) business systems. A few innovative firms had dramatic improvements in customer service and financial performance when QR was successfully implemented. However, full-scale trials to test the effectiveness of various aspects of QR were very expensive and time-consuming. One solution was computer simulation of the merchandise planning and sourcing process (Poindexter, 1991, January).

Computer simulation is one way of estimating the impact of business decisions on potential outcomes. A simulation is an abstraction of reality that makes it possible to focus on key components of a process and examine their relationships. Simulation provides a low-cost, yet powerful analysis tool for evaluating the impact of different business decisions on performance measures, in the case of merchandising, including gross margin, adjusted gross margin, gross margin return on inventory, inventory turns, lost sales, and service level, to name a few.

A computer simulation called ARM (Apparel Retail Model) was developed at North Carolina State University by the Departments of Textile and Apparel Management and Industrial Engineering with funding provided in part by the industry consortium CRAFTM (Consortium for Research into Apparel, Fiber, and Textile Manufacturing) during the late 1980s. ARM was regarded by the developers as the first in a series of integrated simulations that would involve the entire apparel trade matrix. Its purpose was to provide a "hands-on" tool for retail merchandisers/buyers when exploring the significance of ordering, reordering, markdowns, etc., in traditional and QR settings. The simulation of the merchandising process came first because the developers recognized that the apparel manufacturing process was dependent on the merchandise plans and the resulting purchase orders developed by retail buyers. The textile manufacturers were, in turn, dependent on the orders for fabric from apparel manufacturers to fulfill their retail customer's' orders (Nuttle, King, & Hunter, 1991).

The presentation of ARM evolved over the years, but the original model still runs the simulation. ARM was originally designed for use on a DOS-based personal computer. However, during the mid-1990s, ARM was transferred to a Windows operating system and became known as ARMS (Apparel Retail Modeling System). During the late 1990s, Textiles and Clothing Technology Corporation [TC]^2 adopted ARMS and hired Dr. Russell King from North Carolina State University to do more extensive development of ARMS in relation to analysis of apparel production systems. The result was named Sourcing Simulator (SS). ARM, ARMS, and SS have also been used in academic merchandising research. Some of the results are reported in this text.

The various versions of ARM, ARMS, and SS also have been used by some colleges and universities in merchandising classes for many years. And now we have Sourcing Simulator, Student Version, developed specifically to be used with this merchandising textbook. *The primary purpose of using Sourcing Simulator, Student Version is to stimulate essential analysis and critical thinking on the part of faculty and students regarding merchandising processes and decisions.*

ILAs involve two phases: "pencil" merchandise plans and SS tests of selected merchandising decisions included in the merchandise plans. You will research the firm, prepare merchandise plans for it, test the plans on SS, and evaluate the quantitative and financial outcomes as the course progresses. The first phase of "pencil" plans is selecting a retailer or manufacturer that you will assume as your "employer." A detailed assignment for developing retailer profile follows Chapter 2.

You are encouraged to keep all your ILA assignments, including your "pencil" plans and your SS analysis, in your Merchandising Analysis Portfolio (MAP) that you can "tidy-up" and use as an interviewing tool.

Go ahead! Load Sourcing Simulator and experiment with it.

References

Nuttle, H., King, R., & Hunter, N. (1991). A stochastic model of the apparel-retailing process for seasonal apparel. *Journal of the Textile Institute,* 82(2): 247–259.

Poindexter, M. (1991, January). Apparel retail model version 2.0 operating manual (Prepared for CRAFTM). Raleigh: North Carolina State University.

Acknowledgments

I appreciate the on-going support of my colleagues at Iowa State University, as well as many colleagues at other colleges and universities who encouraged me in this 2nd edition. My graduate students, research assistants, and the graduate-level merchandising classes have provided invaluable literature search assistance and lively discussion of merchandising ideas. The research conducted by Dana Rupe, Jeong Won Song, Tiing-Sheng Lin, Ui-Jeen Yu, Brecca Farr, has provided key concepts and clarification of ideas particularly in relation to merchandise planning. Special thanks for Seung-Eun Lee for her merchandising research, conceptual thinking, and review of the first seven chapters including checking my math. Thanks also to Hong Yu for her timely invitation to Oklahoma State University to train faculty on Sourcing Simulator using the new Integrated Learning Activities and the Representative Data Set. Your feedback was invaluable.

Interaction with numerous apparel professionals, including alumni and recruiters, has provided on-going opportunities for testing ideas and implications. Special thanks for Dr. Russell King and his colleagues at North Carolina State University as well as Jim Lovejoy and Textiles and Clothing Technology Corporation [TC]^2 for developing Sourcing Simulator—Student Version. I have really enjoyed working with you over the years. Thanks also to Mike Todaro, Director of AAPN (American Apparel Producers Network) who I originally became acquainted with as members of the Quick Response Leadership Committee of the American Apparel and Footwear Association. AAPN has developed global connections that make it one of the most effective apparel trade associations.

Appreciation goes to Olga Kontzias for supporting the development of the second edition and the inclusion of Sourcing Simulator. Thanks to Elizabeth Marotta for working on the production of the manuscript and thanks to the people who reviewed the prospectus including Fay Gibson, East Carolina University; Pamela S. Norum, University of Missouri—Columbia; Teresa Robinson, Middle Tennessee State University; Laverne Tilley, Gwinnett Technical College; and Scarlett Wesley, University of South Carolina. Your comments and questions provided necessary assistance in manuscript development for the new edition. Special thanks also goes to the reviewers of the prospectus and manuscript for the first edition.

section one ————————————————————————➤

Merchandising Theory

1

Merchandising

Concepts

Learning Objectives

- Define merchandising.

- Introduce the fundamental components of the merchandising process.

- Examine the role of merchandising according to the Behavioral Theory of the Apparel Firm.

T he textiles and apparel business is one of the most globalized industries in the world involving more than 10 percent of world business. The people of the United States consume more textiles and apparel per capita than citizens of any other country — nearly 80 pounds of textile fiber per person in a year. Most of the products imported to the United States are sourced by U.S.-based firms, primarily manufacturers and retailers. Consequently, the majority of the more than 200 countries in the world export textiles and apparel to the United States. At the same time, domestic apparel production has been declining for nearly 10 years and now provides about 25 percent of domestic consumption.

Textile and apparel trade associations have been aggressive in developing standards for technology and **quick response (QR)** business systems (Lowson, King, & Hunter, 1999). Retailers are often the first to benefit from new technology related to acquisition and management of inventory in the trade system. Consequently, those retailers that benefited from apparel QR systems apply the same technology to other consumer products. Thus, technology standards developed and supported by the textiles and apparel industry are now being used by both manufacturers and retailers of a wide variety of consumer products. The leadership provided by the textiles and apparel industry has resulted in much broader application of QR systems than was originally conceived.

The textile industry produces three primary types of consumable goods: home textiles, industrial textiles, and apparel. Home textiles include carpets, draperies, upholstery, kitchen and bathroom towels, table linens, etc. Home textiles have been a growth industry over the last decade due primarily to an active home-building industry. Industrial textiles range from roadbed stabilizers to household insulation, from tents and awnings to heart valves. This application of "soft" materials to industrial and medical problems has also resulted in a growth industry.

The apparel business exists to satisfy fundamental human needs — that of protecting and enhancing the appearance of the human body. Materials used for protecting the body as well as those regarded as aesthetically pleasing differ greatly among ethnic groups worldwide. Still, these materials usually have one characteristic in common — flexibility to comfortably accommodate the shape and movement of the human body. As a result, all production and distribution systems in the apparel business are uniquely adapted to handling **flexible materials.** "Soft" materials influence nearly every phase of the production and distribution process and are probably the greatest deterrent to automation of production processes. Thus, much of apparel production remains labor intensive. Human hands are still often the most effective tools for picking up two pieces of fabric, matching the edges, and guiding them through a sewing machine. Soft materials also influence packaging and distribution methods. In the retail sector, hangers, racks, and display fixtures have to be designed to show garments made of flexible materials in an attractive manner.

Apparel has long been recognized as the most **change-intensive** category of consumer products. In developed countries, the combination of fashion and seasonal influences results in major changes in product offerings at both wholesale and retail levels several times a year. As economies develop, fashion becomes a factor in apparel as soon as people can afford it. Fashion influences are reflected in changes in styling, such as color, line, silhouette, pattern, shape, and acceptable fit. Seasonal influences, including the weather, holidays, and calendar-related events such as the beginning of the school year, impact product change. Some manufacturers and retailers update apparel product offerings every four weeks, others every two weeks, and a growing number every day. The process of planning, developing, and presenting product lines for identified target markets is called **merchandising.**

Merchandising Processes

Merchandising is a necessary business process for most types of products. Automobile merchandisers determine the number of styles, colors, and sizes of vehicles to offer, how many to stock, and when to do price promotions. Grocery merchandisers decide how much space will be devoted to fresh, canned, frozen, and ready-to-eat foods, as well as how assortments and pricing will differ at different times of the year. Video rental store merchandisers determine assortment balance among adventure, romance, and classic movies and video games as well as how many of each title to have on hand. In the textiles and apparel business, merchandisers have a particularly strong role because of the intensive nature of product change.

Merchandising is integral to all parts of textile and apparel trade. Lines of textile fibers, yarns, and fabrics must be planned, developed, and presented. Lines of findings, such as buttons, zippers, and thread, must be merchandised for sale to finished-goods manufacturers. Most apparel manufacturers plan, develop, and present lines to be offered at wholesale markets for selection by retail buyers. At the same time, retail buyers merchandise lines to sell to their retail customers. In these days of vertical integration, many apparel firms are merchandising for both the wholesale and retail sectors.

Some of the newest forms of technology are being applied to merchandising processes. Merchandisers, when working outside their offices, are using palm and hand-held devices that operate with powerful Windows CE Operating Systems instead of laptop computers. These small computers have plenty of RAM and full color and can be equipped with peripherals such as digital cameras and bar code scanners. Another technology that is great for merchandisers is interactive-voice response, the next generation of voice mail. These and many other established forms of technology support merchandising processes (Price, 2003).

Learning Activity 1.1
Role of merchandising

1. Why is merchandising a necessity to nearly every business venture?
2. Why is apparel often regarded as synonymous with merchandising?
3. Read Case 1.1 very carefully. In what sense is Venus vertically integrated?
4. How has Venus maximized the potential sales by developing their product line?
5. In what way does Venus merchandise both for wholesale and retail?

Definitions of Merchandising

There are many definitions of merchandising in print and probably dozens more in use in common practice, particularly in the apparel industry. Perhaps the most confusing practice is using retailing and merchandising interchangeably. **Retailing** is selling goods and services to the ultimate consumer. Retailing is one component of the consumer goods trade

---

📁   *Case 1.1 Making a Wholesale Business Click**   📁

With the luxury of a thriving catalog business carrying the brunt of the revenue and profit load, Venus Swimwear president and majority owner Daryle Scott has built a small, yet profitable wholesale arm. Venus, a 19-year-old cataloger/manufacturer, mails several editions of its racy swimsuit catalog targeted at the junior-miss set as well as spin-off books of women's conservative swimwear and casual apparel each year. Venus now also has a Web site (www.venusswimwear.com) where the primary purpose is retail sales.

The private company, which won't reveal its annual sales, entered the wholesale business 13 years ago as a means of leveraging its manufacturing business. Venus wholesales to surf shops and specialty stores throughout the world. Although the wholesale business makes up about 10 percent of Venus's total revenue, Scott says wholesale brings in steady incremental income. Venus wholesales primarily to mom-and-pop stores rather than to big retail chains. Unlike many wholesalers, Venus doesn't negotiate prices or terms. "We're in a unique position in that our primary business is mail order," Scott says. "So we have our wholesale prices and terms, and that's it."

A spread of Venus swimsuits appears regularly in Kristi's from Overton's, a swimsuit catalog produced by boating supplies mailer Overton's. "We supply Overton's because its target market is a bunch of boaters," Scott says. So that neither book gains a competitive edge, Scott makes sure Kristi's prices are the same as Venus's. Although the two books' lists overlap 15 to 25 percent, "we mostly target different customers," says Overton's vice president of marketing, Jeff Parnell.

Venus Swimwear has grown at an astonishing rate. Today, Venus Swimwear is the world's largest retailer of junior swimwear and is still growing.

*Based on *Catalog Age* (1996, March, p. 24) and www.venusswimwear.com (accessed 2003 August).

---

matrix. The **trade matrix** for apparel includes four major components: materials manufacturers and suppliers, finished goods manufacturers, retailers, and consumers. In contrast, merchandising is one of several functions required to run a business that might operate at any level of the trade channel.

P. H. Nystrom (1932) defined merchandising as "careful planning, capable styling and production or selecting and buying, and effective selling" (p. 4). By this definition, the primary mission of today's merchandisers seems similar. They continue to play an important role in the exchange process by providing products for consumption. Merchandisers must still understand customer demands, analyze sales trends, and select and present salable products (Fiorito & Fairhurst, 1993; Solomon, 1993). However, due to the competitive pressures in the apparel industry and the innovations required under QR business systems, the demands placed on merchandisers are changing.

R. C. Kean (1987) recognized these pressures when she explored the definition of merchandising, calling it one part of a marketing continuum. She said merchandising has usually been defined by function (i.e., planning, buying, etc.), rather than by concepts from which a theory could ultimately be developed. Kean proposed the following definition: "Merchandising is the analysis and response to the changes (transformations) and processes (advances) which occur in the planning, negotiation, acquisition, and selling of products/services from their inception to their reception and use by the target customer" (pp. 10–11). She proposed that perceptions of these functional words were changing due to internal changes in the industry.

As Kean foresaw, merchandisers are becoming more accountable for managing bottom-line profitability in contrast to the traditional measure of gross margin. This means merchandisers may be responsible for inventory turns, carrying costs, in-stock position, and distribution expenses in addition to traditional functions. Therefore, ensuring an in-stock position for the consumer while reducing average inventory is key, as is tailoring merchandise assortments to meet local demand (Solomon, 1993; Troyer & Denny, 1992).

I proposed the Behavioral Theory of the Apparel Firm (BTAF) in which merchandising and marketing are two of six constituencies necessary to operate an apparel firm (Kunz, 1995). Kean saw merchandising as a subpart of marketing, whereas I see merchandising and marketing as interactive yet equivalent functions, particularly within the apparel business. I used the Glock and Kunz (2000) definition of merchandising in the behavioral theory, *planning, developing, and presenting product line(s) for identified target market(s) with regard to pricing, assorting, styling, and timing.* An alternative name for product line is merchandise line; these terms can be used interchangeably. The Glock and Kunz definition of merchandising is used as a foundation for this textbook.

As indicated by the definition, merchandising has three major components—line planning, line development, and line presentation. **Line planning** evolves in six major activities—evaluate merchandise mix, forecast merchandise offerings, plan merchandise budgets, plan merchandise assortments, determine delivery and allocation, and analyze and update merchandise plans. Synthesis of merchandise forecasts, budgets, and assortment plans results in some combination of model stock plans, basic stock plans, and automated replenishment plans. Implicit to these plans is number and types of merchandise classifications, weeks of sale, pricing strategy, price points, size ranges, and size and fit standards.

Line development occurs in several ways: by selecting finished goods at wholesale markets to fill the line plans, by internal product development, or via a combination of buying finished goods, product development, and sourcing. Regardless of the method of line development, initial orders are placed for the desired merchandise and may represent 30 to 100 percent of the total inventory required. Reorders are placed according to agreements with vendors regarding merchandise replenishment, components of which include order processing, shipping, receiving, and distribution.

When product development is a part of line development, three phases evolve — creative design, line adoption, and technical design. Creative design focuses on proposing designs, costs, and performance of merchandisable groups. Line adoption involves analysis of the salability of the proposed groups and deciding which designs should become styles in the line. Technical design prepares the accepted styles for production. The focus is on perfecting garment fit, analyzing materials, doing detailed costing, writing style specifications, and perfecting production patterns.

Line presentation may occur internally within a firm, at wholesale levels, and/or at retail levels depending on the particular firm's strategies. Internal presentation involves evaluating line plans and/or presenting designs for adoption during the product development process. Wholesale presentation involves offering products for sale to retail buyers in show rooms at seasonal markets or by sales representatives when they call on retail buyers in their stores. Retail presentation involves many different types of retail stores as well as catalog, television, and Internet selling. Strategies associated with merchandise presentation include: pricing; preparing visual displays using fixtures, lighting, and space; providing product information via labels, tickets, and signage; serving customers; and managing inventory.

Merchandising as a Business Function

Merchandising was recognized as a key business function as early as 1924 (Copeland, 1924). In firms with a high rate of product change, merchandising is the function that coordinates the planning, development, and presentation of product lines (Glock & Kunz, 2000). While merchandising may not be recognized as a separate business function when focusing on basic/staple goods (since the same styles remain in assortments over long periods of time), in firms that deal with fashion goods, merchandising processes are essential to the firm's operation.

Theoretical Foundations

The fundamental purpose of a **theory** is to describe, organize, and predict happenings in relation to something. Ultimately, the goal of theory development is to understand and describe a phenomenon and to be able to control and predict outcomes based on the presence and interaction of certain variables (Laughlin, 1993). In its simplest form, a theory consists of assumptions, constructs, and relationships among these constructs. **Assumptions** are the foundation from which a theory departs; **constructs** are the fundamental variables; and **relationships among constructs** determine potential outcomes when the theory is applied.

Two types of theories of the firm are used to describe a firm's decision making: economic and behavioral (Cyert, 1988). **Economic theories** emphasize profit maximization as is widely accepted in business practice. These theories play a strong role in business management, but even the best business strategies are limited by the human beings charged with executing them.

Behavioral theories of the firm provide an alternate way of thinking about how and why business firms operate as they do. These emphasize the role of human behavior, rather than economic factors, in explaining the activities of the firm. The key to a firm's survival is the ability to acquire and maintain resources, including people, money, and physical property. Major issues addressed include how organizational objectives are formed, how strategies evolve, and how decisions are reached within those strategies (Cyert, 1988; Cyert & March, 1963).

Fundamental Constructs from Behavioral Theories of the Firm

According to **behavioral theories of the firm,** the business firm is a coalition of individuals who have some common goals in relation to production, inventory, sales, market share, or profit (Cyert & March, 1963). Members of the firm's coalition are also members of interdependent, internal subcoalitions or constituencies (Pfeffer & Salancik, 1978). The **internal constituencies** correspond roughly to the major functional **areas of specialization** within a firm. Each constituency within the firm shares a common frame of reference and a relatively consistent set of goals and objectives, which may not be consistent with the other constituencies or with the overall goals of the firm. "A theory of the firm that does not give explicit recognition to the activities of these functional subunits fails to address their obvious importance in explaining firm behavior" (Anderson, 1982, p. 70).

Goals of the firm are achieved by negotiation to 1) determine the distribution of resources among internal constituencies; 2) resolve conflicts among the internal constituencies; and 3) determine resource exchanges with external coalitions. The power of an internal constituency is related to the importance of resource exchanges that are its responsibility. Contributing and managing the most critical resources results in the ability to direct and control the organization (Pfeffer & Salancik, 1978). The following theory of the apparel firm and the assumptions that emerge are based on fundamental constructs adopted from previously developed behavioral theories of the firm. These constructs are summarized in Table 1.1.

Table 1.1

Fundamental constructs of behavioral theories of the firm. *

1. A business firm is a coalition of individuals who have some common goals.
2. Each firm/coalition is divided into interdependent, internal subcoalitions or constituencies corresponding to the functional divisions of a firm.
3. Constituencies negotiate resource exchanges inside and outside the firm.
4. Conflicting goals develop among the constituencies because of specialization.
5. Negotiation is the primary means of resolving conflicts.
6. The most powerful internal constituencies manage the most critical resources.
7. The most powerful external coalitions offer/control the most critical resources.

*Based on Anderson (1982), Cyert & March (1963), and Pfeffer & Salancik (1978).

Learning Activity 1.2

Applications of constructs of behavioral theories of the firm

1. What constituencies (areas of specialization) have been involved wherever you have been employed, for example, restaurant, childcare facility, retail store, lifeguard? What were the primary goals of each constituency in that organization?
2. Can you think of experiences during your employment when conflicts developed because of different goals related to specialization of constituencies? Were problems resolved? According to the behavioral theory, how would you expect problems to be resolved?
3. How can you apply the concepts of constituencies and specialization from behavioral theory of the firm to situations in family life?
4. What determines the power of a constituency? Does this concept apply in family life?

Behavioral Theory of the Apparel Firm

Apparel is the classic example of a consumer goods industry that experiences demand for rapid product change. Products with rapid change have the greatest need for merchandising processes. Therefore, it is appropriate that **Behavioral Theory of the Apparel Firm (BTAF)** (Kunz, 1995) provides the conceptual foundation for this merchandising textbook. The key economic unit in the apparel industry, as with any industry in the free enterprise system, is the firm. Some apparel firms are primarily manufacturers, while others are primarily retailers. A manufacturer is involved in the formulation of the product; a retailer is involved in distributing goods to ultimate consumers. Some apparel firms are vertically integrated in that they are involved in some aspects of both manufacturing and retailing of apparel. Thus, BTAF must accommodate multi-functional organizations and strategies.

Relationships of Internal Constituencies of the Apparel Firm

It is traditional to represent a firm's organizational structure linearly (Figure 1.1). Organizational structure represented in this way is reflective of top-down communication, limited interaction among divisions, and Theory-X management style. Top-down communication means executives determine what is to be done and instruct accordingly. Interaction among a company's divisions may be limited because the activities of each are primarily dependent upon instructions from the division's executives. **Theory-X management style** is based on the assumptions that 1) employees really don't want to work, and 2) the primary motivation for work is money (McGregor, 1960). This mode of operation is historically typical of the apparel business (Arpan, De La Torre, & Toyne, 1982; Kunz, 1991; Scheller, 1993).

For contemporary apparel firms, particularly those involved in QR business systems, the apparel business does not operate in a linear manner. Instead, these firms utilize a highly **interactive matrix** of complex decision making. To understand this matrix, it is essential to separate sequential events from decisions that cause events to happen. For example, a sequence of events might go as follows: fiber must be made before yarn can be made before fabric can be made. However, determining what type of fiber, what type of yarn, and what type of fabric should be made to satisfy customer needs requires interaction among people with multiple forms of expertise. Decision making is often most effective when it is highly interactive and multidimensional in its impact. **Theory-Y management style** (McGregor, 1960) incorporates multidimensional communication, problem solving, and empowerment

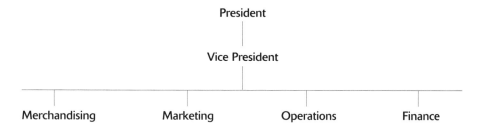

Figure 1.1 Traditional diagram of firm organization.

in all parts of the organization. A behavioral view of the firm provides a more realistic and functionally positive view of these realities.

Apparel firms can be viewed as **coalitions of employees** that share some common goals. The apparel coalition/firm is divided into six necessary internal constituencies, or areas of specialization (Figure 1.2). They are: executive management, merchandising, marketing, operations, finance, and quick response. In the proposed model, these six constituencies encompass all the business functions that must be performed by an apparel firm.

External Coalitions and Environments

The apparel firm's constituencies interact both internally and with constituencies of external coalitions to provide the apparel firm with resources. These **external coalitions** include communities in which the firm resides, competitors, customers, families of employees, shareholders, and suppliers. The apparel firm and its external coalitions operate in many overlapping **environments,** including cultural, ecological, economic, political, regulatory, social, and technological. These environments may enhance or limit firm behavior. The external coalitions are not represented in Figure 1.2, but the permeable nature of the model implies opportunity for influence from external sources.

▯ *Learning Activity 1.3*

Examining theoretical models

1. How do line and shape of the models in Figures 1.1 and 1.2 imply different relationships within the firm?
2. How does the implied working environment differ in each model?
3. In which environment would you, as an employee, have the most independence, authority, and responsibility? Why?
4. In which environment would you rather work? Why?

The Marketing Concept as a Philosophy of the Firm

The central focus of each behavioral model of firm organization (Figure 1.2) is on the target market. This reflects the **marketing concept** in this theory of the apparel firm. Supporting the marketing concept means the ability of a firm to meet its goals is partially dependent on satisfying the needs and wants of external coalitions that are exchange partners, particularly their customers (Houston, 1986). Note that the marketing concept is a philosophy of the

Quick Response System Selectively Implemented

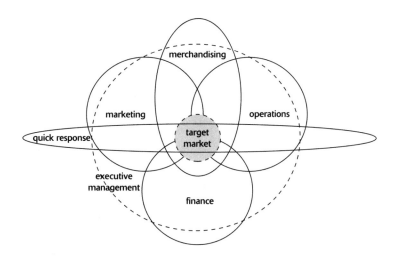

Quick Response System Fully Implemented

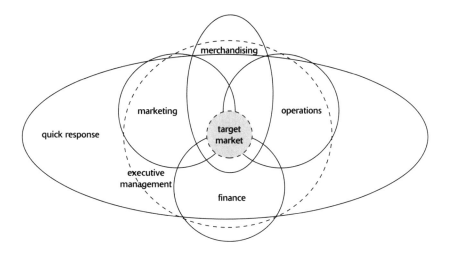

Figure 1.2 Interaction of the functional areas of specialization of an apparel firm operating with selectively implemented and fully implemented quick response business systems.

firm as a whole; this is separate from the activities of the firm's marketing constituency. The marketing concept reflects a mode of operation for the firm that directs the agendas and activities of individual constituencies. Adoption of the marketing concept is a key factor in the success of apparel firms (Arpan et al., 1982; Cline, 1990).

Apparel firms specializing in manufacturing were once production driven, but now many realize the importance of being market driven. As such, they have adopted the marketing concept. **Production-driven** firms make and sell goods that can be produced conveniently and efficiently. Deadlines are determined by the production constituency. In contrast, a **market-driven** company evaluates opportunities in the market in relation to the firm's capabilities, and then merchandises, produces, and markets accordingly. In a market-driven firm, production schedules are planned based on sales forecasts and merchandise planning and development. Delivery deadlines are determined by the merchandising and marketing constituencies (Arpan, De La Torre, & Toyne, 1982).

Some apparel retailers used to believe they were **arbiters of taste**—it was the retailer's job to tell customers what they should buy. Stanley Marcus has said that in the early days of Neiman Marcus, establishing taste level was a merchandising responsibility. Most retailers today recognize their customers are likely to know their own minds. The retailer's success is dependent on figuring out what customers want, presenting it to them when they want it, and at a price they are willing to pay. This presents new challenges because of the willingness of customers to "cross-shop," that is use a variety of types of retail stores from mass retailers to upscale specialty stores, depending on where they believe they will find the best value for their money (Wal-Mart..., 2002). Retail success is dependent on responding to customer wants, not dictating customer needs. This also reflects an adoption of the marketing concept.

The preceding scenarios include some key descriptions of concepts that contribute to the framework for the BTAF. A summary of these concepts is presented in Table 1.2.

Constituencies of the Firm

The six internal constituencies of the apparel firm (executive, merchandising, marketing, operations, finance, and quick response) form the fundamental theoretical constructs of the BTAF. The discussion of each construct includes primary responsibilities of the constituency, job titles that might be associated with each, and common measures of success. In a particular apparel firm, the actual number of areas of specialization and their titles may differ from those used as theoretical constructs in the model.

Table 1.2

Concepts in the apparel scenario of behavioral theory. *

Apparel Firm—a multi-functional and sometimes vertically integrated business involved in manufacturing and/or distributing apparel.

Constituencies of an Apparel Firm—six necessary internal areas of specialization encompassing all business functions including executive management, merchandising, marketing, operations, finance, and quick response.

Environments of an Apparel Firm—the complex of conditions that impact the nature of operation of an apparel firm, including cultural, ecological, economic, political, regulatory, social, and technological surroundings.

External Coalitions of an Apparel Firm—constituencies and coalitions outside the apparel firm that impact its behavior, including communities in which the firm resides, competitors, customers, families of employees, shareholders, and suppliers.

Marketing Concept—management philosophy of the apparel firm that recognizes that achieving a firm's goals is partially dependent on satisfying the needs and wants of the firm's external coalitions, particularly its customers.

Resources—people, money, and physical property required for operation of the firm's business.

*Based on Kunz (1995).

Executive Constituency

Responsible for the management of an apparel firm, the executive constituency is generally comprised of the heads of the other functional areas of specialization/constituencies and the owner/manager or chief executive officer/president. The **executive constituency** establishes goals for the organization and makes decisions that move the organization toward those goals. Fundamental management decisions include development of the firm's mission and business plan, including selection of target markets, identification of product lines, price ranges, and quality levels. The executive constituency sets the tone for the company and provides a foundation that allows employees to build the company and make it successful. Factors that influence the behavior of executives include the formal structure systems, plans, and policies of the firm; management/leadership style; corporate culture; and the environment in which the firm operates (Kotter & Heskett, 1992). Job titles often included in the executive constituency are owner/manager, president, chief executive officer (CEO), chief operating officer (COO), chief financial officer (CFO), vice president, director, and manager. The executive constituency's success is measured by its ability to achieve the firm's objectives and level of return on shareholder investments.

Merchandising Constituency

The **merchandising constituency** interprets customers' apparel preferences for the rest of the firm. Merchandising is a profit center, that is, the merchandising constituency is responsible for the product lines that provide the firm's primary source of income. While other constituencies provide services that are essential to the firm's operation, they are not usually sources of revenue. In fact, they are primarily cost centers. The merchandising constituency establishes the merchandising calendar; plans, develops, and edits product lines; and determines product presentation strategies (Bernard, 1987; Bertrand Frank Associates, 1982; Glock & Kunz, 2000; Technical Advisory Committee, 1982). The merchandising constituency works with, and may also source, materials and production capacity for finished goods.

Merchandising involves directing and overseeing the development of the product lines from start to finish. The content of the line, fabrications, styling, diversity of assortments, pricing, mid-season changes, visual presentations, and timing are all part of the responsibilities and decision making of the merchandising constituency. Positions or job titles that might be a part of the merchandising constituency include buyer, designer, merchandise manager, merchandiser, product development manager, and product manager. Measures of merchandising success may include adjusted gross margin, average inventory, finished goods turnover, gross margin, gross margin return on inventory, maintained markup, markdown percentage, materials cost, piece goods turn, sales-per-square-foot, and sell-through.

Interestingly, as mentioned earlier, not all apparel firms have a defined merchandising constituency. When product lines are defined so that product change is not intense, merchandising responsibilities may be handled by the executive constituency or dispersed among other constituencies. Visualize the models in Figure 1.2 without the merchandising constituency loops. Notice that the models nevertheless appear complete. A model of the behavioral theory of an apparel firm engaged primarily with basic/staple goods may omit the merchandising constituency.

Marketing Constituency

The **marketing constituency** is responsible for broadly defining a company's market, and shaping and strengthening the company's image and its products through promotion, optimizing sales opportunities, and developing alternate strategies for corporate growth (Bertrand Frank Associates, 1982). Marketing constituencies conduct market research, describe target customers, develop marketing strategies, set sales goals, and may sell products at wholesale and/or retail. This constituency also establishes the market position of a firm relative to competing firms, establishes the marketing calendar, and sets advertising and promotional objectives to attain sales goals. In firms without a defined merchandising constituency, the marketing constituency assumes many merchandising responsibilities. Positions or job titles included in the marketing constituency are advertising manager, manufacturer's representative, marketing/communications manager, market researcher, public relations director, and sales manager. The success of marketing is measured by market share, advertising/sales ratios, and rate of sales increase.

Operations Constituency

The **operations constituency** manages the organization's resources of people and physical property. Responsibilities include human resources, inventories, physical facilities and equipment, and quality control. Concerns of the operations constituency include employee turnover, materials and resource utilization, cost control, efficiency, productivity, and quality. Depending on the firm's mission, the operations constituency may be involved in the operation and management of the firm's production and/or retailing facilities. Positions or job titles that might be a part of this constituency include manager of information, inventory controller, receiving manager, distribution manager, personnel manager, college relations manager, and recruiter. Other positions may include plant/store manager, apparel engineer, patternmaker, costing engineer, line manager, quality manager or engineer, and sewing machine operator. Measures of the success of the operations constituency include employee retention, stock/sales ratios, contribution margin, materials utilization, labor productivity, and break-even point.

Finance Constituency

The **finance constituency** personnel are responsible for evaluating the profitability of past business and setting goals for future business. They are additionally responsible for managing accounts receivable and payable, borrowing and spending money, managing investment in resources, and profit. Job titles included in the finance constituency include accountant, financial analyst, and investment manager. Measures of success include return on investment and profit.

Quick Response Constituency

Quick response (QR) embodies the concepts of speed to market and time-based competition. Fundamentally, the purpose of QR is to minimize the time between conceptualizing a product and delivering it to the retail selling floor. Information technology and telecommunications systems tend to be the core aspects of these implementations. As shown in the first model in Figure 1.2, firms with **quick response constituencies** cut across all other divisions and seek teamwork support from other areas via the QR "propeller." Job titles include QR director, QR coordinator, EDI director, UPC supervisor, as well as support positions. QR directors tend to have experience in merchandising or marketing because they must understand the product side of the business. Nevertheless, firms with QR constituencies keep minimal numbers of their people directly involved in QR.

As shown in the second model in Figure 1.2, when firms are fully invested in QR systems, the commitment nearly encompasses the company and the propeller becomes "wings." In this sense, QR is a comprehensive business strategy incorporating time-based competition, agility, and partnering to optimize the supply system, the distribution system, and service to customers. This implies joint decision making and teamwork involving most people and all aspects of the firm's operation with QR business strategies. See Table 1.3 for a summary of the responsibilities, job titles, and measures of success of each constituency.

Learning Activity 1.4

Distinguishing between merchandising and marketing

The roles of merchandising and marketing are frequently confused. Read Case 1.2 carefully considering the definitions and descriptions of merchandising and marketing presented in BTAF.

1. Make two lists related to the case, one of issues primarily associated with merchandising and the other of issues associated with marketing.
2. In what ways might these two areas of specialization conflict with one another?
3. In what ways are these areas of specialization essential to one another?

The Decision-Making Matrix According to Behavioral Theory of the Apparel Firm

According to behavioral theories of the firm, **specialization** causes each constituency of the firm to develop its own goals and objectives. At the same time, constituencies must interact and coordinate their activities to achieve the common goals of the coalition/firm established by the executive constituency. The goals of individual constituencies often conflict with each other because of contrasting responsibilities and priorities. The ability of the firm to reach its goals may be limited by how successful constituents are at resolving conflicts. Although there is a normal human tendency to avoid confrontation, conflicts among constituencies can be resolved through negotiation. Such negotiations emphasize the benefits of collaboration over competition.

Table 1.3

Theoretical constructs of the internal constituencies of the apparel firm including names, primary responsibilities, job titles, and measures of success.

Constituency	Responsibility	Job Titles	Measures of Success
Executive	Establishes the firm's goals and administers activities to achieve them	Owner/manager, president, chief executive or operating officer or financial officer, vice president, director, manager	Achievement of the firm's objectives; return on shareholder investment
Merchandising	Plans, develops, and presents product lines	Buyer, designer, merchandise manager, merchandiser, product development manager, product manager	Adjusted gross margin, average inventory, finished goods turnover, gross margin, gross margin return on inventory, maintained markup/markdown percentage, materials cost, piece goods turn, sales-persquare-foot, sell-through
Marketing	Defines target customer(s) and develops positioning and promotion strategies	Advertising manager, manufacturer's representative, marketing/communications director, market researcher, public relations director, sales manager	Market share, advertising/sales ratios, rate of sales increase, markdowns/sales ratios, growth
Operations	Manages people and physical property	Manager of information, inventory controller, receiving manager, distribution manager, personnel manager, college relations manager, recruiter, plant/store manager, apparel engineer, patternmaker, costing engineer, line manager, quality manager, sewing machine operator	Employee retention, stock/sales ratios, contribution margin, materials utilization, labor productivity, break-even point
Finance	Manages monetary resources	Accountant, financial analyst, investment manager	Return on investment, profit, cash flow
Quick Response	Inspires priorities for speed to market	QR director, QR coordinator, UPC supervisor, EDI director	Reductions in stockouts, reduced inventory on hand, reduced reorder lead-times

---

📁   *Case 1.2*   *Nike laces up Converse deal.**   📁

Converse used to virtually own the U.S. sneaker market with its legendary Chuck Taylor All Star sneakers. Now, onetime upstart Nike owns Converse. During July 2003, Nike agreed to buy Converse for about $305 million. The world's number one athletic footwear company said it also took on undisclosed working capital liabilities. The deal brings to a close the long hoops rivalry between Converse and Nike.

Founded in 1908, Converse dominated the U.S. sneaker market from the 1920s into the 1970s in the same way that Germany's Adidas ruled overseas markets. When running shoe oriented Nike decided to challenge Converse in basketball shoes in the early 1980s, many scoffed. They didn't think the swoosh could make a dent in the consumer market or in the NBA, where most stars — such as Larry Bird, Julius Erving, and Magic Johnson — wore Converse. But Michael Jordan's Air Jordan shoe led Nike's fast break past Converse as king of basketball shoes.

Converse's lowest point may have been in 1997 when it dropped its star endorser, Latrell Sprewell, after he choked his coach, P.J. Carlesimo. The North Andover, Massachusetts-based Converse filed for bankruptcy protection in 2001. A group of investors spent the next two years trying to rebuild the privately held company and its popular high-top Chucks brand, now more fashion item than performance footwear. The divergent fortunes of the two sneaker firms can be seen in their sales: Nike rang up $10.7 billion in revenue in 2002 while Converse's 2002 revenue was $205 million.

Tom Clarke, Nike's president of new business ventures, said in a statement, "Our strategy for growing through non-Nike brands is to identify strong brands with superior management teams where Nike can directly assist in the company's growth." Jack Boys, CEO of Converse, said his new team has "rebuilt and reinvigorated" Converse and that the deal can make Converse a global footwear and apparel brand.

The deal gives Nike a "downstairs brand that they can sell in mass merchandise stores like Wal-Mart," says Terry Lefton, editor-at-large of *Sports Business Daily*. Analysts also say Nike is looking to cash in on the demand for "retro" shoes.

*Based on McCarthy (2003).

Issues that commonly cause conflict among constituencies include sales forecasts, materials selection, number and types of merchandise classes and styles, size and timing of purchase orders or production runs, levels of inventory, and quantities and types of fixtures or equipment. Each constituency's perspective on these issues differs in relation to timing of decisions and levels of investment.

Functional priorities of constituencies also differ. For example, the merchandising constituency recognizes the need for diversity of styling, color, and price to satisfy customers' needs. Yet from the standpoint of the operations constituency, diversity and efficiency are not compatible. The finance constituency usually seeks to limit merchandise investment while marketing may seek brand identity and product differentiation through what may be regarded by the operations constituency as frivolous and costly advertising campaigns. Interactions and conflict resolution among internal constituencies and interactions of internal constituencies with external coalitions and environments provide the basis for the decision-making matrix.

Executive Interactions

Cohesiveness of purpose among constituencies may well depend on the strength of leadership from the executive constituency. As described earlier, the executive constituency provides the glue that cements the functional divisions into a whole. Sam Walton was a classic example of a leader able to inspire unified support for a firm's goals—the goals necessary to grow a small discount shop into Wal-Mart, the world's largest mass retailer.

The executive constituency often establishes the firm's goals with input from the firm's other constituencies. The management/leadership process includes interactions related to planning, coordinating, directing, negotiating, allocating, motivating, and evaluating activities of all the firm's constituencies. The ability of executives to inspire resourceful cooperation among constituencies while carrying out the varied responsibilities required for the firm to reach its goals may determine the firm's overall productivity.

The executive constituency also interacts intensively with external coalitions and environments. Executives are responsible to shareholders first and foremost. They are the primary representatives of the firm in the community at large. Their presence is often required on boards of charitable organizations and chambers of commerce. Their interaction in the economic and political environment of the community may be essential to maintain community support for the firm.

Merchandising Interactions

As illustrated in Figure 1.2, the merchandising constituency provides an integrative function among the five divisions involved with the product line (Bernard, 1987; Bertrand Frank Associates, 1982; Brauth & Brown, 1989; Brown & Brauth, 1989; Glock & Kunz, 2000; Kunz, 1986; Mellon & Brown, 1989). The merchandising constituency is responsible for making decisions with regard to product lines, using input from the other constituencies, and interpreting the needs and wants of the target market while considering the economic, social, and cultural environments of the firm. Merchandising negotiates differences in goals and priorities that exist among the firm's internal constituencies related to product lines.

Responsibilities of the merchandising constituency and its interactions with other constituencies vary according to the size of the firm. Merchandising is sometimes described generally as buying and selling (Copeland, 1924; Kotsiopulos, 1987), and in small firms the merchandising constituency tends to be responsible for both. As firms grow, buying and selling is eventually separated and assigned to different constituencies, with the planning and acquisition remaining the primary function of the merchandising constituency. The selling function may become the responsibility of the marketing or operations constituency. In this scenario, the merchandising constituency loses direct control of presentation and sale of goods. Merchandisers must work with market representatives or retail department managers on an informal basis since merchandisers do not have formal power in the marketing or operations constituencies. This is a source of conflict between merchandisers who plan and develop the goods and the constituency responsible for selling the goods. In addition, the finance constituency may impose strict limits on investment in merchandise, particularly when firms are in financial distress. The merchandising constituency, however, continues to be regarded as the primary revenue source because of its responsibility for planning and developing the product lines (Cyert, 1988).

Another major responsibility of the merchandising constituency is negotiating with external coalitions. Internal constituencies that negotiate vital resource exchanges with external coalitions come to have greater power within the firm (Anderson, 1982). The merchandising constituency's acquisition negotiations are vital to the firm because the product line is the firm's primary profit center.

At the same time, external coalitions that control vital resources have great control and influence over the firm's activities (Pfeffer & Salancik, 1978). Suppliers with well-established product lines or highly desired brand names are in the best position to influence merchandisers. They can demand minimum quantities, floor space, specialized display fixtures, advertising, limited markdowns, etc. External coalitions that offer what merchandising constituencies regard as essential resources (e.g., materials, styles, and brands) have the power to influence allocation of the firm's resources.

Marketing Interactions

The marketing calendar, including the key dates within each selling period, provides a framework for planning strategies for the entire apparel firm. Market research conducted or contracted by the marketing constituency provides the basis for establishing sales goals for the company, product line, departments, and/or classifications. Sales goals are functional in guiding resource allocation within the firm.

Using market research and other interactions with external coalitions, the marketing constituency is in the best position to communicate information to internal constituencies about the nature of the target market, customer preferences, nature of the competition, and positioning strategies. Marketing constituencies interact with and evaluate customer and competitor external coalitions. Sales representatives, manufacturer's representatives, and retail sales associates have the most direct contact with buyers at the retail and consumer levels. The marketing constituency provides feedback from retail buyers, competitors, and consumers to the company's other divisions. Marketing also monitors competitors' business activities and plans and implements appropriate positioning strategies to benefit the entire firm.

Operations Interactions

Interactions of the operations constituency may vary greatly depending on the size of the firm, its mission, and whether it owns retailing and/or production facilities. The latter usually involves significant investment in real estate, requiring interaction by operations with the executive and finance constituencies and perhaps the marketing and merchandising constituencies. Numerous external coalitions and environments may also be involved.

In the BTAF model, the operations constituency also includes the human resources area of specialization. Labor is a strong source of interaction both inside and outside the firm. The performance and productivity of the labor force is of great concern to the entire firm, since both retailing and manufacturing-based apparel businesses tend to be labor intensive. The operations constituency collaborates in the development and administration of remuneration systems and benefits packages for employees. As a result, the operations constituency may also have the most direct interaction with the external coalitions composed of the employees' families. Operations may also strongly influence company policy relative to hours of work per week, overtime pay, types of reimbursement, etc., which may affect all family members. Issues such as labor costs, robotization, and safety regulation stimulate interactions for operations constituencies. Economic, technological, and regulatory external environments particularly affect the operations constituency.

Finance Interactions

The control function of the finance constituency creates extensive and sometimes stressful interactions with the other divisions. Finance prepares reports on which the executive constituency bases productivity assessment of the other constituencies and plans for future development. Finance also provides feedback to all other constituencies regarding their performance through management information systems and/or daily, weekly, monthly, and annual reports. Finance is responsible for paying the bills and collecting accounts receivable.

In addition, the finance constituency examines and acquires the necessary financial resources to operate the firm. Interactions with external coalitions may include borrowing money from financial firms, paying vendors for goods and services, and collecting charge accounts from customers. Firms that have heavy debts may become finance-driven instead of market-driven, which would seem contrary to the success of the firm.

Quick Response Interactions

The QR constituency interacts with all the other internal constituencies of the firm to improve the speed of moving products to market. Merchandising must reduce planning and product development times. Marketing must reduce time for market research and development of advertising and promotions. Operations must speed product handling, production, and delivery times. Finance must understand the need to provide support for technology investment to improve communications within the firm and with its vendors and customers. Executives must provide leadership in multiple environments to support the QR priority.

The interactions of constituencies provide the foundation for the decision-making matrix. These interactions, both within and outside the firm, are summarized in Table 1.4.

Learning Activity 1.5

Application of BTAF to Case 1.3

1. According to BTAF, which constituency should be responsible for changing Sears' image? Explain.
2. According to BTAF, which constituency should be responsible for figuring out what Sears wants to be? Explain.
3. What merchandise categories are included in Sears' product line?
4. Why did Sears acquire Lands' End?
5. According to the behavioral theory of the firm, what constituency is in charge of the product line?
6. What constituency is responsible for building market share?
7. Does it appear that the merchandising, marketing, and executive constituencies are working together effectively? Explain.

Table 1.4

*The likely internal and external interactions of constituencies of the apparel firm as foundations for the decision-making matrix.**

Likely Interactions

Constituency	Internal constituencies	External coalitions	Environments
Executive	foundation of firm merchandising marketing operations finance	shareholders suppliers customers communities	economic social cultural political
Merchandising	integrative function related to product line executive marketing operations finance	suppliers customers competitors	economic social cultural technological
Marketing	executive merchandising operations finance	customers competitors communities ecological	economic social cultural political
Operations	executive merchandising marketing finance	suppliers communities families of employees ecological	economic cultural regulatory technological
Finance	executive merchandising operations marketing	customers suppliers communities	economic political technological regulatory
Quick Response	all constituencies	suppliers customers	technological cultural

*Based on Kunz (1995).

 Case 1.3   *What will it take to get Sears back on track?**

Angela Powell walked out of the main Sears, Roebuck and Co. store in suburban Atlanta, where she had been looking for clothes and a television set. Not finding anything she wanted, she headed for the auto center. "Hardware and auto service," she said. "That's what I think of when I think of Sears."

In Columbus, Ohio, Mo Porven had much the same assessment of her local Sears. "I trust them No. 1 for appliances," she said. That may be Sears' biggest problem as it plans a future solely as a retailer, beset by mounting competition from mass retailers and other stores. The nation's fifth largest retailer with over $23 billion in sales has to change its image before it can resurrect its business. In 2003, Sears announced that it will shed the last of its non-retail businesses by selling its credit card business. Sears also warned that earnings for the year will be weaker than anticipated because of sagging sales at its stores.

"The real problem is that consumers haven't given Sears permission to sell them fashion," said Harry Bernard, an apparel consulting company in San Francisco. He added that Sears "has made attempts in the fashion business, but never stayed with it." What will it take to reverse 22 consecutive months of sales declines during Sears' restructuring? Acquiring more labels? Snappier advertising? Will a new clothing line lure Hispanics?

"Sears is still trying to figure out what it wants to be," said John Champion, vice president at Kurt Salmon Associates, a retail consulting company. "And they have competitors left and right snapping at their heels." Analysts, however, offer kudos to chief executive Alan Lacy, who is spearheading a makeover of Sears' merchandise and its stores.

The company said it is seeing positive results from the acquisition of Lands' End, with overall apparel sales reported to be two to four percentage points higher in stores that have the line than in those without it. Lands' End was planned to be in nearly all of its over 800 stores by the end of 2003. But how much Lands' End can serve as a magnet to draw shoppers remains to be seen.

Meanwhile, Covington—Sears' new store brand that combined eight different labels in hopes of generating $500 million in sales—is still "grossly undermarketed," according to Burt Flickinger, managing partner at the consulting firm Strategic Resource Group of New York. And some experts question Sears' move to get out of cosmetics, believing the category is an essential offering for women.

To court Hispanic customers, Sears plans to unveil Lucy Pereda, a line of dressy women's clothing bearing the Cuban-born TV lifestyle personality, in 200 stores in fall 2003.

Case 1.3 (continued)

But while it tries to become more of a fashion player, Sears faces new challenges in appliances. While it is the sales leader in that area, the company's market share has eroded recently because of competitors like Home Depot and Lowe's. Sears announced a new strategy to fight back by expanding its selection of lower-priced appliances and sprucing up its presentation. Some analysts believe Sears will still need to offer even better prices. Overall, Flickinger said Sears needs "more theatre," given the intensifying retail landscape, particularly in apparel.

Wal-Mart Stores Inc., the world's largest retailer with over $158 billion in sales, is fast becoming a player in fashion apparel with its launch of Levi Strauss & Co.'s new discount brand called Signature. Target Corp. has added names like Liz Lange, Isaac Mizrahi, and Mossimo. And JCPenny Co., under CEO Allen Questrom, has more trendy fashions. Lacy said Sears will differentiate itself in its fall advertising campaign. And he said the company is always looking to add brands, either national or proprietary.

*Based on D'Innocenzio (2003).

Summary of Relationships Among a Firm's Internal Constituencies

1. The apparel coalition is divided into six major constituencies: upper management and five functional areas of specialization including merchandising, marketing, operations, finance, and quick response.

2. Each constituency has goals and responsibilities related to their particular functions within the firm.

3. Goals and responsibilities of one constituency contribute in their own way to those of the total firm, but are not likely to be exactly the same as goals and responsibilities of other areas.

4. Goals and responsibilities of constituencies may conflict with one another.

5. Conflicts are resolved through negotiation.

6. The merchandising constituency negotiates/arbitrates differences among constituencies and provides an integrative function in relation to the product line.

7. The power of a constituency is related to the value of the resource exchanges it negotiates.

8. Business decisions frequently involve a complex matrix of information sources.

9. Business decisions have multi-faceted impact on both internal constituencies and external coalitions.

Fundamental Assumptions of Behavioral Theory of Apparel Firm

1. An apparel firm can consist of any combination of manufacturing and/or distribution functions.
2. A firm is a coalition of individuals with some common goals.
3. The coalition is made up of sub-coalitions or constituencies that conform to the functional areas of specialization of the firm.
4. Six constituencies perform all the business functions required for operation of the apparel firm.
5. Overall goals of the coalition are formulated by the executive constituency.
6. The focus of each coalition is on the customer and satisfying the customer's needs within the limitations of the firm.
7. The inter-relationships among constituencies form the internal decision-making matrix for the firm.
8. Time-based competition changes the firm's decision-making priorities and measures of success.
9. Agility contributes to the ability of the firm to satisfy customer wants and needs.
10. Partnering provides information to optimize the ability to achieve the firm's goals.

Summary

The apparel industry is the classic example of a business operation in an environment of intense product change. Merchandising has a key role and a central business function when product change is frequent. While merchandising has many definitions, they nevertheless have similar meanings. This textbook is based on the Glock and Kunz (2000) definition: "Merchandising is planning, developing, and presentating product lines for identified target market(s) with regard to pricing, assorting, styling, and timing." Merchandise/line planning is a process that results in a framework for line development. Merchandise/line development is a process that determines the actual goods to fill out the line plan. Merchandise/line presentation results in evaluation of the effectiveness of line planning and line development. Merchandise/line presentation may take place internal to a firm, in wholesale markets, or in retail markets.

Behavioral Theory of the Apparel Firm (BTAF) addresses the role of the merchandising process in achieving a firm's goals. According to BTAF, a firm is a coalition of individuals with some common goals. An apparel firm can consist of any combination of manufacturing and/or retailing functions. The focus of the coalition is on the customer and satisfying the customer's needs within the limitations of the firm. The coalition is made up of sub-coalitions or constituencies that conform to the firm's functional areas of specialization. Six constituencies perform all the business functions required for the apparel firm operation. The overall goals of the coalition are formulated by the executive constituency. The merchandising constituency is in charge of coordinating the planning, development, and presentation of the product line(s). The marketing constituency defines target customer(s) and develops positioning and promotion strategies for the firm. The operations constituency manages people and physical property, and the finance constituency manages financial resources. The quick response constituency promotes and supports speeding products to market to improve accuracy of forecasts and reduce stockouts to improve sales at first price. Inter-relationships among constituencies form the internal decision-making matrix for the firm. Members of the constituencies interact with external constituencies including their suppliers and customers to conduct the firms business in the context of multiple environments.

Key Concepts

arbiters of taste
areas of specialization
assumptions
behavioral theories of the firm
Behavioral Theory of the
  Apparel Firm (BTAF)
change-intensive products
coalition of employees
constructs
economic theories of the firm
environments of apparel firms
executive constituency
external coalitions

finance constituency
flexible materials
interactive decision-making
  matrix
internal constituencies of the
  firm
line development
line planning
line presentation
market-driven
marketing concept
marketing constituency
merchandising

merchandising constituency
operations constituency
production-driven
quick response (QR)
quick response constituency
relationships among constructs
retailing
specialization
theory
Theory-X management style
Theory-Y management style
trade matrix

Recommended Resources

Bernard, H. (1987, January). Vertical ventures. *Apparel Industry Magazine*, 56–58.

Brauth, B., & Brown, P. (1989, June). Merchandising malpractice. *Apparel Industry Magazine*, 108–110.

Cline, W. R. (1990). *The future of world trade in textiles and apparel*. Washington, DC: Institute for International Economics.

Houston, F. S. (1986). The marketing concept: What it is and what it is not. *Journal of Marketing*, 50:81–87.

Lowson, B., King, R., & Hunter, A. (1999). *Quick response: Managing the supply chain to meet customer demand*. New York: John Wiley & Sons.

Poindexter, M. (1991, January). *Apparel retail model version 2.0 operating manual* (Prepared for CRAFTM). Raleigh, NC: North Carolina State University.

Price, G. (2003). The A, B, C's of merchandising technology. Premium retail services. (www.premiumretail.com/industry_jk.htm). Accessed August 13, 2003.

References

Anderson, P. E. (1982). Marketing, strategic planning and the theory of a firm. *Journal of Marketing*, 46:15–26.

Arpan, J. S., De La Torre, J., & Toyne, B. (1982). *The U.S. apparel industry: International challenge, domestic response* (Research Monograph No. 88). Atlanta: Georgia State University, Business Publications Division.

Bernard, H. (1987, January). Vertical ventures. *Apparel Industry Magazine*, 56–58.

Bertrand Frank Associates. (1982). *Profitable merchandising of apparel.* New York: National Knitwear & Sportswear Association.

Brauth, B., & Brown, P. (1989, June). Merchandising malpractice. *Apparel Industry Magazine*, 108–110.

Brown, P., & Brauth, B. (1989, August). Merchandising methods. *Apparel Industry Magazine*, 78–82.

Copeland, M. T. (1924). *Principles of merchandising.* Chicago: A. W. Shaw.

Cyert, R. M. (1988). *The economic theory of organization and the firm.* New York: Harvester-Wheatsheaf.

Cyert, R. M., & March, J. G. (1963). *A behavioral theory of the firm.* Englewood Cliffs, NJ: Prentice Hall.

Fiorito, S. S., & Fairhurst, A. E. (1993). Comparison of buyers' job content in large and small retail firms. *Clothing and Textiles Research Journal*, 11(3):8–15.

Glock, R. E., & Kunz, G. I. (2000). *Apparel manufacturing: Sewn product analysis* (3rd ed.). Englewood Cliffs, NJ: Prentice Hall.

Houston, F. S. (1986, April). The marketing concept: What it is and what it is not. *Journal of Marketing*, 50:81–87

Kean, R. C. (1987). Definition of merchandising: Is it time for a change? In R. C. Kean (Ed.), *Theory building in apparel merchandising,* pp. 8–11. Lincoln: University of Nebraska–Lincoln.

Kotsiopulos, A. (1987). The need to identify merchandising content and generalizations. In R. C. Kean (Ed.), *Theory building in apparel merchandising,* pp. 12–14. Lincoln: University of Nebraska–Lincoln.

Kotter, J. P., & Heskett, J. L. (1992). *Corporate culture and performance.* New York: Free Press.

Kunz, G. I. (1986). *Career development of college graduates employed in retailing.* Dissertation Abstracts International, 46, 3619-A. (University Microfilm No. DA604886).

Kunz, G. I. (1991). EDI, JIT, FM, MM, QA, QR, UPS, VAM: The magnitude of change for a new socio-technical interface. *[TC]2 Report*, 6–7.

Kunz, G. I. (1995). Behavioral theory of the apparel firm: A beginning. *Clothing and Textiles Research Journal,* 13(4):252–261.

Laughlin, J. (1993). Toward a contextual understanding of theoretical development of textiles and clothing. Unpublished manuscript, University of Nebraska–Lincoln.

Lowson, B., King, R., & Hunter, A. (1999). *Quick response: Managing the supply chain to meet customer demand.* New York: John Wiley & Sons.

McCarthy, M. (2003, July 10). Nike laces up Converse deal. *USA Today* (www.usatoday.com). Accessed August 12, 2003.

McGregor, D. M. (1960). *The human side of enterprise.* New York: McGraw-Hill.

Mellon, C., & Brown, P. (1989, November). Using real time. *Apparel Industry Magazine,* 54–60.

Nuttle, H., King, R., & Hunter, N. (1991). A stochastic model of the apparel-retailing process for seasonal apparel. *Journal of the Textile Institute,* 82(2):247–259.

Nystrom, P. H. (1932). *Fashion merchandising.* New York: The Ronald Press Co.

Pfeffer, J., & Salancik, G. R. (1978). *The external control of organizations: A resource dependence perspective.* New York: Harper and Row.

Scheller, H. P. (1993). *Apparel quality through the perception of apparel production managers and operators.* Unpublished masters thesis, Iowa State University, Ames.

Solomon, B. (1993, July). Will there be a miracle on 34th Street? *Management Review,* 82:33–36.

Technical Advisory Committee of American Apparel Manufacturers Association. (1982). *Fashion in apparel manufacturing: Coping with style variation.* 1982 Report of the Technical Advisory Committee. Arlington, VA: Author.

Troyer, C., & Denny, D. (1992, May). Quick response evolution. *Discount Merchandiser,* 32(5):104–105, 107.

Wal-Mart wants to be big in fashion, too. (2002, April 15). *Women's Wear Daily,* 1, 14–15.

2

Merchandising

Technology

Learning Objectives

- Define merchandising technology.

- Examine concepts of quick response business systems.

- Discuss the role of merchandising in a quick response universe.

M erchandising has become a global occupation. When apparel firms introduced quick response (QR) related business systems and technologies, the assumptions regarding the firm's purpose and mode of operation had to change. Purveyors of technology have often expressed frustration that, when businesses acquire new technology, they seldom use it to capacity; only a few select functions are utilized. Whether spending a few thousand dollars or a few million on technology, business processes have to be reengineered to optimize the result. Organizational learning is required. Unfortunately, among a firm's primary constituencies, merchandising was among the last to receive serious attention regarding technology development. However, many apparel firms have now invested enough time and other resources to fully implement QR strategies and merchandising technology.

Overview of Merchandising Technology

Up until the 1960s, merchandise planning, line development, and inventory management were done manually in both manufacturing or retailing. Purchase orders, price tickets, inventory records, and sales slips were all hand written. To resupply merchandise, goods on the retail sales floor and in the stockroom were physically counted and reorders were based on sales indicated by remaining inventory. Another method was using a tear-off ticket system where half of the price ticket was removed when an item was sold. Occasionally you will still see this method used. The torn off tickets were put in a bag and sent on a daily or weekly basis to the accounting department to update the perpetual inventory system. Tracking sales at the stock keeping unit (SKU) level was helpful, but extremely time consuming, so it was common for reports to be four to six weeks later.

During the 1960s, large manufacturers and retailers acquired mainframe computers that initially were used primarily for record keeping, while increasingly sophisticated cash registers provided more detailed sales information to retailers. The introduction of microcomputers in the 1970s made point-of-sale data systems more affordable for smaller retail firms. Extensive sales reports began to be provided to merchandisers on a weekly and sometimes a daily basis. Many merchants resisted the new technology and continued to use their traditional "black book" system of merchandise planning and line development. Among other things, "black books" included notes on fashion trends and "hot numbers," sketchy dollar plans, and reminders of reliability of vendors.

At the same time, the introduction of new technology in the manufacturing sector increased the capability for product change. Improved communication technology and increased travel made customers more aware of a broader range of fashion choices. Consequently, frequency of fads increased along with rate of fashion change in general. Shorter selling periods became common—26 weeks to 14 weeks to 10 weeks to even 8 weeks for some products. Demand increased for more diversity of assortments. The retail discount industry became full-blown, throwing traditional department store and specialty store pricing systems into disarray.

In the 1980s, firms focused on expense control to protect profits. More and more merchandise was sourced abroad to reduce merchandise costs. Traditional department and specialty store retailers reduced customer service to control selling costs. At the same time, more forms of retailing became available with increased use of mail order, television shopping, and on-line computer services. It became obvious that cost control was not enough to protect market share and provide for growth.

In the 1990s, in part because of the influence of QR business systems, attention turned to refining business processes beyond cost control. Both manufacturers and retailers were changing their organizational structures to facilitate QR. Some organizations were becoming flatter, with middle management levels disappearing and teamwork becoming the norm. Managers were learning how to become leaders. The development of commitment to QR required executive management's profound endorsement, active involvement, and ongoing support. At the same time, they had to become receptive to and comfortable with the technology that supported QR.

Through executive leadership, all constituencies could come to recognize the common goals related to QR, including improving the performance of QR systems already in place. In addition, technology implementation, forecasting, and merchandise planning had to be improved. Measures of QR success included improved stock turn, gross margin return on inventory, employee retention, customer service, reduced average inventory, and increased merchandise sold at first price.

The merchandising constituency became involved in QR with new forecasting and merchandise planning technology. Effective merchandise planning became recognized as a necessary means of reducing inventory investment and markdowns while increasing customer satisfaction and sales at first price.

Concept of Merchandising Technology

Technology is defined by Schon (1967) as "any tool or technique, any product or process, any physical equipment or method of doing or making, by which human capability is extended" (p. 1). Galbraith (1978) defined technology as "the systematic application of scientific or other organized knowledge to practical tasks" (p. 12). This definition is extended by Pacey (1983) as "the application of scientific and other knowledge to practical tasks by ordered systems that involve people and organizations, living things and machines" (p. 6). Pacey's definition includes social and cultural impacts, as well as technical aspects.

Considering these definitions of technology, merchandising itself is a kind of technology. The impact of merchandising technology may have some effect on consumer behavior, industrial and economic structure and activity, and furthermore, on human life, ideas, and creative activity. Therefore, using a broad definition, we can call merchandising technology the systematic application of scientific knowledge and technique to merchandising in ways that reflect social and cultural value. Or to fully implement the Glock and Kunz (2000) definition of merchandising, merchandising technology may be the systematic application of scientific knowledge and techniques to planning, developing, and presenting product lines in ways that reflect social and cultural value.

The ultimate goal of merchandising technology is to use time effectively, increase merchandising accuracy, and optimize benefits to the firm and the customers. In today's markets, scientific knowledge and techniques relate primarily to use of computers, information systems, telecommunications, and related hardware and software. The operational definition of **merchandising technology** used in this text reflects this more limited perspective: *Merchandising technology is the systematic application of information technology and telecommunications to planning, developing, and presenting product lines in ways that reflect social and cultural value.*

Learning Activity 2.1

Concepts of merchandising technology

1. What are some examples of merchandising technology as experienced by retail customers?
2. How does technology change the nature of the customer/vendor relationship at point of sale?
3. Why is it important that technology "reflect social and cultural value"?

Quick Response Business Systems

In the United States, the textiles and apparel industry has recognized that to survive in a globally competitive environment, firms must become more effective in serving their customers. This means operating within shorter time frames and making more accurate and timely decisions. This movement to compress the apparel time line from product concept to delivery to consumer — and to make more informed decisions based on up-to-the-minute information — was termed quick response (QR). Associations within the American textile and apparel industry have been leaders in developing technology and standard practices to support QR business systems (Blackburn, 1991; Hammond, 1993; Sheridan, 1994).

A related term that has become popular throughout world business in recent years is "supply chain management" (SCM). A problem with SCM, conceptually, is the implied linearity of relationships among suppliers and customers. In fact, the "supply chain" is a complex, multidirectional network of relationships (Lowson, King, & Hunter, 1999). Many large apparel companies have developed their own name for their customized QR/SCM systems. Throughout this textbook we will use the generic QR.

A QR system can trigger a series of benefits. A first and foremost benefit is increased sales due to an increased retail in-stock position. Simply stated, this means having the product the customer wants on the shelf or the rack when the customer wants it. Therefore, more merchandise is sold to ultimate consumers at regular price, resulting in higher financial outcomes. Improved sales at retail benefit the entire supply and distribution system.

QR systems also increase sales with lower inventory levels and reduced carrying costs. Additional advantages include the accuracy of information, time savings due to reduced data entry, and increased distribution efficiency (Lowson, King, & Hunter, 1999). These benefits can be recognized throughout the supply and distribution network, creating a win-win situation for all firms involved.

Fundamentals of Quick Response

The textiles and apparel industry operates in a constantly changing business environment. Factors contributing to the complexity of the industry include low wages in developing countries, the U.S. trade deficit, the formation of the World Trade Organization (WTO), the elimination of the Multi-Fiber Arrangement (MFA), the extension of the North American Free Trade Agreement (NAFTA), currency fluctuations, the surge of leveraged buy-outs and consolidations of manufacturing and retail businesses, as well as increasing global competition. Additionally, U.S. retail markets are saturated with malls, stores, and merchandise, distribution channels are clogged with inventory and customers are more demanding. Stiffening global competition is forcing firms to compress lead and cycle times as a condition of being competitive. In an attempt to combat and manage these factors, QR business systems have been developed, implemented, and updated.

The following definition of quick response, as introduced in Chapter 1, is used in this textbook: *Quick response is a comprehensive business strategy incorporating time-based competition, agility, and partnering to optimize the supply system, the distribution system, and service to customers.* The supply system includes manufacturing and associated activities related to materials and finished goods. The distribution system includes wholesale markets, merchandise handling and transportation, and retailing.

Customer-Driven Business System

The fundamental premise of QR is that merchandise systems are **customer-driven business systems**. Knowing what is selling over the retail counter **real-time** (right now) is essential. The process begins when a customer makes a purchase at a retail store and the sale is recorded via a **point-of-sale (POS)** system using a **scanner** and a **Universal Product Code (UPC).** The style, size, color, and other pertinent data related to the product are relayed via **electronic data interchange (EDI)** or the **Internet** to the retailer's and vendor's data systems and to the vendor's materials suppliers. Action on replacement depends on predetermined agreements and/or automatic replenishment models. In less than a week, the product is manufactured using a flexible production system, then delivered to the retailer shelf-ready, using drop shipment or cross-docking strategies. High levels of collaboration and teamwork are required throughout the process. The goal is to optimize sales at first price based on minimum inventory throughout the supply system.

POS information is available primarily through the use of UPCs and retail scanning, combined with EDI and/or Internet among vendors and their suppliers. A UPC is a 12-digit code representing a unique product. The bar code is scanned electronically at the retail counter when a consumer makes a purchase, providing up-to-the-minute (real-time) sales information including the name of the manufacturer and identification of the specific product. The data can be used for analyzing business and making future decisions on re-orders and new product introductions, as well as for forecasting and inventory management. Other benefits include increased speed and accuracy at checkout by eliminating manual entry.

The real-time sales data captured at POS, in addition to other information, can be transmitted electronically and shared throughout the apparel supply chain via EDI, which is the computer-to-computer exchange of business documents, such as sales information, purchase orders, or invoices. Information is moved electronically in a standard, structured, retrievable format that allows the data to be transmitted without rekeying from one business or location to another. EDI's benefits include reduced order lead times, better customer service, better accuracy, increased information availability, and timely information receipt (Riddle et al., 1995). Many of the benefits of EDI can now be realized via integration with the Internet, which can provide the same services faster and at a lower cost.

Retail sales associates and everyone involved with data entry and management, however, need to understand the importance of accuracy at the UPC level when scanning merchandise. This allows replenishment and other merchandise decisions to be based on accurate data, thus maintaining **data integrity.** Data have integrity when merchandise reality is accurately represented, that is, when every activity relative to a product is correctly recorded: pricing, repricing, receiving, transferring, selling, returning, etc. Maintaining data integrity can be a serious challenge: some tests have reported that as much as 60 percent of data being transferred via EDI are in error. Data integrity is a key in a customer-driven business system based on information technology.

The newest technology that will revolutionize customer service and inventory management is **smart labels,** also known as **radio frequency identification (RFID) tags.** RFID tags will replace bar codes and EDI systems to speed sales and inventory processing by manufacturers, distribution centers, and retailers. RFID tags will soon be tracking trillions of consumer products worldwide. Manufacturers and retailers will be able to know the location of each product they make from the time it is made until it's used and discarded. Here is how RFID tags might work on consumer goods:

- One of the things on your shopping list is milk. The milk containers will have smart labels that store the milk's expiration date and price. You add the milk to your shopping cart and head for the store's door.

- The milk and all the other items in your cart are automatically tallied as you walk through the door that has an embedded tag reader. The information from the purchases you made is sent to your bank, which deducts the amount from your account. Product manufacturers know what products you bought and the store knows what products to reorder.

- Your refrigerator is also equipped with a tag reader so it will keep you up to date on when products should be eaten or discarded, and replaced.

- Placing a carton in the trash or recycle bin will cause the refrigerator to add the product to your grocery list (Bonsor, 1998).

Wal-Mart has assured the acceptance of smart labels by announcing its adoption as shown in Case 2.1.

 Case 2.1 **Wal-Mart will direct top 100 suppliers to use RFID by 2005. ***

Wal-Mart's senior vice president and chief information officer Linda Dillman announced the world's largest retailer will tell its top 100 vendors to have all their cases and pallets "chipped" with smart tags by January 1, 2005. At the present time, the cheapest RFP tag is $0.50 and it is believed they will have to cost no more than $0.01 before they can be widely used on consumer goods. However, Wal-Mart's mandate along with adoption of the radio frequency identification (RFID) standard will speed the use of RFID in the retail industry. The top 100 Wal-Mart suppliers will use approximately 8 billion tags a year. It is likely that the move will spark a new wave of technology spending among manufacturers and retailers since RFID requires a wide range of e-business software, services, and hardware involving wireless system vendors, RFID reader and chip manufacturers, packing vendors, enterprise resource planning (ERP) vendors, warehouse management software providers and logis-

(continued)

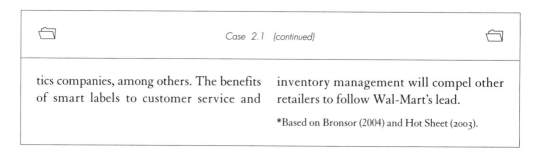

Case 2.1 (continued)

tics companies, among others. The benefits of smart labels to customer service and inventory management will compel other retailers to follow Wal-Mart's lead.

*Based on Bronsor (2004) and Hot Sheet (2003).

Learning Activity 2.2

Smart tags

1. What is the significance of smart tags in the context of QR as a customer driven business system?
2. Make a list of the types of things smart tags might improve related to retail customer service.
3. Make a list of the types of things smart tags might change in relation to inventory management.
4. What unique contribution might smart tags make in relation to merchandising of apparel?

Time-Based Competition

The QR movement is a form of time-based competition that has transformed the way merchandise is conceived, produced, brought to market, and sold. **Time-based competition** means time is recognized as the firm's most fundamental resource (Blackburn, 1991). Much of the development of the global market has been driven by firms seeking the lowest costs for materials and labor. Instead of focusing on doing business at the lowest possible cost, focusing on the increased amount of business that can be generated by shorter time lines requires a great change in the mode of thinking by business executives. In behavioral theory jargon, high levels of cooperation are required among internal business constituencies and with external coalitions to reduce time lines. With time-based competition, business processes and decision making must be prompt, accurate, and agile in adjusting to the needs of target customers and business partners (Fralix & Off, 1993).

Levi Strauss and VF Corp. have been leaders in the QR movement. They implemented EDI with suppliers and customers, changed production to more flexible manufacturing systems, moved production offshore, and adapted EDI to Internet communications. When production trims cycle times, distribution becomes an area of emphasis because there is no point in trimming production time if the product will be held up in warehousing or distribution. Thus, the role of the transportation partner is also critical. Distribution, like retail sales, takes advantage of scanning, UPC, EDI, and Internet technologies, requiring partnerships with transportation companies, as well as close coordination among production plants, distribution centers, and retail stores. The current trend, of course, is toward wireless communication systems.

Agility

A QR system is a market-oriented system wherein merchandise is "pulled" through the system in response to consumer desires (Houston, 1986; Kunz, 1995). It is consistent with the behavioral theory of the firm in that the marketing concept is implicit to the system; the QR system contrasts with traditionally "pushing" goods on consumers (Kurt Salmon Associates, 1994). Agile firms are dynamic, context specific, change-embracing, and growth oriented (Goldman, Nagel, & Preiss, 1995). **Agility** requires information-based decision making along with flexible supply and distribution systems. Agile business systems result in the timely offering of goods desired by customers in the appropriate styles, quantities, and qualities. Determining these factors is primarily a merchandising responsibility. A vision of agile manufacturing follows:

> . . . you hustle over the "QuickFit Tailors" outlet in your local shopping mall. There, after creating the style and selecting the fabric you want, a technician escorts you into a booth where a sophisticated 3-D optical body-scanning device measures and records your precise body dimensions. The data are converted to a 2-D pattern that is transmitted via Internet to an apparel manufacturing plant, where a customized pattern is created. The pattern is relayed to a high-speed single-ply laser cutter that automatically cuts the pieces for your suit. These are immediately routed to a flexible, team-based production line that does the sewing and packages the garment for express shipment to your door. Four days after placing your order, you have a high-quality, custom-tailored suit—at a price comparable to ready-to-wear.

Agile business systems usually include flexible manufacturing systems such as modular and unit production systems. Agility also includes concepts of **Just-In-Time (JIT)** inventory management. JIT is "a business philosophy that focuses on removing waste from all the organization's internal activities and from external exchange activities" (O'Neal & Bertrand, 1991). Principles of Total Quality Management (TQM) are also consistent and in some ways implicit to agility. TQM requires organizing an operation to give timely response, deliver first quality, and get the order right the first time and on time. Technologies inherent to this goal include computer-integrated manufacturing (CIM) and flexible manufacturing in small lots. The use of computer-aided design (CAD) systems allows both the retailer and vendor to quickly and inexpensively alter designs prior to production and engage in joint product development. These technologies and more contribute to agile business systems. Before you drown in acronyms, let's talk about the next component of QR—partnering.

Partnering

QR strategy includes the establishment of business partnerships and procedures to speed the flow of both information within the trade matrix and merchandise to ultimate consumers (Anderson Consulting, 1994; Blackburn, 1991). **Strategic partnering** and value-adding partnership are terms for this relationship. Unusual levels of cooperation, collaboration, and trust are required within firms and among suppliers and customers to make the strategic partnering work. The communication of financial information within and among apparel firms requires a new way of relating to peers, suppliers, and customers—a drastic contrast to traditional adversarial relationships among firms in the trade system. Changing this alienated relationship to a cooperative one is a great challenge.

External Partnering   **External partnering** tactics include timely sharing of sales and inventory information; joint, up-front planning among materials suppliers, manufacturers, and retailers; optimizing logistics to ensure faster processing and transit time; and reducing total inventory by more frequent ordering. The goal of partnerships, like the overall goal of QR, is to optimize the entire supply and distribution system by producing a win-win situation via cooperation. Organizations must extend their narrow view of simply buying and selling to a multi-faceted view of the entire system. They must understand all components involved in producing and moving materials and goods to the ultimate consumer.

Working in an environment where strategic partnerships are the norm requires a paradigm shift (organizational learning) for the apparel industry (Tappscott & Caston, 1993); this change in philosophy must be supported by senior management (Blackburn, 1991; Knill, 1994; Kunz, 1991). This is where the importance of training, education, and learning comes in. Retailers, vendors, suppliers, and manufacturers have made concerted efforts to understand how to work in partnerships. Employees embrace change more readily when they are included in the process from the beginning, especially if their feedback has been solicited (Blackburn, 1991; Kunz, 1991). Many external partnerships are now supported by business-to-business (B2B) electronic/Internet systems.

A recent exploratory study of strategic external partnerships found that the benefits of partnerships included increased speed of delivery of goods resulting in cost savings. Essential elements for the formation of partnerships included the following:

- The potential for mutual benefit of the partners.
- Common interests between the partners in products and markets.
- Compatible business ethics as a foundation of trust.
- Environments for sharing resources and benefits.

They also found that power tended to reside with the retailer in the parternships (Divita & Cassill, 2002).

Internal Partnering   Not only are organizations required to rethink external relationships, but internal functions must also be reevaluated in QR environments. In many firms, developing **internal partnering** is a greater problem than developing partnerships with suppliers and customers. Because QR requires several areas of the apparel firm to function as a whole — sharing, analyzing, and reacting to real-time sales data — management must remove traditional functional barriers so that executives, marketers, merchandisers, production managers, finance managers, and/or store managers can work together toward a unified purpose. Many times this is accomplished through the use of teams — multi-functional and cross-functional teams comprised of members from a firm's different constituencies. Discussion among team members provides perspectives from different areas of specialization for problem solving and policy development. The result is a more comprehensive view of issues and solutions that are easier to implement.

Organizational structures have become flatter and more team-oriented because of access to information. Information provides a foundation for organizational learning.

Merchandising Issues

Despite efforts to move toward QR systems, many business problems persist, including the escalating percentage of markdowns being taken at retail, high levels of stockouts, lowered gross margins, excess inventory, and increasing prices. Many of these problems stem from the lack of adequate forecasting and merchandise planning systems to aid in the merchandising process. *Traditionally, a crystal ball has been a key piece of equipment for merchandisers* (Hartnett, 1993). Today, however, technology is being developed and implemented to take some of the guesswork out of merchandising, providing merchandisers with tangible information upon which to base decisions.

For example, Planalytics helps companies understand and address the impact that weather has had and will have on their businesses, allowing them to eliminate unnecessary surprises and reduce risk. They use artificial intelligence to analyze product sales data to determine the types of weather that drive consumers to buy a particular product, plus temperature thresholds that must be crossed in each geographic market before people in different areas will purchase a particular product (www.planalytics.com). Could Planalytics help Danskin forecast demand in Case 2.2?

 Case 2.2 *Danskin introduces electronic B2B ordering with 7thOnline.* *

Danskin and 7thOnline announced the launch of Danskin's B2B Web presence through 7thOnline. Danskin manufactures and markets leading brands of women's active wear, dance wear, and leg wear. Danskin has expanded its market exposure by offering dance wear through an online product catalog. 7thOnline's technology also provides electronic order transmission capabilities from retailers. Danskin is gearing this new initiative to its large dance specialty store network.

7thOnline is a Web-based supply chain solution providing assortment planning and visual merchandising technology to the global fashion industry. 7thOnline's platform significantly streamlines the merchandising and communication process between manufacturers and their retail trading partners by offering a visual, online product catalog and planning and order management tools. 7thOnline EDI integration gives retailers the capability of electronically transmitting product purchase orders over the Internet, eliminating the high costs associated with manual data entry and order processing.

"We are always looking for business opportunities that help take our business to the next level. 7thOnline's technology gives us the progressive edge to drive our business forward with our retail partners. Our B2B Web presence enhances our customer service by increasing order efficiency, decreasing manual processing time and improving turnover by providing direct access to product availability. At the end of the day, we are providing better customer service to meet our customer's product needs," said Carol Hochman, president and CEO of Danskin, Inc.

7thOnline helps manufacturers like Danskin increase sales in existing channels and facilitates order management by bringing their collections to retailers' desktops, enabling buyers to view products and place orders with the click of a mouse.

"We are very pleased to be partnering in this initiative with Danskin, a leading marketer of women's and children's dance and active wear. This opportunity has expanded our market leadership position in providing Web-based merchandising technology to the global fashion industry," said Max Ma, co-founder and CEO of 7thOnline.

*Based on Danskin press release, April 2, 2002.

 ### Learning Activity 2.3

Read Case 2.2 very carefully.

1. What aspects of QR are exemplified by this case?
2. Is internal or external partnering most evident? Explain.
3. Consider the definition of merchandising that is being used as the foundation of this text. What aspects of merchandising are being facilitated in the Danskin/7thOnline relationship?
4. Think through your work experiences in terms of evidence of the concepts of QR. What experiences can you think of that exemplify time-based competition? Agility? Partnerships among suppliers and vendors?
5. What problems have you experienced that might have been solved had QR been in use?

Theoretical Foundations of Technology Innovation

Four theoretical viewpoints are considered here as a basis for examining innovation of technology: theories of the firm, theories of management style, organizational learning, and diffusion of innovation. Theories of the firm and theories of management style were introduced in Chapter 1. A brief overview of these theories follows.

Theories of the Firm and Theories of Management Style

Behavioral theories of the firm emphasize the role of human behavior in explaining the activities of the firm, while economic theories emphasize profit maximization (Anderson, 1982). According to the behavioral theory of the firm, employees form constituencies related to their areas of specialization within the firm. The executive constituency provides leadership and sets the tone for the firm's operation. Other constituencies develop their own objectives that may or may not directly relate to the objectives of the firm. Conflicts frequently develop between constituencies because of different objectives and responsibilities. Conflicts may be resolved through negotiation. Constituencies that control the firm's key resources tend to have the most power in negotiation. The success of the firm is dependent on the ability of the executive constituency to unify the employees to support the firm's objectives.

Apparel firms, historically, have been autocratically operated firms. Top-down communication has been the norm. Most QR strategies require that executives/managers change from being "bosses" (Theory-X Management Style) to being "leaders" (Theory-Y Management Style). Under Theory-Y management style, leaders engage the whole human being into his/her work based on the assumption that employees are capable, desire respect and responsibility, and want the opportunity to be creative and solve problems. Employees are empowered with both the responsibility and authority to make decisions regarding the use of the firm's resources (McGregor, 1960). Successful implementation of QR technology is dependent on stimulating employees to accept technology, learn to use it, and see it as a positive influence in their work environment.

Organizational Learning

Training is a relatively short-term activity involving teaching how to produce specific, predetermined results as quickly as possible. In training, there is a correct way and an incorrect way to perform the task, one right answer and a lot of wrong ones. In contrast, **learning** is the result of educating for longer-term outcomes (Barr & Tagg, 1995). Benefits of learning may be less immediate; its goals are less clear-cut. Definitions of right and wrong become much less distinct because of asking questions differently and because of problem solving in a more complex manner. It is one thing to teach employees skills that will help them do their present jobs better (training); it is something else to expose them to information or situations that will enable them to perform better in a variety of possible jobs (learning). In the case of training, management expects an immediate payoff. The trained person can go straight back to the job and start to do something differently, and this difference will be a good thing for the organization. In the longer term learning process, exactly when or how the organization will benefit is not as readily apparent.

Firms engage in training when they perceive the short-term benefits to the organization will outweigh the costs. The worth (W) of human performance is equal to or greater than the value (V) of a person's accomplishments on the job divided by the cost (C) of behavior that goes into producing the accomplishments.

$$W \geq V \div C$$
$$\text{worth} \geq \text{value} \div \text{cost}$$

It is impossible to talk about training without measuring a return on the investment. When deciding to train to cure a performance discrepancy, the first step is to figure out how much the discrepancy is costing the firm.

Implementing QR strategies and merchandising technology requires organizational learning. A **learning organization** is "an organization that is continually expanding its capacity to create its future" (Senge, 1990, p. 14). Learning involves vision, critical thinking, and problem solving. Through learning, pupils understand how and why something works the way it does. Understanding *why* is the key difference between training and learning.

For example, firms launch training programs for quality improvement. These programs are designed to teach employees specific processes that will improve quality of products and/or services. Initially, significant improvements occur. But over time many organizations reach a plateau because employees have been trained in only a specific process, not in problem solving for ongoing quality improvement. They have not been empowered to think for themselves. They don't know how or haven't been allowed to take the next steps on their own.

In contrast, a learning organization is one that *continuously improves*. Because employees are encouraged to use their intelligence and implement their own ideas, improvements do not stop when the process they were taught in training is in place. Instead, employees determine the next logical step and initiate ongoing improvements.

Educating for learning involves risk for the firm since the learner/employee may acquire new competencies and be ready to seek out new opportunities when the firm does not have a new job available. If it is not possible to enrich the current job, the employee may seek a new job elsewhere, taking the new learning with him or her. The possibility of this outcome has made some organizations cautious about providing education with learning outcomes. This perspective is extremely short-sighted, because it deprives the firm of the full engagement of employees' intellect during the time they are employed by the firm.

Theory of Diffusion of Innovations

Rogers (1983) identified five characteristics of an innovation or new technology that determine its rate of adoption by members of a social system. These attributes are: relative advantage, compatibility, complexity, trialability, and observability. Relative advantage is the degree to which an innovation is perceived as better than the idea it replaces. Compatibility refers to the perception of how consistent the innovation is with existing values, past experiences, and needs of the potential adopters. Complexity is the perceived difficulty involved in understanding and using the innovation. Trialability describes the ease with which the innovation may be experimented with on a limited basis. Finally, observability refers to the degree to which the results of an innovation are visible to others. Although these are not the only qualities that affect adoption rates, "past research indicates that they are the most important characteristics of innovations in explaining rate of adoption" (Rogers, p. 16).

Rogers also outlines a two-stage process model for the adoption of innovations within the organization. These sequential stages are called initiation and implementation. The **initiation** phase is the decision to adopt the technology; the **implementation** stage occurs as the technology is put to use. Difficulties may result from the fact that the individuals usually involved in the initiation process are often a different group from the implementers. In addition, the organizational structure that supports the initiation may be resistant to implementing an innovation.

Summary of Concepts of Quick Response and Technology Innovation

1. Fundamental concepts of Behavioral Theory of the Apparel Firm (BTAF) are consistent with the fundamental concepts of quick response (QR) and diffusion of innovation.
2. Theory-Y management style and the associated empowerment are essential to successfully implement QR-related business strategies and new technology.
3. Executive leadership is essential to implement change.
4. Modification of both formal and informal organizational structure is necessary to fully implement QR systems.
5. Because of the underlying assumptions related to human behavior, it is unlikely that groups using Theory Y can operate effectively within a Theory-X management structure.
6. The characteristics of a particular technology may limit its rate of adoption.
7. Organizational learning is required for successful innovation.
8. Both initiators and implementors of technology innovation must be adequately educated to support the process.

Case 2.3 *A failure of merchandising technology innovation**

The purpose of this case study is to examine the people and events involved in a technology innovation failure. We were seeking the multiple realities of the many people associated with introduction of new technology throughout the organization; thus, naturalistic, field research methods were employed. Sources of data included interviews based on an interview guide, informal interviews, and field observation.

The Company

The setting is an apparel manufacturer specializing in athletic wear, particularly uniforms and "letter" jackets that identify athletes with certain teams. The firm features a quick response turnaround time from order placement to delivery of finished goods. This is achieved in part by stocking pre-cut basic garment parts that can be assembled in the color combinations specified by different teams.

Sales representatives are part of the marketing department and work from a catalog of styles and selected sales samples. They assist customers in selecting garment styles and color combinations. Logos are custom designed by the art department as desired by customers. The firm does not offer the lowest prices in the market; instead, they provide good quality and the best service as their strategic advantages.

Initiation of Technology

A few of the manufacturing executives identified development of garment design as a bottleneck in the merchandising/product development process. They decided they needed a computer-aided design (CAD) system to create visualizations of garment designs. They believed the illustrations produced on the CAD system would help the company to do the following: provide a "blueprint" for design development, reduce the number of sample garments produced, assist in the development of more innovative design ideas, and maintain and/or improve company image with customers and competition.

As is sometimes the case with companies that deal primarily with basic types of goods, in this company product development is a division of what is called the marketing department. Because garment design ideas are first visualized by product developers, it seemed logical to the technology initiators that the CAD system should be implemented in product development. They acquired over $40,000 worth of hardware and software and put it in place in the product development area. Two years later the system was pushed aside, sitting unused; four years later the system was being used in ways only utilizing a few of its functions.

(continued)

Implementation, Phase One

An enthusiastic, recent graduate of a textiles and clothing program was hired, sent to California for two weeks' training on the CAD system, and then put in place in product development. Numerous problems soon became apparent. It was assumed the other product development people would give the CAD operator work. They didn't. Sales representatives who asked for design development found the CAD operator was not skilled enough to execute what they wanted on the spot. It turned out the person hired to run the CAD system was not very skilled in computer operation nor aggressive in learning how to solve problems. Perceptions of complexity of the system dominated perspectives of the technology. After about six months of frustration on her part and others, she resigned and left the company, taking the California training with her. The CAD system sat idle for several months. The technology initiative was generally regarded as a failure.

Implementation, Phase Two

To get the CAD system operating again, the technology initiators hired a summer intern from a neighboring university who had learned the CAD system as a part of her coursework. She was a friendly, out-going person who was comfortable with her computer expertise. She was quickly able to impress the product developers, the sales representatives, and the art department with the relative advantages of the system. The initiators were pleased with her contributions to the company during her three-month internship. However, none of the product developers were prepared to take up CAD when she left, so once again, the system was idle.

Implementation, Phase Three

The technology initiators decided their mistake had been placing the CAD in the product development area; it should have been placed in the art department. They decided to hire the CAD company to come to the headquarters and train two people on the system: one as the regular operator and one as a backup. Their logic was that the art department was familiar with graphical software and learning new technologies was an ongoing part of their activities.

In addition, the individual chosen as the primary operator would be given "ownership" of the system, and mastering CAD would be his or her sole responsibility. Under this arrangement, marketing (product development and sales) would place orders, so to speak, with the CAD artist to obtain garment illustrations.

Two individuals were chosen for training by the art department manager, who expressed a priority for an individual with a strong personality to be able to deal with the marketing/sales people who were regarded as being unreasonable in their demands on the art department. The art department manager, however, selected the person she thought she could work with most compatibly, and rearranged the department so the CAD would be located close to the manager. That way the manager could assist the CAD operator in dealing with the difficult marketing/sales people. As implementation proceeded, the primary CAD artist attempted to gain competence and the secondary user had little access because he was fully employed elsewhere.

Two years have elapsed. A recent check on the status of the system revealed that it is being used for designing signs and to some extent for catalog layout—certainly not the primary uses to maximize the investment in technology.

Sources of Implementation Problems According to Theory

The initiators started out by placing CAD in product development, then they moved it to the art department, and eventually planned to have still other individuals use it. Even after members of the art department were trained on it, management still saw product development as the primary users. The initiators failed to recognize the rivalry between the art and marketing departments. The two departments were forced to work together everyday. The marketing department thought the art department was too slow and the art department thought marketing was too demanding. Marketing employees did not like the art department manager. These issues went unresolved through negotiation. CAD was moved from marketing, where it failed, and forced on the art department, creating resentment on both sides. All interviewees acknowledged the strain between art and marketing except the director of marketing, who took over the art department just prior to Phase Three of implementation. From the marketing director's perspective, restructuring was viewed as a means of facilitating CAD implementation.

The concept of a firm's internal constituencies having conflicting goals was exemplified by the tension between the art and marketing departments. However, the tension was not acknowledged by management and no effort was made to negotiate a solution to the problems. Theories of management style also lend some insight into the difficulty in implementing CAD. Although employees said they were very

(continued)

happy with their jobs and they all expressed a certain amount of ease in interaction with superiors and other departments, the situation indicates there was not adequate communication within the firm. The firm seemed to be operating primarily with a top-down communication system within the confines of a Theory-X management style. More teamwork in the technology initiation phase may have eased the implementation phase. The first CAD operator may have been screened more carefully for computer skills or a more assertive art department employee might have been selected as the third operator.

There was an obvious need for organizational learning beyond the technical training for CAD operators. The art and marketing departments needed to work out a more productive working relationship. The sales people, the art department, and product development all needed help in understanding what the CAD system could do, how it could help them with their jobs, and how they could expect to work with the CAD operator. Individuals were not relieved of other job responsibilities in order to concentrate on perfecting skills and developing new professional relationships necessary to successful technology implementation.

The case study confirmed the relevance of Rogers' concepts of innovators and implementers and the behavioral theory of the apparel firm. Lack of collaboration between initiators and implementers was decidedly a problem. The excitement and inspiration of the initiators must be transferred to the implementers and their work environment must be modified to support implementation of technology.

*Based on Cosbey & Kunz (1995).

Learning Activity 2.4

Innovation and implementation of technology

Think through Case 2.3.
1. Considering BTAF, what constituencies are involved in this case?
2. What is the central problem in the technology innovation?
3. What types of initiatives might the executive constituency have tried to make the technology productive after the initial failure?

4. Based on the behavioral theory of the apparel firm and Rogers' diffusion of innovation theory, design a process for introduction of a CAD system into the product development area. Be sure to consider management style and organizational learning in the process.

Decision Making in a QR Universe

The addition of the QR construct expands the focus of the BTAF beyond interactions of internal constituencies to interactions of the firm and its constituencies with external coalitions, particularly its trading partners. Words used to describe the apparel industry and industries in general tend to imply linearity: trade channel, pipeline, supply chain, etc. In reality, however, firms within the apparel industry and their associated manufacturing and distribution processes do not have linear relationships with each other. While certain events are sequential (e.g., cotton must grow before it can be harvested and spun into yarn; patterns must be made and fabrics cut before garments can be sewn), products are manufactured and distributed through a complex matrix of integrated decision making within the firm, between the firm and its suppliers and customers, and between the firm and its interlocking environments. Many of the perceived "problems" that arise in the manufacturing and distribution processes are related to violations of an erroneous assumption of linearity (Scheller, 1993). The assumption of linearity is the problem.

If decision making is regarded as interactive and individuals/teams are empowered with information, education, and the right to make decisions, the "problems" become resoluble issues that are a normal part of doing business. Effective solutions can be developed because the people who are dealing with the "problems" have the authority, responsibility, and ability to find solutions.

For QR systems to operate successfully, unusual levels of cooperation, collaboration, and trust are required among suppliers and customers throughout the **trade universe**. In this case, *a universe is defined as all firms, collectively, that are subjects of consideration at one time.* Breaking down traditional adversarial relationships among suppliers and customers to the point of electronically sharing data requires new paradigms in industrial relations. To be involved in time-based competition, business executives and their employees must believe that it is possible to create a win-win situation through collaboration.

Strategic partnering results in a type of vertical integration that does not involve a purchase or takeover. This is occurring at a time when formal vertical integration is also increasing. Manufacturers' outlet malls are one of the most obvious forms of forward vertical integration. At the same time, retailers are adding product development divisions to modify their sourcing capabilities, thus creating backward vertical integration. These vertical integration systems provide control over both product and process, as well as the time required for both. Clearly, control of product and process is regarded as a strategic advantage in today's apparel markets. Figure 2.1 is a graphic example of a multi-dimensional apparel trade universe operating under assumptions of BTAF.

In the trade universe represented in Figure 2.1, some firms are retailers, some are manufacturers of finished goods, and some are manufacturers of materials. Some of the firms have defined merchandising constituencies, while some don't. Some firms (those with QR wings) are fully engaged in QR. Think about the huge amount of information being shared by firms fully engaged in QR. Is it possible that full commitment to QR might actually limit the flexibility of the firm to adjust the other changes in the firm's environment?

For firms partially engaged in QR (those with QR propellers), the QR connections may be primarily electronic: UPC, EDI, and perhaps some automated replenishment. Some firms are isolates: they are not directly connected to other firms in the universe. Firms without propellers or wings are not engaged in QR. Those with propellers but not attached to other firms may have failed in QR partnerships or be new to QR and seeking partnerships. Which firms will be able to optimize the benefits of QR? Will the isolates starve and die?

Merchandising in a QR Universe

Hammond (1993) emphasized the difficulties associated with full implementation of QR business systems. Most firms focus on some aspects of QR and do not attempt full implementation. She particularly identified components of the textile and apparel industry's culture that must change, including:

- the traditional focus on the short term
- hostility of interfirm relationships
- lack of attention to human resources
- inadequate production flexibility

See Table 2.1 for a summary of factors that need to be implemented for QR systems to fully succeed. While some firms have successfully overcome the challenges listed in Table 2.1, some have not. As indicated by the table, merchandising technology is a component of the

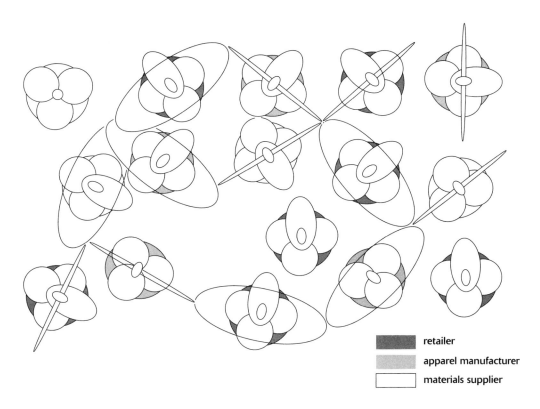

Figure 2.1   Example of a QR universe operating under assumptions of the Behavioral Theory of the Apparel Firm.

QR business system needing more development and implementation. *The problems associated with forecasting and merchandise planning are seen as the greatest challenges in the current market.* For some firms, quick response could be more accurate if firms determined what forecasters can and cannot predict well and redesigned their merchandise planning processes to minimize the impact of inaccurate forecasts (Fisher et al., 1994, p. 84).

   Some merchandisers are using the wealth of information available from technological innovations, such as UPCs, scanning, and EDI, to make more accurate and timely decisions. Such support systems allow merchandisers to react more quickly to definite information, rather than relying on sales representatives, trade journals, fashion magazines, or instinct. But most of the systems, or the *use* of the systems, do not provide adequate usable information. Having a lot of information is not enough; it must be usable information. The textile and apparel industry has come a long way, but much remains to be done to optimize the effectiveness of QR systems.

📖 Learning Activity 2.5

Examine Table 2.1.

1. What are merchandising-related issues for manufacturers regarding QR implementation?
2. What are merchandising-related issues for retailers regarding QR implementation?
3. Are there merchandising-related issues requiring joint activity?
4. How might more accurate forecasting help solve other problems in the apparel business system?
5. What merchandising issues are related to training versus learning?
6. What merchandising problems are related to the nature of the trade universe?

Sources and Capabilities of Merchandising Technology

There are three primary sources of merchandising technology: proprietary systems, commercial systems, and third-party systems. **Proprietary systems** are developed by individual firms for their own use. For example, Sears' SAMS system (Sears Apparel Merchandising System) was among the first integrated systems (Sears' merchandise, 1993). During the late 1990s, Target Corp. developed a proprietary system to unify over 60 different merchandising technology related systems into a single integrated system that could be used in all divisions of Target. Firms usually hire consultants to assist operations/MIS (management information system) and merchandising personnel to tailor the systems to the firm's product lines and priorities. Proprietary systems are usually regarded as trade secrets.

Commercial systems for merchandising technology are available for sale from computer software and consulting firms. The software is often designed in several parts so the buyer can purchase only the components desired for implementation. The cost of the software probably includes some sort of a service package for training, updates, and problem solving. A merchandising technology software system may cost anywhere from a few thousand dollars to many million, depending on its capabilities and the size of the firm it will serve.

Third-party merchandising is the term used to describe professional merchandising services companies that provide outsourced labor to execute merchandising assignments. Third-party merchandisers are generally contracted on a project or program basis and

Table 2.1

*Challenges to quick response business systems. ***
(Items in bold italics are merchandising related issues.)

Manufacturing	Joint Activity	Retailing
• Provide adequate learning opportunities to support QR systems	• Fully implement necessary technology to support QR activities	• Provide adequate learning opportunities to support QR systems
• Improve efficiency by negotiating resolutions of conflicts among internal constituencies	• Replace adversarial customer and supplier relationships with cooperative partnerships	• Improve efficiency by negotiating resolutions of conflicts among internal constituencies
• *Improve basis of forecasting beyond sales history*	• *Incorporate demand uncertainty into planning processes*	• *Improve basis of forecasting beyond sales history*
• Shift production emphasis from direct labor costs to total product costs and bottom line returns	• *Plan merchandise assortments and track inventory at full SKU level*	• *Shift merchandising focus from percent gross margin to bottom line returns*
• Use short-cycle manufacturing so final product decisions can be close to point of sale	• Use automated replenishment systems for basic and staple goods	• *Plan assortments and manage inventory by individual store rather than by aggregate chain*
• Ship merchandise floor-ready		• *Place smaller initial orders and replenish based on POS data*

*Based primarily on Abernathy et al. (1999), Fisher (1994), Hammond (1993), and Reda (1994).

charge clients for actual work performed rather than being paid on a commission basis or percent of sales. Examples include Premium Retail Services, Merchandising Corporation of America, and USA Merchandising Solutions. You can explore their services by looking them up on the Internet. Third-party services tend to be focused on in-store merchandising systems related to planogram visual presentation software for shelves, pegboard, slatwall, and other displays, inventory management, and/or presentation of specific categories such as cosmetics, food, or hardlines. Only a few offer services related to front-end systems such as **merchandise planning.**

Front-end systems help determine what merchandise will be received. Front-end merchandising systems address things like forecasting and merchandise planning. **Back-end systems** address management of the merchandise that is received. Back-end merchandising

systems tend to focus on inventory management. Table 2.2 lists some of the common functions of commercial merchandising technology systems. Merchandise planning and inventory management are frequently used terms in relation to merchandising technology.
Automated replenishment tends to be offered in association with forecasting and ware-
house/distribution center inventory management. Forecasting is often viewed as a component of automated replenishment systems and is based primarily on POS data. Customer
profiling is not always described in relation to forecasting. Store management systems tend
to have strong accounting relationships and do not always include multi-tier applications,
that is, headquarters and stores integration. Space management systems focus primarily on
planogramming for grocery and drug stores. Visual merchandising and assortment planning for soft goods applications are now available.

In 1995, I attended a three-hour workshop featured at a retail technology show with the title
"Assortment Planning: The Next Frontier." The speaker promised to clarify the definitions of
merchandise planning, merchandise management, and assortment planning. The topics were indicative of the primitive level of merchandise planning software in 1995. Now several vendors
claim assortment planning software. However, the premier system of merchandising technology is
Arthur Enterprise Suite of Strategic Merchandise Management from JDA Software Group, Inc.

Arthur Enterprise Suite includes an integrated set of applications:

- *Arthur Planning* is a powerful merchandise planning, decision-assist application that enables manufacturers and retailers to create detailed financial plans and merchandise
budgets from a customer and/or store perspective, analyze valuable information, and
test merchandise strategies before resources are committed.

- *Arthur Planning Portal* is a web-based version of Arthur Planning that enables collaborative planning over the Internet to share plans and up-to-the-minute results with trading partners and field personnel.

- *Arthur Assortment Planning* allows merchants to create plans that take into account store personalities, space, seasonality, and the right mix of product characteristics that matter most to customers.

- *Arthur Allocation* improves the management of inventory and facilitates distribution of
merchandise according to current trends, merchandise plans, and store characteristics.

- *Arthur Performance Analysis* is an enterprise-wide decision support system. It supports the
organized dissemination of the critical information needed to identify trends and uncover
merchandise problems hidden in the data (JDA Software Group, Inc., 2003; Reda 2001).

Table 2.2

Functions of commercial merchandising technology systems.

Assortment Planning	Merchandise Allocation
Merchandise Management	Merchandise Planning
Automated Replenishment	Multi-Tier Applications
Customer Profiling	Space Management
Forecasting	Store Management System
Inventory Management	Visual Merchandising

I once had aspirations of adapting Arthur Planning for classroom use. Unfortunately, the learning curve was too time-consuming — too much class time would have been required to learn how to run Arthur Planning and not enough time would have been available to learn how to make merchandising decisions. That is why Sourcing Simulator accompanies this text. A relatively short learning curve results in generation of realistic outputs related to merchandising scenarios. With Sourcing Simulator, instructors and students can focus on planning merchandising inputs and interpreting and evaluating outputs.

Overview of Potential Outcomes of QR

The outcomes of QR for basic and staple merchandise are obvious. It truly becomes possible to have the right product at the right place at the right time. Salable products are on the retail shelf, salable products are manufactured, and materials for salable products are produced. Automatic replenishment systems based on model stocks can be developed and basic stock models can be automatically modified by computer based on rate of sale.

The benefits related to what is sometimes called the "quick response movement" accrue throughout the consumer goods business systems. These benefits include increased sales, reduced markdowns, increased stock turn, lower average inventories, increased gross margin return on inventory, increased adjusted gross margin, and satisfied customers (Hunter, 1990; Lowson, King & Hunter, 1999). Implementation of QR strategies requires discarding traditional apparel business paradigms in favor of human-empowerment strategies and technology-based systems.

QR systems are more frequently applied to basic/staple goods than to fashion/seasonal goods, although Kincade and Cassill (1993) found no significant difference in the success. Fundamentally, the time period that fashion and seasonal goods are salable is so short, usually less than 12 weeks, that the merchandising process is believed to test even the best of

QR strategies. Those responsible for the planning, developing, and presenting of product lines face more complex expectations and require a broader base of expertise.

Merchandising trends include increasing complexity of line and product development with fewer weeks of sale for individual styles and less defined selling seasons. Channels of distribution in the market are more complex, with multiple sourcing methods including both finished goods and product development with domestic and international sources. At the same time, the new emphasis on QR relationships will have a profound impact on merchandising.

Merchandising Technology Theory

Constructs, assumptions, and propositions are fundamental results of the inductive process of theory development. The constructs and assumptions related to Behavioral Theory of the Apparel Firm have already been discussed. Propositions describe the next level of complexity in theory development: they predict outcomes related to interactions of constructs. **Propositions** are tested through trial and error in the business sector and are sometimes treated as hypotheses in the academic sector becoming the basis of research to test the theory. See Table 2.3.

Table 2.3
Propositions related to merchandising technology.

1. The concept of the selling season will be replaced by weeks of sale, with new merchandise being strategically introduced on a continual basis thoughout the merchandising cycle.
2. Merchandise planning, development, and presentation will extend to the SKU level.
3. Seasonal wholesale markets will be replaced, at least in part, by joint product development and Internet communication.
4. Consolidation will continue to occur in the number of retailers and manufacturers in the market.
5. Consolidation will continue to occur in the number of vendors and customers with which each firm works.
6. Merchandising processes will be adapted based on characteristics of different merchandise classifications.
7. Assortment planning model stocks will provide the basis of initial deliveries; the rest of inventory supply will be customer-driven based on POS.
8. Automatic replenishment model stocks will control flow of basic/staple goods.
9. Measures of merchandising success will include not only an established level of gross margin and/or sales per square foot, but more importantly, gross margin dollars, total revenue, gross margin return on investment, and gross margin adjusted for delivery and carrying costs.
10. All of a firm's products will not necssarily be on QR systems, but QR products will be given priority by both suppliers and buyers.
11. Merchandising decisions will be based on information about products, suppliers, and customers— more information than merchandisers have ever dreamed possible.

Summary

A paradigm shift is required of both people and firms in order to adapt to changes required by implementing merchandising technology consistent with QR business systems. Merchandising technology is one part of the total QR business system. Until now, the focus of merchandising aspects of QR systems has been on "back-end" systems and merchandising processes, including inventory management that is sometimes performed by the operations constituency. "Front-end" systems and processes, including merchandise planning and, in particular, assortment planning, have been slower to be developed. Customer purchases may drive automated re-plenishment, but merchandisers still must decide when merchandise needs to be added or dropped from the line and what, at what price, and how much to include in an assortment.

Technology and technology standards for EDI (electronic data interchange), UPC (universal product codes), POS (point of sale), and inventory management are well established, but not necessarily at the SKU (stock keeping unit) level. Many are planned only to the style level with color and size left in limbo. The newest technology for both commercial and proprietary systems is RFID (radio frequency identification). Inadequate training on new technology systems reduces effectiveness of more information. Education can help reduce employees' resistance to implementation of merchandising technology.

Strategic partnering, both internally and externally, is a top priority for retailers because retailers are the first beneficiaries of improved inventory management. Many firms say they are partnering, but are not truly operating as equals. Establishment of collaborative and coperative relationships among business partners is essential for ongoing success. Human qualities of judgment, insight, and creativity are even more important in the presence of QR technology. Gaining a consistent level of excellence throughout the business system is essential.

Key Concepts

agility	internal partnering	real-time
back-end systems	Internet	scanner
commercial systems	Just-In-Time (JIT)	smart labels
customer-driven business systems	learning	strategic partnering
data integrity	learning organization	technology
electronic data interchange (EDI)	merchandise planning	third-party merchandising
external partnering	merchandising technology	time-based competition
front-end systems	point of sale (POS)	trade universe
implementation of technology	propositions	training
initiation of technology	proprietary systems	Universal Product Code (UPC)
	radio frequency identification (RFID) tags	

Integrated Learning Activity 2.6.1

Retailer profile

Begin a profile of a retailer that you are familiar with and that you would like to work with for the rest of this course. This profile will provide a foundation for the development of your line plans that you will keep in your Merchandise Analysis Portfolio (MAP). Your MAP retailer will provide a context for all your decisions related to your merchandise plans. You will add components to the profile throughout the semester. Your instructor may provide you with guidelines for your choice of a retailer. Reviewing the Representative Data Set in ILA 2.6.2 is a good place to start.

It is helpful to choose brick-and-mortar retailers that are part of your local retail community, so that you can visit the stores and analyze the merchandise as well as the merchandising processes and strategies. The process you use to select retailer(s) is up to your teacher, while resources you might use to choose retailer(s) and develop profile(s) include the following:

1. annual reports available at the library and/or on the Internet
2. the retailer's Web site
3. articles from the trade press such as *Stores, Retail Merchandiser, Women's Wear Daily, Daily News Record,* etc.
4. interviews with the retailer's executives
5. your own critical observation and analysis
6. the Representative Data Set in ILA 2.6.2

(Note: Store managers are not always goods sources of specific information about merchandise plans, especially in chain organizations. Merchandise planning is often carried at headquarters, while store managers are primarily charged with carrying out the merchandise plans by selling the merchandise.)

If your retailer has a catalog, obtain a copy. It can be very useful in developing and understanding the retailer's policies, assortments, and pricing strategies. You should also review their Web site to help understand these things. Put the profile on a word processing system so it can be modified easily as you learn more about the firm.

Complete the following steps for your profile.

1. List and/or describe name, address of headquarters, corporate owner (if there is one), organizational structure, number of stores and locations, and location of local or nearest store.
2. Describe market position including categories of merchandise offered, price/quality levels, and company's mission.

3. Describe target/mass market customer strategy using demographic and lifestyle variables. (The mean family income in United States is about $42,000; middle class is sometimes described with a range of income from $25,000 to $75,000.) Identify competing firms and describe why they are competitors.
4. Describe how merchandise is presented for sale: departments, layout, fixturing, traffic flow, etc. Is this a single channel or multi-channel retailer?
5. Describe social, economic, and fashion trends that might impact sales of the firm.
6. Present a copy of an income statement from a current annual report that includes three or more years of data, so you can see trends in financial productivity.
7. Include a reference list.
8. Present your company profile in an orderly manner in your MAP.

Integrated Learning Activity 2.6.2

Representative Data Set

To assist you in selection of a retailer and analysis of its performance, I have provided a Representative Data Set of Measures of Retail Productivity in Different Retail Channels. It consists of five different tables of data related to the nature and size of retailers, their merchandise, and their financial productivity (see Tables 2.4 through 2.8). Since you will probably refer to it many times throughout this course, you may want to put a tab on the page where the data set is located so it will be easy to find. Most of these data were published in *Retail Merchandiser* and *Stores* online magazine but were supplemented with additional calculations. In some cases, data were added from individual retailers' Web sites.

The retail channels included are broadline mass retailers, mid-market department store chains, category dominant specialty chains, off-price apparel chains, and wholesale chains primarily from *Retail Merchandiser* and upscale department store chains, apparel specialty chains, and other retailers primarily from *Stores* online magazine. The Representative Data Set provides the opportunity to compare various well-known retailers in terms of sales and number of stores, growth, and financial productivity. Additional perspectives of the company (including updating the data presented in the Representative Data Set) can be derived from visiting the individual retailers' Web sites.

In addition to the retailer data, there is a table with the breakdown of sales by merchandise category and class. Apparel, home, and hardlines are included.

Table 2.4

Representative Data Set: Measures of retail productivity in different retail channels. *

Company	Sales (in millions)	% Change in Sales	5 Year CAGR**	# of Stores	Sales/Store (in millions)	Total Sq. Ft. (in thousands)	Sq. Ft/Store (in thousands)	Sales/Sq. Ft.
Top Broadline Mass Retailers								
Wal-Mart	$157,121	12.93	13.39	2,826	$55.60	386,524	136.77	$406.50
Target	36,911	13.28	12.71	1,147	32.19	140,255	122.28	263.21
Kmart	30,762	(14.91)	(0.90)	1,829	16.82	179,242	98.00	171.62
Meijer	10,900	2.83	9.58	156	69.87	35,100	225.00	310.54
Fred Meyer	5,675	3.18	4.61	145	39.14	21,000	144.83	270.24
ShopKo	3,240	(2.35)	9.03	364	8.90	20,000	54.95	162.00
Ames	2,825	(13.18)	4.88	333	8.48	17,649	53.00	160.07
Value City	1,519	2.57	n/a	116	13.09	10,092	87.00	150.52
Top Mid-Market Department Store Chains								
Sears	$23,028	-5.29	0.16	872	$26.40	127,200	145.87	$181.04
JCPenney	15,091	1.91	-1.04	1,049	14.40	107,200	102.19	140.77
Kohl's	9,120	21.78	24.41	457	20.00	40,000	87.53	228.00
Mervyn's	3,816	-5.24	-1.48	264	14.50	21,425	81.16	178.11
Goody's Family Clothing	1,409	18.11	8.34	328	4.30	9,151	27.90	153.97
Stein Mart	1,193	9.62	8.51	265	4.50	9,805	37.00	121.67
Selected Category Dominant Specialty Chains								
Home Depot	$58,247	8.77	19.25	1,532	$38.00	199,160	130.00	292.46
Best Buy	20,946	13.18	18.95	1,895	9.80	73,000	38.52	253.51
Staples	7,166	3.64	3.82	1,300	5.30	26,780	20.60	258.18
CompUSA	4,800	4.35	1.07	225	21.30	5,850	26.00	820.51
Radio Shack	4,577	-4.17	-2.32	7,213	0.70	17,311	2.40	275.89
Barnes and Noble	3,917	4.48	6.03	886	4.20	15,200	17.16	246.64
Bed Bath & Beyond	3,665	25.17	22.6	490	6.00	17,255	35.21	169.69
Michaels	2,856	12.84	11.69	770	3.30	15,900	20.65	159.18
Linens 'n Things	2,185	19.79	15.85	391	4.70	13,607	34.80	134.05
Jo-Ann Stores	1,682	7.13	10.00	919	1.80	15,435	16.80	108.97
Pier 1 Imports	1,677	13.46	9.31	1,008	1.70	9,475	9.40	176.99
Dick's Sporting Goods	1,273	18.42	16.16	141	9.00	6,807	48.28	187.01
Famous Footwear	1,075	2.97	4.81	918	1.20	6,200	6.75	173.39
Franks Nursery & Crafts	315	-15.09	-9.36	170	1.90	6,035	35.50	52.50

Top Off Price Apparel Chains

TJX Companies	$11,981	11.88	10.15	1,559	$7.70	53,826	34.53	$222.59
Ross Stores	3,531	18.21	12.16	507	7.00	29,400	57.99	120.10
Burlington Coat Factory	2,605	7.25	8.29	317	8.20	25,700	81.07	101.36
Men's Wearhouse	1,295	1.73	8.16	575	2.30	3,198	5.56	404.94
Dress Barn	717	3.17	5.26	754	1.00	5,340	7.08	134.27
Factory 2U	535	-7.76	12.19	243	2.20	3,645	15.00	146.78
Loehmann's	349	8.05	-4.48	44	7.90	1,100	25.00	317.27
One Price Clothing Store	332	-2.35	1.91	597	0.60	2,209	3.70	150.29
Filene's Basement	303	3.41	n/a	20	15.20	800	40.00	378.75

Top Wholesale Chains

Costco	$38,762	11.39	9.82	374	$103.60	51,238	137.00	$756.51
Sam's Club	31,702	7.85	8.93	525	60.40	65,747	125.23	482.20
BJ's Wholesale Club	5,860	12.20	15.33	140	41.90	14,868	106.20	394.14

*The Fact Book (2003, pp. 16, 28, 34, 36 & 37).

**Compound Annual Growth Rate

Table 2.5
Representative Data Set: Measures of retail productivity. *

	Sales (in millions)	% Change in Sales	Earnings (in millions)	# of Stores	Sales/Store (in millions)	Total Sq. Ft. (in thousands)	Sq. Ft/Store (in thousands)	Sales/Sq. Ft.
Top Upscale Department Store Chains								
Federated Department Stores	$15,435	−1.45	$818	450	$34.30	83,633	185.85	184.56
May Department Stores	13,491	−2.80	618	867	15.56	78,695	90.77	171.43
Dillard's	7,911	−3.00	(398)	333	23.76	56,700	170.27	139.52
Nordstrom	5,975	6.10	$90	166	35.99	18,428	111.01	324.23
Saks Fifth Avenue	5,911	−2.60	$24	356	16.60	32,800	92.13	180.21
Neiman Marcus	2,948	−2.20	100	35	84.23	6,142	175.49	479.97
Marshall Field's	2,691	−3.13	135	64	42.05	14,845	231.95	181.27
Belk	2,242	0.30	84	214	10.48	n/a	n/a	n/a
Top Apparel Specialty Chains*								
Gap	$14,454	4.40	$478	4,353	$3.32	37,252	8.56	388.01
Limited Brands	8,445	0.30	502	4,036	2.09			
Foot Locker	4,509	3.00	144	3,625	1.24			
Ross Stores	3,531	18.20	201	507	6.96			
Abercrombie & Fitch	1,596	16.90	195	597	2.67			
Talbots	1,595	−1.10	121	895	1.78			
American Eagle	1,463	6.70	89	864	1.69			
Ann Taylor	1,380	6.30	80	588	2.35			
Goody's Family Clothing	1,193	0.10	8	332	3.59			
Famous Footwear	1,075	2.90	46	918	1.17			
Ralph Lauren	1,001	7.80	n/a	n/a	n/a			
Stage Stores	876	2.30	54	354	2.47			
J. Crew	766	−1.50	(41)	194	3.95			
Gymboree	547	0.25	22	583	0.94			
Chico's FAS	531	40.50	67	368	1.44			
Other Retailers								
Spiegel	$2,650	−13.90	$(500)	560	$4.73			
Williams-Sonoma	2,361	13.10	124	478	4.94			
Linens 'n Things	2,185	19.80	69	391	5.59			
Home Shopping Network	1,900	11.80	n/a	n/a	n/a			
Pier 1 Imports	1,755	13.30	129	1074	1.63			
JoAnn Stores	1,682	7.10	45	918	1.83			
L.L.Bean	1,150	3.60	n/a	n/a	n/a			

*Based on *Stores* (2003) and retailers' Web sites.

Table 2.6

Representative Data Set: Sales by merchandise category and class. *

Apparel Category Sales (in millions)			Home/Hardlines (H/H) Category Sales in (millions)		
Category/Class	Sales	% Apparel Sales	Category/Class	Sales	% H/H Sales
Total Sales Women's Wear	$24,909	37.91	Total Sales Housewares	$30,918	39.88
tops	8,430	12.83	cookware, accessories	6,258	8.07
dresses, skirts, suits	4,845	7.37	small electrics	5,642	7.28
bottoms	4,548	6.92	jewelry, watches	4,517	5.83
intimate apparel	4,027	6.13	soaps, cleansers	3,593	4.63
active wear	1,599	2.43	tabletop	3,486	4.50
outerwear	600	0.91	plastic ware storage	2,352	3.03
miscellaneous	860	1.31	paper goods	1,866	2.41
			vacuum cleaners, floors	1,312	1.69
Total Sales Men's Wear	$15,145	23.05	picture frames, art	711	0.92
tops	4,919	7.49	giftware	412	0.53
bottoms	3,875	5.90	major appliances	126	0.16
furnishings	2,586	3.94	miscellaneous	643	0.83
active wear	1,398	2.13	Total Sales Hardware	$21,923	28.28
outerwear	991	1.51	lawn & garden	6,621	8.54
suits, sportcoats	922	1.40	RTA furniture	3,385	4.37
miscellaneous	454	0.69	paint, wallpaper	2,869	3.70
			batteries, flashlights	1,296	1.67
Total Sales Infant's Wear	$5,659	8.61	building supplies	1,215	1.57
boys	2,940	4.47	electrical supplies	897	1.16
girls	2,719	4.14	hand tools	754	0.97
			power tools	733	0.95
Total Sales Boys' Wear	$5,072	7.72	security, hardware	712	0.92
tops	1,874	2.85	fasteners	650	0.84
bottoms	1,127	1.72	plumbing supplies	633	0.82
furnishings	780	1.19	heating supplies	308	0.40
active wear	722	1.10	lighting fixtures	293	0.38
outerwear	383	0.58	miscellaneous	1,557	2.01
suits, sportcoats	46	0.07	Total Sales Home Fashions	$15,031	19.39
miscellaneous	140	0.21	bedding	3,229	4.17
			bed covers	1,807	2.33
Total Sales Girls' Wear	$4,196	6.39	sewing goods, fabrics	1,798	2.32
tops	1,008	1.53	bath goods	1,792	2.31
bottoms	799	1.22	draperies/curtains	1,541	1.99
intimate apparel	651	0.99	crafts/yarns	1,503	1.94
dresses, skirts	581	0.88	shades, blinds	1,422	1.83
active wear	498	0.76	rugs	582	0.75
outerwear	309	0.47	kitchen textiles	491	0.63
miscellaneous	350	0.53	table linens	367	0.47
			window treatments	149	0.19
Total Sales Shoes	$5,000	7.61	miscellaneous	350	0.45
Total Sales Hosiery	$3,066	4.67	Total Sales Auto Accessories	$9,647	12.44
Total Sales Accessories	$2,658	4.05	motor oil	2,366	3.05
			accessories	1,302	1.68
Total Apparel Sales	$65,705	100.00	car stereo	1,004	1.30
			parts	962	1.24
			filters	720	0.93
			batteries	664	0.86
			antifreeze	575	0.74
			waxes, polishes	558	0.72
			ignition electrical	488	0.63
			chemical additives	392	0.51
			DIY books	57	0.07
			miscellaneous	559	0.72
			Total H/H Sales	$77,519	100.00

* *The Fact Book* (2003, pp. 20 & 24).

Table 2.7

Representative Data Set: Major categories and classes of merchandise and measures merchandising success for mass retailers. ＊

Categories and Classes	Sales (in millions)	% Gross Margin	$ Gross Margin (in millions)	Inventory Turn	GMROI＊＊
Home/Hardlines (27.72%)	$77,519	18–35	$20,543		
Housewares	30,918	28–32	9,275	3.2–3.7	1.52
Hardware	21,923	28–33	6,687	2.4–2.8	1.18
Home fashions	15,031	30–35	4,885	2.6–2.9	1.37
Auto accessories	9,647	18–25	2,074	3.2–3.9	1.07
Apparel (23.49%)	$65,705	22–48	$23,654		
Women's wear	24,909	33–38	8,843	4.0–4.5	2.29
Men's wear	15,145	30–35	4,922	3.9–4.3	1.93
Infants' wear	5,659	24–30	1,528	3.5–3.9	1.33
Boys' wear	5,072	22–35	1,446	3.2–3.8	1.78
Shoes	5,000	35–40	1,875	2.5–2.8	1.71
Girls' wear	4,196	28–34	1,301	2.6–3.0	1.29
Hosiery	3,066	30–35	996	3.0–3.6	1.65
Accessories	2,658	40–48	1,170	3.0–3.6	2.60
Entertainment (19.14%)	$53,517	14–34	$10,168		
Consumer electronics	16,519	14–20	2,808	2.8–3.4	0.57
Toys	11,591	24–30	3,130	2.5–2.8	0.95
Sporting goods	9,551	23–28	2,436	2.2–2.7	0.87
Stationery/greeting cards	8,461	32–48	3,384	3.0–5.0	2.82
Photo goods	5,500	15–20	963	4.6–5.2	1.00
Books/magazines	1,895	22–28	474	3.3–4.0	1.28
Health & Beauty (8.01%)	$22,394	13–28	$4,815	3.2–7.8	1.11
Food/Beverages (5.98%)	$16,736	10–48	$4,853		
Food/beverages	7,738	15–22	1,432	6.6–7.4	1.41
Candy	5,135	15–21	924	6.1–6.6	1.36
Tobacco	1,988	10–16	258	11.4–12.4	1.51
Pet supplies	1,875	25–35	563	4.8–5.4	2.18
Food in Super Centers	$40,920	25–38	$12,890		
Total Sales by Major Departments	$279,666	27.30	$76,349		

＊ *The Fact Book* (2001 & 2003).

＊＊Gross Margin Return on Investment

Table 2.8

Representative Data Set: Sales per square foot related measures for selected categories and classes. *

Category/Class	Sales Area in Sq.Ft.	Sales per Sq. Ft.	% of Total Sq. Ft.
Apparel			
Women's wear	8,978	$243	10.0
Men's wear	5,102	261	5.7
Shoes	2,372	185	2.6
Boys' wear	2,210	202	2.5
Infant's wear	2,067	242	2.3
Girls' wear	1,832	201	2.0
Jewelry & watches	941	425	1.0
Accessories	937	248	1.0
Hosiery	696	392	0.8
Home/Hardlines			
Home fashions	5,601	$240	6.2
Cleaners, paper, plastics	3,853	173	4.3
Auto accessories	2,665	318	3.0
Lawn & garden	2,362	239	2.6
Hardware	1,658	471	1.8
Paint & wallpaper	1,037	223	1.2
RTA furniture	924	318	1.0
Small electrics	848	596	0.9
Giftware	674	53	0.7
Entertainment			
Sporting goods	3,157	$243	3.5
Toys	2,657	382	3.0
Stationery/greeting cards	1,726	413	1.9
Consumer electronics	1,075	776	1.2
CDs/tapes	802	564	0.9
Photo goods	545	876	0.6
Luggage	462	119	0.5
Books/magazines	182	868	0.2
Food & Beverage			
Food/beverage	1,650	$393	1.8
Candy	537	818	0.6
Pet supplies	379	442	0.4
Tobacco	106	1,712	0.1
Health & Beauty			
Drugs/cosmetics	2,771	$690	3.1

*Based on an average, full line, mass merchandise store with 90,000 square feet and $27 million in sales.

These data provide important information for merchandise plans in terms of the relative rate of sale of different merchandise classes. Finally, another table presents measures of merchandising success, including sales, percent gross margin, dollar gross margin, inventory turn, and gross margin return on investment presented by merchandise category and class. These measures are extremely hard to find in any sort of comparative manner, so they are presented here as an indicator of merchandising reality.

◉ *Integrated Learning Activity 2.6.3*

Get acquainted with Sourcing Simulator, Student Version

Sourcing Simulator (SS), Student Version runs with Windows 95, 98, ME, NT, 2000, and XP. SS includes five different merchandising folders: Buyer's Plan, Consumer Demand, Cost Data, Markdowns/Premiums, and Sourcing Strategy. Based on the merchandise plan for a particular merchandise group, it fundamentally allows the operator to input the planned quantity of merchandise; an assortment plan according to style, size, and color; a pricing plan including merchandise cost, markups, and markdowns; and a delivery plan including choice of QR or traditional delivery. SS simulates in-store shopping behavior, tracks the prescribed merchandise assortment at the SKU level throughout the selling period, and generates an analysis with over 40 quantitative and financial measures of productivity.

SS includes a complete default data set representing typical quantities, costs, and expenses associated with planning and sourcing apparel. It is possible then to insert a few numbers that represent a particular retailer and merchandise group, use the default data set for the rest of the numbers, and very quickly simulate the potential outcomes. Then you can go back and change one or two numbers to test modifications in the merchandise plan. SS allows testing merchandise plans as you would a scientific chemistry experiment — you can hold all variables constant except the one you want to test. Thus, the potential outcome of one change can be assessed. This is impossible using data in the real retail world, but very useful when trying to understand the relationships among variables in a merchandise plan.

Modeling in-store shopping behavior

SS "simulates in-store shopping behavior…." Consumer behavior in the retail store is modeled as a stochastic process. The program generates a flow of customers that arrive according to a nonstationary Poisson statistical process. The Poisson process results in a "probability distribution useful in describing the number of events that will occur in a specific period of time" (McClave & Benson, 1988, p. 235) or in this case, the flow of purposive and browsing customers during a selling period. The purposive customer has a specific piece of merchandise in mind, while a browsing customer is gathering information for future use but might be tempted for an impulse purchase. The arrival rate of customers is allowed to change from week to week to reflect seasonality. When a customer arrives, s/he either has an item in mind to purchase or s/he browses. The customer is randomly assigned a desired SKU by style, color, and size from discrete probability distributions which describe the consumer preferences. If the desired SKU is in stock, the customer purchases the item. If it is out of stock, the customer may either choose another item or leave (King & Poindexter, 1991). Figure 2.2 illustrates this process.

Because of the Poisson process with random assignment of SKUs to purposive customers, each simulation can create a slightly different output, a very realistic scenario every retailer faces. However, when testing particular merchandising decisions, the SS will perform multiple replications with the same input and provide an average of the results increasing the validity of output. Ten replications are the default for the seasonal model and three is the default for the basic model. (If you want to see the effects of the random variable on the outputs of SS after you run the Simulator, click View and Details of Last Run.)

POS data are collected each week by the Simulator based on the behavior illustrated in the diagram. If the SS is in traditional sourcing mode, reorders are placed based on the original merchandise plan. If the SS is in quick response mode, reorders are placed based on re-estimation of demand based on sales. Upon completion of the simulation, POS data, together with inventory levels, stock outs, and other information collected by the simulation, is used to calculate the performance measures that are printed in an output table.

Operate SS

1. Load SS according to directions on your CD. Unless you tell it to go elsewhere, SS will become a part of your Programs list. The name of the file is SSv12se. Put your cursor on file SSv12se and you will have two options: Sourcing Simulator Help and SSv12se. Click Sourcing Simulator Help.
2. Read the Help screens beginning at the top of the list. This will help you understand what SS can do and how to run it. If you want an operating manual for SS, print out the Help screens. Close SS Help.

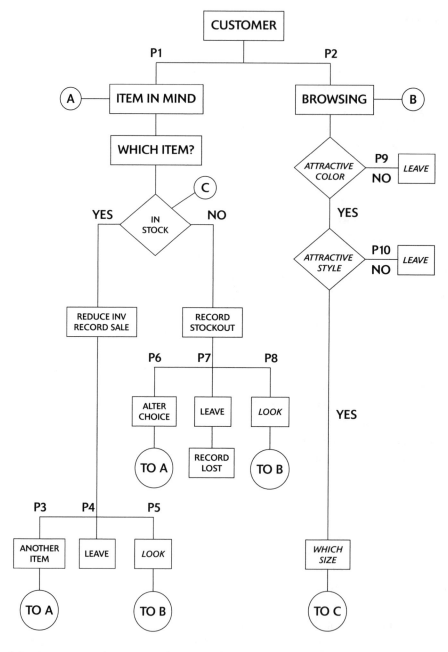

Figure 2.2   Sourcing Simulator in-store shopping behavior branching diagram (Poindexter, 1991, p. 5).

3. Go back to the Programs list and click on SSv12se. Click on Seasonal Model.

4. Get acquainted with the program by clicking on the folders and looking at inputs in the default data set. Try changing numbers to see how SS responds. Be sure to read the error messages and figure out how to correct problems.

5. In the header above the folders, click Simulate. Click the tab that comes down and you will have the opportunity to name the simulation run. Use a name that relates to what is being tested in this simulation as well as your own name. If you are testing assortment volume, the name could be "low volume, Grace," then your simulation activity is identified as your work. Say OK and you can view SS's lengthy but very interesting list of outputs.

6. Print the inputs by reaching back to the main screen and clicking File and then Print Current Inputs. Click View and then Outputs, then print outputs.

7. Close the Seasonal Model. Do not save your inputs or outputs. Reopen the Seasonal Model and the default data set will be restored.

8. Open the Basics Model. Explore it as you did the Seasonal Model, including running the simulation and printing inputs and outputs. How do inputs differ between Seasonal Model and Basics Model? How do outputs differ?

9. You are not expected to understand the meaning of all of the inputs and all of the outputs right away. The series of assignments using SS will gradually expand your understanding of the merchandising process and the variables that provide a foundation for decision making. SS will help you enhance your critical thinking and the understanding of relationships among inputs and outputs.

References

Abernathy, F. H., Dunlop, J. T., Hammond, J.W., & Weil, D. (1999). *A stitch in time: Lean retailing and the transformation of manufacturing—Lessons from the apparel and textile industries.* New York: Oxford University Press.

Anderson, P. E. (1982). Marketing, strategic planning and the theory of a firm. *Journal of Marketing*, 46:15–26.

Anderson Consulting. (1994). *Quick response.* Charlotte, SC: Arthur Anderson & Co.

Barr, R. G., & Tagg, J. (1995, November/December). From teaching to learning—A new paradigm for undergraduate education. *Change,* 13–25.

Blackburn, J. D. (1991). The quick-response movement in the apparel industry: A case study in time-compressing supply chains. In J. D. Blackburn (ed.), *Time-based competition: The next battleground in American manufacturing.* Homewood, IL: Irwin.

Bonsor, K. (2004). How smart labels will work. *How Stuff Works* (electronics.howstuffworks.com/smart-label2.htm). Accessed June 9, 2004.

Cosbey, S., & Kunz, G. I. (1995). A failure of merchandising technology innovation. Unpublished paper. Ames, IA: Iowa State University.

Divita, L.R., & Cassill, N. L. (2002). Strategic partnerships in the domestic textile complex: Exploring suppliers' perspectives. *Clothing and Textile Research Journal*, 20(3):156–166.

The Fact Book. (2003, July). *Retail merchandiser.* New York: VNU Business Publications.

The Fact Book. (2001). *Retail merchandiser.* New York: VNU Business Publications.

Fisher, M. L., Hammond, J. H., Obermeyer, W. R., & Raman, A. (1994, May/June). Making supply meet demand in an uncertain world. *Harvard Business Review*, 72:83–93.

Fralix, M., & Off, J. (1993). A changing soft goods industry: A look at today and tomorrow. *ITAA Proceedings 1993*, 44–47.

Galbraith, J. K. (1978). *The new industrial state* (3rd ed.). Boston: Houghton Mifflin.

Glock, R. E., & Kunz, G. I. (2000). *Apparel manufacturing: Sewn product analysis* (3rd ed.). Englewood Cliffs, NJ: Prentice Hall.

Goldman, S. L., Nagel, R. N., & Preiss, K. (1995). *Agile competitors and virtual organizations: Strategies for enriching the consumer.* New York: Van Nostrand Reinhold.

Hammond, J. H. (1993). Quick response in retail/manufacturing channels. In S. P. Bradley, J. A. Hausman, & R. L. Nolan (Eds.). *Globalization, technology, and competition: The fusion of computers and telecommunications in the 1990s.* Boston: Harvard Business School Press.

Hartnett, M. (1993, September). Buyers: Endangered species? *Stores*, 75:53–55.

Hotsheet (2003, July). *Retail Merchandiser*, 11.

Houston, F. S. (1986, April). The marketing concept: What it is and what it is not. *Journal of Marketing*, 50:81–87.

Hunter, A. (1990). *Quick response in apparel manufacturing: A survey of the American scene.* Manchester, England: The Textiles Institute.

JDA Software Group, Inc. (2003). Arthur Planning: Building optimized plans with an eye on your bottom line (www.jda.com/arthur.asp). Accessed August 11, 2003.

Kincade, D. H., & Cassill, N. L. (1993). North Carolina apparel manufacturers implementation of quick response. *Clothing & Textiles Research Journal*, 11(3): 23–30.

King, R., & Poindexter, M. L. (1991, September). A simulation model for retail apparel buying. North Carolina State Univeristy Industrial Engineering Technical Report #90-9.

Knill, B. (1994). Quick response: Slow but inevitable [Automatic Data Collection Management Section]. *Industry Week*, 243(16):8–15.

Kunz, G. I. (1991, May). EDI, JIT, FM, MM, QA, UPS, VAM: The magnitude of change for a new socio-technical interface. *[TC]² Report*, 6–7.

Kunz, G. I. (1995). Behavioral theory of the apparel firm: A beginning. *Clothing and Textiles Research Journal*, 13(4):252–261.

Kurt Salmon Associates. (1994). *The quick response handbook.* Princeton, NJ: Author.

Lowson, B., King, R., & Hunter, A. (1999). *Quick response: Managing the supply chain to meet customer demand.* New York: John Wiley and Sons.

McClave, J. T., & Benson, J. T. (1988). *Statistics for business and economics.* San Fransisco: Dellen Publishing Co.

McGregor, D. (1960). *The human side of enterprise.* New York: McGraw-Hill.

O'Neal, C., & Bertrand, K. (1991). *Developing a winning JIT marketing strategy.* Englewood Cliffs, NJ: Prentice Hall.

Pacey, A. (1983). *The culture of technology.* Oxford, England: Basil Blackball.

Poindexter, M. (1991, January). *Apparel retail model version 2.0 operating manual* (prepared for CRAFTM). Raleigh, NC: North Carolina State University.

Reda, S. (1994, April). Floor-ready merchandise. *Stores,* 76:41–44.

Reda, S. (2001, May). After 15 years and ownership changes, merchandising software still draws retail fans. *Stores,* 28–30.

Riddle, E. J., Bradbard, D. A., Thomas, J. B., & Kincade, K. H. (1999). The role of electronic data interchange in quick response. *Journal of Marketing and Management,* 3(2):133–146.

Rogers, E. M. (1983). *Diffusion of innovations* (3rd ed.). New York: Free Press.

Scheller, H. P. (1993). Apparel quality through the perception of apparel production managers and operators. Unpublished masters thesis, Iowa State University, Ames.

Schon, D. A. (1967). *The process of invention, technology and change.* New York: Delacorte Press.

Sears' merchandise allocation system helps spur turnaround. (October, 1993). *Chain Store Age Executive,* 69(10):20–23, 26–31.

Sheridan, J. H. (1994, March 21). A vision of agility. *Industry Week* [Supplement], 243:43–46.

Stores. (2003). (www.stores.org/archives). Accessed August 27, 2003.

Tappscott, D., & Caston, A. (1993). *Paradigm shift: The new promise of information technology.* New York: McGraw-Hill.

3

Merchandising

Systems

Learning Objectives

- Introduce multi-channel merchandising systems.

- Explore the Taxonomy of Apparel Merchandising System (TAMS).

- Examine measures of success.

- Relate fundamentals of income statements to merchandise planning and controlling processes.

M erchandising is a function performed by every firm engaged in business-to-business commerce and in selling goods to ultimate consumers. Business-to-business transactions are assumed to be at wholesale prices while sale of goods to ultimate consumers are at retail prices, but regardless of the stage in the trade matrix, every firm has to plan, develop, and present product lines. The ultimate goal, whether the merchandising is taking place in a manufacturing or retailing environment, is to put products in the hands of consumers at prices that make the whole process profitable.

Business-to-Business Relationships—Wholesaling

Historically, business-to-business processes have been heavily dependent on visits by sales representatives who carried sales samples and catalogs representing a product line or lines. A successful sale resulted in a written order mailed in by the sales rep. A complementary event was a periodic and/or annual wholesale market where dozens or even hundreds of vendors had showrooms or set up displays of product lines. Their business customers and potential customers who attended the markets saw new styles, compared models, and evaluated their potential compatibility with their business needs. An apparel business example is the Bobbin Show where textile materials, software, and machinery vendors displayed their wares for purchase by apparel manufacturers. Another example is retail technology shows where dozens of purveyors of software designed to meet retailers' needs displayed their systems. Yet another example is the many apparel wholesale markets that are held in major cities across the United States where apparel manufacturers displayed their lines for purchase by retailers. Many of these wholesale markets continue to take place on a biannual, annual, semiannual, or multi-annual basis.

However, the Internet is changing the marketplace and replacing many traditional business-to-business transactions. The growth of the Internet stimulated coining of the term "B to B," representing wholesale business-to-business transactions. Web sites make it possible for customers to view the product line every time a product is modified or a new product is introduced. It is not necessary to design, print, and distribute a new catalog and/or retrain sales reps to make customers aware of new products. Orders can be placed instantaneously and tracked in their fulfillment. Weeks of time between order placement and delivery of goods have been eliminated and sales reps do not have to be paid a commission on Internet sales. Sales reps are still employed, and wholesale markets with products physically on display are still used, but the numbers and importance of both have declined (Barth, 2001).

Business to Ultimate Consumer Transactions—Retailing

Retailing is selling goods and services to ultimate consumers. A merchant with a cart full of vegetables parked at the side of the road is a retailer as is a super store covering hundreds of thousands of square feet with 100 checkout lanes. Regardless of the size of the retail "store," product lines have to be merchandised. The vegetable merchant planned what vegetables to plant in the garden and when to plant them. He or she developed the plants by cultivating, watering, and feeding them. When perfectly ripe, the vegetables were picked, washed, and finally presented on a colorful blanket in the cart at the side of the road. The super store retailer also had to plan, develop, and present product lines. The processes and priorities differ from the vegetable merchant, but the same merchandising principles apply.

Retailing is the second largest business in the United States, both in number of establishments and number of employees. With more than 1.6 million establishments ranging from automobile dealers and gas stations to apparel and grocery stores, retailers employed more than 22 million people, nearly 20 percent of the U.S. workforce, and generated more than $3 trillion in retail sales annually. Single store businesses account for over 95 percent of all U.S. retailers, but generate less than 50 percent of all retail store sales (Retail trade market USA, 2002). Over 80 percent of all retail companies employ fewer than 20 workers and most of these operate one or two stores. Fifty-six percent of retailers reported profitable online operations in 2001, up from 48 percent in 2000 (Deloitte & Touche, 2002).

A complete description of a retail organization usually requires terms related to assortment definitions, price positioning, business organization, and presentation methods:

- Assortment definitions—boutique, broadline, category killer, department, private label, specialty, variety

- Price positioning—discount, closeout, off price, one price, outlet, warehouse, wholesale

- Business organization—chain, manufacturer owned, mass, retailer owned, vertically integrated

- Presentation methods—big box, brick-and-mortar, catalog, door-to-door

- Miscellaneous—Web site, kiosk, online, party plan, or in case of the vegetable merchant, a cart

Assortment definitions relate to the variety and quantity of goods offered. Price positioning terms relate primarily to communicating low price to customers. Business organization relates to ownership and business structure in the trade matrix. Presentation methods are the means used to show the merchandise to the ultimate consumer. In spite of ongoing technology innovations, brick-and-mortar retailers are expected to continue to dominate the retail sector (Johnson & Longo, 2001). Figure 3.1 lists and describes many of the types of retailers that operate in today's consumer markets. As with most areas of business, the onset of online retailing is having a huge impact on business methods and customer shopping methods. See Case 3.1.

Category killers are big-box retailers that specialize in a wide variety of products in a few merchandise categories. Examples are Borders, Home Depot, and The Sports Authority.

Catalog retailers present their merchandise assortments in printed form delivered to customers' mailboxes. Orders may be placed by mail, telephone, or Internet and merchandise arrives at the customer's door in a few days. Victoria's Secret, Roaman's, and L.L.Bean are examples.

Convenience retailers are small stores in neighborhood locations carrying a small assortment of regularly used auto accessories, beverages, candy, groceries, magazines, pizza, snack foods, and other items. They are often associated with gasoline pumps and/or car washes. Examples include Casey's General Store, Kum & Go, and Kwik Trip.

Department store retailers operate relatively large brick-and-mortar stores offering multiple categories of merchandise usually including apparel for men, women, and children; bed and bath textiles and accessories; kitchen equipment; window treatments; and home furnishings. Sales associates may be available to assist with merchandise selection. Dillard's, Macy's, and Marshall Field's are examples.

Internet/online retailers offer merchandise for sale through a computer network. Types include online catalogs and online auctions. Customers view the merchandise assortment on a computer and place an order via computer, telephone, or mail. The merchandise arrives at the customer's door in a few days. Amazon.com is an example.

Manufacturer outlets offer primarily distressed merchandise (last season, retailer returns, overruns, sales samples, second quality) at less than regular prices. Liz Claiborne, Nike, and Levi Strauss are examples.

Manufacturer owned retailers offer complete assortments of their own product lines at regular prices. Calvin Klein and Ralph Lauren are examples.

Mass merchandise stores are departmentalized retail establishments utilizing many self-service techniques to sell merchandise from the following categories: hard goods, apparel, and other soft goods; health and beauty care products; and other general merchandise with broad appeal across income ranges, ethnic groups, occupations, and lifestyles. Wal-Mart, Target, and ShopKo are examples.

Retailer outlets are operated as clearance centers of last season's and last year's excess merchandise for the retailers department, specialty, catalog, and/or Internet stores. Examples include Spiegel, Saks Fifth Avenue, Lands' End, and J.Crew.

Specialty boutiques are shops or parts of stores that specialize in merchandise that is new and different or where related items from different merchandise categories are gathered together to fulfill special customer requirements.

Specialty retailers offer a large selection of a limited line of consumer goods usually with target customers narrowly defined by demographics and/or lifestyle variables. Victoria's Secret and Brooks Brothers are examples of multi-unit specialty chain retailers.

Warehouse/wholesale clubs are self-service environments where customers pay an annual membership fee of about $35. A primary customer appeal is national brands at low prices. Costco, Sam's Club, and BJ's Wholesale Club are examples.

Figure 3.1 Types of retailers in today's consumer goods markets.

📁   Case 3.1 *Retailers reap rewards of selling goods online.* *   📁

With sales stalled by a sluggish economy, many of the nation's retailers are finding growth opportunities in an unlikely place — online. With over 70 million Internet users around the globe, and over a million more joining each month, the Internet offers retailers a potentially huge market. Started by the U.S. military during the Cold War era and taken over by scientists and academics, the Internet rapidly outgrew its image as a home for computer geeks. By making careful investments in their online businesses and by responding quickly to the changing demands of Web shoppers, many established retail chains have weathered the dot-com bust to collectively generate billions of dollars in sales over the Internet each year.

Some merchants have learned to reach customers who do not live near their stores. Others have found a new channel for getting rid of excess inventory. Still more have discovered a way to reach customers who venture away from home less frequently in the wake of the September 11 attacks and the war in Iraq.

As merchants fine-tuned their online operations, 51.3 million Internet users visited online shopping sites between November 25 and December 23, 2001. Online holiday sales increased 50 percent in 2002 over 2001. Internet sales were expected to jump 26 percent in 2003, accounting for 4.5 percent of total retail sales. By 2007, the portion of retail spending conducted online was expected to reach 5 percent, according to a study by Forrester Research and Shop.org, an e-commerce trade group.

Senior executives tend to get intimately involved in Internet operations because they see it as a growth strategy. Although the Internet remains a relatively tiny source of sales for big chains such as JCPenney, Pier 1 Imports, and Neiman Marcus, executives say it still presents an opportunity for expansion and increased profits. Alongside pioneers such as Amazon.com, the retailers that have best adapted to the Internet are established merchants that invested conservatively in online operations after finding logical reasons to migrate to the Web. For example, JCPenney, Neiman Marcus, and Lands' End applied their know-how from the catalog industry to reach customers online.

Lands' End is globalizing its e-commerce presence for potential double-digit sales growth. Web sites were launched for France, Italy, and Ireland during the latter half of 2000. These were the first markets in which Lands' End had not already established catalog operations. They already had Web sites for Japan, the United Kingdom, and Germany. The UK facilities are being used to service the new European markets.

Meanwhile, Pier 1 shrugged off the pressure from Wall Street in the late 1990s and took its time to develop Internet strategy. Pier 1's Web site opened for business in mid-2000,

(continued)

two months after the NASDAQ stock market began its steep descent to signal the end of the initial Internet boom. The relatively late start shielded Pier 1 from the financial pain that was thrust upon companies that invested too much, too soon, based on industry predictions that never materialized. As a result, the chain did not have to scale back its commitment to the Web, according to Steve Woodward, senior manager of Internet operations at Fort Worth-based Pier 1.

Other stalwart chains got off to a less successful start. Wal-Mart dissolved a partnership with a California venture capital firm that was supposed to help the retailer become a powerhouse on the Web. Borders enlisted Amazon.com to handle its online book business. Macy's parent, Federated Department Stores, drastically scaled back its Internet offerings and abandoned a business that shipped Web orders for chains.

U.S online sales were expected to reach $96 billion in 2003 with at least 7 merchandise categories showing 40 percent growth, according to the Forrester Research and Shop.org study. Home goods were among the products expected to show the strongest growth, working in Pier 1's favor. Americans shifted more of their discretionary spending toward housewares and furnishings, perhaps in an attempt to make their homes more comforting.

*Based on Landy (2003) and Barth (2001).

 ## Learning Activity 3.1

Read Figure 3.1 and Case 3.1 very carefully.

1. Every retailer mentioned in Case 3.1 is a chain organization. Retailer chains have headquarters that include most of the executive, merchandising, marketing, and QR constituencies. They operate dozens and sometimes thousands of individual stores. Why might retail chains be more likely to get involved in online sales?
2. What benefits might single unit retailers realize from online sales? What costs might be exorbitant for single unit retailers?
3. According to the BTAF (Behavioral Theory of the Apparel Firm), what advantages could accrue from having top executives closely involved in Internet operations?
4. What advantages might catalog retailers have in their involvement in online retailing?
5. Traditional department stores have been experiencing declines in business. From your perspective, what might be causes of their reduction in customer appeal?

Merchandising in Multi-Channel Environments

The term *trade channel* has multiple uses and meanings. However, for our purposes here, it is defined as the means manufacturers and retailers use to present merchandise to their customers. As described earlier, historically, apparel manufacturers used primarily two channels to reach their retail customers: traveling sales representatives and wholesale markets. Now most have added an Internet presence.

During the last half of the 20th century, traditional department and some specialty stores had multi-floor buildings set up with the merchandise display fixtures, trained sales associates, and fitting rooms to entice customers to view their merchandise. For the most part, a retail firm focused on brick-and-mortar stores in the department store channel or the specialty store channel. Other firms were in the catalog retail channel. As the 20th century came to a close, more and more retailers operated in multi-channel environments. Many now have the brick-and-mortar stores, a printed catalog operation, retailer outlet stores, and online retail sales. They also are likely to be vertically integrated into private label product development. These channels may all carry similar merchandise but not necessarily the same merchandise or the same prices. Thus, the process of planning, developing, and presenting product lines must take place at both manufacturing and retailing levels and for every channel that reaches for their customers. The merchandise plans are certainly related, but must be customized for each channel to effectively serve customers and result in profitability for the manufacturer or retailer.

The reality is that shopping has changed. Most customers :

- are better educated and have greater access to information, thus have greater expectations from products they purchase.
- enjoy media symbols representing common people rather than glitzy/glamorous types.
- have a newfound craving for goods that afford excellent value and great design — more important than traditional status symbols.
- are less likely to shop as a leisure activity (browsing shoppers) and are more likely to be purposive shoppers with specific products in mind.
- shop less often, spend less time, and spend more per shopping trip.
- are less likely to seek out an enclosed regional shopping mall and more likely to choose power strip shopping centers where parking is available and stores carry improved selections within limited merchandise categories.
- have increased willingness to cross-shop retail channels (Seckler, 2002).

Taxonomy of Apparel Merchandising Systems

The **Taxonomy of Apparel Merchandising Systems (TAMS)** was developed as a comprehensive description of elements of a merchandising system—an extended definition of merchandising within the context of the Behavioral Theory of the Apparel Firm. Think of the egg-shaped merchandising portion of the BTAF model presented in Chapter 1. TAMS describes planning, developing, and presenting product lines as merchandisers interact and collaborate with the firm's internal constituencies and with outside coalitions, particularly vendors and customers. TAMS is based on a series of assumptions related to BTAF. Consider Figure 3.2.

Now take a few minutes to examine TAMS in Figure 3.3. The shaded portions of TAMS detail elements of the merchandising process related to planning, developing, and presenting product lines. These elements are commonly regarded as merchandising responsibilities. The white segments of TAMS represent areas closely associated with merchandising process, but usually not direct responsibilities of merchandisers. In small firms, a single merchandiser may be responsible for the shaded portions of TAMS as well as parts of the white portions. In large firms, a particular merchandiser's job may include only a few elements of one of the shaded portions.

At first glance, TAMS may appear static, but in fact, merchandising is a dynamic process of intense change. Notice the double-ended arrows related to each segment of TAMS. These indicate influence of each segment throughout time. Visualize the TAMS model rolled into a cylinder; the arrows related to line planning circumnavigate the cylinder,

1. Merchandising is a functional constituency of an apparel firm.
2. The apparel firm can be a manufacturer, a retailer, or be vertically integrated.
3. The dynamic merchandising process takes place in the context of a firm's business and financial plans and marketing strategy.
4. The three fundamental components of the merchandising process are line/merchandise planning, line/merchandise development, and line/merchandise presentation.
5. TAMS has vertical and horizontal dimensions; elements located vertically on the model tend to happen simultaneously, while elements located horizontally tend to be sequential.
6. The dimensions of product lines that merchandisers are responsible for include pricing, assortments, styling, and timing.
7. Merchandisers work closely with and may be involved in sourcing materials and production.
8. The merchandising cycle is one year beginning February 1 and ending January 31.
9. A merchandising cycle is divided into several overlapping selling periods depending on the nature of the merchandise and customer demand defined by weeks of sale.

Figure 3.2 Summary of assumptions of the Taxonomy of Apparel Merchandising Systems (TAMS).

reflecting endless change and responsiveness of line plans to influences within and outside the firm. Peer into the center of the cylinder and visualize a spiderweb-like network of electronic data interchange (EDI) and Internet connecting constituencies within the firm, and coalitions outside the firm, with information related to the product line.

The **merchandising cycle** represented by TAMS is 1 year (52 weeks), beginning the first week of February and ending the last week of January. The cycle begins in February because January apparel sales are primarily the clearance of fall and holiday stocks in preparation for the new spring and summer selling periods. A **selling period** is the time period a particular group of merchandise is planned to be available for sale. Traditionally, selling periods were described as selling seasons — spring, summer, early fall, late fall, holiday, and cruise. In many firms, the selling season concept has become more precisely defined as selling periods defined by weeks of sale. For example, at JCPenney, "week 1" is the first week of the merchandising cycle, the first week of February. Thus, certain merchandise groups might be planned for retail sale from week 5 through week 15, that is, four weeks in March, four weeks in April, and two weeks of May. Merchandise groups overlap one another in the merchandise plan to provide adequate variety for customers and a continuous supply of new merchandise.

As a merchandiser, it is common to work on several different selling periods at the same time. As shown in the Line Planning component of TAMS, a merchandiser might be planning delivery and allocation for merchandise to be presented weeks 1 through 12, planning budgets and assortments for merchandise to be presented weeks 13 to 26, and evaluating merchandise mix for merchandise to be offered weeks 27 to 40. This makes for a great deal of variety and challenge in the life of a merchandiser. The merchandising calendar is examined more completely in Chapter 4.

A **product line** consists of a combination of styles that:

- satisfy similar or related customer needs.
- are sold within the targeted price range.
- are marketed with similar strategies.

The terms product line and merchandise line are used interchangeably. Apparel manufacturers and retailers commonly plan, develop, and present two to eight lines a year depending on their fashion focus. A "year" in this case refers to a merchandising cycle that begins in February.

Large apparel firms may have several product lines for each selling period, with each product line marketed at a different price range, under a different label, and targeted to a different market segment. This gives the firm broader market coverage. Each of these lines may have a different merchandise manager.

Line Planning

Marketing Plan	**Evaluate Merchandise Offerings**	**Forecast Merchandise Offerings**	**Plan Merchandise Budgets**
Position the firm Create marketing Plan advertising/ promotions	Categories Classifications Subclassifications Groups	Sales history Selling periods Product types Size ranges Price points	Sales Reductions Required merchandise Prices Initial markup Allowable costs

Line Development

Business Plan	**Line Concept**		**Creative Design**

Mission
Goals
Merchandise mix
Fashion emphasis
Policies and practices
Price range(s)
Quality standards
	Synthesize current
	  issues/trends
	• economic
	• social
	• cultural
	• technological
	• demographic
	• lifestyle
	Describe fashion trends
	• line
	• detail
	• silhouette
	• color
	• pattern
	• fit
		Establish line direction
		• color palette
		• styling guidelines
		Describe materials
		• fiber content
		• yarn type
		• fabric structure
		• finishes
		Identify group concepts
		• separates
		• related separates
		• coordinates
		Analyze current line
		• continued styles
		• modified styles
		• new designs
			Develop designs
			• sketches
			• precosting
			• first patterns
			• design specifications
			• fit standards
			• materials descriptions
			Create design prototypes
			Review prototypes
			• styling
			• fit
			• fabric
			• assembly methods
			Revise patterns
			Create prototypes until
			  designs are perfected

Line Presentation

Sourcing Strategy

Make or Buy	**Process**	**Materials**	**Internal**

Finished goods
Materials
Product development
Production
Domestic
International
Global
Full package
Cut/make/trim
	Screen contractors
	Assign styles
	Place initial orders
	Finished goods
	Materials production
	Style assignment
	Manage trade
	  regulations
	Evaluate vendors
		Product characteristics
		Variety
		Prices
		Lead times
		Minimums
		Quality standards
		Specifications
		Performance standards
			Review for adoption
			• line concept
			• image strategy
			• groups and designs
			• applications to line
			  plan
			• design specs and
			  costing
			• pricing strategy
			• visual merchandising

Figure 3.3 Taxonomy of Apparel Merchandising Systems (TAMS): interactive, concurrent, and sequential components defined as planning, developing, and presenting product lines.

Line Planning

Plan Merchandise Assortments
Model stocks
Basic stocks
Automated replenishment

Determine Delivery and Allocation
Sequence delivery
Allocate to stores
Arrange resupply

Analyze and Update Merchandise Plans
Update budgets
Update assortments
Update delivery plans

Line Development

Line Adoption
Determine styles in line
- wholesale finished goods
- product development
Establish list or first prices
Assign styles/sizes/ colors to line plan
Balance assortments
- variety
- volume
- diversity
- allocation
Produce sales/photo/ catalog samples

Technical Design
Perfect styling and fit
Finalize patterns
Test materials
Test assembly methods
Develop style samples
Develop style/quality specifications
- styling
- fit
- materials
- assembly methods
- labeling
- ticketing
Detailed costing
Grade patterns

Line Presentation

Wholesale

Line preview
- line concept
- image strategy
- assortment strategy
- style appeal
- marketing strategy
- pricing strategy
- visual merchandising

Line/style release
- fashion shows
- wholesale markets
- sales presentations
- trunk shows
Customer service

Retail

Types
- specialty
- department
- mass
- off price
- manufacturer's outlet
- catalog
- television
- Internet

Power of appeal
- display space
- fixtures
- lighting
- signage
- labels
- tickets
- pricing strategy
- customer service
- inventory management

Garment Production

Production Planning
Make to order/make to stock
Cut order planning
Marker making
Engineering specifications
Plant layout/startup
Methods development
Training/ergonomics

Assembly and Finishing
Production scheduling
Work study
Quality control
Spreading/cutting
Sewing
Pressing
Finishing

Packaging and Distribution
Labeling/ticketing
Packaging
Hanger or shelf ready
Loading
Shipping
Quality audits

📖 *Learning Activity 3.2*

Taxonomy of Apparel Merchandising Systems (TAMS)

1. What is an assumption?
2. What is the role of assumptions when using and applying the components of TAMS?
3. What is the purpose of TAMS?
4. What are the major components of TAMS? What components are somewhat sequential? What components are somewhat concurrent?
5. How can you visualize TAMS as being dynamic?

Line Planning

As shown in TAMS, **line planning** is a dynamic, ongoing process throughout the merchandising cycle. Notice that elements of line planning are somewhat concurrent with elements of line development. Line planning requires assessment of the present, analysis of the past, and projection for the future. Line plans are based on and integrated with the overall business and marketing plans, as well as information provided by the operations and finance constituencies. The primary elements of the line planning process are evaluate merchandise mix, forecast merchandise offering, plan merchandise budgets, plan merchandise assortment, determine delivery and allocation, and analyze and update merchandise plans.

Evaluating Merchandise Mix and Forecasting Offerings Evaluating merchandise mix requires objective analysis of productivity of merchandise by category, classification, subclassification, and groups. Classification analysis results in establishing priorities for weeks of sale, price points, size ranges, and size standards.

Forecasting merchandise offerings requires evaluation of past selling periods, usually with detailed analysis of the same selling period last year, as well as an examination of the current selling period for any relevant trends. For the past season, planners seek to understand customer spending patterns in relation to merchandise classifications, identification of hot selling merchandise groups and styles, size ranges, and influences of pricing.

Merchandise Budgets and Assortment Plans **Merchandise budgets** identify planned dollar investment by merchandise category or classification, reductions, required merchandise, pricing, initial markup, and allowable costs. Budgets provide a framework for all subsequent decision making. **Assortment plans** may include model stocks, basic stocks, and automated replenishment incorporating number of stock keeping units and volume per stock keeping unit (SKU).

Delivery and allocation plans determine when, what, and how much merchandise will be received where. Merchandise plans are dynamic and constantly must be reviewed and updated to adjust to changing market conditions. Merchandise plans may identify merchandise to be continued in stock, but only provide criteria for the selection of new merchandise to be introduced into the line. The identification of the actual new merchandise is a function of line development.

Line Development

Line development includes the processes required to translate a line plan into real merchandise. The length of time allowed for line development varies greatly from one firm to the next depending on the nature of the merchandise offered and the types of line development processes used. Sometimes the process is highly formalized, with numerous planning meetings involving a merchandising team; in other firms the process may be almost haphazard in nature. The line plan is a guide for line development and is always subject to review. Adjustments are often needed to make the line more marketable, producible, and salable.

If the line will be sold at wholesale, it must be completed in time for presentation to the sales staff before wholesale markets are held. If the firm is vertically integrated and sells all of its merchandise through its own retail outlets, the wholesale selling process is unnecessary. Line development may be completed with a final internal management review. In any case, the line development timeline is determined by when the merchandise must appear on the retail sales floor. The first phase of line development is formulating the line concept. Once this is agreed upon, there are two means of completing line development: finished goods buying/sourcing and/or product development.

Line Concept   A **line concept** includes the look and appeal that contributes to the identity and salability of the line. Synthesizing current issues and trends might include considering positioning of new local, domestic, or international competitors with similar merchandise classifications, as well as economic, social, and cultural influences on fashion trends and potential sales. Establishing line direction is related to trends in color, styling, and fab-rications as interpreted for the firm's target customers. Group concepts are factors that give unanimity to merchandise groups, enabling manufacturers and retailers to sell them together. Group concepts may be communicated by style features, repetition of color or fabric, coordinated print designs, and so forth. Based on group concepts, sales history, and sales forecasts, decisions are made as to which styles from the past season's line should be carried over and which should be replaced. To minimize product development costs and risks associated with introducing new styles, firms must identify high-volume styles that, with no change or minimal change, can continue to be top sellers.

Finished Goods Buying/Sourcing   Retail buyers/merchandisers often travel to **wholesale markets** or work with manufacturers' representatives in their stores to select merchandise from apparel manufacturers' lines. Wholesale markets provide a setting for linking the work of merchandisers at the wholesale level with those at the retail level. **Sales representatives** are often instrumental in developing retail assortments and writing purchase orders.

Merchandise plans provide the framework for developing balanced assortments. Good coordination within merchandise groups is critical to sales success. The more merchandise groups mix, match, and complement each other, the greater the potential for multiple sales, higher total sales volume, and gross margin. A well-planned variety of styles is essential to make a fashion statement, inspire the retail buyer and ultimate consumer, and make an effective presentation on the retail sales floor.

Both manufacturer and retailer merchandisers may be involved in sourcing finished goods in the world market. More often than not, however, they are also involved in some form of product development.

Product Development   **Product development** is the design and engineering of products to be serviceable, producible, salable, and profitable (Glock & Kunz, 2000). In the apparel industry, product development evolves in three phases: creative design, line adoption, and technical design. The line plan, combined with the line concept, provides the framework for these processes. **Creative design** focuses on analysis, creativity, and the formation of product groups that are unique while reflecting the line concept. Design is an important element in the preadoption phase of product development.

Line adoption may be one of the most stressful periods for designers and merchandisers. In some firms, line adoption occurs during a series of daylong meetings involving elaborate presentations of line concept, group concepts with story boards, design samples, design specifications, fit analysis, and cost estimates. In other firms, line adoption is more gradual, occurring during ongoing short meetings where a few designs or merchandise groups are evaluated at a time. No matter the format, this is when decisions are made about what styles and merchandise groups will be included in the line and how the styles will be applied to the line plan. Decisions are made about what merchandise groups will be adopted, what designs will become styles in the line, model stocks, gross margins, prices, and expected volume for each merchandise group.

Technical design is the key component of post-adoption product development. Styles are prepared for production. The process includes perfecting styling and fit, finalizing patterns, testing materials and assembly methods, developing style and quality specifications, developing detailed costs, and grading patterns. Early phases of production planning are concurrent with post-adoption product development. Merchandisers must be knowledgeable about merchandising, marketing, and production in order to develop products and product lines that are salable and financially productive.

Line Presentation

Line presentation involves evaluating the line in order to make it visible and salable. The power of appeal (Scheller, 1993), also known as hanger or shelf appeal, attracts attention and causes retail buyers and ultimate consumers to stop, take a longer look, and ultimately purchase. Successful merchandise groups have hanger and shelf appeal for both retail buyers and target customers. Customer loyalty develops when expectations are satisfied from one season to the next. Line presentation occurs internally within a firm at line adoption, at wholesale to retail buyers, and at retail to ultimate consumers.

Internal Line Presentation   The purpose of **internal line adoption** presentations is to develop consensus and support for the proposed additions of specific products to the line plan. Product developers often include articulation of the line concept and image strategy for the coming selling period in their adoption presentations. They describe proposed merchandise groups and styles to be carried over into the next selling period, along with any proposed modifications. New groups, and each proposed design within a group, are described and evaluated. Other considerations discussed are the application of the proposed merchandise groups and designs to the line plan, cost estimates, pricing strategies, and visual mer-chandising strategies for the retail sales floor.

Wholesale Line Presentation   There are two aspects of **wholesale line presentation:** line preview and line release. **Line preview** is the presentation of the planned and adopted product line to the sales force. The purpose of line preview is to communicate the line concept and to help sales representatives to effectively sell the line the way it was conceived. Feedback from the sales force with regard to the proposed product line can be very helpful when refining merchandise groups and styles in the post-adoption product development process. **Line release** marks the beginning of promotion for the new selling period. The line may be released via an elaborate fashion show attended by the fashion press. Other firms may release their line by distributing sales samples to the sales force. In any case, line release marks the first opportunity for the public to view the new line.

Retail Line Presentation   The purpose of **retail line presentation** is to sell the line to ultimate consumers. Strategies used for retail line presentation vary depending on the type of retailer.

For example, specialty and department stores have different types of store layout and fixturing than discount, off price, and manufacturer's outlet stores. Obviously, retail merchandise presentation in catalog, television, and computer formats take on very different forms. Issues they have in common, however, include merchandise appeal, use of space, fixturing, lighting, signage, pricing and delivery strategies, customer service, and inventory management.

Learning Activity 3.3
Fundamentals of TAMS

1. How does the Taxonomy of Merchandising System (TAMS) relate to the Behavioral Theory of the Apparel Firm (BTAF)?
2. Write three sentences, one each describing line planning, development, and presentation in your own words.
3. How do line planning, development, and presentation relate to each other in terms of a) control of the process and b) timing?
4. What strategies could help control the time (number of weeks) required to complete the merchandising process?

Context of Merchandising

As explained by the BTAF, merchandising is one of six essential, interactive business constituencies including executive management, marketing, operations, and finance. Executive management is responsible for development of the business plan that defines the business and establishes long- and short-term goals. Marketing defines and describes target customers, shapes the image of the company, and develops strategies for growth. Merchandising plans, develops, and presents product lines. Operations and finance manage the firm's resources: people, property, and money. Quick response focuses on speeding products to market. One of the ways the interactive productivity of a firm's constituencies is assessed is via an income statement, or profit and loss statement, as it is sometimes called.

Income Statements

An **income statement** is a summary of a firm's revenue and expenses for a defined period of time. Income statements are commonly prepared on a monthly, quarterly, and/or annual basis. Frequently assessing revenue and profitability allows a firm to update plans, modify strategies in a timely way, and be proactive rather than reactive in the business environment. For a small firm, a single income statement per time period may suffice. But in large complex organizations, many income statements may be prepared to examine financial productivity of different parts of the firm. Income statements are commonly prepared for each tier in an organization and often for individual components within each tier.

A primary purpose of an income statement is to demonstrate whether the firm has made a profit for the period. **Profit** is an essential component of business operation in a capitalistic system. Profit may be stated in different ways: gross profit, operating profit, net profit, dollar or percentage profit, or before- and after-tax profit. **Gross profit,** commonly called gross margin, is closely associated with merchandising responsibilities.

Basic income statements include 12 basic elements that can be grouped into two categories: income measurements and income modifications.

Income measurements include the following:

- **Gross sales** is total dollar revenue received by a firm from the sale of goods and services.

- **Net sales** is actual revenue from the sale of goods and services (gross sales—customer returns and allowances).

- **Gross margin** is the revenue available for covering operating expenses and generating profit, sometimes called gross profit (net sales—cost of goods sold).

- **Adjusted gross margin** is the revenue available after merchandise procurement costs are paid (gross margin—merchandise procurement costs).

- **Operating profit** is what remains after all financial obligations related to operating the business are met (adjusted gross margin—overhead and operating expenses).

- **Net profit before taxes** is the figure on which the firm pays income tax.

Income modifications include the following:

- **Customer returns and allowances** is cancellation of sales because of merchandise returns and refunds or price adjustments related to customer dissatisfaction.

- **Cost of goods sold** is the amount the firm has paid to acquire or produce the merchandise sold (cost of merchandise available for sale—cost value of remaining inventory).

- **Procurement costs** are ordering and shipping costs associated with acquiring merchandise.

- **Overhead/operating expense** is all costs associated with operating a business other than cost of merchandise sold and procurement costs.

- **Other income and/or expenses** is additional revenue or costs related to operating the firm other than from selling goods and services.

In the first column of Table 3.1, measures of income are left justified; modifications of income are indented. Each measure of income has a corresponding modification in an income statement with the amounts reported in dollars in the second column.

Income statements often also include **merchandising and operating ratios** associated with measures of income and income modifications. See the third column of Table 3.1. The ratios are commonly stated as a percentage of net sales. Cost of goods sold and gross margin ratios are primary responsibilities of merchandisers. Responsibilities for the other ratios in the income statement are shared with marketing and operations constituencies. Ratio analysis often provides the most important information in the income statement besides profit. Past and present ratios can be compared to identify trends (Lewison, 1994). Ratios generated by a particular firm can also be compared to other firms in the same business to identify advantages and disadvantages in the way a firm is conducting its business. Ratios are also reported across industries to identify general trends and problems in business operation.

Table 3.1

Sample of a basic income statement.

Gross sales	$2,200	110%
Customer Returns and Allowances	$ 200	10%
Net Sales	$2,000	100%
Cost of Goods Sold	$1,000	50%
Gross Margin	$1,000	50%
Procurement Costs	$200	10%
Adjusted Gross Margin	$800	40%
Overhead/Expense	$700	35%
Operating Profit	$100	5%
Other Income	$200	10%
Other Expense	$100	5%
Net Profit Before Taxes	$200	10%

Relationships of Income Measurements, Income Modifications, and Associated Ratios

Income measurements are different expressions of revenue gained while running a business for a defined period. Income modifications are the reasons for the differences in income measurements. Table 3.2 demonstrates the mathematical relationships among income measurements, income modifications, merchandising ratios, and operating ratios.

Gross sales is total revenue received from the sale of goods and services in a time period, including both cash and credit sales. Unfortunately, not all goods sold stay sold. There are many reasons why customers return goods for refund or exchange. Many firms have liberal return policies, which grant customers a full refund. Allowances, a reduced price, or other form of credit may be granted to customers because merchandise is unsatisfactory for some

Table 3.2

Calculation of a basic income statement and common merchandising and operating ratios.

Calculating Dollar Values	Calculating Ratios	Common Ratios
Gross Sales	gross sales ÷ net sales × 100	101% to 140%
− Customer Returns & Allowances	customer R & A ÷ net sales × 100	1% to 40%
Net Sales	net sales = 100%	100%
− Cost of Goods Sold	cost of goods sold ÷ net sales × 100	55% to 70%
Gross Margin	gross margin ÷ net sales × 100	30% to 45% of net sales
− Procurement Costs	procurement costs ÷ net sales × 100	5% to 15%
Adjusted Gross Margin	adjusted gross margin ÷ net sales × 100	20% to 40%
− Operating Expense	operating expense ÷ net sales × 100	18% to 35% of net sales
Operating Profit	operating profit ÷ net sales × 100	1% to 15% of net sales
± Other Income and/or Expenses	other income/expenses ÷ net sales × 100	0% to any number
Net Profit Before Taxes	net profit before taxes ÷ net sales × 100	2% to 15% of net sales

reason. Employee discounts are also included in allowances. The ratio of gross sales to net sales is greater than 100 percent because gross sales is more than net sales:

$$gross\ sales = net\ sales + customer\ returns\ and\ allowances.$$

Customer returns and allowances in relation to net sales may vary widely depending on the nature of a firm and its return policies. Internet retailers and catalog operations may have returns that total up to 40 percent of net sales, which is a real problem (Fleischer, 2001). Returns and allowances are a part of manufacturer/retailer relationships, as well as the retailer-customer relationships. Retail merchandisers frequently request to return merchandise to the manufacturer that is unsatisfactory for some reason, i.e., it was shipped late, it was not what was ordered, or the quality was unsatisfactory. Sometimes they negotiate an allowance on the goods, that is, a price reduction, so the merchandise can be sold at a lower price and still provide adequate gross margin for the retailer. In this case, the retailer would not return the merchandise.

Net sales is the foundation of the income statement. It is the amount of merchandise actually sold in dollars during a specified time period: gross sales less customer returns and allowances. Net sales is the most realistic measure of revenue gained from operating a firm. All numbers and merchandising and operating ratios in the income statement relate directly to net sales. Net sales is 100 percent in relation to all ratios.

Cost of goods sold is calculated with consideration for inventory on hand at the beginning of the period, purchases of new merchandise with related transportation charges and cash discounts during the period, and alteration and workroom costs associated with sales. The difference between net sales and cost of goods sold is gross margin.

Gross margin is a measure of the amount of money available to cover all of the firm's expenses, except cost of merchandise, which is the only expense already accounted for. The merchandising ratio of gross margin in relation to net sales commonly runs from 30 to 45 percent in the retail sector depending on type of retail operation. Discounters commonly have lower percent gross margin than department stores, while specialty stores are usually higher. Manufacturers commonly operate on lower percent gross margin than retailers.

Adjusted gross margin is the amount of money available for overhead and expenses after merchandise procurement costs are accounted for. Procurement costs include ordering, shipping, and importing merchandise. Adjusted gross margin became a significant income measurement with the advent of global sourcing. Any excess of adjusted gross margin over remaining overhead and expenses results in operating profit. Adjusted gross margin is especially relevant to financial well-being in the presence of global sourcing.

Overhead and operating expenses cover all general and administrative costs incurred to run the business (rent, utilities, supplies, maintenance, and payroll) other than cost of merchandise and taxes. To realize a profit, operating expense must be less than adjusted gross margin. The ratio of operating expense to net sales is insightful in relation to a firm's profitability. Wal-Mart is known for its low overhead/operating expense ratio of less than 20 percent, which is credited, in part, to its efficient methods of distributing merchandise. For comparison, Nordstrom (as reported in Case 3.3) was seeking an overhead/operating expense ratio of 29 percent. Every dollar a firm reduces its operating expense goes directly to the bottom line operating profit.

Operating profit is the measure of a firm's efficiency in managing the relationship between gross margins and operating expenses. Operating profit is the expression of profit commonly reported in the trade press and referred to when only the word "profit" is used. Firms may have negative operating profit (loss) for some periods for many reasons, for instance, unanticipated shifts in the market resulting in a decline in sales or large capital expenditures. However, successful continuation of a business depends on profit. Firms must show profit in order to grow, and growth is essential in today's market. Growth requires the reinvestment of profits into the business. Operating profits of 2 to 15 percent of net sales are common for apparel firms. But a firm may still be considered successful with a ratio of operating profits in relation to net sales as low as 1 percent.

Other income and expenses are commonly derived from activities associated with the business other than sales of goods and services. One common source of income in the retail sector is selling goods on the retailer's credit card with a service/interest charge on the credit card balance. Other income added to operating profit and/or other expenses subtracted from operating profit results in net profit. *Net profit* is the basis of the firm's tax liability.

Merchandisers play key roles in relation to a firm's income statement because they are usually responsible for planning what and how much merchandise will be acquired or produced, what it will cost, and how it will be priced for sale. These decisions are closely associated with cost of goods sold and gross margin on the income statement. Gross margin is a key factor because it determines how much money is available to pay marketing, operations, and financial expenses.

Learning Activity 3.4

Fundamentals of income statements

1. What does it mean to say the "net sales is the foundation of an income statement"?
2. From a merchandising perspective, higher gross margin is always better than lower gross margin. According to an income statement, what can a merchandiser manipulate to increase gross margin?
3. Why is net sales the foundation of an income statement instead of gross sales?
4. A merchandiser has more control over gross margin and adjusted gross margin than operating profit. True or false? Explain your answer.

Income Statements for Mike's Bikes

Read Company Profile 3.1, Mike's Bikes, Part 1. Mike's Bikes is a company that will be used for examples throughout the following chapters. You may want to put a tab on this page so it will be easy to refer back to the Mike's Bikes profile.

Table 3.3 shows the beginning of an income statement for Mike's Bikes based on the Company Profile. An income statement is like a financial puzzle. Given a few dollar figures and/or ratios, the rest of the statement can be calculated. It is an excellent way to estimate the merchandising effectiveness and the financial well-being of a firm. For example, if you are reading a news report of one of your favorite manufacturers or retailers that includes a few numbers in the financial report, you can quickly calculate a few more to make up a basic income statement. This can be compared with the firm's annual report to check on the accuracy of the news article or compared with competing companies' annual reports for a broader picture of the "health" of the company. This analysis can be very useful when seeking an employer for an internship or for your career initiation after graduation.

Company Profile 3.1

Mike's Bikes, Part 1, Financial Position

Mike's Bikes is a "family"-owned partnership operated by Michelle Gibbs and Kevin Dean, longtime companions and avid cyclists. They met 15 years ago on RAGBRAI, an annual weeklong bike ride across Iowa that attracts 10,000 cyclists annually from around the world. At the time they met, Michelle was a financial analyst for a computer company in Los Angeles, California, and Kevin was a salesman for an aluminum company based in Chicago. Two years later, after developing an extensive business plan, they decided to join forces and turn their hobby into their profession. They resigned their positions and took up housekeeping in West Des Moines, Iowa, surrounded by the highest average income area of the state. They created Mike's Bikes, a specialty store for serious cycling hobbyists. The name "Mike" was created by combining the first two letters of each of their first names.

They chose Des Moines as the site for their shop because the state capital has an

---

extensive bike path system, has a large contingent of dedicated leisure cyclists, and commuters are increasingly using bikes as transportation to work. The State of Iowa and the *Des Moines Register* also host the popular cycling event RAGBRAI (Register's Annual Great Bike Ride Across Iowa), which attracts the attention of national and international serious recreational cyclists each year.

The climate in Iowa allows biking three seasons of the year. Michelle and Kevin planned from the beginning to close the store during late January and early February, when business would be slow anyway, to allow them and their bike riding employees to vacation with their bikes in other parts of the country or the world. Mike's Bikes has been in business 13 years and last year generated $2 million in net sales for the first time with only 1 percent returns and allowances.

Michelle and Kevin brought complementary expertise to the business. Michelle is in charge of the operations and finance; Kevin is in charge of marketing and merchandising. Together they comprise the management team. The 10,000-square foot store is located in a strip mall within a mile of a major regional mall. Other stores in the strip mall include a Lands' End outlet, a computer store, an office supply store, a book store, and a TCBY yogurt store. Mike's Bikes has one full-time and four part-time employees, all dedicated cyclists.

The store is open six days a week, closed Mondays. Hours are 10 to 8 each day. The primary selling period is April through August, followed by fall bike sales and holiday sales in November and December. As originally planned, the store is closed four weeks in January and early February.

The merchandise mix includes three categories: bikes, apparel, and accessories. They also have a bike service department. Gross margin runs at about 41 percent. Because transportation on bikes is relatively expensive, procurement costs are 14 percent. Operating expenses including their own salaries of $39,000 each leaves only 3 percent operating profit. Michelle and Kevin have considered opening a store in another location, since they have no other income, but fear it would limit their time to enjoy their sport.

To complete the Mike's Bikes income statement, insert the easy numbers first, that is, the ones given in the company profile including net sales and percent customer returns and allowances, gross margin, procurement costs, and operating profit. In an income statement, net sales is always 100 percent. To calculate the rest of the numbers:

Table 3.3

Numbers from Company Profile for Mike's Bikes Income Statement.

Gross Sales		
Customer Returns & Allowances		1%
Net Sales	$2,000,000	
Cost of Goods Sold		
Gross Margin		41%
Procurement Costs		14%
Adjusted Gross Margin		
Overhead/Expenses		
Operating Profit		3%
Other Income/Expense	—	—
Net Profit Before Taxes		

customer returns & allowances = net sales × 1% = $20,000

gross sales = net sales + returns & allowances = $2,020,000

percent gross sales = percent net sales + percent returns & allowances = 101%

gross margin = net sales × percent gross margin = $820,000

cost of goods sold = net sales − gross margin = $1,180,000

percent cost of goods sold = cost of goods sold / net sales = 59%

procurement costs = net sales × percent procurement costs = $280,000

percent adjusted gross margin = percent gross margin − percent procurement costs = 27%

adjusted gross margin = net sales × percent adjusted gross margin = $540,000

operating profit = net sales × percent operating profit = $60,000

overhead/expense = adjusted gross margin − operating profit = $480,000

no other income or expense so operating profit and percent operating profit = net profit before
   other income/expenses

This example is one way to develop Mike's Bikes' income statement based on the information given in the profile. A different sequence of calculations could be used to derive the same result; however, it is always safer to work as much as possible from the top down rather than from the bottom up. The sequence doesn't matter as long as all the numbers make sense together. Table 3.4 shows the completed income statement.

Learning Activity 3.5

Income statements

1. Considering Table 3.4, if Mike's Bikes was able to reduce overhead expenses by 5 percent, how would gross margin be affected? How would operating profit be affected? Why?
2. If Mike's Bikes was forced to increase cost of goods sold by 3 percent, how would gross margin be affected? How would operating profit be affected? Why?
3. Read Case 3.3 carefully. Assume that Nordstrom achieved the goals laid out by the President. Create an income statement for Nordstrom from the information given in the case. Use Table 3.1 as a model. Set up the income statement listing the components on the left with a column for dollars and a column for percents on the right. Insert the numbers given in the case and calculate the rest. How can you check to be sure your numbers make sense?

Table 3.4

Income statement for Mike's Bikes.

Gross Sales	$2,020,000	101%
Customer Returns and Allowances	$20,000	1%
Net Sales	$2,000,000	100%
Cost of Goods Sold	$1,180,000	59%
Gross Margin	$820,000	41%
Procurement Costs	$280,000	14%
Adjusted Gross Margin	$540,000	27%
Overhead/Expenses	$480,000	24%
Operating Profit	$60,000	3%
Other Income/Expense	—	—
Net Profit Before Taxes	$60,000	3%

4. How is it possible for Nordstrom to have a 9.2 percent increase in sales but only have a 1 percent increase in same-store sales?

5. In 2003, Nordstrom had net sales of $5.975 billion, gross margin of $2.1 billion, procurement costs of 11 percent, and operating income of $189,736,000. Create an income statement for 2003. (Always set up the framework for the income statement first.) Did they achieve their goals for percentages of overhead/expenses and gross margin?

6. Why might centralized buying result in more markdowns? Why will more markdowns result in lower gross margin?

  Case 3.3 Nordstrom unveils plan for revamping.

On December 8, 2000, Nordstrom announced it was shaking up its business. Decisions on new store openings were reexamined and the three proposed sites were canceled. With $5.5 billion in sales, the company decided to be less deal-oriented with developers and more selective in choosing locations. The company chose to shrink certain back office operations and reduce expenses, including those bloated by an abundance of purchasing agents and consultants and excesses in the areas of travel, energy, and computer purchasing.

On the other hand, millions were allocated to spend on new technology, including merchandising systems, so buyers and sales associates could be on top of the hot items and inventory flow. The legendary sales force was rewarded with compensations built on base salaries and increased commissions to boost morale and productivity. That was just part of the agenda planned to sweep through the Seattle-based specialty chain that is commonly called a department store.

Nordstrom opened 10 stores in 2000, and though sales grew 9.2 percent, same-store sales were up only 1 percent. The company's president, Blake Nordstrom, told analysts the outlook for same-store growth was conservative, projected at 1 to 3 percent for the next 3 years. He also saw overhead and expenses at 18 percent, procurement costs at 11 percent, and gross margins at 35 percent. "These are not aggressive goals, but goals we need and must reach."

In terms of categories, women's apparel had missed plan all year, while men's wear was growing. In general, more centralized buying had led to better deals on merchandise and improved margins, but high markdowns offset any positive results they would have had.

Benchmarks of a Firm's Success

Each constituency in an apparel firm tends to have **measures of success,** particularly related to its responsibilities. Some business executives declare, "You get what you measure." Table 3.5 summarizes some of the issues particularly related to the responsibilities of each constituency and benchmarks that might be used to measure success. **Benchmarks** (points of comparison) provide indicators of levels of success. The merchandising responsibility is to provide a product line that generates revenue to support the necessary activities of the other constituencies to run the business.

As might be expected, the measures of success related to the executive constituency focus on broad issues integrating the entire firm. Marketing measures focus on market position and growth in sales and market share. Operations measures focus on management of people and physical property. Finance measures relate to management and growth of financial resources. Merchandising measures relate to planning, developing, and presenting product lines.

The next three sections of this textbook are based on the definition of merchandising. Section Two deals with line planning, Section Three with line development and presentation, and Section Four with career opportunities. The merchandising measures of success and their benchmarks will be revisited numerous times throughout these discussions. You may want to put tabs on the pages for Tables 3.2, 3.4, and 3.5 so they will be easy to find.

Learning Activity 3.6

Measures of success

1. Examine Table 3.5. What is the nature of the measures of success for each constituency?
2. What is the nature of a benchmark?
3. What does the expression "You get what you measure" mean?

Summary

The Taxonomy of Apparel Merchandising Systems (TAMS) was developed to comprehensively describe elements of a merchandising system. TAMS is viewed as an extended definition of merchandising in the context of the Behavioral Theory of the Apparel Firm

Table 3.5 (continued)

Indicators of business success. *

Executive

Issue for Analysis	Benchmark
1. Has the firm achieved its financial goals?	1. Profit, market share, GMROI
2. Has the firm achieved its goals related to social responsibility?	2. Community support, environmentalism
3. Does return on shareholders' investments meet expectations?	3. Achieved plan
4. Has the firm achieved its goals related to its employees?	4. Employee satisfaction and retention
5. Has the firm achieved its goals in relation to customers?	5. Sales growth, customer loyalty
6. Has the firm achieved its goals in relation to suppliers?	6. Vendor partnerships

Merchandising

1. What is average initial markup?	1. 48 percent might be regarded as minimum; over 58 percent is more and more common
2. What are markdowns as a percent of sales by classification?	2. Markdowns for fashion/seasonal goods (may be over 15 percent) will be much higher than basic/staple goods (less than 5 percent)
3. Are markdowns taken regularly based on rate of sale?	3. A minimum of every 26 weeks, preferably every 2 to 4 weeks
4. What is maintained markup by classification?	4. Under 39 percent is a problem for many firms; over 46 percent is good
5. Is open-to-buy updated as indicated by sales for each classification every few weeks?	5. Open-to-buy needs to be adjusted frequently to reflect rate of sale of various merchandise classifications
6. What is the annual rate of merchandise turnover by classification?	6. Less than 1 is a problem; over 7 is very good
7. How much of present inventory is merchandise purchased for this selling period?	7. Less than 50 percent is a problem; close to 100 percent is best
8. What are the weeks of sale for each selling period for each merchandise classification?	8. Weeks for fashion/seasonal goods: 10–26; weeks for basic/seasonal goods: 52–104
9. What are the peak selling weeks for each selling season for each classification?	9. Usually one-half to two-thirds of the way through the selling period
10. What is the best size scale by classification?	10. Merchandise should be bought in the same size ratios that it sells
11. What is profitability by resource?	11. Gross margin, quality, late deliveries, charge backs
12. What is the common range for gross margin?	12. 30 to 45 percent

(continued)

Table 3.5 (continued)

Indicators of Business Success*

Marketing

1. What are annual advertising costs as a percent of sales?	1. Over 6 percent may be too high; less than 1 percent may be too low
2. What are markdowns as a percent of sales for whole operation?	2. Ten percent may be acceptable; over 20 percent can be a big problem
3. Have goals for market share been achieved?	3. Market share goals met or exceeded
4. Have goals for sales increases been achieved?	4. Sales goals met or exceeded

Operations

1. What are operating expenses as a percent of sales?	1. Over 43 percent is probably a big problem; less than 30 percent is probably good
2. What is the total annual payroll expense as a percent of sales?	2. Over 21 percent is probably a big problem; less than 13 percent is probably very good
3. What are the annual selling costs (sales personnel wages and commissions) as a percent of sales?	3. Over 15 percent is probably a big problem; less than 6 percent is very good
4. What was last year's inventory shrinkage as a percent of sales?	4. Over 4 percent is a big problem; less than $\frac{1}{2}$ percent is probably very good
5. Do you transfer non-selling merchandise from non-selling to selling stores?	5. Yes
6. What is rental costs as a percent of sales?	6. Over 11 percent is a problem; less than 4 percent is probably very good
7. What are annual utility costs as a percent of sales?	7. Over $1\frac{1}{2}$ percent is probably a problem; less than $1\frac{1}{4}$ percent is probably very good
8. What is the annual rate of merchandise turnover for the whole organization?	8. Less than 1 is a big problem; over 7 is very good

Finance

1. Is the level of fixed expense reasonable?
2. Is the level of variable expense reasonable?
3. Is cash flow adequate to cover expenses without reducing resources?
4. Is growth adequate to achieve goals?

*Based in part on criteria developed by Retail Merchandising Services Automation, Inc. (RMSA) and Quick Response Leadership Committee of American Apparel Manufacturer's Association.

(BTAF). Merchandising is a dynamic process of intense change. The merchandising cycle represented by TAMS is 1 year (52 weeks), beginning the first week of February and ending the last week of January. A product line consists of a combination of styles that satisfy similar or related customer needs, can be sold within the targeted price range, and can be marketed with similar strategies. Line planning requires assessment of the present, analysis of the past, and projection for the future.

Line development includes the processes required to translate a line plan into real merchandise. A line concept includes the look and appeal that contributes to the identity and salability of the line. Wholesale markets provide a setting for linking the work of merchandisers at the wholesale level with those at the retail level. Sales representatives are often instrumental in developing assortments and writing purchase orders. In the apparel industry, product development evolves in three phases: creative design, line adoption, and technical design. The line plan and the line concept provide the framework for product development.

Line presentation includes evaluating the line to make it visible and salable. The power of appeal (Scheller, 1993), also known as hanger or shelf appeal, attracts the attention of retail buyers and ultimate consumers, causing them to stop, take a longer look, and finally purchase.

As explained by the BTAF, merchandising is one of six essential, interactive business constituencies; the others are executive management, marketing, operations, finance, and quick response. Each constituency measures its success in relation to its responsibilities. Income statements are common measures of success. Benchmarks provide indicators of levels of success. The merchandising measures of success and their benchmarks will be revisited numerous times throughout the following chapters.

Key Concepts

adjusted gross margin
assortment plans
basic income statement
benchmarks
cost of goods sold
creative design
customer returns and
  allowances
delivery and allocation plans
gross margin
gross profit

gross sales
income measurements
income modifications
income statement
internal line-adoption
line adoption
line concept
line development
line planning
line preview
line release

measures of success
merchandise budgets
merchandising and operating
  ratios
merchandising cycle
net profit
net profit before taxes
net sales
operating profit
other income and/or expenses
overhead/operating expense

procurement costs
product development
product line
profit
retail line presentation

returns and allowances
sales representatives
selling period
Taxonomy of Apparel
   Merchandising Systems
   (TAMS)

technical design
wholesale line presentation
wholesale markets

Integrated Learning Activity 3.7.1

Basic income statement for your MAP retailer

Develop a basic income statement for the most recent year for your MAP retailer, using Table 3.1 as a model. You will be referring back to this income statement many times during the semester so it is important to develop a good one now. Refer to the income statements you copied from the retailer's Web site or annual report to obtain the information. (See ILA 2.6.1.) Presentation of income/profit and lost statements varies among firms. Different terms are used for the same things, order of presentation is different, and sometimes some measures are omitted altogether and others are added. Use the following process:

1. Set up the basic income statement with the list of components and columns for numbers in dollars and percents using Table 3.1 as a model. Be sure to title it with your retailer's name.
2. Examine your retailer's income statements and identify items that fit into your basic income statement. Fill in the numbers in the appropriate spaces.
3. Calculate other numbers on your basic income statement based on the numbers you entered.
4. Look back at your retailer's income statement and see if you find the same numbers. Make note of what they were called.
5. Find or calculate the rest of the numbers so you will have a complete basic income statement.
6. Look for your company in the Representative Data Set. (See ILA 2.6.2.) If your firm is not included, compare its numbers with one of its competitors. How do the numbers in your basic income statement compare to those in the Representative Data Set? Find the page with the gross margin numbers. Is your company high or low within the gross margin range for the merchandise they carry? What do you know about the company that would explain your MAP retailer's gross margin?
7. Add your income statement to your Retailer Profile in MAP.

⊚ *Integrated Learning Activity 3.7.2*

Learn to use Sourcing Simulator (SS), Student Version

This is the first of a series of exercises using SS to test the resulting financial productivity related to merchandising decisions. SS allows you to enter information from a
merchandise plan, including the quantity of merchandise you wish to order, the assortment by style, size, and color, the pricing strategy and merchandise costs, and the
sourcing strategy. The computer simulates in-store shopping behavior and provides a
financial analysis. For each experiment it is possible to use the default data set, changing only a few variables before running each simulation. Thus, it is important to protect the default data set because you will want to use it repeatedly.

   The purpose of this assignment is to generate data using SS and then create income
statements based on the data. The income statement is one important measure of outcome related to the merchandise plan.

1. Begin an SS experiment. Open the SS Seasonal Model. Run SS by clicking Simulate at the top of the screen. SS will create outputs based on the default data set. Include "default" in the title of the output. Leave your output screen open. Reach
   behind your output screen and click on File and then Print Current Inputs to get a
   copy of the inputs for your first simulation. (It is actually the default data set.)
   Mark the input to identify it as your first simulation.
2. Go to the Cost Data tab. Double the Retail Price of your product. Leave other inputs the same. Simulate again. Use "double price" in the title. Print your inputs
   for the second simulation and mark it as your second simulation.
3. Your output for the second simulation will appear on the same screen as the first
   so you can compare results. Print your outputs.
4. Look over the information on the output printout for the two simulations. In particular, highlight total number of customers, total inventory offering, total revenue, $ gross margin, % gross margin, and % gross margin potential. Write out
   the definitions for the terms highlighted. Based on the definitions, use your calculator to derive how the gross margin measures are determined. Be sure you understand what they mean.
5. Go back to the SS output screen. Find the tab for graphs of outputs. Look at the
   different output graphs. Be sure to put outputs from both of your simulations on
   each graph so you can see the comparisons. Print out the gross margin graph.
   Close SS. Do not save inputs in order to preserve the default data set. Why does
   your second simulation have more than twice as much gross margin as your first

simulation? Why is there an even greater difference in adjusted gross margin between the simulations?

6. Make up two income statements, one from each of your simulation outputs. Use
   total revenue as net sales. SS does not include customer returns and allowances.
   Assume overhead and expenses are 29 percent. Calculate the percentages not included in the printout. Which income statement is more realistic considering level
   of gross margin achieved? Why?

7. Present this assignment in an orderly manner in your MAP.

Recommended Resources

Fleischer, J. (2001, May 2). Online apparel buyers wearing down the return key. *Daily News Record*, 12.

Johnson, J. L. & Longo, D. (2001, March). Retailing 2005. *Retail Merchandiser,* 53.

Sproles, G. B. (1985). Behavioral science theories of fashion. In M. R. Solomon (ed.), *The psychology of fashion,* 55–70. Lexington, MA: Lexington Books.

References

Barth, B. (2001, February 12). Blazing a trail to better B2B communcation. *Daily News Record*, 64.

Deloitte & Touche. (2002, October). *Retail trade* (www.retail.ru/biblio/inenglish04-3.htm). Accessed
   August 25, 2003.

Fleischer, J. (2001, May 2). Online apparel buyers wearing down the return key. *Daily News Record,* 12.

Glock, R. E., & Kunz, G. I. (2000). *Apparel manufacturing: Sewn product analysis* (2nd ed.). Englewood
   Cliffs, NJ: Prentice Hall.

Johnson, J. L., & Longo, D. (2001, March). Retailing 2005. *Retail Merchandiser,* 53.

Landy, H. (2003, July 5). Retail giants using Web to build sales. *Knight Ridder News Services.*

Lewison, D. M. (1994). *Retailing* (5th ed.). New York: Macmillan.

Quick Response Leadership Committee. (1996). *Measurements of excellence.* American Apparel Manufacturers Association: Author.

Retail trade market USA. (2002). (www.researchandmarkets.co.uk). Accessed May 1, 2002.

Retail Merchandising Services Automation, Inc. (1995). *Retail intelligent forecasting: Merchandise
   planning for the future.* Riverside, CA: Author.

Scheller, H. P. (1993). *Apparel quality through the perception of apparel production managers and operators.* Unpublished masters thesis, Iowa State University, Ames.

Seckler, V. (2002, April 11). The new consumer: Shopping crossroads of mass and class. *Women's
   Wear Daily,* 183:1 & 10–11.

Stores. (2003). (www.stores.org/archives). Accessed August 27, 2003.

*The Fact Book. (*2001*). Retail Merchandiser.* New York: VNU Business Publications.

*The Fact Book. (*2003, July*). Retail Merchandiser.* New York: VNU Business Publications.

Merchandise Planning

4

Fundamentals of

Merchandise

Planning

Learning Objectives

- Apply concepts of merchandise classification systems to facilitate merchandise planning.

- Examine differences in fashion, basic, seasonal, and staple merchandise.

- Develop merchandise calendars suitable for fashion/seasonal and basic/staple merchandise.

- Explore the fundamentals of Accurate Response and Category Management.

A review of the continuing declines in gross margin, adjusted gross margin, stock turnover, and gross margin return on inventory confirm the existence of inadequate merchandise planning processes in both wholesale and retail sectors. The historic use of line planning processes has always recognized the need for forecasting sales, but today technology is available to support more sophisticated forecasting and line planning. Effective **forecasting,** integrated with classification-level merchandise budgets and assortment plans, provides a necessary framework for productive merchandising systems.

Traditional Line Planning

Line planning processes have often been described as top-down, bottom-up, and occasionally middle-out. **Top-down planning** means the executive constituency develops the business plan and, based on growth projections, prescribes sales goals and dollar investment in merchandise, usually for a six-month period or a year. Funds are then allocated, usually by classification or department, for the acquisition of merchandise for each selling period. The plans developed by the executive constituency often prescribe the goals, levels of dollar investment, and measures of success for each constituency. With top-down planning, the focus is often on sales goals. This may lead the merchandising constituency to over-buy (retail sector) or over-produce (manufacturing sector) because of the penalties related to lost business. Setting goals also for merchandise turnover, maintained margins, and gross margin return on inventory provides a more balanced perspective on merchandising performance. If sales do not meet expectations, across-the-board cuts in inventory might be implemented, resulting in high rates of markdowns because of excess goods in some categories and massive lost sales in other categories where demand is strong.

Bottom-up planning means the analysis begins with what was sold: how much, what kind, when, and at what price. Projections are made for the coming period and investment in merchandise is based on previous sales and the perspectives of store managers and department managers. Classification-level plans are combined into department or line estimates and eventually merged into a company plan. Bottom-up planning may be used particularly in smaller firms where everyone knows the product line and thinks they understand the reasons for cycles in the past selling period. The bottom-up plan may or may not be based on substantive data. Data-based bottom-up plans may be the more realistic, since they match plans to perceived needs at the store level. When bottom-up plans are not merged into a cohesive plan for the entire firm, the constituencies may lack common goals and the firm may appear to lack direction.

Phases of Traditional Line Planning

Traditionally, line plans took the form of two six-month plans a year. **Six-month plans** established available levels of investment for merchandise lines and product classifications for each month of the year. Last year's sales provided the primary basis for six-month plans with possible consideration for the marketing strategy, profit goals, and sales forecasts. Six-month plans required a great deal of time and attention on the part of merchandisers, with much numerical manipulation to develop appropriate numbers before appropriate computer technology was available. Consequently, once the plans were set they tended to be static. The plans were in place and merchandisers were expected to carry them out. Merchandisers were expected to "make plan" regardless of intervening circumstances.

The six-month plans could have two parts: dollar planning and unit planning. **Dollar plans** were usually based on an assumption of improved performance over the same period last year: improved sales, increased turnover, improved profit margins, and reduced markdowns. Dollar **open-to-buy** was usually determined based on the difference between planned sales and the combination of inventory already owned and on order. Open-to-buy determined the amount of merchandise in a particular classification or class that could or should be purchased at a particular time. The primary purpose of open-to-buy was to prevent over-investment in merchandise. A six-month plan did not detail strategies required to achieve the improvements.

The second part of six-month plans—**unit plans**—could be based on bottom-up planning, but was usually based on top-down dollar plans. The quantity (units) of goods that could be made available during the selling period was determined by dividing the dollar allocation by average merchandise price. Unit open-to-buy could also be determined by dividing dollar open-to-buy by average price. Unit plans may have been developed to the SKU level to examine exactly how many styles, sizes, and colors could be made available in each classification.

During the 1980s and 1990s, as the size of retailers exploded through growth, mergers, and consolidations, merchandising systems became more centralized and dependent on dollar plans with less and less planning to the store level or SKU level. Mainframe computers could handle dollar plans but not unit plans because of the number of SKUs involved. Unit planning nearly disappeared from the retail scene. Consequently, store-level assortments were frequently neglected, resulting in lost sales in combination with high rates of markdowns.

The conceptual simplicity of traditional six-month plans is dated in current merchandising environments. Today, dollars should follow merchandise sales rather than using dollar plans to limit merchandise availability.

Contemporary Line Planning

Large and complex firms have many tiers in their organizational structures that influence the levels and the manner in which merchandise might be planned. Figure 4.1 has a pyramid shape, representing a firm with the possibility of five different tiers in its organizational structure. Pyramids can be used to represent a firm's organizational structure for a number of reasons. Numbers of employees are normally relatively few at the top and many at the bottom. At the peak of the **organizational pyramid** is the conglomerate tier, followed by tiers entitled group, corporate, division, and individual store or production unit. The actual number of tiers and the language used to describe them varies by firm.

In 1996, Dayton Hudson Corporation was a retail conglomerate that included several relatively independent corporate units including Target, Mervyn's, and the department stores Dayton's and Marshall Field's. Within both Dayton's and Marshall Field's were dozens of individual department stores.

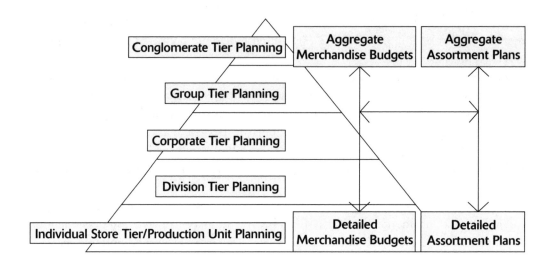

Figure 4.1   Tiers in an organizational pyramid in relation to planning merchandise budgets and assortments. (Model developed by G. I. Kunz.)

In January 2000, Dayton Hudson Corporation changed its corporate name to Target Corporation reflecting the fact that Target Stores was generating 80 percent of the Corporation's revenue. They also merged the department stores into one division under the name Marshall Field's. Target Corporation is now addressing four retail channels—upscale department stores with Marshall Field's, mid-market department stores with Mervyn's, mass market with Target Stores, and the Internet market with target.direct. Target.direct represents all three brick-and-mortar channels. To relate Target Corporation to Figure 4.1 and merchandise planning:

> Conglomerate Tier = Target Corporation
> Group Tier = Target Stores, Marshall Field's, Mervyn's, and target.direct
> Corporate Tier for Target Stores = Greatland, SuperTarget, and Target
> Division Tier for Target Stores = Target regional offices: Los Angeles, Dallas, Minneapolis, Richmond, VA, and Troy, MI
> Store Tier = 1,107 stores in 47 states reporting to five regional offices

(Target Corporation, 2003).

Each channel of Target Corporation has separate but highly related merchandising systems. An example of a merchandising decision made at the conglomerate level was to integrate over 60 different merchandising software packages used by Target Stores into an integrated system that all the channels could use. "Aggregated" is used to describe merchandise plans at the conglomerate level because this tier tends to think in terms of the combined financial generation and results of the entire firm. It is required that quarterly financial results are reported to the media and the stockholders for Target Corporation, not Target Stores, Mervyn's, and Marshall Field's.

VF Corporation is the largest apparel company in the world. The conglomerate includes several business coalitions: Sportswear, Jeanswear, Global Intimates, Outdoor, and Imagewear. Each coalition forms a pyramid and includes several brands. For example, Sportswear includes Nautica, Earl Jean, and John Varvatos. Nautica breaks down into Nautica Sportswear, Nautica Jeanswear/Children's, Nautica Furnishings, and Nautica Retail. Some aspects of merchandise planning occurs in each tier of each pyramid.

In contrast, Mark Shale, a privately owned, upscale, Chicago-based specialty retailer operates seven retail stores, an outlet store, a catalog, and markshale.com. Mark Shale has only two tiers: corporate and individual store. The corporate tier includes merchandising for the brick-and-mortar stores, catalog, and Web site as well as private label product development. Independent retail chains and small retail firms like Mark Shale with one or a few stores may start the merchandise planning process at the corporate or individual store tier levels of the organizational pyramid or both. Mark Shale was aggressive in developing a proprietary merchandise planning and management computer system that supports merchandise planning at the store, classification, sub-classification, and SKU levels. Mark Shale is the exception rather than the rule, as most firms now use commercially available merchandise planning systems.

Contemporary Integrated Planning

Integrated planning is consistent with QR business systems and the use of information technology. **Integrated planning** is a combination of the top-down and bottom-up systems previously described. It is a teamwork approach with input from all of the firm's constituencies. Information technology systems make it possible for everyone in the firm, regardless of organizational tier or constituency, to have access to the appropriate data and reports. However, a common problem with information systems is that data are sometimes not presented in usable form. A retail executive recently stated, "We are over-loaded with data but we don't have any information." Data has to be critically analyzed and interpreted in different forms to become information needed by a firm's constituencies to make business decisions. This often requires "tailor-made" reports developed by a firm's management information system (MIS) team. The information is used very differently by the constituencies because of their areas of specialization.

With integrated planning the executive constituency negotiates broad guidelines in relation to the firm's goals. Estimates for the line plan are also developed by the merchandising constituency using bottom-up planning methods at the merchandise classification level. The marketing constituency develops sales and promotion plans based on the business plan. The finance constituency plans needs for cash flow, revenue, and profit. The operations constituency plans human resource needs, renovation of property, and logistics for handling merchandise.

The plans proposed by each constituency are negotiated into a company-wide plan that provides guidance for the decisions of managers throughout the merchandising cycle. A merchandising cycle is 52 weeks beginning the first week of February and ending the last week of January. Integrated plans result in the most accurate merchandise plans, but are also stressful and time-consuming because of all the negotiation involved. From the perspective of saving time, top-down planning is probably most efficient, but the process may result in unrealistic plans and may alienate the employees who are expected to carry them out. Integrated plans provide opportunities for new initiatives and may increase efficiency and profitability by reducing inventories and markdowns. Top-down and bottom-up plans can be compared, while assortment plans can be reconciled with financial plans (Cristea & Mangit, 2003).

Phases of Contemporary Line Plans

Merchandise budgets identify planned sales, reductions, and merchandise to receive by merchandise category, class, subclass, or group for a merchandising cycle or for a selling period within a merchandising cycle. Merchandise budgets were traditionally called dollar plans. **Assortment plans** may include model stocks, basic stocks, and/or automated replenishment determining merchandise by style, size, and color. Assortment plans were traditionally called unit plans.

The closer to the peak of the pyramid of the corporate structure, the more aggregated the merchandise planning and the more likely that merchandise budgets will be the primary form of planning. The closer to the base of the pyramid, the more detailed the planning and the more likely that assortment-type merchandise planning will be included. The lower in the pyramid the firm plans, the greater the need for a sophisticated merchandise planning computer system and the more power and capacity required of that system. Parts of a firm's merchandise mix may be planned at any or all of the tiers in the pyramid.

Merchandise planning for private label goods that are internationally sourced may take place at the conglomerate, group, or corporate tiers. Desire for economies of scale may encourage high-level coordination of these activities. The larger the quantities the firm buys, the more power the firm has when sourcing in the global market. Private label goods are often intended to offer good value to consumers while contributing to the improvement of overall gross margin; thus, merchandise cost is an important sourcing factor. By combining orders from several divisions or corporate units, economy of scale can often be achieved.

For example, Target Corporation owns Associated Merchandising Corporation (AMC), a buying office specializing in sourcing and private label product development. AMC handles much of the sourcing for the various channels included in Target Corporation as well as providing services for outside retail clients. When smaller firms are members of corporate buying offices, the buying office assists with merchandise planning and buying similar to conglomerate or division-level activity in large firms.

 Learning Activity 4.1

Line planning fundamentals

1. How does line planning relate to line development and presentation?
2. What are the key differences between traditional line planning and contemporary line planning?
3. What is the relationship between organizational structure and merchandise planning processes?

      Case 4.1 Federated to supply goods for Bon-Ton *

Department stores have long regarded each other as fierce competitors. In a first for Federated Department Stores, Inc., the Federated Merchandising Group (FMG) will become a sourcing arm for private label merchandise at Bon-Ton Department Stores, Inc.

Federated Department Stores, Inc. is the largest retail department store conglomerate in the United States, operating

(continued)

460 stores in 34 states. In terms of the organizational pyramid, Federated has Groups that provide support operations: FACS (financial) Group, FS (electronic systems) Group, FASST (logistics and operations) Group, and FMG. The headquarters are in Cincinnati, Ohio, and New York, while the groups are scattered across the country. At the corporate level, the department stores include Bloomingdale's and Burdines as well as multiple divisions of Macy's combined with regional department stores like Rich's and Lazarus.

FMG is responsible for the process of conceptualizing, designing, sourcing, and marketing private label and private branded goods across all of Federated's department store divisions. Networking with its 17 offices in 14 countries, FMG can find the best source for each product to bring definitive value at competitive retail prices.

Bon-Ton Department Stores, Inc. is a regional department store chain with 72 stores in 9 northeastern states. Bon-Ton's strategy is to carve out a niche for moderate and better price merchandise in smaller markets with stores located close to their customers.

The arrangement between FMG and Bon-Ton does not provide for the sale of Federated's own private label brands, including Charter Club, Alfani, and I-N-C, in Bon-Ton stores. The sourcing assistance is for Bon-Ton's own private label goods. FMG may also assist in development of new private label goods. The arrangement with another department store is the first of its kind for Federated. FMG does have similar arrangements with a specialty retailer that is a Federated division. The scope of FMG's global network was one attractive factor in Bon-Ton's choice of FMG. The agreement replaces an arrangement Bon-Ton had with the now-defunct Frederick Atkins Inc., a New York-based retail buying office that closed its doors last month.

Marvin Traub, former CEO of Federated's Bloomingdale's said, "This is a good arrangement for both, with FMG acting as manufacturer in the development of private label merchandise. Traub noted that the arrangement would be a source of revenue production for Federated and provide expertise that Bon-Ton lacks. Emanuel Weintraub, president of Weintraub Associates, a management consulting firm, pointed out that the arrangement makes for more purchasing power in the global market for FMG. The deal is a reflection of how companies are starting to look at their core competencies and how those skills fit in with strategies going forward.

Bon-Ton and Federated are not direct competitors since Bon-Ton operates in secondary markets in Pennsylvania, New

Case 7.1 (continued)

York, New Jersey, and other eastern states. As one of several regional retailers struggling with disappointing results, Bon-Ton is considered a potential takeover target. After a first quarter loss of $5.1 million, the company cut 137 jobs and eliminated 50 unfilled positions in its corporate office and at stores.

*Based on Bon-Ton (2003), Federated Department Stores (2003), and Young (2000).

 Learning Activity 4.2

Federated and Bon-Ton

1. What are the advantages to Bon-Ton in making use of FMG's services?
2. How will using FMG's services affect Bon-Ton's line planning processes?
3. What does it mean to say that FMG is acting as a manufacturer?
4. What core competency is Bon-Ton lacking that FMG can provide?
5. Do you think this "deal" would have happened if Federated and Bon-Ton were direct competitors? Explain your answer.
6. The Federated organizational structure lends itself to the BTAF model. Create a BTAF model for Federated.

Dimensions of Planning Product Lines

Dimensions of product lines identified by Glock and Kunz's (2000) definition of merchandising are "prices, assortments, styling, and timing." These dimensions must be identified, described, and understood before planning merchandise budgets and merchandise assortments.

Pricing Dimensions

Merchandise price is used as an indicator of product quality as well as the amount that has to be paid to buy a product. Of course, product price is not always consistent with intrinsic quality or the value a customer places on a product. Firms use customers' perception of quality in relation to price when they describe their products as being in the budget, moderate, or better price ranges depending on their target customers. Merchandisers select or develop products, select materials, and perhaps recommend performance and quality characteristics that can be executed within a price range. They also help set list prices for manufacturers and first prices for retailers. List prices provide the foundation for pricing in the manufacturing sector; first prices are the basis of pricing in the retail sector. Merchandisers determine markup and the timing and amount of markdowns that are consistent with the firm's pricing strategy. The complexities of the pricing process are addressed more completely in Chapter 5.

Assortment Dimensions

A **merchandise assortment** is a range of choices offered at a particular time. A merchandise assortment is determined by the relative number of styles, colors, and sizes included in the line. A **SKU** is a stock keeping unit determined by a combination of style, size, and color. Apparel merchandise assortments are sometimes structured by related product groupings called collections or stories. Perhaps the most critical merchandising problem is that of having—on demand—the type of merchandise in the SKU sought by a customer at a particular time.

Classifying Merchandise

An effective merchandise classification system contributes to having the right merchandise assortment; it facilitates planning, developing, and presenting product lines, as well as customers' shopping and merchandise selections. Classifying merchandise is the process of arranging the merchandise mix into groups based on the criterion of the end-user. Criterion might include functional use, quality, size range, rate and type of product change, and product characteristics. A classification system organizes many unique pieces of merchandise into manageable groups (Taylor, 1970).

A merchandise classification system consists of a set of names and code numbers for breaking down the total merchandise mix into consistent identifiable groups. A classification system enables the following activities:

- evaluating consistent merchandise groups for sales potential, profitability, or expense reduction

- timing of beginning, peak(s), and end of selling periods
- eliminating unplanned duplication of merchandise
- planning dollar sales and stocks with reasonable precision
- developing realistic dollar open-to-buy
- facilitating communication among managers, sales associates, merchandisers, sales representatives, and distribution managers
- providing appropriate space for storage and/or display (Taylor, 1970)

Effective classification systems may include the following categories:

- class and subclass codes and descriptions
- seasonal indicators for each class and subclass
- age limit/markdown time for each class or subclass
- price lines or price ranges
- allowable cost
- minimum initial markup percentage
- preferred resources (Taylor, 1970, p. 15)

Classification information in relation to inventory and sales records (including when products were sold, at what price, gross margin generated, rates of markdowns, and job off rates) provides a substantive foundation for continuing, increasing, decreasing, or modifying the merchandise in a product class. Classification systems may be modified as types of merchandise are added to the assortment. Over-classifying, or having too detailed a classification system, may generate meaningless information. Think about the characteristic of classification systems as you read Company Profile 4.1, Mike's Bikes, Part 2, Merchandise Mix. If you are not familiar with cycling apparel, do an Internet search to get some pictures and descriptions of various products. Pay particular attention to how products are described and presented in merchandise groups. (You may want to put a tab on the Company Profile page so you can easily refer to it later.)

Mike's Bikes has primarily 2 selling periods a year with 26 weeks each, spring and fall, with a bubble in the middle of the summer for RAGBRAI. Some merchandise groups have 4 or 5 selling periods of 10 to 13 weeks, while other groups have only one 26, 52, or 104 week period.

Company Profile 4.1

Mike's Bikes, Part 2, Merchandise Mix*

Mike's Bikes' merchandise mix includes three categories: bikes, apparel, and accessories. They also have a bike service department. Mountain bikes represent the majority of demand in central Iowa and sales continue to increase. Road bikes are a small but consistent part of the business and sales have shown some growth lately. Hybrid bikes — combinations of mountain, road, and/or racing bikes — tend to be higher priced than mountain and road bikes, but interest has grown with increased availability of both hard service and off-road bike paths. Other bikes include portables, recumbents, and kid's. Portables have either folding frames or separable frames and can be carried on airplanes like luggage or stored in closets. Portables can be broken down in about 30 minutes and re-assembled in about 45 minutes. There is growing interest in portables from people who bike during their travels as well as from apartment-living, bike-riding commuters. Recumbent bikes require the rider to lie back while operating the bike. Mike's Bikes keeps a few recumbents on hand, primarily as a novelty for their customers. Kid's bikes are offered primarily as a convenience to serious recreational biking customers with families.

Bikes are sold in three price ranges: budget, moderate, and better. Budget/starter type bikes are $250 to $450; mid-range, moderate priced bikes are $500 to $800; better and custom bikes are $900 and up. Bikes can be special ordered. Demand is strong for upper-moderate and high-end bikes from customers living in high-income western Des Moines suburbs.

Mike's Bikes has six classifications of apparel: cycling shorts and tights, jerseys and tops, outerwear, shoes, socks, and gloves. Cycling shorts cling to the body and feature chamois pads in the crotch designed to quickly absorb and evaporate sweat and reduce friction on the saddle. They are worn without underwear to prevent chafing from elastic and seams. Baggier shorts with Lycra liners are included in the assortment for people who do not want to appear in public in skintight garments. Shorts are solid colors or solids with side stripes. Tights are usually solid colors and extend past the ankle. They have stirrups under the foot to hold them in place. Tights are worn under shorts for biking in inclement weather.

Cycling jerseys feature long tails so the biker's back will be covered when in biking position. There are usually pockets across the lower back for carrying cell phones and other necessities. Jerseys are made of technical fabrics that wick perspiration and feature bright colors or striking printed designs for riding safety and fashion. Finally, jerseys should have a snug fit so they do not flap in the wind. Jerseys are classified as solids, color blocked, and fancy. They are offered in long, short, and sleeveless styles. Other tops tend to be less expensive than jerseys, are usually solid colors, and may be worn under jerseys in inclement weather.

The size ranges for bottoms and tops are small, medium, large, extra large, and extra-extra large. Average first price is $75 for tops and $65 for bottoms, with women's about $10 higher than men's.

Cycling shoes have hard soles to alleviate pedal pressure that can cause foot pain, tingling in the toes, or numbness. Stiff soled shoes minimize possible foot pressure problems and increase efficiency of energy transfer between legs and bike. For bikes with clipless pedals, biking shoes are required to have cleats to attach to pedals. Some styles have recessed clipless pedal cleats for easier walking. Styles differ for mountain and road biking, although both include sandals and racing shoes. Cycling shoes range in price from $50 to over $200.

Cycling socks are designed to keep feet comfortable and dry. Cycling socks are made of thin, snug-fitting, sweat wicking and evaporating fabrics. For example, a popular quarter sock style is made with a 38 percent ultra-soft Merino wool outer layer, 38 percent stretch nylon for durability, 18 percent four-channel polyester for wicking, and 6 percent spandex for close fit. Bicycling is also a great excuse to wear fun socks with interesting designs and colors. Socks range in price from $6 to over $18.

Cycling gloves have padded palms to reduce the amount of road shock transmitted to your hands. They also minimize pressure on the median nerve of the palm to prevent numb or tingling fingers. Tough fabrics for the palms help avoid "hamburger hands," which is what palms look like when you take that inevitable spill. Fingerless design exposes fingertips given greater "feel" for the road and increases dexterity for shifting gears and adjusting clothing. Some styles have mesh-like backs for air circulation. Cycling gloves range in price from $10 to over $50.

Requirements for outerwear include jackets, wind breakers, and slickers that are wind and rain proof, lightweight, and brightly colored for safety. Some have lightweight mesh liners. Since bikers can't wear underwear, they often wear arm and leg warmers for protection of the extremities. Outerwear is offered in unisex sizes from double extra small to double extra large. Outerwear ranges in price from $95 to $200.

(continued)

Cycling helmets are the most frequently purchased accessory, ranging in price from $30 to over $170. Helmets have been shown to reduce risk of head injury by over 85 percent. Helmets have to be replaced every three or four years because foam padding deteriorates. High-end helmets have aerodynamic design and vents to allow air to flow through your hair. Good fit is important. Some have rear "locking systems" to allow ponytails. Lance Armstrong's red, white, and blue colors have been very popular. Other accessories include backpacks for water bottles and sunglasses for eye protection.

Bike parts include racks, saddles, pedals, and other hardware attachments. Many new designs of saddles are now available. Good fit is essential for comfort on long rides. Other accessories include bike tools and tool kits and computers. Bicycle parts like wheels and tires are part of the service department since the service department has to have those parts on hand.

*Thanks to Team Estrogen (1998) for technical information.

 ### Learning Activity 4.3

Dimensions of product lines

1. Why are merchandise classification systems carefully structured?
2. How might price be used in structuring assortment dimensions?
3. What criteria might be used to set up a classification system?
4. Based on Mike's Bikes, Part 2, what types of criteria are particularly important in classifying merchandise?
5. What assortment dimensions are addressed in the merchandise descriptions at Mike's Bikes?
6. What priorities does Mike's Bikes appear to have relative to selection of merchandise?
7. In what way is Mike's Bikes considering the needs of their customers?

Breaking Down a Merchandise Assortment

There is a great deal of inconsistency in the use of language describing merchandise. Therefore, the terms used here reflect a simple system that makes sense within this context, but may differ from systems you read about in other texts or experience as customers or employees of a manufacturer or retailer. A detailed classification system must be learned in the context of a particular firm because each one is unique to the company.

A total **merchandise mix** is the complete offering of a particular manufacturer or retailer. This mix is comprised of categories of merchandise. For example, the merchandise mix offered by a men's specialty retailer may include the categories of suits, outerwear, casual wear, furnishings, and accessories. **Merchandise categories** may be broken down further into **merchandise classes** and **merchandise subclasses.** Classes within the suit category may be single-breasted, double-breasted, and formal. Subclasses within the single-breasted class may be solids, stripes, and tweeds. Subclasses may, in turn, be broken into **merchandise groups.** Subclasses and groups are described by assortment factors that make up an SKU. For apparel, SKUs are usually defined by style, size, and color. To summarize, the breakdown of a merchandise mix goes from

categories to…
classes to…
subclasses to…
groups to…
assortment factors.

See Table 4.1 for an example of breaking down a merchandise assortment at Mike's Bikes. The table includes all of the categories and classes but not all subclasses and merchandise groups.

A **balanced assortment** is one that has a well-planned variety of styles, sizes, and colors for special appeal to a specific market. A primary goal of merchandise planning is offering balanced assortments. At the same time, the firm must sell each style or merchandise group in adequate numbers to meet volume and profit goals. A balanced assortment results in satisfied customers and meets merchandising goals including the following:

Goal 1. adequate variety to attract target customers
Goal 2. adequate inventory to prevent stockouts
Goal 3. minimum investment in slow-moving goods
Goal 4. minimum investment in total inventory
Goal 5. maximum gross margin
Goal 6. maximum gross margin return on inventory
Goal 7. maximum stock turn

Table 4.1

Fundamentals of the merchandise classification system at Mike's Bikes. *

Merchandise Categories and Classes within a Merchandise Mix

Bikes	Biking Accessories	Apparel
Mountain bikes	Bike parts	Shorts/tights
Road bikes	Helmets	Jerseys/tops
Hybrid bikes	Tools/tool kits	Outerwear
Other bikes	Computers	Cycling shoes
	Sunglasses	Socks
	Backpacks	Gloves

Subclasses within Selected Classes

Other Bikes	Bike Parts	Shorts/Tights	Jerseys/Tops	Cycling Shoes
Portable bikes	Racks	Solid color shorts	Solid jerseys	Mountain cycling
Recumbent bikes	Saddles	Baggy shorts	Color blocked jerseys	Road cycling
Children's bikes	Pedals	Side stripe shorts	Fancy jerseys	Women's cycling
	Other	Tights	Tops	Kid's cycling

Merchandise Groups within Selected Subclasses

Portable Bikes	Solid Color Shorts	Baggy Shorts	Mountain Cycling Shoes
Folding frames	Men's	Men's	Sandals
Separable frames	Women's	Women's	Racing
	Kid's	Kid's	

Assortment Factors for Selected Subclasses and Merchandise Groups

Folding Frames	Saddles	Tops	Mountain Cycling Sandals
Brand	Style	Style	Style
Style	Size	Size	Size
Size	Color	Color	Color
Color			

*Based on Company Profile 4.1, Mike's Bikes, Part 2, Merchandise Mix.

A balanced assortment may contribute more to merchandising success than any other activity. That said, it is also nearly impossible to achieve. In the list of results related to balanced assortments, improvement of one factor decreases the effectiveness of others. For example, minimum inventory (Goal 4) is sure to cause stockouts (Goal 2); an attractive variety of merchandise (Goal 1) may not allow minimum investment in slow-moving goods (Goal 3). Planning and developing balanced assortments is an ongoing merchandising challenge.

Learning Activity 4.4

Merchandise assortments

1. What is a balanced assortment?
2. What does it mean to "breakdown" an assortment?
3. What language is used in this text to describe the "breakdown" of merchandise assortments?
4. A woman is shopping at the sale rack at a favorite store and finds lots of sizes 2, 4, 16, and 18, but few sizes 6 through 14. What does that say about the retailer's assortment balance relative to size?
5. Considering the scenario in the previous question, describe the probable merchandising outcomes in terms of stockouts, lost sales, and markdowns.
6. Using Table 4.1 as a model and the information in Company Profile 4.1, break down the assortment for outerwear at Mike's Bikes from category to class, to subclass, to group, to assortment factors.
7. Using the same process as #6, set up a classification system for helmets.

Styling—Dimensions of Product Change

Styling refers to the appearance of a product. It involves selecting or developing the creative, functional, and fashion aspects of line. Styling must be consistent with the firm's market positioning strategy in terms of the relative number of fashion and/or basic goods in an assortment. If a firm defines itself as fashion forward, most styles it includes in a line must convey fashion leadership. If a firm defines itself as offering classics, then the styles included in the line should reflect time-tested favorites. Style choices for a particular selling period are framed by the development of the line concept. In the line development process, specific styles are selected or developed to fill out the line plan.

Dealing with the demand for constantly changing products may be one of the most challenging and interesting aspects of apparel merchandising. The explanation of the demand for intense product change is often attributed to fashion. However, understanding fashion change is a subject of some complexity. Psychologists speak of fashion as the seeking of individuality; sociologists see class competition and social conformity to norms of dress; economists see a pursuit of the scarce; aestheticians view the artistic components and ideals of beauty; historians offer evolutionary explanations for changes in designs. Literally hundreds of viewpoints unfold from a literature more immense than for any phenomenon of consumer behavior (Sproles, 1985).

The stages of the fashion process are often discussed in relation to a bell-shaped curve representing levels of fashion acceptance. Sproles provides a meta-theory approach to understanding fashion change (see Table 4.2); he emphasizes the complexity of perspectives on what drives fashion change.

Merchandising Perspectives on Product Change

From a merchandising perspective, "fashion is a continuing process of change in the styles of dress that are accepted and followed by segments of the public at any particular time" (Jarnow, Judelle, & Guerreiro, 1981). A second aspect of product change — seasonal change — is often confused with fashion change by both academicians and apparel professionals. The terms "seasonal goods" and "fashion goods" are often used interchangeably, as are the terms "basics" and "staples." However, when fashion change is separated from seasonal change, this clarifies the characteristics of product change with which merchandisers must contend. Essential first steps are distinguishing between "fashion" and "seasonal" and "basic" and "staple."

Fashion goods are products that experience demand for change in styling. **Style** is the characteristic or distinctive appearance of a product, the combination of features that makes it different from other products of the same type (Troxell & Judelle, 1981). **Fashion goods** require frequent change in styling in order to maintain acceptance from consumers. For example, the salable life of junior dress styles may be only about eight weeks and the salable life of some music CDs is less than that.

In contrast, products that have little demand for style change are called **basic goods.** Basic goods, with little or no change in styling, may be salable in the same styles from one year to perhaps several years. White cotton socks and batteries are classic examples of basic goods.

Seasonal goods experience change in demand related to a combination of factors associated with the calendar year, including ethnic and cultural traditions, seasonal events, and weather changes. Holidays and the beginning and ending of the school year have a major

Table 4.2

The framework for a general fashion theory. *

Stages of the Fashion Process	Explanatory Models
Invention and Introduction	Aesthetic (art movements, ideals of beauty) Business (market infrastructure) Cultural (subcultural leadership) Historical (historical resurrection, historical continuity)
Fashion Leadership	Aesthetic (art movements, ideals of beauty, aesthetic perception) Communications (symbolic communications, adoption and diffusion) Cultural (social conflict) Economic (scarcity, conspicuous consumption) Psychological (individuality) Sociological (trickle down)
Increasing Social Visibility	Aesthetic (aesthetic perception) Business (market infrastructure, mass market) Communications (adoption and diffusion) Geographical (spatial diffusion) Psychological (uniqueness) Sociological (collective behavior)
Conformity within and across Social Groups	Communications (adoption and diffusion) Economic (demand) Geographic (spatial diffusion) Psychological (conformity)
Social Saturation	Business (mass market, market infrastructure) Economic (demand) Psychological (individuality) Sociological (collective behavior)
Decline and Obsolescence	Business (mass market, market infrastructure) Communications (adoption and diffusion, symbolic communications) Economic (demand) Historical (historical continuity) Psychological (individuality)

*Based on Sproles (1985, p. 66).

impact on the demand for certain types of products. Some seasonal goods sell only a few weeks out of the year, for example, holiday décor.

In contrast to seasonal products, products that have little change in demand relative to the time of the year are called **staple goods**. Staple goods sell 52 weeks a year and perhaps longer at similar rates. Change in demand related to the time of the year may or may not include a corresponding demand for change in styling. Batteries are basic as well as staple goods and so are white cotton socks.

A Perceptual Map of Product Change

Figure 4.2 is a Perceptual Map of Product Change reflecting a two year time period. This model is an update and expansion of the **Perceptual Map** that appeared in the first edition of this textbook. The same concepts and assumptions support this Perceptual Map except this model relates to a 2-year, 104-week time period and basic/staple goods have a 52- to 104-week selling period instead of a 26- to 52-week selling period. Some apparel products are highly fashionable; others are highly seasonal. Some are both seasonal and fashionable; others are neither. The impact of these aspects of product change on merchandise planning and positioning can be visualized through the use of this Perceptual Map, a graphic means of plotting variation in length of time consumers' demand selected fashion and seasonal products.

Fashion/Basic Continuum   Think of a completely basic product as one with no demand for styling changes through a 104-week time period, two merchandising cycles. At the other extreme, think of a fashion product that experiences weekly demands for styling change. Putting these two scenarios opposite each other on a line results in a continuum related to demand for change in styling. At one extreme are completely basic products with infrequent demand for style change and relatively long selling periods, over 52 weeks. At the other extreme are high-fashion or fad items requiring very frequent changes in styling and relatively short selling periods, usually less than 26 weeks. This continuum is represented horizontally in Figure 4.2 as an arrow from 1- to 104-week time periods.

Seasonal/Staple Continuum   A completely staple product experiences no change in demand related to the time of year and sells at a similar rate throughout the year and perhaps longer. A completely seasonal product would be salable for only one week. The seasonal/staple continuum is represented vertically in Figure 4.2 as an arrow from 1- to 104-week time periods.

Four sectors are created by the intersection of the fashion/basic and seasonal/staple continuums. These are useful in describing product characteristics in relation to length

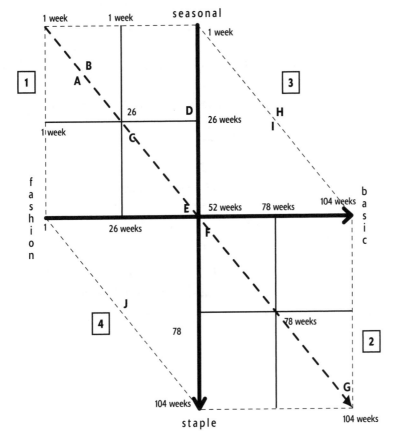

Figure 4.2 Perceptual map of product change.

Types of Mike's Bikes Products in Each Sector

<u>Sector 1</u>

A. Jerseys (13 weeks)—both fashion and seasonal influences

B. Cycling Gloves (13 weeks)—both fashion and seasonal influence

C. Outerwear (26 weeks)—both fashion and seasonal influence

D. Mountain Biking Sandals (26 weeks)—strong seasonal influence, some fashion influence, carried only half the year

E. Mountain Biking Racing Shoes (52 weeks)—some influence of both fashion and seasonal

<u>Sector 2</u>

F. Road Bikes (52 weeks)

G. Tools (104 weeks)—very basic, very staple

<u>Sector 3</u>

H. Solid Colors Cycling Shorts (52 weeks)—basic but seasonal

I. Arm and Leg Warmers (52 weeks)—basic but seasonal

<u>Sector 4</u>

J. Backpacks (52 weeks)—staple with occasional color or style change of selling periods and the associated demand for product change. Table 4.3 provides a summary of definitions that have been developed so far relative to merchandise planning, merchandise mix, and product change. These definitions relate to the Perceptual Map.

Assessment of Product Change and Length of Selling Periods

Mike's Bikes' Company Profile 4.1 describes their merchandise while the merchandise mix is broken down in Table 4.1. Merchandise classes and subclasses used for examples on the Perceptual Map include solid color cycling shorts, mountain biking sandals, mountain biking racing shoes, road bikes, outerwear, jerseys, arm and leg warmers, backpacks, and tools. To place items on the Perceptual Map, answer the following questions:

1. Does a class or subclass have demand for change in styling and how often?

2. Does the same class or subclass have change in demand related to the time of the year?

3. Where should this same class or subclass be placed on the Perceptual Map to understand the balance between fashion and seasonal influences and the length of the selling period?

Table 4.3

Summary of definitions related to merchandise planning.

Merchandising—the planning, development, and presentation of product line(s) for identified target market(s) with regard to prices, assortments, styling, and timing.

Merchandising Cycle—one-year period from February 1 to January 31.

Weeks of Sale—time period during the merchandising cycle that a particular classification of merchandise is salable.

Merchandise Classification—group of products that are reasonable substitutes for each other from the perspective of customers; similar in function, selling period, and price.

Styling—characteristic or distinctive appearance of a product; the combination of features that makes it different from other products of the same type.

Fashion Goods—classifications that experience frequent demand for change in styling during a merchandising cycle.

Basic Goods—classifications that experience little demand for change in styling during a merchandising cycle.

Staple Goods—classifications that are in continuous demand throughout a merchandising cycle; demand is not greatly affected by the time of the year.

Seasonal Goods—classifications that experience changes in market demand during a merchandising cycle related to ethnic and cultural events, holidays, and weather changes.

Sector 1, fashion/seasonal, includes classes or subclasses with selling periods from 1 to 52 weeks. Many classes/subclasses of products, particularly in the apparel category, fall into the fashion/seasonal sector. Most selling periods for fashion/seasonal goods are between 1 and 26 weeks with some groups extending to 39 or 52 weeks. Retailers are increasingly striving to position selling periods so they are consistent with customer use of seasonal garments. Instead of relying on the decades-old strategy of stocking winter clothes in July and summer clothes in January, retailers including Old Navy, Payless Shoe Source, Express, American Eagle, and Abercrombie & Fitch are seeking to increase sales by offering clothes more in sync with the climate (D'Innocenzio, 2003).

At Mike's Bikes, cycling jerseys and gloves have both fashion and seasonal influences that demand new styles at least 4 times a year, thus each selling period is about 13 weeks. Jerseys are positioned at A and cycling gloves at B. Both jerseys and gloves require inspired design innovation to keep merchandise fresh and exciting to customers.

Outerwear is influenced by season as well as fashion. Spring and fall are the primary selling periods, so there are two selling periods a year, each consisting of about 26 weeks; therefore, outerwear is positioned at C. Mountain biking sandals have only one 26-week selling period a year so they are positioned at D. Designers and merchandisers have to consider cycling needs, fashion trends, and type of protection needed for both outerwear and cycling sandals.

Products that experience subtle fashion change from one year to the next are sometimes called "fashion basics." ("Fashion basics" is an apparel industry term for what are commonly called "classics" in the fashion literature.) They have both fashion and seasonal influences with one or two selling periods a year of 26 to 52 weeks each. At Mike's Bikes, some styles of mountain cycling racing shoes might be regarded as fashion basics. These might be positioned at E in Sector 1 in the Perceptual Map. Modification of fabrications and color assortments are the primary merchandising design tactics.

Sector 2, basic/staple, represents merchandise classes or subclasses that are basic and staple with 52- to 104-week selling periods. Products in this sector experience the least demand for product change and have a relatively stable rate of sale throughout a year or more. The same or similar styles can be stocked and sold for an extended period. Examples of products that are usually basic/staple products include underwear t-shirts, men's white boxer shorts, pajamas, athletic socks, work clothes, and budget nylon hosiery. AtMike's Bikes, a group of moderate-priced road bikes might be successfully carried for 52 weeks with only a few changes in color for the second 52 weeks. These bikes would be positioned at F in the Perceptual Map. Another basic/staple product at Mike's Bikes is bike tools. The same styles of bike tools could be sold through two merchandising cycles — 104 weeks — so, tools are positioned at G on the Perceptual Map. Basic/staple merchandise lends itself to standardized stocks and computer-based reordering systems.

Sector 3 includes basic/seasonal products that have selling periods from 1 to 104 weeks. Holiday merchandise tends to be somewhat stereotypical in styling from year to year but limited in selling period around each particular holiday. Merchandise for each major holiday (Valentine's Day, Easter, Halloween, Thanksgiving, and Christmas) tends to be sold during only a short four- to six-week selling period each year. An important basic and seasonal category in Mike's Bikes' apparel category is solid color cycling shorts positioned at H for 52 weeks. They could carry the same styles of solid color shorts for 52 weeks, a complete merchandising cycle. Winter underwear is another product that fits the basic/seasonal description; however, serious cyclists wear arm and leg warmers instead of underwear. Arm and leg warmers might be positioned at I with a 52-week selling period.

Sector 4 represents products that are fashion and staple with a potential selling period of 1 to 104 weeks. Solid color sheets may be a fashion/staple; the same styles stocked year-round with a slightly different fashion color palette each year with a 52-week selling period for each. But Mike's Bikes doesn't carry sheets. Backpacks might fit into fashion/staple with a 52-week selling period positioned at J. Relatively few categories of goods tend to fall into the fashion/staple sector.

Determining the Length of Selling Periods

Merchandise classifications could be more accurately placed on the Perceptual Map by analyzing sales figures that reflect changes in rate of sale during each week of the year. Clearly, the length of time that a particular style or classification is salable may be limited either by consumer expectation for fashion change or by the seasonal nature of the product. Merchandisers must understand what aspect of product change limits salability and makes merchandise plans accordingly.

Point-of-sale (POS) data combined with EDI makes appropriate information easily accessible to both manufacturers and retail merchandisers. Raw sales figures reflect two things:

- the results of decisions made by merchandisers and marketers related to selection, presentation, and promotion of goods
- customers' preferences relative to the merchandise offered

Fashion and seasonal changes are two aspects of product change that strongly influence merchandisers' decisions, who often have their salaries and/or number of assigned departments or classifications varied according to the "difficulty" of the merchandise. Difficulty of the assignment is highly related to the amount of change in the merchandise.

⬚ *Learning Activity 4.5*

Determining causes of product change and length of selling periods

1. What are the two primary causes of consumer demand for product change?
2. What determines the length of a selling period?
3. How long is a merchandising cycle?
4. According to the Perceptual Map of Product Change, what is the maximum length of a selling period for products that are in the fashion/seasonal sector?
5. What are the most common selling periods for fashion/seasonal merchandise?
6. What causes selling periods for fashion/seasonal goods to be so short?
7. According to the Perceptual Map of Product Change, what is the shortest selling period for products that are in the basic/staple sector? Is it easier for merchandisers to make decisions about fashion/seasonal or basic/staple products? Why?

Timing—Merchandising Calendars

Timing is determined by the nature of merchandise classifications in relation to the merchandising cycle. Timing of merchandise presentation at the wholesale and retail levels determines merchandise, marketing, and production schedules. The merchandising calendar for a manufacturer who sells wholesale is likely to be based on key market dates relating to major selling periods in the retail sector. A retail merchandising calendar defines the total merchandising cycle into selling periods for particular merchandise classifications. It also considers the timing of major selling periods and special promotions. A **selling period** is defined by an opening date, a closing date, and the overall selling trend. The calendar also might identify the potential for extending the selling period beyond the initial plan.

A component of timing that is extremely important for both manufacturers and retail merchandisers is the turnaround time between order placement and delivery of the goods to the retail sales floor. For both branded and private label goods, the time required from developing a concept for new merchandise to having the group ready to go into production is crucial, as is the time from beginning production until the goods can be delivered to the retail sales floor. Timing is a key factor in merchandising success.

For most merchandise classifications, the merchandising cycle is divided into selling and **transition periods** reflecting the buying cycles of customers. All other merchandising activities are planned backwards from the selling periods. Manufacturers' merchandisers plan backward from wholesale market dates and the wholesale market dates are planned backward from the retail selling periods. Retail merchandisers also plan backwards from retail selling periods. Key questions to answer when doing a merchandising cycle selling analysis for a particular merchandise classification include the following:

- During which weeks in the merchandising cycle does each selling period begin?
- During which weeks does each selling period end?
- How many peaks are in each selling period?
- During which weeks do the peaks occur in each selling period?
- What merchandising activities influence the sales per week?

Figure 4.3 shows selling periods in the merchandising cycle superimposed with buying cycles for cycling jerseys, a fashion/seasonal product. Jerseys have strong sales throughout the merchandising cycle because they can be worn alone during hot weather and worn with a long sleeve top underneath in cool weather. But demand for fashion and seasonal product change creates four selling periods a year. The vertical axis is weekly sales for the classification and the horizontal axis is weeks in the merchandising cycle beginning with week number one as the first week of February. The line segments in Figure 4.3 represent four different selling periods and four transition periods:

Selling period #1	=	11 weeks
Transition period #1	=	2 weeks
Selling period #2	=	11 weeks
Transistion period #2	=	3 weeks
Selling period #3	=	12 weeks
Transistion period #3	=	2 weeks
Selling period #4	=	7 weeks
Transistion period #4	=	4 weeks

The total is 52 weeks. Traditional semiannual merchandise clearance is included in transition. #2. The second semiannual clearance runs before transition #4 because the store is closed three weeks in January and the first week of February. The buying cycles indicate that four selling periods are appropriate for merchandise planning.

Figure 4.4 shows the sales during the selling period in the merchandising cycle for solid colored cycling shorts, a basic/seasonal product. The length of a selling period for these styles commonly is a single 52 weeks. Sales during the merchandising cycle increase for Father's Day and RAGBRAI, but it is not necessary to bring in new styles to support the rate of sale. The product is well developed to suit its end use and fashion influences are minimal. If the

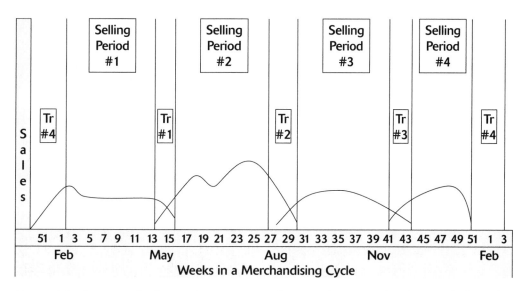

Figure 4.3 Illustration of selling and transition periods imposed on a merchandising cycle for cycling jerseys (a fashion/seasonal product).

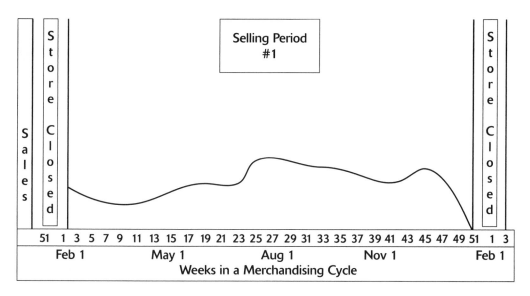

Figure 4.4 Illustration of a selling period with the buying cycle for solid color cycling shorts (a basic/seasonal product).

same merchandise is carried into the second merchandising cycle, then there is no clearance and no transition period at the end of the merchandising cycle. The biggest challenge to merchandisers is to select the right styles and colors and have merchandise in stock to avoid lost sales.

Developing a Merchandising Calendar

A **merchandising calendar** brings together multiple dimensions of merchandising decision making in relation to the merchandising cycle for particular merchandise classes, subclasses, or groups. A calendar commonly includes the following information in relation to the merchandising cycle for a particular merchandise group: months of the year, weeks in the merchandising cycle, seasonal events, selling and transition periods, pricing plan, and delivery plan.

Table 4.4 is a merchandising calendar for cycling jerseys by weeks in the merchandising cycle. The merchandising cycle shown here is consistent with the 4-5-4 calendar commonly used by retailers for accounting purposes. The 4-5-4 calendar defines the fiscal year from February through January, the same as the merchandising cycle; 4-5-4 stands for the number of weeks in each month for each quarter. For example, for the first quarter, the days of the month are manipulated so that there are four weeks in February, five weeks in March,

Table 4.4

Calendar-related events and selling periods by weeks in the merchandising cycle for jerseys/tops.

Month	Week	Event	Selling Periods	Pricing Plan	Delivery Plan
Feb	1	Groundhog Day	Transition period #4		
	2	Valentine's Day	Period #1/Peak#1		
	3	Presidents Day			
	4	**Bicycle Ride to Rippey**			
Mar	5				
	6				
	7	St. Patrick's Day			
	8	Spring begins			
	9				
Apr	10	**April Fool's Ride**			
	11	Jewish Passover			
	12	Easter Sunday	End Period #1		
	13	Admin. Prof. Day	Clearance		

(continued)

Table 4.4 (continued)

Calendar-related events and selling periods by weeks in the merchandising cycle for jerseys.

Month	Week	Event	Selling Periods	Pricing Plan	Delivery Plan
May	14	**Black Earth to Hyderseek**			
	15	Mother's Day	Period #2/Peak#1		
	16	Armed Forces Day			
	17	Memorial Day			
June	18				
	19	**Blast to Blanchardville**			
	20	Father's Day			
	21	**Recumbent Roundup**			
	22	**Just Pedal Faster**			
July	23	Independence Day			
	24	**Iowa Games**	RAGBRAI promo		
	25	**RAGBRAI**	Sales Peak #2		
	26		Semiannual Clear		
Aug	27				
	28		Preseason Sale		
	29		Begin Period #3		
	30	**Sugar Bottom Scramble**			
Sep	31	Labor Day			
	32	**Tour de Metro**			
	33				
	34	Autumn begins	Sales Peak #3		
	35	Jewish New Year			
Oct	36	Yom Kippur			
	37	**Columbus Day Drag**			
	38	End Daylight Savings Time			
	39	**Halloween Haggle**			
Nov	40	Fall Classic	End Period #3		
	41	Veterans Day	Transition #3		
	42				
	43	Thanksgiving	Begin Period #4		
Dec	44	**Big Wheel Rally**			
	45	**Winter to Wanker**			
	46	Hanukkah	Sales Peak #4		
	47	Christmas			
	48		Semiannual Clear		
Jan	49	**New Year's Day Recovery**	End Period #4		
	50		Transition #4		
	51	M.L. King Jr.'s Birthday			
	52				

and four weeks in April. To accomplish this, week one of the merchandising 4-5-4 calendar actually includes a few days of January (Donnellan, 1996).

National holidays and religious events that commonly influence sales or are used as a basis for promotional events (special purchases of merchandise or price promotions) are identified in relation to weeks of sale. The beginning and the end of each selling period are identified by week. In addition, timing of major promotional activities is identified along with timing of semiannual clearances. Columns are also indicated for pricing and delivery strategies. These will be addressed in future chapters.

Notice that for jerseys, Valentine's Day and Mother's Day both occur in the beginning of selling periods. The sale of men's and children's apparel responds to different seasonal holidays and events. The merchandising calendar for each merchandise group has to be customized to recognize natural events in relation to the time of the year as well as promotional events created by the merchandiser. In the case of Mike's Bikes, major regional biking events are always a factor when planning sales. They are shown in bold on the merchandise calendar.

An experienced merchandiser can look at spreadsheets of data, graphs, and tables and understand the significance of a particular week in the merchandising cycle, and with a little practice, you can, too. Relationships to holidays or cultural events, as well as merchandising activities that might have influenced sales in different weeks, are readily recalled. But even excellent merchandisers can't synthesize outcomes for forecasting without some systematic analysis of a variety of data. The current season needs to be compared to a similar interpretation of selling periods for last year and for previous years' merchandising cycles. Look for similarities and differences in timing and rate of sale for the same weeks. Statistical analysis can help interpret when differences really matter. Then, consider reasons for similarities and differences and determine which information provides the best foundation for planning for the coming merchandising cycle.

Many aspects beyond the sales history need to be considered to determine what aspects of sales history are unique to a particular selling period and which should be considered for future planning. These include:

- What factors influenced the beginning and end of the selling periods?
- Did the timing of merchandise delivery influence sales?
- Were inventory levels appropriate?
- Were sales lost because of unbalanced assortments?
- Were sales lost because of missed reorder opportunities?
- Were weather conditions a factor in any of the selling periods?

- What caused selling peaks?
- Would similar selling peaks be expected this year?
- For multi-store operations, were distribution plans effective by classification?
- How much and what kind of merchandise remains from the past season by store?
- How much and what kind of merchandise was transferred among stores?
- How might distribution plans be modified to balance assortments?
- Is remaining merchandise salable at regular price?

Learning Activity 4.6

Merchandise calendars

1. What is the purpose of a merchandise calendar?
2. If a merchandise group is carried year-round and has selling periods lasting 26 weeks, how many selling periods are there in the merchandising cycle?
3. If a merchandise group is carried year-round and has selling periods lasting 13 weeks, how many selling periods are there in the merchandising cycle?
4. What might cause sales peaks within a selling period? What is the importance of sales peaks in terms of merchandise planning?
5. Create a merchandise calendar for outerwear at Mike's Bikes. Reviewing Company Profile 4.1, Table 4.1, and Learning Activity 4.4, #6 before you begin. These will provide the necessary information. (You can use Table 4.4 as a guide, but remember that the selling periods for outerwear are not the same length as the selling periods for jerseys/tops.)

Forecast-Based Merchandise Plans

Members of the Supply Chain Leadership Committee of the American Apparel and Footwear Association frequently express frustration with the inaccuracy of forecasting. They were frustrated because their own merchandisers could not present merchandise plans that incorporated accurate forecasts for sales at wholesale to facilitate efficiency in production processes. They were also frustrated that their retail partners were ineffective in forecasting demand, even with the short time lines associated with QR systems.

One of the realities of being a professional merchandiser is that you are always wrong. There are many potentially "right" ways to do things and some have better results than others. But, there is always room for improvement in decisions related to dimensions of product lines — prices, assortments, styling, and timing. The purpose of merchandise forecasts is to provide a foundation for planning product lines to satisfy customers while achieving the firm's goals for each selling period in the merchandising cycle.

A mistake that is often made in the merchandise planning process is not looking beyond what can be directly derived from sales data. The Behavioral Theory of the Apparel Firm identifies essential external coalitions and environments that influence a firm's success. The **external coalitions** include communities in which the firm resides, competitors, customers, employees' families, shareholders, and suppliers. A systematic analysis for forecast-based merchandise plans includes these coalitions. Market research, focus groups, and brief telephone surveys can provide insights into the firm's perceived role in the community and what creates satisfied customers.

Regional and Local Economic and Cultural Influences

The apparel firm and its external coalitions operate in many overlapping environments, including cultural, ecological, economic, political, regulatory, social, and technological. During certain times these environments require particular attention in the merchandise planning process. Blackenterprise.com has identified five forces operating in these environments that will be present in the 21st century and will complicate apparel forecasting. These include the casually dressed workforce, the decreasing popularity of department stores, the emergence of urban wear, the stronger voice of youth, and the integration of technology into the fashion arena (blackenterprise.com, 2004).

According to Brannon (2000), forecasting must proceed in a systematic manner. To be effective, it includes the following steps:

1. Identify the basic facts about past trends and forecasts.

2. Determine the cause of change in the past.

3. Examine the differences between past forecasts and results.

4. Determine factors that are likely to affect trends in the future.

5. Apply forecasting tools and techniques, paying attention to issues of accuracy and reliability.

6. Follow the forecast continually to determine the reasons for significant deviations from expectations.

7. Update the forecast as changes are indicated.

During-the-Period Trend Analysis

Merchandise planning and forecasting is an ongoing, dynamic process. A merchandise plan is only good as long as it meets the needs of the firm and its customers. Plans should be reviewed at least every four weeks and modified as the need becomes apparent. Trend analysis needs to be conducted during the current selling period, because after the period ends, it may be too late for planning the same selling period for next year. Trend analysis might develop during the season as follows:

Evaluate fast sellers
- Determine the appeal of the product—quality, style, color, fit, price, other.
- Reorder for continued sales potential, if time permits.
- Rework merchandise presentation to feature similar and related merchandise.
- Update trend analysis.

Evaluate slow sellers
- Determine problem(s) with the product—quality, style, color, fit, price.
- Rework merchandise presentation to better display merchandise.
- Mark down promptly if price is too high.
- Consider stage of fashion cycle.
- Update trend analysis.

End-of-Period Trend Analysis

Analyzing overall productivity by classification is the final component of classification analysis. In a multi-store operation, it may be useful to look at combined statistics for a classification by store (Table 4.5). The evaluation criteria include sales volume, turnover, markdown percentage, maintained markup, and current sales trend. The means are presented for each criteria at the bottom of the table. **Sales volume** is total sales for the classification during the selling period being evaluated. Turnover is the number of times average inventory on hand was sold. **Percent markdown** is markdown dollars as a percent of net sales. Maintained markup is the difference between cost of merchandise, including its transportation, and selling price. Percent change in sales reflects the sales trend as compared to the same selling period last year. Other criteria might be included depending on the firm's goals.

Table 4.5

History of merchandise classfication by store. *

History of		Classification		Selling Period	
Store	Sales Volume	Turnover	% Markdown	% Maintained Markup	% Change in Sales
1	20,500	2.0	22.0	41.0	+16.6
2	18,700	3.1	10.7	50.3	+8.5
3	48,500	4.2	12.2	49.9	−5.9
4	67,000	4.3	10.9	52.1	−6.4
5	52,000	3.7	18.7	46.6	+11.0
6	48,000	3.3	15.5	45.1	+5.1
Mean	*42,450*	*3.43*	*15.0*	*47.5*	*+4.82*

*Based on *Retail Merchandising Services Automation, Inc.* (1995).

It is clear that a quick perusal of these figures does not reveal how the classification should be planned for the next selling period. Additional analysis, including serious reflection, is required to make merchandising decisions. A similar comparison should be made among classifications to evaluate their relative productivity.

📁   *Case 4.2   Merchandise planning with Accurate Response* *   📁

The academic expertise of Marshall L. Fisher from the Wharton School at University of Pennsylvania and Janice H. Hammond and Ananth Raman at Harvard University combined with Walter R. Obermeyer, principal of Sport Obermeyer, Ltd. in Aspen, Colorado, and other manufacturers and retailers has resulted in re-engineering the merchandising planning process.

Accurate Response combines QR practices with a new planning paradigm that maximizes profit by explicitly measuring forecast risk and then optimizing production to minimize stockouts and markdowns. Accurate Response appropriately *focuses attention on the result* (accurately producing the styles and colors customers want by responding to early market signals), *rather than the means* (lead time reduction). Costs associated with implementing Accurate Response are less than one-tenth of 1 percent of sales and the savings are at least 20 times that. Profits in the apparel industry average 3 percent of sales, so the savings are

---

---

great enough to increase profits at Sport Obermeyer by 66 percent.

Sport Obermeyer designs and manufactures fashion skiwear, including parkas, pants, suits, shells, jackets, sweaters, turtlenecks, and accessories. The merchandise is sold primarily through specialty ski shops. The primary retail selling period is about 26 weeks long, depending on the length of the ski season in different parts of the country.

Obermeyer is a dominant company in the fashion skiwear market. More than 95 percent of Obermeyer's products are new styles each year. Clearly, Obermeyer ski jackets are short life-cycle products. If you see an Obermeyer jacket you can't live without, buy it — you will not see it on the rack next year.

Obermeyer works with long lead times. The design process begins two years ahead of the retail selling period, and line adoption one year ahead. Production of components and garments begins in January in a variety of locales, including Hong Kong, China, Japan, Korea, Jamaica, Bangladesh, and the United States. Retail orders are received between February and May. Finished goods are shipped to Obermeyer's distribution center in Denver, then allocated to stores according to purchase orders in time for the beginning of the retail selling period in November. Obermeyer implemented numerous QR projects related to order processing and materials management to improve overall performance.

Perfecting Forecast-Based Merchandise Plans

Traditionally at Obermeyer each November, shortly after line adoption (about one year prior to the retail selling period), a six-member buying committee (president, vice president, merchandiser, and managers of marketing, production, and customer service) reviewed the new line. Through a consensus process, forecasted sales are determined for each style and color. Analysis of the forecasts relative to sales revealed the forecasts were accurate for about half of the company's products. The problem was, before the season began, there was no way of knowing which half of the products were accurately forecast.

In an attempt to improve the buying committee's forecasts, they modified the process so each member of the committee forecasts independently, rather than through consensus. They found the independent forecasts were better predictors of sales than those formed by consensus. They also were able to indicate which styles were being accurately forecasted by looking at the standard deviation among the independent forecasts for a single style (Table 4.6).

Table 4.6 shows the results of forecasting by committee. The forecasts made by each member of the buying committee are

(continued)

for a portion of the adult outerwear line. The overall forecast is the mean of the individual forecasts. The **standard deviation** for a style is estimated as twice the square root of the variance. A scale factor of two was chosen to equal the actual forecast errors from previous periods. Some styles were not forecast by all members of the committee; these are shown as blanks on the table and all calculations are done on the available individual forecasts. Obermeyer offers each style in about four colors, so the buying committee members also forecast the demand for each style/color

Table 4.6

Computing Forecast and Standard Deviation from Buying Committee Estimates. *

| | INDIVIDUAL FORECASTS | | | | | | Overall | Standard |
STYLE	Carolyn	Malinda	Laura	Kenny	Wally	Klaus	Forecast	Deviation
Women's Parkas								
Nell	4,000	3,000	3,500	3,200	4,100	2,200	3,333	1,284
Stardust	3,500	2,800	3,300	2,300	2,700	2,800	2,900	792
Tantric	2,500	2,600	2,000	2,100	1,500	1,800	2,083	761
Blue Ribbon	1,000	1,200	1,200	1,000	700	1,200	1,050	361
Shells								
Blondie	4,100	4,000	3,400	4,200	3,000	4,000	3,783	867
Pamela	2,000	1,800	2,200	2,100	2,000	2,000	2,017	243
Taylor	1,100	1,000	800	850	1,400	1,600	1,125	577
Suits								
Ruthie	1,200	1,000	1,300	1,800	1,400	1,500	1,367	499
Switchback	1,200	800	1,100	950	1,100	1,200	1,058	285
Audacious	700	1,000	800	450	600	600	692	348
Men's Parkas								
Ski Chute	800	1,200	800	850	1,000	1,000	942	285
Helicopter	1,800	1,000	800	1,150	900	1,600	1,208	736
Snowcat	1,100	1,200	1,100	1,150	900	1,000	1,075	198
Big Burn	800	1,400	1,500	1,350	800	1,700	1,258	684
Shells								
Quad	1,000	800	900	1,100	600		880	344
Zermatt	600	300	600	550	400		490	240
Suits								
Gondola	1,800	1,200	1,200	1,700	1,500		1,480	496
Innsbruck	800	600	500	800	1,000		740	349
Ravine	500	1,000	900	650	650		740	366
Cirque	400	500	300	250	400		370	174
Snowbird	500	700	1,100	600	450		670	463

*Fisher et al. (1994, February).

Case 4.2 (continued)

combination. The same method is used to compute the forecast and standard deviation for style/color combinations.

As shown in Table 4.6, the more the members of the buying committee disagreed about the sales potential of a style, the larger the standard deviation. The hypothesis is that if the buying committee disagrees on the sales potential of a style, demand uncertainty is greater for that style. Standard deviation provides a way to identify those styles and colors that are accurately forecast and can be produced with low risk of bad production forecasts. These styles are put into production early, reserving production capacity later in the merchandising cycle for products with uncertain forecasts. Forecast error on high-risk products have been shown to range from 50 to 100 percent (Fisher & Raman, 1999).

A program called Early Write is specifically directed toward improving merchandise forecasts for styles where the buying committee did not agree or had high standard deviations. Early Write invites a select group of customers, representing about 20 percent of sales, to the home office to place orders a month earlier than everyone else. Obermeyer uses these orders to reevaluate the accuracy of their forecasts. The Early Write orders represent a very small amount of sales data, but provide information that substantially improves forecasts. The retail buyers are closer to the ultimate consumer than the Obermeyer buying team; thus; they provide additional insight into the salability of the styles. The Early Write orders have priority for shipping, so these retailers receive their merchandise earlier than other retailers. Early Write also gives Obermeyer the potential to increase the "square-footage days" that goods are displayed by retailers. This is a key to achieving excellent sell-through for short life cycle products.

Performing Style Tests

Another option for perfecting potentially error-prone forecasts for short life cycle products is performing style tests. Merchandisers have observed that one week of pre-selling period exposure in a prominent place on a retail sales floor provides significant insight into customer preferences for a new product. Orders for the regular selling season can be modified by style, size, and color to greatly reduce merchandise planning error.

An experiment with a catalog company sought to reduce 55 percent of forecast error on their short cycle products. Sophisticated statistical analysis of the first two weeks of catalog sales reduced forecast error to eight percent of sales (Fisher & Raman, 1999). The greatest limitation of both style testing and analysis of early catalog sales is having QR suppliers that can produce the appropriate quantities and assortments quickly enough to resupply and support sales.

(continued)

Case 4.2 (continued)

Based on their creative and extensive research related to forecast error in merchandise plans, Fisher and Raman (1999) have created a company called 4R Systems that offers "product lifecycle intelligence." 4R helps calculate the risks and costs of stockouts vs. closeouts and then recommends what to buy, when to have it, and at what price (4R Systems, 2003). Stockouts mean you have the wrong merchandise in stock; closeouts mean you have excess stock left over after the selling period. Both problems increase average inventory, reduce stock turn, reduce gross margins, and reduce gross margin return on inventory.

The following are accurate response principles for reducing forecasting error:

- Invest technology and people's time into forecast-based merchandise plans.

- Identify what can and cannot be accurately forecast.

- Early in the process, seek diversity of opinion rather than consensus.

- Put accurately forecast products into early production.

- Reserve later production for less accurately forecast goods.

- Provide opportunities for experts and/or ultimate consumers to assist with poorly forecast goods.

- Use appropriate, systematic methods for ongoing analysis of effectiveness of forecasts.

*Based on Fisher & Raman (1999), Fisher et al. (1994, May/June), Fisher et al. (1994, February), and Obermeyer (2003).

 Learning Activity 4.7

Forecast-based merchandise plans

1. What is merchandise forecast error?
2. Why is forecast error such a problem?
3. In the Sport Obermeyer experiment, how does standard deviation help distinguish between good forecasts and bad forecasts?
4. Can the principles demonstrated by the Sport Obermeyer experiment be applied to forecast-based merchandise plans in the retail sector? How?

Category Management

Accurate Response addresses short life cycle merchandise and fashion/seasonal merchandise with relatively brief selling periods. Category management is now trying to extend its expertise beyond food and other consumables to fashion/seasonal, SKU intensive, lower turn merchandise. Food and consumables like soap and shampoo commonly have relatively low unit cost and relatively high stock turn (15 to 25 turns a year). They sell a high number of units per SKU and have relatively low forecasting error (less than 5 percent of sales). Apparel has a relatively high unit cost and a relatively low stock turn (1 to 4 turns a year), sells a relatively low number of units per SKU, and has high forecasting error (commonly over 50 percent of sales).

Category management has been developing as an art and a science for over a decade in food and other commodities. Category management is a sophisticated form of merchandise planning that, until recently, has had little application in fashion and seasonal goods. A fundamental problem with fashion/seasonal goods is how to define a category. One thing the experts do agree on is that categories should be defined by how the customer buys, not how the retailer buys. For example, yogurts are usually presented by brand name and customers shop by yogurt type: diet, low fat, thick, and creamy. Within these broad classifications, customers then shop for flavors. A study by Marsh Supermarkets found that sales and profits increased when cake mixes were displayed by microwavable and non-microwavable instead of by brand name. Other factors relevant to defining categories include unique aspects of a product's end use, products that are substitutable, and products that are complementary and likely to be purchased together (Karczewski, 2001). Each product should appear in only one category to minimize duplication in inventory and confusion on the part of customers.

Within a category, products should be assigned subcategory roles. Some examples include the following:

- Traffic Builders — products with high market share
- Transaction Builders — add-on type purchases; impulse items that increase total average sale.
- Cash Generators — popular items with higher margins and stock turn
- Image Creators — designer names or other things that impart prestige
- Excitement Creators — fashion or fad items with impulse appeal (Karczewski, 2001)

In the Mike's Bikes merchandise mix discussed earlier (Table 4.1), the color blocked jersey/tops subclass might include nine different styles chosen according to their role in the assortment: traffic builder, transaction builder, cash generators, etc. Perhaps bike racer Lance Armstrong licensed jerseys could be the image creator. However, this is not necessarily the way apparel merchandisers think.

The key to effective category management is the technology that supports the systems. The systems as they are now functioning contribute to merchandise planning and micro-marketing. They can handle vast amounts of data to zero in on consumer subgroups and determine where the merchandising opportunities lie. Many names are being used for the current systems including consumer-based category marketing, efficient consumer response, and customer relationship management. Customers want the merchandise they want to buy in stock. This requires daily restocking of merchandise sold yesterday or an hour ago (Schwartz, 2000).

Advancements in technology now allow market basket analysis. Store data is used to determine what types of products customers buy together. This allows retailers to plan promotions and adjacencies in store layout for convenient customer shopping. Fully functioning partnerships between retailers and their suppliers are essential for effective category management. See Case 4.3.

   Case 4.3 *Applying category management to SKU intensive,*
low turn merchandise*

It's tough enough to apply category management to fast turning consumables like food. But when it comes to apparel, housewares, home furnishings, and consumer electronics, the challenges are compounded multi-fold. As compared to consumables, these categories are beset by lower turns, higher unit costs, and longer lead times. In addition, they can quickly fall victim to seasonal variances, technological obsolescence, and the whims of fashion and consumer tastes. Retail leaders, however, often cite VF Jeanswear as the benchmark of successful category management. VF Corporation offers a portfolio of jeans brands that includes Lee, Wrangler, Riders, Rustler, Brittania, Chic, and Timber Creek. VF Jeanswear works with their retail customers on assortments at the style, size, and color levels.

They are more concerned about how it sold rather than what was shipped. VF Jeanswear once focused vendor managed inventory on what was shipped. Vendor managed inventory improved sales and profitability for both VF and the retailer because it reduced stockouts and average inventory while increasing sales. But category management does much more.

Rather than looking at shipments, the company now looks at what consumers choose to buy. One retailer reports, "Ten years ago, we had one fixture with 300 pieces in one color. Today, that same fixture has four or five colors in the same 300 piece inventory, and we probably have 100 different planograms of that fixture related to the store's sales and based on data generated through consumer research. You sell more when you give customers a better selection." VF has invested $50 million in technology, the people, and the resources over the last five years to manage the complexity inherent to category management of apparel.

VF starts the category management process by ascertaining the merchandise mix based on demographic and psychographic information determined by zip code, along with data on what is selling at the store. A trading profile is developed for each store based on which of the 15 different consumer-based store clusters it fits into, such as urban, rural, retirement area, or college town. A college town store may get cargo and carpenter jeans while a store that serves an elderly population will get stretch jeans. Determining where zip legs and techno fabrics fit in is worlds away from replenishing five-pocket basics.

They are combining the science of technology with the art of fashion. VF uses extensive testing, focus groups, and research to pick up on trends, especially as boys' and girls' jeans move quickly and closely mirror trends in juniors, and the latest styles almost immediately jump from trendy mall stores to the mass market stores. VF's expertise extends to the retail sales floor. Their research includes effectiveness of space management and fixturing in relation to the stores' customers' shopping preferences.

VF's category management has paid off. Over the last 4 years, their jeans business has grown by 40 percent. They are often driving the retailer's total jeans business, not just their own.

*Beyond Shampoo. (2000).

 Learning Activity 4.8

Category management

1. Why has apparel had less attention from category managers than food and other consumables?
2. Why is stock turnover such a concern of category managers?
3. How has VF Corporation improved forecasting of jeans?

4. What measures of merchandising success have VF improved for jeans?

5. Why is it a merchandising problem to have five colors of jeans in 300 units instead of one color of jeans in 300 units? What merchandising measures are likely to be affected?

Summary

Computerization of merchandise planning and other merchandising-related processes has had a profound effect on merchandising systems, even though this planning technology has not until recently kept pace with the other functions of a firm. The development of intense competition in both manufacturing and retailing global markets during the 1980s resulted in a focus on price competition. Merchandisers traveled the world seeking lower merchandise costs. In the 1990s, quick response (QR) business systems focused on the benefits of saving time and recognized the essential need for forecast-based merchandise plans.

An effective merchandise classification system is an essential foundation for merchandise planning. The language used for merchandise classification varies greatly among firms. Therefore, a simple system of commonly used terms is presented in this text. The merchandise mix is made up of categories, which can be further broken down into classes and subclasses. Subclasses may be divided into merchandise groups. Groups are described according to assortment factors; for apparel these are usually style, size, and color.

Two primary contributors to demand for product change are fashion change and the time of year. The terms "seasonal goods" and "fashion goods" are often used interchangeably, as are the terms "basics" and "staples." However, when fashion change is separated from seasonal change, this clarifies the characteristics of product change with which merchandisers have to deal. The length of selling periods for fashion, seasonal, basic, and staple merchandise can be determined by thinking in terms of a Perceptual Map of Product Change. A merchandising calendar incorporates the concepts of a merchandising cycle, selling periods, and seasonal events that contribute to sales peaks during a selling period. A merchandise calendar incorporates a time frame into merchandise plans.

The dimensions of product lines considered by both manufacturers and retail merchandisers include prices, assortments, styling, and timing. Merchandisers select or develop products, select materials, and perhaps recommend performance and quality characteristics that can be executed within the price range. A merchandise assortment is determined by the relative number of styles, colors, and sizes included in the line. Styling refers to the appearance of a product and involves selecting or developing product design, the creative, functional, and fashion aspects of line, as well as product development. Styling needs to be consistent with the firm's positioning strategy in terms of the relative number of fashion and basic goods in an assortment. Timing is determined by the nature of merchandise classifications in relation to the merchandising cycle. Timing of merchandise presentation at wholesale and at retail determines merchandise, marketing, and production schedules.

Forecasting is the most frequently requested feature in merchandise technology systems. Early forms of merchandising technology had forecasting based primarily on sales history. Today's firms focus on planning merchandise budgets and merchandise assortments based on more diverse forms of information, for example: 1) priorities of each of the firm's constituencies in relation to the firm's goals, 2) events impacting the firm's external coalitions, and 3) influences of a firm's environments.

Sport Obermeyer has developed a forecasting system based on the concept of identifying what goods can be accurately forecast and sourcing them early and by developing additional information on goods that cannot be accurately forecast and sourcing them later. Obermeyer uses standard deviation among individual forecasts as a measure of forecast accuracy. Now VF Corporation has perfected the art of category management with sophisticated planning and management systems.

Key Concepts

Accurate Response
assortment plans
balanced assortment
basic goods
bottom-up planning
category management
dollar plans
external coalitions
fashion goods
forecasting

integrated planning
merchandise assortment
merchandise budgets
merchandise categories
merchandise classes
merchandise groups
merchandise mix
merchandise subclasses
merchandising calendar
open-to-buy
organizational pyramid
percent markdown

perceptual map
sales volume
seasonal goods
selling period
six-month plans
SKU
standard deviation
staple goods
style
top-down planning
transition periods
unit plans

Integrated Learning Activity 4.9.1

Line analysis and merchandise calendars

1. Review and update the company profile for your MAP retailer in ILA 2.6.1 and the basic income statement that you created in ILA 3.7.1.
2. Who are the primary suppliers and/or what are the brand names carried by your retailer? Does your company use private label merchandise? If so, what are their private labels?
3. Make a table of the merchandise mix for your store including categories, classes, subclasses, merchandise groups, and assortment factors (use Table 4.1 as a model).
4. Draw a Perceptual Map of Product Change (use Figure 4.2 as a model) and plot your retailer's merchandise subclasses and/or merchandise groups considering change according to fashion or seasonal factors as well as the length of the resulting selling periods.
5. Choose two merchandise subclasses or merchandise groups based on your perceptual map for your retailer, one that is fashion/seasonal and one that is basic/staple. Develop a merchandise calendar for each using Table 4.4 as a model. Determine the number of selling periods, sales peaks, etc., to suit your selected merchandise groups.

◎ Integrated Learning Activity 4.9.2

Use Sourcing Simulator (SS) to analyze selling period seasonality in a merchandise calendar.

Objectives

- Apply information from your merchandise calendars to SS inputs.
- Consider differences in inputs and outputs considering fashion/seasonal and basic/staple merchandise.
- Test potential impact of errors in sales peaks on sales forecasts.
- Develop a better understanding of significance of sales peaks, length of selling periods, and measures of gross margin.

Resources to use for this assignment

- Integrated Learning Activities 2.6.3, 3.7.1, and 4.9.1 from this textbook and class notes
- SS Help screens
- Your teacher, lab assistant, and/or other class members

Procedure

1. Correct any errors from your line plans from ILA 2.6.3, 3.7.1, and 4.9.1. Think in terms of the fashion/seasonal and basic/staple merchandise groups for which you developed merchandising calendars.
2. Open SS Seasonal Model. Conduct the first experiment with your fashion/seasonal merchandise group in mind:
    a) Use the default data set for everything but instructions for changes in b through n.
    b) Fill out the Buyer's Plan with your fashion/seasonal product name, weeks in selling period, and pre-defined sales peak according to your merchandise calendar. Use 250 units to sell.
    c) Use the default assortment plan for style, sizes, and colors, but increase the number of styles to five and reallocate the planned percent to equal 100.
    d) On the Consumer Demand folder, use 0% error from plan for both volume and SKU mix; check same as presumed seasonality for the sales peak.
    e) On the Sourcing Strategy folder, use the traditional replenishment strategy and set initial stocking to 100%.
    f) On the Cost Data folder, use the default pricing plan or, based on your merchandise group, input the merchandise price and the probable cost (think in terms of keystone markup). Use the relationships in the default prices as a model.
    g) On the Markdown folder, use one 50% markdown three weeks before the end of the selling period.
    h) Run the simulation. Put the sales peak and your name in the title.
    i) Print your inputs and mark them with your name and highlight the "sales peak" inputs.
    j) On Consumer Demand folder, click Pre-Defined and then an appropriate peak to change actual seasonality so it differs from your merchandise plan.
    k) Run the simulation again and print your inputs again. Highlight sales peak inputs.
    l) Print your outputs. Highlight Customers, Total Offering, Lost Sales, Total Revenue, % Gross Margin, and Gross Margin Return on Inventory.
    m) Click View and Graphs. Print Number of Purchases, GMROI, Gross Margin, Lost Sales, and Average Inventory.
    n) Close SS; do not save inputs as default. Organize your printouts from your seasonal experiment in an orderly manner.

3. Open SS Basics Model. Conduct the second experiment with your basic/staple merchandise group in mind.
   a) Use the default data set for everything but instructions for changes in b through i.
   b) Fill out the Buyer's Plan folder with your basic/staple product name and Early Peak predefined sales peak. Use planned annual volume of 1,000 units. Use the default assortment plan for style, sizes, and colors.
   c) On the Consumer Demand folder, use 0% error from plan for volume and style, color, and size error, and click Early Peak.
   d) On Cost Data folder, use defaults unless you want to enter more appropriate Wholesale Costs and Retail Prices.
   e) On the Sourcing Strategy folder, use default.
   f) On the Promotions folder, use default.
   g) Run the simulation. Title it early/early.
   h) Print out the data input for the simulation.
   i) On the Consumer Demand folder, change Seasonality to Mid Peak.
   j) Run the simulation. Title it early/mid.
   k) Print out the data input for the simulation.
   l) On the Consumer Demand folder, change Seasonality to Late Peak.
   m) Run the simulation. Title it early/late.
   n) Print out the data input for the simulation.
   o) Examine the graphs of your output data. Be sure to put all three data sets on each graph. Print out Gross Margin and Lost Sales. Note: The graphs show three years of data.
   p) Print out your outputs. Note: Your outputs apply to one year of data.
   q) Highlight Customers, Total Offering, Total Revenue, and % Gross Margin.
4. Close SS. Do not save inputs as default.
5. Examine your Outputs and Output Graphs and write out answers to the following questions:
   a) Examine the highlighted outputs for your fashion/seasonal and basic/staple merchandise groups.
   b) Review the definitions of terms so you are sure what they mean. Use these to explain the appearance of the graphs in the following questions.
   c) Examine the number of purchases graph for the fashion/seasonal group. Does it look like a double-humped camel? Why or why not?
   d) Examine the lost sales graph. Why is there lost sales at the end of the selling period when both the merchandise plan and consumer demand have an early peak?

e) Why does the gross margin graph start out negative?

f) Why is gross margin lower when there is an error in forecasting seasonality?

g) Why is average inventory higher when there is an error in forecasting seasonality?

h) Why is gross margin return on inventory lower when there is an error in forecasting seasonality?

i) Are the same trends shown in your output graphs for both merchandise groups? Why or why not?

6. Assemble your inputs, outputs, graphs, and explanations in an orderly manner in your MAP.

Basis of Evaluation

1. Present this assignment in an orderly manner in your MAP. Be sure to include your merchandising calendars for each merchandise group identifying selling periods and sales peaks.

2. Include four simulation input printouts and two simulation output printouts and copies of graphs prepared according to your SS assignment.

3. What are the primary financial outcomes resulting from error in forecasting sales peaks? Specifically, what causes these outcomes?

4. How can forecasting sales peaks be improved?

Integrated Learning Activity 4.9.3

Read Case 4.4 very carefully. Assume you are going to open a "gently used" children's clothing store.

1. Develop a classification system for the merchandise you will carry.

2. Will each classification be consigned or purchased outright? Why?

3. Establish business policies for accepting goods and disposing of unsalable goods.

Case 4.4 *Second-hand items, first-rate bargains*

Some people turn their noses up at used clothes, some people consider these their best clothes, and some buy used items just for play clothes. It's no secret to parents, grandparents, and gift-givers that kids' clothes don't come cheap. That's one reason the children's consignment business involves a lot of loyal, repeat customers.

(continued)

Outfitting children from head to toe — tops, bottoms, socks, shoes, hair accessories, coats — can be both expensive and tedious. Then, quicker than you can capture the Kodak moment, the clothes are too small. Still, if there is no one to pass on the "previously loved" outfits to, there are good alternatives.

Charitable organizations like Disabled American Veterans (DAV), Goodwill, and the Salvation Army accept good used clothing as well as household items. In many cases, you can claim a portion of the value of donated merchandise as a deduction on income taxes if you itemize your return and get a receipt. Garage sales are another option. All you need is the ambition to clean up the items, set prices, sweep out the garage, make signs, place ads, and hang around the house all day waiting for customers to take interest in your merchandise.

But increasingly consumers are turning to consignment stores — to cash in on outgrown or unwanted stuff and to buy the "next size up" or a different version in bargain-priced used goods. For example, in the Des Moines, Iowa, area (population 250,000), there are nearly a dozen stores that resell children's apparel. Some cater exclusively to the kiddie market, others accept adult clothing, and many also take books, toys, baby equipment, and other children's paraphernalia. Assortments may include clothing for newborns to preteens,

plus children's furniture, books, toys, decorations, and miscellaneous articles.

Most consignment store operators are very selective about items they accept. Some specialize in items like dance wear and take mainly higher-priced clothing and name-brand items rather than play clothes. Some avoid casual clothes and playwear because they are so affordable from Wal-Mart, Target, and other mass retailers. Consigners are usually required to wash and iron clothing and hang it. If the clothing required dry cleaning, consigners may be required to provide a receipt.

In typical consignment agreements, whether a store deals in children's clothing exclusively or family apparel, the store contracts to keep items for 90 days and pay consigners 50 percent of the resale price of the item. If they don't sell, the price is reduced. If they still don't sell, they are donated to emergency shelters or other charitable agencies or must be reclaimed by the owners. A few stores will keep items indefinitely and store them off-season, then offer them for sale the following year.

ABC Children's Store in Johnston, Iowa, is one such shop. Out-of-season clothing is kept in a basement storage area but remains handy if needed out of season, say, for a vacation. Kay Wieland, who co-owns ABC with daughter Gail Bates, said the store does a mixture of buying outright and taking

Case 4.4 (continued)

consignments. However, in outright purchases, the seller is offered a price that is "just a little more than garage sale prices"—about a fourth to a third of what the store will mark them. That's in comparison to consignments, where the seller gets 50 percent of the selling price. Wieland said that often ABC will buy a customer's consignment "leftovers" and put the items on a sale rack. The store also takes the loss on any items that are shoplifted. "The customer can't use a loss, but we can take it off our taxes," she said.

Once Upon a Child, a franchise outlet in Clive, Iowa, is run by Shari Balberg. She handles children's clothing, toys, and accessories. Items are purchased outright, never consigned. Other Iowa Once Upon a Child stores are in Cedar Rapids, Waterloo, and Sioux City. Her main requirements for items are that they are freshly laundered and not stained or torn. Baby equipment and toys, equally big sellers, are checked against a list of manufacturers' recalls, so a customer can be sure that although the merchandise has "previous experience," it is of good quality.

Another franchise operation is Play It Again Sports, which, like Once Upon a Child, is a division of Minneapolis' Grow Biz International. There are two Des Moines outlets, both owned by Joe Schneider and his father, Dennis. Joe Schneider said a lot of used sporting goods for such children's activities as Little League and hockey are purchased outright. The stores also take in larger items—bicycles and fitness equipment—on consignment. Some athletic clothes for children and adults are available, but they must show only minimal wear to be accepted for resale.

Hand Me Downs are big in southern Ontario, Canada. Stephanie Jukes opened her first children's second-hand store in 1991, and with her husband's assistance, the second in 1993. With ongoing demand to open more stores, they decided to expand the operation through franchising. Franchising allowed continuity and integrity of their corporate mission, while involving other select entrepreneurs.

*Based on Hand Me Downs (2003) and Myers (1996).

Recommended Resources

Cristea, K., & Mangit, J. (2003). Fairchild's executive technology (www.executivetechnology.com). Accessed February 13, 2003.

D'Innocenzio, A. (2003, July 5). Time fashions: Stores pump up sales by keeping in sync with the climate. *The Tribune,* C7.

Fisher, M., Obermeyer, W., Hammond, J., & Raman, A. (1994, February). Accurate response: The key to profiting from QR. *Bobbin*, 35:48–62.

Fisher, M., & Raman, A. (1999, April 15). Managing short life-cycle products (www.ascet.com/documents.asp?d_ID=201). Accessed May 11, 2004.

Reda, S. (2002, February). On-line retail grows up. *Stores,* 30 & 34.

Target Corporation. (2003). (www.target.com). Accessed September 18, 2003.

References

Beyond Shampoo. (2000, October). *Retail Merchandiser* [Supplement], 24–25.

blackenterprise.com. (www.blackenterprise.com). Accessed June 18, 2004.

Bon-Ton. (2003). (www.bonton.com). Accessed September 22, 2003.

Brannon, E. L. (2000). *Fashion Forecasting*. New York: Fairchild Books.

Cristea, K., & Mangit, J. (2003). Fairchild's executive technology (www.executivetechnology.com). Accessed February 13, 2003.

D'Innocenzio, A. (2003, July 5). Time fashions: Stores pump up sales by keeping in sync with the climate. *The Tribune*, C7.

Donnellan, J. (1996). *Merchandise buying and management.* New York: Fairchild Books.

Federated Department Stores. (2003). (www.fds.com). Accessed September 23, 2003.

Fisher, M., & Raman, A. (1999, April 15). Managing short life-cycle products. (www.ascet.com/documents.asp?d_ID=201). Accessed May 11, 2004.

Fisher, M., Obermeyer, W., Hammond, J., & Raman, A. (1994, February). Accurate response: The key to profiting from QR. *Bobbin,* 35:48–62.

Fisher, M. L., Obermeyer, W., Hammond, J., & Raman, A. (1994, May/June). Making supply meet demand. *Harvard Business Review,* 72:83–90.

4R Systems. (2003). (www.4rsystems.com). Accessed August 23, 2003.

Glock, R., & Kunz, G. I. (2000). *Apparel manufacturing: Sewn Product Analysis* (3rd ed.). Upper Saddle River, NJ: Prentice Hall.

Hand Me Downs. (2003). (www.handmedowns.com). Accessed September 26, 2003.

Hart, E., Salfin, C., & Spevach, R. (1993, April 7). Matrix remakes marketing methods. *Daily News Record,* 11.

Jarnow, J. A., Judelle, B., & Guerreiro, M. (1981). *Inside the fashion business* (3rd ed.). New York: Wiley.

Karczewski, S. (2001). Category management (http://www.planfact.co.uk/catman.htm).

Kunz, G. I. (1988). Apparel merchandising: A model for product change. In R. C. Kean (Ed.), *Theory building in apparel merchandising*, pp. 15–21. Lincoln: University of Nebraska.

Karczewski, S. (2001). Category management (http://www.planfact.co.uk/catman.htm).

Myers, M. (1996, April 1). *Des Moines Register,* 1T & 2T.

Obermeyer, (2003). (www.obermeyer.com). Accessed September 9, 2003.

Reda, S. (1994, March). Planning systems. *Stores,* 76:34–37.

Retail Merchandising Services Automation, Inc. (1995). *Retail intelligent forecasting: Merchandise planning for the future*. Riverside, CA: Author.

Schwartz, E. (2000, October). A new chapter for category management. *Retail Merchandiser* [Supplement], 7–14.

Sears' merchandise allocation system helps spur turnaround. (1993, October). *Chain Store Age Executive,* 69(10):20–23, 26–31.

Skinner, R. C. (1992). Fashion forecasting at Oxford Shirtings. Proceedings of the Quick Response '92 Conference, 90–107.

Solomon, B. (1993, July). Will there be a miracle on 34th Street? *Management Review,* 82:33–36.

Sproles, G. B. (1985). Behavioral science theories of fashion. In M. R. Solomon (Ed.), *The psychology of fashion*, p. 66. Lexington, MA: Lexington Books.

Target Corporation. (2003). (www.target.com). Accessed September 18, 2003.

Taylor, C. G. (1970). *Merchandise assortment planning: The key to retailing profit*. New York: National Retail Merchants Association.

Team Estrogen. (2003). (www.teamestrogen.com). Accessed October 6, 2003.

Troxell, M. D., & Judelle, B. J. (1981). *Fashion merchandising*. New York: McGraw-Hill.

Young, V. (2000, October 17). Federated to supply goods for Bon-Ton. *Women's Wear Daily*, 2 & 4.

5

Merchandising

Perspectives

on Pricing

Learning Objectives

- Analyze the intricacies of pricing language.

- Examine the relationships among manufacturer pricing, retailer pricing, and customer perceptions of pricing.

- Evaluate components of pricing strategies as administered by consumer goods firms.

- Apply pricing mechanics to pricing processes.

*P*rices and pricing became major issues in consumer goods merchandising as increasing quantities were sold at less than the original ticketed price. At the peak of price-cutting practices that were particularly pervasive with apparel and in department stores, over 75 percent of goods were being sold "on sale" (Kaufmann, Smith, & Ortmeyer, 1994). A major contributor to retail price deflation was the perceived heightened price sensitivity of consumers (Levy, 1994, p. 1). Since then, consumers are commonly described as being "value conscious."

Price had become the primary component of consumer goods advertising. Selling at less than "regular" retail price had become so common that many consumers had been conditioned not to buy if a product was not "on sale." Firms had to recognize that price was an important component, but not the only component of merchandising. Research demonstrated that only 10 to 15 percent of customers were so focused on product cost that they would sacrifice convenience to find the lowest price. The others were satisfied with a fair price along with selection, quality, and fast checkout (Reda, 1994). More recently, because of application of merchandise planning technology, pricing has become more scientifically focused on balancing outcomes measured by net sales, stock turn, gross margin, and other measures depending on the firm's goals.

Pricing Relationships in the Trade Matrix

Merchandise price is the amount asked for or received in exchange for a product. **Merchandise cost** is the value given up to receive goods or services or the amount invested to have a product. The relationship between selling price and merchandise cost determines gross margin, the traditional measure of merchandising success. Firms engaged in consumer goods businesses administer the prices of their products with regard to market conditions, merchandise costs, and what they perceive to be customers' priorities. For the most part, consumer goods are **differentiated products,** that is, a particular firm's products are identifiable from similar products produced or distributed by competing firms. The individual firms set the prices, not impersonal market forces that establish prices for commodities such as steel, corn, or cotton. Effective pricing assists in meeting gross margin goals, meeting volume goals, and covering other costs. Achievement of these goals contributes to accomplishing the firm's mission.

Pricing practices in wholesale and retail sectors are based on a combination of legal regulation, tradition, and strategic marketing. A combination of federal, state, and local laws determines what types of pricing practices are legal. Table 5.1 includes a list of federal laws regulating pricing activity. The impact of these laws is discussed within context of the appropriate pricing practices.

Table 5.1

Federal laws regulating pricing. *

Sherman Antitrust Act, 1890
- Prevents development of monopolies.
- Protects competition.
- Makes horizontal price fixing illegal.

Federal Trade Commission Act, 1914, Amended 1938
- Established Federal Trade Commission as a regulating body.
- Regulates truth in price advertising.

Robinson-Patman Act, 1936
- Removed advantages of large companies.

Consumer Goods Pricing Act, 1975
- Terminated all interstate resale price maintenance and fair trade regulations.
- Made it illegal for manufacturers to specify retail prices and take action to be sure distributors and retailers use them.

*For an extended discussion of ethical and legal issues related to pricing, see Nagle & Holden (2002, pp. 369–392).

Control of Price

The issue of who should control the price of a product offered to the ultimate consumer is an ongoing debate between manufacturers and retailers. A 1977 lower court decision was upheld in 1988 by the U.S. Supreme Court allowing manufacturers to "reasonably decide to protect some dealers from price competition so that the favored dealers would be profitable enough to promote the products adequately and to provide good display, service, and repair facilities." The court said a manufacturer restricting distribution to price-cutting retailers would not necessarily be violating the Sherman Antitrust Act. The decision was regarded as especially relevant to apparel and electronic industries (Manufacturers can refuse..., 1988). More recently the Federal Trade Commission announced the settlement of a case against Reebok International Ltd. related to charges that Reebok coerced retailers into restricting price reductions to the amounts and time periods specified by Reebok (Novak & Pereira, 1995). Prosecuting restraint-of-trade cases was a low priority for the Reagan administration, but the Federal Trade Commission became much more active during the Clinton administration. Case 5.1 provides a more extensive example of this issue.

 Case 5.1 **States settle CD price-fixing case.** *

The five largest music companies and three of the U.S.'s largest music retailers agreed to pay $67.4 million and distribute $75.7 million in CDs to public and non-profit groups to settle a lawsuit led by New York and Florida over alleged price fixing in the late 1990s. The Final Judgment and Order was issued July 9, 2003. CD customers submitted claims during July 2003. Each CD customer filing a claim could be paid a maximum of $20 plus free CDs. Notices of appeal were filed by those objecting to the settlement. Payments will not be made to customers until the appeals are resolved.

Attorneys general in the two states, who were joined in the lawsuit by 39 other states, said that the industry kept consumer CD prices artificially high between 1995 and 2000 with a practice known as "minimum-advertised pricing." The settlement will go to all 50 states, based on population. Consumers may be able to seek compensation.

Under minimum-advertised pricing, the record companies subsidized ads by retailers in return for agreement by the stores to sell CDs at or above a certain price. "This is a landmark settlement to address years of illegal price-fixing," New York Attorney General Eliot Spitzer said in a statement. "Our agreement will provide consumers with substantial refunds and result in the

(continued)

Case 5.1 (continued)

distribution of a wide variety of recordings for use in our schools and communities."

The companies, including Universal Music Group, Sony Music, Warner Music Group, Bertelsmann's BMG Music, and EMI Group, plus retailers Musicland Stores, Trans World Entertainment, and Tower Records, admitted no wrongdoing. The companies have not practiced the pricing agreement since 2000. At that time, they agreed in settling a complaint by the Federal Trade Commission (FTC) that they would refrain from minimum-advertised pricing for seven years.

Former FTC chairman Robert Pitofsky said at the time that consumers had been overcharged by $480 million since 1997 and that CD prices would soon drop by as much as $5 a CD as a result. In settling the lawsuit, Universal, BMG, and Warner said they simply wanted to avoid court costs and defended the practice.

"We believe our policies were pro-competitive and geared toward keeping more retailers, large and small, in business," Universal said in a statement. Previously, the companies said that minimum-advertised pricing was needed to protect independent music retailers from rising competition from discount chains such as Wal-Mart, Circuit City, and Best Buy. They had slashed CD prices, below cost in some cases, in the hope that once consumers were in their stores, they would buy other, more expensive products.

The music companies said that minimum-advertised pricing did not directly help them because it didn't affect wholesale prices. Retailers added that they needed support to keep prices up because their rents, particularly for stores in malls, were higher than the discount chains.

*Based on Lieberman (2002) and Music CD Settlement (2003).

  Learning Activity 5.1

Read Case 5.1 very carefully.
1. What are the central pricing issues in the CD case?
2. What were the firms doing that was illegal?
3. How will the resolution of the case impact the music companies (the manufacturers)?
4. How will the resolution of the case impact the music retailers?
5. How will the resolution of the case impact consumers?

A Language of Price

A firm's business plan usually includes the price range(s) within which it plans to compete. For apparel, general price ranges are commonly described as **low-end, budget, moderate, better, bridge,** and **designer.** Apparel is generally manufactured to be retailed within a particular price range; retail merchandisers select products at wholesale to be retailed within a similar price range.

When customers are not well informed about product attributes, they may use price as a surrogate for quality. They may assume that if the price is high, the quality is high. This may allow merchandisers to exploit their customers by buying lower quality goods and selling them at a higher price, at least until customers find product performance is inadequate.

Perry Ellis-Supreme is a wholesale "men's sportswear house…a one-stop shop" for retailers. It was formed when a private label men's apparel manufacturer began buying up branded men's sportswear companies. As shown in Table 5.2, they offer known brand names of men's sportswear in price ranges budget through better. Each brand is identified by appropriate type of retailer and positioning related to target customers. Positioning well-known brands at different price levels allows the company to supply many different types of retailers.

Pricing terminology is not used consistently throughout the trade and academic literature. For purposes of clarity in this text, a set of commonly used pricing terms are defined and used throughout. Readers are encouraged, however, when reading other publications or talking with merchandising professionals to keep in mind the context in which the language relative to price is offered to clearly understand its meaning. To make it easier to refer back to the definition of terms, they are presented in Table 5.3 in alphabetical order.

Learning Activity 5.2

Using the list of definitions in Table 5.3:
1. Identify all of those that include the word *price*. How do these terms relate to each other?
2. Identify all the terms that include the word *discount*. How do these terms relate to each other?
3. Identify all the terms that include the word *cost*. How do these terms relate to each other?
4. Identify all the terms that include the word *markdown*. How do these terms relate to each other?
5. Identify all the terms that include the word *markup*. How do these terms relate to each other?

Table 5.2

Brands, merchandise categories, and distribution in relation to price range and market positioning at Perry Ellis-Supreme. *

Brand	Merchandise Categories	Distribution	Price Range	Position
Ping Collection	Golfwear: golf shirts, sweaters, shorts, outerwear	Golf pro shops, specialty stores, corporate market	Better	High-income, 25–50 year old men who are fashion-conscious
Perry Ellis Collection & Portfolio	Complete collection: sportswear, clothing, dress shirts, outerwear, furnishings, fragrance	Department stores, corporate market	Upper moderate	High-income, status-conscious, 25–50 year old men; licensed to third parties
Perry Ellis America	Jeanswear, activewear, footwear, eyewear, swimwear, clothing, accessories	Department stores, young men's specialty stores	Upper moderate	New "vintage classic" point of view, 18–30 year old men; jeanswear produced in-house
John Henry	"Dress casual" sportswear, dress shirts, knits, footwear, accessories	Middle market chains, primarily Mervyn's	Moderate	Middle-income, 25–45 year old men
Crossings	Sportswear: shirts, sweaters, pants, shorts	Department stores	Moderate	Middle income, 25–65 year old men
Grand Slam	Sportswear & golfwear: shirts, vests, jackets, pants, shorts	Department stores	Moderate	Middle-income, 30–70 year old men, golf enthusiasts
Natural Issue	Sportswear & golfwear: shirts, vests, jackets, pants, shorts	Chain stores	Lower moderate	Middle income, 25–55 year old men
Penguin Sport	Dress casual collections: sportswear, dress shirts, knits, footwear, accessories	Chain stores	Lower moderate	Middle-income, 30–70 year old men, golf enthusiasts
Munsingwear	Sportswear & golfwear: shirts, vests, jackets, pants, shorts	Regional department stores	Mass, budget	Middle-income, 30–70 year old men, golf enthusiasts
Manhattan	"Dress casual" collections: sportswear, dress shirts, knits, footwear, accessories	Mass market, primarily Kmart	Mass, budget	Middle-income, 25–45 year old men

*Based on Cunningham (2001).

Table 5.3

Definitions of pricing terms.

- above-market—price set in the upper range of prices for a particular product type; includes additional markup on first price or higher than average initial markup
- additional markup cancellation—reduction in above-market/premium price to first price
- additional markup—difference between first price and above-market/premium price
- adjusted gross margin—gross margin less transportation and distribution expense
- at-market price—similar to competitors offering the same products
- below-market price—less than competitors offering the same products; may be based on lower than normal markup
- better price—above average pricing for product class, implying higher quality but not exclusive design; widely used in upscale department and specialty stores
- billed cost—list price less quantity and trade discounts as stated on an invoice
- bridge price—the price line between better and designer; some features of couture goods; featured in designer boutiques in department stores and in designer named specialty stores
- budget price—below average price for the product class; widely used by mass and discount retailers
- cash discount—reduction in billed cost as incentive to pay the invoice on time
- clearance price—price asked when increasing the appeal of goods to customers for purposes of inventory management
- comparison price—price offered in advertising or on price tickets as representative of "regular price" or the value of the product
- contract dating—terms of a purchase agreement that determine when an invoice is due to be paid
- designer price—the highest relative price for the product class; sold in exclusive department store boutiques and specialty stores
- distressed goods—merchandise unsalable during a selling period using established outlets for first quality goods
- first price—original retail price; may or may not be the same as list price or the price the customer first sees on a price ticket; base price for retail price structures
- initial markup—difference between wholesale price (billed cost) and first price
- job-off price—price for liquidating distressed goods to a jobber or diverter; may be sold by the piece or by weight
- keystone markup—traditional markup on apparel; 50% markup on retail; 100% markup on cost
- liquidation price—see job-off price
- list price—suggested retail price used in manufacturer's/wholesaler's catalogs and price sheets; an estimate of the value of the product to the ultimate consumer; list price is the base price for wholesale price structures
- loss-leader pricing—advertising prices below cost to increase customer traffic and sell more products are regular price
- low-end price—the lowest relative price for the product category; used by flea markets, outlets, street vendors, and one-price discount stores; high risk of poor quality merchandise

(continued)

Table 5.3 (continued)

Definitions of pricing terms.

- manufacturer's wholesale price—list price less quantity, seasonal, and trade discounts
- markdown—difference between first price and promotional or clearance price
- markdown cancellation—elimination of a markdown to restore first price; may be accompanied by another markdown or an additional markup to establish the next price a customer will see
- moderate price—goods sold at average price for the product class; also decribed as upper moderate and lower moderate; widely used in department and specialty chain stores
- permanent markdown—reduction in price reflecting decline in merchandise value based on salability; the markdown will not be cancelled
- predatory pricing—illegally selling items at very low markup or below merchandise cost to eliminate competition
- premium price—see above-market price
- price lining—"offering merchandise at a limited number of price points that should reflect differences in merchandise quality" (Mason, Mayer, & Ezell, 1984); selling items of varying costs for the same price
- price points—specified prices representing a price line
- pricing strategy—particular combination of pricing components designed to appeal to a firm's target customers and contribute to achieving a firm's goals
- promotional price—price intended to increase total revenue by generating additional customer traffic
- quantity discount—reduction from list price related to efficiencies of volume of purchase
- reference price—see comparison price
- regular price—price perceived to be the "usual" or "normal" price for a product
- retail merchandise cost—wholesale price less discounts and allowances; may include transportation costs
- sales promotion—a marketing strategy intended to increase total revenue
- seasonal discount—reduction from list price relating to time of purchase in a selling period; a manufacturer may offer pre-selling period, late-selling period, and end-of-the-selling-period discounts
- selling price—price a customer pays for a product; wholesale price in the manufacturing sector; may be higher or lower than first price in the retail sector
- shipping terms—determines who pays the freight costs and when ownership of products is transferred; free on board (FOB); cost, insurance, and freight (CIF); free alongside the ship (FAS)
- temporary markdown—reduction in price for sales promotion; markdown will be canceled at end of sale period
- trade discount—reduction from list price granted to a firm that performs some marketing or distribution function
- wholesale price—list price less quantity, seasonal, and trade discounts

Perceptions of Price

Quick response (QR) business systems require that merchandisers are informed about pricing throughout the trade matrix in order to be effective negotiators of contracts and agreements related to development, acquisition, and sale of merchandise. The fundamental premise of QR is partnering, including collaboration and cooperation in all processes required to improve speed of processing and service to consumers.

QR has improved communications among firms actively participating, but price structures within the textiles and apparel trade matrix remain based primarily on industry tradition. In spite of their interdependence, apparel manufacturers and retailers may be intolerant of one another's pricing practices when each has little understanding of the other's cost structures and pricing strategies. At the same time, retail customers are often shocked to find out that what retailers call 50 percent markup (keystone markup) actually represents a retail price that is double and sometimes more than double the billed cost of the merchandise.

Table 5.4 demonstrates relationships among pricing factors as viewed by manufacturers, retailers, and consumers. The pricing factors are accompanied by a mathematical example to clarify the relationships. Table 5.4 can be interpreted both vertically and horizontally. Note in this scenario that the list price and the first price — the manufacturer's and retailer's planning prices — are not seen by the retail customer because a premium price is used. The customer sees a premium price and the consumer sees the markdowns as related to that premium price — not the first price, which is the retailer's basis of determining price. What the customer perceives as a bargain price may be the retailer's planned average selling price, one that is expected to provide adequate gross margin for successful business. Some regard retail pricing practices such as this to be deceptive, yet the practice has become widespread in what is known as high-low or promotional pricing. The average selling price indicates that the retail merchandiser plans that most merchandise will be sold at substantially less than the premium/comparison price offered to the customer.

Wholesale price, in the manufacturing sector, may be reduced to billed cost in the retail sector. After two substantial markdowns in the retail sector, the clearance price still exceeds the billed cost of the merchandise. This means the clearance price will cover the cost of the merchandise and make some small contribution toward other business expenses.

The gross margin realized on the merchandise is the difference between the average selling price and merchandise cost. (Review the Income Statement discussed in Chapter 3.) Gross margin is a common measure of merchandising success. The significance of the pricing relationships demonstrated in Table 5.4 will become more apparent as you work your way through this chapter and the following chapters.

Table 5.4

Relationships among pricing factors as viewed by manufacturers, retailers, and consumers.

Manufacturer Pricing		Retailer Pricing		Retail Customer's View of Pricing	
ist price	$105[1]	premium price	$110	regular price	$110
quantity/seasonal discounts	−5%	additional markup	+10%		
reduced list price	$100	first price	$100[5]		
		planned average markdown	−20%	special sale	−27%
		planned average selling price	$ 80	bargain price	$ 80
trade discount	−50%	initial markup	−50%	great sale	−55%
wholesale price	$ 50	planned cost	$ 50	clearance price	$ 49.50[10]
advertising/mark-down discounts	−10%	advertising/mark-down discounts	−10%		
billed cost	$ 45	billed cost	$ 45		
production cost	−$ 32				
$ gross margin	$ 13	$ gross margin	$ 35[6]		
% gross margin	28.89%[2]	% gross margin	43.75%[7]		
cash discount on billed cost	−8%	cash discount on billed cost	−8%		
reduced billed cost	$ 41.40[3]	reduced billed cost	$ 41.40[3]		
reimbursed ship-ping expense	+$ 2	shipping expense	+$ 2		
amount received	$ 43.40	amount remitted	$ 43.40		
other expenses	−$ 2	other expenses	+$ 3		
production cost	−$ 32	net cost of goods	$ 46.40		
$ adjusted gross margin	$ 9.40	$ adjusted gross margin	$ 33.60[8]		
% adjusted gross margin	21.66%[4]	% adjusted gross margin	42%[9]		

[1] price changes in wholesale sector are based on list price or reduced list price

[2] [(billed cost − production cost) / billed cost] × 100

[3] billed cost − cash discount

[4] [amount received − (production cost + other expense) / amount received] × 100

[5] all price changes in the retail sector are based on first price

[6] planned average selling price − billed cost

[7] [(planned average selling price − billed cost) / planned average selling price] × 100

[8] planned average selling price − net cost of goods

[9] [(planned average selling price − net cost of goods) / planned average selling price] × 100

[10] regular price − great sale percent

Learning Activity 5.3

Pricing in the trade matrix

1. Use the definitons of terms in Table 5.2 to interpret the pricing relationships displayed in Table 5.3. Examine particularly how the bold faced items relate to each other from the manufacturer's, retailer's, and customer's perspective.
2. Think through how the numbers within the "retailer" columns relate to each other mathematically. In particular, examine $ and % gross margin and $ and % adjusted gross margin. Use the footnotes to clarify calculations.

Company Profile 5.1

Mike's Bikes, Part 3, Pricing Policy

Mike's Bikes has a pricing policy that guides decisions about retail pricing. They have found that systematic pricing reduces errors in setting and changing prices as well as handling sales and keeping records. Mike's Bikes thinks about their pricing strategy as everyday-fair price (EDFP) with quick markdown for slow selling items. Price promotions are infrequently used, mostly reserved for 20 percent temporary markdowns before RAGBRAI and holidays. They use even dollar price endings on regular price merchandise, $0.97 price endings on clearance merchandise, and $0.67 price endings on promotional merchandise. The price ending is a quick identifier of the status of the merchandise.

Mike's Bikes keeps extensive records of customer purchases including styles, sizes, and colors. They also record family events like birthdays and anniversaries and send emails with reminders and suggestions for gifts based on their sales records.

Since they are both in the store nearly every day, it is easy to observe customers' response to merchandise and the prices. Reducing prices on slow selling merchandise and getting it sold reduces investment in slow selling merchandise and increases turnover while making cash available for investment in more desirable items.

Most merchandise is sold in three price ranges — budget, moderate, and better — with a strong focus on moderate and an appealing representation of strong brands in better. Application of new technology in design and materials is a strong selling point for better price merchandise. Price lining is used within each price range.

The merchandise mix includes three categories: bikes (50 percent of sales), apparel (20 percent of sales), and accessories (15 percent of sales). They also have a bike service department that accounts for 15 percent of sales. Most of the bike inventory

(continued)

Company Profile 5.1 (continued)

on hand is in the moderate price range with a few tantalizing better bikes. Colorful catalogs are always ready at hand for special orders. Markup on bikes is 50 percent on retail.

Cycling shorts and tights have an average first price of $65. Moderate jerseys are price lined at $50, $60, and $70. Outerwear is offered in the moderate price range at $140 and $160. Markup on apparel is 60 percent on retail except shoes; markup on shoes is 50 percent.

Helmets are the most frequently purchased accessory with an average first price of $90. Backpacks are next in frequency of purchase. Table 5.5 presents the merchandise category, classes, price ranges, and average first prices.

 ### Learning Activity 5.4

Pricing at Mike's Bikes

1. What aspects of Mike's Bikes' pricing policy needs to be communicated when training new part-time sales associates?
2. Why does knowing the average first price for merchandise classes help make merchandising decisions?
3. How might the average first price be misinterpreted?
4. Is it unusual to find three different price ranges for the same classes of merchandise in the same store?
5. What are advantages and disadvantages of having three different price ranges for merchandise in one store?
6. Mike's Bikes thinks about their pricing strategy as everyday-fair price (EDFP) but they use 60 percent markup. Nordstrom also thinks of their pricing strategy as EDFP and Wal-Mart is the master of everyday-low price (EDLP) with closer to 50 percent markup. From a shopper's perspective, what are the issues here?

Pricing Mechanics

Merchandisers set and manipulate prices on merchandise within the context of a firm's pricing strategy. They also frequently negotiate contracts for purchase of materials to be made into finished goods and/or merchandise to be sold either at wholesale or retail. Meth-

Table 5.5

Merchandise categories, classes, features, price ranges, and average first price at Mike's Bikes.

Category & Class	Use	Budget	Moderate	Better	Average First Price
Bikes					
Mountain bikes	Off-road riding	$250	$500–$600	$650 & up	$750
Road bikes	Highway and hard surfaces	$450	$650–$1,000	$2,000 & up	$850
Hybrid bikes	Any surface		$700–$1,100	$3,500 & up	$1,000
Portable bikes	Fold for transport and storage	$550		$2,500 & up	$2,500
Recumbent bikes	Lay back and ride	$800		$2,500 & up	$2,500
Kid's bikes	Variety of styles for boys and girls	$150	$250–$300		$2,50
Apparel					
Shoes	Recessed cleat pockets, stiff soles	$50–$80	$100–$180	$220 & up	$120
Socks	Thin, sweat-wicking, snug fit	$6–$7	$10–$14	$18 & up	$12
Gloves	Padded palms, fingerless	$10	$20–$25	$36–$50	$25
Shorts/tights	Snug fit reduces saddle friction	$25–$40	$65–$80	$90–$130	$65
Jerseys/tops	Back pockets, wicking, snug fit	$30–$45	$50–$70	$75–$100	$75
Outerwear	Midlayer or outer layer	$95–$125	$140–$160	$180–$200	$140
Accessories					
Helmets	Mountain bikers wear visors	$30	$50–$100	$170 & up	$90
Saddles	Difficult to find the right one	$30–$45	$60–80	$90–$125	$80
Sunglasses	Protect eyes from bug and debris	$70	$100–$180	$220–$275	$180
Backpacks	Water, necessities	$35–$50	$60–$80	$100–$125	$80
Tool kits	Tire pump, wrenches	$40	$60–$70	$85–$125	$70
Computers	Reports time, distance, speed		$100	$150	$125

ods used to calculate costs and prices are sometimes very elaborate and other times very simple. The methods often reflect an accounting perspective of inventory management rather than a merchandising perspective of planning, developing, and presenting product lines. The key elements of retailer's pricing from a merchandising perspective have been selected for discussion here. Factors related to manufacturer's pricing and wholesale price structures are discussed in Chapter 8, Developing Product Lines. Detailed studies of the many mathematical manipulations that relate to pricing are left to a merchandising mathematics course.

Retail Pricing Policies

When establishing merchandise prices and price changes, merchandisers must consider their employer's pricing policy, planned cost, and amount of markup needed to achieve gross margin goals, as well as the perceived value customers will place on the merchandise. Most retailers have **pricing policies** that provide a framework for setting and changing prices. Pricing policies may include descriptions of application of pricing strategies. For example, the mass retailer ShopKo uses every-day-low-pricing (EDLP) for pharmacy and promotional pricing (high-low) on the rest of their merchandise. Other stores may use a price matching strategy, guaranteeing prices will match or be lower than their competitors. This may require regular price comparison shopping by the store's employees and modification of prices accordingly. Retail interns are sometimes assigned the comparison shopping task. Sometimes pricing policies establish a specific level of markup and timing and amount of markdowns.

Normally, retail prices are set before merchandise is delivered. Therefore, the exact amount to be paid for the merchandise is not yet determined; thus, price planning considers planned cost. **Planned cost** is determined by the wholesale price offered by the manufacturer or the cost estimates provided by product developers and sourcers of privately developed merchandise. The percent markup needed to achieve gross margin goals is often documented in data related to previous selling periods. Fundamentally, for Mike's Bikes cycling jerseys that retail for $70,

$$\$ \text{ retail price} = \$ \text{ planned cost} + \$ \text{ markup}$$
$$\$70 = \$28 + \$42$$
$$\$ \text{ planned cost} = \$ \text{ retail price} - \$ \text{ markup}$$
$$\$28 = \$70 - \$42$$
$$\$ \text{ markup} = \$ \text{ retail price} - \$ \text{ planned cost}$$
$$\$42 = \$70 - \$28$$

If the retailer includes **price lining** in its pricing policy, groups of styles with different wholesale prices are sold at the same retail price. The retail prices of the merchandise are predetermined and the merchandise is selected to fit into the price lines. For example, moderate cycling jerseys are price lined at $50, $60, and $70. Styles are assigned to each price line based on their wholesale price and how the merchandiser believes customers will respond to the various styles. For example, a lower wholesale priced style could be assigned to a higher price line because of strong shelf appeal. A higher wholesale priced style might be assigned to a lower price line to add "spark" to the assortment. Price lining simplifies selection for the consumer. If the customer is concerned about price, he or she can focus on the appropriate price group and then focus on size, style, and color.

But how about the merchandiser's price plan? The retail price for the cycling jerseys is set by the price line and 60 percent markup on retail is needed to make gross margin goals. What could be the average merchandise cost of the $70 merchandise group?

$$\text{merchandise cost} = \text{\$ retail price} - \text{\% markup}$$
$$\$28 = \$70 - 60\%$$

However, from the merchandiser's perspective, the pricing process has only begun. Table 5.6 itemizes the manipulations of price that might occur during the selling period for a particular group of merchandise including first price, markups, and markdowns.

Table 5.6

Manipulation of retail price throughout the selling period.

	wholesale price
+	initial markup
=	first price
+	additional markup
=	premium price
−	markup cancellation
=	first price
−	temporary markdown
=	promotional price
+	markdown cancellation
=	first price
−	permanent markdown
=	clearance price

First Price

First price is the original retail price and/or the base price for retail price planning. First price is a key component of the pricing plan because all price changes are based on first price. First price may or may not be the same as list price (the manufacturer's suggested retail price) or the price the customer first sees on a price ticket. In calculations of merchandise price, merchandise cost, markups, and markdowns, it is common to say markup is 50 percent or markdown is 25 percent. These are percentages of first price, thus first price is 100 percent in these equations. If you are purchasing the cycling jerseys for Mike's Bikes without a price lining policy, you would be told by the manufacturer that the merchandise cost is $28 and you would know percent markup needed is 60 percent. With this information you can find first price after you find percent merchandise cost:

$$
\begin{array}{rcl}
\% \text{ cost} &=& \% \text{ first price} \; - \; \% \text{ markup} \\
40\% &=& \quad 100\% \quad - \quad 60\%
\end{array}
$$

$$
\begin{array}{rcl}
\$ \text{ first price} &=& \$ \text{ cost} \; \div \; \% \text{ cost} \\
\$70 &=& \quad \$28 \quad \div \quad 40\%
\end{array}
$$

📖 Learning Activity 5.5

Practice pricing basics.

1. Considering the price lined group of cycling jerseys/tops discussed earlier, find the appropriate merchandise cost for the $60 price line when using 60 percent markup. Use the calculations above as a model.
2. Assume you are buying the cycling jerseys/tops without a price line policy. You know the dollar merchandise cost is $15.75 and you are using 55 percent markup. What is the first price?

Markups

Initial markup (IMU) establishes the difference between wholesale price (planned cost) and first price. Initial markup is often planned and reported both in terms of percentage and dollars. To interpret %IMU correctly, it is essential to know how it was calculated. Two methods of calculating initial markup may be used, resulting in very different implied results: initial markup based on retail and initial markup based on cost. %IMU based on cost implies a much higher level of $IMU than %IMU based on retail when, in fact, $IMU is the same (see Table 5.7). An initial markup of $7 results in 58.34%IMU based on retail and 140%IMU based on cost. The financial impact for the firm is the same, but appearance is very different.

Initial markup based on cost is commonly used on non-apparel, basic/staple type of goods that are stocked year-round and have few price changes. Consumer goods with a very high price-per-item, such as fur coats and automobiles, also often use markup based on cost. It is common for manufacturers to use initial markup based on cost when thinking of their wholesale prices and use markup based on retail for list prices representing recommended retail prices. **Initial markup based on retail,** in both dollars and percents, is the system commonly used in the retail sector, particularly for apparel and other products that experience high rates of fashion and seasonal change. Markup based on retail is consistent with the retail method of calculating inventory where merchandise value is recorded at retail rather than cost. Permanent price reductions result in the reduction of the retail value of inventory as an asset, a much more realistic assessment for fashion and seasonal goods. Remember, initial markup is the difference between merchandise cost and first price.

Additional markup (AMU) is the difference between first price and premium price. Premium prices are sometimes used for status/prestige pricing strategies and as a comparison price for high-low/promotional and quick markdown pricing strategies. Retailers that use additional markup sometimes call it **two plus two pricing.** They use 50 percent initial markup that doubles the merchandise cost (the first "two" in two plus two) and then add 20 percent additional markup (the second "two" in two plus two). The premium price thus created shows as the original price on the price ticket. For example, assume that you want to use

Table 5.7

Comparison of percent initial markup (%IMU) when calculated as based on retail and based on cost.

$ Initial Markup	% Initial Markup Based on Retail	% Initial Markup Based on Cost
first price $12 − initial markup $ 7 merchandise cost $ 5	$\%IMU = \dfrac{\text{first price} - \text{planned cost}}{\text{first price}} \times 100$	$\%IMU = \dfrac{\text{first price} - \text{planned cost}}{\text{billed cost}}$
	$58.34\%IMU = \dfrac{\$12 - \$5}{\$12} \times 100$	$140\%IMU = \dfrac{\$12 - \$5}{\$5} \times 100$

two plus two promotional pricing on your cycling jerseys that cost $28. Determine the first price and then the premium price but first find percent cost so you can get first price:

$$\% \text{ cost } = \% \text{ first price } - \% \text{ markup}$$
$$50\% = 100\% - 50\%$$

$$\$ \text{ first price } = \$ \text{ cost } \div \% \text{ cost}$$
$$\$56 = \$28 \div 50\%$$

$$\$ \text{ premium price } = \$ \text{ first price } + \% \text{ additional markup}$$
$$\$67.20 = \$56 + 20\%$$

Since premium prices are usually even dollar prices, $67.20 may be presented as $67 or $68 depending on the merchandiser's perspective on the products shelf or hanger appeal.

Premium price is adjusted downward by canceling additional markup and recalculating with a lower percent additional markup and/or taking a markdown on first price. From the perspective of the consumer, the premium price including additional markup was the original retail price. Thus, the new lower price, a "bargain" price, provides incentive to buy. Technically this is not a markdown; it is a **markup cancellation**. All price changes are based on first price.

Markdowns

Once first price is established based on initial markup, all price changes are based on first price. Markdowns are calculated as a percent decrease in first price. There are two types of markdowns—temporary markdowns and permanent markdowns. **Temporary markdowns** are used to stimulate customer traffic and sales during selected time of the selling period. The merchandise is marked down for a prescribed number of days and then the markdown is cancelled so the price returns to first price. Temporary markdowns could be taken for price promotion several times during long selling periods.

Permanent markdowns are taken for clearance of inventory. If a series of permanent markdowns are to be taken, the original markdown is canceled and a greater markdown is taken based on first price. For example, assume a firm has a pricing strategy where it uses 30 percent, 40 percent, and 50 percent markdowns for clearance, each for one week during the last 3 weeks of a 10-week selling period. Table 5.8 shows a correct system for calculating a series of markdowns.

Table 5.8

Markdown calculation (based on first price of $30, 50%IMU on retail).

	1st Markdown		2nd Markdown		3rd Markdown
First Price	$30	1st	$30	2nd	$30
% Markdown	−30%	markdown is	−40%	markdown is	−50%
Clearance Price	$21	canceled	$18	canceled	$15

Each time a new clearance price is calculated, it is based on the first price of $30. Assuming 50 percent markup on retail for first price, a 50 percent markdown on first price means the merchandise is being cleared at cost based on the third markdown. Using first price as the base price for all price changes provides a systematic, logical method of price change. Ignoring the concept of markdown cancellation causes serious problems.

The results of an inexperienced merchandiser calculating markdowns without understanding the concept of **markdown cancellation** is shown in Table 5.9. When reviewing the financial records of the sale, a merchandising manager would find the merchandise being sold at well below cost with both the second and third markdowns. While customers may find these uncommonly low prices very gratifying, they would have devastating effect on the gross margin produced by the merchandise group.

Pricing in Relation to the Merchandising Calendar

A complete **pricing plan** includes planned merchandise cost, dollar and percent initial markup, first price, price promotions including percent temporary markdowns, promotional prices, permanent markdowns, and clearance prices—all set to weeks of sale during the selling period considering planned sales peaks. If premium price will be used, percent

Table 5.9

Incorrect markdown calculation (based on first price of $30, 50%IMU on retail).

	1st Markdown		2nd Markdown		3rd Markdown
First Price	$30	1st	$21	2nd	$12.60
% Markdown	−30%	markdown is	−40%	markdown is	−50%
Clearance Price	$21	not canceled	$12.60	canceled	$6.30

additional markup, additional markup cancellation, and reapplication of additional markup will also be included if appropriate.

Refer back to Table 4.4 and think through the pricing plan for the first two selling periods of Mike's Bikes cycling jerseys/tops in relation to the merchandising calendar. Notice the column for the pricing plan. Assume you are planning 60 percent markup with $70 first price. The first selling period begins with a 20 percent temporary markdown and markdown cancellation. The only permanent markdown for clearance is in weeks 13 and 14. During the second selling period, there will be a 20 percent promotion for weeks 23 and 24. Week 26 begins a 30 percent permanent markdown with an additional 10 percent for week 27 and 15 percent for week 28. The pricing plan for the merchandise calendar might look like this:

Weeks 2–3	20% temporary markdown, promotional price $56 (presented as $55.67); cancel temporary markdown
Weeks 4–12	first price $70 with 60% markup; $28 cost
Weeks 13–14	40% permanent markdown, sale price $42 (presented as $41.97)
Weeks 15–22	first price $70 with 60% markup; $28 cost
Weeks 23–24	20% temporary markdown, promotional price $56 (presented as $55.67)
Week 25	travel with RAGBRAI; cancel temporary markdown
Week 26	30% permanent markdown, clearance price = $49 (presented as $48.97)
Week 27	cancel 30% markdown; begin 40% permanent markdown, clearance price $42 (presented as $41.97)
Week 28	cancel 40% markdown, begin 55% permanent markdown, final clearance price $31.50 (presented as $30.97)

The clearance price might even be marked $29.97 because it puts the price in the 20s instead of the 30s. Notice that, in this case, the final clearance price is still higher than the $28 merchandise cost. That is not always the case, especially if the retailer is overstocked or if the style or merchandise group seriously lacked customer appeal.

Many retailers are trying to simplify and clarify their pricing strategies. For example, Younkers, a division of Saks, Inc., used to post "50% off" signs on merchandise already marked down. Customers would carry the merchandise to checkout expecting to pay half the markdown price, only, to their embarrassment or chagrin, to find it was 50 percent off of the original price. Recently, a newspaper ad demonstrated that Younkers has changed the way they present markdowns to customers. The ad included the following explanation of pricing:

```
Original Price  . . . . . . . . . . . . . . . . . . . . .      $50
Sale   . . . . . . . . . . . . . . . . . . . . . . . . . .  $29.99
Extra 50%   . . . . . . . . . . . . . . . . . . . . . .      $15
You Pay Only (excludes tax)   . . . . . . . . . .  $14.99
A Total Savings of 70%
```

Younkers changed their markdown presentation so it was consistent with how customers think instead of how merchandisers think (Younkers, 2001).

Federated Department Stores also has new price initiatives. It has created a "Best Value" program for key items offered at EDLP. They are eliminating coupons on many promotional events and ensuring that prices are very competitive (Federated Department Stores, 2003). JCPenney has observed that sales and promotions are confusing for customers. Customers have been "trained" to wait for sales, eroding margins and movement of goods. JCPenney is now using one cohesive promotional plan based on one calendar to eliminate confusion for customers. They are using fewer promotions, selecting distinct classifications to promote, using lower levels of markdowns to protect gross margin, and offering better signage so customers will know what they have to pay when they reach the register (Stankevich, 2000).

Learning Activity 5.6

Markups and markdowns

1. Examine the differences in results when percent initial markup is based on cost and on retail. Set up three different experiments based on the following examples using Table 5.7 as a model:
   - 14-karat gold chain with a planned cost of $140 and a markup of $150
   - baseballs with a first price of $6 and planned cost of $4
   - video tapes with a dollar markup of $0.90 and a first price of $2.99
2. Which method of calculating markup is commonly used by most retailers, markup based on cost or markup based on retail? Why?
3. If a group of boys' shirts had no price changes and all sold at first price, what would be the relationship between initial markup and gross margin?
4. Correctly calculate the clearance prices for a camera with a first price of $50 and merchandise cost of $30 with sequential permanent markdowns of 20, 30, and 40 percent. Is the final clearance price below cost?
5. What is first price if merchandise cost is $16 and markup is 50%? 45%? 55%?

6. Develop a pricing plan for the 3rd and 4th selling periods for Mike's Bikes cycling jerseys/tops from weeks 29 through 52. Use the merchandise calendar in Table 4.4 as a guide. Decide how much you will take for temporary and permanent markdowns, what the prices will be, and when markdown cancellations will occur. Explain the reasoning for your decisions. Be sure to consider the previously presented pricing plan for weeks 1 through 28.

Strategic Pricing

The type of pricing strategy employed by a firm is a key business decision determined by executive management with input from the merchandising and marketing constituencies. The goal of many firms now is to build a price image that is consistent with their target customer's needs. The merchandising constituency is then responsible for selecting merchandise that can be priced according to the strategy and sold in adequate quantities to meet the firm's goals. Merchandisers determine list or first price, depending on whether they are working in the wholesale or retail sector, and subsequent price changes according to the pricing strategy. The marketing constituency helps carry out the pricing strategy by developing and managing appropriate advertising and promotions.

Six to 12 different pricing strategies, or policies as they are sometimes called, are frequently itemized in the pricing literature and retailing textbooks. A pricing strategy is a particular combination of pricing components designed to appeal to a firm's target customers and contribute to achieving the firm's goals. For purposes of discussion here, a taxonomy of pricing was developed relating six different pricing strategies with six different pricing components. Pricing components are variables of pricing strategies that can be applied in different ways. The mode of applying these pricing components determines their internal consistency and their ability to support the firm's mission and strategic goals. There are three fundamental purposes for the development of a consistent pricing strategy:

1. Stimulate regular shopping by target customers.
2. Optimize sale of available merchandise.
3. Provide guidelines for consistent administration of price.

With rare exceptions, firms are dependent on regular, established relationships with suppliers and customers. Customer loyalty has been seriously undermined by the prevalence of promotional pricing in today's retail markets. If a firm wants to be known as a "purveyor of fine quality merchandise in a high-service environment," then their pricing strategy should support that image. If a firm wants to be known as a "source of better than average quality/ status merchandise at less than average price," then their pricing strategy must correspond. If the firm wants to be known as a "source of a wide variety of serviceable consumer goods available everyday at good value," then the pricing strategy should reflect this.

"Optimize" means to make the most effective use of, to make as good or as effective as possible considering relationships among factors involved. Discussions of pricing strategies are usually placed within the economic assumption that the purpose of pricing is to maximize profit. To maximize is to make as great as possible. However, at any given time, maximizing profit may or may not contribute to the firm's other goals. Therefore, the purpose here — to optimize sale of available merchandise — recognizes the behavioral context and the complexity of interactions that must occur to successfully distribute merchandise to ultimate consumers. In a merchandising environment, all desirable things cannot be maximized, but outcomes can be optimized by making strategic use of opportunities.

Price administration is a profound challenge because of the variety of people involved in establishing, publishing, and changing prices. Consistent pricing practice improves communication with customers. For example, some retailers may consistently use even dollar prices on regular merchandise and odd-price endings on sale merchandise. This practice can become quickly apparent to new customers, making it easy for them to identify the desired merchandise. From a record-keeping perspective, consistent application of a pricing system helps prevent and detect errors.

Strategic Pricing Fundamentals

Pricing strategies face the economic reality of a downward sloping demand curve. There may be very rare instances where increasing a price results in increased quantities purchased in the market. For the most part, however, the higher the price for a particular product, the smaller the quantity purchased; conversely, the lower the price the larger the quantity purchased. The fundamental questions are: How high should the price be set? How much and how often should prices change? What will happen to unsold merchandise?

Setting Prices

The relationship between price and quantity purchased is called the price elasticity of demand. When price is inelastic, the quantity purchased is relatively unaffected by a small price change. Thus, a slightly higher price results in an increase in total revenue because only a few less items are purchased and the higher price more than compensates for this. At the same time, a slightly lower price results in a decrease in total revenue because, while only a few more items are purchased, it is nevertheless not enough to compensate for the lower price.

When price is elastic, a slightly higher price results in a decrease in total revenue; the number purchased is noticeably less because of the higher price. A slightly lower price results in an increase in total revenue because of the increase in the number purchased. When price is elastic, price elasticity is greater than one. Unit elasticity means a higher or lower price has no impact on total revenue; a higher price results in a proportional quantity decrease and a lower price results in a proportional quantity increase so that total revenue is unaffected. The price elasticity is equal to one. Assuming other things being equal, price elasticity of demand determines the financial impact of the price level at which a price is set.

Apparel and other differentiated products are generally regarded as relatively inelastic in relation to price, which in price elasticity jargon means the elasticity is less than one. A small increase or decrease in price will have relatively little impact on the quantity purchased in a particular time period. This means if a merchant desires a large increase in quantity sold, a much larger discount must be taken than when dealing with goods with elastic demand. Consequently, a "sale" of apparel is seldom advertised with less than 20 percent discount.

Sourcing Simulator includes price elasticity as one component of the in-store shopping behavior model to control consumer behavior in relation to price. Appropriately, price elasticity of demand is included in the Markdowns/Premiums folder. The price elasticity default in Sourcing Simulator is set at 0.7 which represents inelastic demand. This is the price elasticity frequently found in research related to apparel expenditures.

Price elasticity is evaluated against total revenue, while merchandising success tends to be evaluated against gross margin. Fundamentally, assuming merchandise costs stay the same and merchandise is salable, a price increase results in greater gross margin and a price decrease results in less gross margin on a per-item basis. Gross margin determines the number of dollars available to pay the firm's expenses beyond the cost of the merchandise. Consequently, price changes must be planned into the pricing strategy to consider both total revenue and gross margin. Setting the price and changing the price are among the many components of a complete pricing strategy.

Changing Prices

Women's apparel has long been regarded as the primary domain of fashion change because of customer demand for frequent change in styling. Fashion influence has expanded to include most apparel and many other consumer products, such as toys. Historically, women's apparel has had higher levels of markup and higher levels of markdowns than men's apparel, although the difference has narrowed since the 1960s. By the 1980s the magnitude of markups and markdowns were greater for juniors and teens than any other apparel group (Pashigian, 1988). This is still the case. The role of fashion in men's wear has increased significantly in recent years and teen and junior apparel are sometimes regarded as fashion leaders in today's markets.

The rate of fashion change has increased over time, as has the variety of products available. Pashigian (1988) suggested the increase in fashion influence was due to the supply side rather than the demand side. Improvements in technology and ready access to global markets make a wider variety of goods available, increasing the complexity of merchandise selection for both retail buyers and ultimate consumers. Now, with wide consumer access to the Internet, immeasurable amounts of information are readily available to consumers, no doubt increasing the demand for fashion change as well as increasing the number of consumers who expect it.

Based on uncertainty theory, Pashigian and Bowen (1991) attributed the difference in markup and markdown rates to: 1) rate of product change associated with fashion, 2) the time of the year, and 3) the variety of product offering. A retail buyer faces greater uncertainty in product selection and in price-setting when dealing with fashion/seasonal goods. Fashion goods require higher rates of markdowns than basic goods because of their greater uncertainty relative to choosing the most desirable items, judging what price customers will pay, and judging volume of demand. Seasonal influences also require judgment in determining when and how long a product will be salable at what price. Increasing variety of product offerings increases risk of incomplete assortments and stockouts. Merchandisers must decide how much of each group of goods to order, where to set the price, when and how much to reorder, and when to markdown broken assortments.

There are three times during a selling period when markdowns are commonly taken: pre-selling period, main or within-selling period, and end-of-selling period or clearance. Price elasticity of demand may vary at different stages of the selling period. Markdowns have to be higher to stimulate sales for clearance than for pre-selling period sales. For apparel, pre-selling period price promotions may be 10 percent off, main selling period price promotions may be advertised at 20 percent off, and clearance prices at the end of the selling period are frequently 50 percent off. The characteristics of products sold on clearance differ from those sold during the pre-selling and main selling periods. The most desirable goods sell early, while the less desirable goods remain for clearance sales. It takes a larger discount to move leftover merchandise and broken assortments at the end of the selling period. Markdowns peak in July and January, which are the primary clearance periods for the main spring and fall selling periods.

"... the relative profitability of shorter markdown periods is greater than longer markdown periods" (Levy and Howard, 1988, p. 56). When merchandise is marked down for an extended period and still no one buys it, customers may conclude there is something wrong with it. When the markdown period is short, customers may perceive they are in competition for scarce resources and thus place more value on the merchandise. These observations provide support for brief pre-selling period price promotions, limited times for main selling period promotions, and limited times for clearance.

Handling Unsold and Distressed Merchandise

A clearance sale toward the end of the selling period is a common way to sell discontinued merchandise and broken assortments. This often involves a series of markdowns over a specified period of time. However, some merchandise usually remains at the end of the clearance period. Some retailers leave the unsold merchandise on the sales floor and continue to mark it down until someone buys it. To do that, space has to be allocated on the selling floor, which takes away from space for selling more desirable and profitable merchandise.

Another option is available to get rid of old merchandise, to **liquidate** or **job-off** the leftover merchandise to a diverter or wholesaler. The advantage to the retailer here is a relatively short clearance period can be followed by removing all unwanted merchandise from inventory. This frees space to display new merchandise for customers to focus on. The disadvantage is the job-off price seldom exceeds merchandise cost and may be as low as 10 percent of merchandise cost. Both manufacturers and retailers liquidate or job-off excess merchandise (see Case 5.2).

 Case 5.2 *Slowdown in retail sales creates overstock glut.* *

Excess men's spring dress shirts bound for Nordstrom? Men's button down shirts originally slated for Kmart at $2 instead of the usual wholesale of $6 to $7? Forty-eight thousand men's Hawaiian shirts intended for Montgomery Ward? A slowdown in retail sales can cause a backup in the apparel pipeline and overstocked clothing makers have to "dump" excess goods, that is, sell them below cost. The rising excess stock

Case 5.2 (continued)

was a boon to wholesalers, diverters, and brokers in the business of buying and selling excess inventory and other distressed goods. The result can be more higher-quality labels showing up on the racks of discount and off-price retailers.

Mark Zandi, chief economist with Economy.com, says that when apparel inventory-to-sales ratios (the number of weeks of inventory on hand is high in relation to weekly sales) are high, overstocks occur. The result is delayed or cancelled orders to their suppliers. The clothing makers are stuck holding the goods and may turn to wholesale intermediaries to unload the merchandise. First, they try to adjust the rate of production, then they have to liquidate. Off-pricers (Ross, Marshalls, and T.J. Maxx) eat up the deals. Mass retailers including Wal-Mart also may be beneficiaries. For example, Ross buys primarily close-out, end-of-season, and discontinued styles.

There are some restrictions on where liquidation products can go. For example, Lands' End does not allow its dress shirts to be sold to off-pricers. Certain designers do not allow goods to go to Costco stores. At the same time, some discounters and off-pricers carry Coach handbags, The Sak accessories, in-season Anne Klein women's apparel, and Bloomingdale's dresses with labels still in. I-N-C, a Federated Department Stores private brand, and Kohl's branded apparel has been seen on some racks.

A Kohl's spokesperson said Kohl's private label merchandise is proprietary, and therefore should not be appearing on off-price racks. Merchandise overflow can cause excess goods to get into the hands of black market dealers, an industry-wide concern. Manufacturers and retailers do surveillance to prevent licensed brands from being diverted illegally.

*Based on Degross & Staff (2001).

A third option for disposing of unwanted merchandise is consolidation in a few stores or into a single area of a store. For example, Paul Harris used consolidation of distressed merchandise in stores where demand was high for high-value merchandise. The merchandise was shipped to stores in college towns for a consolidation sale at very low prices. Consolidation may allow the retailer to recover more total revenue than from a job-off, but staging the consolidation sale may involve considerable expense. During the 1990s, Spiegel made a practice of staging consolidation sales in several areas of the country before they established their own outlet stores. They rented huge auditoriums and ran the sale for a number of weeks. They added inventory to the selection frequently to maintain interest in the sale. They used a system of highly publicized price reductions for each week of the sale. Some independent consolidators are still using this practice.

A fourth option is establishing outlet stores designed to unload merchandise that cannot be sold in the original retail environment. Eddie Bauer has set up temporary outlet stores for a clearance period from January through March. Most manufacturers and retailers with outlet store divisions operate year-round. They make or buy merchandise specifically for the outlets, as well as use these stores to dispose of distressed goods from their production floors or other retail divisions. The manufacturers' outlet system that was thriving during the 1990s was established based on the premise of disposing of unwanted manufacturer-owned inventory at wholesale prices. As a result of their success, some manufacturers have become highly vertically integrated and now sell more than over 50 percent of their merchandise through their own retail outlets.

A final option is to carry over merchandise to the next selling period. This might be acceptable for basic/staple goods, as some revenue may be recovered through carryover; however, it is unsuitable for fashion/seasonal goods. Disadvantages include the necessity of storing the goods in a clean, secure area. It is unlikely that fashion goods can be presented the following year without looking out of date and shopworn. Having money invested in goods of questionable value for an extended period of time is not good business practice.

Learning Activity 5.7
Strategic pricing fundamentals

1. Compared to department or specialty stores, how might pricing differ for off-price retailers who are selling distressed merchandise purchased from diverters or wholesalers?

2. What factors influence how much and when prices should be changed?

3. Collect a group of retailer "Sunday supplements," the advertising inserts commonly included in Sunday newspapers. Look for a statement of pricing policy in each in relation to the time frame the advertised prices are in effect. Is the merchandise featured in the ads regular inventory, inventory purchased especially for the sale, or distressed merchandise? What clues are given to customers as to the type of merchandise featured?

4. Does each Sunday supplement include a statement of a price matching policy for merchandise offered by other retailers? Is a price-matching policy fair to consumers who do not ask for the lower price that might be available through price matching?

5. Make a list of the different terminology that is used to describe regular and reduced prices. What is the advantage of using different language from your competitors? What are the disadvantages?

Components of Pricing Strategies

Many decisions must be made about how to price goods in relation to a firm's mission, image, and goals. To be effective, the pricing strategy a firm chooses to use must result in a mode of doing business consistent with the firm's other business strategies. The strategic components listed here include many of those pricing decisions. The particular combination of pricing components determines a particular firm's pricing strategy.

Table 5.10 is a taxonomy of pricing strategies. These pricing strategies are commonly used in consumer goods markets, particularly for textiles and apparel products. Each includes a different application of pricing components to express a unique communication to customers. The horizontal axis represents the names of different types of pricing strategies, along with the fundamental, strategic concept of each. The vertical axis of the taxonomy shows the components of pricing strategies. The interior of the taxonomy describes the application of each pricing component in relation to each pricing strategy.

Choices in market price position include above-market, at-market, and below-market. An **above-market price** position is usually associated with products of high quality and/or performance, customers who are relatively insensitive to prices and a strong customer service strategy. The above-market price is possible because customers get more than just the product and they value the associated product attributes and services.

At-market price position means the firm intends to offer products at prices similar to other firms in the same markets. Merchandisers may do frequent comparative price shopping to be sure prices are comparable on similar merchandise, and they adjust prices when they are out of line. The firm may guarantee any competitor's price for exactly the same item.

Below-market price position means the firm intends to sell goods for less than its competitors in the same markets. If the firm has the same product costs as its competitors, it must have lower operating expenses so it can survive on lower gross margin. This may be evident in self-service/warehouse types of merchandise presentation.

Price Lining

As discussed earlier, price lining is the practice of "offering merchandise at a limited number of price points that should reflect differences in merchandise quality" (Mason, Mayer, & Ezell, 1984). **Price points** are the specified prices within a price line. Price lining simplifies

Table 5.10

Taxonomy of selected pricing strategies. *

Components of Strategies	Pricing Strategies		
	Prestige Pricing	Everyday-Low Pricing	High-Low Pricing
Concept of Strategy	Quality/value/service image for people willing to pay "regular" price	Focus customers on value at their convenience	Periodic price promotions to stimulate customer traffic
Market Price Position	Prices may be above competitors'; appeal to customers desiring special service and/or quality/performance.	Price may be negotiable through price matching policy.	Pricing may focus on or match competitors' prices; prices change when competitors' prices change.
Price Lining	Likely to be used.	Can be used.	Likely to be used.
Price Endings	Even price endings used on first and premium prices; odd price endings on clearance prices.	Odd price endings will probably be used on all prices.	Odd price endings are very likely to be used during price promotion.
Role of First Price	Basis of additional markup for premium price and markdowns for clearance; promotional and below-market prices not used.	Most merchandise sold at first price with slightly below average markup; premium and promotional prices seldom used.	Basis of additional markup for comparison price and temporary markdowns; below-market prices may be used for sales promotion.
Role of Markdowns	Permanent markdowns used for inventory management at seasonal or semiannual clearance.	Permanent markdowns used for inventory management at seasonal or semiannual clearance.	Temporary markdowns used weekly to stimulate customer traffic; permanent markdowns for clearance.
Price Advertising	Institutional and image advertising promotes brands, fashion, quality, service, and functional design.	Advertise value, convenience, and regular prices.	Constant advertising of temporary markdowns.

*Developed by G. I. Kunz.

Pricing Strategies		
Quick Markdown Pricing	**Penetration Pricing**	**Cost-Plus Pricing**
High value for bargain shoppers	*Establish value image and market share*	*Realize a specified markup from each product sold*
Prices are fixed in each time period; most merchandise sold at first price or less.	First price set slightly below competitors' on highly visible items; first price may increase after reputation is established.	Price is determined by multiplying unit cost by some "reasonable" markup.
Can be used.	Can be used.	Not likely to be used.
Odd price endings will probably be used on all prices.	Odd price endings will probably be used on all prices.	Even price endings are not possible.
Basis of additional markup and permanent markdowns; premium price establishes comparison price.	Most merchandise sold at first price with slightly lower than average markup; below-market prices used on highly visible items.	Price at which merchandise is sold; traditional level of markup.
Permanent scheduled markdowns administered throughout selling period.	Temporary markdowns to match competitors' prices; permanent markdowns for inventory management.	As desired; inventory value does not change with price.
Frequent advertising of percent off or may depend on word of mouth.	Advertise value.	As desired.

the pricing scenario for customers, reducing concern about price and allowing customers to focus on selecting the desired product based on style, color, fit, or coordination with a desired outfit. Price lining results in selling items of varying costs for the same price. Consequently, actual IMU might vary within the price line, but average markup is planned to achieve gross margin goals.

Price Endings

Consideration for **price endings** determines how prices are stated, for example $99.99, $99.98, $99.95, $99.49, or $99.00. Two outcomes are related to the way prices are stated:

1. What is the impact on customers' perceptions of price?
2. What is the impact on accuracy of accounting?

Traditionally, odd-cents price endings have commonly been used based on the assumption that sales will be higher when odd price endings are used because the customer perceives the price to be lower. This assumption is unproved by research. **Even-dollar pricing** is not necessarily a deterrent to sales. Regardless of this reality, odd-price endings are deeply ingrained in traditional pricing systems.

Customers have been trained by viewing prices to recognize **odd-price endings** as representing lower priced or bargain goods. In apparel, better, bridge, and designer, goods are more likely to be even-dollar priced, while low end, budget, and moderate goods are more likely to have odd-price endings. Upscale goods with even-dollar prices for regular prices are likely to have odd-price endings used for promotional and clearance goods.

Role of First Price

Types of prices mentioned in previous discussions have included first, premium, comparative, promotional, and clearance. As previously defined, first price is the basis of determining subsequent prices. While customers may never see it, first price is the planning price. It is the basis for additional markups for premium or comparative price, for temporary markdowns for price promotion, and for permanent markdowns for clearance price. In these cases, first price may also represent a targeted average selling price. In other scenarios, first price may be what the customer perceives as "regular" price and may be the price at which most merchandise is sold.

Role of Markdowns

In the simplest of all apparel pricing environments, basic/staple goods would have one price, a regular price, and fashion/seasonal goods would have two prices, a regular price and a clearance price. The basic/staple goods have little styling change and would be stocked year-round at the same price. Fashion/seasonal goods have demand for regular change in styling or according to the time of the year, so merchandisers must plan zero-to-zero inventories several times a year. Clearance prices are necessary to move out unwanted merchandise so new, fresh merchandise can be acquired and displayed.

Most of today's pricing strategies are more complex than the description above. Customers are perceived as being price sensitive, and merchants find that sales increase when they advertise price reductions. Some retail firms advertise special prices several times a week, so often that some statistics show that department stores sell up to 80 percent of their merchandise at less than "regular" price.

From a merchandising perspective, there are three primary functions of markdowns: inventory management, sales promotion, and financial management. For inventory management, markdowns are intended to get rid of unwanted merchandise, including out-of-season goods, broken assortments, overstocks, and distressed merchandise. Clearing unwanted and unsalable goods makes room for new, fresh, exciting merchandise. Markdowns for inventory management are permanent markdowns and reflect decline in merchandise value both to the customer and the merchant.

Markdowns for sales promotion and financial management may be temporary markdowns for a specified period to motivate customers to buy more merchandise than they would at regular price. These are followed by markdown cancellations so the price goes back to the earlier price. The expectation is a price elasticity that will result in increased total revenue (but at a lower gross margin) based on more units sold at a lower price. From a financial management perspective, the markdowns generate cash flow which makes money available to invest in new merchandise.

Price Advertising

Firms may choose from many forms of advertising media or can rely primarily on word-of-mouth advertising among customers. Among those that use advertising, they may or may not mention price. Firms wishing to focus customer attention on quality and service are unlikely to use price advertising. Instead, they use institutional or image types of advertising as a reminder of the firm's presence in the market. Firms that frequently use temporary markdowns must advertise so customers will know the timing available for the special prices. Firms that use selling period-based quick markdown schedules may or may not advertise their special values. Some rely entirely on customer knowledge of their strategies and word-of-mouth advertising between customers.

📖 Learning Activity 5.8

Components of pricing strategies

Three images of firms were mentioned earlier that might be supported by pricing strategies. They are: a purveyor of fine quality merchandise in a high service environment, a source of better-than-average quality/status merchandise at less than average price, and a source of a wide variety of serviceable consumer goods available every day at good value.

1. Give examples of firms that embody each of the images described above. Explain why each example represents the image.
2. Pick one of the images described above and describe how the six components of pricing strategies relate to the image you selected.

Types of Pricing Strategies

A **pricing strategy** is a particular combination of pricing components designed to appeal to a firm's target customers and contribute to achieving a firm's goals. Some firms have very clearly defined pricing strategies and practice them religiously; others use combinations of strategies and/or a combination of pricing tactics.

Prestige Pricing

This strategy is intended to reflect a quality/value/service image for people willing to pay "regular" price. Prestige pricing, as it is called here, is also known as status, psychological, or above-market pricing. Nordstrom is known nationally for its success with a prestige pricing strategy, although they would rather call it an EDFP (everyday-fair price) strategy. Von Maur, in the Midwest, has also been successful with prestige pricing. Both Nordstrom and Von Maur use full-time, well-trained, well-paid sales associates. Prestige pricing is usually associated with an intensive customer service environment that includes personal selling services.

Personal selling services may include wardrobe consultation, assisted product selection and fitting, notification of new merchandise, and personal thank-you notes for shopping.

Firms may empower customer service associates to do anything to support the development of satisfied customers. A sales associate at Nordstom once received a customer service award and a lifetime customer because the customer wanted a blue men's dress shirt with white collar and cuffs when Nordstrom had none in stock. With the assistance of the sales associate, the customer selected the desired blue shirt and appropriate white shirt with the desired collar and cuffs. The sales associate took the shirts to the tailor who transferred the white collar and cuffs to the blue shirt. The happy customer paid the price for the blue shirt, but Nordstrom gained a customer for life.

Other services might include free gift wrapping, home delivery, interest-free credit cards, records of purchases and preferences, email notification of family birthdays and special occasions, and invitations to trunk shows and other special events. In these stores, merchandise presentation frequently involves spacious aisles, live music, particularly attractive visual merchandising, and large fitting rooms with telephones and beverage service.

Customers of firms that use prestige pricing are usually of two relatively distinct types — those that shop regular price and those that shop sales. Both groups of customers are essential for the success of this pricing strategy. The regular-price customers value the services offered, as well as the quality, performance, and fashion offered by the merchandise. The sale customers are more price sensitive and value the merchandise, but cannot afford or do not choose to shop at regular price.

The clearance sales associated with prestige pricing are often highly celebrated events that occur only a few times a year. Sales are typified by hundreds of customers waiting for the doors to be opened on the mornings of the sale. Nearly every store employee may be engaged in the selling process, from president and CEO to secretaries and stock keepers. Clearance is essential to get rid of unwanted inventory to make space for new merchandise to sell at regular price. Clearance also generates good will with the sale customers and produces cash flow for investment in the new merchandise. (See Tables 5.11 and 5.12 for examples of prestige pricing by weeks of sale as viewed by customers.)

Everyday-Low Pricing

Everyday-low pricing (or EDLP) focuses the customer's attention on fair value at their convenience. Wal-Mart, Toys "R" Us, and The Home Depot have succeeded using primarily EDLP. Its primary feature is absence of promotional pricing and the presence of a low "regular" price. EDLP requires control of both merchandise and operating costs so the firm can operate at slightly less than normal gross margin because up to 10 percent less than normal markup may be used (Reda, 1994). This pricing strategy invites customers to shop regularly at their convenience with the assurance that prices will be reasonable and fair. Firms that

Table 5.11

Examples of pricing strategies for fashion/seasonal goods with a 10-week selling period as viewed by customers.

	(Billed Cost—$50; First Price—$110; Markup on Retail—54.55%)			
Selling Period	Prestige Price Strategy	Quick Markdown Strategy	High-Low Price Strategy	EDLP Strategy
Week 1	$140	$140	$140	$110
Week 2	$140	$130	$120	$110
Week 3	$140	$130	$100	$110
Week 4	$140	$110	$120	$110
Week 5	$140	$110	$ 90	$110
Week 6	$140	$110	$120	$110
Week 7	$140	$100	$ 80	$110
Week 8	$140	$100	$ 70	$110
Week 9	$ 70	$ 60	$ 70	$ 55
Week 10	$ 70	$ 50	$ 50	$ 55

are successful with EDLP usually start with it and stay with it. Both Sears and Montgomery Ward tried unsuccessfully to change their businesses over to this strategy. It is a long and expensive process to retrain customers who have been accustomed to frequent price promotions. EDLP flattens out fluctuations in sales and promotes partnerships with vendors. (See Tables 5.11 and 5.12 for examples of EDLP by weeks of sale as viewed by customers.) The primary difference between EDLP and prestige pricing is the level of markup and the fringe benefits related to customer service.

High-Low (Promotional) Pricing

High-low pricing involves periodic and sometimes very frequent temporary markdowns to stimulate customer traffic. Deception of consumers is a primary issue in the use of a high-low pricing strategy. Over the past 25 years, most U.S. department stores and some specialty stores have moved to high-low pricing in an effort to compete with discount and off-price stores. The common practice with high-low pricing is to establish a premium price as a comparison or reference price, then advertise the product at 20 to 50 percent off the comparative price. Another option used for presenting the price promotion is just stating "40 percent off" without stating the comparison price. This pricing practice might be deceptive,

Table 5.12

Examples of pricing strategies for basic/staple goods as viewed by customers.

(Billed Cost—$50; First Price—$100; Markup Based on Retail—50%)

Selling Period	Prestige Price Strategy	High-Low Price Strategy	EDLP Strategy
Week 1	$120	$120	$ 98
Week 2	$120	$100	$ 98
Week 3	$120	$100	$ 98
Week 4	$120	$120	$ 98
Week 5	$120	$120	$ 98
Week 6	$120	$120	$ 98
Week 7	$120	$ 95	$ 98
Week 8	$120	$ 95	$ 98
Week 9	$120	$ 95	$ 98
Week 10	$120	$110	$ 98
Week 11	$120	$110	$ 98
Week 12	$120	$110	$ 98
Week 13	$120	$ 90	$ 98
Week 14	$120	$ 90	$ 98
Week 15	$120	$ 90	$ 98
Week 16	$120	$110	$ 98
Week 17	$120	$110	$ 98
Week 18	$120	$110	$ 98
Week 19	$120	$ 85	$ 98
Week 20	$120	$ 85	$ 98

according to the FTC Guides Against Deceptive Pricing. Consumers are deceived if they assume the comparison price represents a product's intrinsic value and is thus a fair price, or if they assume the comparison price is the product's "regular" price. More sophisticated consumers might assume that the sale price is really the "regular" price. In this case, the comparison price is the "penalty price paid only by those unable to wait even a short time for the retailer's frequent sale events" (Kaufmann, Smith, & Ortmeyer, 1994). (See Tables 5.11 and 5.12 for examples of high-low pricing by weeks of sale as viewed by customers.)

Manufacturers may support retailers' high-low pricing by offering certain product lines at lower prices for sale during price promotions. Retailers pay less than regular price so the merchandise can be sold to customers for less than regular inventory at nearly full markup; thus, the customer gets a good deal while the retailer achieves planned gross margin. Retail merchandisers may also pressure vendors for increased allocations of markdown discounts on purchase contracts. Some manufacturers do not allow their goods to be advertised at reduced prices during the main selling period.

Quick Markdown Pricing

This approach is designed to provide high value for the bargain shopper. Quick markdown is used for fashion and seasonal goods that have several selling periods per year. Merchandise may be upscale, first-quality goods; a mix of upscale, moderate, and budget goods; or a combination of first quality and distressed merchandise as presented by off-price retailers such as T.J. Maxx. It is common for prices to be reduced on a set time schedule. Customers that shop early in the selling period find more complete assortments with a comparison price plus the current selling price on the ticket. As the selling period proceeds, multiple markdowns may appear on the ticket. Assortments become broken so, even though the price may be comparatively low, it will be difficult to find companion pieces. (See Table 5.11 for an example of quick markdown pricing by weeks of sale as viewed by customers.)

Penetration Pricing

This strategy is designed to establish a value image in the mind of the customer while increasing market share. Wal-Mart is well-known for using market penetration pricing strategies on high visibility items when entering new markets. The Arkansas Supreme Court overturned a lower court decision ruling that Wal-Mart did not engage in illegal predatory pricing when one of its pharmacies sold products below cost. The court found that competition was thriving in the town despite Wal-Mart's pricing strategy. "The maximum price for any item sold at Wal-Mart is set at the company's headquarters in Bentonville, Ark. The individual store managers may reduce prices to match or undercut competitors' prices without regard to the cost to Wal-Mart of individual items" (Lee, 1995, p. B8).

Cost-Plus Pricing

"Cost-plus pricing is, historically, the most common pricing procedure because it carries an aura of financial prudence" (Nagle & Holden, 2002, p. 2). This method makes it possible to realize a specified level of markup from each product offered for sale. Initial markup is based on cost, rather than retail; it is not necessary to use a retail method of inventory. There is a certain security in cost-plus pricing with the expectation that each product is initially expected to make an equal percentage contribution to gross margin. Conceptually, the process is simpler and requires less judgment in the pricing process but is not very strategic. It leads to overpricing in weak markets and underpricing in strong markets. It neglects consumer demand and the concept of value. It ignores the reduction of fashion/seasonal merchandise value because of time passing during the selling period. Cost-plus pricing is generally not effective in today's consumer goods markets.

Other Pricing Strategies and Combinations of Pricing Strategies

Every retailer knows that the right pricing strategy can dramatically increase profits. Some apparel retailers have been successful with a single price strategy, that is, "everything in the store for $10.99." These firms focus on an assortment of low-end and budget goods. Several firms have been successful using single prices with fashion goods in pre-teens and juniors (Corwin, 1990).

Some firms use EDLP on some merchandise and rely on high-low pricing on other merchandise to generate traffic (Reda, 1994). Many firms using prestige or EDLP have scheduled markdowns related to the rate of sale of merchandise. For example, the rule may stipulate a mandatory markdown if sales are two weeks behind plan. The marked-down garments may be hung back on the rack with the regular-price merchandise as a bargain for regular shoppers.

 Learning Activity 5.9

Pricing strategies

1. What makes pricing strategies fundamentally different?
2. How many different prices is a product likely to have during a single selling period?
3. What calculations are required to determine the prices?

Understanding the Pricing Game/Application of Pricing Mechanics to Pricing Strategies

Pricing strategies differ greatly in the way prices are manipulated over the course of a selling period for a particular product or merchandise group. Table 5.13 demonstrates the different prices a product with a merchandise cost of $30 might carry, depending on the pricing strategy and levels of markup(s) and markdown(s). Four pricing strategies are included: everyday-low pricing (EDLP), prestige pricing (PP), quick markdown pricing (QMD), and high-low pricing (Hi/Lo).

Table 5.13

Life of a price when merchandise cost is $30 and four different pricing strategies are applied.

Life of a Price in an Everyday-Low Pricing (EDLP) Strategy

$First Price (SMC/%MC)	$MC (given)	%MC (100% − %IMU)	%IMU (given)	$IMU ($FP − $MC)	%PermMD (given)	%PermMD ($FP × %PMD)	$Clear Price ($FP − $PMD)
55	30	55	45	25	40	22	33
60	30	50	50	30	40	24	36
67	30	45	55	37	40	27	40

Life of a Price in a Prestige Pricing (PP) Strategy

$First Price ($MD/%MC)	$MC (given)	%MC (100% − %IMU)	%IMU (given)	$IMU ($FP − $MC)	%PermMD#1 (given)	$PermMD#1 ($FP × %PMD)	$ClearPrice#1 ($FP − $PMD#1)	Can$PermMD#1 $FirstPrice
67	30	45	55	37	35	23	43	67
75	30	40	60	45	35	26	49	75
86	30	35	65	56	35	30	56	86

Life of a Price in a Quick Markdown (QMD) Pricing Strategy

$First Price ($MC/%MC)	$MC (given)	%MC (100% − %IMU)	%IMU (given)	$IMU ($FP − $MC)	%PermMD#1 (given)	BarPrice#1 ($FP − %PermMD#1)	%PermMD#2 (given)	BarPrice#2 ($FP − %PermMD#2)
67	30	45	55	37	20	54	30	47
75	30	40	60	45	20	60	30	53
86	30	35	65	56	20	69	30	60

Life of a Price in a High-Low (Hi/Lo) Pricing Strategy Using Only Initial Markup

$First Price ($MC/%MC)	$MC (given)	%MC ($MC/$FP) × 100)	%IMU (given)	$IMU ($FP − $MC)	%TempMD#1 (given)	PtomoPrice#1 ($FP − %TempMD#1)	CanTempMD#1 ($FirstPrice)	%TempMD#2 (given)
67	30	45	55	37	20	54	67	25
75	30	40	60	45	20	60	75	25
86	30	35	65	56	20	69	86	25

Life of a Price in a High-Low (Hi/Lo) Pricing Strategy Using Both Initial and Additional Markup

$First Price (given)	$MC (given)	%MC ($MC/$FP) × 100)	%IMU ($FP − $MC/ $FP) × 100)	$IMU ($FP − $MC)	%AMU (given)	$AMU ($PP − $FP)	$CompPrice ($FP + %AMU)	CAN$AMU ($PremPrice − $AMU)
60	30	50	50	30	10	6	66	60
60	30	50	50	30	20	12	72	60
60	30	50	50	30	30	18	78	60

%PermMD#2 (given)	$PermMD#2 ($FP × %PMD#2)	$ClearPrice#2 (SFP − $PMD#2)
50	33	34
50	38	38
50	43	43

%PermMD#3 (given)	BarPrice#3 (SFP − %PermMD#3)	%PermMD#3 (given)	BarPrice#4 (SFP − %PermMD#4)
40	40	50	34
40	45	50	38
40	52	50	43

PromoPrice#2 (SFP − %TempMD#2)	CanTempMD#2 (SFirstPrice)	%TempMD#3 (given)	PromoPrice#3 (SFP − %TempMD#3)	CanTempMD#3 (SFirstPrice)	%PermMD (given)	$ClearPrice (SFP − %PermMD)
50	67	35	44	67	50	34
56	75	35	49	75	50	38
65	86	35	56	86	50	43

$PromoPrice#1 (SFirstPrice)	%TempMD#1 (given)	$PromoPrice#2 (FP − %TempMD#1)	CanTempMD#1 (PromoPrice#1)	%TempMD#2 (given)	$PromoPrice#3 (SFP − %TempMD#2)	CanTempMD#2 (PromoPrice#1)	%PermMD (given)	$ClearPrice (SFP − %PermMD)
60	20	48	60	25	45	60	45	33
60	15	51	60	20	48	60	40	36
60	10	54	60	15	51	60	35	39

The "given" elements that provide the basis of calculation for each strategy are presented in italics and the prices customers will see are presented in boldface. The equation/explanation for calculating each element appears under the title of each column. All numbers are rounded to even numbers to simplify presentation. Notice that there are no time periods specified for each price so these examples of pricing strategies could be applied to selling periods of different lengths.

Three different levels of initial and/or additional markup are used for each pricing strategy to show each part of the price calculations and the resulting prices. EDLP, PP, QMD, and the first Hi/Lo are based only in initial markup. The second Hi/Lo is based on both initial and additional markup. For purposes of comparison, PP, QMD, and the first Hi/Lo all have the same levels of initial markup and thus the same first prices.

The examples for EDLP and PP strategies are similar (because the strategies are similar) except prestige has higher levels of initial markup resulting in higher first prices and two permanent markdowns. These two examples are simple and straightforward, both from merchandisers' and consumers' perspectives. The consumer sees only two prices during the selling period for EDLP and three prices for PP. The merchandiser only has to determine the first prices and the clearance markdowns. For the PP strategy, notice that $ Permanent Markdown #1 for $ Clearance Price #1 is cancelled to restore First Price before Permanent Markdown #2 is taken. A permanent markdown means the customer will not again be expected to buy the product at a higher price. The first markdown is cancelled to allow the merchandiser to calculate the second clearance price based on first price. The customer sees the price go from Clearance Price #1 to Clearance Price #2. Given the levels of markups and markdowns, both pricing strategies have clearance prices that exceed merchandise costs. Sometimes a few temporary markdowns for promotional prices are used within EDLP and PP strategies.

The QMD strategy uses Initial Markup and Permanent Markdowns while Hi/Lo with Initial Markup has Temporary Markdowns for Promotional Prices and Markdown Cancellations to return to First Price. QMD and Hi/Lo have high rates of initial markup, the same as for the PP strategy. The permanent markdowns go from 20 percent to 30 percent to 40 percent to 50 percent with a markdown cancellation in between each markdown to allow correct calculation of the next one. The customer only sees the price go down the longer he or she waits to buy the lower price. With Hi/Lo, the price goes up and down during the selling period. In this case both PP and QMD end up with a 50 percent permanent markdown for clearance but have different routes getting there.

The Hi/Lo strategy with both Initial and Additional Markup includes the a comparison or reference price. The strategy uses 50 percent Initial Markup and 10 percent, 20 percent, and 30 percent Additional Markup. Early on the Additional Markup is cancelled leaving the "premium price" established by the Additional Markup as a value representing the "actual value" of the product. A series of Temporary Markdowns for Promotional Prices are intended to further tempt customers by the "good values." Temporary markdowns are followed by markdown cancellations when First Price is resumed until another Temporary Markdown or Permanent Markdown is taken for Clearance. It would be interesting to set up an experiment on the Sourcing Simulator and test these pricing strategies to see which would be most financially productive.

Strategic Pricing Software

Pricing is the largest lever on profitability. A percent increase in price can result in over an $\frac{1}{8}$ percent increase in profitability. A 1 percent improvement in fixed costs results in less than 2 percent increase in profitability. Applying computer software to pricing has opened a whole new perspective on outcomes related to price changes. The Professional Pricing Association has been founded for business professionals engaged in applying information technology (IT) to pricing. DHL Global uses IT to boost revenues on express shipping; Ford Motor Co. uses it to refine promotional pricing. It is immediately possible to see that prices can be set higher, fewer units will be sold, and more profit can be made (Cortese, 2002). Variable pricing such as that used by the airline industry, based on IT, is being tested by other creative businesses. Consumers may soon face a whole new world of pricing (Leonhardt, 2002).

Learning Activity 5.10

Apply pricing mechanics to pricing strategies.

1. Pick three out of the first four examples of pricing strategies from Table 5.13 and calculate another row of numbers to add to the table for each. Use the numbers in italics as a guide to get started. Use 5 percent more or less initial markup than is already included in the table and the equations that are at the top of each column to create the row of numbers.
2. What insights on pricing strategies have you gained from studying Table 5.13?

Summary

Market tradition continues to define pricing relationships between the manufacturing and retailing sectors despite the implementation of quick response business systems, although new technology is offering insights. Prices and pricing involve an intricate language related to interrelationships in the trade matrix. Key concepts include list price, first price, wholesale price, billed cost, gross margin, and adjusted gross margin. Common price changes in both the wholesale and retail sectors reflect differences in price elasticity throughout the selling cycle. Customers' perceptions of price may vary greatly from those of manufacturers and retailers.

A body of federal law beginning in the 1890s frames the legality of pricing practices. Resale Price Maintenance has been a point of particular contention over the past 30 years. Deceptive retailer pricing has more recently become a legal issue.

Pricing policies developed and applied by individual firms are the result of decisions made by executive management with input from the other constituencies of the firm. The most common pricing strategies applied by merchandisers are everyday-low, prestige, quick markdown, and high-low. Merchandisers commonly select or develop products that can be sold within the firm's price range, at their price points, and within their price lines. Pricing strategies are comprised of particular applications of six pricing components: market price position, price lining, price endings, role of first price, role of markdowns, and price advertising. Pricing mechanics are applied to determine first prices, premium prices, markups, and markdowns. Pricing technology is now being tested for applications on consumer goods. To be effective, pricing strategies must uphold a firm's image, mission, and business goals.

Key Concepts

above-market price	distressed goods	merchandise cost
additional markup (AMU)	even-dollar pricing	merchandise price
additional markup cancellation	everyday-low pricing (EDLP)	moderate price range
at-market price	first price	odd-price ending
below-market price	high-low pricing	penetration pricing
better price range	initial markup (IMU)	permanent markdown
billed cost	initial markup based on retail	planned cost
bridge price range	job-off	predatory pricing
budget price range	liquidate	premium price
comparison price	list price	prestige pricing
cost	low-end price range	price
cost-plus pricing	manufacturer's wholesale price	price endings
designer price range	markdown	price lining
differentiated products	markdown cancellation	price points
	markup cancellation	pricing plan

pricing policy
pricing strategy
promotional price
quick markdown pricing
regular price

retail merchandise cost
seasonal discount
selling price
shipping terms

strategic pricing software
temporary markdown
trade discount
two plus two pricing

Integrated Learning Activity 5.11.1

Application of pricing strategies

1. Review, update, correct, and present the company profile that you began developing with ILA 2.6.1 and continued with ILA 3.7.1 and 4.9.1. Be sure to include your corrected income statements and merchandising calendar in your Merchandising Analysis Portfolio (MAP).

2. Develop descriptions for two of the following pricing strategies that are used by or could be appropriate for your MAP retailer: prestige price strategy or every-day-low-price strategy and high-low strategy or quick markdown strategy. Complete your description of one strategy before beginning the other. Include in your description of each strategy:
   - role of first and premium price
   - role of initial and additional markup
   - role of permanent and temporary markdowns
   - number of price changes
   - timing of price changes
   - role of merchandise cost
   - role of cancellation of markup and markdown

3. Which pricing strategy is most consistent with your retailer's image? Why? In what ways might these pricing strategies be unfair or misleading to customers?

4. Apply the two pricing strategies to your fashion/seasonal product calendar and two pricing strategies to your basic staple merchandise calendars (ILA 4.9.1). Be sure to base two strategies for each product on the same merchandise cost. Add an extra column for pricing to each calendar so you can use one column for each pricing strategy. Decide on merchandise cost and initial markup, amount of additional markup (if used), timing of temporary and permanent markdowns, and markup and markdown cancellations. Show amount of first price, merchandise cost, $ and % initial markup, $ and % additional markup (if used), premium price (if used), markup cancellations, markdown cancellations, and $ and % markdowns. Refer to Table 5.13 for help with calculations.

⊚   *Integrated Learning Activity 5.11.2*

Using Sourcing Simulator (SS) to analyze pricing strategies

Objectives
- Develop and apply two different pricing strategies to both fashion/seasonal and basic/staple merchandise groups.
- Test pricing strategies on SS and compare and evaluate selected outcomes of pricing strategies.

Resources for this assignment
- Merchandising text and class notes
- SS Help screens
- Integrated Learning Activities to date
- Your teacher, interactive lab tutor, and/or other class members

Procedure
1. Correct and update your Line Plans resulting from ILA 3.7.1, 4.9.1, and 5.12.1 including two pricing strategies for each merchandise group. Think in terms of your pricing plans for your fashion/seasonal and basic/staple merchandise groups in your merchandise calendars.
2. Open SS Seasonal Model. Conduct the first experiment with your fashion/seasonal merchandise group pricing plan in mind:
   a) Use default data set for everything but instructions for changes in b through n.
   b) Fill out the Buyer's Plan with your fashion/seasonal product name, weeks in selling period, and pre-defined sales peak according to your merchandise calendar. Use 250 units to sell.
   c) Use the default assortment plan for style, sizes, and colors except increase the number of styles to 5 and reallocate the planned percent to equal 100.
   d) On the Sourcing Strategy folder, use the traditional replenishment strategy and set initial stocking to 100%.
   e) On the Consumer Demand folder, use 0% error from plan for both volume and SKU mix; check same as presumed seasonality for the sales peak.
   f) On the Cost Data folder and the Markdowns/Premiums folder, based on your pricing plan in your merchandise calendar, input one pricing strategy. Run the simulation. Check the Planned Average SKU Price graph to be sure your prices are as you intended. Be sure to include the name of the pricing strategy in the title of your outputs.

g) Print your inputs. Examine inputs and outputs. Repeat your simulation if necessary to correct inputs and improve outputs.

h) If you wish to save your inputs for your first pricing strategy, click File and Save As and use the name of the pricing strategy.

i) Input your other pricing strategy for your fashion/seasonal group and repeat the simulation procedure.

j) Examine inputs and outputs. Repeat simulation if necessary. Print inputs and outputs and graphs for total revenue, gross margin, planned average SKU price, and % gross margin potential.

k) Close SS Seasonal Model. Do not save inputs as default.

3. Open SS Basics Model. Conduct the second experiment with your pricing strategy on your merchandise calendar for your basic/staple merchandise group.

a) Fill out the Buyer's Plan folder with your basic/staple product name and planned sales peak according to your merchandise calendar. Use planned annual volume of 1,000 units. Use the default assortment plan for style, sizes, and colors.

b) Use the default Sourcing Strategy.

c) Repeat inputs described in e through k above. Use the default data set for everything else.

d) Organize your printouts. Be sure each is clearly marked with your name and pricing strategy.

Basis of Evaluation

1. Present this assignment in an orderly manner in your MAP. Be sure to include your merchandising calendar that includes your planned pricing strategy.

2. Include four simulation input printouts and two simulation output printouts and copies of graphs prepared according to your SS assignment.

3. Based on your input printouts, calculate and/or report in table form the following inputs per unit for each pricing strategy for both merchandise groups: retail planning price, merchandise cost, $ initial markup, % initial markup, $ additional markup, % additional markup, premium price, and $ for each % markdown.

4. Highlight the following outputs on your printout: total units received, revenue per unit offered, % sell through, $ gross margin, % gross margin, and % gross margin potential. Review definitions of output terms. Which pricing strategy was most successful for each merchandise group? How do you know?

5. Why are % sell through, revenue per unit offered, and % gross margin potential particularly useful when evaluating pricing strategies?

6. Is your % gross margin realistic for both pricing strategies for each product? If not, what adjustments need to be made in your pricing strategy to make it more realistic? Describe other change(s) in your pricing plan that could improve the output measures in your table.

Recommended Resources

Cortese, A. (2002, March 1). Price flexing: How the Web adds new twists. *CIO Insight* (www. Khimetrics.com/Articles_CIO_Insight_0302.htm). Accessed June 11, 2002.

Kaufmann, P. J., Smith, C., & Ortmeyer, G. K. (1994). Deception in retailer high-low pricing: A 'rule of reason' approach. *Journal of Retailing,* 70(2):115–138.

KhiMetrics and The Professional Pricing Society. (2002). Retail revenue management: Improving financial performance through strategic pricing (www.Khimetrics.com). Accessed June 11, 2002.

Nagle, T. T., & Holden, R. K. (2002). *The strategy and tactics of pricing: A guide to profitable decision making* (3rd ed.). Upper Saddle River, NJ: Prentice Hall.

Shugan, S. M., & Desiraju, R. (2001). Retail product-line pricing strategy when costs and products change. *Journal of Retailing,* 77:17–38.

Stankevich, D. G. (2000, May). In the heat of battle. *Retail Merchandiser,* 109–112.

References

Carlson, P. G. (1983, Spring). Fashion retailing: The sensitivity of rate of sale to markdown. *Journal of Retailing*, 59(1):67–76.

Cortese, A. (2002, March 1). Price flexing: How the Web adds new twists. CIO Insight, (www. Khimetrics.com/Articles_CIO_Insight_0302.htm). Accessed June 11, 2002.

Corwin, P. (1990, April). Finessing the one-price strategy. *Discount Merchandiser,* 66–72.

Cunningham, T. (2001, July 23). Bargain hunter. *Daily News Record,* 16:26.

Degross, R., & Staff. (2001, May 12). Economy's swelling surplus: Overstock glut trickles down to discounters. *Atlanta Journal-Constitution.*

Federated Department Stores. (2003). (www.fds.com/company/strategies.asp). Accessed September 24, 2003.

Kaufmann, P. J., Smith, C., & Ortmeyer, G. K. (1994). Deception in retailer high-low pricing: A 'rule of reason' approach. *Journal of Retailing,* 70(2):115–138.

Kunz, G. I. (1995). Behavioral theory of the apparel firm: A beginning. *Clothing and Textiles Research Journal,* 13(4):252–261.

Lee, L. (1995, January 10). Wal-Mart wins ruling on pricing policy. *Wall Street Journal,* B8.

Leonhardt, D. (2002, May 12). Tiptoeing toward variable pricing. *New York Times,* 4.

Levy, W. K. (1994, November). Beware, the pricing genie is out of the bottle. Retailing Issues Newsletter: Arthur Andersen and Center for Retailing Studies, Texas A&M University.

Levy, W. K., & Howard, D. J. (1988). An experimental approach to planning the duration and size of markdowns. *International Journal of Retailing,* 3(2):148–158.

Lieberman, D. (2002, September 30). States settle CD price-fixing case. *USA Today* (www.usatoday.com). Accessed October 3, 2003.

Manufacturers can refuse to sell to discounters, Supreme Court says. (1988, May 3). *The Daily Tribune,* B4.

Mason, B. J., Mayer, M. L., & Ezell, H. F. (1984). *Foundations of retailing.* Plano, TX: Business Publications, Inc.

Music CD Settlement. (2003). Compact disc minimum advertised price antitrust litigation settlement (www.musiccdsettlement.com). Accessed August 13, 2003.

Nagle, T. T., & Holden, R. K. (2002). *The strategy and tactics of pricing: A guide to profitable decision making* (3rd ed.). Upper Saddle River, NJ: Prentice Hall.

Novak, V., & Pereira, J. (1995, May 5). Reebok and FTC settle price-fixing charges. *Wall Street Journal,* B1 & B8.

Pashigian, B. P. (1988, December). Demand uncertainty and sales: A study of fashion and markdown pricing. *American Economic Review,* 78(5):936–953.

Pashigian, B. P., & Bowen, B. (1991, November). Why are products sold on sale? Explanations of pricing regularities. *The Quarterly Journal of Economics,* 1015–1038.

Reda, S. (1994, October). Is E.D.L.P. coming up short? *Stores,* 76(10):22–26.

Rupe, K., & Kunz, G. I. (1995). Building a financially meaningful language of merchandise assortments. *Clothing and Textiles Research Journal,* 16(2):88–97.

Stankevich, D. G. (2000, May). In the heat of battle. *Retail Merchandiser,* 109–112.

Younkers. (2001, March 4). Red dot sale. *Des Moines Register,* 18A.

6

Planning and Controlling Merchandise Budgets

Learning Objectives

- Explore static vs. dynamic budgets.

- Examine components of merchandise budgets.

- Practice the mechanics of merchandise budgets.

- Explore the integrated relationships among the components of a merchandise budget.

*F*irms commonly generate numerous financial statements at the end of each quarter and fiscal year to assess the firm's financial position and establish goals for the coming year. These may include balance sheets, income statements, merchandising ratios, marketing ratios, operating ratios, and financial ratios. Of these, income statements (discussed in Chapter 3) with their corresponding ratios are most closely associated with merchandise planning processes. Merchandise budgets determine the levels of dollar investment in goods for a selling period in the merchandising cycle. Merchandise budgets are formulated within the context of a firm's business plan and goals for the selling period. Budgets are the primary means of controlling investment in merchandise.

Components of Merchandise Budgets

Effective firms systematically make and evaluate plans related to all aspects of their businesses. They make marketing plans, operation plans, finance plans, merchandising plans, overall business plans, and annual goals. **Merchandise plans** primarily cover the planning of merchandise budgets, pricing, assortments, and deliveries. The income statement is a report of a firm's past performance. It provides one of many sources of information that might be used to modify a firm's strategic plans and set its annual productivity goals. A merchandise budget is designed to provide a foundation for implementing merchandising plans and to help the firm meet those goals. Merchandise budgets take different forms depending on the nature of the firm's business and its strategic priorities.

The retail merchandise budgets discussed here assume the firm uses the **retail method of accounting for inventory,** which means that the value of inventory is determined by retail prices. So when merchandise price is permanently changed, the value of inventory is changed. For many products, the retail price is a better reflection of merchandise value than merchandise cost. Fashion/seasonal goods, for example, decline in value as the selling period progresses. Reduction in price can mean one of two things from the merchant's perspective: customers won't buy it at the original price because the price is too high or the merchandise needs to be cleared from inventory because of broken assortments or end of the selling period. In any case, the permanent price change is a conscious business decision on the part of the merchandiser with the purpose of increasing the rate of sale of the goods. A permanent price reduction reflects a reduction in the retail value of the merchandise.

The merchandise budget discussed here is dynamic and forecast-based (see Table 6.1). The budget is based on detailed sales and inventory forecasts for individual stores for each merchandise classification. This budget is designed to show the investment in merchandise for a merchandising cycle for a fashion/seasonal merchandise class or subclass that has four 13-week selling periods such as Mike's Bikes jerseys/tops. With minor modifications, this type of a budget can be used for fashion/seasonal goods with 26-week selling periods or basic/staple goods with 52-week selling periods or longer. It also could also be used as a merchandise plan for a manufacturer. The manufacturer would plan by classification but not plan for individual stores unless they had their own retail outlet operation. They might, however, use a plan like this for each major retail customer.

When computerized, the **dynamic budget** can be set up to allow immediate comparison, where appropriate, of actual figures for last year, last month, last week, yesterday, or this morning to plan for this year, this month, this week, today, or this afternoon. The actual figures for this time this year can be shown with percent change from last year. Comparisons to last year demonstrate progress toward achieving goals related to sales growth. The major elements of the budget relate to:

- sales at retail for last year, planned sales, and actual sales for this year
- inventory (stock) at the beginning of each day, week, or month and stock/sales ratios

- reductions last year, reductions as a percent of planned sales this year, and actual reductions this year
- merchandise to receive/planned purchases
- merchandise on order at retail and at cost
- open-to-buy at retail and at cost
- average first price per unit
- number of units (merchandise volume) required to meet sales goals

Budgets commonly focus on these elements, often in this order because of the mathematical relationships among the elements.

As the dynamic budget is updated weekly, daily, hourly, or continuously, it consistently shows history for the same period in the past and projected sales, inventory, and other information for planning the next time periods. The budget for the same selling period next year is commonly developed before the completion of the period this year. Thus, with a dynamic budget, modifications of plans for the coming time period can be updated based on present sales trends.

Implementing this dynamic merchandise budget means the firm must have an integrated, computerized information technology system or a contract with a third-party service to process the data. The more frequently the system can update the budget, the better merchandisers can plan. Most systems can now update weekly and some can update daily, some hourly, and some "right now" with the touch of a key.

Top-down budgets based on planned sales for the whole organization can be split into budgets for categories, classes, and subclasses to provide a detailed view sometimes down to the SKU (stock keeping unit) level. Bottom-up budgets based on departments or merchandise classes can be aggregated to show the resulting overall view of the category, for the whole store, and/or for the whole chain of stores. Budgets show how money is being invested in merchandise and the results of that investment.

Learning Activity 6.1

Dynamic merchandise budget

1. What is the retail method of accounting?
2. What is the fundamental purpose of a merchandise budget?
3. Why should a merchandise budget be dynamic as opposed to static?
4. What is required to make a budget forecast-based?

Table 6.1

*Example of an expanded merchandise budget related to a merchandising calendar with 13-week selling periods. ***

Dynamic, Forecast-Based Merchandise Budget

Store _____   Class/Subclass/Group _____

Elements of Budget	Selling Period #1			Selling Period #2	
	Feb weeks 1–4	Mar weeks 5–9	Apr weeks 10–13	May weeks 14–17	Jun weeks 18–22
Sales					
Last year actual					
Next year plan					
Next year actual					
Inventory First of Week					
Last year actual					
Next year plan					
Next year actual					
Inventory/Sales Ratio					
Last year actual					
Next year actual					
Reductions					
Last year actual					
Next year plan					
Next year actual					
Merchandise to Receive/Retail					
Last year actual					
Next year plan					
Next year actual					
Merchandise to Receive/Cost					
Last year actual					
Next year plan					
Next year actual					
Percent Initial Markup					
Last year actual					
Next year plan					
On Order (Retail)					
On Order (Cost)					
Open-to-Buy (Retail)					
Open-to-Buy (Cost)					
First Price					
Number of Units					

*Based on Retail Mechandising Services Automation, Inc. (1995).

Square Feet _____ Year _____

	Selling Period #3			Selling Period #4			Total or Average
Jul weeks 23–26	Aug weeks 27–30	Sep weeks 31–35	Oct weeks 36–39	Nov weeks 40–44	Dec weeks 45–49	Jan weeks 50–52	

5. How would the budget in Table 6.1 be modified if planning investment in a basic/staple merchandise class?
6. How would the budget in Table 6.1 be modified if planning investment in a fashion/seasonal merchandise class such as Mike's Bikes outerwear with 26-week selling periods?
7. Why are last year's sales usually a key component of merchandise planning?

Mechanics of Merchandise Budgets

To begin to understand the conceptual relationships among the elements of a merchandise budget, focus on the fundamental elements of a budget in relation to the totals for a selling period or merchandising cycle. Allocation across weeks of sale during the selling period is discussed later.

The elements are similar for the dynamic budget in Table 6.1; however, the comparative figures for each element are omitted to make the process easier to interpret. All of the formulas and calculations in this section are presented in an outcomes type format, that is, the unknown element being sought is listed first followed by the formula. The components of a **fundamental merchandise budget** include the following:

- Last Year's Sales
- % Increase or Decrease
- Planned Sales
- Planned Reductions
- Merchandise to Receive
- First Price
- Number of Units

The information needed to plan merchandise budgets for Mike's Bikes is presented in Company Profile 6.1, Part 4 and a discussion of the steps involved in developing a merchandise budget follows.

Company Profile 6.1

Mike's Bikes, Part 4, Merchandise Budgets

The outlook for Mike's Bikes is bright. Cycling is predicted to continue to grow in popularity. Sales have increased about 5 percent every year except one, and they have made a profit every year since the third year. A 5 percent increase in sales is planned for next year. Last year, for the first time, Mike's Bikes achieved $2 million in net sales. A Sports Authority store opened last year in the West Des Moines area, but it has only slowed sales of some of the budget priced merchandise at Mike's Bikes. Michelle and Kevin are active, visible members of local and regional cycling clubs. The store regularly supports cycling activities in the area and the state. This gives them the opportunity to observe not only what the cyclists buy in their own store, but also what they are buying elsewhere. They are active in the Chamber of Commerce and meet regularly with other entrepreneurs.

Kevin maintains an extensive database of email addresses of current customers and their purchases at the SKU level, and uses these as the primary form of advertising. He sends three primary emails a year — early spring, pre-RAGBRAI, and holiday. He also sends individualized emails reminding regular customers of birthdays, anniversaries, and other events.

Kevin estimates that RAGBRAI alone contributes 15 percent of sales.

The merchandise mix includes three categories: bikes (about 50 percent of sales), apparel (20 percent), and accessories (15 percent). In addition, bike service accounts for 15 percent of sales.

They stock both men's and women's mountain bikes, road bikes, and hybrid bikes. They also have a few portable, recumbent, and kid's bikes. Mountain bikes are 55 percent of sales, road bikes are 20 percent, hybrids are 15 percent, and the others are 10 percent of sales. Bikes take up 6,200 square feet of space.

The apparel assortment is about 50 percent men's, 30 percent women's, 13 percent kids, and 7 percent unisex (outerwear). They carry six classifications of apparel. Cycling shorts and tights are 50 percent of apparel sales. Basic/seasonal solid color cycling shorts dominate sales of bottoms with 75 percent of sales and they have a 52-week selling period. Shoes are 20 percent, jerseys and tops 20 percent, and socks and gloves 3 percent of apparel sales. Jerseys/tops have four 13-week selling periods. Outerwear is 7 percent of apparel sales and has two 26-week selling periods with 60 percent of sales in the second period. Apparel is crowded into 1,000 square feet of space.

(continued)

Company Profile 6.1 (continued)

Four hundred square feet of the apparel space is devoted to bottoms, that is, cycling shorts and tights.

Accessories include six classifications: bike parts; helmets; tools and tool kits; backpacks, water bottles, and bags; sunglasses; and computers to track distance, time, heart rate, etc. Initial markup on accessories is 60 percent and has 500 square feet of space.

The service department assembles bikes for display, as well as assembles and repairs bikes for customers. The service department sells bike parts, tires, wheels, and other hardware. It has 2,000 square feet of space. Three hundred of Mike's Bikes' 10,000 square feet are used for the office. Table 6.2 organizes last year's sales and pricing information in an easily understandable form.

At Mike's Bikes, reductions include markdowns, shoplifting, damaged goods, employee discounts, and accounting errors. Fifty to 55 percent of markdowns are used for final clearance of discontinued apparel and biking accessories. Twenty percent of temporary markdowns are taken on solid colored biking shorts and selected bikes during the three weeks in July including RAGBRAI. A series of quick markdowns—30, 40, and 50 percent—are taken during the selling period on slow-moving styles or colors. Reductions of inventory value because of theft, inventory damage, and accounting error is estimated at 5 percent of sales, primarily because of theft of small biking accessories. They do provide 30 percent employee discounts on both regular and sale prices on all merchandise. Overall, reductions are estimated last year at $300,000. The development of a fundamental budget for a merchandise subclass for a merchandising cycle follows.

Planning Sales

Planned sales are the foundation of a merchandise budget just like net sales are the foundation of an income statement. The first challenge is to break down last year's sales to provide a point of departure to determine planned sales. Table 6.2 provides an example of the levels at which a merchandise budget might be planned. You could develop budgets for each

Table 6.2

Breakdown of Mike's Bikes $2 million in sales last year by merchandise category, sales per square foot, and class.

% Sales by Category		$ Sales by Category	Square Feet	Sales per Sq. Ft.	% Sales by Class		$ Sales by Class	Average First Price
Bikes	50%	$1,000,000	6,200	$160	Mountain	55%	$550,000	$ 750
					Road	20%	$200,000	$ 850
					Hybrid	15%	$150,000	$1,000
					Other	10%	$100,000	$2,000
Apparel	20%	$400,000	1,000	$400	Shorts/Tights	50%	$200,000	$ 65
					Jerseys/Tops	20%	$ 80,000	$ 75
					Shoes	20%	$ 80,000	$ 120
					Outerwear	7%	$ 28,000	$ 140
					Socks/Gloves	3%	$ 12,000	$ 20
Accessories	15%	$300,000	500	$600	Helmets	35%	$105,000	$ 90
					Bike Parts	30%	$ 90,000	$ 70
					Backpacks	15%	$ 45,000	$ 80
					Sunglasses	10%	$ 30,000	$ 180
					Tools/Tool Kits	8%	$ 24,000	$ 70
					Computers	2%	$ 2,000	$ 125
Service	15%	$300,000	2,000	$150	Parts	50%	$150,000	
					Repair	35%	$105,000	
					Assembly	15%	$ 45,000	

merchandise category using last year's sales for each. Each of those budgets could be split into budgets for each class and then each subclass. Be sure to keep the following in mind:

- Sales for a category are a percent of total sales.
- Sales for a class are a percent of sales for the category.
- Sales for a subclass are a percent of sales for the class.

The data in Table 6.2 are based on Mike's Bikes' last year's sales ($2 million), the percent of sales by category, the square feet allocation, and the percent of sales generated by class. Using the apparel category and shorts/tights class as an example, the sequence of calculations for the data in the table was as follows:

$$\text{sales for category} = \text{total sales} \times \text{\% of sales for category}$$
$$\$400,000 = \$2,000,000 \times 20\%$$

$$\text{sales per square foot for category} = \text{sales for category} \div \text{square feet for category}$$
$$\$400 = \$400,000 \div 1,000$$

$$\text{sales for class} = \text{category sales} \times \text{\% of sales for the class}$$
$$\$200,000 = \$400,000 \times 50\%$$

These calculations demonstrate the relationships between the amount of sales and the merchandise classification system.

Ultimately, planning sales often comes down to last year's sales plus some **percent increase or decrease.** Businesses always prefer to plan sales increases because a firm has to grow in order to accommodate common levels of inflation that reduce buying power, provide employees with raises in their paychecks, and maintain or increase profitability. Sometimes planned sales increases are top-down from executive decrees—other times they are carefully planned, realistic considerations.

The forecasting process that determines the percent increase or decrease may consider the following:

- sales for the previous year(s), same selling period
- sales percentages by month or week of the selling period
- recent trends in sales
- changes inside the store, such as remodeling
- factors outside the store, such as new competition

- comparisons of productivity with competitors
- trends in demographic and lifestyle priorities of target customers
- planned marketing strategies for the selling period
- short- and long-term goals of the firm

Whatever the source of the decision, merchandisers are committed to generating merchandise plans that will achieve the sales increase and thus **make plan,** that is, planned sales so the income statement can declare a successful year. Success of the selling period and the generation of the planned productivity figures are highly dependent on achieving the planned sales level. Planned sales therefore become the **sales goal** for the selling period.

We are going to develop a merchandise budget for solid color cycling shorts (SCS) at Mike's Bikes. (We are using an abbreviation for "solid color cycling shorts" in this discussion because solid color cycling shorts is repeated many times, but remember SCS stands for solid color cycling shorts, a basic/seasonal product.)

Look back at Company Profile 6.1. What information is relevant to a budget for SCS? Solid color cycling shorts are a subclass of the shorts/tights class in the apparel category. They are a basic/staple product so they have at least a 52-week selling period. Last year's sales of cycling shorts and tights were $200,000 and SCS sales were 75 percent of the class.

sales of subclass	=	total sales of the class	×	% of sales of subclass
sales of SCS	=	total sales of shorts/tights	×	% of sales of SCS
$150,000	=	$200,000	×	75%

Thus, last year's sales for SCS were $150,000. Now we are ready to determine planned sales for next year.

According to the profile, Mike's Bikes is planning a 5 percent increase in sales. The calculation of planned sales for next year for an ongoing business comes down to the following formula:

planned sales for the year	=	last year's sales	×	$(1 \pm$ % change in sales$)$
planned sales for SCS	=	last year's sales of SCS	×	$(1 \pm$ % change in SCS sales$)$
$157,500	=	$150,000	×	$(1 + 5\%)$

To plan and achieve the sales goal for the merchandising cycle, sales of SCS next year must equal or exceed $157,500. Now we have the first entries in Mike's Bikes Fundamental Merchandise Budget for SCS (see Table 6.3).

Table 6.3

Mike's Bikes Fundamental Merchandise Budget Plan.

Category/Class/Subclass   Solid color cycling shorts

Product type basic/staple   selling period   52 weeks

Last year's sales	$150,000
Planned % increase/decrease	5%
Planned $ increase/decrease	$ 7,500
Planned sales	$157,500
Planned % reductions	
Planned $ reductions	
Merchandise to receive	
Average first price	

Learning Activity 6.2

Planning sales based on percent increase or decrease

1. Calculate planned sales at the category level for bikes at Mike's Bikes using the percentage increase/decrease method assuming their 5 percent planned sales increase and a 52-week selling period. Follow the series of steps demonstrated in the discussion of the SCS planned sales for the budget.
2. Calculate planned sales for hybrid bikes based on planned sales for bikes in #1.
3. Based on Table 6.2, calculate planned sales for the apparel category for next year's merchandising cycle and then planned sales for outerwear. (Tip: Be sure you include the 5 percent sales increase only once.)

Planned Sales for Selling Periods, Months, Weeks, or Days

Sales can be allocated to months and/or weeks of the merchandising cycle or a selling period based on last year's percent of sales per month or week, unless forecasts indicate that adjustments are necessary. Based on last year's merchandise budget, percent of sales for SCS last year by month are shown in Table 6.4.

Based on their sales forecast, Michelle and Kevin agreed to use the same sales percentages per month from last year for this year's merchandise plan. Planned sales by month for next year for SCS are shown in Table 6.5. To plan by selling period use the same process

Table 6.4

Percent of sales by month for solid color cycling shorts (SCS) last year.

Percent Sales per Month		=	Monthly Sales	÷	Sales for Selling Period	×	100
Feb	2%	=	$ 3,000	÷	$150,000	×	100
Mar	2%	=	$ 3,000	÷	$150,000	×	100
Apr	3%	=	$ 4,500	÷	$150,000	×	100
May	5%	=	$ 7,500	÷	$150,000	×	100
Jun	8%	=	$ 12,000	÷	$150,000	×	100
Jul	17%	=	$ 25,500	÷	$150,000	×	100
Aug	15%	=	$ 22,500	÷	$150,000	×	100
Sep	14%	=	$ 21,000	÷	$150,000	×	100
Oct	12%	=	$ 18,000	÷	$150,000	×	100
Nov	9%	=	$ 13,500	÷	$150,000	×	100
Dec	12%	=	$ 18,000	÷	$150,000	×	100
Jan	1%	=	$ 1,500	÷	$150,000	×	100
Total	100%		$150,000		$150,000		

shown in Table 6.5, but substitute "sales percent per selling period" for "sales percent per month." If you have two selling periods, you would have two rows of numbers. If you planned by week, you would have 52 rows of numbers. Remember, the percent allocations have to add up to 100 percent. Since the Fundamental Budget only includes totals for the year or selling period being planned, we will not add the monthly distribution of sales, but they will be useful later when developing the extended budget for the merchandising cycle and when planning merchandise deliveries.

Learning Activity 6.3

Planning sales for multiple selling periods

1. According to Figure 4.2, Perceptual Map of Product Change, outerwear is a fashion/seasonal product with two 26-week selling periods. Sixty percent of outerwear sales are in the second selling period. Calculate planned sales for the outerwear class for next year's two selling periods with planned sales based on Learning Activity 6.2, #3.

2. Using planned sales for outerwear's second selling period from problem #1, plan sales by month for outerwear's fall selling period. Assume the following rate of

Table 6.5

Planned sales for solid color cycling shorts for next year by month.

Monthly Planned Sales	=	Planned Sales for Next Year	×	Sales Percent per Month
Feb	$ 3,150	=	$157,500	×	2%
Mar	$ 3,150	=	$157,500	×	2%
Apr	$ 4,725	=	$157,500	×	3%
May	$ 7,875	=	$157,500	×	5%
June	$ 12,600	=	$157,500	×	8%
July	$ 26,775	=	$157,500	×	17%
Aug	$ 23,625	=	$157,500	×	15%
Sep	$ 22,050	=	$157,500	×	14%
Oct	$ 18,900	=	$157,500	×	12%
Nov	$ 14,175	=	$157,500	×	9%
Dec	$ 18,900	=	$157,500	×	12%
Jan	$ 1,575	=	$157,500	×	1%
Total	$157,500		$157,500		100%

sale by month: August 15 percent, September 19 percent, October 19 percent, November 20 percent, December 22 percent, and January 5 percent. Use Table 6.4 as a model for presenting your results.

3. Table 6.2 shows jerseys and tops had $80,000 in sales last year. The jerseys/tops class breaks into subclass solid color jerseys (15 percent of jerseys/tops), color-blocked (45 percent of jerseys/tops), fancies (15 percent of jerseys/tops), and tops (15 percent of jerseys/tops). According to the merchandising calendar (Table 4.4), jerseys/tops are a fashion/seasonal product with four selling periods. Assume first selling period last year had 16 percent of sales, second had 34 percent, third had 26 percent, and the fourth had 24 percent. Calculate planned sales for color-blocked jerseys for the four selling periods next year. Be sure to include Mike's Bikes' planned sales increase.

4. Before Mike's Bikes could implement their sales plan demonstrated in the previous discussion, it was announced that RAGBRAI would not be held next year. Refer to Company Profile 6.1. How might that affect their sales plan? Recalculate Mike's Bikes' total planned sales for next year for SCS without RAGBRAI sales. Be sure to account for both the planned sales increase and the lost sales from

RAGBRAI. There are two or three different ways to do this. The results will be different but not necessarily wrong, just different. The challenge is to decide which method results in the most appropriate planned sales numbers. Explain the method you used and why.

Planning Sales Based on Space Productivity

Space is a resource that must be used productively for a firm to succeed. Grocers allocate shelf space by the inch or centimeter and measure productivity of shelf space by the linear inch or centimeter. Farmers measure productivity of space in bushels per acre; retailers measure productivity of space in sales per square foot. Retail display fixtures are evaluated based on how many dollars per square foot in sales a fixture should be able to generate. In New York City, the value of real estate is assessed by the square foot, so McDonald's restaurants sometimes utilize vertical space, with sales on the street-level and seating upstairs. Space can be analyzed using multiple perspectives, for example, catalogs analyze sales per square inch by page, by item profitability, product category, and price point (Schmid, 2001, June).

The retail floor space allocated to a particular merchandise classification is expected to generate a planned number of dollars so the firm can meet its sales goals. The firm must balance sales productivity of the classification with the amount of space allocated to the classification. Merchandise categories differ greatly in **sales per square foot,** as indicated by industry averages. There are also wide ranges among specialty, department, and mass retailers. Tables 2.4 and 2.5 of the Representative Data Set located at the end of Chapter 2 include average sales per square foot for retailers in different channels. Table 2.8 presents average sales per square foot for different merchandise categories and classes. In addition, Table 6.6 provides ranges of sales per square foot for different merchandise classes across retail channels. A useful number to keep in mind is *$250 per square foot.* This is an average sales per square foot across retail channels and merchandise categories. When asked whether a sales per square foot number is high or low, think first of the average, $250 per square foot. If it is $500 per square foot, it is very high; if it is $100, it is very low. When sales per square foot is above average, it increases the retailer's opportunity for profitability; when sales per square foot is low, it decreases the ability to operate profitably.

Sales per square foot can be used as a zero-based or a bottom-up merchandise planning tool. **Zero-based budgeting** means no previous levels of sales or productivity are assumed. The budget begins with a blank sheet of paper. Bottom-up planning means plans are based on numbers generated at the store and classification level. Zero-based plans are sometimes more innovative than history-based plans; bottom-up plans may be regarded as more realis-

Table 6.6

Ranges of sales per square foot by merchandise category across retail channels.

Category or Classification	Sales per Square Foot	
	Low	High
women's and girl's apparel	$150	$640
men's and boy's apparel	$110	$410
women's accessories	$140	$415
footwear	$250	$450
cosmetics/health & beauty	$190	$345
sporting goods	$150	$280
home furnishings	$ 50	$170

tic than top-down plans, while top-down plans are more likely to be related to company goals.

To determine planned sales for a classification for a defined period using the **space productivity method** based on sales per square foot:

1. Examine annual sales per square foot being generated by competing stores as well as industry-wide annual sales per square foot generated by merchandise classification. (These are included in the Representative Data Set.)

2. Determine the number of square feet allocated to the classification.

3. Decide on a reasonable estimate of sales per square foot based on your research related to merchandise class and retail channel.

If you are planning for a basic/staple product, annual sales per square foot would be planned sales for the selling period and the merchandising cycle because the selling period is the same length as the merchandising cycle (52 weeks). The annual planned sales can then be broken down to sales per week, sales per month, or, if planning for a fashion/seasonal product, sales per selling period. Planned sales for a selling period could be determined based on sales per square foot as follows:

$$\text{sales for the selling period} = \text{sales per week} \times \text{weeks of sale}$$
$$\text{sales per week} = \text{square feet for the class} \times (\text{annual sales per square foot} \div 52 \text{ weeks per year})$$

The method above assumes that sales are relatively uniform from week to week because each week has the same amount of sales. Another way to plan by selling period is to divide annual sales per square foot by number of selling periods instead of number of weeks per year. This assumes the selling periods will have equal sales. If selling periods have similar lengths but differ in rate of sale, multiply annual sales per square foot by percent of sales per selling period. There are many ways to develop a planned sales number depending on the conditions that influence sales.

To plan sales for Mike's Bikes SCS using the sales per square foot method, refer to Table 6.2 and Company Profile 6.1. According to the profile, the shorts/tights class had 400 square feet of the apparel space and, as Table 6.2 shows, they generated 50 percent of apparel sales, $200,000. What is the sales per square foot for the shorts/tights class?

sales per sq. ft. for class	=	*sales for the class*	÷	*number of sq. ft. for class*
sales per sq. ft. for shorts/tights	=	*sales for shorts/tights*	÷	*number of sq. ft.*
$500	=	200,000	÷	400

Thus, the shorts/tights class is very productive on a sales per square foot basis. If Mike's Bikes decided they wanted to plan a 5 percent increase in sales per square foot for the SCS subclass, what is planned sales? First determine number of square feet for the subclass.

sq. ft. for subclass	=	*sq. ft. for the class*	×	*subclass percent of sales*
sq. ft. for SCS	=	*sq. ft. for shorts/tights*	×	*SCS percent of shorts/tights sales*
300	=	400	×	75%

planned sales per sq. ft.	=	*last year's sales per sq. ft.*	×	*(1 ± percent change)*
planned sales for SCS	=	*last year's sales per sq. ft. for SCS*	×	*(1 + 5%)*
$525	=	$500	×	*(1 + 5%)*

planned sales for subclass	=	*planned sales per sq. ft.*	×	*sq. ft. for subclass*
planned sales for SCS	=	*planned sales per sq. ft. for SCS*	×	*sq. ft. for SCS*
$157,500	=	$525	×	300

Thus, planned sales for SCS using the sales per square foot method and the process above is the same as planning sales using the percentage increase/decrease method because we used the same ratios.

Planning sales based on space allocation is an alternate method to the percent increase or decrease method previously described. Both methods may be used for the same selling periods using different assumptions, then the results can be compared to evaluate the effectiveness of sales planning methods. For example, you might question whether it is realistic to plan to sell another $25 a square foot of SCS when sales per square foot is already very high. If they want the sales increase, it may be necessary to allocate more space to SCS. Thus, planning sales based on sales per square foot might be used as a way to test the realism of a sales plan based on the percentage increase method. Space productivity can also be used to estimate the sales of privately owned competitors or firms that do not reveal their financial status. In addition, space productivity may also provide the basis of a business plan for an entrepreneur starting a new business.

 Learning Activity 6.4

Planning sales based on space productivity

1. Create two sales plans for the bike category at Mike's Bikes, one using the percentage increase/decrease method and the other the sales per square foot method. Use Table 6.2 for your data.
2. How is it possible for the shorts/tights class to have half of apparel sales with less than half of apparel square feet?
3. Plan sales for SCS with a 5 percent increase in its 400 square feet and a 5 percent increase in last year's sales of $200,000. What will be the expected sales per square foot for SCS? What justification is there to give SCS more square feet?

Planning Reductions

Reductions are anything other than sales that reduce the value of inventory. When merchandise is sold, it is usually assumed that the value of inventory is reduced and new merchandise must be purchased to replace it so the firm can remain in business. When the value of merchandise is reduced by some means other than sales, merchandise must be purchased to replace the lost value or sales goals cannot be met. Reductions of inventory value by means other than sales is an implicit aspect of operating a manufacturing or retailing business. Therefore, reductions must be planned into merchandise budgets. Reductions take three forms:

-   markdowns for purposes of sales promotion or inventory clearance
-   markdowns as employee discounts
-   inventory shortage because of shoplifting, employee theft, damaged merchandise, or record-keeping errors

Markdowns are the largest portion of reductions but vary greatly by classification of merchandise. Fashion/seasonal goods may be planned with **zero to zero inventories.** That means merchandise is purchased specifically for a particular selling period and anything not sold during the selling period is marked down for clearance. Goods not sold on clearance are liquidated. This process happens two to eight times in a single merchandising cycle because of selling periods that are usually 7 to 26 weeks long. In contrast, basic/staple goods have long selling periods, 52 weeks or more, and some merchandise is usually carried over from one selling period to the next. Markdowns for clearance are only for styles or colors that are being discontinued.

Shoplifting rates also vary by merchandise class. Some types of merchandise are easier to conceal than others. Fad merchandise and hot brands are primary targets for some shoplifters for their own use or for the black market value. Did you know that more merchandise is shoplifted by employees than by customers? Unfortunately, data from retailers and manufacturers regarding the total amount of reductions is very hard to find. See Table 6.7 for indicators of levels of reductions for different classes of merchandise. You may want to put a tab on this page so you can refer back to it.

Reductions can be planned for the merchandising cycle, a series of selling periods, months, or weeks. As reported in Company Profile 6.1, Mike's Bikes estimates their reductions at $300,000. Reductions are usually calculated as a percent of net sales. Plan reductions for SCS as follows:

Table 6.7

Guidelines for estimating reductions.

Merchandise Class	Reduction Rate
books	Less than 5% of sales.
cosmetics	Less than 5% of sales.
costume jewelry	About 10% of sales.
drugs	About 5% of sales.
highly seasonal goods	May be more than 30% of sales.
holiday décor	May be more than 30% of sales.
men's suits	May be as high as 20% of sales.
shoes	May be as high as 30% of sales.
swim suits	May be more than 30% of sales.
women's dresses	May be as high as 30% of sales.

$$
\begin{aligned}
\textit{percent reductions} &= \textit{reductions for a period} \div \textit{net sales for same period} \times 100 \\
\textit{percent reductions/Mike's Bikes} &= \textit{reductions for period} \div \textit{net sales for same period} \times 100 \\
15\% &= \$300{,}000 \div \$2{,}000{,}000 \times 100
\end{aligned}
$$

$$
\begin{aligned}
\textit{planned reductions} &= \textit{planned sales} \times \textit{planned reduction percent} \\
\textit{planned reductions SCS} &= \textit{planned sales SCS} \times \textit{planned reduction percent} \\
\$23{,}625 &= \$157{,}500 \times 15\%
\end{aligned}
$$

Now we have more entries for the Mike's Bikes Fundamental Merchandise Budget Plan (Table 6.8).

Table 6.9 shows one way to plan reductions by month. If you have last year's monthly sales by percents, then the center two columns can be replaced with those numbers. Simply multiply the percent times the planned monthly sales.

If Mike's Bikes could reduce its reductions, gross margin would increase because sales would be higher with no increase in merchandise cost. Options for reducing reductions include decreasing employee discounts, trying to sell more merchandise at regular price, improving surveillance to prevent shoplifting, and reducing accounting errors.

Table 6.8

Mike's Bikes Fundamental Merchandise Budget Plan

Category/Class/(Subclass)   Solid color cycling shorts

Product type basic/staple   selling period   52 weeks

Last year's sales	$150,000
Planned % (increase)/decrease	5%
Planned $ (increase)/decrease	$ 7,500
Planned sales	$157,500
Planned % reductions	15%
Planned $ reductions	$ 23,625
Merchandise to receive	
Average first price	
Allowable cost	
Number of units	

Table 6.9

Planning reductions by month for solid color cycling shorts.

	Planned Monthly Reductions	=	Last Year's Monthly Reductions	÷	Last Year's Monthly Sales	×	Planned Monthly Sales
Feb	$ 472	=	$ 450	÷	$ 3,000	×	$ 3,150
Mar	$ 472	=	$ 450	÷	$ 3,000	×	$ 3,150
Apr	$ 709	=	$ 675	÷	$ 4,500	×	$ 4,725
May	$ 1,183	=	$ 1,125	÷	$ 7,500	×	$ 7,875
Jun	$ 1,890	=	$ 1,800	÷	$ 12,000	×	$ 12,600
July	$ 4,016	=	$ 3,825	÷	$ 25,500	×	$ 26,775
Aug	$ 3,544	=	$ 3,375	÷	$ 22,500	×	$ 23,625
Sep	$ 3,307	=	$ 3,150	÷	$ 21,000	×	$ 22,050
Oct	$ 2,835	=	$ 2,700	÷	$ 18,000	×	$ 18,900
Nov	$ 2,126	=	$ 2,025	÷	$ 13,500	×	$ 14,175
Dec	$ 2,835	=	$ 2,700	÷	$ 18,000	×	$ 18,900
Jan	$ 236	=	$ 225	÷	$ 1,500	×	$ 1,575
Total	$23,625		$22,500		$150,000		$157,500

Learning Activities 6.5

Planning reductions

1. Plan 15 percent reductions on planned sales for the bike category based on Learning Activity 6.2, #1.
2. Why does every retailer want to reduce reductions?
3. Plan 15 percent reductions for the outerwear class based on the planned sales figures developed in Learning Activity 6.2, #3.
4. Options for reducing reductions at Mike's Bikes include decreasing employee discounts, selling more merchandise at regular price, and improving surveillance to prevent shoplifting. What are the advantages and disadvantages of each method? Which is best for Mike's Bikes?

Planning Merchandise to Receive

Planning the amount of **merchandise to receive** to achieve planned sales involves incorporating planned reductions. Since reductions reduce inventory value and revenue from sales, the amount of inventory available for sale must equal planned sales plus planned reductions since planned sales is based on first price. More merchandise must be sold than the value of planned sales in order to achieve planned sales. For example, consider Mike's Bikes' SCS. If planned sales is $157,500, and if $157,500 in merchandise is on hand to sell at the beginning of the selling period and it is all sold considering 15 percent in reductions during the selling period, only $133,875 would be realized in sales. This is true because 15 percent of $157,500 is $23,625.

$$\$133{,}875 \;=\; \$157{,}500 \;\times\; (1 - 15\%)$$

$$
\begin{aligned}
\textit{realized sales} &= \textit{planned sales} - \textit{reductions} \\
\$133{,}875 &= \$157{,}500 - \$23{,}625 \\
&\text{or} \\
\$133{,}875 &= \$157{,}500 \times (1 - 15\%)
\end{aligned}
$$

There is no way to realize planned sales unless more merchandise is sold than the value of planned sales at first price to compensate for the inevitable reductions. Thus, reductions are planned into the merchandise budget. Planned reductions are *added* to planned sales to determine the amount of merchandise to receive in order to achieve planned sales. For Mike's Bikes' SCS, planned merchandise to receive for the selling period is calculated as follows:

$$
\begin{aligned}
\textit{planned merchandise to receive} &= \textit{planned sales} + \textit{planned reductions} \\
\textit{planned SCS to receive} &= \textit{SCS planned sales} + \textit{SCS reductions} \\
\$181{,}125 &= \$157{,}500 + \$23{,}625 \\
&\text{or} \\
\$181{,}125 &= \$157{,}500 \times (1 + 15\%)
\end{aligned}
$$

Remember to *add* reductions. It sounds like a paradox but determining the amount of merchandise to receive is the only way to achieve planned sales. In order to achieve the sales goal of $157,500 for SCS for the selling period, Mike's Bikes needs to receive a total of $181,125 in inventory at first price. Now we can add another number to the Mike's Bikes Fundamental Budget Plan (Table 6.10).

To plan merchandise to receive for SCS by month, refer back to Table 6.9. The actual amount of merchandise that needed to be received last year is the sum of the two center columns (last year's monthly sales + last year's monthly reductions). To determine planned merchandise to receive for next year, sum the two outer columns (planned monthly reductions + planned monthly sales).

Table 6.10

Mike's Bikes Fundamental Merchandise Budget Plan.

Category/Class/Subclass Solid color cycling shorts

Product type basic/staple   selling period   52 weeks

Last year's sales	$150,000
Planned % increase/decrease	5%
Planned $ increase/decrease	$ 7,500
Planned sales	$157,500
Planned % reductions	15%
Planned $ reductions	$ 23,625
Merchandise to receive	$181,125
Average first price	
Allowable costs	
Number of units	

Learning Activity 6.6

Planning the amount of merchandise to receive

1. Assuming 15 percent reductions, plan the amount of bikes at the category level to receive for next year at Mike's Bikes. You can use planned sales and reductions from Learning Activity 6.5, #1 or use Table 6.2 for the data.
2. Plan total merchandise to receive for outerwear assuming 15 percent reductions based on planned reductions from Learning Activity 6.5, #3.
3. Why should the merchandise to receive number be larger than planned sales?
4. Set up a table showing Mike's Bikes SCS merchandise to receive by month for last year and next year. Be sure your numbers add up to total merchandise to receive for each year.

Planning First Price, Allowable Cost, and Number of Units to Receive

As discussed in Chapter 5, first price is the original retail price established by the merchandiser. It may be determined by adding initial markup to merchandise cost or a retailer's pricing strategy that prescribes levels of markup, type of price endings, and/or price lining.

With several styles in a merchandise class, subclass, or group, each style may have different merchandise cost and have its own first price assuming the same level of markup. If the retailer uses price lining, the merchandiser assigns styles of varying costs to the appropriate price line depending on what s/he believes the customer will be willing to pay. Thus, styles of varying costs and levels of markup will be sold for the same price. But the merchandiser will pay attention to what the average markup is within the group.

For purposes of the Fundamental Merchandise Budget, it is useful to estimate how many units (pieces) of merchandise will be received for the number of dollars planned for purchase for a category, class, subclass, or group. Knowing the number of units, the merchandise volume, is also necessary for planning merchandise assortments, the topic of the next chapter.

Determining average first price last year for a merchandise category, class, subclass, or group can be precisely calculated by determining first prices of each style, multiply the price of each style by the number of units of each style. Add up the total dollar value of first prices and then divide by the total number of units for all the styles. When dealing with large quantities of merchandise, average first price might be estimated by assessing what the mid-price point is, assessing if there is more merchandise above or below the mid-price point, and then determining a reasonable estimate of the average first price. A sophisticated computer system could easily determine the number exactly.

Table 6.2 provides average first prices for some of Mike's Bikes' merchandise classes. Many of them are above their middle price line to match the needs of their upscale customer base. This makes it easy to determine the number of units and the merchandise volume Mike's Bikes will receive. Remember to use *Merchandise to Receive* rather than *Planned Sales* to determine *Number of Units to Receive*. For example, the average first price for the shorts/tights class is $65. Using this as average first price, calculate units of SCS as follows:

number of units to receive	= $ merchandise to receive	÷ average first price
number of units of SCS to receive	= $ SCS to receive	÷ average first price
2,787	= $181,125	÷ $65

Units always have to be rounded to even numbers because you can't buy half a shirt or even half a pair of shorts. The same calculation can be used to determine merchandise to receive by month.

The last number to determine for the Fundamental Merchandise Budget Plan is allowable merchandise cost for SCS. Allowable cost can be determined either for total merchandise to receive or for a single unit. Unit cost may be particularly useful if private label product development is part of the sourcing strategy. Planned markup is 60 percent.

$$\text{allowable cost} = \text{average first price} \times \text{percent merchandise cost}$$
$$\$26 = \$65 \times 40\%$$

Allowable cost per unit for SCS is $26. Total allowable cost for SCS is

$$\text{total allowable cost} = \text{allowable cost} \times \text{number of units in assortment}$$
$$\text{total allowable cost SCS} = \text{SCS unit allowable cost} \times \text{number of SCS units}$$
$$\$72,462 = \$26 \times 2,787$$

Now the Fundamental Merchandise Budget for solid color shorts can be completed (see Table 6.11).

One way to think about the number of units is relative to the average number to sell each week and each day. To sell all the SCS merchandise Mike's Bikes plans to receive, it means they will have to sell an average of 58 units each week they are open (2,787 ÷ 48). Remember, Mike's Bikes is closed for 4 weeks of the year and on Mondays. Each day they will have to sell about 10 units (58 ÷ 6). Thinking about the numbers in this way makes the meaning more real. It is important to also recognize that sales in late summer are at least triple the spring months so inventory has to be planned accordingly. It is financially ineffective to have money invested in more inventory than necessary to support current sales.

Table 6.11

Mike's Bikes Fundamental Merchandise Budget Plan.

Category/Class/(Subclass) Solid color cycling shorts

Product type basic/staple   selling period   52 weeks

Last year's sales	$150,000
Planned % (increase)/decrease	5%
Planned $ (increase)/decrease	$ 7,500
Planned sales	$157,500
Planned % reductions	15%
Planned $ reductions	$ 23,625
Merchandise to receive	$181,125
Average first price	$ 65
Allowable cost	$ 26
Number of units	2,787

Learning Activity 6.7

Merchandise budgets including first price and number of units to receive

1. Calculate number of units to receive by month for Mike's Bikes' SCS. Be sure the total equals total units to receive from the Fundamental Merchandise Budget.

2. Assemble Fundamental Merchandise Budgets for bikes, outwear, and/or jerseys/tops. You have calculated most of the numbers through your learning activities. It is just a matter of organizing them into a formal budget so you can see how they relate to each other. Calculate the missing numbers to finish the Fundamental Budgets. What is the sales goal for each of the budgets?

3. Mill's Fleet Farm, a well-established farm store, has decided to add flannel shirts to its product offerings for the fall selling period. The first price of the shirts is $30. Fleet Farm expects to devote about 36 square feet to display the shirts in each store. Mill's expects the shirts to generate $95 per square foot during the fall selling period. Reductions are expected to be 10 percent of sales. Determine how each of the following merchandise budget figures were calculated and write out the formula for each:

   a) What is the sales goal for the sale of flannel shirts in each store? $3,420

   b) What is the total dollars in reductions? $342

   c) How much merchandise will Fleet Farm have to receive in each store in order to make their sales plan? $3,762

   d) How many units of merchandise will have to be sold in each store? 126

4. You are a children's wear merchandiser for Duber's, a small regional department store that specializes in interesting children's apparel at good value. The store's mission is to provide serviceable fashion goods at a reasonable price. You are planning sales, reductions, and merchandise to receive for spring girl's tops. The economy is flat and sales are not expected to increase.

   Last year's net sales for the store is $2,500,000. Children's apparel is about 20 percent of sales. Girl's apparel represents 40 percent of children's apparel and tops are 35 percent of girl's apparel. The four selling periods for girl's tops and the distribution of sales are as follows: spring (15 percent), summer (10 percent), back-to-school (60 percent), and holiday (15 percent). The selling periods are approximately equal in length. The average first price is $10. They use 50 percent markup. Reductions are 18 percent of sales and there is no inventory on hand.

   Determine how the following merchandise budget figures were found and write out the formula and the calculations for the following:

a) Last year's children's sales? $500,000
b) Last year's girl's sales? $200,000
c) Last year's girl's tops sales? $70,000
d) Last year's spring girl's tops sales? $10,500
e) Next year's planned spring girl's tops sales? $10,500
f) Reductions on planned spring tops? $1,890
g) Planned spring tops to receive to make the sales plan? $12,390
h) Total units of tops for spring? 1,239
i) Sales goal for planned spring tops? $10,500
j) Allowable cost per unit? $5

Developing an Expanded Merchandise Budget

It is now possible to develop an **Expanded Merchandise Budget** for SCS using all our calculations so far. Table 6.12 is a modified form of Table 6.1 at the beginning of the chapter. SCS is a basic/staple product with a 52-week selling period, whereas Table 6.1 was designed for fashion/seasonal goods with 13-week selling periods. The selling period divisions were removed from the chart.

To begin creating the expanded budget, the top of the form was filled out with appropriate information. Then the Fundamental Budget previously completed was filled into the "Total" column and the appropriate "Next Year Plan" rows. Table 6.9 provided "last year actual" and "next year plan" sales and reductions. Learning Activity 6.6, #4 provided last year and planned merchandise to receive. Learning Activity 6.7, #1 provided the "first price" and "number of units to sell." The Inventory/Sales Ratios and Inventory First of Month are given so they can be used later. Now you can complete the Expanded Budget (see Table 6.12).

Planning Inventory and Purchases During the Selling Period

Planning and controlling inventory to support planned sales during specified periods should accomplish four things:

- Fulfill sales goals.
- Avoid stockouts.
- Prevent overstocks.
- Minimize inventory investment (Lewison, 1994).

Table 6.12

Example of an expanded merchandise budget related to a merchandising calendar with a 52-week selling period as calculated so far.

Dynamic, Forecast-Based Merchandise Budget

Store _____ *Mike's Bikes* _____ Class/Sub-Class/Group _____ *solid color biking shorts* _____

Elements of Budget	Selling Period #1			Selling Period #2	
	Feb weeks 1–4	Mar weeks 5–9	Apr weeks 10–13	May weeks 14–17	Jun weeks 18–22
Sales					
Last year actual ($)	3,000	3,000	4,500	7,500	12,000
Next year plan ($)	3,150	3,150	4,725	7,875	12,600
Next year actual					
Inventory First of Month					
Last year actual ($)	4,500	9,300	13,500	21,750	33,600
Next year plan ($)	9,450	10,080	14,175	22,838	35,280
Next year actual ($)					
Inventory-to-Sales Ratio					
Last year actual	1.5	3.1	3	2.9	2.8
Next year planned	3	3.2	3	2.9	2.8
Next year actual					
Reductions					
Last year actual ($)	450	450	675	1,125	1,800
Next year plan ($)	472	472	709	1,183	1,890
Next year actual ($)					
Merchandise to Receive/Retail					
Last year actual ($)	3,450	3,450	5,175	8,625	13,800
Next year plan ($)	3,622	3,622	5,434	9,058	14,490
Next year actual ($)					
Planned Purchases (PP)					
Last year actual ($)					
Next year plan ($)					
Next year actual ($)					
On Order (65% of PP)					
On order at retail ($)					
On order at cost (60%IMU) ($)					
Open-to-Buy (35% of PP)					
Open-to-buy at retail ($)					
Open-to-buy at cost (60%IMU)					
First Price ($65)					
Number of Units to Sell	56	56	84	139	223

Square Feet ___400___ Year ___next___

	Selling Period #3			Selling Period #4			
Jul weeks 23–26	Aug weeks 27–30	Sep weeks 31–35	Oct weeks 36–39	Nov weeks 40–44	Dec weeks 45–49	Jan weeks 50–52	Total
25,500	22,500	21,000	18,000	13,500	18,000	1,500	150,000
26,775	23,625	22,050	18,900	14,175	18,900	1,575	157,500
58,650	56,250	52,500	46,800	35,100	46,800	2,850	381,600
64,260	61,425	55,125	43,470	28,350	28,350	2,993	375,795
2.3	2.5	2.5	2.6	2.6	2.6	1.9	
2.4	2.6	2.5	2.3	2	1.5	1.9	
3,825	3,375	3,150	2,700	2,025	2,700	225	22,500
4,016	3,544	3,307	2,835	2,126	2,835	236	23,625
29,325	25,875	24,150	20,700	15,525	20,700	1,725	172,500
30,791	27,169	25,357	21,735	16,301	21,735	1,811	181,125
							$65
474	418	390	334	251	334	28	2,787

The means of accomplishing these goals is different depending on how and why products change. The fashion/basic continuum relates to frequency of demand for changes in styling and the seasonal/staple continuum relates to changes in rate of sales associated with time of the year. When merchandise classifications are well defined by a manufacturer or retailer, the subclasses and groups of merchandise in the classification will fall mostly into Sector #1, fashion/seasonal or Sector #2, basic/staple. A few groups, because of their characteristics, may fall into Sector #3, basic/seasonal or Sector #4, fashion staple. Planning inventory and purchases for goods in each quadrant differs because of the nature of the merchandise in relation to customer demand related to fashion change and the time of the year.

The following discussion is organized according to the sectors in Figure 4.2. The examples of different methods of planning inventory and purchases during selling periods in the following discussion uses Mike's Bikes' solid color cycling shorts as an example throughout. Thus, it is possible to compare the outcomes related to different methods of calculations.

Sector 1, Fashion/Seasonal Goods

Fashion/seasonal goods experience frequent demand for change in styling and rate of sale because of the time of the year; thus, the total selling period is usually 26 weeks or less. Defined weeks of sale for particular styles in a classification result in the need to plan zero-to-zero inventory for each selling period. In other words, you bring in new merchandise at the beginning of each selling period and clear it at the end of the same selling period. The ideal condition is when inventory for the class, subclass, or merchandise group starts with no stock and ends with no stock. The **inventory-to-sales ratio method** of planning inventory is most appropriate for fashion/seasonal goods (Mason, Mayer, & Ezell, 1984, 1994) that have variation week to week, month to month, and/or selling period to selling period in the rate of sales. The assumption is that the merchant should maintain a certain ratio of goods on hand to monthly sales (Lewison, 1994). The terms *inventory* and *stock* are used interchangeably throughout these discussions.

The formula for calculating inventory-to-sales ratios is as follows:

inventory-to-sales ratio = total inventory for the period ÷ sales for the same period

An inventory-to-sales ratio states the amount of inventory on hand to support the amount of sales. An inventory-to-sales ratio of 2 means that $6,000 of inventory was on hand to support $3,000 in sales. If ratios were very low for a month (less than 1), it may indicate shortage of stock, low planned sales, or clearance for end-of-selling period. If ratios are high (more than 3), it may indicate too much inventory on hand, sales were planned too high, a long lead time for orders, or that inventory is being built up in anticipation of a sales peak. The monthly inventory-to-sales ratios are useful guides for planning necessary first-of-the-month (FOM) inventory. To have merchandise available for sale on the first of the month, it must be received during the previous month.

First-of-the-month is the traditional time period for planning inventory using the inventory-to-sales ratio method. With quick response business systems and computerized merchandise planning, plans may be made for the first of each week, or even daily plans for stock needed to support sales for each day. It depends on arrangements the retailer makes with vendors and/or distribution centers for resupply. The sophistication of their merchandise planning software also could be a limitation. If merchandise can be delivered weekly or daily and if demand can be re-estimated based on sales weekly or daily, the inventory on hand at any given time can be much smaller while avoiding lost sales because of stockouts.

For Mike's Bikes, the monthly inventory-to-sales ratios are reported in Table 6.12. For example, the inventory-to-sales ratio for February last year was calculated as follows:

$$\textit{inventory-to-sales ratio} \; = \; \textit{total inventory for the period} \; \div \; \textit{sales for the same period}$$
$$1.5 \qquad = \qquad \$4,500 \qquad \div \qquad \$3,000$$

The inventory-to-sales ratios for SCS vary month by month throughout the period with the lowest levels at peak sales in July. Notice that the stock-to-sales ratio for January is 1.9, which provides only enough merchandise to cover sales and reductions because it is a clearance period. Ending inventory for the selling period is low so less is invested in inventory during the Mike's Bikes closing during late January and early February. The next selling period begins with a majority of fresh merchandise. Notice Mike's Bikes changed some of the planned inventory-to-sales ratio because they were short of stock and had lost sales or had excess inventory last year.

For example, the February planned inventory-to-sales ratio is 3. This means they are planning three times as much inventory as sales in February next year to reduce lost sales from last year. Using the inventory-to-sales ratio method, planned FOM stock for *February next year* is determined by:

$$\textit{planned FOM inventory} \; = \; \textit{planned sales} \; \times \; \textit{planned inventory-to-sales ratio}$$
$$\$9,450 \qquad = \qquad \$3,150 \quad \times \qquad 3$$

The rest of the months were calculated in a similar manner and the results are shown in Table 6.12. Notice that FOM inventories using the inventory-to-sales ratio method have less merchandise for months with low sales and more merchandise for months with high sales.

Sector 2, Basic/Staple Goods

Products that fall into Sector 2 of Figure 4.2 are basic/staple goods that change little in styling over time and also change little in rate of sale related to the time of the year. New products are introduced infrequently. The length of the selling period range is a minimum of 52 weeks, one merchandising cycle, and may extend to 2 or 3 years. Planning inventory, then, is primarily a matter of determining the quantities of current goods required to maintain complete assortments throughout the selling period being planned.

The **periodic replenishment method** of planning inventory lends itself to merchandise that can be automatically replaced through computer-generated orders. The formula for periodic replenishment is:

$$\textit{maximum inventory} \ = \ (\textit{lead time} \ \times \ \textit{rate of sale}) \ + \ \textit{reserve stock}$$

where

> *maximum inventory* is the amount of merchandise needed on hand during the period;
>
> *lead time* is a combination of 1) time between placing orders and 2) time between placing and receiving an order;
>
> *rate of sale* is the retail value of units commonly sold during a reorder period; and
>
> *reserve stock* is additional stock kept on hand to prevent stockouts if sales exceed plan.

The formula for reserve stock is

$$2.3 \ \times \ \textit{square root of } (\textit{lead time} \times \textit{rate of sale})$$

(Donnellan, 1996).

Periodic replenishment inventory planning assumes the rate of sale is relatively uniform throughout the selling period and that there is an ongoing need for similar merchandise in inventory. It is common to replenish basic/staple goods at least weekly, and sometimes daily. These strategies greatly reduce stockouts and increase sales. Reductions are infrequent and may be less than 2 percent of sales, since they are related primarily to employee discounts, damaged merchandise, and inventory shrinkage. Clearance is seldom required because the same styles, sizes, and colors are continuously included in the assortment. At Mike's Bikes, parts for bike repairs could be set up with a periodic replenishment system to keep parts continuously in stock with the lowest possible average inventory. The formula for periodic replacement calculates the maximum inventory of inventory required considering the lead time of each period.

For purposes of comparing the periodic replacement method of inventory planning with the stock to sales ratio method for SCS, consider the following example. It uses four weeks lead time, similar to adding merchandise once a month with the inventory-to-sales ratio method:

$$
\begin{aligned}
\textit{maximum inventory} \quad = \quad & \textit{(lead time x rate of sale)} \; + \; \textit{reserve stock} \\
= \quad & [(2 + 2) \times (\$181,125 \div 24 \text{ weeks})] \\
& + [2.3 \times \text{square root of } (2 \times 7,547)] \\
= \quad & (4 \times \$7,547) + \$400 \\
= \quad & \$30,587
\end{aligned}
$$

where

Four weeks lead time = (two weeks between placing orders + two weeks between placing the order and receiving the order);

$7,547 rate of sale = $181,125 merchandise to receive ÷ 24 reorder periods of one week each = the retail value of merchandise planned to be sold during a reorder period; and

$400 reserve stock = 2.3 × square root of (4 weeks lead time × $7,547 rate of sale)

As shown in Table 6.12, with the inventory-to-sales ratio method of inventory planning, planned FOM inventories range from less than $10,000 to over $60,000 as related to variance in rate of planned sales. With the periodic replenishment method, maximum inventory is $30,587, which would appear to overstock the lower sales months and understock the high sales months. If periodic replenishment were going to be used for SCS, it would have to be adapted to accommodate variance in rate of sale.

For purposes of observing the benefits of shorter lead time using periodic replenishment in inventory planning, assume that SCS at Mike's Bikes could be ordered every week with one week between placing and receiving an order. Inventory would be calculated as follows:

$$
\begin{aligned}
\textit{maximum inventory} \quad = \quad & \textit{(lead time x rate of sale)} \; + \; \textit{reserve stock} \\
= \quad & [(1 + 1) \times (\$181,125 \div 48 \text{ weeks})] \\
& + [2.3 \times \text{square root of } (2 \times 3773)] \\
= \quad & (2 \times \$3,773) + \$200 \\
= \quad & \$7,746
\end{aligned}
$$

where

Two weeks lead time = (one week between placing orders + one week between placing the
                        order and receiving the order);

$3,773 rate of sale = $181,125 merchandise to receive ÷ 48 reorder periods of one week each
                     = the retail value of merchandise commonly sold during a reorder period; and

$200 reserve stock = 2.3 × square root of (2 weeks lead time × $3,773 rate of sale)

If Mike's Bikes used the periodic replenishment method to calculate inventory with a 2-week lead time, they would keep a maximum of $7,746 in SCS on hand for each 2-week reorder period or $15,492 for a month. That is half the maximum inventory for a 4-week reorder period. It suggests that throughout the merchandising cycle half as much money would have to be invested in inventory for the subclass SCS. Imagine how much less money would have to be invested in inventory for the entire store if there were 2-week lead times on deliveries of new merchandise.

An estimate of the number of units of biking shorts on hand can be determined by dividing maximum inventory by average first price:

number of units in inventory = *maximum inventory* ÷ *average first price*
          119 units   = $7,746   ÷ $65

as compared to

          470 units   = $30,587   ÷ $65

Only 119 units in inventory with a 2-week lead time; 470 units on hand with a 4-week lead time to achieve the same level of planned sales. Think about how much less space is necessary for merchandise display and storage with shorter lead time. This demonstrates one of the primary benefits of quick response business systems.

Sector 3, Basic/Seasonal and Sector 4, Fashion/Staple Goods

To produce more realistic results when stock turnover is high (more than six times a year) or relatively stable, basic/seasonal and fashion/staple goods (Sectors 3 and 4 respectively in Figure 4.2) may be planned using the **percentage variation method.** Applying this method results in inventories that are closer to average than the other inventory planning methods

(Berman & Evans, 1995). This method attempts to adjust stock levels in relation to actual variations in sales (see Table 6.13) (Lewison, 1994). The formula is:

planned FOM stock = average inventory × 1/2 [1 + (planned sales for the month
÷ average monthly sales)]

Compare the FOM inventories resulting from the percentage variation method with those resulting from the inventory-to-sales method in Table 6.12. The percentage variation

Table 6.13

Planned first of the month (FOM) inventory for solid color cycling shorts using the percentage variation method. *

Planned FOM Stock	=	Average × 1/2 Inventory [1	+	(Planned Sales	÷	Average Monthly Sales)]
Feb	$20,176	=	$32,542 × 1/2 [1	+	$ 3,150	÷	$13,125]
Mar	$20,176	=	$32,542 × 1/2 [1	+	$ 3,150	÷	$13,125]
Apr	$22,128	=	$32,542 × 1/2 [1	+	$ 4,725	÷	$13,125]
May	$26,034	=	$32,542 × 1/2 [1	+	$ 7,875	÷	$13,125]
Jun	$31,891	=	$32,542 × 1/2 [1	+	$12,600	÷	$13,125]
Jul	$49,464	=	$32,542 × 1/2 [1	+	$26,775	÷	$13,125]
Aug	$45,559	=	$32,542 × 1/2 [1	+	$23,625	÷	$13,125]
Sep	$43,606	=	$32,542 × 1/2 [1	+	$22,050	÷	$13,125]
Oct	$39,701	=	$32,542 × 1/2 [1	+	$18,900	÷	$13,125]
Nov	$33,844	=	$32,542 × 1/2 [1	+	$14,175	÷	$13,125]
Dec	$39,701	=	$32,542 × 1/2 [1	+	$18,900	÷	$13,125]
Jan	$18,224	=	$32,542 × 1/2 [1	+	$ 1,575	÷	$13,125]

*First of month and end of month (EOM) inventory numbers and planned monthly sales are from Table 6.6 where

average inventory = FOM inventory for each month + EOM inventory for last month ÷ number of months + 1

and

end of month inventory = first of month inventory from next month.

Average inventory = sum of BOM inventories + EOM of the last month ÷ 13

= $423,045 / 13

= $32,542

and

average monthly sales = total monthly sales ÷ number of months

= $157,500 /12

= $13,125.

method has more inventory during low sale times and less during high sale times. Which would work best? Many factors have to be considered, especially for a product like solid color cycling shorts that is an essential element in apparel sales, basic in styling, but varies widely in rate of sale during the selling period.

Planning inventory is clearly a challenging activity. The first step is to analyze the merchandise in terms of the nature of change (fashion, seasonal, basic, and/or staple) and then choose what appears to be the most appropriate method of planning inventory. The amount of inventory required for the first of each month depends on what assumptions are made about the needs for inventory; these assumptions differ for each method of calculation.

Learning Activity 6.8

Planning inventory during the selling period

1. Plan inventory for outerwear for the fall selling period using the inventory-to-sales ratio method. Use planned sales from Learning Activity 6.3, #2. Use the same inventory-to-sales ratios for the months of August through January that are presented in Table 6.12 for SCS.
2. Assume that Mike's Bikes was able to work out QR partnerships with their outerwear suppliers so they could reorder every week with a 1-week lead time between order placement and delivery. Using the periodic replenishment system, calculate maximum inventory per month when placing orders every week with a 1-week lead time. How does the maximum inventory on QR compare to inventories on the first of the month calculated in #1?
3. What are the advantages and disadvantages of placing orders more frequently? Of a shorter lead time? Of automating an ordering system?

Planning Purchases, Merchandise On Order, and Open-to-Buy

A retail merchandiser first determines **planned purchases,** followed by planned merchandise on order, and then planned open-to-buy. The amount of merchandise that you plan to purchase for a selling period, month, week, or day depends on the relationship among:

- How much merchandise do you plan to receive (planned sales + reductions)?
- How much do you want to have on hand at the end of the period?
- How much do you plan to have at the first of the period?

Purchases can be planned for any time period with the following formula but, to be consistent with previous examples, we will plan by the month. The formula for calculating planned purchases by month is as follows:

planned purchases by month = *planned merchandise to receive*
+ *planned EOM inventory*
− *planned FOM inventory*

where

EOM stock = *FOM stock of the following month*

The terms *inventory* and *stock* are used interchangeably in this discussion.

Table 6.14 is a completed merchandise budget for SCS, including the information previously presented in Table 6.12 plus Table 6.13 and the results of the following discussions. As shown in Table 6.14:

planned purchases of SCS for Feb = (*planned merchandise to receive*
+ *planned Feb EOM inventory*)
− *planned Feb FOM inventory*
$4,252 = ($3,622 + $10,080) − $9,450

The same formula was used to calculate planned purchases for each month as shown in Table 6.9. Total planned purchases is the sum of planned purchases by month. Total planned purchase is the same as total planned merchandise to receive. However, monthly planned purchases have dollars redistributed to accommodate planned FOM inventory.

Open-to-buy is a means of controlling merchandise investment before and during a selling period. Total dollar open-to-buy is the difference between planned purchases and merchandise on order:

dollar open-to-buy = *planned purchases* − *merchandise on order*

Calculation of planned total open-to-buy for next year for cycling shorts is as follows:

dollar open-to-buy = *planned purchases* − *merchandise on order*
$63,394 = $181,125 − $117,731

Open-to-buy during the selling period means money is available to provide flexibility to adjust the receipt of stock to the rate of sale. Open-to-buy can make money available for

Table 6.14

Example of a completed merchandise budget related to a merchandising calendar with a 52-week selling period.

Dynamic, Forecast-Based Merchandise Budget

Store ____*Mike's Bikes*____ Class/Sub-Class/Group ____*solid color biking shorts*____

Elements of Budget

	Feb weeks 1–4	Mar weeks 5–9	Apr weeks 10–13	May weeks 14–17	Jun weeks 18–22
Sales					
Last year actual ($)	3,000	3,000	4,500	7,500	12,000
Next year plan ($)	3,150	3,150	4,725	7,875	12,600
Next year actual					
Inventory First of Month					
Last year actual ($)	4,500	9,300	13,500	21,750	33,600
Next year plan ($)	9,450	10,080	14,175	22,838	35,280
Next year actual ($)					
Inventory-to-Sales Ratio					
Last year actual	1.5	3.1	3	2.9	2.8
Next year planned	3	3.2	3	2.9	2.8
Next year actual					
Reductions					
Last year actual ($)	450	450	675	1,125	1,800
Next year plan($)	472	472	709	1,183	1,890
Next year actual ($)					
Merchandise to Receive/Retail					
Last year actual ($)	3,450	3,450	5,175	8,625	13,800
Next year plan ($)	3,622	3,622	5,434	9,058	14,490
Next year actual ($)					
Planned Purchases (PP)					
Last year actual	8,250	7,650	13,425	20,475	38,850
Next year plan	4,252	7,717	14,097	21,501	43,470
Next year actual					
On Order Next Year (65% PP)					
On order at retail	2,764	5,016	9,163	13,975	28,256
On order at cost (60%IMU)	1,106	2,006	3,665	5,590	11,302
Open-to-Buy Next Year (35% PP)					
Open-to-buy at retail	1,488	2,701	4,934	7,525	15,215
Open-to-buy at cost (60%IMU)	595	1,080	1,974	3,010	6,086
First Price ($65)					
Number of Units to Sell	56	56	84	139	223

Square Feet ___400___ Year ___next___

Jul weeks 23–26	Aug weeks 27–30	Sep weeks 31–35	Oct weeks 36–39	Nov weeks 40–44	Dec weeks 45–49	Jan weeks 50–52	Total
25,500	22,500	21,000	18,000	13,500	18,000	1,500	150,000
26,775	23,625	22,050	18,900	14,175	18,900	1,575	157,500
58,650	56,250	52,500	46,800	35,100	46,800	2,850	381,600
64,260	61,425	55,125	43,470	28,350	28,350	2,993	375,795
2.3	2.5	2.5	2.6	2.6	2.6	1.9	
2.4	2.6	2.5	2.3	2	1.5	1.9	
3,825	3,375	3,150	2,700	2,025	2,700	225	22,500
4,016	3,544	3,307	2,835	2,126	2,835	236	23,625
29,325	25,875	24,150	20,700	15,525	20,700	1,725	172,500
30,791	27,169	25,357	21,735	16,301	21,735	1,811	181,125
26,925	22,125	18,450	9,000	27,225	(23,250)	3,375	172,500
27,956	20,869	13,702	6,615	16,301	(3,623)	8,269	181,125
18,171	13,565	8,906	4,300	10,596	(2,355)	5,375	117,731
7,269	5,426	3,563	1,720	4,238	(942)	2,150	47,093
9,785	7,304	4,796	2,315	5,705	(1,268)	2,894	63,394
3,914	2,922	1,918	926	2,282	(507)	1,158	25,358
							$65
474	418	390	334	251	334	28	2,787

yet-to-be-determined merchandise, for instance, hot-selling or popular merchandise not included in initial orders. But if sales are not up to plan, open-to-buy may not be invested in merchandise at all.

Last year, Mike's Bikes held about 35 percent of planned purchases by month in open-to-buy. Thus, 65 percent of planned purchases was for merchandise on order for delivery in specified months or weeks during the selling period. They plan to use the same strategy for next year. Calculate planned on order by month as follows:

planned on order at retail by month	=	*planned purchases*	×	*% on order*
planned on order at retail for Feb	=	planned purchases for Feb	×	65%
$2,764	=	$4,252	×	65%

Open-to-buy by month at retail is 35 percent of planned purchases. Thus, open-to-buy at retail can be determined by using the same formula as planned on order but use 35 percent of planned on order by month.

planned open-to-buy at retail by month	=	*planned purchases*	×	*% open-to-buy*
planned open-to-buy at retail for Feb	=	planned purchases for Feb	×	35%
$1,488	=	$4,252	×	35%

Proportion of merchandise on order is often greater early in the selling period; proportion of open-to-buy may be greater late in the selling period allowing more flexibility related to actual rate of sale. Based on the merchandise plan so far for SCS, see Planned Purchases, On Order, and Open-to-Buy in Table 6.14.

Planning Initial Markup

Initial markup is the difference between merchandise cost and first price. First price is a retailer's planning price and the basis of all price changes. Initial markup is part of the merchandise plan, but is closely associated with the income statement, specifically gross margin. The amount of money available for reductions, expenses, and profit is largely dependent on initial markup as the selling period progresses. For accounting purposes, over the entire selling period,

percent initial markup = (reductions + expenses + profit) ÷ (merchandise to receive)

The above equation itemized the measures of business that initial markup is expected to cover. Merchandise purchased for and sold during the selling period being planned needs to have an average initial markup according to plan in order to achieve profitability goals. If the necessary percent initial markup seems too high to be realistic given competition in the market, adjustments must be made in planned reductions, expenses, or profits.

Mike's Bikes had an average initial markup on apparel of 60 percent on retail. Since planned purchases are stated in Table 6.14 in retail value, to calculate *planned on order at cost* and *open-to-buy at cost* you have to consider level of markup. To calculate planned on order per month at cost for SCS, do the following:

$$
\begin{aligned}
\text{planned on order at cost} &= \text{planned on order at retail} \times (1 - \% \text{ markup}) \\
\text{planned on order at cost for Feb} &= \text{planned on order at retail for Feb} \times (1 - 60\%) \\
\$1{,}106 &= \$2{,}764 \times (1 - 60\%)
\end{aligned}
$$

To calculate *planned open-to-buy at cost by month* do the following:

$$
\begin{aligned}
\text{planned open-to-buy at cost by month} &= \text{planned open-to-buy by month} \times (1 - 60\%) \\
\text{planned open-to-buy at cost for Feb} &= \text{planned open-to-buy at retail for Feb} \times (1 - 60\%) \\
\$595 &= \$1{,}488 \times (1 - 60\%)
\end{aligned}
$$

Open-to-buy at cost is the actual dollar amount planned for spending in the wholesale market. For dynamic budgeting, merchandise to receive, planned on order, and open-to-buy need to be updated based on sales at least weekly and preferably daily for effective merchandise management.

The completed merchandise budget for SCS based on the stock-to-sales ratio method of inventory planning is presented in Table 6.14. This provides guidelines for pricing strategy and developing merchandise assortments.

Learning Activity 6.9

Planning purchases, on order, and open-to-buy

1. Based on Learning Activity 6.8, #1, plan purchases, on order, and open-to-buy for outerwear.
2. Assuming an average first price of $140, plan number of units to sell for outerwear.
3. Assemble all of your data for outerwear into an expanded merchandise budget using Table 6.14 as a model.

Summary

Firms often incorporate some sort of "management by objectives" philosophy into their business plans. This means that goals are set for business success. Short-term goals may relate to expectations for a merchandising cycle or a selling period within a merchandising cycle. Measurements of success often take the form of ratios that relate to the responsibilities of merchandising, marketing, operations, finance, and QR. Merchandising success is reflected on the firm's income statement, particularly in relation to cost of merchandise sold and gross margin.

Planned percent gross margin is achieved through planning and controlling the merchandise budget, pricing, and assortments. Operating profit is determined by the relationship between gross margin and operating expenses. Operating expenses relate to the management of people and physical property and are primarily the responsibility of the operations constituency; gross margin is the result of acquisition and sale of goods and services, the primary responsibilities of merchandisers.

Merchandise budgets are tools for planning and controlling dollar investment in inventory so the firm can meet its sales goals. With today's information technology systems, it is possible for budgets to be forecast-based and dynamic. It is tempting to plan sales for the coming period based primarily on sales history, since it is comparatively easy to calculate percent increase or decrease. However, good forecasts are based on a wide range of variables that are chosen because of their relevance to a particular firm's business environment. A dynamic budget is one that is updated frequently, preferably daily, to help identify the most recent historic trends. A dynamic budget assists with merchandise decisions before, during, and after a selling period.

A merchandise budget incorporates an integrated system of numbers representing dollars and merchandising ratios including sales, reductions, inventory, merchandise to receive, merchandise on order, open-to-buy, and number of units to sell. Outcomes related to each part of the budget affects all other parts of the budget. The mathematics calculation of each budget component helps explain these interdependencies.

Key Concepts

dynamic budget
expanded merchandise budget
fundamental merchandise
  budget
initial markup

inventory-to-sales ratio
  method (of planning
  inventory)
make plan
merchandise plans
merchandise to receive

open-to-buy
percent increase or decrease
  (method of planning sales)
percentage variation method
  (of planning inventory)

periodic replenishment method
  (of planning inventory)
planned purchases
planned sales
reductions

retail method of accounting for
  inventory
sales goal
sales per square foot

space productivity method (of
  planning sales)
zero-based budgeting
zero to zero inventory

Integrated Learning Activity 6.10.1

Create Fundamental Merchandise Budgets for your basic/staple and fashion/seasonal merchandise groups.

1. Review, update, correct, and present the company profile for your MAP retailer. Add the beginning of your merchandise plan including income statement, merchandising calendar, and pricing plan that you have developed based on ILA 2.6.3, 3.7.1, 4.9.1, and 5.12.1 for your fashion/seasonal and basic/staple merchandise groups. Keep the plans for your merchandise groups separate.

2. Based on your company profile, identify and/or estimate annual sales for your retailer and for a single store owned by your retailer for last year.

3. Estimate the size of a single store in square feet and annual sales per square foot (based on and/or compared to industry averages). Also, estimate the number of square feet that is used for your fashion/seasonal and basic/staple merchandise groups in a single store. (If possible, visit your MAP retailer and observe how your merchandise groups are displayed and how much space is allocated.) It is also useful to use the Representative Data Set at the end of Chapter 2 to get an idea how much space is commonly used for different types of merchandise.)

4. Estimate annual and selling period sales for your basic/staple and fashion/seasonal merchandise groups for which you have developed merchandise calendars. You might calculate these as a percent of total store sales or based on your sale per square foot information.

5. Based on your company profile, what is a reasonable increase in sales to plan for the coming year? Develop planned sales figures for next year for your fashion/seasonal and basic/staple merchandise classes as well as planned selling period sales.

6. Based on industry averages (Table 6.7) and your pricing strategies, identify an appropriate reduction rate for each of your merchandise classes. Calculate total merchandise to receive at retail for each merchandise group in order to achieve your annual sales goals.

7. Based on your merchandise budget, determine merchandise to receive for each selling period for each of your merchandise groups.
8. Based on the first price for each merchandise group, determine the number of units to receive for each merchandise group.
9. Based on the data developed above, assemble a merchandise budget for a single store and selling period for each of your merchandise groups using Table 6.11 as a model.

◉ Integrated Learning Activity 6.10.2

Using Sourcing Simulator (SS) to examine the financial impacts of Fundamental Merchandise Budgets

Objectives
- Examine financial productivity of merchandise budgets for fashion/seasonal and basic/staple merchandise groups.
- Simulate two different levels of volume for each merchandise group, one based on your merchandise budget and the other with volume doubled from your merchandise budget.
- Compare and evaluate financial outcomes related to volume for each merchandise group.

Resources for this assignment
- Class notes, textbook, and Integrated Learning Activities
- Your teacher, interactive lab tutor, and/or other class members

Procedure
1. Correct any errors in your merchandise plans and Fundamental Merchandise Budgets. Decide which pricing strategy from ILA 5.12.2 you will use for each merchandise group (fashion/seasonal and basic/staple). Determine number of units to receive if planned assortment volume for fashion/seasonal and basic/staple merchandise groups were doubled.
2. Open SS Seasonal Model. Conduct the first experiment based on the Fundamental Budget for your fashion/seasonal merchandise group.
   a) Use the default data set for everything but instructions for changes in b through k.
   b) Fill out the Buyer's Plan with your fashion/seasonal product name, weeks in selling period, and pre-defined sales peak according to your merchandise calendar.

Use the planned annual volume according to your Fundamental Merchandise Budget.

c) Use the default assortment plan for style, size, and colors, but increase the number of styles to five and reallocate the planned percent to equal 100.

d) On the Consumer Demand folder, use 0% error from plan for both volume and SKU mix; check same as presumed seasonality for the sales peak.

e) On the Sourcing Strategy folder, use the traditional replenishment strategy and set initial stocking to 100%.

f) On the Cost Data and Markdowns/Premiums folders, enter the pricing strategy you decided to use from ILA 5.12.2 for the fashion/seasonal group.

g) Run the simulation. Print inputs. Leave the output screen open.

h) Enter the doubled volume for fashion seasonal group in the Buyers Plan folder.

i) Run the simulation again. Print inputs for second simulation.

j) Examine printed inputs and outputs on the screen. Repeat simulation if necessary to correct errors or improve outputs.

k) Print outputs and highlight customers, total offering, service level %, sales revenue, revenue per unit offered, cost of goods, gross margin, % gross margin, and % gross margin potential.

l) Click view and graphs; print graphs of actual cumulative sales, purchases, gross margin, and GMROI.

m) Close SS; do not save inputs as default. Put your name on your printouts from your seasonal experiment and organize in an orderly manner.

3. Open SS Basics Model.

a) Use the default data set for everything but instructions for changes in b through k.

b) Fill out the Buyer's Plan for your basic/staple merchandise plan. Use the planned annual volume determined by your Fundamental Budget.

c) Use the default assortment for styles, sizes, and colors.

d) On the Consumer Demand folder, use 0% error from plan for both volume and SKU mix; check same as presumed seasonality for the sales peak.

e) On the Sourcing Strategy folder, use the default.

f) Enter your selected pricing strategy in your Cost Data and Promotions folders.

g) Repeat 2g to 2k to complete your second experiment.

Basis of Evaluation

1. Present this assignment in an orderly manner in your MAP, including an updated Company Profile for your store with pricing plans and corrected merchandise budgets.

2. Include four simulation input and two output printouts with your name in the title of the outputs and four graphs for each prepared according to your line plan and the instructions above. Separate the information so everything for each merchandise group is together.

3. Focus on the highlighted items in your outputs for your fashion/seasonal group. Which ones stayed nearly the same and which ones nearly doubled when you doubled your planned annual volume? Look at the number of customers. Since you specified no error on the Consumer Demand folder, SS gave you nearly the same amount of customers as merchandise. Thus, sales also nearly doubled. Does that explain the other numbers that doubled?

4. Focus on the outputs that stayed nearly the same. Review their definitions. How can volume double while these outputs stay the same?

5. Based on the highlighted measures, discuss how the increase in your assortment volume impacted outcomes for each merchandise group. Look at your graphs as well as your tables. Be sure to use merchandise budget language. Be specific in using the numbers.

6. Evaluate your total revenue generated by SS in relation to planned sales in your Merchandise Budget. Did you make your sales plan when you used the volume specified in your budget? Why or why not? If you didn't make your sales goal, what changes in your merchandise plan could help you make your sales goal?

Integrated Learning Activity 6.10.3

Merchandise planning challenges in the catalog business

Read Case 6.1 carefully and discuss the following issues.

1. What is the relationship between what is called "rebuying" in Case 6.1 and the inventory planning systems like inventory sales ratios and percentage variation method discussed earlier in this chapter?

2. According to Table 6.15, which of the apparel items are most likely to have lost sales because of unavailable inventory? Explain.

3. What product has the most excess inventory available? Given the information in the table and assuming a similar rate of sale, through how many selling periods will the present inventory last? Thinking about the nature of these products, what are the advantages and disadvantages of having this quantity of product on hand?

4. Examine the rate of sale for spring indicated by the percentages by week in Table 6.16. Would you describe the rate of sale as early peak, mid-peak, or late peak? How does the rate of sale for fall, in general, differ from the rate of sale in spring?

5. With the information in Table 6.16, what justification could you make that the catalog company should have four selling periods in the merchandising cycle instead of two?

Case 6.1 *Manage that inventory!* *

Every catalog business has its unique inventory challenges. Apparel catalogs can expect high returns and cancellations — often 25 to 30 percent of sales — and typically have few items repeated each selling period. Conversely, many business-to-business mailers have a high number of repeated items from catalog to catalog, introducing 20 to 25 percent of new products with each book. Regardless of your market sector, though, your inventory is a major asset, and it needs careful attention and management.

Forecasting Reports

Most catalog merchandising systems have some inventory forecasting subsystems and reports that can help the rebuyer, the person responsible for resupplying merchandise in the current catalog, project consumer response based on results from just one or two weeks. A sample of a forecasting report is shown below in Table 6.15. The report has the following columns:

- item number, the actual product number in the catalog or on the Internet
- color and size
- description, a simplified product description
- on order, open orders with vendors

- quality assurance (Q/A) hold, any item that has a quality question that remains unresolved
- accumulated returns, returned items from customers during the selling period
- on hand, product in the warehouse ready to ship
- accumulated issued, products that have ordered and sent to customers
- total B/Os, items in backorder awaiting either an additional shipment of merchandise or cancellation
- HFC, hold for confirmation, product being held by vendor to support the catalog mailing. Usually HFC orders are time-dated as to when the cataloger must give the vendor a yes or no answer.
- 86, 89, 95, or 99 percent, based on the seasonal response curve and how many units have been sold at the time the report was compiled, the computer's estimate of how many units you'll have sold at the end of the order curve. For instance, according to the report below, 36 silver caddies have been sold. If the report was compiled when the response curve was 86 percent complete, the report predicts that 41 caddies will be sold by the end of the catalogs's selling period. If the curve was already 89 percent

(continued)

when the report was compiled, only 40 caddies are likely to be sold in all.

This type of catalog inventory forecasting report is tied into a stock status report and a historical weekly response curve. Marrying the two reports gives the rebuyer an effective tool to project total sales of any item in the catalog and to manage inventory on a week-to-week basis during the catalog selling cycle.

A sample of an actual catalog response curve is shown in Table 6.15, but you cannot assume that this response curve is appropriate for your company. You must build a response curve for your catalog, and it is important to be aware of seasonal variations in your catalog's response.

Rebuying Activity

Sometimes the rebuying of inventory, also called control buying, is considered a function of the merchandising constituency; other times, catalogers consider it an analytical operations function. Regardless of who handles it, rebuying starts the first week that order activity begins. Three types of product situations quickly become apparent:

1. Products will be on forecast, or generating as many orders as were forecast in the merchandise plan. You'll typically place the second or third order for the product in weeks three or four.

2. Products will be ahead of forecast. These "high flyers" need immediate attention. As soon as you can quantify the extra demand, the overpull of these items, alert the vendor and activate reorders or HFC orders. Take action at the earliest time so that you minimize backorders and lost sales.

3. Product will be underpulling, or behind forecast. As soon as you can quantitatively confirm the underforecast response, cancel HFC orders and start planning how to dispose of excess product.

Control buying is a vitally important function for most catalogers, and using a forecasting report with a stock status report and order curve history will make this task easier and more efficient. Keep in mind that the more volatile the product line, with multiple colors and sizes, and the longer the vendor lead time in replenishing orders, the more important control buying is.

*Based on Schmid (2001, October).

Table 6.15

"Catalog Forecasting Report, Catalog #22, page 8."

Item #	Color	Size	Description	On Order	Q/A Hold	Accum return	On Hand	Accum Issued	Total B/Os	HFC	86%	89%	95%	99%
6606	white	6	KGM blouse	11				8	14		25	24	23	22
6606	white	8	KGM blouse	14				12	10		25	24	23	22
6606	white	10	KGM blouse	7		1		24	10		39	38	35	34
6606	white	12	KGM blouse	2				20	8		32	31	29	28
6606	white	14	KGM blouse	6		1		16	2		20	20	18	18
6606	white	16	KGM blouse	5		1		11	4		17	16	15	15
6607			Bird vase	24		2	3	291	4		343	331	310	297
6608			Calla lily candle	750		37		1,971	437		2,800	2,705	2,534	2,432
6612			BK side table				18	2			2	2	2	2
6613	black	L	Beaded sweater			4	57	32			37	35	33	32
6613	black	M	Beaded sweater			7	80	31			36	34	32	31
6613	black	S	Beaded sweater				43	17			19	19	17	17
6614			Crown bookmark			1	1,678	227			263	255	238	229
6615			Pendulum clock			1	17	4	1		4	4	4	4
6617	peacock	4	Silk dress			3		13			16	15	14	14
6617	peacock	6	Silk dress			5		25			29	28	26	25
6617	peacock	8	Silk dress			9	9	27			31	30	28	27
6617	peacock	10	Silk dress			8	7	37			43	41	38	37
6617	peacock	12	Silk dress			7		47	8		63	61	57	55
6617	peacock	14	Silk dress			14	6	38			44	42	40	38
6617	peacock	16	Silk dress			10	6	40			46	44	42	40

Table 6.16

Catalog response curves based on percent orders received.

Week	Spring Year 2	Spring Year 3	Fall Year 1	Fall Year 2	Fall Year 3
1	2.7	7.1	1.2	1.7	2.8
2	18.1	20.9	10.7	10.6	10.2
3	18.1	14.1	15.8	15.3	18.5
4	12.2	8.4	10.8	13.0	12.8
5	6.4	7.0	7.6	9.0	10.7
6	9.1	9.5	5.9	6.5	9.5
7	8.3	7.4	7.0	6.6	7.1
8	5.3	6.6	7.1	6.4	6.0
9	3.8	4.3	4.8	5.8	4.1
10	3.2	2.9	4.3	5.2	3.5
11	2.7	2.5	3.4	3.7	3.1
12	2.1	2.6	2.6	3.2	2.4
13	1.9	2.0	2.4	2.7	1.9
14	1.4	1.3	1.7	1.0	1.4
15	1.4	1.3	2.2	2.1	1.6
16	1.0	1.1	1.6	1.8	1.8
17	1.0	1.0	1.6	1.5	1.2
18	0.1	1.5	1.4	0.8	
19	0.6	1.4	1.4	0.5	
20			1.4		
21			1.4		
22			1.0-		
23			1.3		
24			0.8		
25			0.4		
26					
Total	100%	100%	100%	100%	100%

Recommended Resources

Gable, M., & Topol, M. T. (1987, Fall). Planning practices of small-scale retailers. *American Journal of Small Business,* 12(2):19–32.

Merchandise Planning Resources. (2003). The Planning Factory Limited (www.planfact.co.uk/ mp_resou.htm). Accessed February 13, 2003.

Rupe, D., & Kunz, G. I. (1998). Building a financially meaningful language of merchandise assortments. *Clothing and Textiles Research Journal,* 16(2):88–97.

Schmid, J. (2001, May). Determining your product winners—and losers. *Catalog Age,* 95–96.

Schmid, J. (2001, June). Taking "squinch" a step further. *Catalog Age,* 162–164.

Schmid, J. (2001, July). Preplanning merchandising. *Catalog Age,* 63.

Schmid, J. (2001, October). Manage that inventory. *Catalog Age,* 57–59.

References

Berman, B. B., & Evans, J. R. (1995). *Retail management.* Englewood Cliffs, NJ: Prentice Hall.

Donnellan, J. (2002). *Merchandise buying and management.* New York: Fairchild.

Lewison, D. M. (1994). *Retailing,* 5th ed. New York: Macmillan.

Mason, J., Mayer, M., & Ezell, H., (1984). *Foundations of retailing.* Plano, TX: Business Publications, Inc.

Mason, J., Mayer, M., & Ezell, H., (1994). Foundations of retailing, 2nd ed. Plano, TX: Business Publications, Inc.

Retail Merchandising Services Automation, Inc. (1995). Retail intelligent forecasting: Merchandise planning for the future. Riverside, CA: Author.

Schmid, J. (2001, June). Taking "squinch" a step further. *Catalog Age,* 63.

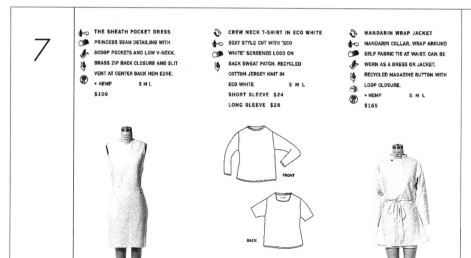

THE SHEATH POCKET DRESS
PRINCESS SEAM DETAILING WITH
SCOOP POCKETS AND LOW V-NECK.
BRASS ZIP BACK CLOSURE AND SLIT
VENT AT CENTER BACK HEM EDGE.
• HEMP   S M L
$100

CREW NECK T-SHIRT IN ECO WHITE
BOXY STYLE CUT WITH "ECO
WHITE" SCREENED LOGO ON
BACK SWEAT PATCH. RECYCLED
COTTON JERSEY KNIT IN
ECO WHITE   S M L
SHORT SLEEVE $24
LONG SLEEVE $28

MANDARIN WRAP JACKET
MANDARIN COLLAR. WRAP AROUND
SELF FABRIC TIE AT WAIST. CAN BE
WORN AS A DRESS OR JACKET.
RECYCLED MAGAZINE BUTTON WITH
LOOP CLOSURE.
• HEMP   S M L
$165

Planning and Controlling Merchandise Assortments

Learning Objectives

- Examine a model of in-store shopping behavior in relation to stockouts.

- Learn a language of assortments.

- Introduce the concept of assortment diversity.

- Plan receipt of merchandise to optimize sales and inventory levels.

*T*he best form of quick response should be customer response (Lewis, 1996). A customer response system (CRS) means that merchandise assortments are truly customer-driven. Effective customer response is dependent on:

- determining what customers want in advance
- understanding customers' activities while they are in the process of shopping, whether they are shopping in a retail store or via catalog or electronic media
- planning assortments so the merchandise the customer wants is available when he or she wants it

The challenge relative to assortments faced by manufacturers and retail merchandisers has some surprising similarities. Manufacturers compete in a global market where an over-abundance of products can be sourced competitively in several countries; retailers, particularly in the United States, face over-malled and over-stored markets where the greatest challenges include getting purposive customers into your store and having the merchandise they want while they are there. Balancing assortments at both the wholesale and retail levels reduces stockouts. As with many aspects of merchandising, manufacturers' problems with stockouts have not been addressed by research, so the focus of the following discussion is on the problem of stockouts in the retail sector.

In-Store Shopping Behavior

Sales increases of 10 to 50 percent resulting from introduction of quick response (QR) business systems are indicators of the magnitude of the retail stockout problem (Hunter, 1990; Nuttle, King, & Hunter, 1992). Stockouts result from inadequate assortments of merchandise. Researchers have conducted hundreds of studies of consumer behavior, but until recently the few studies of customer in-store shopping behavior have focused on grocery stores. Song and Kunz, in collaboration with a regional, upscale, specialty retailer, conducted a 1996 study to examine customer reactions to stockouts. The code name "Ramal" was used to protect the confidentiality of the retail collaborator. Ramal's product line includes career and dressy/casual wear for men and women. Ramal provided demographic and purchase information on a random sample of 250 credit card and 250 non-credit card customers for one year, one and a half years of sales, and assortment data from multiple stores, as well as access to their customers for a survey.

Ramal has a unique customer group as defined by demographics. They are mostly white, middle aged, highly educated, married, and employed with high income. Average family income in the United States is about $42,000. For 41 percent of Ramal customers, the average individual income was between $100,000 and $200,000 per year, and 18 percent of the sample had annual income over $200,000. With regard to education, 34 percent had bachelor's degrees and 38 percent had advanced degrees. The average annual apparel expenditure for individuals in the sample ($3,783) was more than twice the average annual expenditure of a family in the U.S. population ($1,710) (Bureau of the Census, 1994).

The model of in-store shopping behavior resulting from the Ramal research is based on the Behavioral Theory of the Apparel Firm (BTAF) (see Figure 7.1). An important concept of BTAF is the interactive relationships among functional areas focused on the target market, thus the link to in-store shopping behavior. The dark box in Figure 7.1 indicates the relationship of the proposed in-store shopping behavior model to BTAF.

Syntheses of previous research directly related to **in-store shopping behavior** resulted in the identification of four constructs that provide the structure of the in-store shopping behavior model: demographics and situational factors, shopping intentions, stock situations, and purchase decisions (see Figure 7.2).

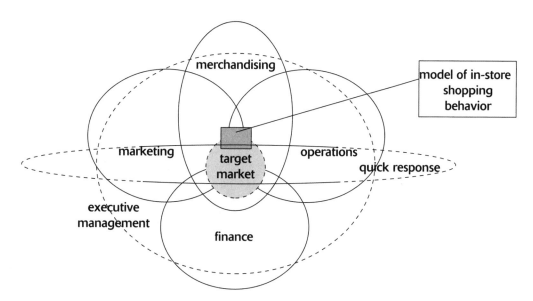

Figure 7.1 Interaction of the functional areas of specialization within an apparel firm combined with the Model of In-Store Shopping Behavior.

Situational Factors

Situational factors are defined as all those factors particular to a time and place, excluding personal preferences and choice alternatives, that have a demonstrable and systematic effect on current behavior (Belk, 1975). Five situational factors that may influence an apparel shopper's in-store shopping behavior are identified in the model: demographics, store knowledge and loyalty, time available for shopping, type of shopping trip, and social surroundings.

Considering demographics, previous research reported that the younger a customer is, the more likely he or she is to buy something at the first store they shop in. The reasoning is that it would take too much time to shop around (Meet the new competition, 1994). At the same time, customers over 65 years old may be more likely to shop at department stores for clothing because they believe department stores have better prices and selections than discount or specialty stores (Chowdhary, 1989).

For Ramal customers, age, education, income, level of clothing expenditure, gender, and possession of a Ramal credit card were all found to be significantly related to some aspect of in-store shopping behavior. Price was more likely to be an important consideration for the

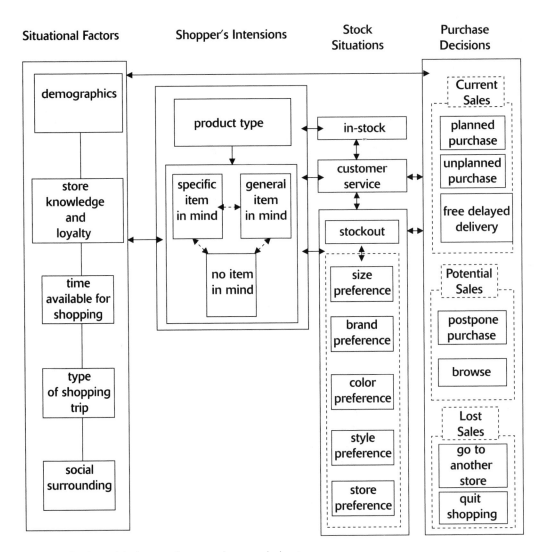

Figure 7.2 A model of apparel in-store shopping behavior.

customers 18 to 34 years old and customers over 55. Females were more likely to be concerned about price than males. Strong relationships were found between holding a Ramal credit card and level of expenditure at Ramal.

In terms of reactions to stockouts, Ramal customers with higher levels of apparel expenditures were significantly more likely to postpone a purchase after experiencing a stockout than those with lower levels of clothing expenditure. A higher level of apparel expenditure may mean more shopping trips or more multiple purchases. Thus, the customer who spent more money for apparel may have had more chance to buy the stockout item on a later shopping trip or decided to buy another item instead.

Situational factors/store knowledge and loyalty refers to the information a customer has about a specific store's attributes and the perceived reliability of the store as a source of goods. Shopping trips and expenditures at Ramal were compared for three groups: the random sample of 250 credit card and non-credit card customers provided by Ramal and the survey sample of 95 credit card customers (see Table 7.1).

Customers with Ramal credit cards visited the store nearly twice as often, bought nearly twice as many items, and spent nearly three times as much money per year as non-Ramal credit card customers. Loyalty to Ramal was also exhibited in terms of product type—customers significantly preferred Ramal as a source for business suits, as compared to casual shirts. About 13 percent of customers answered that they only shopped in Ramal for business suits, while about 2 percent of customers answered that they only shopped in Ramal for casual shirts.

For situational factors/time for shopping, 30 percent of Ramal customers shopped every month and 52 percent shopped a few times a year. The average frequency of customers' shopping for their clothes was four times a year. There were no significant differences between males and females.

Situational factors/type of shopping trip is categorized as major shopping trip and fill-in shopping trip (Kahn & Schmittlein, 1989, 1992; Kollat & Willett, 1967). A major shopping

Table 7.1

Shopping patterns of the sample, credit card customers, and non-credit card customers based on Ramal sales records.

	Credit Card Customers (N5250)	Non-Credit Card Customers (N5250)
Average number of items purchased per person per year	9.79	5.15
Average sales volume per person per year	$1,026.38	$383.81
Average frequency of visiting Ramal stores per person per year	3.82	2.02
Average number of items purchased per trip	2.56	2.55
Average expenditure per trip	$268.69	$190.00

trip is an extended excursion for seasonal or annual needs. A fill-in shopping trip is a quick excursion for a current need. More unplanned purchases may be made during major shopping trips than fill-in trips. About 70 percent of Ramal customers engaged in major shopping trips to update their wardrobes.

Situational factors/social surroundings refer to how other people influence an individual's purchase behavior (Runyon & Stewart, 1987). Among Ramal customers, men were significantly more likely to shop with their spouse than women, and women were significantly more likely to shop alone or with other family members than men. About half of respondents shopped with someone when they shopped for their clothes.

Recent reports from the Commerce Department's Census Bureau suggest significant changes in nature and structure of U.S. households that could influence in-store shopping behavior. Between 1970 and 2000:

- Median age for women increased 4.3 percent to 25.1 years.
- Median age for men increased 3.6 years to 26.8 years.
- The proportion of women never married 20 to 24 years old doubled from 36 to 72 percent and tripled for women 30 to 34 years old from 6 to 22 percent.
- The average size of a household decreased from 3.14 to 2.62 persons.
- The percent of persons living in households with five or more persons decreased from 21 percent to 10 percent.
- The percent of persons living in households with one or two persons increased from 46 to 59 percent.
- The number of single mothers increased from 3 million to 10 million.
- The number of single fathers increased from 400,000 to 2 million.
- In 2000, 12 percent of wives were two or more years older than their husbands, while 15 percent earned at least $5,000 more than their husbands annually.

Learning Activity 7.1

Situational factors in relation to in-store shopping behavior

1. Think through the situational factors that influence in-store shopping behavior. How do your shopping experiences compare to the findings? According to your observations, what situational factors influence your parents, your grandparents, and your peers?

2. What situational factors might need to be included in a model of catalog shopping behavior? Electronic shopping behavior?

3. Think about demographics recently reported by the Census Bureau included above. In what ways might these trends influence situational factors related to in-store shopping behavior?

4. Read Case 7.1. How is Wal-Mart attempting to change in-store shopping behavior? What factors included in Figure 7.2 are key components of Wal-Mart's success in appealing to upscale customers?

 Case 7.1 *Wal-Mart eyes BMW crowd.* *

Wal-Mart is the world's largest retailer. It got there by sounding a single note — low prices — that attracted millions of mostly working-class Americans in search of everything from toilet paper to fishing rods. Now, after leveling discount chains from Kmart to Caldor and Ames to Bradlee's, Wal-Mart executives are setting their sights on a fresh target: more affluent shoppers who pride themselves on snagging bargains and who discovered stores such as Target, Costco, and Kohl's some time ago.

Many of the 178 stores Wal-Mart has opened in the last year are in well-off suburbs such as Plano, Texas, and Alpharetta, Georgia. All of them include grocery sections the size of a supermarket, with gourmet desserts and fresh herbs to attract people with money to spend. Wal-Mart is also adding pricier products, from big-screen televisions and digital cameras to more glamorous cookware.

But reaching for new customers holds risks for Wal-Mart. In the past, the company has succeeded by selling to penny-wise shoppers. Experts warn that the company might alienate these customers if it replaces too many private label slacks and run-of-the-mill sheets with European cookware and personal computers.

"As they add these new customers, as they trade up, the risk is that a new Sam Walton in some place that you and I have never heard of says, 'Hey, I'm going to buy it low, stack it high and sell it cheap,'" said Richard Tedlow, a professor of business administration at the Harvard Business

(continued)

School the author of *Giants of Enterprise,* a study of Wal-Mart and other companies.

Founded in Arkansas 40 years ago by a five-and-dime merchant, Sam Walton, Wal-Mart built its empire with stores in rural areas where land was cheap and shoppers looking for variety and low prices saw few alternatives. By the time Walton died 10 years ago, Wal-Mart was the largest discounter. In 2002, Wal-Mart became this nation's largest company with over $217 billion in sales. Wal-Mart is the nation's largest private employer with more than 1.2 million employees.

Despite its formidable size, attracting and keeping more affluent shoppers is a battle that Wal-Mart must wage with great care. Their new customers are coming in on a distinctly different mission. "Everything you need for a summer house, you can certainly get at Wal-Mart," said Kathy Sullivan, a New York resident who mainly shops for food and paper products at Wal-Mart. She was pleasantly surprised by the selection and the prices. Pursuing upscale customers increases the cost of doing business, but Wal-Mart has no choice. They have run out of places to build stores where they reach their traditional customers and like all businesses, if they are going to stay in business, they have to grow.

*Based on Hays (2002).

Shopper's Intentions

Shopper's intentions relate to the purpose of the shopping trip. Shopper's intentions were found to relate to product type and have three forms: specific item in mind, general item in mind, and no item in mind. Specific or general item in mind means the customer is *purposive*—he or she intends to make a purchase. Specific item in mind means the customer has a type of product and brand in mind; general item in mind means the customer has only the type of product in mind. No item in mind means the customer is *browsing* for pleasure or to collect information for future shopping trips. The three shopping intentions may interact. A customer who has no item in mind may recognize a need for a specific or general item during the shopping trip. A customer who has a general or specific item in mind can lose purchase intention and move to no item in mind because of the stock situation or influence of other situational factors.

Jarboe and McDaniel (1987) reported that browsers in regional malls are more likely to be employed females. Females and customers over 55 years old may be more likely to regard shopping as fun. Ramal customers were much more likely to be purposive customers (89 percent) with a specific or general item in mind than browsers (11 percent). Males were significantly more likely to have a specific item in mind than females, and females were significantly more likely to have a general item in mind than males. About 84 percent of customers purchased multiple or coordinated items.

Stock Situations

Stock situations refer to the presence or absence of an item a customer wants to buy: in-stock or stockout. **In-stock** means the particular stock keeping unit (SKU), defined by style, size, and color, is immediately available to buy. **Stockout** means the particular SKU is not immediately available to the customer who wants to buy it. The stock situation is the point at which a shopper's intentions meet merchandising strategy. **Customer service** is any interaction between the customer and store personnel. It is a component in stock situation because customer service is required for a customer to make a purchase or to provide alternatives that might be available to compensate for a stockout. The components of the stockout element in the model are ordered in terms of the willingness of Ramal customers to adjust their preferences to make a purchase in spite of the stockout.

Ninety-three percent of Ramal customers experienced stockouts, and 72 percent of these stockouts were because of size (see Table 7.2). Females were significantly more likely to experience stockouts because of size than males. Males were significantly more likely to experience stockouts because of other reasons (brand, style, and color) than females. Customers were significantly less flexible with regard to size of business suits (94 percent) or casual shirts (87 percent) than any other response to stockouts. It follows then that a stockout because of size was most likely to result in a lost sale. Customers were more likely to change style or color than size and even more likely to change brand. Customers had a little more flexibility to change size in casual wear than business wear, even though most customers were not likely to change size when they encountered stockouts.

Purchase Decisions

The purchase decisions construct is configured into three merchandising related elements: current sales, potential sales, and lost sales. *Current sales* occur when a customer makes a purchase and the store records the sale. Current sales could be recorded for planned

Table 7.2

Frequency of customer reactions to stockouts for business suits and casual shirts.

Reactions to Stockouts	Business Suits			Casual Shirts		
	% less likely	% not sure	% more likely	% less likely	% not sure	% more likely
Change Size	93.55	5.38	1.06	87.31	7.35	6.31
Change Style	64.51	9.68	25.80	52.63	25.26	22.10
Change Color	59.14	10.75	30.11	50.52	25.26	42.10
Quit Shopping	55.91	16.13	27.96	60.00	16.84	23.14
Browse	41.93	13.98	44.09	28.42	16.84	54.94
Postpone	41.93	13.98	44.06	23.16	13.68	63.16
Change Brand	40.86	13.98	45.16	50.53	14.74	43.73
Delayed Delivery	30.11	8.60	61.29	03.16	2.11	94.74
Other Store	26.89	9.68	63.44	38.42	12.63	58.94

purchases, unplanned purchases, and buying the item with free delayed delivery. The latter was a more acceptable option for casual wear than for business suits and more acceptable for women than for men (in the Ramal study the delay was specified as being within three days). For business suits, 61 percent of customers were likely to accept free delayed delivery of the stockout item, but 95 percent would accept free delayed delivery for casual shirts.

Potential sales exist if the customer postpones purchase or browses. Potential sales may result when a customer experiences a stockout. Store-loyal customers are more likely to change brands or products within the store, while brand-loyal customers were more likely to go to another store, resulting in a lost sale. Non-loyal customers were more likely to buy available stock considering convenience, efficiency, or economic factors. Ramal customers were significantly more likely to postpone purchase or browse when they experienced a stockout while shopping for casual wear than business wear.

Lost sales result when a customer goes to a different store or quits shopping. Customers may perceive a less urgent need of a purchase of casual wear when they encounter stockout than business wear, for which customers would be more likely to go to another store for the same item. Higher income customers were significantly less likely to quit shopping for casual wear than business wear when they encountered stockouts.

Implications for Merchandising Strategy

Most Ramal customers were purposive shoppers, as is the trend nationwide. Customers are making fewer shopping trips, spending less time in each shopping trip, and spending more money. They may make relatively few shopping trips per year, but make multiple purchases with high-dollar expenditures per trip. Considering these customers' shopping patterns, several important implications for merchandising strategy are suggested from the Ramal research. The implications are as follows:

1. According to the results of this study, the most frequent reason for stockouts is unavailability of a particular size the customer wants. Furthermore, most customers do not want to change size when they encounter a stockout. It is unlikely, particularly with suits, that a garment of a different size will fit adequately. Thus, an appropriate range of sizes must be considered a priority to reduce stockouts. Taylor (1970) pointed out the importance of size in assortment planning. He called it the least flexible assortment dimension. The findings of this study confirm his position. Both manufacturers and retailers of apparel need to set up sizing systems so that size is a customer-driven assortment dimension rather than a merchandiser- or production-determined one.

2. Offering free delayed delivery service to customers can result in eliminating lost sales and getting current sales. Offering fast replenishment of stockout items can change potential sales to current sales when the customer shops again for the stockout item. However, if replenishment is not made by the time the customer visits again, potential sales become lost sales. Researchers have found that repeated stockouts increased the percentage of customers who would go to another store. Delayed delivery may help sustain store loyalty, thus justifying the cost of the service.

3. Considering customer service in relation to stockouts, if a salesperson knows a customer encounters a stockout, he or she can offer the customer three options: helping the customer find alternatives, resulting in current sales; offering delayed delivery service, resulting in current sales; and offering to call the customer when the item is restocked, resulting in potential sales, thus, possibly avoiding a lost sale.

4. Casual wear continues to be an important category of business attire. The results in this study reported that Ramal customers tended to have less preference for Ramal as a source for casual wear than business wear. This can cause a critical loss of sales. Adjusting assortments to accommodate the business casual trend is a very difficult merchandising problem. However, free delayed delivery could help prevent lost sales in casual wear where the problem may be more prevalent because of diverse assortments.

5. A priority for Ramal should be persuading credit card customers to make more trips to Ramal each year to satisfy a larger proportion of their clothing needs. It is impossible to keep all items customers might want and need in stock. Therefore, careful merchandise planning and fast replenishment is essential.

To prevent stockouts and to support delayed delivery service and other stockout compensation policies, merchandisers need better merchandise planning and replenishment systems. Assortment planning systems have improved as compared to other retail and production technology, but inadequate assortment planning is still the primary cause of stockouts. Effective resupply of current merchandise is dependent on accurate information, cooperation, and speed. Cooperation among a firm's five internal constituencies, as well as collaboration with external coalitions (suppliers), is required. The ability of the firm to achieve its goals may depend on how all constituencies interact, coordinate, and resolve conflicts among internal constituencies and external coalitions.

Learning Activity 7.2

Merchandising issues related to stockouts

1. What do stockouts have to do with planning, developing, and presenting product lines?
2. How can stockouts be prevented?
3. Are stockouts ever desirable?
4. Is it possible that a complete assortment is undesirable?
5. Is it possible to address the problem of stockouts because of size?
6. What are the implications of providing free three-day delivery service for stockout items?
7. Based on these findings, what should be the particular concerns of merchandisers as they plan assortments?

Language of Assortment Planning

The foundation for planning assortments is the same as the foundation for planning budgets — classification analysis. A clear understanding of what categories of merchandise make up the merchandise mix and regular analysis of the classes and subclasses within each keep the framework for the assortment current. At the same time, a well-planned pricing system strategically and consistently applied supports the merchandise budget and assortment plan. An interactive, dynamic merchandise budget and assortment plan provides the best opportunity to satisfy customers and optimize sales and financial productivity.

A **balanced assortment** is every merchandiser's goal. An assortment is balanced when it meets customers' needs and accomplishes the firm's goals with a minimum investment in inventory. It is nearly impossible to have completely balanced assortments but some assortments are more balanced than others. Assortment balance is one of the purposes of the processes of classification analysis discussed in Chapter 4, pricing strategies discussed in Chapter 5, and planning merchandise budgets discussed in Chapter 6. Another step in balancing assortments is more direct—assortment planning.

Assortment planning, the determination of the range of choices to be made available at a given time, is a primary merchandising function (Bohlinger, 1977; Glock & Kunz, 2000; Mason, Mayer, & Ezell, 1994; Risch, 1991). Assortment planning occurs at many different times and for a variety of purposes throughout the apparel business. For example, in apparel manufacturing, assortment planning is conducted by designers, merchandisers, and product managers during line planning and product development; by sales representatives as they communicate a line to potential buyers and write purchase orders for customers; and during cut order planning for production (Glock & Kunz, 2000). In the retail sector, assortment planning occurs when executive management determines merchandise categories, when retail buyers select product offerings, when merchandise controllers allocate goods to individual stores, when department managers merchandise the retail floor, and when visual merchandisers create displays and fill fixtures (Kunz & Rupe, 1999).

Measures of merchandising success may include adjusted gross margin, cash flow, finished goods turnover, percent gross margin, gross margin return on inventory, maintained markup, markdown percentage, materials cost, piece goods turn, sales per square foot, and/or sell-through. The success of a selling period, for both manufacturers and retailers, is often greatly dependent on effective assortment planning. An assortment plan, when used as a framework for line development, provides control over merchandise investment. However, until recently, there were no quantifiable guidelines for assortment planning that relate to potential financial outcomes.

Traditional Dimensions of Assortments

The most traditionally used terms for assortment dimensions are breadth and depth (Bohlinger, 1977; Brown & Davidson, 1953; Berman & Evans, 1995; Davidson & Doody, 1966; Dunne, Lusch, & Gable, 1995; Gillespie & Hecht, 1970; Mason, Mayer, & Ezell,

1994; Risch, 1991). Although the terms *breadth* and *depth* of assortment are widely used throughout the manufacturing and retailing sectors, the definitions of these terms that appear in merchandising and retailing textbooks are inconsistent and provide little quantitative meaning to merchandisers for planning profitable assortments (see Table 7.3). Each of these definitions offers a slightly different meaning, while none provides adequate quantitative measurement of breadth. Similar discrepancies exist for defining depth.

These traditional definitions are one-dimensional in that they look at only one aspect of the assortment. For example, they may consider the number of SKUs or number of brands in an assortment, but never both dimensions at once. To get any meaningful understanding of an assortment using these terms, the merchandiser must compare one assortment plan to another using phrases such as "more broad than" or "less deep than," etc. The plan cannot be considered in isolation, but must always be accompanied by another frame of reference.

Table 7.3

Examples of definitions found in the literature for assortment breadth and depth. *

Definitions for Assortment Breadth	Definitions for Assortment Depth
"characteristic of an individual assortment offering a large number of different categories" (Bohlinger, 1977, p. 369)	"characteristic of an inventory assortment offering limited versions of proved styles" (Bohlinger, 1977, p. 368)
"description of the different categories available in a store" (Jernigan & Easterling, 1990, p. 548)	"description of quantity of each item available in the assortment" (Jernigan & Easterling, 1990, p. 548)
"the number of merchandise brands found in the line" (Dunne et al., 1992, p. 475)	"average number of SKUs within each brand" (Dunne et al., 1992, p. 476)
"the number of product lines carried" (Clodfelter, 1993, p. 361)	"number of choices offered within each brand" (Clodfelter, 1993, p. 362)
"refers to the number of different styles" (Rath et al., 1994, p.487)	"how many pieces of each style carried" (Rath et al., 1994, p. 487)
"number of product lines" (Lewison, 1994, p. 423)	"number of product items within each product line" (Lewison, 1994, p. 423)
"refers to the number of distinct goods/service categories with which a retailer is involved" (Berman & Evans, 1995, p. A63)**	"refers to the variety in any one goods/services category with which a retailer is involved" (Berman & Evans, 1995, p. A51)

*Rupe & Kunz (1998).

**This definition is referred to as width of assortment.

This demonstrates the incongruous uses of the assortment dimension words of breadth and depth and indicates the lack of guidance available to merchandisers when carrying out assortment planning processes (Kunz & Rupe, 1999).

Learning Activity 7.3

Assortment fundamentals

1. What is an assortment?
2. What is a balanced assortment?
3. Think through the definitions of breadth and depth of assortments. How are the meanings similar and how are they different? What seems to be the fundamental meaning of breadth? What seems to be the fundamental meaning of depth?
4. Since the terms *broad, shallow, narrow,* and *deep* are widely used by the industry but vary greatly in meaning, how can you know the meaning in a particular instance of use?
5. Carefully read Company Profile 7.1, Mike's Bikes, Part 5, Merchandise Assortments. It is used as the basis of examples throughout the rest of this chapter.

Company Profile 7.1

Mike's Bikes, Part 5, Merchandise Assortments

The target customers at Mike's Bikes are young and young-in-spirit individuals and families who have average to above average income and pursue cycling as their primary form of recreation. Most of their customers are in the upper middle income class with incomes of $75,000 and more. Many live in the surrounding 15-mile radius that includes the highest average income area of Iowa. They include dual income families in the 20 to 50 age range that support their children's school activities and enjoy outdoor entertainment. Their fringe customers have similar demographics but pursue cycling more casually. The majority of their customers are members of

(continued)

local cycling clubs and know each other as well as the other cycling stores in the area. They tend to develop loyalty to the local cycling store that best meets their needs, but shop multiple stores.

Company Profile 6.1 included a breakdown of Mike's Bikes' sales by category and class including average first prices. Overall, the apparel assortment is about 50 percent men's, 30 percent women's, 13 percent kid's, and 7 percent unisex (outerwear). Outerwear lends itself to unisex presentation and allows them to offer more styles in the same number of SKUs because the duplication of sizes is eliminated. Outerwear is sized extra small, small, medium, large, extra large, and extra extra large with the majority of sales in medium and large. Subclasses in outerwear include jackets, windbreakers, slickers, and arm and leg warmers. Outerwear has two selling periods — spring (40 percent of sales) and fall (60 percent of sales).

According to Table 4.1, the shorts/tights class is broken down into subclasses of solid color shorts, baggy shorts, side stripe shorts, and tights. Solid color shorts has 400 square feet of space and breaks into merchandise groups of men's (50 percent), women's (40 percent), and kid's (10 percent). The actual first price of men's solid color shorts last year was $59.50. Men's run lower in price than women's. They are planning to experi-

ment with $10,000 of women's knickers. Average first price is planned at $90 with an assortment of four styles, four sizes, and three colors.

The jersey/tops class has four subclasses: solid jerseys (25 percent), color blocked jerseys (45 percent), fancy jerseys (15 percent), and tops (15 percent). Jerseys have four selling periods: spring (16 percent), summer (34 percent), early fall (26 percent), and late fall (24 percent).

Helmets are the most frequently ordered accessory purchase, ranging in price from $30 to over $170. Water bottles and bags are next in frequency of purchase. Accessories have 500 square feet of space and sales are $600 per square foot.

Vendor sales representatives visit the store and help plan assortments. Kevin is very comfortable with the marketing aspects of the business, but is still working on the merchandising part. Many vendors leave catalogs so customers can special order merchandise. This means the store can stock a smaller variety of styles, sizes, and colors. Even so, assortments are diverse, with only five or less units stocked in each SKU on the average. Ordering is done four to six months out; the goods are usually delivered in a single shipment except solid color shorts that are regularly replenished. Branded merchandise is important, but there are few opportunities to reorder hot sellers.

Measurable Assortment Dimensions

Measurable assortment dimensions that can provide a basis for assortment planning include assortment factors, SKUs, volume, and assortment variety. **Assortment factors** are dimensions that define characteristics of a product for purposes of identifying and describing it. Assortment factors for apparel are commonly style, size, and color. For example, these are appropriate assortment factors for cycling apparel. Assortment factors for groceries might be brand, size (grams, ounces, or liters), and type (fresh, canned, or frozen). Assortment factors for automobiles might be model, color, and accessories package. Assortment factors for shoes might be style, color, length, and width. (The term might be used because firms use different systems for defining product characteristics.)

Stock Keeping Unit

The combination of assortment factors embodied in a single product determines a **stock keeping unit (SKU).** A SKU is a unique piece of merchandise. A SKU is distinct from other similar merchandise because of its particular combination of assortment factors. For example, a baby's romper in pink, size small is a different SKU than the same style and size of romper in blue. The larger the number of SKUs in an assortment, the more difficult it is to keep all unique pieces of merchandise in stock.

Assortment Variety

Assortment variety can be determined by the total number of SKUs in the assortment. For example, an apparel assortment might include 6 styles, 5 sizes, and 12 colors for an assortment variety of 360 SKUs.

assortment variety	=	*number of SKUs*	= *numbers of assortment factors multiplied together*
assortment variety	=	*360 SKUs*	= *6 styles* × *5 sizes* × *12 colors*

Reducing the number of SKUs means fewer unique pieces of merchandise to order, manufacture, ship, sort, stock, and display. It also means customers—either retail buyers if the firm is a manufacturer or ultimate consumers if the firm is a retailer—have a more limited selection to choose from. Identifying the appropriate level of variety is an ongoing struggle.

Assortment variety is an indicator of the magnitude of the inventory management challenge. For example, it is conceivable that one retailer would have a merchandise mix with a variety of 20,000 SKUs; others might have a merchandise mix with 60,000 or 160,000 SKUs. Absence of any single SKU at a given moment can result in a stockout and a lost sale. The greater the variety, the greater the challenge of consistently having all planned merchandise in stock.

Assortment Volume

Assortment volume is the total number of units in an assortment. A unit is a single piece of merchandise. Assortment volume has to be matched to the level of demand. Assortment volume cannot be increased by ordering or manufacturing more products, unless there is some sort of unsatisfied demand for the goods. The purpose of the merchandise budget is to match merchandise investment to expected demand. For example, if the merchandise budget specifies planned receiving at retail of $100,000 and if the merchandise class is sable coats or sports cars, the assortment volume could be one unit if the retail price of the product is $100,000 ($100,000 ÷ $100,000). With the same merchandise budget of $100,000 for t-shirts that will retail for $10, the assortment volume would be 10,000 units ($100,000 ÷ $10).

assortment volume	=	planned receiving for a selling period	÷	average retail price of a single unit
1	=	$100,000	÷	$100,000
10,000	=	$100,000	÷	$10

Table 7.4 shows a copy of the fundamental budget for solid color cycling shorts (SCS) developed in Chapter 6 (Table 6.11). A merchandise budget is a plan for how much merchandise can be sold. The budget determines assortment volume.

According to the merchandise budget, receiving at retail for SCS total subclass at Mike's Bikes is $181,125. With an average first price of $65, the assortment volume is 2,787 units. Remember, receiving at retail is planned sales plus reductions. According to Company Profile 7.1, SCS are 50 percent men's with an actual average first price last year of $59.50. Men's tends to have a lower retailer price than women's. The volume for men's solid color cycling shorts (MSCS) merchandise group, then, can be determined by first calculating planned receiving of MSCS:

planned receiving MSCS	=	receiving at retail SCS	×	% MSCS
$90,563	=	$181,125	×	50%

volume of MSCS	=	planned receiving MSCS	÷	average retail price
1,522 units	=	$90,563	÷	$59.50

Table 7.4

Mike's Bikes Fundamental Merchandise Budget Plan

Category/Class/Subclass *Solid color cycling shorts*

Product type *basic/staple* selling period *52 weeks*

Last year's sales	$150,000
Planned % increase/decrease	5%
Planned $ increase/decrease	$ 7,500
Planned sales	$157,500
Planned % reductions	15%
Planned $ reductions	$ 23,625
Merchandise to Receive	$181,125
Average first price	$ 65
Allowable cost	$ 26
Number of Units	2,787

Learning Activity 7.4

Assortment volume and variety

1. Mike's Bikes decided to test adding cycling knickers for women to their total merchandise assortment. These cropped pants are great for those who want to bypass the Lycra look but want full-performance cool-weather wear. They decided on planned sales for next year of $10,000 with 15 percent reductions. With an average first price of $90, what is the volume of the assortment? How many units are in the assortment?

2. What assortment factors do you think are relevant for cycling knickers? Why? Given your assortment factors for cycling knickers, what are the dimensions of a SKU? How many SKUs will be in your assortment?

3. Read Case 7.2. Explore how much difference the "fourth dimension" width makes in total number of SKUs a shoe store carries for a single style. Why is width called the fourth dimension?

4. How many SKUs are required if a store has a fashion boot in 3 colors and 15 sizes as opposed to the same fashion boot in 3 colors, 15 lengths, and 8 widths? What if there were only 3 widths—narrow, medium, wide? Think about how much storage space is required to accommodate customers' good fit considering width.

5. If a particular shoe style has an assortment plan that requires 150 SKUs, what is the minimum number of pairs of shoes that must be in stock to have one pair of each SKU?

📁   *Case 7.2   Famous Footwear is winning the battle of widths. **   📁

Famous Footwear, a division of St. Louis-based Brown Shoe, has made some great strides in comp-store sales increases lately, an accomplishment credited in part on new technology initiatives. The company saw a 5.8 percent increase in December 2000 comp-store sales, a hefty jump over its 0.7 percent comp-store increase the year before. Earl Fischer, Famous Footwear's vice president of information services, attributes the increases in large part to a technology project. According to Fischer, the stores are seeing improvements because they have the right stock in the right sizes and widths, thanks to more accurate purchasing forecasts and assortment planning, and hence more accurate allocation to specific stores.

The solution is an integrated financial and merchandising planning solution from JDA Software. Fischer said the software, which pulls point-of-sale information from datamarts on servers from IBM, Armonk, New York, helps to solve footwear's most vexing twist of complexity — the added product attribute of width. This "fourth dimension" must be taken into consideration along with style, size, and color in generating assortments. The width variable can bring a single style of shoe to as many as 150 stock keeping units, Fischer explained.

These four attributes — style, size, color, and width — are being sorted weekly. The information coming back to headquarters on size and width is improving same-store numbers, thanks to knowledge that there are "smaller feet in San Francisco, narrow feet in Dallas, and wider feet in Chicago," according to Fischer. "The trick is to have just the right assortment in each store so you don't have massive inventory and low turns," Fischer said, adding that assortment planning will become even more critical going forward in new-store planning. Data mining will be used to project both location and merchandise assortment for the 100 new stores projected to open soon. "But," Fischer added, "It's a constant challenge to optimize mix and flow."

The retailer, with over 900 stores in 50 states as well as Guam and Puerto Rico,

Case 7.2 (continued)

prides itself on its ability to work well with big brands like Nike and Reebok. Those suppliers get a steady stream of detailed point-of-sale data for forecasts and ongoing fine-tuning of orders. Suppliers can generate economies of scale by ramping up for specific volumes for each style six months in advance, then making adjustments at the size and width levels as often as every two weeks.

"The better our buyers can work for our vendors, the better service we are likely to get in exchange," said Fischer. "They appreciate accurate detail."

*Based on Conrad (2001) and Famous Footwear (2003).

Integration of Assortment Dimensions into Assortment Plans

Assortment plans can take a number of forms depending on a firm's priorities. Combinations of assortment dimensions can result in model stocks, assortment distribution, volume per assortment factor, and volume per SKU.

Model Stock

A **model stock** is a plan for a merchandise assortment according to assortment factors. The model stock identifies how many of each assortment factor should be included in the assortment, but it does not specifically identify what merchandise will fill out the merchandise plan. Determining the specific merchandise is a line development process and right now the focus is still on line planning. The model stock, in and of itself, is simply the number of each relevant assortment factor that is planned for the assortment. Assortment variety can be controlled via a model stock since the number of SKUs is controlled by the combination of assortment factors. A model stock for apparel commonly includes three assortment factors (style, size, and color) but does not always include three assortment factors. For example, as discussed in Case 7.2, a model stock for bras and shoes usually requires four assortment factors including two related to size: style, color, cup or width, and circumference or length. It is common for a department store assortment of bras to include over

50,000 SKUs. An assortment with that much variety is very difficult to manage. Examples for model stocks for different classifications are in Table 7.5.

The purpose of a model stock is to balance assortment factors relative to demand and to control the variety offered within a classification. Because of limited dollars available to invest in inventory and limited space for display or capacity for production, decisions have to be made about what combinations of assortment factors will best help the firm meet its goals. For example, when merchandisers go to market, they may look at hundreds of styles of cycling shorts; the inclination normally is to buy more than the nine styles, five sizes, and nine colors specified in the assortment plan in Table 7.5, thus increasing the assortment variety. The model stock helps the merchandiser stay within the space available for merchandise display and within the merchandise budget. The merchandise budget and the model stock, of course, are based on projected/forecasted customer demand.

Assortment Distribution

Assortment distribution is the allocation of volume across assortment factors at the classification level. It is an estimate of the relative rate of sale of each style, size, and color in the assortment. Assortment distribution determines the proportion of unit allocation to each assortment factor. The assortment must be distributed so available merchandise will meet customer demand. Assortment distribution usually takes place in the context of a model stock (see Table 7.6).

The nine styles of MSCS are distributed for a total 100 percent of MSCS based on forecasted customer preferences. The size distribution is allocated as a bell-shaped curve with

Table 7.5

Examples of model stock plans by merchandise classification with assortment variety stated as number of SKUs.

Classification	Model Stock	# of SKUs
Cycling shorts	9 styles, 5 sizes, 9 colors	405
Junior jeans	8 styles, 5 sizes, 3 colors	120
Turtlenecks	1 style, 4 sizes, 12 colors	48
T-shirts	3 styles, 5 sizes, 9 colors	135
Bras	12 styles, 5 cup sizes, 6 circumference sizes, 5 colors	1,800
Earrings	2 types, 50 styles, 5 colors	500
Skillets	4 brands, 7 styles, 3 sizes	84

Table 7.6

Example of a combination of model stock for men's solid color cycling shorts at Mike's Bikes with assortment distribution.

Assortment Factor		Assortment Factor		Assortment Factor	
Style	Distribution	Size	Distribution	Color	Distribution
1 — 6 panel	30%	1 — small	10%	1 — ebony	20%
2 — 4 panel	20%	2 — medium	25%	2 — color spliced	20%
3 — 6 panel PCL	15%	3 — large	40%	3 — fuchsia	13%
4 — 8 panel	10%	4 — extra large	15%	4 — plum	12%
5 — double duty	10%	5 — extra extra large	10%	5 — red	10%
6 — bib short	5%			6 — cobalt	8%
7 — short short	5%			7 — screaming yellow	6%
8 — bikeatard	3%			8 — navy	6%
9 — aerosuit	2%			9 — lime	5%
Total Volume	100%		100%		100%

the largest percentage in the center of the size range. Sales history and experience with customers in relation to stockouts and special orders should be the basis of size distribution. Colors are allocated based on fashion trends identified in the line plan. Note that each assortment factor must be planned relative to the total assortment volume.

Learning Activity 7.5

Measurable assortment dimensions

1. Refer back to the model stocks in Table 7.5. How many SKUs would be in the assortment if the merchandisers decided to carry only seven styles of junior jeans instead of eight? How many SKUs would there be if they carried seven styles and four sizes instead of five? How many SKUs would there be if they carried seven styles, four sizes, and two colors instead of three?

2. What would happen to the number of SKUs if they decided to carry three different lengths of junior jeans in addition to the seven styles, four sizes, and two colors? What are the advantages and disadvantages of carrying a greater variety in an assortment? What are the advantages and disadvantages of a lesser variety in an assortment?

3. Refer back to Learning Activity 7.4, #1 and #2. Given the assortment factors you chose for women's cycling knickers, create a model stock. Based on your model

stock, how many SKUs are in the assortment you created? What is the variety of the assortment?

Volume per Assortment Factor

An assortment distribution plan can be used to reveal volume per assortment factor. **Volume per assortment factor** is the relationship between total number of units planned for the classification and the percent distribution. Using a planned volume of 1,522 units and percent distributions to determine units per style, per size, or per color for MSCS, do the following:

$$\text{volume per style, size, or color} = \text{units planned for the classification}$$
$$\times \text{ percent distribution for the assortment factor}$$

volume for style #1	=	456 units	=	1,522	×	30%
volume for style #2	=	304 units	=	1,522	×	20%
volume for size #1	=	152 units	=	1,522	×	10%
volume for size #2	=	380 units	=	1,522	×	25%
volume for color #1	=	304 units	=	1,522	×	20%
volume for color #2	=	304 units	=	1,522	×	20%

As you will see in Table 7.7, since style #1 is 30 percent of the assortment, Mike's Bikes will order 456 pieces of style #1. Style #1 had better be very popular with their customers. In contrast, style #9 is planned to be only two percent of the total classification, only 31 pieces. If this style is more popular than planned, stockouts and lost sales are likely. If style #1 is less popular than planned, quick markdowns will have to be applied to create open-to-buy to acquire more of style #9.

Volume per SKU

To determine the number of units for each unique SKU in an assortment, you can develop a volume per SKU plan, based on a combination of the model stock, units per assortment factor, and the assortment distribution plan. It is calculated on a style-by-style basis, one table for each style. Once you calculate a few volume per SKU plans, you will appreciate the fact that volume per SKU plans are fundamental to the operation of the Sourcing Simulator. Better yet, Sourcing Simulator calculates them for you based on volume, model stock, and assortment distribution; however, you never see them.

Table 7.7

Volume per assortment factor based on the model stock and assortment distribution in Table 7.6 and the volume based on the merchandise budget for men's solid color cycling shorts (1,522 units).

Number	Style	Units per Style	Size	Units per Size	Color	Units per Color
1	30%	456	10%	152	20%	304
2	20%	304	25%	380	20%	304
3	15%	228	40%	609	13%	198
4	10%	152	15%	228	12%	183
5	10%	152	10%	152	10%	152
6	5%	76			8%	122
7	5%	76			6%	91
8	3%	46			6%	91
9	2%	31			5%	76
Total	100%	1,521*	100%	1,521*	100%	1,521*

*Rounding error.

To calculate **volume per SKU** for styles in Table 7.7 (as demonstrated in Tables 7.8 and 7.9), do the following:

volume per SKU	=	*volume per style*	×	*% size*	×	*% color*
volume per SKU for style #1	=	volume for style #1	×	% for size #1	×	% for color #1
9 units	=	456	×	10%	×	20%
volume per SKU for style #1	=	volume for style #1	×	% for size #1	×	% for color #2
9 units	=	456	×	10%	×	20%
volume per SKU for style #1	=	volume for style #1	×	% for size #1	×	% for color #3
6 units	=	456	×	10%	×	13%

Each cell in each table represents the number of units of a unique piece of merchandise, a SKU. The percentage distribution plan demonstrated in Table 7.7 seems reasonable until

Table 7.8

Volume per SKU for style #1 based on 30% of total men's solid color cycling shorts
456 units, with model stock and assortment distribution as indicated in Table 7.7.

Color	Size #1	Size #2	Size #3	Size #4	Size #5	Total
#1	9	23	36	14	9	91
#2	9	23	36	14	9	91
#3	6	15	24	9	6	60
#4	6	14	22	8	6	55*
#5	5	11	18	7	5	46
#6	4	9	15	5	4	37
#7	3	7	11	4	3	28
#8	3	7	11	4	3	28
#9	2	6	9	3	2	22
Total	47	115	182	68	46*	458*

*Rounding error.

the volume per SKU plan for style #9 is examined in Table 7.9. The volume per SKU plan is very insightful in terms of what kind of an assortment will be available to display on the sales floor. The assortment for style #9 will obviously be incomplete given the assortment plan. Some SKUs have none, one, or a few units. A stockout can result in a lost sale and a lost customer.

Learning Activity 7.6

Assortment planning

1. As determined in Learning Activity 6.7, #3, Mill's Fleet Farm has a merchandise budget that includes $3,420 in planned sales for flannel shirts, $342 in planned reductions, and $3,760 in planned merchandise to receive. The assortment includes two styles, two colors, and four sizes. First price on the shirts is $30. Mill's expects to devote about 36 square feet to displaying the shirts in each store and the shirts to generate $95 per square foot during the fall selling period. Markdowns are expected to be 10 percent of sales.

Table 7.9

Volume per SKU for style #9 based on 2% of men's solid color cycling shorts, 31 units, with model stock and assortment distribution as indicated in Table 7.7.

Color	Size #1	Size #2	Size #3	Size #4	Size #5	Total
#1	1	2	3	1	1	8
#2	1	2	3	1	1	8
#3	0	1	2	1	0	4
#4	0	1	2	1	0	4
#5	0	1	1	0	0	2
#6	0	1	1	0	0	2
#7	0	0	1	0	0	1
#8	0	0	1	0	0	1
#9	0	0	1	0	0	1
Total	2	8	15	4	2	31

How are the following numbers determined for the merchandise plan? Write the formula or explanation for the answer.

a) What is the planned volume of the assortment? 126

b) How many SKUs are in this assortment? 16

c) What is the model stock? Two styles, two colors, four sizes

d) How was volume per style determined in the following volume-per-assortment factor plan?

e) Calculate volume per color and volume per size to fill out the following table.

Plan for Volume per Assortment Factor for Mill's Fleet Farm Flannel Shirts for Fall

#	Style	Volume per Style	Color	Volume per Color	Size	Volume per Size
1	60%	76	75%		10%	
2	40%	50	25%		20%	
3					40%	
4					30%	
Total		126 units		126 units		126 units

f) How was volume per SKU determined for style #1 in the following table?

Volume per SKU for Flannel Shirts for Style #1

Color	Size #1	Size #2	Size #3	Size #4	Total
#1	6	11	23	17	57
#2	2	4	8	6	19*
Total	8	15	30*	23	76

*Rounding error.

g) Develop a volume per SKU plan for style #2 to fill out this table.

Volume per SKU for Flannel Shirts for Style #2

Color	Size 1	Size 2	Size 3	Size 4	Total
#1					
#2					
Total					

2. Develop volume per SKU plans for men's solid color cycling shorts, styles #2 and #8 based on Table 7.7.

3. Considering your model stock of women's cycling knickers (Learning Activity 7.5, #3), how would you distribute volume across assortment factors? Develop a volume per SKU plan to evaluate your assortment distribution.

The Concept of Assortment Diversity

The concept of assortment diversity (Rupe & Kunz, 1998) resulted from research using the Apparel Retail Model (ARM) (Nuttle, King, & Hunter, 1991), a computer simulation of the merchandising process now called Sourcing Simulator (SS). Included in ARM/SS's capabilities is the capacity to perform rapid merchandising analysis of specific assortment situations. As you know, ARM/SS allows the user to plan a merchandise assortment, a pricing strategy, and a delivery strategy. The computer program simulates customer demand and provides a financial analysis of the impact of the chosen strategies. ARM/SS can be configured so that it can operate under the assumption that the merchandise is salable by planning assortments so there is one customer for each unit of merchandise. Consequently, it is possible to eliminate issues related to merchandise selection and customer shopping behavior and instead focus on outcomes related to the nature of the assortment. ARM/SS tracks the prescribed assortment of merchandise, at the SKU level, throughout a selling period. The fundamental finding of the research was that the more diverse the assortment, the lower the financial productivity (Rupe & Kunz, 1998).

Assortment diversity is the range of relationships that can exist between assortment *volume* and assortment *variety*. Thus, assortment diversity is a combination of the total number of units in the assortment (assortment volume) and the number of SKUs in the same assortment (assortment variety). Assortment diversity, then, is measured by **volume per SKU for the assortment (VSA).** The VSA is the average number of units available per SKU. The actual number of units per SKU will depend on the assortment distribution plan. If the t-shirt assortment described in Table 7.5 was planned for 10,000 units, then the VSA would be 74 (10,000 units ÷ 135 SKUs). The VSA for the Mike's Bikes MSCS is 3.76 (1,522 units ÷ 405 SKUs).

assortment diversity	=	volume per SKU for the assortment		
volume per SKU for the assortment	=	# of units	÷	# of SKUs
74	=	10,000	÷	135
3.76	=	1,522	÷	405

The ARM/SS experiments revealed one reason why traditional definitions of assortment dimensions have been ineffective as assortment planning tools: They neglect to identify a relationship between assortment volume and assortment variety. Under the definitions of breadth and depth previously discussed, an assortment could not be defined without being compared to another assortment. They had to be vaguely defined as more broad, less shallow, more narrow, less deep, etc., than another assortment of comparison. Using the VSA, how diverse or focused an assortment is can be meaningfully described in and of itself:

- 100 units with 50 SKUs = VSA of 2 = more diverse
- 100 units with 20 SKUs = VSA of 5 = diverse
- 100 units with 10 SKUs = VSA of 10 = focused
- 100 units with 5 SKUs = VSA of 20 = more focused

The smaller the VSA, the more diverse the assortment will be; the larger the VSA, the more focused the assortment will be. Given the same number of units in the assortment, a smaller VSA indicates more variety in the assortment (more SKUs) and fewer items per SKU on the average. The larger the VSA, the less variety in the assortment (fewer SKUs) will be and the more items per SKU on the average.

The concept of assortment diversity adds the following to the assortment planning language:

- *assortment diversity* = the range of relationships that can exist between assortment volume and number of SKUs in an assortment
- *volume per SKU for an assortment* = assortment volume divided by the total number of SKUs in the same assortment

The Relationship of VSA to Financial Productivity

The ARM/SS simulation experiments also revealed that the nature of the assortment matters from the standpoint of financial productivity. Assortments, particularly with a VSA of less than five, can be potentially detrimental to financial productivity simply because of the diversity of the assortment. Tables and graphs of VSA relative to percent gross margin (%GM) indicate that as VSA increases, the %GM increases (see Figure 7.3).

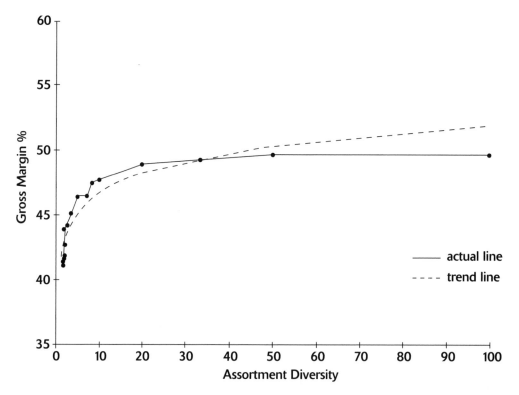

Figure 7.3 Graph of assortment diversity determined by VSA of 1 to 100 in relation to percent gross margin (%GM) (Rupe & Kunz, 1998).

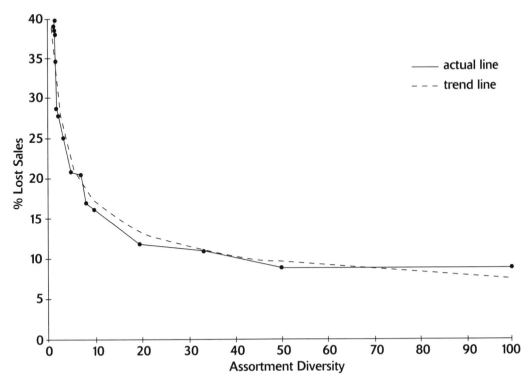

Figure 7.4 Graph of assortment diversity determined by VSA of 1 to 100 in relation to percent lost sales (%LS) (Rupe & Kunz, 1998).

The graph shows that the lower the VSA, the lower the financial productivity and the higher the VSA, the greater the financial productivity, at least up to a point. The change in financial performance related to VSA is attributed primarily to lost sales in relation to stockouts. Figure 7.4 indicates that as an assortment has fewer units allocated per SKU on the average, the chances of not having the right SKUs for customers increase; therefore, stockouts increase, resulting in **lost sales**. This is especially prevalent with a VSA of less than two. As fewer customers find what they are looking for, fewer purchases are made, leaving more merchandise unsold at the end of the selling period. In actual retail settings, this merchandise must either be marked down from first price and sold at a lower selling price and/or jobbed off at the wholesale price or less (the latter was the option in the simulation data sets). In either case, merchandise is sold at lower than first price, resulting in less total revenue and lower financial performance. With low VSAs, what appears to be a merchandise shortage can result in more units being left at the end of the selling period.

Table 7.10

Computer simulation inputs and outputs of analysis of specialty store and discount store assortments.

	VSA	Variety in SKUs	Volume in Units	% Gross Margin	% Lost Sales
Specialty Store	0.81	108	87	37.75	23.4
	2.00	40	80	42.93	12.0
Discount Store	3.30	80	264	32.60	4.0
	9.00	120	1,080	32.67	0.8
	12.61	240	3,026	32.99	0.6

The results were similar when financial outcomes from simulations based on the specialty and discount assortments were examined (see Table 7.10). For example, two specialty store assortments had VSAs of 0.81 (there were more SKUs than units in the assortment) and 2. As expected, the assortment with a VSA of 2 had better financial outcomes (that is, %GM) than the assortment with a VSA of 0.81. Similar results were obtained with the discount store's assortments. The three assortments had VSAs of 3.3, 9, and 12.61. (The assortment with the VSA of 12.61 had the highest VSA in the store data we examined.) As expected, the assortment with the VSA of 12.61 had a higher %GM. The assortment with a VSA of 3.3 exhibited the poorest %GM for the discount store assortments, while the assortment with the VSA of 9 fell in the middle of the %GM performance range.

Because of the recent development of the assortment diversity concept, little is known about the diversity of "normal" store level assortments other than those reported in Table 7.10. If these assortments reported are typical, then VSAs would range below 15.

Learning Activity 7.7

Volume per SKU for the assortment (VSA)

1. How does VSA differ from volume per SKU?
2. Explain the logic behind the concept that as VSA is smaller, financial productivity is less.
3. If you have 1,000 units planned for an assortment distributed across 20 SKUs, what is the VSA for the assortment? How many units per SKU are in the assortment? What is the volume of the assortment? What is the variety of the assortment?
4. Why is an assortment with a lower VSA likely to have more stockouts?
5. According to Learning Activity 6.7, #4, Duber's has a merchandise budget for girl's tops for the spring selling period that includes receiving 1,208 girl's tops for a total of $12,075 in merchandise to receive to make their sales plan of $10,500. The

sizes carried and distribution of sales by size for last spring were as follows: 6 (8%), 7 (25%), 8 (40%), 10 (20%), 12 (5%), and 14 (2%). You are planning to apply the fashion trend of wearing body-conforming tops. Since Duber's is the primary source for children's wear in this town, the store normally carries a diverse assortment. You are developing an assortment plan with a model stock of eight styles, six colors, and six sizes for girl's tops.

a) Create a volume-per-assortment factor plan for tops.
b) Create a volume per SKU plan for style # 4. (You have to decide on percent distribution of styles and colors. Do not distribute uniformly.)
c) How many SKUs are in this assortment?
d) What is the VSA of this assortment?
e) How will the VSA impact potential stockouts?

a) Plan for volume-per-assortment factor for girl's tops for spring.

#	Style %	Units per Style	Color %	Units per Color	Size %	Units per Size
1						
2						
3						
4						
5						
6						
7						
8						
Total						

b) Volume per SKU plan for style # 4.

Color	Size #1	Size #2	Size #3	Size #4	Size #5	Size #6	Total
#1							
#2							
#3							
#4							
#5							
#6							
Total							

Assortment Diversity Index

The **assortment diversity index (ADI)** is a predictor of the impact of VSA on financial productivity. An index is "something that serves to guide, point out, or otherwise facilitate reference . . . something that reveals or indicates" (*The American Heritage Dictionary*, 1994). According to the simulation experiments, three ranges of VSAs were identified in relation to financial outcomes to form the basis of an ADI. The following words and definitions were developed to describe these segments:

- **Diverse assortments**—assortments with few units allocated per SKU, five or less on the average for an individual store assortment
- **Transition assortments**—assortments with a moderate number of units allocated per SKU, between six and 10 on the average for an individual store assortment
- **Focused assortments**—assortments with many units allocated per SKU, usually 10 or more

Two of the VSA segments have been further refined. The diverse assortment is broken down into two areas: very diverse, with VSAs of 2 or below, and diverse with VSAs of 2.01 to 5. The focused assortment is broken down into three parts: focused with VSAs of above 10 to 20, very focused with VSAs of 20 to 50, and unaffected with VSAs above 50. Assortments with VSAs above 50 are so focused that they exhibited no impact on financial outcomes. The six segments defined as parts of the ADI are shown in the first three columns of Table 7.11.

The key VSA points in the ADI are 2, 5, 10, 20, and 50. As VSA increases, the greatest change in financial productivity (%GM) occurs within very diverse assortments, those with a VSA of 2 or less. Within the diverse segment, VSAs of 2 to 5, sizable improvements in financial productivity are also realized as VSA increases. Percent gross margins improved almost 1 percent per index point, for example, an assortment with a VSA of 3 had a %GM about 1 percent greater than an assortment with a VSA of 2. In the merchandising world, a one 1 increase in gross margin is an important accomplishment.

With transition assortments, or those with VSAs of between 5 and 10, the rate of %GM increase was not as great as when VSAs were below 5, but greater than when VSAs were above 10.

As assortments became focused, VSAs of 10 to 20, the rate of increase in financial productivity is considerably less. For the very focused segment, VSAs of 20 to 50, the rate of increase in financial productivity is very small; after 50, increases in financial productivity nearly disappeared. In general, as the VSAs increased to 50, the financial productivity increased.

Table 7.11

Assortment diversity index (Rupe & Kunz, 1998) with markup adjustments for assortment diversity based on 50 percent initial markup. *

Assortment diversity	VSA	Total impact on %GM	Total Impact on Percent Markup				
			Target financial productivity: Percent gross margin with VSA of 10		Target financial productivity: Percent gross margin with VSA of 5		
			Required additional markup	Converted to initial markup	Required additional markup	Converted to initial markup	
very diverse	2 or less	3.5%	27%	7.8%	22%	7.3%	
diverse	2.01 to 5	2.3%	13%	5.3%	12%	5.2%	
transition	5.01 to 10	1.3%	5%	2.4%			
focused	10.01 to 20	1.1%					
very focused	20.01 to 50	0.7%					
unaffected	50.01 to 100	0.0%					

*Numbers have been rounded to simplify presentation. Lee (1999, p. 78).

Conversely, as the VSAs decreased from 50, financial productivity decreased (Rupe & Kunz, 1998).

So what is the practical application of the assortment diversity index? When apparel professionals discuss the ADI, their first inclination is to find ways to make assortments less diverse because that will help reduce stockouts and improve gross margin. However, many assortments are necessarily diverse because consumers want great variety in the assortment to choose from and want unique garments to wear. Thus, it is not possible to make all assortments less diverse and also satisfy customers.

The other option is to increase markup on items that need to be offered in diverse assortments. If diverse assortments are going to generate similar financial productivity (%GM) as less diverse assortments, then markup has to be higher.

Lee (1999) examined how much additional markup would be required for diverse assortments to achieve the same gross margins as assortments with VSAs of 5 and 10. Lee also converted the additional markup to initial markup so markup could be applied in a more traditional manner. Focus on the last four columns of Table 7.11.

If an assortment has a VSA of 2 or less (very diverse), a 50 percent initial markup plus 27 percent additional markup is required to achieve the same gross margin as an assortment with a VSA of 10 using only 50 percent markup. In the next column, the additional markup has been converted initial markup. The initial markup of 50 percent plus 8 percent means a total initial markup of 58 percent will achieve the same gross margin as the previous calculation using additional markup. *The overall point is, diverse assortments cramp financial productivity and little attention has been paid to this reality in the world of merchandise planning.*

⬚ Learning Activity 7.8

Assortment diversity index (ADI)

1. What is the purpose of an index like the ADI? How might a merchandiser use the ADI to plan more financially productive assortments?
2. What is the VSA for the assortment of MSCS in Table 7.7? According to the VSA, what is the level of assortment diversity according to the ADI? What are the implications for financial productivity of the assortment?
3. Style #9 in Table 7.7 is part of the MSCS assortment. How does the VSA for MSCS explain the empty cells in the volume per SKU plan in Table 7.9?
4. What is the VSA and ADI of the assortment you created in Learning Activity 7.6, #3 for women's cycling knickers at Mike's Bikes? Based on the ADI, how much impact would you expect the diversity of the assortment to have on financial productivity?

Integrated Merchandise Plans

Integrating company profiles, merchandise budgets, assortment dimensions, and assortment diversity into complete merchandise plans is a great merchandising challenge. Few merchandising technology systems have accomplished it, so merchandisers continue to face the challenge of developing merchandise plans and interpreting their results. As with merchandise budgeting processes, the assortment planning process applied to a particular merchandise class is determined by demand for product change and change in the rate of sale:

- *basic/staple goods planned at SKU level*—basic stock or automated replenishment plan with an item replenishment system with a goal of continuous inventory throughout the merchandising cycle
- *basic/seasonal and fashion/staple goods planned at classification level*—model stock plan with assortment distribution with a goal of zero-to-zero inventory for the selling period; automated replenishment systems may be used
- *fashion/seasonal goods planned at classification level*—model stock plan with assortment distribution with a goal of zero-to-zero inventory for the selling period

Basic stock and automated replenishment systems were discussed in Chapter 6. A strategy for synthesizing the merchandise planning systems and practices discussed in Chapters 4, 5, 6, and 7 appears in Figure 7.5. The key to good planning is ongoing systematic analysis of past, present, and future opportunities.

Summary

Planning and controlling merchandise assortments has been the least sophisticated area of merchandising. The magnitude of the retail stockout problem has had little study, but it is a serious problem in today's markets as shoppers spend less time shopping in fewer shopping trips but spend more money in each. Competition for consumer dollars is so great that merchants must provide appropriate merchandise assortments to optimize sales from merchandise offerings. A better understanding of in-store shopping behavior is essential to create effective assortments

Effective assortment planning is dependent on recognizing the interrelationships among the merchandise classification system, the pricing system, and the merchandise budget. The most effective plans are dynamic and interactive. Assortment plans are based on the measurable dimensions of volume, variety, and distribution. From those dimensions, model

1. Develop a profile of the firm including its mission, goals, market positioning, target customers, product line, financial status, and current issues and trends.
2. Determine last year's sales for an individual store if the firm is multi-stored and/or multi-tiered.
3. Develop a general forecast for next year for the individual store, sales up or down, general trends, etc.
4. Break down the merchandise mix into categories, classes, subclasses, and groups.
5. Apply merchandise classes to a Perceptual Map of Product Change.
6. Select a merchandise class, subclass, or group as a focus of your planning.
7. Evaluate the role of the selected merchandise in the product line and create a merchandise calendar.
8. Determine the pricing strategy, level of markup, average first price, and allowable cost.
9. Determine last year's sales and planned sales based on sales history, sales forecasts, and/or space productivity.
10. Determine planned reductions based on sales history or industry averages for the classification.
11. Determine receiving at retail for the classification adequate to cover reductions and achieve your planned sales goal.
12. Determine assortment volume.
13. Develop a model stock and determine number of SKUs.
14. Distribute the assortment across the model stock.
15. Develop a volume per SKU plan.
16. Determine the VSA and rank of the plan according to the ADI.
17. Evaluate potential of plan in relation to stockouts.
18. Are changes needed in pricing, receiving at retail, model stock, or assortment distribution?

Figure 7.5 Developing merchandise plans for a selling period for a merchandise category/class/sub-class/group at the individual store tier.

stocks, volume per assortment factor, and volume per SKU plans can be developed. Merchandise budgets are the source of volume error; assortment plans are the source of variety error.

Volume per SKU for the assortment (VSA) is a means of measuring assortment diversity. The assortment diversity index (ADI) is an indicator of the impact of the assortment on potential financial productivity. Calculating assortment plans by hand is very labor intensive. Implementing computer-based merchandising plans at the SKU level on computer systems that can handle a huge number of SKUs is essential to improve the effectiveness of merchandise planning.

Key Concepts

assortment distribution	balanced assortment	shopper's intentions
assortment diversity	customer service	stock keeping unit (SKU)
assortment diversity index	diverse assortments	stockout
(ADI)	focused assortments	transition assortments
assortment factors	in-stock	volume per assortment factor
assortment planning	in-store shopping behavior	volume per SKU
assortment variety	lost sales	volume per SKU for the
assortment volume	model stock	assortment (VSA)

Integrated Learning Activity 7.9.1

Integrated merchandise plans including assortment plans

Based on corrected merchandise budgets developed in ILA 6.10.1 and tested in ILA 6.10.2, complete assortment plans for the merchandise classes you have defined as your fashion/seasonal group and your basic/staple group. To be realistic, make your fashion/seasonal group have a VSA of less than 5 and your basic/staple have a VSA of more than 10. Use Figure 7.5 as an overall guide for completing your merchandise plans. You have already completed many of the steps. Complete all of these steps for one merchandise group and then proceed to the other.

1. Update, correct, and present your merchandise calendar and budget developed for ILA 6.10.1 including assortment volume.
2. Develop a model stock that will satisfy the VSA requirements. Rank the plan according to the ADI.
3. Determine the VSA and rank the plan according to the ADI.
4. Distribute the assortments across the model stock and determine the volume per assortment factor.
5. Develop volume per SKU plans for each style.
6. Evaluate potential of plan for stockouts considering each style.
7. Which merchandise group has the most potential for lost sales? Why?
8. Are changes needed in pricing, reductions, receiving at retail, model stock, or assortment distribution to improve potential financial productivity?

⊚ *Integrated Learning Activity 7.9.2*

Using Sourcing Simulator (SS) to analyze financial impacts of assortment diversity

Objectives of this simulation exercise

- Develop, describe, and apply assortment diversity strategies to fashion/seasonal and basic/staple merchandise groups.
- Compare and evaluate financial outcomes related to focused and diverse assortments.

Resources for this assignment

- Merchandising text , class notes, and Integrated Learning Activities (ILA)
- Your teacher, your lab assistant, partner, and/or class members

Procedures

1. Correct any errors in your merchandise plans in ILA 6.10.1, 6.10.2, and 7.9.1. Use assortment *volume* (number of units) based on merchandise to receive in your merchandise budget from ILA 6.10.1 and *model stock* from ILA 7.9.1.

2. Develop two additional assortment plans so that you have one that is *focused* and one that is *diverse* for your fashion/seasonal group and one that is *focused* and one that is *diverse* for your basic/staple group. Use your planned assortment volume for both groups based on merchandise to receive in your budget in ILA 6.10.1. (Note: SS will not accept more than 500 SKUs. If your diverse assortments require more than 500 SKUs, reduce the volume on both your diverse and focused assortments so VSA is 5 or less when using no more than 500 SKUs for your diverse assortment.)

3. Open SS Seasonal Model. Conduct the first experiment based on the diverse assortment plan for your fashion/seasonal merchandise group.

    a) Use the default data set for everything but instructions for changes in b through k.

    b) On the Consumer Demand folder, use 0% error from plan for both volume and SKU mix; check same as presumed seasonality for the sales peak.

    c) Fill out the Buyer's Plan with your fashion/seasonal product name, weeks in selling period, and pre-defined sales peak according to your merchandise calendar. Use the planned annual volume according to your Fundamental Merchandise Budget unless you have modified volume because your assortment plan had more than 500 SKUs.

d) Also enter in the Buyer's Plan folder your fashion/seasonal diverse assortment by style, size, and color. (If you have more than five styles, you can enter styles in Size, and sizes in Style.)

e) On the Sourcing Strategy folder, use the traditional replenishment strategy and set initial stocking to 100%.

f) Based on ILA 6.10.2, enter a pricing strategy for your fashion/seasonal group in the Cost Data and Markdowns/Premiums folders.

g) Run simulation using fashion/seasonal diverse in the title. Print inputs. Leave the output screen open.

h) Check inputs and outputs for effectiveness. Modify and rerun if necessary or desired.

i) In the Buyer's Plan folder, enter focused assortment for fashion/seasonal merchandise group.

j) Run the simulation again. Print inputs for second simulation.

k) Examine printed inputs and outputs on the screen. Repeat simulation if necessary to correct errors or improve outputs.

l) Print graphs for both simulations for service level, gross margin, stockouts, empty shelves, and average inventory.

m) Print outputs. Highlight total offering, average inventory, % offering sold, % liquidated, % sell-through, lost sales, service level, total revenue, revenue per unit offered, gross margin, and % gross margin.

4. Open SS Basics Model.

a) Use the default data set for everything but instructions for changes in b through k.

b) Fill out the Buyer's Plan for your basic/staple merchandise group. Use the planned annual volume determined by your Fundamental Budget.

c) Use the assortment plan for styles, sizes, and colors based on ILA 7.12.1.

d) On the Consumer Demand folder, use 0% error from plan for both volume and SKU mix; check same as presumed seasonality for the sales peak.

e) On the Sourcing Strategy folder, use the default.

f) Enter your pricing strategy based on your pricing plan for basic/staple merchandise group in your Cost Data and Promotions folders.

g) Repeat 3g to 3m to complete your second experiment.

h) Close SS; do not save inputs as default. Put your name on your printouts from your basic/staple experiment and organize in an orderly manner.

Basis of grading

1. Present this assignment in an orderly manner in your MAP, including an updated merchandise plan for the store and the classification.
2. Include four simulation input and output printouts and the requested graphs marked for identification.
3. Examine the highlighted outputs on your printouts and the associated graphs. Write out definitions for stockouts, lost sales, average inventory, and empty shelf. Changes in volume tend to make large changes in outputs, whereas changes in variety make smaller but very important changes. To a merchandiser, every increase in percent gross margin is important, no matter how small.
4. Discuss how your assortment strategies impacted outcomes. What are the most noticeable differences between diverse and focused assortments for each merchandise group? Be sure to use assortment dimensions language.
5. Evaluate total revenue in relation to planned sales from ILA 6.10.1. Did you make your sales plan? Why or why not? What changes should you make to bring you closer to your sales goal?

Integrated Learning Activity 7.9.3

Merchandise plans for Tommy Jeans

1. Read Case 7.3 very carefully. Make notes as you read of ideas that will impact how a retailer's merchandise plan for Tommy Jeans could be set up. What clues are there about the merchandise classification system, the budget, the calendar, the assortment plan, and assortment diversity?
2. What moves has Tommy Jeans made to improve service to their retail customers?

📁   *Case 7.3*   **Tommy Jeans makes major line changes. ***   📁

Tommy Jeans is becoming more nimble. The label had made several dramatic moves aimed at increasing sales by enabling it to react more quickly to changes in the market.

Under the tutelage of Todd Howard, who recently added the men's jeans line to his duties, Tommy Jeans has cut product-development times, made it easier to inject new styles into the line, implemented out-of-season testing to get a read on fashion trends, overhauled the replenishment business, and, most significantly, changed the market date.

These "adjustments," as Howard calls them, essentially move men's to the same merchandise calendar as junior's. Tommy Jeans will now open its New York showroom to men's wear retailers March 4, some two months after the other major labels debuted their collections. Howard was able to revise the market dates because he has cut the label's development and production time. The space between market and first delivery will now be three to four months instead of five to six months as it was in the past, he said. The calendar shift is the most visible element of a revitalization strategy orchestrated by Howard, who also oversees the junior's and children's components of Tommy Jeans.

"This jeans business didn't need an overhaul," Howard said. "It just needed an adjustment. We're still in progress in men's. It took three seasons in the junior's business, and we're in our second season in men's."

The designer Tommy Hilfiger has been deeply involved in re-creating the brand Tommy Hilfiger since the label's sales started to slow in the fall of 1999. His junior's business was the first to bounce back and now his attention has shifted to men's.

On the runway earlier this month, the payoff for that focus was evident in Hilfiger's fall collection, which faultlessly combined denim, sportswear, and tailored clothing for a fresh take on his signature all-American style. Now the challenge for Tommy is to turn that excitement into dollars on the sales floors of America's department stores.

By showing men's jeans in March, it will give retailers (and Tommy Jeans) more time to watch the market for trends before they commit their dollars, Howard said. "Retailers can analyze Christmas and early spring sales before they buy back-to-school," he said. "And they can make it through Labor Day before they buy spring. It gives them more information and more flexibility."

Retailers might have some complaints about the later calendar since they'll have to make a special trip to buy Tommy Jeans, after buying the other big brands earlier in the year. They'll also have to allocate dollars to other brands before they buy Tommy Jeans. Regardless, Howard feels that the additional buying flexibility more than makes up for the initial inconveniences for his retail customers. "With any new initiative there are going to be challenges, but you have to make decisions and move forward. And I believe every retailer wants to make their buying decisions with the best possible information. And, of

(continued)

Case 7.3 (continued)

course, there is a possibility that Howard's move will force the other big labels like Polo Jeans Co., Calvin Klein, and Nautica to advance their calendars as well.

Tommy Jeans has also completely revamped its core men's replenishment group, which now has six denim fits, each offered in several washes, including sandblasted or whiskered. Some key fits are the Liberty, a loose fit, low-rise; Field Patriot, a low-rise carpenter; and the classic five-pocket Freedom jeans. The bulk of the core jeans will retail between $49 and $59.

Tommy Jeans also has two khakis and a track pant on replenishment, as well as a selection of stretch t-shirts and knit polos.

The label will focus on delivering new fashion for men every month during the fall season, Howard said. That will give customers more fresh looks and keep giving them reason to come back to the stores, he said. "Newness at all times, that's the goal."

*Based on Cunningham (2002).

Recommended Resources

Kitchel, D. B., & Leibowitz, S. (2001, May). Assortment planning, turning strategy into action. *Bobbin,* 63–65.

Kunz, G. I., & Rupe, D. (1999). Volume per stock-keeping unit for an assortment: A merchandise planning tool. *Journal of Fashion Marketing and Management,* 3(2):118–125.

Lewis, R. (1996, May). Power to the consumer. In *DNR Infotracs,* a supplement to *Daily News Record.*

Taylor, C. G. (1970). *Merchandise assortment planning.* New York: Merchandising Division, National Retail Merchants Association.

References

The American Heritage Dictionary. (1994). Boston, MA: Houghton Mifflin.

Anderson, P. E. (1982, Spring). Marketing, strategic planning and the theory of a firm. *Journal of Marketing,* 46:15–26.

Belk, R. W. (1975). Situational variables and consumer behavior. *Journal of Consumer Research,* 2:157–164.

Berman, B., & Evans, J. R. (1995). *Retail management: A strategic approach.* Englewood Cliffs, NJ: Prentice Hall.

Bohlinger, M. (1977). *Merchandise buying: Principles and applications.* Dubuque, IA: Wm. C. Brown.

Brown, P., & Davidson, W. (1953). *Retailing principles and practices.* New York: Ronald Press.

Bureau of the Census. (1994). Statistical abstract of the United States 1994 (114th ed.). Washington, DC: Author.

Chowdhary, U. (1989). Apparel shopping behavior of elderly men and women. *Perceptual and Motor Skills,* 68:1183–1189.

Conrad, A. (2001, March 2). Famous Footwear's winning the battle of widths. *Daily News Record,* 8.

Cunningham, T. (2002, February 25). Tommy Jeans makes major line changes. *Daily News Record,* 1 & 8.

Davidson, W., & Doody, A. (1966). *Retailing management.* New York: Ronald Press.

Dunne, P., Lusch, R., & Gable, M. (1995). *Retailing.* Cincinnati, OH: South-Western.

Famous Footwear. (2003). (www.famousfootwear.com). Accessed December 9, 2003.

Fisher, M. L., Hammond, J. H., Obermeyer, W. R., & Raman, A. (1994, May/June). Making supply meet demand in an uncertain world. *Harvard Business Review,* 83–93.

Gillespie, K., & Hecht, J. (1970). *Retail business management.* New York: McGraw-Hill.

Glock, R. E., & Kunz, G. I. (2000). *Apparel manufacturing: Sewn product analysis (*3rd ed.). Englewood Cliffs, NJ: Prentice Hall.

Hays, C. L. (2002, February 24). Built on the working class, Wal-Mart eyes the BMW crowd. *New York Times,* 1 & 24.

Hunter, A. (1990). *Quick response in apparel manufacturing: A survey of the American scene.* Manchester, England: The Textiles Institute.

Hunter, N., King, R., & Nuttle, H. (1991). Comparison of quick response and traditional retailing performance through stochastic simulation modeling (NCSIU-IE Technical Report #91-6). Raleigh, NC: North Carolina State University, Department of Industrial Engineering.

Jarboe, G. R., & McDaniel, C. D. (1987). A profile of browsers in regional shopping malls. *Journal of the Academy of Marketing Science,* 15:46–53.

Kahn, B. E., & Schmittlein, D. C. (1989). Shopping trip behavior: An empirical investigation. *Marketing Letters,* 1(1):55–69.

Kahn, B. E., & Schmittlein, D. C. (1992). The relationship between purchase made on promotion and shopping trip behavior. *Journal of Retailing,* 68(3):294–315.

Kollat, D. T., & Willett, R. P. (1967, February). Customer impulse purchasing behavior. *Journal of Marketing Research,* 4:21–31.

Kunz, G. I., & Rupe, D. (1999). Volume per stock-keeping unit for an assortment: A merchandise planning tool. *Journal of Fashion Marketing and Management,* 3(2):118–125.

Lee, S. E. (1999). An analysis of assortment diversity in relation to merchandising performance measures and markup. Unpublished Master's thesis, Iowa State University, Ames.

Lewis, R. (1996, May). Power to the consumer. In *DNR Infotracs*, a supplement to *Daily News Record.*

Mason, J. B., Mayor, M. L., & Ezell, H. F. (1994). *Retailing* (5th ed.). Burr Ridge, IL: Irwin.

Meet the new competition: Emerging home shopping alternatives. (1994, February). *Stores,* S3–S22.

Nuttle, H., King, R., & Hunter, N. (1991). A stochastic model of the apparel-retailing process for seasonal apparel. *Journal of the Textile Institute,* 82(2):247–259.

Nuttle, H. L. W., King, R E., & Hunter, N. A. (1992). An apparel supply system for QR retailing. *Journal of the Textile Institute,* 93(3):462–471.

Risch, E. (1991). *Retail merchandising.* New York: Macmillan.

Runyon, K. E., & Stewart, D. W. (1987). *Consumer behavior.* Columbus, OH: Merrill.

Rupe, D., & Kunz, G. I. (1998). Building a financially meaningful language of merchandise assortments. *Clothing and Textiles Research Journal,* 88–96.

Schary, P. B., & Becker, B. W. (1978). The impact of stock-out on market share. *Journal of Business Logistics,* 1(1):31–44.

Taylor, C. G. (1970). *Merchandise assortment planning.* New York: Merchandising Division, National Retail Merchants Association.

section three ———————————————————➤

Developing and Presenting Product Lines

8

Developing

Product Lines

Learning Objectives

- Discuss the relationships between merchandise planning and line development.

- Examine line development through purchase of finished goods and product development.

- Examine issues in buyer/vendor negotiations.

L ine development processes have become more diverse as quick response (QR) business systems have been implemented and the textile and apparel industry has become more globalized. **Line development** is the process of determining the actual styles, sizes, and colors that will fill out the line plan (Glock & Kunz, 2000). In today's markets, line development is closely associated with sourcing. **Sourcing** is determining the most cost efficient vendor of materials, production, and/or finished goods at a specified quality and service level with delivery within an identified time frame. Both manufacturer and retailer merchandisers are commonly responsible for line development. Merchandisers are either responsible for sourcing or work closely with those who are responsible for sourcing.

Fundamental Methods of Line Development

In its purest form, a line plan (merchandise plan) is a bunch of words and numbers. The words describe relevant socioeconomic, cultural, environmental, fashion, and technological trends that impact a firm's target customers. The numbers reflect analysis of sales history, interpretation of trends, and forecast of future customer demand. They provide a dollar investment and quantitative framework for forecasting sales for specific merchandise classifications and time frames. The merchandise plan also guides variety and diversity of the line, but does not necessarily identify the actual merchandise that will be offered to customers.

Line development results in the determination of the actual styles, sizes, and colors customers will have the opportunity to view, examine, consider, and purchase. As shown in Figure 3.2, Taxonomy of Apparel Merchandising Systems (TAMS), line development is closely integrated with line planning and line presentation. The relationship is not linear; line planning does not necessarily come first, followed by line development and line presentation. Many activities among planning, development, and presentation may be simultaneous and, perhaps more important, interactive. Effective use of QR:

- Requires simultaneous and interactive processes to reduce the time required for merchandising decisions
- Moves the key decisions closer to the point of sale to the ultimate consumer.

Simultaneous and interactive decisions through the use of multifunctional merchandising teams streamline the merchandising process and reduce redundancy. There are two primary forms of line development—purchase of finished goods and product development.

Purchase of Finished Goods

Finished goods include merchandise ready for use by the ultimate consumer. The **purchase of finished goods** may come from both manufacturer and retailer merchandisers. Manufacturers usually specialize in producing certain types of products. For example, an athletic shoe manufacturer is likely to offer socks but doesn't own any knitting machines to make socks. A jeans manufacturer may want to offer matching shirts, vests, or jackets, but they may have neither the production capacity nor the expertise to do so. Merchandisers, then, may be charged with searching the market for appropriate finished goods to fill out the product line. The finished goods purchased from another manufacturer are sold at wholesale to retail buyers as if the shoe or jeans manufacturer had produced the items themselves.

Retail Organization for Line Development

Purchase of finished goods by retailer merchandisers is often regarded as the traditional form of retail line development. Merchandisers view and evaluate lines when presented by sales representatives that call on them in their stores or offices. Retail merchandisers might also visit local, regional, national, or international wholesale markets to view dozens or even hundreds of product lines that may be synthesized into the total retail product offering for a particular selling period. Now, merchandisers can also view and purchase finished goods online. From a manufacturer's perspective, wholesale markets provide the opportunity to identify new prospects, service current customers, introduce new and modified products, enhance corporate image, test new products, improve corporate morale, gather competitor information, and sell merchandise. Web sites now offer manufacturers a focused and flexible means of presenting and updating product lines.

The merchandising constituency of a retail firm is usually charged with the responsibility for supplying merchandise to the firm's retail stores. The merchandisers responsible for this effort were traditionally called buyers. According to Figure 3.2, TAMS, buyers of finished goods make line plans, develop line concepts, interact with sales representatives at wholesale line presentations, adopt styles to fill out the line plan, and determine delivery strategies for the goods. The process of choosing among thousands of potential styles at wholesale markets is challenging and can be confusing, expensive, and time consuming.

Buyers commonly purchase designer or brand name goods to fill out their line plans. They also may purchase private label goods. **Private label** is "merchandise that bears a retailer's own name brand rather than that of a designer or manufacturer" (Jernigan & Easterling, 1990, p. 565). Private label goods are now known as the retailer's brands. A retailer's brand(s) may be the retailer's own name, another copyrighted name, and/or a designer with whom the retailer has an exclusive license for the use of the name. Brands are acquired in many ways. Some manufacturers develop lines to be sold especially for private label. The retailer selects styles and specifies sizes and quantities and the manufacturer inserts the retailer's brand into already manufactured goods. Other times retailers are involved in the development of the products.

Private brand merchandise has increased as a proportion of total assortment for most merchandise categories. Women's and girl's apparel has had a slightly larger increase than men's and boy's. Private label, as a portion of total assortments, ranges from 0 to 100 percent, but 15 to 30 percent is very common for classifications in mass and department store retailers.

For example, at Saks Incorporated, private brands have increased from 5 percent in 1998 to 18 percent of men's wear in 2001. Prices run 15 to 20 percent lower than national brands. While the space allocated to private brands is increasing, they have to earn their space just like any other brand. Saks makes sure they have the most productivity per square foot they can achieve. "Saks DSG (department store group) is merchandising the private brands as they would national brands with signage, fixturing, and a shop-like ambience" (Lloyd, 2001, p. 5).

Purchasing finished goods requires an individual who is organized, able to take risks, energetic, and capable of performing under pressure (Wickett, 1995). The life of a buyer is exciting, tedious, and stressful. Buyers commonly spend at least one week of every month attending wholesale markets in search of new merchandise and negotiating with vendors. While buyers may visit many exotic parts of the world, they may not be able to enjoy them very much. A buyer's time is fully consumed by the duties involved in line development. Then, after devoting much time and attention to merchandise selection, most buyers must get the approval of his or her divisional merchandise manager for the finished goods selected.

In recent years, large retailers commonly have used **matrix buying** to improve the effectiveness of its line development processes. The merchandising group identifies its best and/or most dominant suppliers and creates a matrix of preferred vendors for each merchandise classification. In order to have a chance to show their product line to buyers, the vendor's name must be on the list. Matrix buying creates much greater interdependence between buyers and vendors. The buyer is limited by what the vendors in the matrix offer; and the vendor is likely to have a larger portion of the business committed to fewer retail customers.

Role of Manufacturer Sales Representatives

Part of the role of manufacturer merchandisers and the product development team is to train sales representatives on how to present, assort, and sell a line. In Figure 3.2, TAMS, this training session is called **wholesale line preview.** The training includes a summary of overall trends that influenced line development, how trends evolved into line concept, the nature of the merchandise plan, and how the merchandise groups and individual styles are expected to appeal to the target customer. Pricing strategies and assortments are reviewed with emphasis on key styles and colors to balance merchandise plans with sales. Merchandisers train the sales reps on how to plan assortments for their customers that will be consistent with sales forecasts for the selling period.

The **wholesale market** is an external line review, and is represented by the "wholesale" component in line presentation in Figure 3.2, TAMS. Two-thirds or fewer of the styles in a line presented at wholesale may generate adequate purchase orders to justify putting products into production. This means that the retail buyers who placed orders for goods with low demand will not receive the goods or will have other merchandise substituted by the manufacturer. The wholesale market system is highly inefficient from a product development standpoint because it is common for nearly half of the product development effort to be wasted because of inadequate quantities ordered by retailers. On the other hand, the system provides an opportunity to test the acceptability of styles according to the retail buyers' perceptions of the ultimate consumers' wants and needs. Wholesale markets provide opportunities for new firms to display innovative product lines. Some become instant successes. Others are ignored and may never be heard from again.

Retail merchandisers/buyers are notorious among manufacturers for trying to engage in the product design process. They tell sales representatives they want a long sleeve or a short sleeve, a collar or no collar, and a change in fabric. A classic example of buyer/vendor design conflict relates to a situation recently reported by a buyer regarding the design of little girls' velveteen holiday dresses. The manufacturer designed the dresses with short sleeves to control product costs. The velveteen fabric was very expensive compared to other fabrics being used for holiday dresses. Putting long sleeves on the dresses increased fabric costs by nearly two-thirds. The result would have been an increase in the wholesale price of $10 and an increase in suggested retail price of $22. The retail buyers were frustrated because they knew their customers wanted long sleeves on holiday dresses. The higher price might put off some customers, but the short sleeve would make most of the dresses unsalable. The manufacturer's concern about cost was interfering with the buyer's need to satisfy the holiday dress customer.

Professional manufacturers' sales representatives (reps) are invaluable resources for retail buyers, particularly inexperienced buyers. In a study to identify sources of information used by buyers to reduce the uncertainty of their buying decisions, manufacturers' representatives were identified as the most important source, followed by trade journals and top management (Shim & Kotsiopulos, 1991). Reps are storehouses of information about industry trends, competitors, and customers. Sales representatives are commonly required to purchase the sales samples that provide the visual and tactile aspects of showing a line. Manufacturer sales representatives are usually paid a commission based on how much merchandise they sell. In the short term, the more merchandise they sell, the more money they make. In the long term, the more merchandise that successfully sells through at retail the better the relationship the sales rep will have with the buyer and the stronger the relationship between the two companies. Read Case 8.1 about Wal-Mart's buyer's electronic relationship with one of its sock suppliers.

📁   *Case 8.1   To sell goods to Wal-Mart, get on the net. ⃰*   📁

Using a system called electronic data interchange (EDI), the sock buyers for Wal-Mart Stores Inc. send electronic files to Candor Hosiery Mills Inc. twice a day, telling the Robbins, North Carolina, company such things as how many pallets of white and multicolored crew socks to deliver to stores. It used to take Candor employees six hours, spent sitting at desktop computers hooked to a dial-up modem, to receive the data from Wal-Mart, based in Bentonville, Arkansas. If the connection was disrupted, the whole transmission had to be sent again, making the transaction even longer.

Then Wal-Mart, the world's biggest retailer, told its suppliers they would have to start sending and receiving electronic data over the Internet. Today, more than 90 percent of Wal-Mart's EDI exchanges with suppliers are done over the Internet using AS@, a software package from Isoft Corp., Dallas, that suppliers must purchase and install if they wish to continue selling to the chain. (The package can cost as little as $300 if the supplier wishes to connect with only Wal-Mart but can cost six figures for links to more than 100 companies.)

The change at Wal-Mart underscores the way the Internet and simple off-the-shelf business software are overhauling the retail-distribution system, making transac-

tions cheaper and faster for both retailers and their suppliers. With razor-thin profit margins that recently have been pressured further by deflationary prices and rising costs, these industries find saving even a few hours a day and a few thousand dollars a month important to their bottom lines.

"We have more time to prepare and get orders together," said Dorenda Kidd, chief of information officer for Candor. That time bonus in turn gets goods out quicker and allows the company to ship more merchandise. All that helps as retailers ask more of their manufacturers. For example, Wal-Mart asks Candor to mix about 40 different styles and sizes of socks into a single pallet for direct-to-store delivery, bypassing the distribution center. "That means a lot more people are touching the product [to assemble the diverse assortment], and it costs us an additional 15 cents a dozen in labor," Ms. Kidd says. "But we still get the same $2 a pair for the socks."

Candor has seen several of its customers adopt Internet EDI, including Meijer Stores LLP, a Grand Rapids, Michigan, based superstore and Kohl's Corp., a thriving, mid-market department store based in Milwaukee, Wisconsin. The purpose of the conversion to EDI Internet by Wal-Mart was to provide a cheaper, faster, and more accurate method

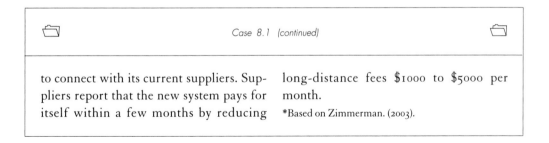

Case 8.1 (continued)

to connect with its current suppliers. Suppliers report that the new system pays for itself within a few months by reducing long-distance fees $1000 to $5000 per month.

*Based on Zimmerman. (2003).

Learning Activity 8.1

Traditional forms of line development

1. How does line development via purchase of finished goods relate to the merchandise budget and the assortment plan?
2. In what way might a sales representative be a link between manufacturer and retailer merchandisers?
3. According to Case 8.1, what are the primary advantages of EDI Internet vs. traditional EDI?
4. Why would Wal-Mart buyers order socks twice a day?
5. How much more does it cost Wal-Mart per pair of socks to have socks packed on pallets for single store shipment? Why is that a concern to Candor? Why is it a benefit to Wal-Mart?

Product Development as a Means of Line Development

Product development is the design and engineering of products to be serviceable, producible, salable, and profitable (Glock & Kunz, 2000). The line plan combined with the line concept provides the framework for product development. According to TAMS, product development has three phases: creative design, line adoption, and technical design. The time frame and actual sequence of events related to product development may differ considerably from one firm to another and from one product line to another. Through application of CAD systems and modification of processes, product development time from concept to consumer has been reduced from 56 weeks in 1982 (American Apparel Manufacturers Association, 1982) to 26 weeks in 1997, and some firms now have reduced it further.

The process of product development involves planning, creating, copying, modifying, sampling, costing, testing, reviewing, adopting, and rejecting. Some steps may take weeks, while others may take only a few hours. But a small time investment makes a process no less important. The execution of the process differs depending on whether the products will be wholesaled and how they will be retailed.

Product Development by a Manufacturer for Wholesale Distribution

Product development for wholesale distribution represents traditional processes where the timeline for product development is determined by merchandising and marketing calendars. Sales samples must be prepared in time for wholesale line preview and presentation at seasonal wholesale markets. Sales samples are not made until the creative design and line adoption phases of product development have been completed. Other deadlines are backed up and planned forward from the timing of wholesale markets.

The amount of time required for product development is a central issue in QR. For example, at Wrangler, 18 cross-functional teams were challenged with reengineering 18 major processes. As a result, they reduced product development times by almost 75 percent (Black, 1995). Improvements of this sort impact creative design, line adoption, and technical design. Review these phases in Figure 3.2, TAMS.

The pre-adoption, **creative design** phase of product development focuses on analysis, creativity, and the formation of product groups with commonalties such as piece goods, design features, or trim. The nature of the groups that are created depends on how the manufacturer defines its business. If it is a coordinates house, merchandise groups might consist of jackets, skirts, pants, blouses, and perhaps accessories. If it is a separates house, merchandise groups might include short-sleeve tops, knit tops, dressy blouses, and shirts. New designs are created, design specifications developed, first patterns are made, design samples are sewn, materials are evaluated, and cost estimates are made. Designs may be modified and sampled several times before a design is finalized and presented for line adoption.

If a firm planned for 60 styles in their line, historically, up to 200 new designs might have been created—the "best" of which were adopted and became styles in the line. Less than two-thirds of the 60 styles were likely to represent over 90 percent of the sales for the selling period. Recent modifications of product development processes have focused on providing more focus and more effective trend analysis to reduce costs and time required for product development. Depending on where in the world materials will be purchased, materials sourcing often occurs simultaneously with creative design. To have goods on hand for production, orders often have to be placed early in the product development process.

The purpose of **line adoption** is to determine which designs will become the styles to fill out the line plan, the styles for which sales and catalog samples will be made, and the styles that will go forward into technical design. Line adoption forces designers and merchandisers to articulate their reasons for their line plans, line concepts, and proposed designs. They must persuade the decision makers that their proposed line is well founded, salable, and potentially profitable.

The purpose of **technical design** is to perfect styling and fit and make it possible to engineer perfect production patterns. Adapting fit to the target customer is very important as garment shapes must be adapted to the body shapes of different ethnic groups (Giddings & Boles, 1990). Merchandisers must ensure quality and performance of materials and develop detailed style specifications, including descriptions of assembly methods. Detailed costs are developed and patterns are graded in preparation for the development of markers. Technical design will proceed immediately for styles for which forecasts are very certain. Other styles will not move into the post-adoption product development phase until after sales potential is confirmed at wholesale markets. A manufacturer may or may not have its own factories, but in any case production planning often proceeds simultaneously with technical design.

Learning Activity 8.2

Stages of product development

1. If a manufacturer is forward vertically integrated by having its own retail stores, how would the product development process be different than product development for wholesale distribution?
2. If a manufacturer is backward vertically integrated by having its own materials production, how might the product development process differ?

Product Development by a Retailer

Retail product development is "the process of creating research-based private label merchandise manufactured or sourced by a retailer for its exclusive sale to an identified target market" (Wickett, 1995, p. 59). Many retailers have assumed responsibility for product development by creating their own product development divisions. These groups often work closely with and/or report to the merchandising division. Based on a case study of such a retailer, Gaskill (1992) proposed a model of retail product development (see Figure 8.1). The components of Gaskill's model are similar to some of those identified in TAMS. Gaskill's

A. Product Development Model

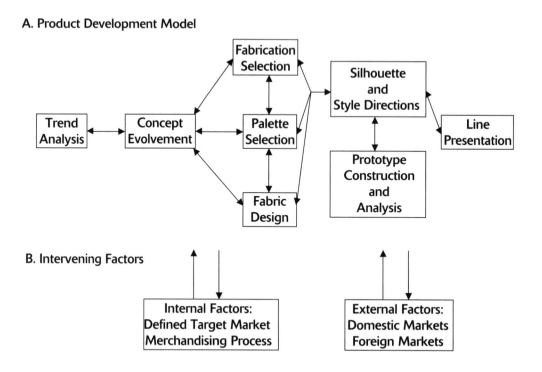

Figure 8.1   Model of retail product development from Gaskill (1992).

trend analysis, concept evolvement, fabrication selection, palette selection, fabric design, and silhouette and style directions are included in line concept in TAMS. Gaskill's prototype construction and analysis are part of creative design in TAMS.

Gaskill's line presentation is part of internal line presentation in TAMS and results in line adoption. Line presentation is described as presentation of the line by the product developers to the merchandisers. Interaction of product development with merchandising is also implied in Gaskill's intervening factors where the merchandising process is recognized as an internal factor related to the product development process.

Interestingly, Gaskill's model does not include any indicators of technical design. Historically, retail product development groups did not always include people trained as technical designers or have patternmaking technology available. Therefore, technical aspects of patternmaking for sample development may have been lacking in the retail firm.

Retail product developers commonly have been responsible for private label goods where style development depends on **knockoffs** of competitors' lines or other higher-priced merchandise. Finished goods purchased at retail by the product developers were often supplied to contractors along with fabric and a few instructions for style modification. The contractor then developed a pattern based on the ready-to-wear garment or from a style block they already had in their computer system. The resulting sample was then sent to the retail product developers for approval. Samples and instructions were often mailed back and forth several times before the style was approved. The knockoff system of product development is still common for many retailers and is also used by many manufacturers, as well.

Retailers engaging in product development have no need for sales samples but they may need samples for advertising and promotion photographs. Catalogers need photographs for catalog layout. They may use design or style samples for this purpose; consequently catalog presentation does not always perfectly represent the garment as it is mass produced. Color is a very important factor. Usually the color shown in the photograph has by far the best sales potential. If the wrong color is chosen for the catalog picture, the style may not sell at all. Decisions are also made about catalog layout and catalog copy by merchandisers or catalog specialists.

The current trend in retail product development is to develop product development divisions complete with designers and CAD systems of all kinds, including patternmaking. The Gap has been regarded as a model of product development strategy. The Gap sells only its own designs and restocks its stores every six weeks throughout the year. Under this system, core products (basic goods) are stocked continuously with only occasional modifications in style and color. At the same time, the selling period for fashion goods is six weeks. Every six weeks, new merchandise replaces goods from the last selling period (Schultz, 1997). The product line includes everything from underwear to casual professional apparel. The Gap corporation also includes Banana Republic at upper-moderate price points and Old Navy at lower-moderate price points, each intended to appeal to different target markets. Jeans at Banana Republic might retail at $55, while jeans at Old Navy retail at $22. Each has its own product development group.

The Gap product development team has grown from 10 to 80 designers in just a decade. The challenge to the designers is to interpret European fashions for the average American consumer. The product development team receives assistance with the color palette from a fashion consultant. They also travel to European fabric and fashion shows looking for inspiration. Members of the team take extensive notes and collect samples. Design ideas are copied, developed, and modified to suit the Gap's customer. The team also decides which styles will be continued, dropped, or modified, and what new styles will be introduced (Schultz, 1997).

Line adoption occurs four times a year at the Gap when Chief Executive Millard Drexler and a group of merchandising executives fly from the headquarters in San Francisco to New York to evaluate the proposed line. They decide what will be offered at retail eight months later. The 1997 fall show, for instance, consisted of over 1,000 samples of men's, women's, and children's apparel, which were displayed in a room arranged like a Gap store. The product development team works on the line for 10 weeks. Their presentation includes the line concept (theme) and an overview of the line plan, for example, the change in the number of styles and colors offered. Individual designs are critiqued by the executive group; some are dropped, others modified. Endorsement by The Gap executives means the styles are prepared for production (Schultz, 1997).

Other retailers are imitating the Gap's product development success. Federated Department Stores has a design/product development team of more than 400. Retailers are trying to increase the uniqueness of their assortments by doing their own product development, which often translates into private label goods. Private label used to be thought of as "bargain" merchandise, but now it is regarded as exclusive brand name merchandise. JCPenney's Arizona line is a classic example. Sears has developed Canyon River Blues to counter the success of Arizona and bought Lands' End to become the exclusive retail store selling the brand. Other retailers are following the Gap's premise that image and customer demand are dependent on the goods' design.

A retailer vertically integrated into product development is providing some of its own manufacturing services. A reality of retailers taking on the complete product development process is that they must bear the cost of design, sourcing, and inventory. Retailers bear the risk of bad sales forecasts and being over- or underinventoried. They also have to find ways to dispose of unsalable merchandise. Under traditional product development systems that included wholesale markets, manufacturers shared these risks.

Another result of this trend is that demand by retailers for product development expertise has driven up designer salaries. Base salaries for design directors have risen 30 percent to $250,000. Demand for graduates with product development expertise is high. Retailers are hiring both creative and technical designers away from apparel manufacturing firms (Berner, 1997).

Retailers are also experiencing conflicts between their merchandisers who set budgets and their designers, who develop products. As predicted by Behavioral Theory of the Apparel Firm in Chapter 1, constituencies develop conflicts because of differing in responsibilities and priorities. Joint-product development teams may be the answer.

Signing exclusive licensing deals with well-known designers to have private brands with status is another retailer private label strategy. Target Stores has scored big with Mossimo and other now privately held designer labels. Read Case 8.2.

📂   Case 8.2   *Target-Mossimo sales generate $700M—*   📂
                            *and designer copies. **

Target Stores Inc. is part of the mass market retail revolution. In the process, it is becoming a designer haven. Call Target the hassle-free way for designers to build huge volume. Industry analysts and observers hold up the deals the mega-retailer has made with Mossimo Giannulli, Michael Graves, and Stephen Sprouse as models for the future of designers and apparel retailing.

Giannulli was among the first to ditch capital-intensive inventory, markdown hassles, and global production nightmares in favor of direct-to-retail licensing. Giannulli pursued Target because he believes this model is the future. And he's glad he did. In the first year since signing a three-year exclusive license for his namesake brand to Target, the gamble has raked in more than $700 million for the chain, according to industry sources.

Unlike Giannulli's old mega-headquarters in Irvine, California, the new digs are a row of ivy-covered buildings where Giannulli and eight employees dream up product for the style-minded masses. "This last year it was about rolling up our sleeves, putting our heads down, and proving to everybody that brand equity could remain." Based on sliding-scale royalty percentages, Mossimo Inc. raked in roughly $15 million from Target in the year ending February 2002. That's nearly double the $8.5 million on volume of $300 million guaranteed in his contract.

Chalk one up for the Cherokee Group, too. CEO Robert Margolis used his connections with Target to broker the deal. A 15 percent finder's fee on Mossimo revenues added roughly $2.2 million to Cherokee Group's coffers. The Van Nuys, California-based licensing company has become an adept matchmaker, hooking major retailers up with broad audience brands. Its first big deal six years ago put the Cherokee brand exclusively into Target domestically. Revenues of Cherokee landed apparel in Target reached $1.4 billion in the first three quarters of 2001. The company is currently working on global licensing deals for Gotcha, BUM Equipment, and Candies.

Target's competitors also have been keenly interested in the designer partnerships at Target. Other major mass mer-

(continued)

Case 8.2 (continued)

---

chants are taking close note because apparel has been a stumbling block for that market. "Apparel is critically important to the mass merchant formula. It turns over. It drives traffic with newness. And it can be very high margin," said retail analyst Jeffrey Klinefelter. "Target has demonstrated that customers will buy first-run fashion at mass retailers."

There are two Mossimo-branded collections: Red Label, an active, youth-oriented line that plays directly into Giannulli's design strengths and Black label, a casual career wear collection aimed at a slightly older demographic. Red has outperformed Black and will be expanded accordingly. Giannulli and his staff design much the way they always have, creating concept boards they present to the retailer. He flies to Minneapolis each month to meet with the Target team.

"They ask me to push them. They'll ask if they are going far enough, said Giannulli. "And in their defense, they know very well what works for them." You talk to anyone in the junior market and they are shopping Target for inspiration. They are doing a fantastic job of merchandising.

Mitch Kummetz, a senior analyst of A.G. Edwards & Sons, observed, "Anytime you drop a brand down in distribution, the consumer still associates it with the previous distribution at higher price points. It's almost as if they perceive they're getting a good deal. The perception may change the longer it stays in the lower channel." Some industry professionals question whether fashion brands can last beyond two or three years in a mass channel.

*Based on Bowers (2002).

 ## Learning Activity 8.3

Retailer apparel product development

1. What are the primary advantages of a retailer engaging in its own product development?
2. What are the primary disadvantages of a retailer engaging in its own product development?
3. Considering Case 8.2, how does licensing a brand differ from a privately developed brand?

4. What percent of retail sales has Mossimo Inc. realized on the licensing agreement? (You will have to calculate the number.)

Joint Product Development

Joint product development is a key component of merchandising in a QR environment. Joint product development means that retailer merchandisers are working with manufacturer merchandisers and designers to develop the line concept, to establish line direction, and to develop products. The goal of the retailer may be to buy the finished goods produced by the manufacturer. However, by having the retailer's early input in the product development process, the manufacturer can reduce the number of unsalable styles that are developed under traditional product development systems, hence saving both time and money. The manufacturer benefits from the retailer's experience in directly serving the target customer. The line developed by the manufacturer more closely reflects the retailer's interpretation of the customer's needs.

As with traditional product development, joint product development also includes creative design, line adoption, and technical design, but the need for the wholesale market is eliminated. The result is similar to what the Target/Mossimo licensing deal has achieved. The breadth of perspective provided by the combination of both retailer and manufacturer merchandisers provides an excellent foundation for line analysis and the development of new styles. The proximity of the retailer merchandisers to their customers and the retail sales history is otherwise unavailable to the manufacturer merchandisers.

Integrating the manufacturer's and retailer's perspectives into creative design should reduce the number of inappropriate designs and improve the development of successful ones. But the methods used in pre-adoption processes may differ. For example, design development may be based primarily on computer-generated images and product specifications, rather than on design samples. Sampling to test patterns may be delayed until after electronically developed designs are approved for the line. By reducing the number of samples required, time and money is saved since samples are often made in another part of the world.

Under joint product development, line adoption may focus more on developing the retailer's line plan than on choosing styles for the line. Most of the style decisions have been made before line adoption. No sales samples, and possibly no photo samples, are necessary since the wholesale market process has been eliminated although samples may be needed for print advertising. Styles with certain sales forecasts can go immediately into technical design and then into mass production. Firms may decide to test more risky styles with short production runs. A few days, well-positioned on a retail selling floor, is regarded as an excellent predictor of sales potential.

Technical design needs to be closely integrated with production planning. A short production run for style testing should serve as a test of style specifications, assembly methods, and plant layout. Considerable redundancy may exist between post-adoption product development and production planning under traditional product development systems. A multifunctional product development team may be able to eliminate those redundancies.

▯ Learning Activity 8.4

Joint product development

1. From the perspective of Behavioral Theory of the Apparel Firm (BTAF), what kinds of problems are likely to develop during an effort to do joint product development?
2. Saving what resource provides the primary motivation for engaging in joint product development?
3. In what way is the Target/Mossimo licensing deal (Case 8.2) an example of joint product development?

Negotiating with Vendors

Both manufacturer and retailer merchandisers, whether engaging in acquisition of finished goods or product development, are often responsible for negotiating contracts with their vendors. To be effective, they must understand wholesale price structures and how these interrelate with retail price structures. Retail price structures were discussed in Chapter 5 (Table 5.3). It is reproduced here as Table 8.1 to examine the **wholesale price structure** portion of the pricing relationship. The concepts represented in Table 8.1 are discussed throughout the following section. The numbers in Table 8.1 are rounded to even dollars to simplify presentation. However, when buying thousands of units of merchandise, every penny counts.

Focus first on the retail customer's view of pricing in Table 8.1. Assume a customer at Nordstrom has just bought a pair of pants for the clearance price at $49.50, the original retail at $110. Now focus on manufacturer pricing and the costs that might have been considered by the Nordstrom's buyer/merchandiser when buying the same pants at wholesale.

Table 8.1

Relationships among pricing factors as viewed by manufacturers, retailers, and consumers.

Manufacturer Pricing		Retailer Pricing		Retail Customer's View of Pricing	
		premium price	$110	regular price	$110
list price	$105[1]				
quantity/seasonal discounts	−5%	additional markup	+10%		
reduced list price	$100	first price	$100[5]		
		planned average markdown	−20%	special sale	−27%
		planned average selling price	$ 80	bargain price	$ 80
trade discount	−50%	initial markup	−50%	great sale	−55%
wholesale price	$ 50	planned cost	$ 50	clearance price	$ 49.50[10]
advertising/markdown discounts	−10%	advertising/markdown discounts	−10%		
billed cost	$ 45	billed cost	$ 45		
production cost	−$ 32				
$ gross margin	$ 13	$ gross margin	$ 35[6]		
% gross margin	28.89%[2]	% gross margin	43.75%[7]		
cash discount on billed cost	−8%	cash discount on billed cost	−8%		
reduced billed cost	$ 41.40[3]	reduced billed cost	$ 41.40[3]		
reimbursed shipping expense	+$ 2	shipping expense	+$ 2		
amount received	$ 43.40	amount remitted	$ 43.40		
other expenses	−$ 2	other expenses	+$ 3		
production cost	−$ 32	net cost of goods	$ 46.40		
$ adjusted gross margin	$ 9.40	$ adjusted gross margin	$ 33.60[8]		
% adjusted gross margin	21.66%[4]	% adjusted gross margin	42%[9]		

[1] price changes in wholesale sector are based on list price or reduced list price

[2] [(billed cost − production cost) ÷ billed cost] × 100

[3] billed cost − cash discount

[4] [amount received − (production cost + other expense) ÷ amount received] × 100

[5] all price changes in the retail sector are based on first price

[6] planned average selling price − billed cost

[7] [(planned average selling price − billed cost) ÷ planned average selling price] × 100

[8] planned average selling price − net cost of goods

[9] [(planned average selling price − net cost of goods) ÷ planned average selling price] × 100

[10] regular price − great sale percent

Manufacturer's Wholesale Price and Cost Structures

Market tradition has established and perpetuated a series of discounts in relation to list price that determine how much a retailer pays for apparel at wholesale. The focus is on list price, discounts on list price, shipping terms, and negotiation with vendors.

List Price

List price is the base price for wholesale price structures. It is the **suggested retail price** used in manufacturer/wholesaler catalogs and price sheets. It is also the manufacturer's estimate of the value of the product to the ultimate consumer. List price is useful to retail merchandisers because it allows comparison of the style and quality of the product to the price lines and price points included in merchandise plans.

List price is the suggested retail price because resale price maintenance is illegal in the United States. The Consumer Goods Pricing Act of 1975 terminated the right of manufacturers to control the retail prices of their products. **Resale price maintenance** is also known as vertical price fixing and fair trade. Manufacturers may seek to fix prices to protect the firm's quality image and to prevent retailers from using well-known brand names to draw customers into promotional sales. Resale price maintenance is regarded as anticompetitive and thus it is illegal for manufacturers to require that retailers sell their products at a particular price.

Discounts on List Price

The Robinson-Patman Act, 1936, prohibits manufacturers from discrimination in price to purchasers of products of "like quality" if the effect of such discrimination is to injure competition. This law seeks to prevent large, influential retailers from using their market power to obtain discounts that are not justified by cost savings. In other words, discounts allowed to retail buyers must be justifiable in terms of economies to the manufacturer. Proportional promotional allowances must be available to all customers related to economies of scale. In light of this legal scenario, three types of discounts may be applied to list price to determine a manufacturer's wholesale price: seasonal discount, quantity discount, and trade discount.

A **seasonal discount** is a reduction from list price that relates time of purchase to the stage of the selling period. A manufacturer may offer pre-selling period, late selling period, and end-of-the-selling period discounts. A **pre-selling period discount** may be allowed when the retail merchandiser commits to merchandise well ahead of the traditional buying period. This allows the manufacturer to spread production for a fashion/seasonal line over a longer time period, hence easing production schedules, while still being assured that the merchandise being produced is sold. With flexible production systems, the early selling period discount teamed with early delivery may allow style testing prior to delivery of the most salable merchandise.

The pre-selling period discount may also be offered in combination with a requirement for early payment for the goods. Traditional payment terms frequently allow retailers to pay for merchandise several weeks or even months after the merchandise has been produced and shipped. This means the manufacturer may be paying interest on loans used to purchase materials and cover production expenses for the line over a prolonged period of time, which greatly increases merchandise costs. The pre-selling period discount, then, can provide financially justifiable benefits to both retailer and manufacturer.

A **late-selling period discount** might be used to extend production and the sale of items where the manufacturer had already invested in materials. It can also help clear finished goods still in stock. An **end-of-selling period discount** is used to clear the manufacturer's inventory of finished goods and distressed merchandise at the close of the selling period. Distressed goods owned by the manufacturer might include design samples, sales samples, experimental goods, production test runs, production overruns, second-quality goods, and retailer returns.

A **quantity discount** is used to provide incentive for retail merchandisers to make large or multiple purchases. Large orders usually provide manufacturers with the benefits of economy of scale. Production systems require considerable investment in nonvariable costs such as buildings and utilities, as well as setup costs for producing particular products. Increasing the quantity sold from a given production setup allows distribution of nonvariable costs over more finished goods. The result is lower average production costs for all goods produced. The application of seasonal and quantity discounts results in a **reduced list price,** which becomes the foundation of the trade discount for a particular retail buyer.

Purchases made by the Nordstrom buyer qualified for a 2 percent seasonal discount and a 3 percent quantity discount resulting in a reduced list price as shown in Table 8.1. It is calculated as follows:

$$\text{reduced list price} = \text{list price} - (\text{seasonal discount} + \text{quantity discount})$$
$$\$99.75 = \$105 - (2\% + 3\%)$$

A **trade discount** is a reduction from list price or reduced list price. Sometimes a trade discount is granted to a firm who performs some marketing or distribution function. A trade discount to a wholesaler may be 30 percent at the same time the trade discount to a retailer is 50 percent. The amount of trade discount is proportional to the perceived services to be rendered. A wholesaler may assemble merchandise assortments to offer to small retailers who lack the skill or the resources to travel to markets to develop the assortments on their own. Thus, the service provided to a manufacturer by a wholesaler translates to getting finished goods into the hands of retailers. Wholesalers provide a substitute mechanism for the apparel wholesale market system in which most manufacturers and retailers participate.

The trade discount offered directly to retailers is higher than that for wholesalers because the retailer will sell the goods to the ultimate consumer. Ownership of merchandise must be transferred to the ultimate consumer before the distribution system is complete. Ultimate consumers bear all the manufacturing and distribution costs. Manufacturers sell goods by the group, dozen, pre-pack, or shipping container. Retailers sell goods to consumers, for the most part, one piece at a time, a very expensive process. If retailers did not buy goods at wholesale to sell in their stores, then manufacturers would have to invest in catalogs, electronic shopping, or retail stores to get their goods to ultimate consumers. Some form of retailing is an essential aspect of merchandise distribution.

A trade discount to a retailer tends to be roughly comparable to initial markup in the retail sector. Trade discounts to apparel retailers have traditionally been 50 percent. Now, with retail markups more in the 60 percent range, list prices are proportionally higher, as are trade discounts. Applying the trade discount to list price or reduced list price results in the wholesale price and billed cost reported on an invoice. However, the billed cost is not necessarily what the retailer will pay for the merchandise. The final payment is dependent on invoice payment terms and on discounts and allowances on the wholesale price.

The pants the Nordstrom buyer purchased had a planned trade discount of 50 percent. The wholesale price was calculated as follows:

$$\text{wholesale price} = \text{reduced list price} - \text{trade discount}$$
$$\$50 = \$100 - 50\%$$

Other Discounts and Allowances

A variety of discounts and allowances to reduce the wholesale price may be a part of buyer/vendor negotiations. **Promotional discounts** or allowances may be included to support the retailer's advertising of the style or styles. **Markdown money** is increasingly negotiated into the purchase contract to compensate retailers for markdowns necessary to clear inventory. Markdown money reduces the cost of the merchandise and helps retailers achieve their financial goals. **Stocking or introductory allowances** may be used to persuade retail buyers to stock certain merchandise for the first time.

The Nordstrom buyer negotiated a 10 percent discount on wholesale for a combination of markdown money and advertising. Subtracting discounts and allowances from wholesale price results in billed cost, amount that actually appears on the invoice the retailer receives:

$$billed\ cost\ =\ wholesale\ price\ -\ discounts\ and\ allowances$$
$$\$45\quad =\quad \$50\quad -\quad 10\%$$

Invoice Payment Terms

The purchase negotiation is not over yet. **Invoice payment terms** determine when and how much of the billed cost will be paid by the retailer. Most sales of finished goods to retailers are made on credit and the retailer pays for the goods after they have been received in the retail store, perhaps even after they have been sold to the ultimate consumer. Three common types of invoice payment terms are cash discounts, contract dating, and shipping terms.

A **cash discount** is a reduction in billed cost as incentive to pay the invoice by the time specified by contract dating. Common terms for women's wear are 8 percent cash discount on billed cost payable within 10 days of receipt of invoice, with total billed cost due in 30 days. Cash discounts for men's wear have commonly been 2 percent.

Contract dating determines when a cash discount can be taken and when an invoice is due to be paid. Unauthorized extension of the time period in which cash discounts can be taken is a common source of conflict between retailers and vendors. Vendors frequently complain about retailers waiting 60, 90, or even 120 days before paying bills and then taking discounts anyway. Mass merchandisers commonly now regard standard terms for all products as no less than 60 days and often 90 days instead of the traditional 30. This practice metes particular hardships on small manufacturers who depend on prompt payment of invoices to maintain cash flow.

Invoice due dates may be specified as COD, DOI, ROG, or EOM. **COD (cash on delivery)** means the merchandise must be paid for in full in cash or certified check when delivered or the goods will be returned to the vendor. COD terms are only used when the buyer has a poor credit rating or no credit rating, as might be the case with a new firm. Retailers that are involved in bankruptcy proceedings (for example, Chapter 11) may be required by vendors to pay COD. **DOI (date on invoice)** is regarded as normal or ordinary dating. DOI is assumed when no other terms are stated.

ROG (receipt of goods) dating means the cash discounts and due dates relate to the date the goods are received by the store or distribution center. Receipt of goods dating may be appropriate when goods are being shipped from foreign ports. Because of shipping delays, an invoice may be received well ahead of the merchandise. With DOI dating on foreign-made goods, the bill might have to be paid before the merchandise is received and quantity and quality can be verified.

EOM (end of month) dating means discounts and due dates are calculated from the end of the month when the invoice is dated rather than the invoice date itself. Other forms of dating that might be negotiated include the following: **extra dating,** or extending credit for an additional period; **advanced dating,** or setting the invoice due date at some future time; **anticipation,** or allowing a discount for paying the invoice early; and **loading** to adjust billed cost so the same discount rate will be applied to all invoices. Clearly invoice payment terms can have a profound impact on merchandise costs. See Table 8.2 for examples of invoice payment and shipping terms as they might appear on an invoice.

Shipping Terms

Shipping terms determine who bears the transportation costs and when the buyer takes title/ownership of the merchandise. **FOB (free on board)** origin or factory means ownership is transferred when goods are loaded on a transporting vehicle and the buyer bears the shipping costs. FOB distribution center or FOB store means ownership is transferred when the goods are delivered at their destination and the vendor bears the freight costs. **CIF (cost, insurance, freight)** means the billed cost includes merchandise cost, insurance, and freight. All are due to the vendor according to other contract terms. **FAS (free alongside the ship)** means the vendor will pay for transportation of goods to the dock where the ownership is transferred to buyer. All shipping costs are borne by the buyer.

The Nordstrom pants buyer negotiated a cash discount and contract dating of *8/10, n/60* meaning an 8 percent cash discount could be taken if the invoice was paid within 10 days of receipt; otherwise the invoice could be paid in full in 60 days. The 8 percent cash discount on billed cost reduces the billed cost to $41.40.

$$reduced\ billed\ cost\ =\ billed\ cost\ -\ cash\ discount$$
$$\$41.40\ =\ \$45\ -\ 8\%$$

The shipping terms were *FOB manufacturer's distribution center* meaning the Nordstrom buyer assumed ownership of the pants when they are loaded on the truck at the distribution center and had to reimburse the manufacturer for freight to the store. The shipping expense for the shoes is $2. The retailer sends the manufacturer/vendor a check for $43.40 to pay for the shoes.

Table 8.2

Examples of invoice payment and shipping terms.

COD	No discounts are allowed; merchandise must be paid for in cash or by certified check when delivered.
3/10, n/30, FOB factory	Three-percent discount allowed if bill is paid within 10 days of date on invoice; otherwise n/30 (net 30) means total billed cost is due within 30 days of date on invoice; retailer pays the freight; ownership is transferred when goods are loaded on the truck at the factory.
8/10 EOM, FOB store	Eight-percent discount allowed within 10 days of the end of the month in which the invoice is received (n/30 is implied, meaning 30 days from end of the month); manufacturer pays freight costs and ownership is not transferred until goods reach the store.
6/10 ROG, FAS	Six-percent discount allowed within 10 days of receipt of goods (n/30 days from receipt of goods [ROG] is implied); manufacturer pays for delivery of goods to the dock or airport where ownership is transferred and the remainder of freight costs are borne by the retailer.
2/10, n/60 CIF	Two-percent discount on billed cost if paid within 10 days of date of the invoice; otherwise n/60 (net 60) means total billed cost is due within 60 days from date of the invoice; CIF means ownership is transferred as soon as merchandise is shipped; billed cost includes merchandise cost, insurance, and freight, hence the term CIF.

$$
\begin{array}{ccccc}
\textit{amount remitted} & = & \textit{reduced billed cost} & + & \textit{transportation costs} \\
\$43.40 & = & \$41.40 & + & \$2
\end{array}
$$

Learning Activity 8.5

Manufacturer pricing

1. Why is a retail merchandiser concerned about contract terms?
2. Why is an apparel manufacturer/vendor concerned about contract terms?
3. What contract terms reduce list price?
4. What contract terms reduce merchandise cost?
5. Read Case 8.3 very carefully. What are fundamental negotiation strategies?
6. What skills are required to be a successful negotiator?
7. What kind of experiences do you need in order to be an effective negotiator?

Case 8.3   *Negotiating with your vendors.* *

A wise catalog merchant once advised me that margin is the difference between what I am willing to pay for a product and what my customer is willing to pay; if the margin is not sufficient, I have only myself to blame for paying too much. Too many buyers compromise their judgment and end up overpaying by first looking at the cost of a product, then applying a margin formula and deciding if the customer will pay the resulting retail price.

Instead, you need to first look at a promising product through the eyes of the customer and decide the appropriate retail price. Next you apply your margin formula to the retail price in order to determine an acceptable cost. Only then should you look at the wholesale price to see if it would allow you to meet the goal. If the answer is no, you have two options — walk away or negotiate for an appropriate wholesale price.

Successful Negotiation

Negotiating for price is a fundamental part of the buyer's responsibility. Successful negotiation requires a positive attitude, adequate time or priority, appropriate role definition between the buyer and the purchasing staff, and excellent negotiation skills.

Some buyers find negotiation to be distasteful and an impediment to their relations with suppliers. While this may be true of "confrontational" negotiation, where one party is a loser and the other a winner, it should not be the case when working with merchandise vendors. Negotiation with vendors must be a cooperative process in which both parties search for a win-win solution.

Because the negotiating process requires a full discussion of all issues, you will rarely be successful negotiating at a merchandise show where there are frequent interruptions, little privacy, the need to "keep moving," and, perhaps, only a product rep who is not empowered to modify price or terms on behalf of the vendor. You're better off negotiating, sampling, and ordering in subsequent weeks, even if it means doing so by phone.

The merchant should have primary responsibility for selecting products and negotiating the initial price and terms. Frequently, however, the merchant shares this responsibility with the purchasing staff, which can compromise the process in favor of the vendor.

For one thing, by the time the staff has decided to pursue a purchase, the vendor is likely to perceive a strong commitment to the product and a reduced likelihood that they will "walk away." For another, the staff may know less about the vendor's financial objective and costs than the lead merchant does. Finally, the purchase staff is less likely to have the personal relationship with the vendor that facilitates understanding, trust, and partnership.

The Fundamental Skills

Negotiation has developed into such a sophisticated art form that you should invest in formal training. In the meantime, here are several basic concepts:

- *Be willing to walk away.* Keep in mind that the vendor is almost always more eager to sell than you are to buy and is therefore motivated to seek acceptable terms. You lose this edge if you show any degree of commitment to the product. This is why you need to spell out to the vendor that you both must agree to the price and the terms before you'll even consider the product.
- *Know the product.* Don't assume that the asking price bears any relation to what the product costs the vendor. To properly assess the fairness of the vendor's asking price and her/his flexibility in negotiating, ask about the product's country of origin, manufacturing minimums, lead times, methods of shipment, packaging, quality control, royalties, licenses, and anything else of relevance you can think of.
- *Know the vendor.* Again, to understand avenues for negotiation, learn as much about the vendor as possible, including sales commissions, inventory levels, capitalization, credit line, and whether you would be a big account or a small one.
- *Take your time.* To avoid being hurried into paying a higher price than you can afford, you must allow yourself time for give and take. Aim high. Request a price and terms that are much better than what you realistically expect to achieve. This leaves room for compromise.
- *Remember that money has many forms.* While you may need to ask the vendor to lower the price, it is more likely that you will negotiate around the price through discounts, terms, and related benefits to you or the vendor.

Points of Negotiation

The crux of win-win negotiation is finding combination of terms that has high value to both you and the vendor: You try to give concessions that cost you little but are valuable to the vendor, and vice versa. Here are

(continued)

everal methods many catalogers have used, and several ways to implement each of them. Any one could impact the true cost of the product.

Reduce the vendor's expense in order to justify price reductions or discounts.

- Guarantee a purchase volume so that the vendor can negotiate volume discounts for materials or production.
- Place orders sufficiently early to allow the vendor to produce and ship the goods (particularly from Asia) at the lowest cost.
- Order case packs to save the vendor labor and materials and eliminate fancy retail-display packaging, but be sure the size ratios are appropriate for your customers.
- Accept delivery directly from overseas rather than through the vendor's warehouse.
- Agree not to return damaged or defective product unless such problems exceed an agreed upon percentage.

Finance your vendor in exchange for a discount.

- Pay in less than 30 days to receive a discount — perhaps a 2 percent discount for payment within 10 days.
- Pay prior to shipment.

- Accept early delivery, saving the vendor storage expense and allowing it to borrow against a receivable.

Require the vendor to share the financial risk, protecting your long-term margin.

- Secure the right to return unsold inventory for credit, perhaps paying only a restocking fee.
- Request that the vendor provide "markdown dollars" to reserve your planned margin should you need to sell the product at a reduced price.
- Agree that there will be no price increase on the product for a set period, at least for the life of the catalog, but preferably for the typical life cycle of similar products.

Have the vendor finance your business.

- Receive extended net payment terms; net 30 days may be normal, but 60 days, 90 days, or more is frequently available for the asking.
- Participate in a "dating program" that allows you to pay at the end of the selling season.
- Accept inventory on consignment, eliminating your investing in product and the need to liquidate unsold goods.
- Request the vendor to drop ship your orders, which not only has the benefits

Case 8.3 *(continued)*

of inventory on consignment but can also save on fulfillment costs.

Have the vendor enhance the product value and, in turn, retail price and margin.
- Persuade the vendor to give you a total or catalog exclusive.
- Have the vendor create a private label product with your brand name.
- Work with the vendor to add special features, such as packaging or companion items that can add substantial value at minimal cost.

Reduce your secondary merchandise costs.
- Request that the vendor pay for insurance and freight to your distribution center.
- Ensure that the individual product cartons supplied by the vendor can be used as the shipping cartons, minimizing your pick and pack costs.
- Require the vendor to mark products or include any necessary information such as bar codes, safety warnings, or instructions that will save you expense or increase your efficiency.

Secure advertising support from the vendor.
- Request an advertising allowance of at least 10 percent (the industry norm).
- Ask for an advertising fee based on the size and location of the catalog space given to the product and on the catalog's circulation.
- Request an initial placement fee to offset all or a portion of the catalog photography, copywriting, and film costs associated with the product.
- Ask for support materials such as transparencies to save you photography costs, or printed promotional material that can be mailed or used as package inserts.

As the pressures on the bottom line increase, many catalog executives cut advertising or expenses, rather than address what is their single greatest expenditure, the product they sell. Yet every point of additional margin achieved is a point that goes straight to the bottom line. And it's certainly more pleasant to negotiate your way into an additional point of margin than it is to lay off staff and enforce other reductions in order to cut a point of expenses.

Other Contract Terms

Numerous other contract terms may be negotiated by either the manufacturer or retailer. Manufacturers may specify minimum-order quantities. Assortments may be confined to prepacks prescribed by the manufacturer that contain a set combination of

(continued)

Case 8.3 (continued)

styles, sizes, and colors. Manufacturers may require a minimum of retail display area in terms of number of square feet and may supply special fixtures (for a fee) and point-of-purchase displays. Manufacturers may also provide free or co-op advertising, offers of free goods, and/or "push" or prize money for sales contests for sales associates. Retailers may negotiate markdown allowances for merchandise unsalable at first price, guarantees of refunds on damaged or defective goods, and guarantees of shipping dates or discounts on late shipments.

The manufacturer's wholesale price must cover a great variety of identified costs, as well as only vaguely defined costs associated with the manufacture of goods and the transfer of ownership of the merchandise. Establishing a wholesale price that is at once adequate to cover expenses, produce a profit, and regarded as reasonable by the retail buyer is clearly a challenge.

*Lenser (1996).

Summary

Line development provides the means of filling out a line plan. Common methods of line development for apparel are buying finished goods and engaging in product development. Both manufacturer and retailer merchandisers may buy finished goods to develop a line. Retailers may exclusively purchase finished goods while manufacturers are more likely to supplement the product development process by purchasing finished goods.

Sales representatives provide key linkages between manufacturer and retailer merchandisers. Manufacturer merchandisers train sales representatives on how to sell a line; retailer merchandisers use the knowledge and skills of sales representatives in developing their retail product lines.

Product development evolves in a series of phases. Who is responsible for what depends on the relationships among materials vendors, apparel manufacturers and/or contractors, and retailers involved. Retailers engaged in product development have probably had more effective forecasting processes than manufacturers doing product development. Today, there is a strong trend toward retailers assuming more and more of the product development responsibilities.

Acquisition of materials and finished goods for line development requires merchandisers to negotiate contracts with vendors. Key points in contract negotiations include contract terms and delivery systems.

Key Concepts

advanced dating	joint product development	resale price maintenance
anticipation	knockoff	retail product development
buyer	late-selling period discount	ROG (receipt of goods)
cash discount	line adoption	seasonal discount
CIF (cost, insurance, freight)	line development	shipping terms
COD (cash on delivery)	list price	sourcing
contract dating	loading	stocking or introductory
creative design	markdown money	allowances
DOI (date on invoice)	matrix buying	suggested retail price
EOM (end of month)	pre-selling period discount	technical design
end-of-selling period discount	private label	trade discount
extra dating	promotional discounts	wholesale line preview
FAS (free alongside the ship)	purchase of finished goods	wholesale market
FOB (free on board)	quantity discount	wholesale price structures
invoice payment terms	reduced list price	

◉ Integrated Learning Activity 8.6.1

Use Sourcing Simulator (SS) to test initiating a private label line

Your MAP retailer has decided to test implementing a private label line (sourced abroad) for the product classes you have been using for your analysis. Of course, lower merchandise cost and exclusive merchandise are primary benefits of private brands. Unfortunately, international sourcing results in many increased costs. Your retailer expects inventory carrying costs to be 25 percent, handling to be 10 percent, and shipping per unit costs to double. Program overhead will be 2 percent of planned sales (you will have to calculate it as an input for SS).

Using your best merchandise budget and assortment plan, set up an SS experiment to determine how much lower merchandise cost will have to be to generate more adjusted gross margin than with the merchandise you have been planning. Why is adjusted gross margin a more important measure of profitability than gross margin in this case?

Integrated Learning Activity 8.6.2

Using merchandise planning and line development to satisfy customers

1. Read Case 8.4 carefully. Why is there an apparel sizing problem?
2. Why is the apparel market so slow to adjust to something as fundamental as a disconnect between the sizes of people in their target market and the sizes of merchandise being offered?
3. What is the nature of the problem that prevents merchandisers from offering goods in an adequate range of sizes to satisfy a wide range of customers?

     Case 8.4   *Solving the special-size puzzle**

Throughout the 20th century, Americans got progressively larger and larger. Medical advances, a better diet, and an increasingly sedentary lifestyle all contributed. But by all appearances, that growth has accelerated over the past decade. And it has required businesses, from Southwest Airlines to fashion designers, to react to a rapidly changing market.

While department stores were trying to do a better job of catering to shoppers, a 1996 survey made it clear that it was no time for anyone to be resting on their laurels. The survey, conducted by Kurt Salmon Associates, revealed that both large size and petite shoppers were highly dissatisfied with product availability, fashion/styling, and brand offerings across all retail tiers. A resounding 84 percent of large size customers and 62 percent of petites felt that fashion/styling selection was less in their size than any other. When asked if the choice of brand names is too limited in their size, 70 percent of large size customers and 48 percent of petites agreed.

Mary Duffy, executive director of special sizes for the Ford Modeling Agency and a frequent speaker on apparel retailing for large size women, said the future of the business rests on standardized sizing. "I've grown accustomed to taking my tape measure to determine whether or not they'll fit," says Duffy. "In some cases, the same size varies by a matter of inches," "Fifty-two percent of American women are 5'4" or under, and 37 percent wear size 16 or above," she says. "Yet 95 percent of floor space, man-

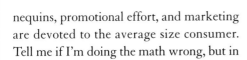

nequins, promotional effort, and marketing are devoted to the average size consumer. Tell me if I'm doing the math wrong, but in my book that doesn't add up."

It wasn't just America's love affair with the double cheeseburger that created this problem. Latinos are now the second largest ethnic group in this country, and they tend to be far smaller in stature than do Caucasians and African Americans. The growing Asian market also tends to be more petite than average. Average sizes, in contrast, are on the decline, leading to a flattening of the demand curve in relation to size. While the Latino ethnic group tends toward petite sizing, the average size is a 14 in many cases.

Plus sizing has become so commonplace that retailers as disparate as Wal-Mart and higher-end specialty retailer J Jill Group have renamed the department to the more generic "women's" and eliminated the term plus size altogether. Changing the nomenclature hardly addresses the issue, however.

"Just because you make a large size dress doesn't mean you satisfy this customer," said Mara Urshel, president of brand development for August Max Woman and Petite Sophisticates. "There are fit, quality, and fabric issues that must be addressed. Because the yield is less when

you're laying patterns in sizes 14 to 24, the price per item jumps dramatically to cover the cost of the fabric." Typically, retailers and manufacturers have traded down in fabric to meet desirable retail prices, but doing so compromises quality. Sizes 14 and 16 are now the average sizes, up from 12 and 14 five years ago. Somewhere between a third and half of American women now wear what historically has been called plus size.

"When a large size shopper walks past misses sportswear and sees a bunch of new looks in pastels, then walks into her department and sees everything looks cheap and cheerful, she gets upset—and rightly so," says Wendy Banks, president of Banks Strategic Marketing and New Business Consultancy. "For years she's been asking for the same looks and the same quality as the misses shoppers, but there are a lot of folks who still haven't listened."

Retailers are now in the position of having to manage yet another expensive variable in the SKU-management nightmare. What used to be fairly simple and straightforward is now a tangle of hundreds of sizes, colors, cuts, and formulations, as new fabrics come online, and women of all sizes seek similar fits and fashions. Vendors are supplying larger, color-coded tags to help customers find the appropriate size and fit.

(continued)

Case 8.4 *(continued)*

What vendors can't supply, however, is more floor space to make room for the ever-expanding selections of styles, sizes, and colors expected by "regular size" and "special size" markets.

*Based on Hisey (2002), Hisey (2003), and Reda (1996).

Recommended Resources

Berner, R. (1997, March 13). Now the hot designers on Seventh Avenue work for Macy's, Sears. *Wall Street Journal,* B1 & B13.

Gaskill, L. R. (1992, Summer). Toward a model of retail product development: A case study analysis. *Clothing and Textiles Research Journal,* 10(4):17–24.

Glock, R. E., & Kunz, G. I. (1997). Angelica's uniform busines (videotape). Ames, IA: Iowa State University Media Resources Center.

Schultz, L. (1997, March 13). How Gap's own design shop keeps its imitators hustling. *Wall Street Journal,* B1 & B13.

Shim, S., & Kotsiopulos, A. (1991, Summer). Information-seeking patterns of retail apparel buyers. *Clothing and Textiles Research Journal,* 10(1):20–30.

References

American Apparel Manufacturers Association Technical Advisory Committee. (1982). *Fashion apparel manufacturing*. Arlington, VA: Author.

Berner, R. (1997, March 13). Now the hot designers on Seventh Avenue work for Macy's, Sears. *Wall Street Journal,* B1 & B13.

Black, S. S. (1995, July). AAMA touts globalization. *Bobbin,* 36(11):22–24.

Bowers, K. (2002, March 6). Target-Mossimo sales generate $700M—and designer copies. *Women's Wear Daily,* 1 & 7.

Gaskill, L. R. (1992, Summer). Toward a model of retail product development: A case study analysis. *Clothing and Textiles Research Journal,* 10(4):17–24.

Giddings, V. L., & Boles, J. F. (1990, Spring). Comparison of anthropometry of black males and white males with implications for pants fit. *Clothing and Textiles Research Journal,* 8(3):25–28.

Glock, R. E., & Kunz, G. I. (2000). *Apparel manufacturing: Sewn product analysis.* Upper Saddle River, NJ: Prentice Hall.

Hisey, P. (2003, March). Is there any such thing as a regular size anymore? *Retail Merchandiser*, 24.

Hisey, P. (2002, March). Not by size alone. *Retail Merchandiser*, 59–60.

Jernigan, M. H., & Easterling, C. R. (1990). *Fashion merchandising and marketing*. New York: Macmillan.

Lenser, J. (1996, June). Negotiating with your vendors. *Catalog Age*, 89–90.

Lloyd, B. (2001, March 7). Saks Incorporated planning private-brand assault. *Daily News Record,* 4–5.

Reda, S. (1996, June). Showering the special-size puzzle. *Stores*, 22–24.

Schultz, L. (1997, March 13). How Gap's own design shop keeps its imitators hustling. *Wall Street Journal,* B1 & B13.

Shim, S., & Kotsiopulos, A. (1991, Summer). Information-seeking patterns of retail apparel buyers. *Clothing and Textiles Research Journal,* 10(1):20–30.

Wickett, J. L. (1995). Apparel retail product development: Model testing and expansion. Master's thesis, Iowa State University.

Zimmerman, A. (2003). To sell goods to Wal-Mart, get on the net. *Wall Street Journal* (www.wsy.com). Accessed January 3, 2004.

9

Presenting
Product Lines

Learning Objectives

- Examine concepts of merchandise presentation.

- Discuss merchandise replenishment and its impact on merchandise presentation.

- Explore multiple delivery strategies in relation to productivity.

The line plan establishes merchandise budgets and assortment plans for a specified time period. Line development through the purchase of finished goods and/or product development determine the actual merchandise, styles, sizes, and colors that will be offered. Line presentation may occur internally within a firm, at wholesale, and/or at retail, depending on the product line and a particular firm's strategies. Merchandise presentation includes processes required to evaluate the line and make it visible and salable.

Concepts of Merchandise Presentation

Merchandise presentation is stereotypically associated with retail merchandise visual display, which may actually be the last commercial presentation of the merchandise. If the goods are purchased from a retail display by the ultimate consumer, the next time the goods are presented may be in the consumer's home or on the consumer's body. The final time the goods are offered for sale may be at the ultimate consumer's yard sale or, if the merchandise is donated to charity, it may be displayed for sale at a thrift store.

Merchandise, however, is presented for evaluation many times before it reaches the retail selling process. The presentations prior to the retail display determine what will be offered by retailers. Taxonomy of Apparel Merchandising Systems (TAMS, Figure 3.1) identifies three components of merchandise presentation: internal, wholesale, and retail. Merchandise presentation is a fundamental part of the merchandising process intended to enhance sales by offering products for consideration in a consciously designed environment that positively affects attitudes and behaviors toward the products and the presenter(s) (Yan, 1996).

Offering Merchandise for Consideration

Offering merchandise for consideration leads to line evaluation. Merchandise lines are evaluated internally by executives in both manufacturing and retailing firms, by retail buyers at wholesale, and by ultimate consumers at retail. Executive reviews are a form of evaluation that is used often in the line planning and development process to assess progress and appropriateness of decisions. Executive reviews of merchandising processes, particularly for line adoption, commonly involve comprehensive presentation of line plans including demand forecasts, line concepts, and creative design. These presentations commonly include persuasive visualization of the line through the use of story boards, videos, live models, and/or runway fashion shows. In addition, persuasive rhetoric by the presenter iterates the line's features in terms of the wants, desires, and needs of the target market, the firm's market positioning, and the actions of its competitors. Merchandise budgets and assortment plans are also summarized and pricing strategies are discussed, including allowable merchandise costs. Estimates of the production costs of new designs are presented, along with quality and performance of materials and assembly methods.

The presentation to sales representatives, often called a line preview, is sometimes the most elaborate internal merchandise presentation for manufacturers. Merchandisers and designers are challenged to persuade sales representatives (reps) to sell the line the way it was conceived and approved by executives. How they communicate assortment plans is particularly important. Purchases of materials and commitments for production capacity often have to be made before purchase orders are received. Since sales representatives frequently plan assortments for retail buyers, the reps have a profound opportunity to influence how much of what gets ordered. The effectiveness of the line preview may determine the success of the wholesale selling period.

Although JCPenney has now centralized most of its buying function, it used to have a very special form of internal line review (Stankevich, 2000). Merchandisers/buyers at the JCPenney headquarters periodically presented lines via CD-ROM to merchandisers at individual JCPenney stores. The goods were usually presented on live models and the merchandisers at headquarters discussed the merits of merchandise groups and each style including retail price and planned percent initial markup. Store merchandisers placed orders based on the relationship between the merchandise presented, their current inventory, and what they saw as local trends, wants, and needs of their local customers. Case 9.1 addresses issues related to retail merchandise presentation.

Case 9.1 *Lifting store sales: Value-added gives a leg up to U.S. hosiery sector. ***

In recent years, the women's sheer hosiery sector has suffered some serious knocks from the casual wear trend, as women cast off their pantyhose and opted for bare legs or trousers, even in the office. According to Mintel Research, sales fell by 39 percent from 1998 to 2002, and Mintel anticipates that hosiery will continue to lose out as a wardrobe basic, declining by around 21 percent through 2007. But if traditional hosiery finds itself out on a limb, novel and niche products are providing fresh opportunities for brands and suppliers.

"New technology and innovations, through machinery or raw materials, is really expanding our industry's capabilities," says Sally Kay, President of America's Hosiery Association. Developments include figure-enhancing body-shaper products, moisturizing or anticellulite pantyhose, footless and Capri styles, low-rise hosiery to be worn under low-rise jeans, thong-toe pantyhose to wear with thong sandals, nonslip soles to wear with mule-style shoes, and products targeting ethnic and fuller-figured women.

Then there's compression hosiery, which helps improve the wearer's circulation, a particularly dynamic market and one that Mintel expects to grow an annual 13 percent by 2007. These added value products command premium prices and fit perfectly in the well-being trend, as hosiery becomes more of a health and lifestyle choice.

With consumers still showing no great inclination to crowd the stores these days, legwear manufacturers feel there are a number of strategies retailers could use to get more out of their legwear business including greater support of best-selling brands, improved customer service, and hosiery outposts. Some acknowledge their ideas are basic, but still useful and often overlooked in the general angst of the current retail clime. Consumers can forget they need socks, and retailers need to remind them, according to the vice president of marketing for Auburn Hosiery Mills,

(continued)

Case 9.1 *(continued)*

which produces licensed Wilson, Coke, and Converse socks.

Part of the big problem is that some retailers do not cross-merchandise. Outposting hosiery in other departments such as sportswear with coordinating apparel increases impulse sales. Wal-Mart does it and it increases volume. When the outpost is simply for display, it is helpful to place small signs indicating where the displayed merchandise can be purchased in the store. It is essential to put new looks front and center as much as possible.

Sometimes hosiery is the most forgotten category, even though it's profitable. Consumers are not likely to purchase anything they have to hunt for. Therefore, retailers should improve merchandising and maintain neatly organized hosiery departments. Many hosiery vendors have [vendor employed] merchandisers in the stores every month, but it's not enough.

Vendors believe retailers should support best-selling brands by allotting more space. Retailers should clean out leftover merchandise from previous seasons to keep current with emerging fashion trends such as sport-influenced looks, according to Karen Bell, president of K. Bell, Culver City, California. The firm provides "must have" silhouettes for sports, juniors, girls/"tweens," and everyday casual legwear.

"This is time for fashion, not for basics. Stores need to be pared down on basics to make a fashion statement," she said. "They can't be afraid to get behind merchandise that's selling by offering it in volume."

The legwear manager for Pennaco Hosiery, a division of Danskin, also pointed out the necessity of maintaining stocks for their core brands. Pennaco has many licensed brands including Givenchy, Evan-Picone, and Ellen Tracy. He further stressed the importance of in-store training through round robins where several vendors teach sales associates about the benefits of each product. Sales training requires increased costs and travel for the manufacturer's representatives, but a trained salesperson sells more products. To create more interest in the category among consumers, stores should offer new products on a regular basis, he said.

Improving customer service is essential to better business. Salespeople need to be friendlier to make shopping more inviting. Shoppers want to know they can find what they need with a good level of service to simplify their shopping. Many retailers also need to improve lighting to make the product look more attractive to consumers.

Newness is key. Many retailers should try new products in a variety of price points. They have to do something creative, whether it's boxed socks or multipacks. To

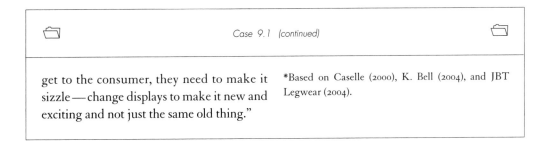

Case 9.1 (continued)

get to the consumer, they need to make it sizzle — change displays to make it new and exciting and not just the same old thing."

*Based on Caselle (2000), K. Bell (2004), and JBT Legwear (2004).

Learning Activity 9.1

Merchandise presentation fundamentals

1. Make a comprehensive list of the recommendations vendors have made to improve hosiery presentation. Identify principles of merchandise presentation reflected in these recommendations.
2. Why are retailers not already carrying out the vendors' recommendations given that they seem to be in the retailer's best interest?
3. Review the vendors' innovations in hosiery design. What is there about the innovations that make "outposting" of hosiery a merchandising essential?
4. According the Roger's theory of diffusion of innovation (introduced in Chapter 2), the innovators of change might be regarded as the vendor's merchandising executives, while the implementers would be retail merchandisers. How might this dual but separated responsibility impact success of innovation in merchandise presentation?
5. Based on your own observations, what suggestions can you make for improving hosiery presentation?

Consciously Designed Environments

Merchandise presentation takes place in environments that are manipulated to provide the desired impression. "The environment is the multisensory setting that surrounds and interacts with the product" (Fiore & Kimle, 1997, pp. 10–11). The aesthetic experience associated with merchandise presentation enhances participants' perceptions of the products by providing pleasure and/or satisfaction. Both utilitarian and aesthetic benefits of products are usually featured. **Utilitarian benefits,** including comfort, protection, quality, social acceptance, status, efficiency, and value, provide social or economic gain (Fiore & Kimle, 1997). Line plans, merchandise budgets, assortment plans, materials specifications, and product specifications provide cognitive assessment of utilitarian benefits.

Aesthetic benefits, including sensual pleasure, beauty, aroused emotion, creative expression, and identity, result in pleasure or satisfaction (Fiore & Kimle, 1997). Of the different forms of line presentation, a fashion show may be the most effective in providing aesthetic benefits because it is a multisensory experience. All the human senses may be stimulated, including visual, tactile, kinesthetic, olfactory, auditory, and gustatory. Aesthetic benefits are magnified by multisensory merchandise presentation (Fiore & Kimle, 1997; Yan, 1996). A complete aesthetic experience can create a positive influence on executives, sales representatives, customers, and sales.

What is commonly called display or visual merchandising in the retail sector is more successful when it is regarded as multisensory merchandising. The senses easily targeted in a retail store are visual, tactile, auditory, and olfactory (sight, touch, sound, and smell). The combination of the sensory and cognitive perceptions defines a customer's image of the store.

Retail chain organizations often control images created by retail display through the use of **planograms.** Planograms are the result of space management technology first developed for grocery stores. Sears was a leader in developing merchandise planning technology for general merchandise that "take the buyer's recommended assortment and customize it right down to the specific store, complete with printed planogram" (Sears Maps, 1990, p. 62). Sears now has two systems: MAPS for general merchandise and SAMS for apparel. Sears markets the planogram software under the name Spaceman. Before Spaceman, Sears did planograms by manually setting up the displays, photographing them, and sending the pictures to each store. The process was time consuming and expensive. Now a computer generates planograms based on the assortments planned for each store. Plans are electronically transmitted to stores, reducing both cost and time. Case 9.2 itemizes some of the other decision-making factors related to consciously designed retail environments.

📁   Case 9.2   *The art of store layout: Enhancing retail presentation**   📁

Did you know over 80 percent of all people move to the right when entering a store?

According to human behavior researchers, this has to do with the orientations of the brain. So, why do so many retailers place low-profit, low turning items or their cash-wrap in this so-called oceanfront real estate area instead of prime merchandise? Mostly it's because so little is understood about retail space layout and how to maximize your investment. Yet, with a basic understanding of predictable customer behavior, you'll gain an edge in any retail climate. Creating the right environment is the best way to help customers really experience the product, the store, and the brand. Creative use of lighting, signage, graphics, and customized displays transforms space into areas that inform, entertain, and reinforces the customer's relationship with the products.

The Control Zone

Your store's entrance area is where you turn customers on enough for them to either come in or turn back to the street. So what does it take? Give 'em some space. Primarily, a customer needs enough room not to feel crowded. Avoid placing merchandise all the way up to your lease line — customers associate this tactic with discounters. Leaving open an area between 60 and 80 square feet is appropriate for a 2,000 square-foot store.

Focus

Here your feature or focal display should be the first thing your customers see. It

should always be trimmed neatly and with some frequency — every week or two.

The Right Direction

Your store's front third is the most critical sales area. If you don't keep the customer's interest here, then you've most likely lost them. The front right wall should contain your expensive and most complete groupings. Keep the psychology of layout in mind here — it is easier to go from high to low prices than the other way around. Most stores tend to place merchandise along the walls with a corresponding aisleway that is parallel. The problem here is that the merchandise is not perpendicular with the customer's line of eyesight. Angle merchandise to the entrance so customers will see and be drawn to key merchandise assortments.

Fixtures

Use of the right fixtures might increase incremental and impulse sales as much as 25 percent. One approach is moving from two-dimensional to three-dimensional presentation. The integration of graphics, lifestyle imagery, and product on updated fixtures plays on all the customer's senses. Fixtures need to be durable and flexible to be frequently adapted to new merchandise.

Service Areas

The most important decision here is where to place your cash-wrap. The center is convenient

(continued)

Case 9.2 (continued)

because of the control it affords the retailer. A centrally placed cash-wrap also helps to promote the desired circular traffic pattern. Otherwise, its location will vary depending upon space size and the number of employees. Dressing rooms should be placed in convenient, but not prime, real estate locations. Back corners or the rear right wall often work best but give easy exit to shoplifters.

Placement of Promotional and Clearance Merchandise

Merchandise featured in advertising should be prominently placed within the department where similar goods are presented. Thus, customers can find the advertised goods as well as examine related options. *Sales associates should be well-informed about what is currently being advertised so they can help customers effectively.* At the beginning of seasonal clearances, sale goods are best presented at the front of the store because most customers have sales on their minds. As clearance progresses and new merchandise is received, clearance can be moved to the rear of the store giving sale customers the opportunity to view new merchandise on the way to the clearance racks.

Must Haves and Resources

Merchandise display and product evaluation are key elements in every store's layout. First capture the customer's attention with creative and stimulating displays; then give them enough room to touch, try on, and evaluate the merchandise. Have you allowed for sufficient movement at this critical time? The effective use of your square footage is indeed a critical area that all retailers need to master. Otherwise, with rents being what they are today, you pay dearly for space not fully utilized.

*Based on Diamond (2000) and Dyches (1996).

 Learning Activity 9.2

Consciously designed environments

1. What utilitarian benefits are derived from following the guidelines provided in Case 9.2?
2. What aesthetic benefits are derived from following the guidelines provided in Case 9.2?

3. Which of the utilitarian and aesthetic benefits will enhance sales?
4. From your observation of retail store layout and displays, what utilitarian benefits are most likely to be neglected? Why?
5. From your observation of retail store layout and displays, what aesthetic benefits are most likely to be neglected? Why?

Sales Enhancement

The fundamental purpose of merchandise presentation is sales enhancement and, thus, contribution to the success of the firm. From the first evaluation of line concept, the purpose is to create a line that will be highly desired by customers. Each additional evaluation has the same goal—to enhance sales. Selecting merchandise desired by customers, of course, is a key component of salability. The risk of selecting unsalable merchandise is reduced by using effective forecasting techniques, market research, and positioning strategies. Acquiring the right amount of merchandise at the right time and replenishing assortments with the right amount of merchandise at the right time are two of merchandise presentation's greatest challenges. Read Case 9.3 for a view of men's wear merchandise presentation.

  Case 9.3 *Fashion first when it comes to space in Midwest**

As real estate costs continue to climb, Midwest men's wear retailers say sales per square foot are only one factor when deciding what goes where on the selling floor. Others that are important to a greater or lesser degree are minimum-square footage levels set by key vendors and the display requirements of different categories. Also important for most stores is being perceived as a "headquarters" store—a place where men can take care of all their wardrobe needs.

In general, fashion merchandise is perceived as a category that requires more space than basic classifications in order to maximize sales. With fashion goods, it is important to show customers a lifestyle setting with the right props, and fixtures, and that takes more space than basics.

Wally Naymon, owner of Kilgore Trout, an upscale specialty store in the Cleveland suburb of Beachwood, said, "With basic merchandise you can do it in several colors and stack it high and it looks

(continued)

---

fine. But fashion merchandise takes more space and also more thought about the location of the space. You want people to know you're in the fashion business."

The demands of vendors are also playing an increasingly important role in determining the amount and location of space. The Big Three sportswear collections—Tommy Hilfiger, Polo, and Nautica—have certain minimum requirements in both areas. Most stores say that, given the financial returns, it's not a problem.

According to the men's senior vice-president of Carson Pirie Scott in Milwaukee, "The Big Three do a great job of putting a lot of units into a fairly small space while still maintaining a fashion presentation. One of their secrets is making the walls work. Overall, it's a great package—you get a good assortment of core merchandise and regular deliveries of fresh goods, and the productivity and margins are there."

Collection sportswear, dress shirts, and neckwear are all picking up more space while clothing (suits and sportcoats) is declining. Better return on investment is being realized with those areas, so when stores are remodeled or new stores built, those are the areas that get more space. While clothing is not picking up space, Naymon said space with the category is shifting. "Opening price is no longer a factor for us. Better clothing is getting more space."

At Hubert White in Minneapolis, owner Bob White said clothing currently leads the store in terms of productivity for several reasons. The key one is that Hubert White is primarily a clothing store. But also important is that clothing is a category that can be merchandised vertically and does not require elaborate displays. "We do a lot with vertical racks with suits, but that's not really possible with sportswear or with furnishings. Both of those require more space. They need to be right in front of the customer."

Outerwear is a category that is productive about three months of the year. It's important to be able to downsize that business during the rest of the year. At Kilgore Trout, Naymon said outerwear is an example of a marginal category that he still has to carry in order to offer a balanced assortment. "My customers drive from heated garage to heated garage and outerwear just isn't that important to them. Fashion outerwear sells, but not much else."

Space for the Big Three has doubled or more in many cases. In the past those lines would have gotten anywhere from 500 to 800 square feet each, but in new and renovated space, they're getting 1,000 to 1,800 square feet and it could increase in the future to as much as 3,000 square feet. However, it is still important to offer customers a full selection. Just because one brand is

Case 9.3 (continued)

performing well doesn't mean you can cut everything else back and just sell that one brand. A store still needs a full presentation on the floor. It is appropriate to first look at increasing capacity before automatically giving more space to top-performing areas. Spinners can be added on counters or four-ways can be replaced with cube units or tables, all of which give you more capacity without changing the basic makeup of the floor.

*Based on Kilgore Trout (2003) and Sharoff (1996).

 Learning Activity 9.3

Retail floor space allocation

1. According to Case 9.3, what are the fundamental principles guiding the allocation of space?
2. What are the productivity measures of space allocation?
3. What is the relationship between space allocation and merchandise presentation?
4. Can these principles of space allocation and productivity measures be applied to other merchandise categories and classifications?

Merchandise Replenishment

Merchandise replenishment systems are key factors in merchandise presentation. They determine what merchandise is available for customers to buy at any particular point in time. Complete assortments prevent stockouts and thus increase sales. **Quick response (QR) replenishment systems** provide competitive advantages and they are a pull-through, instead of the traditional push-through system (Blackburn, 1991; Glock & Kunz, 1995). In the traditional retail environment, there was little opportunity to adjust merchandise assortments offered during a selling period because of lengthy lead times. Retailers ordered and received most merchandise ahead of the selling period (Hunter et al., 1993; Taylor, 1970). Only one or two shipments were delivered during the selling period. For fashion merchandise, it was uncommon for any shipments to be received. If there was remaining inventory not delivered as part of the initial shipment, it was sent in weeks predetermined by merchandise plans. No demand reestimation was employed during the selling period. QR multiple delivery strategies solve this problem by frequently reestimating customer preferences based on up-to-date POS data (Nuttle, King, & Hunter, 1991). Production capability and merchandise offered is adjusted to respond to customer demand based on POS information and style testing (Glock & Kunz, 1995).

Multiple delivery strategies are one means of merchandise replenishment. Multiple delivery strategies employ an initial delivery followed by a series of reorders to accommodate customer needs and preferences and to adjust for merchandise planning errors (Measuring the impact, 1991; Nuttle, King, & Hunter, 1991; Setren, 1993). Replenishing merchandise by reordering best sellers during the selling period may increase the store's profit (Troxell, 1976) and reduce merchandisers' plan errors (King & Poindexter, 1991). Plan errors include assortment error and volume error. **Assortment error** represents differences in distribution of assortment factors (usually style, size, and color for apparel) between planned and actual demand; **volume error** represents a difference between the actual demand volume and the planned volume. Both errors can be reduced by reestimating customer demand after evaluating point of sale (POS) feedback during the first few days of a selling period. Merchandisers may revise the original plan and replenish with merchandise that customers want. Table 9.1 provides a set of terms required for understanding multiple delivery strategies and merchandise replenishment.

Merchandise Replenishment Model

In academic literature, there have been few descriptions of the process of merchandise replenishment. Hughes (1994) indicated that merchandise replenishment is the process of moving stock from suppliers to the retail sales floor. Setren (1993) indicated that the merchandise replenishment process involves purchase order creation, approval, vendor receiving, and shipping, as well as retailer receiving and processing. For purposes of this textbook, merchandise replenishment is defined as the process of planning and placing reorders, as well as handling, shipping, receiving, distributing if necessary, and displaying merchandise. A model of the merchandise replenishment process is presented in Figure 9.1.

Placing the Initial Order

The **initial order** may be based on basic stock, model stock, or automated stock plans depending of the type of merchandise being planned and the technology available. The quantity of the initial order should be sufficient to meet sales until a reorder can be placed

Table 9.1

Terms for multiple delivery strategies and merchandise replenishment.

assortment error—difference in distribution of assortment factors between planned and actual demand.

average inventory—the average number of units in stock during the selling period.

demand reestimation—recalculation of sales forecasts and merchandise plans based on POS data.

frequency of additional deliveries (FAD)—the number of additional deliveries in a selling period.

gross margin return on inventory (GMROI)—the financial ratio that shows the relationship between the gross margin in dollars and the average inventory investment.

initial order—a request to receive merchandise not previously stocked.

lead time—the time between placing the initial order or reorder(s) and receiving the merchandise on the retail sales floor.

merchandise replenishment—the process of planning and placing reorders, as well as handling, shipping, receiving, distributing if necessary, and displaying merchandise.

multiple delivery—using more than one shipment of a given merchandise assortment based on an initial order and reorder(s).

order—a request to receive merchandise.

performance measures—the indicators that help a firm judge the efficiency and effectiveness of their strategies.

quick response (QR) merchandise replenishment—a customer-driven process of planning and placing reorders, as well as handling, shipping, receiving, distributing if necessary, and displaying merchandise with the shortest possible lead time.

reorder—a request to replenish merchandise previously stocked.

single delivery—shipment of 100 percent of a given merchandise assortment based on an initial order.

stock turnover—the number of times the average inventory is sold within a given period of time.

stockout—the particular SKU desired by the customer is not immediately available (Kunz & Song, 1996).

volume error—difference between the quantity planned and actual sales.

volume per SKU for the initial delivery (VSID)—the number of units allocated on the average for each SKU in the initial delivery.

and received (Taylor, 1970) if additional merchandise is desired. Retailers may place small initial orders for a variety of merchandise to observe customer reactions. Preferred products can then be reordered in larger quantities to reduce plan errors.

Initial delivery refers to part or all of the initial order shipped to an individual store at the beginning of the selling period. Traditionally, initial delivery has been determined as a percentage of total inventory (Nuttle, King & Hunter, 1991). The initial delivery usually consisted of the styles and/or sizes and colors that the manufacturer put into production first, thus, it was unlikely to represent the total assortment. Under QR systems, the initial

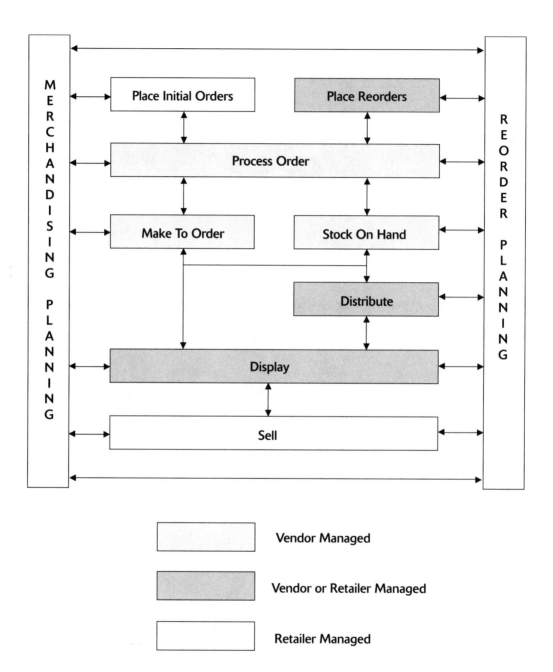

Figure 9.1   A model of merchandise replenishment process (Lin, 1996, p. 18).

delivery needs to include at least one unit of each SKU so that it can be reordered by an automated system. Since re-estimation of demand is based on POS data, each SKU has to be present in the assortment so a customer has the opportunity to buy it. A SKU has to be sold to become part of POS data so a reorder can be placed.

Reorder Planning

Reorder planning is as important as original merchandise planning (Allen, 1982, August). This happens when an initial order is placed and part or all of the initial order is sold. Its objectives involve correcting errors between merchandise plans and actual customer demand (Nuttle, King & Hunter, 1991; Troxell, 1976), as well as keeping complete assortments during the selling period and minimizing residual inventory at the end of the selling period. These objectives are accomplished by regularly monitoring inventory positions; carefully comparing actual sales against merchandise plans; identifying best-selling styles, colors, and sizes (Taylor, 1970); accurately re-estimating customer demand; and incorporating these re-estimations into reorders (Nuttle, King, & Hunter, 1991; Troxell, 1976).

Many factors affect reorder planning, including:

- The length of the selling period limits the number of reorders (Hunter, 1990). Merchandise with short selling periods is usually more difficult to plan.

- Merchandise with considerable fluctuation in the rate of sale during a selling period needs more time and effort to plan (Troxell, 1976). The rate of sale is determined by analyzing past sales performance and predicting new trends (Allen, 1982, September).

- The frequency of updating information affects the ease and accuracy in analyzing customer preferences and determining the quantities of reorders (Allen, 1982, September). Daily updates of purchase orders, sales records, merchandise transfers, returns from customers, returns to vendors, order cancellations, and price changes are necessary for re-estimating customer demand and adjusting merchandise plans.

- Lead time for delivery of merchandise depends on the geographic location of vendors, the overall demand of the specified item among competing retailers, and the vendor's perception of the importance of the retailer among the vendor's customers (Bhat, 1985). Lengthy lead time forces retailers to reorder merchandise when a full inventory still exists (Berman & Evans, 1995).

- The firm's expected customer service level determines the quantity of safety stock (Bohlinger, 1977). **Safety stock** is the amount of merchandise required to be on hand to prevent stockouts until the reorder can be received. Maintaining safety stock may overcome uncertainty in demand and/or supply of merchandise (Lewison, 1991).

- Large purchases may have quantity discounts and thus reduce per-unit costs. Smaller orders may increase the cost per unit, but reduce inventory carrying costs (Berman & Evans, 1995).

Placing the Reorder

Reorders can be created by retailers or suppliers. Reorders generated by suppliers may be prepared and shipped with or without retail merchandiser review and modifications (Buzzell & Ortmeyer, 1995; Gray, 1993). Traditionally, most reorders are created by retailers (Setren, 1993).

Reorders are preferably placed only after actual sales have given sufficient indication of the quantity customers are likely to buy (Taylor, 1970). Reorders are usually placed with current suppliers for previously purchased goods under terms and conditions specified by the initial order (Allen, 1982, September; Lewison, 1991). Reorders can be placed via mail, telephone, electronic transmission, or computer-to-computer transmission (Lambert & Stock, 1993).

Order Processing

Order processing includes entering the order, checking the customer's credit, assembling, packing, invoicing, and arranging to ship (Buzzell & Ortmeyer, 1995; Lambert & Stock, 1993). Suppliers are responsible for this process.

Make-to-Order/Stock on hand

Purchase orders may be assembled from stock on hand or by production if not currently in inventory (Lambert & Stock, 1993). Producing products after receiving the purchase orders is sometimes called **make-to-order.** From the manufacturers' perspectives, the goal of make-to-order is to have zero inventory at both the beginning and end of the selling period. Traditionally, basic and staple goods are assembled from **stock on hand** (Taylor, 1970); fashion and seasonal goods are often make to order (Glock & Kunz, 1995).

Distribution

Distribution is the process of receiving, sorting, storing, allocating, picking, and shipping merchandise. Receiving may take place in the individual store or distribution centers or both. Receiving consists of checking and marking merchandise. The checking activities involve comparing the supplier's invoice and a shipment's physical contents against the original purchase order, inspecting the incoming shipment for defects, and recording any disagreement (Buzzell & Ortmeyer, 1995).

Marking is the process of affixing or tagging the individual items with a price and other identifying information for stocking, controlling, and selling (Lewison, 1991). Merchandise is now often shipped floor ready, with the appropriate hangers in place and tickets attached by the vendor. This saves time in the distribution center and/or the retail store.

The methods for receiving merchandise include direct store delivery, distribution center delivery, and cross-docking (Lewison, 1994). Direct store delivery means that merchandise is received directly in the individual stores. This is the quickest way to move merchandise to individual stores, since merchandise is never stored in a distribution center (Gray, 1993). Distribution center delivery means that merchandise is first received in distribution centers and then shipped to individual stores after it is sorted and allocated. The time merchandise is stored in distribution centers depends on distribution plans and real sales data. Receiving merchandise at a distribution center permits retailers to adjust the allocation of merchandise based on sales during the time between preparing an order and its receipt (Buzzell & Ortmeyer, 1995). **Cross-docking** means that "merchandise is received, sorted, and routed directly from receiving to shipping without spending any time in storage" (Lewison, 1994, p. G-4). The distribution center becomes a sorting area instead of a holding area (Lalonde, 1994).

Displaying

Displaying is the process of making merchandise available for purchase by the customer. Displaying takes place in the individual store and involves moving merchandise to the sales floor for presentation, or to the stock rooms for storage. For reordered merchandise, merchandisers may use the same sales displays designed for original orders.

Selling

Selling is the process of changing ownership of merchandise from the retailer to the ultimate customer. POS data provide information for merchandisers to identify the characteristics of fast sellers, to invest more money on up-trending categories, to manage down-trending categories to minimize markdowns (Setren, 1993), and to make decisions on reorders and new product introductions (Kunz & Rupe, 1995).

The model (see Figure 9.1) delineates the merchandise replenishment process, interactions among elements and possible interactions among retailers and suppliers. It shows that all the elements of the merchandise replenishment process are interdependent. Any change or result in one element impacts the others. Merchandise planning and reorder planning play dominant roles in merchandise replenishment. Those making those plans receive information from both inside and outside the model, coordinate information into the respective reorder plans, and provide guidelines for ongoing interaction. See Case 9.4 for a different perspective on managing sales and reorders.

---

     *Case 9.4   Nike's LeBron James sneaker makes
rapid strides in sales. **

Nike Inc., the world's No. 1 athletic shoe maker, said its sneaker designed for professional basketball player LeBron James was the biggest selling new footwear in at least two years. Customers stood in waiting lines outside stores waiting for the "Midnight Madness" opening of the Nike's Air Zoom Generation of shoes featuring the LeBron James style.

Retailers sold about 33 percent of the $110 Air Zoom Generation shoes the first day of sales. The Beaverton, Oregon-based company has considered other releases successful if 25 percent of the stock sells by the end of the first week. The shoes, designed for the top pick in 2003 National Basketball Association draft, gave Nike sales a boost for the quarter. Sales in the athletic shoes segment rose for the first time in 5 quarters in the period ending Nov. 30, 2003.

Nike signed the 18-year-old James, who plays for the Cleveland Cavaliers, in May 2003 to the richest endorsement contract ever for a rookie — reportedly more than $90 million. Nike outbid its chief competitors, Reebok and Adidas, for James' endorsement. Nike declined to reveal how many pairs of the black-red-and-white-combination shoes Nike introduced. The company released a new color combination in February 2004.

At the time of the release James was averaging a team-leading 18.1 points a game. His jersey has been the top seller of the season at NBA's New York store and Web site.

*Bloomberg News (2003).

 Learning Activity 9.4

Merchandise presentation at Nike

1. Think through the component parts of the process of presenting the LeBron James shoes in retail stores across the country at midnight based on the model in Figure 9.1. Focus on the components that were vendor managed vs. retailer managed.

Which firm would have been the primary player in this case, vendor or retailer? Why?

2. If Nike and its retailers planned to sell 25 percent of the total stock for the selling period at the end of the first week but sold 33 percent, how much of the stock for planned sales for the selling period do you think they had on hand when the doors opened at midnight? Why?

3. The model in Figure 9.1 looks pretty blasé in relation to the dramatic marketing event associated with the LeBron James shoe. Does the model need to be modified to reflect this type of product presentation? If so, how?

Merchandise Replenishment in Relation to BTAF

The merchandise replenishment model is based on the following assumptions of Behavioral Theory of the Apparel Firm (BTAF) discussed in Chapter 2. According to BTAF, an apparel firm consists of six constituencies: quick response, merchandising, operations, marketing, finance, and executive management. Satisfying target customer desires and needs within the limitations of the firm is the central focus of decision making among the six constituencies. Both merchandising and operations constituencies take major responsibilities for replenishing merchandise to satisfy customer demand, all while considering the firm's limitations. Merchandisers plan, develop, and present product lines to satisfy customer demand. Operations personnel manage human resources, physical facilities, equipment, and inventories to maximize the efficiency and profitability of operations.

The dark box in Figure 9.2 indicates the relationship between the model of the merchandise replenishment process and BTAF. The box overlaps the merchandising and operations constituencies because they cooperate both with each other and with external coalitions regarding merchandise replenishment. The box overlaps the target market because POS data are the source of information for predicting future demand and determining the SKUs and quantities to reorder. Only part of the box overlaps the QR constituency because not all firms use the QR concepts to replenish merchandise or may not use them for all merchandise. Some firms may still use traditional methods. The model provides a framework for developing and testing research questions related to merchandise replenishment and developing merchandise replenishment technology.

Merchandise Replenishment Technology

In QR, time is regarded as a firm's primary competitive resource (Blackburn, 1991). Shortening the cycle time of the entire soft-goods production and distribution process helps

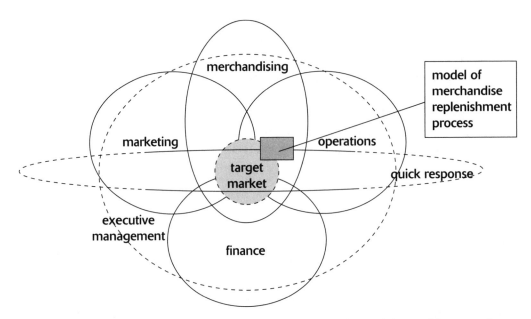

Figure 9.2 The merchandise replenishment process in relation to Behavioral Theory of the Apparel Firm (BTAF) (Lin, 1996, p. 51).

textile, apparel, and retail firms to acquire competitive advantages. Quick decisions made closer to the time of sale in response to actual customer demand can be more accurate and, consequently, more profitable (Blackburn, 1991; Hunter, 1990).

The process of converting raw materials into apparel includes both a product flow from the suppliers to the retailers and an information flow from the retailers to the suppliers (Blackburn, 1991) (see Figure 9.3). Product flows forward from textile producers to customers in value-added processes. Information flows backward from customers to apparel and textile manufacturers by using electronic data interchange (EDI) (Blackburn, 1991).

Conventional approaches to shorten the cycle time of the entire apparel chain from fiber production to the retail sales floor emphasize *speeding product flows* through the pipeline. QR strategies pay attention to speeding not only product flows, but also information flows (Blackburn, 1991; Quick response technologies, 1991). The methods used to speed both flows include changing operating procedures, using technology, and developing cooperative partnerships (Blackburn, 1991; Hammond, 1993).

In terms of changing operating procedures, Buzzell and Ortmeyer (1995) identified four key issues: 1) using information technology to automate manual activities; 2) eliminating

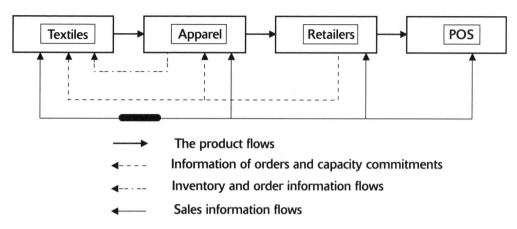

Figure 9.3 Product and information flows in the apparel chain (Blackburn, 1991).

redundancies in operating procedures; 3) reassigning tasks for maximum apparel chain efficiency; and 4) reducing or eliminating control steps in operating procedures.

The benefits of using technology include improving the response time of transmitting customer preferences back to all members of the apparel chain (Blackburn, 1991; EDI and quick response, 1991); reducing the amount of paper work and data entry for both vendors and retailers; improving the efficiency of creating, communicating, and tracking purchase orders (Gilman, 1989; Measuring the impact, 1991); and increasing the efficiency and effectiveness of merchandising, producing, and distributing (Buzzell & Ortmeyer, 1995; Hammond, 1993).

EDI, Internet, bar coding, and scanning are the most common QR technologies used to support time-based competition. EDI (electronic data interchange) is computer-to-computer communication that exchanges business information directly between vendors and customers in a standard electronic format without any human intervention (Baker, 1991; Quick response technologies, 1991). The information exchanged by computers may include product catalogs, product planning schedules, sales, purchase orders, advance ship notices, invoices, functional acknowledgment, and capacity commitments (Blackburn, 1991; Gordon, 1993; Gray, 1993; Quick response technologies, 1991). Internet exchange of information is also computer-to-computer, provides the opportunity for continuous flow of data as opposed to intermittent flow with EDI, and is less expensive. EDI and the Internet have now been united to take advantage of apparel firms' investments in EDI as well as the speed of the Internet.

Bar coding, used in conjunction with scanning devices, facilitates merchandise tracking and inventory control at the SKU level by automatically capturing all relevant information for each product. (Hammond, 1993; Gilman, 1989, Measuring the impact, 1991). Universal product code (UPC) and shipping container marking (SCM) are the two important bar coding systems for retail firms. UPC is the dominant bar coding system used at POS (Hammond, 1993, Quick response technologies, 1991). This is a 12-digit merchandise code that includes a 5-digit vendor number, a 5-digit merchandise number, and leading and trailing digits. This code is scanned and translated by an optical scanning device at POS when a customer makes a purchase (Hammond, 1993). POS information helps firms analyze customer preferences, forecast sales trends, make future decisions on reorders and new product introductions, manage inventory, and speed customer flow at checkout (Rupe & Kunz, 1998).

SCM increases the speed and accuracy of merchandise distribution processes (Hammond, 1993). SCM supplied by the manufacturer provides information on vendors, orders, destinations, and carton numbers for each shipping carton. This information allows containers to be received, verified, and sent to the sales floor without being opened (Hammond, 1993; Quick response technologies, 1991). By pre-ticketing merchandise with UPC and cartons with SCM, retailers may reduce the labor force handling merchandise and accelerate the flow of merchandise through the distribution center (Gilman, 1989). With the use of SCM, shipments may flow constantly and consistently and merchandise may be restocked directly from the manufacturer to the sales floor (Setren, 1993). Radio frequency identification (RFID), a wireless form of merchandise identification, will soon replace manual scanning methods.

Multiple Delivery Strategies in Relation to Merchandise Planning

Merchandise planning and appropriate delivery strategies are major tools for achieving balanced assortments to satisfy customer needs and desires. Previous research (Hunter, King, & Nuttle, 1991; Nuttle, King, & Hunter, 1991) indicated that frequently re-estimating customer demand and replenishing merchandise is one way to increase stock turnover and reduce stockouts. Lin (1996) identified two performance measures and quantitative guidelines for developing delivery strategies in fashion and seasonal goods with two different selling periods. Tables 9.2 and 9.3 provide examples of how multiple deliveries might be timed for 10- and 20-week selling periods. The last delivery in the 10-week selling period is

Table 9.2

Examples of timing additional deliveries for a 10-week selling period. *

Frequency of additional deliveries	Weeks in the selling period					
	2	3	4	5	6	7
1			X			
2		X				X
3	X		X			X
4	X	X		X		X
5	X	X	X	X		X
6	X	X	X	X	X	X

*Lin (1996).

in week 7; and the last delivery in the 20-week week selling period is in week 14. Assuming the merchandise plan includes zero-to-zero inventory, ending deliveries in weeks 7 and 14 allows time to sell as much of the remaining inventory as possible before the merchandise is replaced with fresh goods.

Table 9.3

Examples of timing additional deliveries for a 20-week selling period. *

Frequency of additional deliveries	Weeks in the selling period												
	2	3	4	5	6	7	8	9	10	11	12	13	14
1						X							
2						X							X
3			X					X					X
4		X			X				X				X
5	X			X			X			X			X
6	X		X		X		X			X			X
7	X		X		X		X		X		X		X
8	X	X	X		X		X		X		X		X
9	X	X	X	X	X		X		X		X		X
10	X	X	X	X	X	X	X		X		X		X
11	X	X	X	X	X	X	X	X	X		X		X
12	X	X	X	X	X	X	X	X	X	X	X		X
13	X	X	X	X	X	X	X	X	X	X	X	X	X

*Lin (1996).

Measures of Performance in Relation to Multiple Delivery Strategies

Lin (1996) evaluated the performance of multiple delivery strategies in relation to volume per stock keeping unit for an assortment (VSA). He introduced the concept of **volume per SKU for initial delivery (VSID)** as a companion concept with VSA. He generated data using the apparel retail model (ARM) computer simulation (now known as Sourcing Simulator) and examined performance for two selling periods, 10 weeks and 20 weeks. Lin used Anova and least significant difference (LSD) multiple comparisons (two statistical techniques) to identify two performance factors based on nine performance measures generated by ARM for both selling periods. The performance factors and their respective performance measures are defined in Table 9.4.

The first factor was labeled *revenue and service (RS)*. The measures in the RS factor were influenced primarily by reduced percent total stockouts. Reduced stockouts led to decreased percent lost sales and increased gross margin and total revenue because more customers got merchandise they wanted. Revenues increased because of improved in-stock position. Based on RS measures, the fewer the stockouts, the higher the revenues.

The second factor developed by Lin (1996) is composed of five measures: percent jobbed off, percent gross margin, percent adjusted gross margin, **gross margin return on inventory**

Table 9.4

Definitions of performance measures. *

---

1. Revenue and Service (RS)

Percent total stockouts	=	the amount of total stockouts divided by total inventory.
Percent lost sales	=	the amount of total lost sales divided by total inventory.
Gross margin	=	total revenue (or net sales) minus total cost of goods.
Total revenue	=	sales revenue plus job off revenue.

2. Inventory and Profitability (IP)

Average inventory	=	the average number of units in stock within a specified selling period.
Percent jobbed off	=	residual inventory at the end of the selling period divided by total inventory.
Percent gross margin	=	total revenue minus total cost of goods divided by total revenue.
Percent adjusted gross margin	=	gross margin minus distribution and inventory carrying costs divided by total revenue.
Gross margin return on inventory	=	gross margin dollars divided by the average dollar investment in inventory.

*Lin (1996).

(GMROI), and average inventory. This factor was called *inventory and profitability (IP)*. The components of the IP factor reflected reduced average inventory, resulting in decreased percent jobbed off as well as increased percent gross margin, percent adjusted gross margin, and GMROI because less merchandise was stocked on the average while the same merchandise or more was sold during the selling period. Reduced average inventory was the major reason for the improved performance in IP.

In order to understand the influence of considering both factors at the same time for different strategy combinations, Lin created a third performance measure named *overall performance (OP)*. The scores of OP for selected strategy combinations were determined by totaling the scores of RS and IP since both factors had a similar percentage of variances. The results indicated that when RS and IP factors were considered together, multiple delivery strategies were useful only for the 20-week selling period. For a selling period of 10 weeks or less, multiple delivery strategies did not improve OP.

The Value of Product Velocity

Product velocity is the speed with which a product passes through the industry matrix. The measure of product velocity is average inventory during a selling period. Gilreath, Reeve, and Whalen Jr. (1995, March) explained the product velocity advantage, focusing on GMROI as the measure of productivity. Their example compared Hare (the QR company) and Tortoise (the traditional company). Table 9.5 itemizes their logic.

The scenario begins with a comparison of Tortoise and Hare where the two firms have generated identical total revenue (TR), merchandise cost (MC), gross margin (GM), and percent gross margin (%GM). Tortoise has an average inventory (AI) of $240,000. At the same time, Hare, through use of QR business systems that include smaller initial deliveries and more frequent smaller shipments for merchandise replenishment, has an average inventory of $100,000. Consequently, Tortoise's inventory turnover is 2.5, meaning the average quantity of stock on hand during the selling period was sold two and a half times. Hare, with a much lower average inventory, has inventory turnover of 6.0.

inventory turnover	=	*merchandise cost*	÷	*average inventory*
(Tortoise) 2.5	=	$600,000	÷	$240,000
(Hare) 6	=	$600,000	÷	$100,000

In this scenario, Tortoise has GMROI (gross margin ÷ average inventory) of 167 percent. Gross margin was 167 percent of average inventory for Tortoise. At the same time,

Table 9.5

Time is money, the concept of product velocity. *

	Tortoise	Hare	Formula
Total revenue (TR)	$1,000,000	$1,000,000	
Merchandise cost (MC)	$600,000	$600,000	
Gross margin (GM)	$400,000	$400,000	TR-MC
Percent gross margin (%GM)	40%	40%	(GM/TR) × 100
Average inventory (AI)	$240,000	$100,000	
Inventory turns	2.5	6.0	MC/AI
Gross margin return on inventory (GMROI %)	167%	400%	(GM/AI) × 100
Inventory carrying costs (ICC)	$48,000	$20,000	AI × 20%
Profit	$50,000	$50,000	(5% × TR)
Potential profit		$78,000	(P + ICC savings)

*Based on Gilreath, Reeve, & Whalen Jr. (1995).

Hare had GMROI of 400 percent. The realized gross margin was four times as great as average inventory investment.

$$\text{gross margin return on inventory} = (\text{gross margin} \div \text{average inventory}) - 100$$
$$\text{(Tortoise)} \quad 167\% = (\$400,000 \div \$240,000) - 100$$
$$\text{(Hare)} \quad 400\% = (\$400,000 \div \$100,000) - 100$$

Level of average inventory is a primary determinant of inventory carrying costs, including interest, storage, and insurance. Tortoise has carrying costs of $48,000, while Hare has carrying costs of $20,000. In this example, carrying costs are 20 percent of average inventory. Since Hare has much lower average inventory, carrying costs are also much less.

$$\text{inventory carrying costs} = \text{average inventory} \times 20\%$$
$$\text{(Tortoise)} \ \$48,000 = \$240,000 \times 20\%$$
$$\text{(Hare)} \ \$20,000 = \$100,000 \times 20\%$$

Savings in carrying costs translate directly to the bottom line. If the profit generated is five percent of total revenue given merchandise cost and gross margin, then potential profit with QR is profit plus inventory carrying cost savings. Inventory carrying cost savings is the reduction in ICC related to the reduction in average inventory. Potential profit is profit plus ICC savings.

$$
\begin{array}{llll}
\textit{profit} & = & \textit{total revenue} & \times & 5\% \\
\$50,000 & = & \$1,000,000 & \times & 5\%
\end{array}
$$

$$
\begin{array}{lllll}
\textit{potential profit} & = & \textit{profit} & + & \textit{inventory carrying cost savings} \\
\text{(Tortoise) } \$50,000 & = & \$50,000 & + & (\$48,000 - \$48,000) \\
\text{(Hare) } \$78,000 & = & \$50,000 & + & (\$48,000 - \$20,000)
\end{array}
$$

Thus Hare experiences a 56 percent increase in potential profits ($78,000 − $50,000 ÷ $50,000) based solely on savings in inventory carrying costs because of lower average inventory using QR systems.

Product Velocity at Mike's Bikes

Assuming Mike's Bikes achieves planned sales according to the merchandise budget in Table 6.14, the Tortoise and Hare product velocity concepts can be applied to solid color cycling shorts. The results are summarized in Table 9.6. The scenario begins with a comparison of traditional (Trad) and quick response (QR) business systems where the two scenarios

Table 9.6

Product velocity at Mike's Bikes.

	Traditional	QR	Formula
Total revenue (TR)	$157,500	$157,500	planned sales in Table 6.4
Merchandise cost (MC)	$72,450	$72,450	planned merchandise to receive − initial markup
Gross margin (GM)	$85,129	$85,129	TR-MC
Percent gross margin (%GM)	47%	47%	(GM÷TR) ×100
Average inventory (AI)	$29,634	$11,834	
Inventory turns	2.6	6.1	MC÷AI
Gross margin return on inventory (GMROI %)	287%	719%	(GM÷AI) ×100
Inventory carrying costs (ICC)	$5,927	$2,367	AI × 20%
Profit (P)	$4,725	$4,725	profit = (3% × TR)
Potential profit with QR		$8,285	PP = P + ICC savings

have generated identical total revenue (TR), merchandise cost (MC), gross margin (GM), and percent gross margin (%GM). As indicated in Table 6.14 for solid color cycling shorts with inventories calculated using the inventory to sales ratio method, Mike's Bikes' traditional business system has an average inventory (AI) of $29,634. Average inventory for the traditional business system was determined as follows:

$$
\begin{aligned}
\textit{average inventory} \quad &= \quad \textit{(FOM inventory for each month + EOM inventory for the last month)} \\
&\div \textit{(number of months in the selling period + one month)} \\
\$29{,}634 \quad &= \quad (\$375{,}795 \; + \; \$9{,}450) \; \div \; 13
\end{aligned}
$$

Through the use of QR, including smaller initial deliveries and more frequent, smaller shipments for merchandise replenishment, research has shown the Mike's Bikes might achieve an average inventory that is 40 percent of average inventory with the traditional system, thus, $11,834. According to the merchandise budget, planned merchandise received is $181,125 with an initial markup of 60 percent. Consequently, merchandise cost is $72,450 (planned merchandise to receive − initial markup).

Under the traditional system, inventory turnover is 2.5 (merchandise cost ÷ average inventory), meaning the average quantity of stock on hand during the selling period was sold not quite two and one-half times. QR, with a lower average inventory, has an inventory turnover of 6.1.

$$
\begin{aligned}
\textit{merchandise cost} \quad &= \quad \textit{planned merchandise received} \quad - \quad \textit{initial markup} \\
\$72{,}450 \quad &= \quad \$181{,}125 \qquad\qquad - \qquad 60\%
\end{aligned}
$$

$$
\begin{aligned}
\textit{inventory turnover} \quad &= \quad \textit{merchandise cost} \quad \div \quad \textit{average inventory} \\
\text{(Trad) } 2.5 \quad &= \quad \$72{,}450 \qquad\quad \div \qquad \$29{,}634 \\
\text{(QR) } 6.1 \quad &= \quad \$72{,}450 \qquad\quad \div \qquad \$11{,}834
\end{aligned}
$$

Traditional has GMROI (gross margin ÷ average inventory) of 143 percent. At the same time, QR had GMROI of 230 percent. The realized gross margin with QR is two and one-half times as great as average inventory investment.

$$
\begin{aligned}
\textit{gross margin return on inventory} \quad &= \quad \textit{(gross margin} \; \div \; \textit{average inventory)} \; \times \; 100 \\
\text{(Traditional) } 287\% \quad &= \quad (\$85{,}129 \quad \div \quad \$29{,}634) \quad \times \; 100 \\
\text{(QR) } 719\% \quad &= \quad (\$85{,}129 \quad \div \quad \$11{,}834) \quad \times \; 100
\end{aligned}
$$

As with the Tortoise and Hare example, the level of average inventory is a primary determinant of inventory carrying costs. Using the assumption that carrying costs are 20 percent of average inventory, Traditional has carrying costs of \$11,270, while QR has carrying costs of \$7,000. Since QR has lower average inventory, carrying costs for QR are less than Traditional.

$$
\begin{array}{rcl}
\textit{carrying costs} & = & \textit{average inventory} \times 20\% \\
\textit{(Traditional)} \ \$5{,}927 & = & \$29{,}634 \times 20\% \\
\textit{(QR)} \ \$2{,}367 & = & \$11{,}834 \times 20\%
\end{array}
$$

As indicated in the income statement (Table 3.4), profit generated at Mike's Bikes is three percent of total revenue. Planned sales (total revenue for SCS) according to Table 6.14 is \$157,500. Potential profit with QR is profit plus savings in inventory carrying cost.

$$
\begin{array}{rcl}
\textit{profit} & = & \textit{total revenue} \times \% \textit{ profit} \\
\$4{,}725 & = & \$157{,}500 \times 3\%
\end{array}
$$

$$
\begin{array}{rcl}
\textit{savings in inventory carrying costs} & = & \textit{Traditional carrying costs} - \textit{QR carrying costs} \\
\$3{,}560 & = & \$5{,}927 - \$2{,}367
\end{array}
$$

$$
\begin{array}{rcl}
\textit{potential profit with QR} & = & \textit{profit} + \textit{savings in inventory carrying cost} \\
\$8{,}285 & = & \$4{,}725 + \$3{,}560
\end{array}
$$

Thus QR experiences a 75.3 percent increase in potential profits ((QR potential profit − Traditional profit) ÷ Traditional profit × 100).

The Tortoise and the Hare scenario was developed to demonstrate the benefits of lower average inventory increasing stock turnover thus reducing handling cost and improving adjusted gross margin and sequentially, profit. The reality is that QR systems commonly improve sales and gross margin as well as adjusted gross margin and profit. Sales increase because QR delivery systems are able to make adjustments for volume and assortment error increasing sales and reducing quantities of merchandise sold at less than first price. The challenges include developing delivery plans compatible with the type of merchandise and the production and delivery systems.

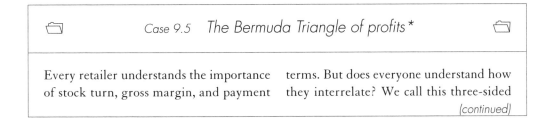

Case 9.5   *The Bermuda Triangle of profits* *

Every retailer understands the importance of stock turn, gross margin, and payment terms. But does everyone understand how they interrelate? We call this three-sided

(continued)

Case 9.5 (continued)

relationship the Bermuda Triangle of Profits, because failure to completely exploit these interactions causes profit to disappear.

Suppose you pay your suppliers every 30 days and you turn your stock 12 times a year. You effectively run your business on free inventory. More than 12 turns and your suppliers bank with you for part of every month. Wal-Mart maintains it can sell diapers (nappies) at less than cost and still make a profit. The stockturn is so high that the interest they make on the suppliers' money is greater than the discount on cost price.

Retailers with lower stockturns, such as specialty stores, will typically pay suppliers on 60 or more days and turn their stocks three to eight times a year. With three turns a year, 100 percent sell through is achieved, on average, in 4 months. With a straight line sell through, a 50 percent gross margin and 60 day payment terms, enough money has been taken in about 2 months to pay the supplier in full. Improving the turn and maintaining the payment terms reduces the cost of financing the stock. It allows the retailer to operate on lower margins if necessary. Achieving this optimum balance between margins, turns, and contract terms is a crucial aspect of profitable retailing.

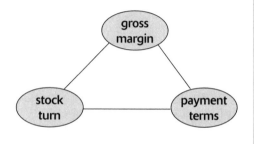

The Bermuda Triangle of profits

*Hume (2001).

Learning Activity 9.5

Developing product velocity

1. What is the meaning of product velocity? How is product velocity measured?
2. How does product velocity relate to gross margin?
3. Contract payment terms were discussed in Chapter 8, Developing Product Lines. What are some examples of payment terms?
4. Why are product velocity, gross margin, and payment terms interrelated?

Developing Merchandise Delivery Plans

A key component of a merchandise delivery plan is the merchandising calendar. Notice that Table 4.4 in Chapter 4, Fundamentals of Merchandise Planning, the merchandising calendar for fashion/seasonal cycling jerseys/tops with 13-week selling periods, has a column for a delivery plan. The calendar provides a number of factors relative to the merchandise plan that must be considered in relation to merchandise delivery including the beginning and end of selling periods, position in the selling period of planned promotions and sales peaks, and timing of merchandise clearance. It is important to have goods delivered a few weeks ahead of clearance to give it a chance to sell at regular price.

Decisions that have to be made relative to delivery plans include the following:

- What are volume and diversity of the assortment (VSA and VSID)?

- Are you going to use traditional or QR deliveries?

- How much of the planned merchandise should be included in the first delivery?

- When should each additional order be placed considering sales peaks, promotions, and clearance?

- What is the lead time between order placement and order delivery?

- When will each order be received?

Traditional deliveries for fashion/seasonal goods commonly include delivering 100 percent of the planned merchandise before the selling period starts. One hundred percent delivery assures all styles are present and assortments are complete according to the merchandise plan. The retailer places an order, the vendor makes the goods to order, and the goods are shipped. A strong limitation of 100 percent delivery is that it does not allow for accommodation for volume error (quantity of units) or variety error (style, size, and color). If too many of certain colors were ordered or too few of a hot-selling style, the result is markdowns and stockouts reducing sales and gross margin. Sometimes it is possible to order additional units of hot sellers if the vendor overproduced according to orders but there usually is not time to manufacturer produce more within a 13- or 26-week selling period.

Traditional delivery is now sometimes modified by using multiple deliveries within a selling period to add new merchandise. For example, for a 13-week selling period with nine styles planned, four styles might in included in the initial delivery (about 40 percent of the merchandise) with four styles added in week 3 (40 percent) and two styles added in week 6 (20 percent) depending on when promotions and sales peaks are planned. The strategy keeps the merchandise fresh for frequent shoppers but keep in mind, with traditional delivery systems, all deliveries are based on the original merchandise plan. Making changes during the selling period, based on customer demand, in the quantity of merchandise or its assortment is difficult if not impossible because the vendor may have already produced the merchandise ordered or may not have the necessary materials available.

Table 9.7 is Mike's Bikes' merchandising calendar for cycling jerseys/tops first presented in Chapter 4. It includes the pricing plan and two options for delivery plans, Traditional and QR. Notice that Mike's Bikes has planned a pre-season sale resulting in an early season sales peak, thus the traditional delivery plan calls for 100 percent of the planned merchandise to be delivered before the selling period starts. No reorders are planned.

Quick response (QR) deliveries are characterized by smaller initial deliveries with subsequent deliveries based re-estimation of demand in relation to in-season POS data. This requires special agreements with vendors who are either willing to make to stock to resupply desired merchandise and/or use flexible production systems that can quickly make goods to order. Sometimes vendors make goods to stock in anticipation of reorders and then make to order the goods that were not already made to stock.

The *volume* and *diversity* of assortment are key components in deciding whether traditional or QR deliveries will be most effective. For example, at Mike's Bikes, solid color biking shorts dominate shorts sales with 75 percent of the total and almost 3000 units. Since the selling period is 52 weeks long, having a single delivery would pose a huge inventory storage and management problem for a single unit store like Mike's Bikes. However, their baggy style shorts are only 10 percent of the volume and would be only about 300 units. Thus, it might be appropriate to set up weekly orders and deliveries on solid color shorts and order baggies only four times a year.

On the other hand, the assortment of baggies may be more diverse than the assortment of solid color shorts. Therefore the baggy assortment would be more subject to volume and assortment errors. Small, more frequent orders could help replace baggies that were selling well and avoid ordering more of those that were not.

Assortment diversity, measured by volume per SKU for the assortment (VSA), is an indicator of potential for stockouts. When VSA is less than 5, risk of stockouts drastically increases and some tests with Sourcing Simulator would probably reveal that the best delivery system is traditional delivery.

Table 9.7

Complete merchandising calendar for cycling jerseys/tops including pricing and alternative delivery plans.

Month	Week	Event	Selling Periods	Pricing Plan	Traditional Delivery Plan	Quick Response Delivery Plan
Feb.	1	Groundhog Day	Transition period #4	Preseason sale	Receive PO #1, 100%	Receive PO #1, 70%
	2	Valentine's Day	Period #1-preseason sale	$55.67 promotion		
	3	Presidents' Day	Peak#1-end sale	Cancel 20% temporary MD		Place PO #2, 30%
	4	BRR Bicycle, RidetoRippey		$70 first price (60% markup, $28 cost)		
Mar	5					
	6					Receive PO #2
	7	St.Patrick's Day				
	8	Spring begins				
	9					
Apr.	10	April Fool's Ride				
	11	Jewish Passover				
	12	Easter Sunday	End period #1			
	13	Admin. Prof. Day	Clearance	$41.97 (40% permanent markdown)		
May	14	Black Earth to Hyderseek			Receive PO #1, 100%	Receive PO #1, 60%
	15	Mother's Day	Period #2/Peak#1	$70 first price (60% markup, $28 cost)		
	16	Armed Forces Day				Place PO #2, 20%
	17	Memorial Day				
June	18	Blast to Blanchardville				Place PO #3, 10%
	19	Father's Day				Receive PO #2
	20	Recumbent Roundup				
	21	Just Pedal Faster				Receive PO #3
	22					
July	23	Independence Day	RAGBRAI promo	$55.67 promotion		
	24	Iowa Games	Sales peak #2	Cancel 20% temporary MD		
	25	RAGBRAI				
	26		Semi-annual clear	$41.97 (40% permanent markdown)		
	27		Final clearance	$$30.97 (55% permanent markdown)		

For example, assume that Mike's Bikes open to buy for cycling jerseys/tops was as follows:

$92,000 for the merchandising cycle.

$14,720 (16% of the total for merchandising cycle) for the first selling period,

$31,280 (34%) for the second selling period,

$23,920 (26%) for the third selling period, and

$22,080 (24%) for the fourth selling period.

The average first price was $75 so they needed to purchase 196 units for the first selling period and 417 units for the second (open to buy ÷ first price). The assortment plan was for four styles, six sizes, and two colors (48 SKUs) for the first selling period and four styles, six sizes, and three colors (72 SKUs) for the second selling period. The volume per SKU for the assortment (VSA) for each selling period was as follows:

	VSA	=	number of units	÷	number of SKUs
1st selling period VSA	=	4.1	=	196 ÷	48
2nd selling period VSA	=	5.8	=	417 ÷	72

The VSA tells us that, on the average, there are about four units per SKU in the assortment for the first selling period and six units per SKU for the second. According to the Assortment Diversity Index, the first selling period has diverse assortments with high risk of stockouts while the second is a transition assortment with lower risk of stockouts. Mike's Bikes regards these assortments as desirable because their customers like a variety to choose from so that bikers have unique outfits (see Table 9.7).

When planning delivery strategies, traditional 100 percent delivery is logical considering a short 13-week selling periods and the early sales peaks. The VSID (volume per SKU for initial delivery) for 100 percent delivery is the same as the VSA.

	VSID	=	# of units in the shipment	÷	# of SKUs in the assortment
1st selling period	=	4.1	=	196	÷	48
2nd selling period	=	5.8	=	417	÷	72

When considering QR multiple deliveries, a key decision is the volume of goods to include in the initial delivery. VSID can be a very useful indicator of whether or not multiple deliveries are likely to improve sales. It might be logical to consider one additional delivery for the first selling period and two additional deliveries for the second selling period because of the difference in volume but what will happen to VSID?

For the first selling period, using 70 percent for the initial delivery followed by 30 percent in a second delivery what will be the VSID of each delivery?

1st selling period 1st delivery	=	$ open to buy	×	% first delivery
$10,304	=	$14,720	×	70%
Units in 1st delivery	=	$ first delivery	÷	first price
137	=	$10,304	÷	$75
VSID	=	# of units in the shipment	÷	# of SKUs in the assortment
2.8	=	137	÷	48

A VSID 2.8 means on the average there will be about three units per SKU included in the order. It also means that some styles, sizes, or colors with low percentage allocations may not be included in the initial order unless the order specifies that at least one unit per SKU should be shipped. Re-estimation of demand for SKUs in a QR system is dependent on sales to show demand for the SKU. If a SKU is not included in the initial order it is not available to be sold so it will not be included in the next order. VSIDs for the second selling period can be determined using the same process.

▢ *Learning Activity 9.6*

Multiple delivery strategies and product velocity

1. How do multiple delivery strategies increase product velocity?
2. Calculate VSID for cycling jerseys during the second selling period using the numbers defined above and the QR delivery strategy detailed in Table 9.7.
3. Set up an experiment using Sourcing Simulator and compare the financial productivity of cycling jerseys/tops for the 1st and 2nd selling periods. Compare traditional and QR for each selling period. Consider inventory turns, lost sales, sales revenue, gross margin $ and %, adjusted gross margin. What factors have influenced each of these productivity measures?
4. Plan delivery strategies for selling periods #3 and #4 for cycling jersey/tops. You will need to decide how many styles, sizes, and colors to use for each. Calculate the VSID for each and test using Sourcing Simulator.

Summary

Merchandise presentation includes processes required to evaluate the line and make it visible and salable. In Chapter 3, TAMS, Figure 3.2, identifies three components of merchandise presentation: internal, wholesale, and retail. Merchandise presentation is a fundamental part of the merchandising process intended to enhance sales by offering products for consideration in a consciously designed environment that positively affects attitudes and behaviors toward the products and the presenter(s).

The fundamental purpose of merchandise presentation is sales enhancement and, thus, contribution to the success of the firm. Merchandise presentation takes place in environments that are manipulated to provide the desired impression. The aesthetic experience associated with merchandise presentation enhances participants' perception of the products by providing pleasure and/or satisfaction. From the first evaluation of line concept the purpose is to create a line that will be highly desired by customers.

A multiple delivery strategy means an initial delivery and several additional deliveries based on re-estimation of POS data. The purpose of developing multiple delivery strategies is to help retailers order in smaller quantities on a more frequent basis to reduce inventory investment, stockouts, and markdowns, and to improve salability. The primary decision elements of multiple delivery strategies involve the number of deliveries, the quantity of each delivery, and the timing of additional deliveries. The advantage compared to single delivery is that customer preferences can be more accurately accommodated. The disadvantages are increased costs of merchandise order processing, handling, and transportation. Multiple delivery strategies have been extensively applied to basic and staple goods. The research and practical execution of multiple delivery strategies on seasonal and fashion goods is more limited.

Key Concepts

aesthetic benefits	make-to-order	selling
assortment error	multiple delivery strategies	stock on hand
cross-docking	planograms	traditional deliveries
displaying	product velocity	utilitarian benefits
distribution	quick response deliveries	volume error
gross margin return on inventory (GMROI)	quick response replenishment systems	volume per SKU for initial delivery (VSID)
initial delivery	reorder planning	
initial order	safety stock	

Integrated Learning Activity 9.7.1

Developing merchandise delivery plans

Within the context of your merchandise plans (income statement, pricing, budget, assortment, and development) for your MAP retailer, develop a total of three merchandise delivery plans for your diverse assortment for your fashion/seasonal and three for your focused assortment for your basic staple merchandise groups.

Each merchandise group will have three delivery plans—one traditional and two QR.

- Make the traditional plans have a single initial delivery of 100 percent of the planned merchandise to receive.

- Make one of the QR strategies for each merchandise group have additional deliveries arriving about two weeks before the sales peak(s) of the selling period.
- Make the other QR strategy for each merchandise group have nearly as many deliveries as weeks in the selling period.

For each plan, determine the percent initial stocking.

- Use a VSID of at least two for the fashion/seasonal group.
- Use a VSID of at least ten for the basic/staple group.

Determine for each delivery plan

- The number of reorders.
- Week of the first reorder.
- Weeks between reorders.
- Reorder lead time.

Incorporate your delivery plans into your merchandise calendar for each merchandise group.

⊚ Integrated Learning Activity 9.7.2

Testing delivery plans with Sourcing Simulator

Objectives
- Test financial effectiveness of traditional and QR delivery plans for fashion/seasonal and basic/staple goods developed in ILA 9.7.1.
- Evaluate the cause and effects of outcomes.

Resources for this project
- Your merchandise plans for pricing, budgets, assortments, and delivery.
- Your teacher, interactive tutor, and/or other class members.
- Your SS CD.

Procedure
Use a similar systematic procedure used for other SS assignments to generate data to compare outcomes for each of your merchandise groups. Compare total revenue, gross margin, lost sales, adjusted gross margin, stockturn, and average inventory.

Integrated Learning Activity 9.7.3

Product presentation in the furniture business

1. Read Case 9.6 carefully. How is the Flexsteel's furniture business different than the apparel business in terms of line development and presentation? How is it similar?
2. How could QR systems be applied to furniture?

📁   Case 9.6   *Flexsteel finds niches in embattled industry.* *   📁

Deep in the heart of the Flexsteel plant, Tom Baldwin pulls a customer order slip from a newly upholstered creamy-white leather loveseat. It's bound for the largest furniture retailer in Detroit. He checks a pricey floral tapestry sofa. It's headed to Luxemburg, Wisconsin, a small town east of Green Bay. A plain blue sofa with basic padding sitting on the conveyer belt next to these two beauty queens will be shipped to Edwards Air Force Base. "We're one of the largest suppliers of upholstered furniture to the U.S. government," said Baldwin, a company spokesman. Despite the inviting look of these comfy sofas rolling off the manufacturing lines, this is no time for Flexsteel Industries Inc. officials to lounge.

Sales Up, Profit Down

The Dubuque, Iowa-based furniture manufacturer, one of the ten largest in the country, finds itself in a business paradox: The company had record sales during the mid-1990s, but posted sharp drops in profitability. That this decline in profits is an industry-wide trend is little comfort, Flexsteel officials say.

"It's been a very tough year," said Baldwin. The first quarter of the new fiscal year looked even gloomier. Sales were down from last year's first quarter. There appears to be several reasons for the slump. Rising interest rates meant it costs more for consumers to fi-nance furniture purchases. During the early 2000s, interest rates are down, home sales are up, and so are sales at Flexsteel.

Raw material price increases for fabric, wood, and foam padding "have risen far beyond what could be passed on to the consumer," said Baldwin. Topping off the profit picture, is the competitive market for scarce consumer dollars. "We are a very deferrable item. A $699 sofa in 1989 is probably selling for $699 or less today," Graham said. "Manufacturers have had to squeeze the fat out of their processes. The entire supply chain has to be extremely efficient to be profitable."

Furniture trends used to hit the East and West coasts and take a year or two to hit the Midwest. "Today, that is no longer true," he said. "The consumer is much more cognizant of color, design, and what they want. We're a fashion-oriented business, and we have to react to changes of consumer lifestyle much quicker."

To capture that ever-changing market, Flexsteel has been helping its gallery dealers with special programs and offers 400 of its 1,000 fabrics choices exclusively to those galleries. Video design catalogs allow customer to custom-order a sofa in a particular fabric and see ahead of time what it will look like. Those are important selling tools for a company that gets 50 percent of its business from custom orders.

Case 9.6 (continued)

Flexsteel responds to what's hot in the retail furniture world right now: wing-back chairs, leather goods, "motion furniture," and furniture covered in a collage look of fabrics or designs. "Leather is just out of this world. In residential sales, leather is more than 20 percent of our volume. I'd see it hitting 25 percent in the next three to four years."

Buyers want more casual, softer furniture to fit in a relaxed, homey lifestyle look. Dual purpose furniture, like motion furniture and sleepers, has become very important and takes away from our sofa sales." Flexsteel initiated a fresh concept in retail furniture display, the Comfort Seating Program that has now become the Flexsteel Comfort Gallery. It showcases Flexsteel upholstered furniture within independent dealer showrooms across the country.

Flexsteel officials say they've tried to position themselves for the future through diversification of products and tightening up supply and production costs. The most recent initiative is teaming with Christopher Lowell, Emmy-award winning host and designer, for the Christopher Lowell Home Collection™. "Studies show the customers will stop at five stores before they buy, and their first stop will only be 8 to 10 minutes. It had better be good if you want them to come back."

*Based on Flexsteel (1996) and Wiley (1995).

Recommended Resources

Allen, R. L. (1982, August). Planned assortments: Buying what sells. *Chain Store Age, General Merchandise Edition*, 90 & 95.

Allen, R. L. (1982, September). Plan a strategy for reordering goods. *Chain Store Age, General Merchandise Edition*, 94–95.

Buzzell, R. D., & Ortmeyer, G. (1995). Channel partnerships streamline distribution. *Sloan Management Review*, 36(3):85–96.

Gilreath, T. L., Reeve, J. M., & Whalen Jr., C. E. (1995, March). Time is money: Understanding the product velocity advantage. *Bobbin*, 50–55.

Kunz, G. I. (1995). Behavioral theory of the apparel firm: A beginning. *Clothing and Textiles Research Journal*, 13(4):252–261.

Lalonde, B. J. (1994, January). Distribution inventory: More speed, less cost. *Chain Store Age Executive*, 18MH–20MH.

Stankevich, D. G. (2000, May). In the heat of the battle. *Retail Merchandiser*, 109, 110, & 112.

References

Allen, R. L. (1982, August). Planned assortments: Buying what sells. *Chain Store Age, General Merchandise Edition*, 90 & 95.

Allen, R. L. (1982, September). Plan a strategy for reordering goods. *Chain Store Age, General Merchandise Edition*, 94–95.

Baker, C. (1991, April). EDI in business. *Accountancy*, 121–124.

Berman, B., & Evans, J. R. (1995). *Retail management: A strategic approach* (6th ed.). Englewood Cliffs, NJ: Prentice Hall.

Bhat, R. R. (1985). *Managing the demand for fashion items* (2nd ed.). Ann Arbor: University of Michigan.

Blackburn, J. D. (1991). The Quick-Response movement in the apparel industry: A case study in time-compressing supply chains. In J. D. Blackburn (Ed.), *Time-based competition: The next battleground in American manufacturing*. Homewood, IL: Irwin.

Bloomberg News. (2003, December 24). Nike's LeBron James sneaker makes rapid strides in sales. *Des Moines Register*, D1.

Bohlinger, M. S. (1977). *Merchandise buying: Principles and applications*. Dubuque, IA: Wm. C. Brown.

Buzzell, R. D., & Ortmeyer, G. (1995). Channel partnerships streamline distribution. *Sloan Management Review*, 36(3):85–96.

Caselle, T. (2000). Value-added gives a leg up to US hosiery sector. tdctrade.com www.tdctrade.com/ mne/garment/hosiery002.htm). Accessed January 19, 2004.

Diamond, C. (2000, March). The fix is in. *Discount Merchandiser*, 55–58

Dyches, B. (1996, January). WWD Specialty Stores/a Business Newsletter.

EDI and quick response: Easy money. (1991, March). *Chain Store Age Executive*, 20B.

Fiore, A. M., & Kimle, P. A. (1997). *Understanding aesthetics for the merchandising and design professional*. New York: Fairchild.

Flexsteel. (1996) History (www.flexsteel.com/about). Accessed January 27, 2004.

Gilman, A. L. (1989, May). Assessing quick response benefits. *Chain Store Age Executive*, 314.

Gilreath, T. L., Reeve, J. M., & Whalen Jr., C. E. (1995, March). Time is money: Understanding the product velocity advantage. *Bobbin*, 50–55.

Glock, R. E., & Kunz, G. I. (1995). *Apparel manufacturing: Sewn products analysis* (2nd ed.). Englewood Cliffs, NJ: Prentice Hall.

Gordon, P. (1993). Rapid replenishment. Proceedings of the Quick Response '93 Conference, 197–204.

Gray, S. B. (1993). Foundation for quick response strategies: A retail point of view. Proceedings of the Quick Response '93 Conference, 41–56.

Hammond, J. H. (1993). Quick response in retail/manufacturing channels. In S. P. Bradley, J. A. Hausman, & R. L. Nolan (Eds.), *Globalization, technology, and competition: The fusion of computers and telecommunications in the 1990s*. Boston, MA: Harvard Business School Press.

Hughes, S. (1994). How to build and maintain a management team to manage stock replenishment. Quick Response 1994 Conference Proceedings, 55–66.

Hume, B. (2001). The Bermuda Triangle of profits. The Planning Factory Limited www. planfact .co.uk/bermuda.htm). Accessed February 13, 2003.

Hunter, A. (1990). *Quick response in apparel manufacturing: A survey of the American scene*. Manchester, England: The Textiles Institute.

Hunter, N. A., King, R., & Nuttle, H. (1991). Comparison of quick response and traditional retailing performance through stochastic simulation modeling (NCSIU-IE Technical Report # 91-6). Raleigh: North Carolina State University, Department of Industrial Engineering.

Hunter, N. A., King, R. E., Nuttle, H. L., & Wilson, J. R. (1993, February). The apparel pipeline modeling project at North Carolina State University (paper presented at the 4th Annual Academic Apparel Research, Raleigh, NC).

JBT Legwear. (2004). About us (www.pennacohosiery.com/about.html). Accessed January 20, 2004.

K. Bell. (2004). About K. Bell socks (www.kbellsocks.com). Accessed January 20, 2004.

Kilgore Trout. (2003). (www.kilgoretrout.net). Accessed January 20, 2004.

King, R., & Poindexter, M. (1991, September). A simulation model for retail buying (NCSU-IE Technical Report #90-9). Raleigh: North Carolina State University.

Kunz, G. I., & Rupe, D. (1995). The status of merchandising technology, part 1: Definition of merchandising technology and literature review. Unpublished manuscript, Iowa State University.

Kunz, G. I., & Song, J. (1996). The influence of stockouts on in-store shopping behavior. Unpublished manuscript, Iowa State University.

Lalonde, B. J. (1994, January). Distribution inventory: More speed, less cost. *Chain Store Age Executive,* 18MH–20MH.

Lambert, D. M., & Stock, J. R. (1993). *Strategic logistics management* (3rd ed.). New York: Richard D. Irwin.

Lewison, D. M. (1991). *Retailing* (4th ed.). New York: Macmillan.

Lewison, D. M. (1994). *Retailing* (5th ed.). New York: Macmillan.

Lin, T. (1996). The effectiveness of multiple delivery strategies in relation to retail apparel assortments. Master's thesis, Iowa State University.

Measuring the impact: Quick response and the bottom line. (1991, March). *Chain Store Age Executive*, 8B–9B.

Nuttle, H., King, R., & Hunter, N. (1991). A stochastic model of apparel retailing process for seasonal apparel. *Journal of the Textile Institute*, 82(2):247–259.

Quick response technologies. (1991, March). *Chain Store Age Executive*, 6B–7B.

Rupe, D., & Kunz, G. I. (in press). Building a financially meaningful language of merchandise assortments. *Clothing and Textiles Research Journal*.

Sears' MAPS' customized assortments. (1990, October). *Chain Store Age Executive*, 62–69.

Setren, M. (1993). Changing measures of performance. Proceedings of the Quick Response '93 Conference, 253–260.

Sharoff, R. (1996, August 19). *Daily News Record,* 72.

Stankevich, D. G. (2000, May). In the heat of the battle. *Retail Merchandiser*, 109, 110, & 112.

Taylor, C. G. (1970). *Merchandising assortment planning: The key to retailing profit*. New York: Merchandising Division National Retail Merchants Associations.

Troxell, M. D. (1976). *Fashion merchandising* (2nd ed.). New York: McGraw-Hill.

Wiley, D. (1995, February 4). *Des Moines Register*, 4S–5S.

Yan, X. (1996). Effect of environmental fragrancing on customers' attitude and purchase intention toward apparel product and aesthetic experience. Master's thesis, Iowa State University.

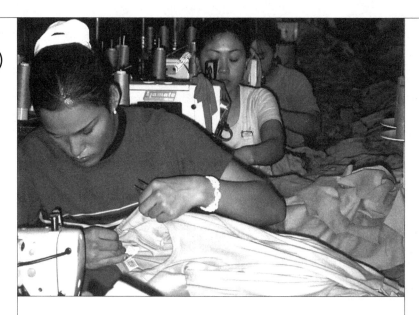

10

Global Sourcing

Learning Objectives

- Examine the concepts of globalization.

- Explore U.S. textiles and apparel sourcing from major suppliers.

- Discuss the sourcing process.

- Examine labor and exploitation issues.

Merchandising decisions frequently include not only what, how much, and when merchandise should be acquired, but also where. At any given time, a major apparel company like The Limited or Liz Claiborne is probably sourcing materials, production, and/or finished goods in more than 30 countries. **Sourcing** is determining the most cost efficient vendor of materials, production, and/or finished goods at the specified quality and service level with delivery within an identified time frame. Sourcing may be domestic or foreign and thus may result in imports. Most of the more than 200 countries in the world export textiles and apparel to the United States. At the same time other markets around the world offer huge potential for export of U.S.-made goods. Sourcing finished goods, materials, or production is closely associated with and may be a part of the merchandiser's responsibilities depending on the size and organization of a firm.

The Concept of Globalization

Imagine if you will the requisite label of origin in the year 2095 after we have colonized other planets in our solar system. Just as we now say "Made in America" or "Made in Sri Lanka," chances are the label of 2095 may say "Made on the Planet Earth" to distinguish the products made on the third planet from the sun (Made on Planet Earth, 1996).

Globalization may be simple compared to solarization! To say something is **global** means it relates to or includes the whole earth. To globalize is to organize or establish worldwide. From a business standpoint, the term **globalization** is associated with viewing multiple sites in the world as markets and/or sources for producing or acquiring merchandise or services. Global firms use advanced communication and transportation technology to simultaneously coordinate manufacturing and distribution and perhaps retailing in multiple locations (Bonacich et al., 1994). Power of global firms may transcend and sometimes overwhelm the power of political states. Some global firms command more capital and economic power than entire countries.

Successful global competitors are characterized by less bureaucracy and more communication. Vertical control and hierarchy of command are being replaced by more horizontal, peer-oriented relationships across borders and boundaries (Kanter, 1994). As with quick response (QR) business systems, the greatest challenge to global firms is "developing new organizational capabilities and managerial mindsets" (Kanter, 1994, p. 232). Agile production for QR is inherently global production, whereas mass production is merely international, i.e., between countries (Goldman, Nagel, & Preiss 1995).

But not only large firms are impacted by globalization. Small firms are both suppliers and buyers in the global market. Many textiles and apparel industry participants believe that globalization favors large firms because of capitalization requirements, economies of scale, breadth of product lines, and sophistication of technology and communications systems. At the same time, globalization factors that favor smaller firms include flexibility, ability to serve niche markets, focus on unique and differentiated products, and higher margin products (Made on Planet Earth, 1995). More disperse locations of production units have resulted in using more functional, smaller scale, and less expensive production equipment (Goldman, Nagel, & Preiss, 1995). The reality of the global market and world trade in textiles and apparel is so pervasive that it is impossible to be an apparel manufacturer or retailer without participating in it.

Regulation of Trade

Countries have always felt the need to regulate commerce between countries, often to protect domestic industries. Until recently, the primary source of textiles and apparel trade regulation was the **General Agreement on Tariffs and Trade (GATT)** operating along with the **multifiber arrangement (MFA).** Through extended negotiations of the Uruguay Round, GATT was replaced by the **World Trade Organization (WTO).** The fundamental purpose of GATT and WTO, its successor, is to increase international trade by reducing trade barriers, which include **tariffs,** taxes on goods that are imported or exported, and **quotas,** limitations on quantities of goods that can be imported. The United States now uses the **Harmonized Tariff Schedule of the United States (HTSA)** to tax imports of all kinds of products, including textiles and apparel, while the MFA imposes quotas on textiles and apparel.

The MFA has been operated as a system of quotas for textiles and apparel based on bilateral agreements among over 60 member countries. These countries are the world's largest producers of textiles and apparel. *The MFA was designed to protect the textile and apparel industries in developed countries from excessive imports from low-wage developing countries.* Since the MFA violates the fundamental purpose of GATT—to promote free trade—the WTO includes a phase-out of MFA bilateral agreements beginning in 1992 and ending in 2005. The result is intended to be freer trade of textiles and apparel throughout the world. It is as yet unknown what will happen in 2005 when the quota phase-out is complete, although China is regarded as the primary benefactor and the worldwide industry has been trying to prepare for it.

During the time the GATT was being renegotiated into the WTO, the **U.S./Canadian Free Trade Agreement** (1988) came into being, followed in 1994 by the **North American Free Trade Agreement (NAFTA).** The development of these trade agreements, along with the dissolution of the Soviet Union and the formation of the **European Union (EU),** has reformed world order. The result is three major trading blocs: The Americas, Europe, and Asia/Pacific Rim. While trade may be freer within each of these trading areas, trade is not necessarily freer among the trading areas (Marlin-Bennett, 1994).

Each trading bloc includes some countries that are relatively developed with higher average incomes and some countries that are developing with relatively lower incomes. As an indicator of the economic power of these trading blocs, Table 10.1 reports their populations, retail sales, and retail sales per capita. Notice in the **Americas trading bloc** the population of Latin America (Mexico, Central, and South America) is larger than North America (United States and Canada), but the retail sales are far less. Retail sales per capita are 12 times larger in North America than in South America. In the **Europe trading bloc,** Western Europe has a larger population than Eastern Europe and Eastern Europe's retail sales are far less. Per capita retail sales are seven times greater in Western Europe than in Eastern Europe. The population in the **Asia/Pacific Rim trading bloc** is huge compared to the other trading blocs. The Asia trading bloc includes some more developed countries (Hong Kong, Japan, South Korea, and Singapore) as well many developing countries. Thus, the average

Table 10.1

Population and total retail sales in world markets. *

Continent/ Trading Bloc	Population (millions)	Retail Sales (millions $)	Retail Sales per Capita ($)
Americas			
North America	290.0	$2,385.2	$8,226
Latin America	340.6	226.7	666
Europe			
Western Europe	357.8	1,971.0	5,509
Eastern Europe	192.0	154.0	802
Asia			
Asia/Pacific Rim	1,669.6	2,030.1	1,216
Australia	21.3	96.2	4,516
Total	2,871.3	6,853.2	
Rest of World	2,862.8		
World Total	5,734.1		

*Management Ventures, Inc. (1996).

retail sales per capita is higher than Latin America and Eastern Europe but are still a fraction of North America and Western Europe. The population of Australia is tiny although per capita retail sales are close to Western Europe.

International trade agreements are only a few of the laws that impact opportunities for importing and exporting goods. Case 10.1 provides an example of complexities that can develop as a result of international sourcing and operation of a transnational corporation like Wal-Mart.

Learning Activity 10.1

Complexities of international business activity

1. From the perspectives of the Americas and Europe trading blocs, what is the significance of the huge population of the Asian/Pacific Rim trading block?
2. What do the relative retail sales per capita indicate about the trading blocs?
3. Read Case 10.1 very carefully. What is the problem from Wal-Mart Stores' perspective?
4. What is the problem from Wal-Mart Canada's perspective?

5. What is the problem from the U.S. government's perspective?
6. What is the problem from the Canadian government's perspective?
7. How could this problem have been avoided?

     Case 10.1 *Wal-Mart puts on pajamas, lies down*
in king-size mess. *

The case of the Cuban pajamas, already at the vortex of a trade dispute between the United States and Canada, also produced a revolt within the management ranks of mega-retailer Wal-Mart.

The incident began when Wal-Mart Canada pulled Cuban-made sleepwear from its stores, apparently in the mistaken belief that selling them violated the Helms-Burton Act. Helms-Burton, passed in 1996, forbids companies anywhere in the world from "trafficking" in property confiscated from U.S. citizens or companies by the Castro regime after it took power in 1959. However, the law has sparked global outrage with the United States' trading partners charging it violates their sovereignty.

As it turns out, the pajamas may not have violated Helms-Burton. However, they likely violated the embargo-tightening Cuban Democracy Act of 1992, which prohibits foreign subsidiaries for U.S. companies from buying or selling most Cuban goods. When Wal-Mart Canada pulled the Cuban pajamas off its shelves, it sparked widespread protests in that country. And Canadian officials said the move violated a Canadian law, the Foreign Extraterritorial Measures Act, which is designed to prevent other countries from extending their laws into Canada.

Wal-Mart Canada relented — executives faced potential fines of up to $1 million Canadian and up to 5 years in prison — and said it would start stocking the pajamas again. Wal-Mart had 136 stores in Canada, with a commanding 45 percent share of the discount merchandise market. But its actions drew the ire of Wal-Mart Stores, the Bentonville, Arkansas, parent, which had ordered its Canadian subsidiary to abide by U.S. laws.

"Wal-Mart Canada made a decision to return that stock to the shelves," said Wal-Mart spokesman Dale Ingram. "They did that in conflict with the directive from Wal-Mart Stores Inc. We had asked them to follow any applicable U.S. law."

As a result, Wal-Mart, the world's largest retailer, finds itself in conflict with Washington, Ottawa, and its own rebellious division. Although the company has been cooperating with the U.S. Office of Foreign Assets control since the incident

(continued)

Case 10.1 (continued)

first erupted, it was nonetheless held accountable for Wal-Mart Canada's actions.

The pajamas "must be a pretty funky
little creation," said Washington lawyer
Robert Muse, who has closely followed the

Helms-Burton Act. "But the legal issues
involved in this case are quite serious."

*Wal-Mart puts on pajamas (1997).

The Americas

Table 10.2 lists the countries in each area of the Americas trading bloc. The U.S. population consumes nearly half of world production for most products (Stone, 1994). According
to sales per capita, the North American segment of The Americas trading bloc has considerably more spending power than the Latin American segment, but Latin America has a
larger and more rapidly growing population, as well as a grand supply of low-cost labor.
With favorable trade regulations and the implementation of QR, U.S. apparel firms are
sourcing in Central and South America and the West Indies as well as the rest of the
world.

Before NAFTA in 1992, the **Caribbean Basin Initiative (CBI)** in 1987 and the **Special
Regime (SR)** in 1988 were already in place providing incentive for doing business within the
Americas. CBI affects a combination of countries located in Central America and the West
Indies. CBI took advantage of a special provision in the U.S. tariff schedules, **Item 807** in the
Tariff Schedules of the United States that was replaced by Chapter 9802 in the Harmonized
Tariff Schedule of the U.S. Item 807, as it is commonly known since 1965, allowed products to
be designed and cut in the United States, exported, sewn in a foreign country, and then imported with tariffs assessed only on value added. **Value added** was determined primarily by
labor costs for sewing. **Item 807, Chapter 9802** allowed manufacturers to take advantage of
low labor costs in foreign countries, particularly those in close proximity to the United States.
CBI also provided **guaranteed access levels (GALS)** to U.S. markets as a part of what is
known as 807A. GALS eliminated the problem of quota limitations on U.S. imports from
specified countries. Mexico was not included in CBI so the SR was developed to provide
Mexico with access to the U.S. market similar to CBI. By 1990, 10 percent of U.S. apparel imports were via 807, 807A, and SR and increased to as high as 34 percent of imports by the late
1990s but has declined dramatically since because of new legislation.

Table 10.2

Countries in Americas trading area.

Central America	North America	South America	West Indies
Belize	Canada	Argentina	Antigua
Costa Rica	Mexico	Bolivia	The Bahamas
El Salvador	United States	Brazil	Barbados
Guatemala		Chile	Cuba
Honduras		Colombia	Dominican Republic
Nicaragua		Ecuador	Grenada
Panama		Galapagos Islands	Guadeloupe
		Guyana	Haiti
		Paraguay	Jamaica
		Peru	Martinique
		Suriname	Puerto Rico
		Uruguay	Trinidad and Tobago
		Venezuela	Virgin Islands

Eighty percent of trade between Canada and the United States was already unrestricted prior to the U.S./Canadian Free Trade Agreement (Wall & Dickerson, 1989). The trade restrictions in place, however, included automobiles, textiles, and apparel. Some U.S. firms like Ford Motor Company built production plants in Canada because tariffs were prohibitive for exporting to Canada. In general, Canada's wages and costs of living were higher than in the United States (Millstein, 1993). When the tariffs were eliminated by the free trade agreement, these plants were closed to take advantage of lower labor costs in the United States. Production costs in the United States and Canada are now very similar.

Before the free trade agreement between the United States and Canada, trade in textiles and apparel was restricted by tariffs and also by quotas from the MFA. The impact of the free trade agreement on textiles and apparel was less immediate because of provisions for phasing out of the quota restrictions between the two countries over a 10-year period. The U.S./Canadian Free Trade Agreement also has a **fabric forward rule** of origin clause. This means that in order to qualify for free trade, apparel must be made from fabric manufactured in the United States or Canada. Canada has long imported high-quality fabrics from Europe, tariff free. Garments made from these fabrics do not qualify for free trade with the United States because of the rule of origin clause. Canada has little textile production so the U.S./Canadian Free Trade Agreement was favorable toward the U.S. textile producers.

Many Canadian apparel manufacturers had to buy fabric from U.S. mills in order to qualify for free trade of apparel.

Negotiation of NAFTA, including United States, Canada, and Mexico, was concluded in 1992 with implementation beginning in 1994. Formulation of NAFTA was extremely controversial (Ellis, 1992) and its impact continues in this vein. It is very clear that many U.S. apparel companies are producing in Mexico. An executive of a major U.S. jeans producer claims that each pair of jeans produced in Mexico costs $1 less than the same jean produced in the United States. The result is millions of dollars in total annual savings that can be passed on to ultimate consumers. Many of the jeans' companies use the same modern technology, production processes, and quality standards to run their plants in Mexico as they do in the United States.

NAFTA also has a **rule of origin** clause but it is "yarn forward" rather than "fabric forward." The **yarn forward rule** of origin means that all yarn manufacturing, fabric manufacturing, and garment manufacturing processes must take place in Mexico, United States, or Canada (Antoshak, 1992). Since little textile manufacturing takes place in either Canada or Mexico, the rule of origin clause also strongly favors the U.S. textile industry.

Benefits of NAFTA to the U.S. apparel industry include the following:

- The ability to cut garments in Mexico. Under the special regime, as with 807 and 807A, firms had to export cut parts in order to benefit from reduced tariff on imported finished goods.

- The ability to do stone-washing, pressing, and other finishing operations in Mexico. Under the special regime, as with 807 and 807A, finishing operations were not allowed to be included in value added. Thus, these operations had to be performed in the United States after the goods were sewn in Mexico or a CBI country.

- Under NAFTA, firms can both import goods and sell directly to Mexico from Mexican operations. Mexican customers can have access to the same products that are being exported to the United States. Under 807 and 807A, all garment parts exported had to be accounted for when sewn garments were imported.

- Much less paper work is required under NAFTA than under the special regime (De-Witt, 1995).

From an apparel perspective, one advantage Canada has over the United States, because of its close historical connections to Great Britain and France, is access to better and designer European made fabrics without import tariffs. Read Case 10.2.

Case 10.2   U.S. firms a force in Canadian apparel market*

The Americanization of Canada's apparel market continues to grow unabated and U.S. companies now account for about 45 percent of Canadian retail sales, according to an industry research consultant. And competition will only get tougher when Old Navy opens up 12 stores in Canada, said Randy Harris, president of Toledo-based Trendex North America. With its relatively low prices, trendy styles, and wide demographic appeal, Harris believes Old Navy is ideally suited for the Canadian market, and some industry observers believe it will become Canada's largest apparel retailer in five years.

"Canadian retailers are woefully behind their U.S. counterparts," Harris said at the recent North American Apparel and Consumer Market Review conference in Montreal. While U.S. retailers are not as fashion forward in their product offering as their Canadian counterparts, Harris said they put more emphasis on logistics, ticketing, hangtags, and inventory turns. In addition, American retailers have more-focused and better-executed price label programs and are more concerned with territorial exclusivity.

As a result, sales per square foot in Canadian department stores and discount sores are 44 percent and 52 percent lower, respectively, than in the United States. The spread in apparel specialty stores is only 7 percent less in Canada.

With fewer domestic retailers to sell to, Canadian apparel manufacturers were given some tips on how to crack the U.S. market, which has 10 times the population and at least 15 times the retail sales, according to Harris. On the marketing side, Canadian companies must develop a unique selling proposition, target upscale midsize retailers and independent specialty stores, offer exclusivity, and prepare a multiyear export marketing plan.

In terms of merchandising, Harris said Canadians need to leverage, where possible, their access to unique fabrications. This can help ensure higher margins and product uniqueness, emphasize European styling and quality without the inflated European pricing, and reinforce high-diversity/short-run plant capabilities.

*Dunn (2000).

Extending NAFTA to CBI and other Central and South American Countries has been a goal of U.S. apparel manufacturers and retailers over the past 10 years. The U.S. Congress and President Clinton signed into law the **Caribbean Basin Trade Partnership Act**

(CBTPA) and **African Growth and Opportunity Act** in 2000. In 2001, the Bush administration picked up the banner promoting Free Trade Area of the Americas (FTAA) including 34 democracies in the western hemisphere. Chile was identified as the first country that could be added because of its political and economic stability. In 2003, the United States signed free trade agreements with Chile and Singapore and Andean/Panama free trade agreements were under development. The U.S./Chile free trade agreement was the first between the United States and a South American country. Canada and the European Union already had free trade agreements with Chile. Trade between the United States and Chile stands at about $6 billion a year.

During the last 10 years, both the U.S. Department of Labor as well as manufacturers and retailers have been very concerned about labor exploitation in both domestic and foreign markets. The result has been development of codes of conduct relative to relationships with vendors, particularly production contractors. **Codes of conduct** establish commitment to fair and responsible business practices that protect the rights of production employees. The American Apparel Manufacturers Association (now called American Apparel and Footwear Association) created the **worldwide responsible apparel production (WRAP)** that established a globally applicable code of conduct as well as a system of certification of production facilities. WRAP now has 1,398 participating factories in 83 countries with 609 factories certified. WRAP continues to expand its presence through an extensive program of training seminars throughout all regions of the world (International Trade Update, 2004).

Since the early 1970s, when employment in the U.S. textiles and apparel industry peaked, total employment had declined by one-third, from 2.4 million to 1.6 million by 1995 (Good, 1997). However, textile and apparel output had not declined in similar proportion. Because of improvements in technology, particularly in textile production, the U.S. industry had remained globally competitive (Cline, 1990).

Between 1995 and 2003 employment in textiles and apparel in the United States dropped by 54 percent to 731,000 (American Textile Manufacturers Institute, 2003). Some textile production, particularly denim, had been moved to Mexico and Caribbean Basin so textile production is closer to garment product to facilitate QR. NAFTA, among other things, is frequently blamed for the decline in employment in textiles and apparel.

📖 Learning Activity 10.2

Textile and apparel trade and the Americas

1. Make a list of the primary trade regulations that are currently in effect that affect the Americas.

2. Why is trade regulated?
3. How do exports affect the economy of a country?
4. How do imports affect the economy of a country?
5. Why is NAFTA so controversial?
6. According to Case 10.2, what advantages do U.S. apparel firms have in the Canadian market?
7. According to Case 10.2, what advantages do Canadian apparel firms have in the U.S. market?

Many U.S. companies have new priorities relative to exports. At an American Apparel Manufacturers Association (AAMA) annual meeting, 81 percent of executives attending reported that their firms were selling internationally (Black, 1995). Unfortunately, exports of U.S. made finished goods have also declined 26 percent from 1998 to 2003 from $1,528 million to $1,128 million. A group of U.S. women's fashion apparel firms have developed export connections in United Kingdom (UK), Germany, and Kuwait. Successful development of export markets is dependent on strategic marketing and great persistence (Abend, 1996, August). Case 10.3 describes the efforts of one U.S. fashion firm that is entering European markets.

---

 *Case 10.3   U.S. firms exporting to Europe**

Sigrid Olsen doesn't manufacture in New York. The New York, N.Y.-based women's casual sportswear house that does about $50 million produces primarily offshore, with factories in Hong Kong, Taiwan, Israel, Greece, and Bulgaria. It makes a small portion of its lines in the United States and Canada, and sells mostly in the States.

Why, then, does the company take part in Fashion Exports/New York (FE/NY) at the Düsseldorf, Germany, Igedo Exhibition, and subsequently, a London, England, trade mission? Because it is keen to break into Europe. Sigrid Olsen's president and CEO, Edward Jones III, explains: "The whole purpose of the trip was to scout the market and see if what was happening in the United States, in terms of sportswear, was happening in Europe in general. And what I learned by talking to a number of retail buyers and potential agents and distributors was, the movement of the market and the way it was changing for us in the States was almost a carbon copy of Europe."

That's good for his type of multiproduct sportswear, which encompasses lots of knits and sweaters and different lifestyles items,

(continued)

---

including t-shirts, with retail prices that range from $18 to $85. What's not so good, he explains, is having to bring the merchandise into the United States from his multi-country sourcing network and then ship it to Europe. As Jones puts it, "The prices would be so high that I wouldn't be able to accomplish what I'm out to accomplish."

Jones' strategy, as a part of his plan to enter the European marketplace, is to be able to offer the same products globally at prices that are as consistent as possible with those in the United States by bringing the goods in directly.

As a result of his participation in the London trade mission program, the CEO already is set up in the United Kingdom Jones says, "The embassy staff in London was incredible. They did such a great job of organizing things that in two days I had 17 appointments. I had four of the best re-

tailers and then a number of potential agents and distributors. I could never have done it without it being organized the way it was."

By the time Jones got to London from Germany, he was "75 percent sure" that he wanted to go through a distributor, not an agent. He selected one — out of five possibilities — that he met at the embassy, who is starting distribution for all of the United Kingdom for holiday. The firm will do shows in Ireland, Scotland, Manchester, and London. Jones notes, "They have already written some orders."

From the trip the CEO found that, "There's an amazing amount of similarity between the United States and Europe in regard to value. It's just as important throughout Europe as it is for us."

*Based on Sigrid Olsen (2004).

Europe

In many ways Western Europe and Eastern Europe are similar to the United States and Mexico. Western Europe includes many of the most developed countries in the world that are similar in size to some states in the United States, while Eastern Europe includes developing countries. A contrast is that the population of Western Europe is far greater than Eastern Europe.

The European Economic Community (EEC), also known as the Common Market, was formed in 1952 followed by the European Free Trade Association (EFTA) in 1960. The EEC provided for elimination of tariffs and quotas on all trade between member nations. Member nations also agreed to implement common policies regarding transportation, agriculture, and social insurance, and to permit free movement of people and financial resources within the boundaries of the community.

The EFTA was formed because the United Kingdom objected to the loss of control over national policies implied by the EEC. The original members included United Kingdom, Norway, Sweden, Denmark, Switzerland, Austria, and Portugal. The EFTA treaty provided only for elimination of tariffs on industrial products among member nations.

But the Western European economy and European competitiveness "passed through a deep trough" in the late 1970s and early 1980s. The combined profits of Europe's 100 largest corporations were zero. Unemployment, especially among the young, was very high. Growth in productivity had lagged behind wage increases. Social costs (health care, unemployment, and disability compensation, education, etc.) were twice that of either Canada or the United States (Stone, 1994). It was very apparent changes had to be made to revitalize European business. The effort became focused once again on attempting to create a unified Western Europe. Meanwhile many countries of Eastern Europe were in turmoil in the throws of recovery from the breakup of the Soviet Union during the early 1990s.

In 1993, the EEC evolved into a 12-nation group known as the European Union (EU) and later into a 15-nation group known both as the EC (European Community) and EU-15 (European Union) (see Table 10.3). The addition of Austria, Finland, and Sweden to the original EU members created the EU-15.

In 1994, the EU and EFTA joined in a cooperative arrangement to form the European Economic Area (EEA). EEA's purpose is to promote a continuous and balanced strengthening of trade and economic relations between the contracting parties with the view to creating a homogenous European economic area. Accomplishments include development of common product standards and reduction of trade barriers among countries to a so-called "single-document" structure. Truck drivers previously had to carry more than 35 documents to be processed when going from one country to another.

Nationalistic policies within countries had created internal monopolies in services, particularly in telecommunications. These monopolies were in a position to continue to charge their customers for the inefficiencies that had become common in their operations. Monopolies were abandoned in favor of competition. Government procurement has also been opened up to all countries in the group instead of being confined to within individual countries. It is now possible to access the whole Western European market and take advantage of economies of scale (Stone, 1994).

As Eastern European countries recovered from the dissolution of the Soviet Union, they recognized the benefits of trade with Western Europe. The developing countries of Europe had an abundance of skilled labor, low wages, and high unemployment rates. Providing

Table 10.3

Members of the European Union (EU) and the European Free Trade Association (EFTA) and developing countries of Eastern Europe.

European Union-15	New EU Members 2004	European Free Trade Association	Potential EU Member Countries
Austria	Czech Republic	Iceland	Belarus
Belgium	Republic of Cyprus	Liechtenstein	Bulgaria
Denmark	Republic of Estonia	Norway	Romania
Finland	Republic of Hungary	Switzerland	Russia
France	Republic of Latvia	Austria	Turkey
Germany	Republic of Lithuania		
Greece	Republic of Malta		
Ireland	Republic of Poland		
Italy	Republic of Slovenia		
Luxembourg	Slovak Republic		
The Netherlands			
Portugal			
Spain			
Sweden			
United Kingdom			

production of consumable goods for Western European countries supplied much needed jobs. Then they began to apply for admission into the EU to gain unfettered access to Western European markets.

EU-15 solidified the European Union when it gained support from the membership to use the **Euro currency** in everyday transactions in 2001. In 2004, EU-15 was enlarged to include 10 new member states from Eastern Europe that also participate in the EEA. Five Eastern European countries remain as potential EU members (see Table 10.3) while EFTA now includes three northern European countries, as well as Switzerland and Austria.

The EEA potentially could control up to 40 percent of world trade, including some of the highest income countries in the world. Western Europe is not yet completely united with Eastern Europe as a trading bloc, but economic power would be clearly increased if they were. The goal of many participants in the evolution of the relationships among the European countries has been to create a United States of Europe. They aren't there yet but they have made a great deal of progress over the past 10 years.

As the EU developed and became more open to trade within, trade barriers remained to exporters from around the world. Case 10.4 provides an example of how controversial trade regulations can be for a seemingly minor product — bananas.

🗁   *Case 10.4   U.S. government ends "Banana War"*   🗁
                    *with European Union. ***

Washington and the European Union announced a settlement in the 9-year "banana war" trade dispute that gives more access to U.S. companies such as Chiquita Brands International to markets in Europe. Since the European Union market was created in 1993, new rules were imposed against fruit imports from Latin America — where U.S. companies have plantations — to protect investments by European capitalists in their former colonies in Africa and the Caribbean.

During the 1980s and early 1990s, Chiquita Brands and Dole Foods, the leading U.S. banana enterprises, raked in profits from European sales because bananas could be sold at twice the price of those in the United States. U.S. grocers have traditionally marketed bananas as "loss leaders" (selling them below cost) to stimulate store traffic greatly limiting the wholesale price they were willing to pay. Chiquita alone had 40 percent of the banana market in Europe. With the 1993 regulations, Chiquita's profits plummeted and market share dropped to only 20 percent by 1997.

Dole's market share was 26 percent in 1993 and 24 percent in 1997.

Chiquita filed suit against the European Union in 2001 accusing it of failing to reduce trade barriers in response to a 1997 World Trade Organization ruling. Chiquita said it was pushed to the brink of bankruptcy by the EU's system of tariffs and quota's, which restricted the sales of bananas marketed by U.S. companies.

According to the new agreement between the United States and the European Union, the European Union will institute a transition period of modified quotas and tariffs to end in 2006. U.S. trade officers said Washington agreed to lift a range of punitive tariffs imposed on some other European products by July 1, 2001.

Dole contends the new deal favors Chiquita because the new European import licenses will be based on import levels from 1994 to 1996 when Chiquita had the bigger market share.

*EC & US... (2001).

European Textiles and Apparel

Among the European countries, Germany and Italy have assumed unique roles in the global textiles and apparel industry. Germany is a global leader in the development and export of textile-and-apparel production machinery. Italy is the leading exporter of upscale, fashion forward, apparel and shoes with the United States as its primary customer. Production of high-value garments tends to be concentrated around sources of high-quality fabrics produced in Europe. Demands of sophisticated Italian consumers and the Italian fashion sense perpetuated by brands like Giorgio Armani, Gianni Versace, Valentino, and others have solidified Italian dominance in the high-value market (Appelbaum, Smith, & Christerson, 1994). Case 10.5 describes the status of textile and apparel markets in the United Kingdom.

🗀   Case 10.5   *Textiles and apparel in the United Kingdom** 🗀

There is currently a competitive retail market in the United Kingdom, which has consequently affected the clothing sector. The UK retail clothing market is estimated to be worth 30.07 billion pounds in 2000, having grown by just 3.8 percent over the past year.

Textile manufacturing, once a stalwart of the UK economy, is in serious decline. Clothing retailers continue to find trading conditions difficult in the face of weak consumer demand and heavy discounting. Marks and Spencer PLC, Arcadia Group PLC, BhS Ltd, and Moss Bros Group PLC are among well-known High Street names struggling to maintain their position. Meanwhile, the chain of C&A admitted defeat and withdrew completely from the British market in early 2001.

It is companies such as these competing in the middle market which are finding business so hard, since the market favors either value or premium brands. Those that are thriving include value chains such as Matalan PLC, Peacock's Stores Led., and Primark Stores Ltd. which are expanding rapidly and are predicted to increase their market share. Furthermore, the upmarket Ted Baker PLC has recently recorded a pretax profit margin of almost four times that of the industry average.

Women's, girl's, and childrens' clothing accounts for the major share of the market with 68.7 percent of the value attributable to same. On the one hand, the increase in working women might be expected to cause an upsurge in demand for smart clothing but, on the other hand, a major feature of the market has been the trend toward dressing down. Men's tailors, such as Moss Bros Group PLC and Austin Reed

Case 10.5 (continued)

Group PLC, have suffered from the demise of the formal suit, while Ted Baker PLC has embraced the trend with the opening of a "Ted's the Business" shop in London's Canary Wharf. The store is devoted to "smart casual wear, which has been developed to meet the needs of the dress down market," and initial reaction to the store is described as extremely favorable. Certainly, in the world of fashion, it is the ability to identify and respond immediately to trends that is all-important.

With depressed demand and the prevalence of discounters, UK clothing retailing is expected to see modest growth. A value of 36.41 billion pounds is expected to be reached by the year 2005.

*Research and Markets (2000).

 Learning Activity 10.3

Trade in Europe

1. What are similarities between the European and the American trading areas?
2. What are differences between the European and the American trading areas?
3. Considering Case 10.5, why do you think the U.S. government became involved in the "banana war"? What did the United States have to give up in order to settle it?
4. In terms of the "banana war," what was the issue between Chiquita and Dole?
5. Considering Case 10.5, now is the textile and apparel markets in the United Kingdom similar to U.S. markets?
6. How are the U.S. and UK markets different?
7. Look up descriptions of the retailers named in Case 10.5. Identify U.S. retailers that are similar to each.
8. Find a business dictionary and determine the meanings of the terms associated with the retailers' names (PLC, Ltd., etc.). Do these terms have comparable language in the United States?

Asia

The Asia/Pacific Rim trading bloc clearly represents the largest segment of the world population and great variety of levels of economic development. Asia is often described in according to geographic sections that relate to physical location. Southeast Asia includes both mainland and island countries. Members of the Association of Southeast Asian Nations (ASEAN), formed in 1977, include Brunei, Cambodia, Indonesia, Laos, Malaysia, Myanmar, Philippines, Singapore, Thailand, and Vietnam. These countries have dominated textile and apparel trade from this region of the world because of investment by Japan, Hong Kong, Taiwan, and Korea (Dickerson, 1995). The ASEAN countries have a free trade agreement. Recently, ASEAN+3 (China, Japan, and South Korea) have been collaborating to promote tourism in Southeast Asia (ASEAN+3, 2004).

Countries involved in textiles and apparel in East Asia include Hong Kong, Korea, Taiwan, China, and Japan. Hong Kong, Korea, and Taiwan became known as the "Big Three" apparel exporters dominating world trade until the early 1970s when trade was opened between the United States and China. By the late 1980s, China became the largest apparel exporter in the world. Countries in each region of Asia are summarized in Table 10.4.

Japan aggressively entered textiles and apparel markets following World War II and became a dominant force in the 1950s. Beginning in the 1970s Japan experienced a huge influx of imports of textile fibers, fabrics, and apparel made at lower cost elsewhere in the world. Imports have continued to grow and Japan now has a huge apparel trade deficit. The Japanese response to the import competition is a strategy of globalization, quality improvements, and technology to expand in overseas markets. Japanese manufacturing of

Table 10.4

Countries located in different regions of Asia involved in the global trade of textiles and apparel.

East Asia	South Asia	Southeast Asia
China	Afghanistan	*Mainland Countries*
Hong Kong	Bangladesh	Kampuchea (Cambodia)
Korea	Bhutan	Laos
Japan	India	Myanmar (Burma)
Taiwan	Nepal	Thailand
	Pakistan	Vietnam
	Sri Lanka	Western Malaysia
		Island Countries
		Brunei
		Eastern Malaysia
		Indonesia
		Malaysia
		Philippines
		Singapore

finished consumer goods has gradually moved to China, Southeast Asia, and to some extent Europe. Japanese efforts have focused on a long-term vision: How to improve the product and its quality and reduce costs. The development of ultrafine, microfiber polyester yarns is one example of the outcomes of this effort. Japan has assumed technical development leadership of the global textiles and apparel industry (Good, 1997) while China has focused on leadership in production.

In 2001, China was admitted to the WTO while China is successfully moving from a centrally planned to a market economy (Zhang, Dickson, & Lennon, 2002). Membership in the WTO provides the opportunity for Chinese textile and garment producers to export goods tariff and quota free after 2005. Retail competition within China is also expected to become much more intense with many foreign retailers entering a potentially huge market (Kwan, Yeung, & Au, 2003). It also makes it possible for Chinese retailers to expand into foreign markets. Case 10.6 describes the risks and opportunities for Chinese retailers related to membership in the WTO.

Case 10.6 *For Chinese retailers, entry into WTO is not risk-free.* *

Sun Guoyin and her daughter Hou Foufang once led a dreary existence as employees of a drab, state-owned department store in Hengshui, China. The mother was a manager, the daughter a clerk. But after Mao Zedong died in 1976 and China began building a market economy, everything changed. Relying on connections as much as cunning, Sun and Hou engineered the store's privatization and grabbed 70 percent of the shares with the help of a $10 million government loan.

Now they are enjoying the good life. Hou's daughter just enrolled in a $25,000-a-year boarding school. The store is booming, with a new 5-story building and a virtual monopoly in this city of 4 million about 150 miles south of Beijing. And Hou landed a job as head of the city government's purchasing department, an ideal position to guarantee business for her store. So why is she frowning?

"The WTO," replied Hou, 39, a stylish divorcee who cruises around in a shiny black Buick. "We built this business playing by China's rules. But now the rules are changing." China's entry into the World Trade Organization promises to do more than rewrite the rules of the nation's freewheeling economy. It could bring about

(continued)

changes as revolutionary as those that resulted from the market reforms beginning in 1978, redefining once again how business is conducted, how success is achieved, and how power is distributed in the world's most populous nation.

As the Chinese economy opens to greater foreign competition, millions of farmers and workers could be forced to look for new jobs. But accession to the global trade body could also force the country to push ahead with difficult reforms in its transition from socialist planning to a market economy, overhauling a banking system and legal structure that remain skewed in favor of those with power or connections. China's Communist leadership is so skittish about the potential shocks that it has yet to publish the terms of its accession to the WTO in public. Many government ministers have not been informed of agreements that will directly affect their ministries, government sources say.

"Of course we are concerned," said Hou. "Up until now, I have felt that we Chinese could somehow control our relations with the outside world. We had competition, but not too much. Now it seems that our whole country is going to be opened up. I worry that we're not ready." To join the WTO, China promised to lift most restrictions on foreign retailers in three years, and Hou worries that stores like hers will become fodder for big international chains.

"Look what happened to China's domestic soft drink companies," she said, sipping a Coke. "A few years ago every town, even Hengshui, had two or three factories. Now, it's just Coke and Pepsi." Wal-Mart already has over a dozen stores in China. The French retailer Carrefour operates 26 outlets. All five of Japan's top retailers have plans to expand quickly here. In addition, Kmart has begun sourcing goods at a factory near Hengshui.

There is another problem: Hou's dual identity as store owner and municipal purchasing chief is viewed as normal in China's hybrid economy. But such a conflict of interest might violate China's promise to eliminate favoritism in government purchasing. Sun and Hou are trying to prepare for changes. But their international strategy consists primarily of a plan to invest in Poland, a country they selected because a trusted friend lives there. They have no market research and do not understand European tastes.

"I am not exaggerating to say that I feel a sense of crisis," Hou said. "A lot of successful people feel the same way."

*Pomfret & Pan (2001).

📁 *Learning Activity 10.4*

Opportunities in Asia

1. Read Case 10.6 very carefully. How will the retail environment for a Chinese retail entrepreneur differ after WTO membership?
2. In the United States, would it be legal for a retail owner to hold a government buyer position and source his/her own store? Why? Would it be ethical?
3. What is the relationship between development of retail markets in Asia and the use of Asian firms as sources of textiles and apparel?
4. With regard to China, what is the meaning of the term "hybrid economy"?

South Asia has assumed much greater importance in the global textile and apparel markets since it includes some of the worlds lowest cost suppliers. India has become a major world supplier with planned exports of $15 billion in 2003. At the same time low manufacturing productivity is a major stumbling block for India (Bheda, Narag, & Singla, 2003). There are also concerns about competition from China, Pakistan, and Bangladesh (International News Digest, 2003). When fiber, yarn, fabric, and finished goods are considered, Pakistan is the largest exporter of cotton and cotton goods in the world.

Tiny Sri Lanka (formerly known as Ceylon), located off the coast of India, is one of the poorest island countries in the world but it has thriving apparel industry that has grown over 16 percent per annum over the past two decades. Apparel provides over 30 percent of manufacturing employment and almost half of its foreign earnings. Unfortunately it has been devastated by civil war lasting over 20 years. In spite of these limitations, Sri Lanka has a strong record of compliance with international standards in terms of labor laws, environmental protection, and human rights, especially as compared to its much larger neighboring countries. Sri Lanka and many other countries in South Asia intend to continue to expand their role in the global apparel market (Burtin & Erguney, 2003).

Globalization of Apparel Sourcing

A little over two-thirds of apparel sold in the United States is now imported. This means that less than a third of apparel is produced by firms in the United States and the other two-thirds are imported from firms in nearly every country in the world. Ten years ago, companies were already operating in an increasingly interconnected world. Global competitors were learning to develop and manufacture products that could be introduced and marketed simultaneously in many countries. And in so doing, they found themselves sourcing materials, components, and technology from sites and suppliers worldwide. Entry-level management positions were being filled by a computer literate group of young people—setting the course for our electronic future. Moreover, computer-to-computer communication, generally called e-mail, was increasing at a rate of 10 percent per month in the United States and has become nearly universal. Every business professional is assumed to have access to e-mail.

Historically, firms have used networks of personal contacts and printed directories of suppliers and trade associations to identify potential sources of materials and production. Determining the appropriate sources meant numerous phone calls and trips to production sites to examine capabilities. Some companies, including Mast Industries (a subsidiary of The Limited) and JCPenney, gained the competitive edge by developing their own electronic sourcing systems. Specifications, costing, and distribution forms were the first sourcing information to be communicated electronically (Anderson & Todaro, 1995).

Rapid increases in reasonably priced microcomputer capability made electronic sourcing a reality. Numerous on-line sourcing databases have been developed. The development of sourcing networks allowed materials and production sourcing to become an integrated aspect of product development. For example, firms developing new fabrics in several different countries might be accessed via the Internet as the product development process evolves. Materials orders can be placed and delivery dates negotiated. Sourcing of production might include electronic displays of plant layouts, production statistics, and capacity availability.

Most of the textiles and apparel imported into the U.S. is sourced by U.S. apparel manufacturers and retailers. Table 10.5 provides numerous ways to think about trends in quantities of U.S. apparel imports. The table is organized by level of square meter equivalent (SME) imports from the top 25 exporting countries to the U.S. Exporting regions and related economic development trade legislation are also reported including the Caribbean Basin, Sub-Saharan Africa, and the Andean Region.

The table summarizes imports from the 25 countries that were the largest exporters of textiles and apparel to the U.S. from 2000 to 2002. Data are reported in SMEs, in dollar value for each year, and by percent change from 2001 to 2002 in SME and in dollars. The impressions garnered from each of these measures differ considerably. Unless the figures are examined closely, they can be very misleading.

Square Meter Equivalents and Dollar Values

The amount of fabric required to make a garment or a group of garments is measured in SMEs for purposes of determining quantities of apparel that are exported and imported. The number of square meters required for a garment can vary from a small fraction of a square meter if the garment is a bikini bathing suit or a baby's shirt to several square meters if the garment is a pair of workwear coveralls. The wholesale price or merchandise cost is used as a measure of quantity traded in dollars. Thus, if the firms in a country are primarily engaged in the manufacture of better lingerie, the measure of SMEs may be relatively low compared to the dollar value of garments exported. The dollar value may be comparatively low if low price/quality of fabric is used.

It is quickly apparent that firms in China are the largest suppliers of apparel for U.S. imports, followed by Mexico. Notice that Mexico was the dominant supplier for several years up until 2003. China had a 46 percent increase in SMEs and a 30% increase in dollars from 2002 to 2003. China also had increases of 60 percent in SMEs and 22 percent in dollars from 2001 to 2002 (these numbers are not in the table). Many apparel industry experts believe these increases reflect the anticipation of expiring of quota restraints in 2005. A wide variety of apparel products are sourced in China and many good quality fabrics are also readily available.

Mexico was established as a major U.S. supplier before NAFTA and became the dominant supplier following the implementation of NAFTA in 1994. A variety of products are sourced in Mexico from lingerie to men's suits to jeans with well-established QR systems. The Mexican textile and apparel industry is very concerned about loss of U.S. apparel market share to China. Mexico initiated a major project three years ago to determine a strategy for holding on to its dominant export role as supplier for U.S. textile and apparel markets, but has continued to gradually lose market share. Comparing the quantities of SMEs exported year to year helps establish the trends in growth and market share. Comparing quantities in dollars provides another trend.

Labor rates have increased in some of the more established apparel supplying countries including Mexico, Hong Kong, and South Korea, prompting low-cost producers to move sourcing to other parts of the world. The countries that have had explosive growth as U.S. suppliers are Vietnam with over 134 percent increase between 2002 and 2003 and Russia with 69 percent increase. Vietnam went from 315 million SMEs/$895 million in 2002 to 739 million SMEs/$2.375 billion in 2003. Russia went from 130 million SMEs/$357 million in 2002 to 219 SMEs/$480 million in 2003.

The CBTPA (Caribbean Basin Trade Partnership Act) also had an influence on rates of imports. Many companies switched to the import incentives provided by CBTPA with a steady increase in country participation since it went into effect in 2000.

Sub-Saharan Africa is showing the benefit of the AGOA (African Growth and Opportunity Act) passed in 2000 with a 44 percent increase in SMEs per 38 percent increase in dollars between 2002 and 2003. Six African countries are major contributors dominated by the growth in Swaziland and South Africa.

Table 10.5

U.S. imports of apparel by country and trade program in square meter equivalents (SMEs) and dollars, top 25 countries based on 2003 SME data (dollar and SME data in millions). *

Rank	Country	2001 SMEs	2001 $	2002 SMEs	2002 $	2003 SMEs	2003 $	% Change 2002–2003 SMEs	% Change 2002–2003 $	% of Imports 2003 SMEs	% of Imports 2003 $
1	China	976	$ 4,602	1,565	$ 5,594	2,290	$ 7,258	46.3%	29.7%	12.1%	11.9%
2	Mexico	2,290	$ 7,811	2,157	$ 7,424	1,977	$ 6,904	-8.3%	-7.0%	10.5%	11.3%
3	Honduras	1,021	$ 2,344	1,090	$ 2,440	1,152	$ 2,503	5.7%	2.6%	6.1%	4.1%
4	Bangladesh	966	$ 2,201	928	$ 1,883	913	$ 1,848	-1.6%	-1.9%	4.6%	3.0%
5	El Salvador	724	$ 1,612	777	$ 1,675	856	$ 1,720	10.2%	2.7%	4.5%	2.8%
6	Hong Kong	917	$ 4,211	821	$ 3,877	785	$ 3,701	-4.4%	-4.5%	4.2%	6.1%
7	Dominican Republic	753	$ 2,252	730	$ 2,162	750	$ 2,124	2.8%	-1.8%	4.0%	3.5%
8	Vietnam	28	$ 48	315	$ 895	739	$ 2,375	134.4%	165.3%	3.9%	3.9%
9	Indonesia	594	$ 2,215	595	$ 2,042	618	$ 2,157	3.9%	5.7%	3.3%	3.5%
10	Taiwan	614	$ 1,811	576	$ 1,576	591	$ 1,611	2.6%	2.2%	3.1%	2.6%
11	South Korea	632	$ 2,182	650	$ 2,062	576	$ 1,807	-11.4%	12.4%	3.1%	3.0%
12	Philippines	553	$ 1,891	551	$ 1,815	546	$ 1,853	-0.9%	2.1%	2.9%	3.0%
13	India	403	$ 1,717	509	$ 1,902	532	$ 2,002	4.6%	5.3%	2.8%	3.3%
14	Cambodia	359	$ 935	440	$ 1,043	528	$ 1,240	20.0%	18.9%	2.8%	2.0%
15	Thailand	453	$ 1,818	490	$ 1,719	496	$ 1,712	1.2%	-0.4%	2.6%	2.8%
16	Guatemala	388	$ 1,604	415	$ 1,658	445	$ 1,762	7.0%	6.3%	2.4%	2.9%
17	Pakistan	347	$ 932	382	$ 878	444	$ 1,016	16.1%	15.6%	2.4%	1.7%
18	Sri Lanka	403	$ 1,505	394	$ 1,413	395	$ 1,436	0.3%	1.6%	2.1%	2.3%
19	Macau	268	$ 1,127	319	$ 1,146	376	$ 1,282	17.8%	11.8%	2.0%	2.1%
20	Turkey	306	$ 1,045	347	$ 1,190	374	$ 1,257	7.8%	5.7%	2.0%	2.1%
21	Costa Rica	350	$ 749	362	$ 725	332	$ 589	-8.2%	-18.7%	1.8%	1.0%
22	Canada	281	$ 1,585	292	$ 1,610	262	$ 1,569	-10.1%	-2.6%	1.4%	2.6%
23	Russia	102	$ 333	130	$ 357	219	$ 480	69.0%	34.3%	1.2%	0.8%
24	Malaysia	193	$ 761	193	$ 720	191	$ 686	-0.7%	-4.8%	1.0%	1.1%
25	Nicaragua	96	$ 374	120	$ 432	150	$ 484	25.1%	11.8%	0.8%	0.8%
	World	16,103	$56,460	17,255	$56,963	18,864	$61,164	9.3%	7.4%	100%	100%

Caribbean Basin	3,570	$ 9,375	3,714	$ 9,471	3,920	$9,611	5.6%	1.5%	20.8%	15.7%
% Under CBTPA[1]	59.3%	54.5%	68.1%	63.7%	70.9%	65/0%	—	—	—	—
CAFTA + DR[1]	3,331	$ 8,934	3,494	$ 9,093	3,685	$9,182	5.5%	1.0%	19.5	15.0%
CAFTA	2,578	$ 6,683	2,764	$ 6,931	2,935	$7,058	6.2%	1.8%	15.6	11.5%
Sub-Saharan Africa	218	$ 951	277	$ 1,098	399	$1,511	43.9%	37.7%	2.1	2.5%
% Under AGOA[1]	34.2%	37.4%	71.8%	72.7%	77.9%	79.2%	—	—	—	—
Andean Region	142	$ 754	153	$ 751	204	$1,051	34.2%	40.0%	1.1	1.7%
% Under ATPDEA[1]	N/A	N/A	N/A	N/A	65.9%	71.9%	—	—	—	—

[1] % Under Program = Percentage of imports from the region entered under the applicable trade preference program. CBTPA = Caribbean Basin Trade Partnership Act, effected October 2000. CAFTA + DR = countries included in proposed U.S./Central America Free Trade Agreement (Costa Rica, Dominican Republic, El Salvador, Guatemala, Honduras, and Nicaragua). AGOA = Sub-Saharan African countries covered by African Growth and Opportunity Act, effected October 2000. ATPDEA = four ANDEAN countries (Bolivia, Colombia, Ecuador, and Peru) covered by Andean Trade Promotion & Drug Eradication Act, effected October 2002.

*American Apparel & Footwear Association (2004).

Dollars per Square Meter

Other countries of interest are Canada and Italy. Canada ranks among the top 25 countries but Italy does not. Canada lost 10% in SMEs and almost 3 percent in dollars, indicating they were exporting fewer SMEs but at a higher dollar value per SME. Canada's exports to the U.S. address a more upscale market involving men's and women's upper moderate and better sportswear and outerwear. Some Canadian firms have been very successful in securing U.S. market share. Canada's exports grew rapidly following the passage of NAFTA, but growth has tapered off. From 2001 to 2003, Canada's exports to U.S. markets were relatively flat at about 280 million SMEs/$1.58 billion. These numbers reflect the high value of products coming from Canada at about $6 per square meter (number of dollars of imports ÷ number of SMEs).

In general, the textiles and apparel industry in Western European countries, with the exception of Italy, has experienced extreme downsizing in both numbers of employees and overall sales. Labor costs have risen and productivity has not kept up with the rest of the world (Cline, 1990). Italy alone has been successful in continuing to grow market share by focusing on an upscale market. If Italy were included in Table 10.5, we could calculate dollars per square meter. We would find that Italy's apparel exports to the U.S. have an average value per square meter of over $10, far exceeding all other countries. Other countries are mostly in the range of $2 to $4 per square meter. Italy is the only European country that falls within the top 30 exporters to the U.S. High labor costs are commonly blamed for low rates of imports from other European countries. Nevertheless, design, fashion, and quality are still desirable attributes of European-made products.

As shown in Table 10.5, dollars per square meter in 2003 ranged from a low of $1.77 per square meter (Costa Rica) to a high of $5.99 (Canada). The only other country over $4 per square meter is Hong Kong. Most of the countries are in the $3 to $4 range. Considering dollars per square meter in Table 10.5 provides an understanding of the relationship between the dollar value of the shipments and the quantity measured in SMEs.

📖 **Learning Activity 10.5**

Trends in U.S. apparel sourcing

1. Create another set of columns for Table 10.5 entitled "Dollars per Square Meter" for 2003. Calculate dollars per square meter for each country represented in Table 10.5 for 2003.
2. What countries have the highest dollars per square meter? Do other countries in the same region of the world also have higher dollars per square meter? Do you

have any clothes in your closet from those countries? What types of apparel would you expect to find coming from that area of the world?

3. What countries have the lowest dollars per square meter? Do other countries in the same region of the world also have lower dollars per square meter? Do you have any clothes in your closet from that part of the world? What types of clothes would you expect to find coming from that part of the world?

4. What part of the world has the greatest portion of the U.S. market? Consider the Americas, Europe, and Asia. What other new information about U.S. apparel imports does market share information provide?

The Sourcing Process

At least two firms are the key ingredients in an apparel sourcing relationship: the sourcing company, which may be a manufacturer or a retailer, and the contracting company, which may be located domestically or anywhere in the world. The manufacturer or retailer decides what and when the goods are to be acquired; the contracting company provides the merchandise. If goods are being sourced in a foreign country it is common for an export trading company and/or an agent to act as an intermediary between the sourcing company and potential contractors. The export trading company may provide merchandise planning as well as product development and production sourcing. The export trading company may also hire the agent. The agent is often native to the country or region when the product(s) will be sourced and is knowledgeable about the companies, their products, production capacities, and quality levels. The export trading companies are paid a fee for their services that becomes a part of the product cost while an agent is paid a commission for services that may be 5 percent of the cost of the goods produced (Birnbaum, 2000).

As sourcing companies become well-established in foreign countries, they sometimes establish their own offices or even a subsidiary that takes over the duties of the agent. Sourcing takes two primary forms: full package sourcing (FPS), and cut, make, trim (CMT) sourcing.

Full Package Sourcing

Full package sourcing (FPS) means the contractor provides everything required to make the garments. The contractor purchases materials, develops samples, makes garments, and ships first-quality goods to the sourcing company. Under FPS, no fabric or findings are owned by the sourcing company; instead, these are sourced and purchased by the contractor. Full package sourcing is facilitated by having materials of appropriate type and quality locally available. Import fees for materials may be included in costs if materials have to be sourced from another country.

The contractor may also make and perfect all the patterns and samples. It is fairly common for contractors to subcontract part or the entire sewing portion of manufacturing. For example, when a full package contractor is Hong Kong-based, product development activities including materials sourcing and patternmaking may take place in Hong Kong while garment assembly is subcontracted to firms in China or Indonesia where labor costs are lower.

Some sourcing companies place detailed orders that include product specifications, quality standards, assortments, quantities, and shipping dates. Contract terms may specify that no seconds are to be shipped by the contractor. The sourcing company backs order commitments by an irrevocable **letter of credit.** When finished goods are shipped and order requirements are satisfied, payment is made automatically from the sourcing company's bank to the contractor's bank. Production and quota reservations are often needed six months in advance of production. Quota rent is determined by market conditions and can vary greatly by time and country. The time required for transit and customs processing is likely to be 60 days. When an export trading company is included in the sourcing process, it may assume many of the responsibilities of the sourcing firm including specification writing.

FPS is well-established in Hong Kong, Korea, and Taiwan where U.S. department stores have long standing relationships with contractors. Many Caribbean Basin contractors are now able to provide FPS after being exclusively CMT and contractors around the world are trying figure out how they can do full package.

At the same time, **business ethics** have become a primary concern for firms collaborating in the apparel manufacturing process. Some have attempted to standardize operating relationships by establishing standards of conduct for sourcing relationships. Table 10.6 reports standards of conduct for business partners of Nordstrom.

Cut, Make, Trim (CMT)

With **cut, make, trim (CMT) sourcing,** the sourcing company is responsible for product development, including development of designs, patterns and product specifications, and sourcing of materials. The primary contribution of the contractor is sewing. The materials are purchased by the sourcing company and may or may not be cut into garment parts when they are delivered to the contractor. No fabrics are owned by the contractor. In some countries, findings are included in the contractor's price. Second-quality garments may be shipped along with those of first quality depending on the purchase agreement.

Table 10.6

Standards of conduct for business partners. *

1. Legal Requirements: Nordstrom expects all of its partners to comply with applicable laws and regulations of the United States and those of the respective country of manufacture or exportation. All products must be accurately labeled and clearly identified as to their country of origin.
2. Health and Safety Requirements: Nordstrom seeks partners who provide safe and healthy work environments for their workers, including adequate facilities and protections from exposure to hazardous conditions or materials.
3. Employment Practices: Nordstrom firmly believes people are entitled to equal opportunity in employment. Although the company recognizes cultural differences exist, Nordstrom pursues business partners who do not discriminate and who demonstrate respect for the dignity of all people.
4. Environmental Standards: Partners must demonstrate a regard for the environment, as well as compliance with local environmental laws. Further, Nordstrom seeks partners who demonstrate a commitment to progressive environmental practices and to preserving the Earth's resources.
5. Documentation and Inspection: Nordstrom intends to monitor compliance with our Partnership Guidelines and to undertake on-site inspection of partners' facilities. Nordstrom will review and may terminate its relationship with any partner found to be in violation of the Partnership Guidelines.

*Based on Spector & McCarthy (1995).

CMT is common in the Caribbean Basin and in countries where apparel production is just being established. For Item 807/Chapter 9802 production, CMT is appropriate because assembly is all that is allowed with duty assessed on value added. Because of the new CBI trade legislation that does not require garments to be cut in the United States, the use of 807 type sourcing is rapidly declining. Freight costs vary by point of departure and point of entry. Other variable costs borne by sourcing companies might include broker's fees, inland freight, bank charges, and insurance. The latter may be about 18 percent of merchandise cost.

🗋 *Learning Activity 10.6*

Full package and cut, make, trim sourcing

1. What is the difference between FPS and CMT?
2. Why might a sourcing firm prefer FPS?
3. Why might a sourcing firm prefer CMT?
4. Why might the contractor prefer CMT?

Sourcing Decisions

Sourcing proceeds in several stages with different requirements of the sourcing company and the contractor at each stage. In Chapter 8, Line Development, we looked at terms related to negotiating contracts with vendors. Those terms are certainly part of sourcing language since contracts are an essential outcome of sourcing. In addition, however, there is the language of the sourcing process related to product descriptions, international trade regulation, transportation systems, and contracts. Table 10.7 itemizes some of the terminology used in sourcing.

Choosing a Country or Countries

Contractors in one or more countries might be necessary in order for the sourcing company to provide adequate quantities of a particular style or merchandise group for their customers. Contractors in particular countries tend to be specialized in certain types of products: knits or wovens; top- or bottom-weight fabrics; budget, moderate, or better price ranges; and simple or complex assembly methods. Thus, the type of product desired (jeans, jackets, sweaters, shirts, etc.) is a primary criteria in determining likely countries for sourcing.

A second consideration also relates to type of product, that is, whether it is a basic or fashion good. Type of styling, quantity required, and lead time are often related to whether goods are basic or fashion. Basic goods often require larger quantities and lead time may be less of a factor. Fashion goods may be more complex in design and construction and require smaller quantities and shorter lead times. Fashion goods may also have a greater likelihood of change in quantity desired, which would have to be written into the garment purchase agreement (GPA).

Type of fabrication is another determining factor. Availability of materials varies greatly by country. Some countries have little domestic materials production, thus all fabrics and findings must be imported. Others have well-developed textile industries. Availability of appropriate materials can significantly reduce costs, and timelines. Fiber content is an important factor, because it is a determinant of the quota category of the finished goods. Garment finishing requirements (e.g., stonewashing, bleaching, and garment dying) may be other determining criteria. Consideration must also be given to whether estimated landed costs are appropriate to planned list or first price, allowable costs, and quota availability.

Choosing a Contractor or Contractors

Sourcing companies provide agents in selected countries with a development package (sometimes called a bid package). A **development package** is the outcome of creative design and the line adoption processes. A development package may be as simple as a sketch and fabric description with size specifications and size range, or a fully developed prototype with fabric swatches, size specifications, and size ranges. Packages may be sent simultaneously to several countries and several contractors in each country. The contractors prepare **counter samples** and costs as a basis for a bid on the contract. Based on the counter samples and the bids, the agent recommends the best contractor(s). Buyers representing the sourcing company then usually visit the contractors to evaluate facilities, working conditions, production capacity, etc.

The sourcing company evaluates samples, costs, and information from plant visits. **Garment purchase agreement(s) (GPAs)** are drawn up with the desired contractor(s). GPAs are legal contracts among the sourcing company, the contractor, and the agent. A letter of credit to the contractor is opened for the value of the order. This letter of credit specifies the ship date and other requirements indicated in the GPA.

Prepare for Production

A detailed **technical package** is prepared by the sourcing company or its export trading company, including materials and findings specifications, graded size specifications, pattern check run requirements, assembly and quality inspections specifications, labeling and ticketing, packing specs, lab dips for fabrics, etc. Technical packages are the result of the technical design process. For goods that will be sold at wholesale, sales samples and swatches must be completed immediately — and they need to be a good representation of the finished goods but to save time, sometimes they are not exactly the same.

Pattern check runs (PCR) are samples that help ensure all aspects of construction and sizing have been clearly communicated and can be properly executed by the contractor. Sometimes the production of sales samples serves as a PCR. PCRs are done for each new combination of fabric, style, and contractor. Production fabric is also tested to ensure quality and performance of finished goods and to determine final care instructions. Approval of a final production garment test using the approved materials, findings, assists, patterns, and assembly methods results in a release to cut order, then production begins.

Production

Production is the process of spreading and cutting materials and assembling garments. There are three common types of garment assembly systems: progressive bundle, unit production, and modular production. The progressive bundle system gets it name from bundles of cut parts being moved from one sewing process to another until the garment is

Table 10.7

Definition of terms for a merchandising language for sourcing. *

Product Description	Trade Regulation
assists—an item or service supplied free of charge (or at reduced cost) to a contractor (e.g., rivets, buttons).	**certificate of origin**—a document that certifies that the goods referred to were manufactured in a specific country.
audit—methodical quality and/or quantity examination applying pre-established company guidelines.	**clearing a shipment**—process involving Customs to validate duty rates and ensure quota is available for goods subject to quota restriction.
care label—a label sewn into a garment showing the care instructions and plant identification code; may also contain product code, fiber content, size, country of origin, etc.	**Customs house broker**—an agent in a port who facilitates Customs clearing on behalf of a company; a person or a firm licensed by the Treasury Department to prepare and file Customs entries, arrange payment of duties due, take steps to release goods from Customs, and represent clients in Customs matters.
carton tag—coded tags attached to cartons of finished garments identifying contents.	
counter sample—a copy of the prototype garment made by the contractor.	**duty**—a tax levied on articles of foreign manufacture imported into a country.
development package—basis of counter sample and costing; sketch and fabric descriptions or prototype and swatches along with sample size specifications and size range.	**duty classification**—one element of a system for applying taxes related to importing goods.
	port of entry—a port having Customs authorities and designated as a place for the entry and clearance of vessels and goods; major ports include Oakland, Los Angeles, New York City, and Miami.
fabric testing—series of lab tests to identify a fabric's characteristics (shrinkage, tear strength, fading, water absorption, etc.) so that appropriate care instructions can be determined and to ensure standards are met.	**quota rent**—purchase of quota from a firm that has excess quota for import of a specific classification of goods from a specific country; cost depends on market demand at a particular time.
pattern check run (PCR)—production of samples to ensure all aspects of construction and sizing have been clearly communicated and can be properly executed by the contractor.	**style sheet**—describes products to Customs for establishment of duty rates and quota classifications; requires merchandiser input to describe garment's construction and fabric.
technical package—product specifications supplementing the GPA detailing construction, measurement, patterns, and markers.	**U.S. Customs Service**—agency responsible for establishment of duty rates and quota classification.

*Based on *Levi Strauss and Company.*

Transportation

airway bill of lading (AWB)—a written receipt given by an air carrier for goods accepted for transporation.

bill of lading (B/L)—a written receipt given by a carrier for goods accepted for transportation.

brokers delivery order—instructions issued by a Customs house broker to an inland carrier to move cargo that has been cleared through U.S. Customs from the dock, to the port of entry, to a specified location.

conference carriers—an organization of ocean carriers that fixes rates and sailing times.

freight forwarder—an agent who facilitates the movement of goods from Customs to inland transportation.

freight on board (FOB)—the cost of the goods up to the time they are shipped.

on the water or shipping report—a report notifying merchandisers that products are being shipped.

preliminary inspection certificate (PIC)—authorizes shipment of goods when they have passed a final audit at the offshore contractor; required by the bank to release funds to pay the contractor.

ship date—the date a bill of lading is signed and the goods are physically in transit.

Contract Terminology

CMPQ—cut, make, pack, and quota.

CMQ—CMT and quota.

CMT—cut, make, trim.

consignee—one to whom goods are shipped or consigned.

contractor evaluation—a procedure to evaluate a potential contractor's ability to meet standards of quality, cost, delivery reliability, and financial stability.

cost and freight (C&F)—seller includes price of the merchandise and freight charge in the price to the buyer.

cost, insurance, freight (CIF)—seller includes cost of merchandise, insurance, and freight charge in price.

fabric booking confirmation—letter of intent used to block or book fabric for use by specified contractors when a merchandiser requires a unique fabric for use by several contractors (e.g., for coordinates).

garment purchase agreement (GPA)—legal contract to purchase a stated quantity of goods, at a certain price, within specified dates, and on stated terms and conditions.

landed cost—the cost of goods up to the time they are delivered to the distribution center of the buyer.

letter of credit—written document issued by a bank at the request of a buyer authorizing a seller to claim payment in accordance with certain terms and conditions; may or may not be irrevocable or transferable.

production activity report (PAR)—a status report summarizing contractor production activity for use by merchandisers.

completely assembled. A unit production system uses a computer managed overhead trans-
porter that moves cut parts from one sewing operator to another. A modular production
system is a team-based group of people and machines that perform assembly operations on
selected parts of garments or assemble entire garments (Glock & Kunz, 1995). The different
production systems have different advantages and disadvantages relative to speed of assembly, product quality, and training required of operators. Progressive bundle systems are
most likely to be used in developing countries.

Quality assurance inspections usually take place during and following production. In-
line inspections evaluate the quality of sewing operations and materials. Quality audits of
finished goods are also conducted. When the goods pass inspection, a **preliminary inspection certificate (PIC)** is issued by the sourcing company. The PIC authorizes shipment of
the goods to the sourcing company. The contractor presents the PIC and the **bill of lading**
to the bank for payment based on the letter of credit. The bill of lading is a written receipt
from the carrier that the goods have been received for shipment.

Customs

Merchandise arrives at **port of entry,** where **U.S. Custom Service** authorities examine **style
sheets** and **certificates of origin** in relation to duty rates and quota availability. If there is
some question about the style sheets, the merchandise itself may be inspected. Inspection
can result in days or weeks of delay in making goods available for sale. **Customs house
brokers** are often used to facilitate the process.

Labor Availability and Cost

Production costs are a major consideration in making sourcing decisions. Retail buyers believe foreign sources provide better quality for the price than domestic sources (Sternquist,
Tolbert, & Davis, 1989). A comparison of cost from selected countries in dollars for each
standard allowed hour (SAH) of production time is shown in Table 10.8. A SAH is an expression of a production standard that "reflects the normal time required to complete one
operation or cycle using a specified method that will produce the expected quality" (Glock
& Kunz, 1995, p. 297). By using SAHs for the table, it is possible to compare the cost of one
hour of the same operations in multiple countries.

The first three listings illustrate the high costs of manufacturing in developed countries.
Germany's rates are nearly double those in the United States and the United Kingdom.
Hong Kong is close to the United Kingdom. The comparison then moves to less developed
countries. It is apparent that production costs can vary markedly depending on the part of
the world where sourcing occurs.

Table 10.8

Apparel manufacturing costs in dollars per standard allowed hours (SAH). *

Country	$/SAH
Germany	31.41
United States	16.56
United Kingdom	13.82
Hong Kong	12.67
Hungary	10.22
Costa Rica	7.74
Thailand	7.63
Russia	6.31
Mexico	6.00
China	5.09

*Does not include freight and import duty. Kurt Salmon Associates.

Issues of Exploitation

Exploitation of labor in developing countries by the apparel industry has had higher visibility than other industries, but it is by no means unique. **Labor exploitation,** in this sense, is to make unethical use of for one's own advantage; to make a profit from the labor of others without giving just return. Exploitation often occurs when the opportunity is available. Levi Strauss is a company that has made a comprehensive effort to improve business ethics. Levi's ethics statement encompasses decision making and relationships in all aspects of the business (see Table 10.9). Applying these business ethics in a domestic market is challenging; applying them in the global market is extremely complex. Levi's is applying all their ethical aspirations to the global market because they closed their last domestic plants engaged in production of jeans in 2003. Many other manufacturers and retailers including Wal-Mart have established policies intended to prevent exploitation of labor.

Each country in the world has a unique mix of customs, laws, values, and ways of doing business (Nichols, 1993). What is regarded as exploitation in one part of the world is standard practice in another. Most countries have laws and regulations regarding exploitation of labor, particularly child labor. For example, it is common in many countries for age 14 to be the minimum age for employment. Major differences, however, lie in the effectiveness of enforcing the law, in the cultural standards and expectations relative to employment, and in the socioeconomic conditions under which people live. Case 10.7 describes efforts in one country to provide "fair" employment.

Table 10.9

*Levi's ethical aspirations.**

New Behaviors: Management must exemplify "directness, openness to influence, commitment to the success of others, and willingness to acknowledge our own contribution to problems."

Diversity: Levi's "values a diverse workforce (age, sex, ethnic group, etc.) at all levels of the organization. . . . Differing points of view will be sought; diversity will be valued and honestly rewarded, not suppressed."

Recognition: Levi's will "provide greater recognition—both financial and psychological—for individuals and teams that contribute to our success. . . . Those who create and innovate and those who continually support day-to-day business requirements."

Ethical Management Practices: Management should epitomize "the stated standards of ethical behavior. We must provide clarity about our expectations and must enforce these standards throughout the corporation."

Communications: Management must be "clear about company, unit, and individual goals and performance. People must know what is expected of them and receive timely, honest feedback. . . ."

Empowerment: Management must "increase the authority and responsibility of those closest to our products and customer. By actively pushing the responsibility, trust, and recognition into the organization, we can harness and release the capabilities of all our people."

*Reproduced from Mitchell (1994).

      Case 10.7   *Kids trade sweatshops for school.* *

At 13, Rina Begum is a veteran seamstress who has worked 10-hour days in a sweatshop [in Dhaka, Bangladesh] for $16 a month, stitching clothes destined for the discount chains of the United States. Now, she's going to school for the first time in her life, under an agreement by Bangladesh's garment industry to end child labor by October 31, 1996.

"I always wanted to go to school, but two years ago my parents sent me to work for money," said Rina in her classroom, a tin shed in a poor Dhaka neighborhood where she studies with a dozen other young ex-laborers.

Threatened with an international boycott of their products, garment manufacturers signed an accord in 1995 with the International Labor Organization (ILO) and UNICEF to end child labor in Bangladesh's highest earning export industry. Under the accord, the indus-try cannot employ children younger than 14.

Case 10.7 (continued)

Revenue from the United States

Bangladesh earns $2.4 billion a year on garments, 66 percent of the country's export earnings during the mid-1990s. Nearly half the revenue came from garments exported to the United States. After the agreement was reached to end child labor, a joint survey by UNICEF and the ILO—both U.N. organizations—and Bangladesh's manufacturers found more than 10,000 children in the garment industry, most of them girls under 14. By the 1996 deadline, about 3,000 of the workers were estimated to have reached the age of 14 and could stay at work. Of the 7,000 others, nearly 4,000 already had been enrolled in 180 schools across Bangladesh.

Two-thirds of the 1,171 garment factories surveyed in mid-October 1996, were found to have no child workers, the ILO's Dhaka office said. The others planned to dismiss their child workers in November, when education arrangements were to be ready. The accord said no child worker could be fired unless the child had a place in school.

Monthly Stipend

In the schools run by voluntary agencies, each child gets a monthly stipend of $7 to compensate for lost wages. The children also learn wage-earning skills such as handicrafts. Some, like Rina Begum, supplemented the stipend with after-school work. But that doesn't come close to her previous $16 a month, a pretty good salary in a country where the average monthly wage for an adult industrial worker is $23. The drop in income has hurt many families.

Aklima, another 13 year old who lost her job, has three brothers and sisters—all too young to work. Her mother is a widow, and until 6 months ago, the family depended on Aklima's $23 per month.

*Kids trade sweatshops for school (1996).

Exploitation of labor is not confined to developing countries (Headden, 1993). Every developed country has "pockets" of apparel sweatshops often made up of immigrants and illegal aliens. The U.S. fast-food industry has also been charged with the exploitation of teenagers because of long hours and unsafe conditions with inadequate training. The telemarketing system has potential to be another "sweatshop." Some parts of the retail sector might also be challenged as exploiting its sales force with unreasonable hours and low pay although the working conditions may be better than in apparel manufacturing. Resolution of the labor exploitation problem is incredibly complex from economic, social, and cultural perspectives.

The apparel industry combines some of the most sophisticated product development, production, communication, and transportation technologies in some of the least developed countries of the world (Bonacich et al., 1994). The primary activity that takes place in the least developed countries is garment assembly. Sewing continues to be a labor-intensive activity that does not require formal education. In apparel, contracting or licensing tends to be the method by which foreign labor is acquired. The result is little long-term commitment to the contracting firms or their locations. The scenario is ripe for exploitation of labor by local management and remotely by global corporations. The electronic industry also has assembly taking place in the world's least developed countries. In electronics, however, assembly tends to take place in subsidiaries of transnational corporations (TNC). A subsidiary means considerable investment by the global corporation and longer commitment to the area (Bonacich et al., 1994).

In 1980, The United Nations reported that women, half the world's population, did two-thirds of the world's work, earned one-tenth of the world's income, and owned one-one hundredth of the world's property. In spite of many changes in world politics, women remain victims of abuse and discrimination (War against women, 1994). Employees in the least developed countries tend to be young women, often in their first and perhaps only opportunity for regular employment. Unemployment and poverty rates tend to be very high. Parents often need their children to work so the family can have basic necessities. Deciding on a "fair" employment policy under these conditions is extremely difficult. Case 10.8 reports the one of the choices being made by the apparel industry to resolve exploitation related issues in the United States.

     Case 10.8   *Who's making the clothes?* *

Although there's plenty of pressure to keep apparel manufacturing costs down, the discovery of modern-day sweatshop conditions in garment factories [in the United States] has stunned both consumers and marketers. The problem has touched many including upscale women's apparel cataloger/retailer Talbots. Two subcontractors manufacturing Talbots merchandise were cited for Labor Department violations, says spokeswoman Margery Brandfon.

Unfortunately, it's not easy to control who's making your clothing or under what conditions. Most apparel suppliers farm out manufacturing to subcontractors, which may in turn send the work to other subcontractors without the marketer knowing — until there's a problem. As Brandfon says, "The labor problem is not with the supplier — it's further down the {manufacturing} chain."

In November 1995, the Labor Department notified Talbots that a subcontractor for supplier David Brooks was cited for a technical infraction involving overtime. "The situation had already been resolved, so it was an informational call, not an active notice," Brandfon says. But when another subcontractor of David Brooks was cited for unpaid overtime in May, Talbots took action.

In June, Talbots, a Hingham, Massachusetts-based company announced that its suppliers must work with Los Angeles-based independent garment auditing firm Cal Safety Compliance Corp., an independent external monitor of subcontracts accredited by the Fair Labor Association. As of August, all merchandise received by Talbots had to be accompanied by a certificate stating that it was made under the subcontractor monitoring program. All of Talbots' top suppliers have so far agreed to comply.

What's more, Talbots and several other catalogers — including Frederick's of Hollywood, JCPenney, J. Crew, Lands' End, and Spiegel — have endorsed the National Retail Federation's Statement of Principles on Supplier Legal Compliance, which warns that "appropriate action" will be taken if a factory used by a supplier has committed legal violations. Actions may include refusing shipments, terminating the relationship with the supplier, or taking legal action in the event of labor violations.

*Dowling (1996) and Fair Labor Association (2004).

  ## Learning Activity 10.7

Labor issues

1. What are the central issues of labor exploitation?
2. What makes a labor policy "fair"?
3. Give an example of applying one culture's standards in another culture. Why might this be a problem?
4. What is a "fair" wage in a developing country?

Summary

The textiles and apparel industry is one of the most globalized, involving most of the more than 200 countries in the world. World trade is regulated by a multitude of laws and trade regulations. Recent agreements have defined three major textile and apparel trade areas: The Americas, Asia, and Europe.

East Asia for many years dominated apparel trade. Now, apparel exporters to the United States include three primary groups: CBI (Caribbean Basin) countries, ASEAN (Association of Southeast Asian Nations) countries, and other Asian countries. Mexico was the largest exporter to the United States, but China quickly became the world's largest apparel exporter because the MFA (Multifiber Arrangement) has quotas phasing out in 2005.

Countries in addition to China that are now showing marked increases in the share of U.S. imports are Cambodia, Pakistan, Macau, Russia, Nicaragua, Vietnam, Sub-Saharan Africa, and the Andean Region. Some are part of trading areas favored by U.S. trade preference programs including CBTPA and AGOA. Dollars per square meter of imported goods range from $1.77 to $5.99 among the 25 countries that are the sources of the most imports.

Two firms are usually involved in the sourcing process: the sourcing firm (a manufacturer or retailer) and a contracting company. In addition, these companies may employ an agent and/or an export trading company. Two major methods of sourcing apparel are full package sourcing (FPS) and cut, make, trim (CMT). Firms in East Asia are known for FPS, while CMT is still predominant in Caribbean Basin and Mexico. Caribbean Basin countries are becoming more expert with FPS. Labor exploitation in apparel production is an ongoing problem that must be addressed by the sourcing firms involved.

Key Concepts

African Growth and
  Opportunity Act
Americas trading bloc
Asian/Pacific Rim trading bloc
Association of Southeast Asian
  Nations (ASEAN)
bill of lading
business ethics
Caribbean Basin Initiative
  (CBI)

Caribbean Basin Trade
  Partnership Act (CBTPA)
certificate of origin
codes of conduct
counter sample
Customs house broker
cut, make, trim sourcing
  (CMT)
development package
Euro currency
European trading bloc

European Union
fabric forward rule
full-package sourcing (FPS)
garment purchase agreement
  (GPA)
General Agreement on Tariffs
  and Trade (GATT)
global
globalization
guaranteed access levels (GALS)
harmonized system of tariffs

Item 807/Chapter 9802
labor exploitation
landed cost
letter of credit
Multifiber Arrangement (MFA)
North American Free Trade
  Agreement (NAFTA)
pattern check run (PCR)
port of entry

preliminary inspection
  certificate (PIC)
quota
rule of origin
sourcing
special regime
square meter equivalents
  (SME)
style sheet
tariff

technical package
U.S. Customs Service
U.S./Canadian Free Trade
  Agreement
value added
World Trade Organization
  (WTO)
worldwide responsible apparel
  production (WRAP)
yarn forward rule

 Integrated Learning Activity 10.8.1

Responsive sourcing

1. Read Case 10.9 very carefully. What is the fundamental meaning of responsive sourcing?
2. What factors should have primary attention when making responsive sourcing decisions?
3. Review your SSSV output printouts from previous Integrated Learning Activities. Which have the best GMROISL? What inputs have contributed to the desired outcomes? Which have the poorest GMROISL? What inputs have contributed to poor outcomes? Why is GMROISL a key factor in the determination of effective sourcing?
4. Design and carryout a SS experiment to test generation of GMROISL? What inputs will be manipulated? What inputs will be held constant?

Case 10.9

Time is money: Responsive sourcing brings big returns for merchandisers and brand managers. The semiannual meeting of the American Apparel and Footwear Association (AAFA) Supply Leadership Committee (SCLC) revalidated major technology issues for merchandisers and brand managers. One that received particular attention was *responsive sourcing* (also called quick response).

The Bottom Line: Responsive sourcing evaluates lead time and cost considerations

(continued)

Case 10.9 (continued)

---

to create the most profitable but consumer-satisfying scenario. Merchandisers and brand managers need more robust measurements to quantify overall performance. *What it Means:* Merchandisers' and brand managers' endless search for least cost alternatives has proven to be ineffective over the long term. This cost consciousness creates the perception that the coming end of import quotas in 2005 will be a boon for China and Vietnam (the cheapest providers of apparel and footwear). Some companies report that they expect to source more than 90 percent of finished goods from China once quotas are lifted. At the end of the day, though, reducing lead times and smoothing flows through the supply chain are as important as cost considerations. The use of different merchandise performance metrics show that there may be great value in sourcing fashion product geographically and temporally closer to the point of sale.

One application, the Sourcing Simulator, brought from academia to commercial use by Textiles and Clothing Technology Corporation [TC]², incorporates the robust measurement and is designed to let merchandisers and brand managers calculate the implications of different sourcing scenarios. The classic retail measurements are ineffective in performing this evaluation, such as the following:

- *What's wrong with gross margin?* Gross margin, which solely measures the retail price-merchandise cost relationship, misses the concept of velocity, opportunity costs (from out of stocks), and effective use of capital.

- *Isn't turnover a better measure?* On its own, turnover, which measures the relationship between sales and average inventory, can force merchandise and systems to bring in all product at the beginning of a month or a selling period. This conceptually provides the maximum amount of selling time, but can lead to crowded aisles and generally an unfriendly environment for consumers. Alternatively, ratcheting turn up too quickly can lead to empty shelves and poor customer service levels.

- *Gross margin return on investment (GMROI) is more meaningful, but still incomplete.* GMROI measures the relationship between gross margin and average inventory. This math helps a retailer evaluate whether taking a position in a particular product was an effective use of capital or not. Its weakness (like turn) is that it fails to capture opportunity costs associated with inventory levels that are too low.

- *Enter the concept of gross margin return on investment service levels (GMROISL).* This calculation multiples the GMROI

---

times (cumulative) in stock percent. In stock percent is an indicator of service level since it measures that average percent of SKUs that were in stock each week. This captures opportunity costs incurred through out-of-stocks caused by "lumpy" receipt patterns and reveals the true value of corporate investment in a product.

Measuring merchandise performance through GMROISL will typically demonstrate that metering product in to the supply chain in a steady stream in response to customer demand patterns is superior to the big bang approach that has developed the overcome long lead times in getting a product from the Far East to the Western hemisphere, despite cost differences.

Conclusion: Merchandisers and brand managers must begin measuring their merchandising investments in new ways. The time has come to end the tyranny of turn and incorporate new metrics into merchandiser and brand manager performance evaluation. Business intelligence (BI) vendors should include new metrics in their packaged reports. All corporate stakeholders would benefit from looking at their companies in this way.

Recommended Resources

Bheda, R., Narag, A. S., & Singla, M. L. (2003). Apparel manufacturing: A strategy for productivity improvement. *Journal of Fashion Marketing and Management,* 7(1):12–22.

Burtin, A., & Erguney, O. (2003, April/May). Sri Lanka: A prospect for peace. *Fashion Business International,* 24–35.

Des Marteau, K. (1995, December). U.S. contractors seek survival solutions. *Bobbin,* 37(4):16–18.

DeWitt, J. W. (1995, February). Home away from home. *Apparel Industry Magazine,* 56(2):42–44.

Fralix, M. T. (1996, August). Into the Far East: A perspective on quality, globalization & fried goose. *Bobbin,* 37(21):80–84.

Nichols, M. (1993, January/February). Third-world families at work: Child labor or child care? *Harvard Business Review,* 12–23.

Zhang, L., Dickson, M. A., & Lennon, S. J. (2002). The distribution channels for foreign-brand apparel in China: Structure, government's role, and problems. *Clothing and Textiles Research Journal,* 20(3):167–180.

References

Abend, J. (1996, August). Sigrid Olsen on a roll. *Bobbin, 76.*

American Apparel & Footwear Association. (2004). *Trends: Annual 2003*, pp. 12-13. Arlington, VA.

American Textile Manufacturers Institute. (2003, December). Textile HiLights. Washington, DC.

Anderson, L. J., & Todaro, M. (1995, May). Sourcing in the year 2000. *Bobbin, 74–80.*

Antoshak, R. P. (1992, August). NAFTA rule of origin: A help or hindrance? *ATI, 46–49.*

Appelbaum, R. P., Smith, D., & Christerson, B. (1994). Commodity chains and industrial restructuring in the Pacific Rim: Garment trade and manufacturing. In G. Gereffi & M. Korzeniewicz (eds.), *Commodity chains and global capitalism.* Westport, CT: Greenwood Press.

ASEAN+3 to continue cooperation in tourism. (2004). (www.chinaview.cn). Accessed February 4, 2004.

Bheda, R., Narag, A. S., & Singla, M. L. (2003). Apparel manufacturing: A strategy for productivity improvement. *Journal of Fashion Marketing and Management, 7*(1):12–22.

Birnbaum, D. (2000). *Birnbaum's global guide to winning the great garment war.* Hong Kong: Third Horizon Press.

Black, S. S. (1995, July). AAMA touts globalization. *Bobbin, 36*(11):22 & 24.

Black, S. S., & Cedrone, L. (1995, July). Americas focus on trade opportunities. *Bobbin, 36*(11):74–79.

Bonacich, E., Cheng, L., Chinchilla, N., Hamilton, N., & Ong, P. (1994). *Global production: The apparel industry in the Pacific Rim.* Philadelphia: Temple University Press.

Burtin, A., & Erguney, O. (2003, April/May). Sri Lanka: A prospect for peace. *Fashion Business International, 24–35.*

Cline, W. R. (1990). *The future of world trade in textiles and apparel* (rev. ed.). Washington, DC: Institute for International Economics.

DeWitt, J. W. (1995, February). NAFTA: One year later. *Apparel Industry Magazine, 56*(2):34.

Dickerson, K. G. (1995) *Textiles and Apparel in the global economy* (2nd ed.). Englewoond Cliffs, NJ: Merrill.

Dowling, M. (1996, October 15). Who's making the clothes? *Catalog Age, 6.*

Dunn, B. (2000, December 15). U.S. firms a force in Canadian market. *Daily News Record, 2.*

EC & US agree to end eight-year banana war. (2001, April 18). *Bridges Weekly Trade News Digest* (www.ictsd.org). Accessed June 22, 2004.

Ellis, K. (1992, October). *The great North American free trade debate.* Reprinted from *Chicago Apparel News.*

Fair Labor Association. (2004). FLA Accredited Monitors (www.fairlabor.org/all/monitor/accredmon.html). Accessed February 6, 2004.

Fralix, M. T. (1996, August). Into the Far East: A perspective on quality, globalization & fried goose. *Bobbin, 37*(21):80–84.

Glock, R., & Kunz, G. I. (1995). *Apparel manufacturing: Sewn product analysis.* Englewood Cliffs, NJ: Prentice Hall.

Goldman, S. L., Nagel, R. N., & Preiss, K. (1995). *Agile competitors and virtual organizations: Strategies for enriching the customer.* New York: Van Nostrand Reinhold.

Good, M. L. (1997, January 30). *The U.S. textile industry outlook: Competitive and technology challenge.* Remarks at the 5th Annual National Textile Center Forum, Myrtle Beach, SC.

Headden, S. (1993, November 22). Made in the U.S.A. *U.S. News and World Report*, 48–55.

International News Digest. (2005, April/May). India expects export hike of 25% plus. *Fashion Business International*, 4.

International Trade Update. (2004, January). Arlington, VA: American Apparel and Footwear Association.

Kanter, R. M. (1994). Afterword: What "thinking globally" really means. *Global strategies*. Boston, MA: Harvard Business School Press.

Kids trade sweatshops for school. (1996, November 2). *Des Moines Register*, 7A.

Kwan, C. Y., Yeung, K. W., & Au, K. F. (2003). A statistical investigation of the changing apparel retailing environment in China. *Fashion Marketing and Management*, 7(1):87–100.

Made on Planet Earth. (1996). *Daily News Record*.

Management Ventures, Inc. (1996, May). Population and retail sales in world markets. *Discount Merchandiser*, 78–79.

Marlin-Bennett, R. (1994, Winter). Camouflaged trade restrictions in the 1990s: Trends in international trade policy. *Futures Research Quarterly*, 61–77.

Milstein, A. G. (1993, September). U.S. manufacturers bringing home the Canadian bacon. *Bobbin*, 100–104.

Mitchell, R. (1994, August 1). Managing by values. *Business Week*, 46–52.

Munk, N. (1994, January). The Levi straddle. *Forbes*, 44–45.

Nichols, M. (1993, January/February). Third-world families at work: Child labor or child care? *Harvard Business Review*, 12–23.

Olsen, Sigrid. (2004). (www.sigridolsen.com). Accessed July 1, 2004.

Planning and implementing an apparel sourcing strategy. (1986) 1986 report of the Technical Advisory Committee of the American Apparel Manufacturers Association, 1–3, 37, 39–41.

Pomfret, J., & Pan, P. (2001, November 10). For China, entry into WTO isn't risk-free. *Washington Post Foreign Service*, A01.

Ramey, J. (1993, June 10). Wal-Mart sets sourcing rules to monitor labor conditions. *Women's Wear Daily*, 14.

Research and Markets. (2000). Clothing Retailing Market Report 2000 (www.researchandmarkets.co.uk). Accessed January 12, 2000.

Spector, R., & McCarthy, P. D. (1995). *The Nordstrom way*. New York: Wiley.

Sternquist, B., Tolbert, S., & Davis, B. (1989, Summer). Imported apparel: Retail buyers' reasons for foreign procurement. *Clothing and Textiles Research Journal*, 35–40.

Stone, N. (1994). The globalization of Europe: An interview with Wisse Dekker. *Global strategies*. Boston, MA: Harvard Business School Press.

Wall, M., & Dickerson, K. (1989, Winter). Free trade between Canada and the United States: Implications for textiles and clothing. *Clothing and Textiles Research Journal*, 1–10.

Wal-Mart puts on pajamas. (1997, March 16). *Des Moines Register*, 2G.

War against women. (1994, March 28). *U.S. News and World Report*, 42–56.

Zhang, L., Dickson, M. A., & Lennon, S. J. (2002). The distribution channels for foreign-brand apparel in China: Structure, government's role, and problems. *Clothing and Textiles Research Journal*, 20(3):167–180.

11

Customer/Vendor

Relationships

Learning Objectives

- Examine the concept of customer service in customer/vendor relationships.

- Discuss the role of personal selling service in customer service.

- Examine the components of an effective personal selling process.

A customer/vendor relationship exists any time materials or finished goods change ownership. The vendor is selling the product and the customer is buying. Some types of customer service are provided and expected along with the transaction. The concept of strategic partnering between vendors and their customers was introduced in Chapter 2 as a component of quick response business systems. Partnering fosters interdependence and on-going business relationships. Retailers have a problem trying to foster a similar interdependence with ultimate consumers. Customer loyalty is sought in the retail sector, but retail customers seem to exhibit less and less of it. In response, many retailers are returning to more intensive forms of customer service to stimulate sales.

The Concept of Customer Service

Customer service has become a key competitive strategy for both manufacturers and retailers. Global competition for manufacturers, overstoring for retailers, and intensive price competition have driven firms to find productive ways to draw and retain customers (Gaskill & Kunz, 1991). Davidow and Uttal (1989), management consultants and authors of

Total Customer Service, state that "good old-fashioned service, plus newer, more innovative ways of winning and keeping customers, may be the ultimate competitive weapon in the 1990s."

Customers have the ultimate power — the power to reject. Consequently, customers have become a primary focus in modern business environments (Goldfarb, 1989). From a vendor's perspective, "the key is getting closer to our customers and making it easier for them to do business with us" (Anton, 1996, p. 4). Retailers equate effective customer service with the willingness of customers to pay more for products, the opportunity for repeat business, lower advertising costs due to positive word-of-mouth advertising (Lele, 1987), and subsequent increases in bottom-line profits (Zemke, 1986). From the retail buyer/merchandiser's perspective, good customer service helps get merchandise into the hands of customers, the people for whom it is planned, developed, and presented.

Customer needs, whether in a business-to-business relationship or business-to-ultimate consumer relationship, seem to be relatively simple: responsiveness, promptness, knowledgeable people, accuracy, and accessibility. When customers are lost, shortcomings in customer service are the cause 75 percent of the time; dissatisfaction with products 13 percent of the time, and other reasons 12 percent of the time (Anton, 1996).

Levels of Customer Service

Components of customer service offered by manufacturing and retailing firms vary greatly. When firms are involved in QR partnerships, technology plays a key role in the type and quality of customer service. Technology is also a key player in retailer customer service, particularly in relation to visual merchandising, inventory management, and database management. "Customer-oriented information technology can empower an employee to manage successful interactions with customers . . . . One of the most important attributes driving customer satisfaction is the availability of accurate information on a timely basis" (Anton, 1996, p. 5). Many components of customer service are dependent on information.

Table 11.1 demonstrates the components of four different levels of retail customer service. While most of the components are applicable to many different types of retail operations, the components related to fitting rooms are unique to apparel. The components include the role of sales associates, training sales associates, assistance with merchandise selection, operation of fitting rooms, alteration services, packaging and wrapping services, methods of payment, merchandise return, and other amenities, including availability of parking (Berman & Evans, 1995; Lewison, 1994; Spector & McCarthy, 1995). An individual firm may use any combination of these components, depending on its overall business strategy.

Self Service

Self service means just what it says: customers provide their own selling service. The retailer records the sales and may provide minimal display, or the merchandise may simply be set out on the sales floor in shipping boxes. Customers roam about looking for what they want to buy. They depend on labels or printing directly on packing cartons for product information. When customers find something, they carry it to the checkout; or if the product is too large, they rip a ticket off the box and take it to the checkout, where they pay for the product, probably in cash. Customers then figure out how to get the merchandise home. Warehouse markets and wholesale clubs probably are closest things to self-service environments, although many accept credit cards.

Limited Service

Limited service combines some aspects of self-service and full-service environments. Limited service usually requires customers to self select merchandise, although greeters may be available at the door to direct customers to appropriate areas. Visual merchandising techniques may be used to help customers find and choose appropriate merchandise. Labels and hang tags are the primary source of product information, although stores may post comparisons of product features. Credit card services and liberal exchange policies are likely to be in place, but the trend is toward more limited return policies. According to Kurt Salmon Associates, a retail consulting company, apparel returns are among retailing's highest, averaged 10 to 12 percent of sales while catalogers and online retailers are much higher at 20 to 40 percent (D'Innocenzio, 2003; Fleischer, 2001). Delivery, alterations, and gift wrap may even be available in limited-service environments for a fee. Most super stores and mass retailers, many department stores, and some specialty stores provide some combination of limited customer service.

Full Service

Full service incorporates a personal selling service into the customer service environment along with other amenities such as free gift wrap, alterations, delivery, and convenient parking. Knowledgeable sales associates may keep personal selling books to assist customers in both wardrobe development and with purchases for friends and family. Stores make a considerable investment selecting, training, and updating sales associates, who are a primary source of product information. Full-service stores display less merchandise on the sales floor since ensembles may be developed for personal presentation to individual customers. The sales

Table 11.1
Levels of retail customer service.

	Self Service	Limited Service
Store Hours	May be limited	Long hours including evenings and weekends
Parking	Free parking	Free parking
Checkout Facilities	Centralized	Centralized or decentralized
Role of Associates	Greet and thank customers, check out, clean, count, reprice, fill racks	Greet and thank customers, check out, fill shelves and racks, clean, count, reprice, may assist customers within department
Training of Associates	Trained on purchase, return, and exchange	Trained on purchase, return, and exchange; may have basic sales training
Customer Information	Signs, hang tags, and labels	Greeter, signs, hang tags, and labels
Merchandise Selection	Customer finds and chooses items from self-service displays	Customer finds and chooses items/may have some assistance from sales associate
Fitting Rooms	Merchandise is counted in and out of fitting room; customer returns merchandise to racks	Merchandise is counted in and out of fitting room; may have some assistance from sales associate; sales associate returns merchandise to racks
Alterations	None available	May be available for a fee
Packaging/Wrapping	Customer provides own bag	Bags or boxes provided
Methods of Payment	Cash only	Cash or credit cards accepted
Delivery Service	Customer carries or arranges delivery	May be available for a fee
Merchandise Return	No exchange/no refund or exchange only in limited time with sales receipt	Exchange or refund on charge purchases; delayed refund on cash purchase
Other Amenities		

Full Service	Premier Service
May meet in customer's home	Location and time at customer's convenience.
Adjacent parking ramp	Valet parking available
Decentralized	Decentralized
Greet, assist, check out, and thank customers in department; other activities if time allows; maintain customer contact book	Empowered associates assist customers in any way possible; generate sales in any department; maintain customer book; send personal letters/thank you notes
Trained on purchase, return, and exchange; selling strategies, product information	Extensive training on cash register, wardrobe analysis, multiple sales strategies, fashion trends, fit, and satisfying customers
Sales associates, signs, hang tags, and labels	Concierge's desk, sales associates, signs, hang tags, and labels
Customer is assisted with merchandise selection if desired; may use personal shoppers; customers may be called when new merchandise comes in	Assisted merchandise selection and personal selling service by appointment, personal consultant presents entire ensembles after wardrobe analysis; merchandise may be charged and mailed to customer for approval
Fitting room is larger so sales associate can assist customer with dressing and additional merchandise; sales associate may gather and return merchandise to inventory	Spacious fitting room equipped with telephones as well as food and beverage service; sales associate gathers merchandise, assists customer, and returns merchandise to inventory
Available free or for a fee	Available free
Signature bags and boxes, free gift wrap	Signature bags and boxes, free gift wrap
Cash or credit cards accepted	Cash or credit cards accepted
Merchandise delivery for a fee	Free merchandise pick up or delivery
Exchange or refund on any purchase	Exchange or refund on any product, any time
Comfortable waiting areas for shoppers' companions	Child care and entertainment for shoppers' companions

floor may include a pianist to contribute to a relaxed, comfortable ambiance. Specialty stores are more likely than department stores to provide full customer service.

Premier Customer Service

Premier customer service involves intensive interaction with customers; indeed, there are few limits on what sellers can do to satisfy customers. The first priority of the company is to satisfy customers. As such, sales associates are empowered to do whatever it takes to reach that end, and are, in fact, rewarded for unusual customer service efforts. Numerous amenities accompany customer service, including entertainment for shopping companions; food, drink, telephones, e-mail, computers, and television sets in dressing rooms; availability of travel consultants; and on-the-spot alterations, delivery, shipping, and gift wrapping services. Sales associates are usually full-time, commissioned, professional employees who may make $60,000+ annually. They culture their relationship with their customers with personal calls and thank-you notes to keep them abreast of purchasing opportunities and to show appreciation for patronage. Only a few upscale stores offer premier customer service, Nordstrom probably being the most notable.

Role of Personal Selling Services

Emphasis on personal selling and knowledgeable sales people remains a critical competitive component of customer service for the nation's top firms. Employees who provide **personal selling services** play major roles in a firm's merchandising efforts. Consider the following:

- Sellers are the most direct means by which the firm communicates with their customers. They facilitate the exchange process by providing information and matching product offerings to customers' needs.
- The quality, ability, and cooperation of sellers have a major influence on how customers perceive a firm.
- In the retail sector, sellers increase sales by turning browsers into shoppers and by building long-term relationships with customers.
- Sellers have direct responsibility for executing most aspects of customer service: the speed of transactions, handling complaints, and providing security (adapted from Ghosh, 1990).

Poorly trained and unmotivated personal service employees affect business through alienation of customers, frequent mistakes in processing, lack of initiative, and low productivity. Some studies suggest it takes 12 positive experiences with customers to rectify one bad experience (Cathcart, 1988). Davidow and Uttal (1989) claim that, "by far the largest costs that outstanding service saves are those of replacing lost customers."

Recognizing the need for good personal service is easy; developing, executing, and evaluating an effective personal-service system in a firm is time consuming, frustrating, and potentially expensive. However, for many firms, the benefits of personal service outweigh the costs. Establishing and maintaining excellent customer service requires commitment that permeates the entire organization. Case 11.1 highlights the level of on-going investment required to provide excellence in customer service and, in particular, personal selling services.

Case 11.1 *Keys to customer service at Nordstrom*

The Nordstrom culture sets employees free. The company believes that people will work hard when they are given the freedom to do their job the way they think it should be done, and when they can treat customers they way they like to be treated. Nordstrom believes that too many rules, regulations, paperwork, and strict channels of communication erode employee incentive. Without those shackles, Nordstrom people can operate like entrepreneurial shopkeepers.

- Nordstrom is informally organized as an "inverted pyramid," with the top positions occupied by the customers and the salespeople, and the bottom position filled by the co-chairmen. Every tier of the pyramid supports the sales staff.
- Empowering the people on the sales floor with the freedom to accept re-

turned merchandise is the most obvious illustration of the Nordstrom culture because it directly impacts the public.

- The unconditional money-back guarantee is designed for the 98 percent of customers who are honest.
- Nordstrom tears down barriers. Salespeople are free to sell merchandise to their customers in any department throughout the store. This promotes continuity in the relationship between the salesperson and the customer.
- Like everyone at Nordstrom, department managers begin their career as salespeople to learn what's required to take care of the customer. This sends the signal that management values the role of salesperson.
- Managers are encouraged to have a feeling of ownership about their department. They are responsible for hiring,

(continued)

training, coaching, nurturing, and evaluating their sales team, and are expected to spend some of their time on the selling floor, interacting with the customers and the selling staff.

- Buying at Nordstrom is partially decentralized, which means that buyers in each region are given some freedom to acquire merchandise that reflects local lifestyles and tastes. Because buyers are responsible for fewer stores, they can afford to take a chance on a unique item without fear of jeopardizing the bottom line.

- Empowerment for getting the right merchandise in the store begins not in the buying office, but on the floor — at the point of sale. Nordstrom encourages entrepreneurial salespeople to provide input to their manager and buyer on fashion direction, styles, quantities, sizes, and colors.

- Employee compensation is based on sales commissions. The Nordstrom brothers felt that the best way to attract and retain self-starters was by paying them according to their ability. An em-

ployee profit-sharing retirement plan inspires motivation and encourages loyalty. Because contributions are made to the plan directly from the company's net earnings, employees have an incentive to be productive and cost conscious.

- Goal-setting is essential to the culture. Employees at every level are perpetually striving to meet or surpass personal, departmental, store, and regional goals for the day, month, and year. Peer pressure and personal commitment push competitive employees toward constantly higher goals.

- Employees have access to sales figures from all departments and stores in the chain, so they can compare their performances.

- Outstanding sales performances are rewarded with prizes and praise, as are good ideas and suggestions.

- Top salespeople are encouraged to help others with sales techniques and building a customer base.

*Spector & McCarthy (1995, pp. 129–130).

Learning Activity 11.1

Concepts of customer service and personal selling service

1. What is the relationship between planning, developing, and presenting product lines and customer service?

2. Identify two stores that you frequent and, using the components of customer service identified in Table 11.1, would you classify them as self service, limited service, full service, or premier service?
3. Based on Case 11.1, what are the fundamental leadership principles underlying the Nordstrom customer service strategy?
4. How do the Nordstrom principles relate to the Behavioral Theory of the Apparel Firm (BTAF) presented in Chapter 1?

Why Customers Buy

Customers, whether materials buyers for manufacturers, finished goods buyers for retailers, or ultimate consumers shopping retail stores, catalogs, or the Internet, do not buy merchandise. On the contrary, they buy what the merchandise will do for them:

- Materials buyers/merchandisers are concerned about appearance, serviceability, handling, minimums, and price.
- Retail buyers/merchandisers are concerned about suitability to fashion trends, styling, color, sizing, quantity discounts, markdown money, delivery dates, gross margin potential, and contract terms.
- Ultimate consumers are concerned about wardrobe coordination, fit, styling, color, durability, and care.

Customers are looking for something to meet their needs and desires. They may be seeking some of the following:

- To gain time, prestige, health, professional advancement, the feeling of personal worth, or a better life.
- To be professional, hospitable, influential, efficient, kind, an outstanding merchant, a good parent, or recognized as important.
- To achieve his or her own goals, expression of themselves, balanced assortments, his or her sales goals, satisfaction of curiosity, acquisition of things, and emulation of others.
- To save time, money, energy, work, and personal embarrassment.

The success of the interaction between the seller and the buyer may determine the success of the transaction. Factors that inhibit customer contact and create sales resistance include the following:

- Fear of being pushed or being pushy. Potential customers in both wholesale and retail markets may avoid direct contact with sellers because they fear being talked into buying something that is not consistent with their needs and wants. Sellers who are sensitive to this fear may hesitate to make customer contact because they do not want to be perceived as being pushy. Refining the seller's skills can overcome this problem and benefit both the buyer and the seller.

- Uncertainty related to benefits and features of products/services. Customers who are uncertain of their product knowledge need help to make an appropriate choice. When sellers also are inadequately informed about how products can meet customers' needs, potential customer satisfaction is lost. Well-trained sellers know their products and can match products to the potential customer's desires.

- Doubt about the ability to make a wise purchase or about the ability to sell. Potential customers may have difficulty making decisions or lack confidence in their ability to make the right decisions. Effective sellers find ways to build confidence in the buyer. However, when sellers are inadequately trained, they may lack the professional confidence required to assist the potential customer with decision making.

The seller's greatest challenge is to identify the potential customer's needs and wants and to show how he or she will benefit from purchasing of the seller's products and/or services. Both buyers and sellers benefit by a complete understanding of the selling process.

The Personal Selling Process

Understanding the fundamentals of selling is useful for both sellers and the buyers. Basic expectations of sellers are similar regardless of product type or stage in the trade matrix. Sellers, whether selling industrial sewing machines, automobiles, buttons, life insurance, fabrics, budget lingerie, or designer apparel, are expected to generate business. Selling is a percentage business; the more potential customers approached the more sales that are made. But sales may be improved even more by effective selling processes. Effective selling processes improve the well-being of both the buyer and the seller. Fundamentally, there are seven stages in the selling process: prospecting, approaching, determining needs, presenting merchandise, handling objections, closing the sale, and follow-up.

Prospecting

Prospecting includes two phases, personal preparation, including developing product knowledge, and evaluating potential customers.

Personal Preparation

Personal preparation includes appearance, improving selling practices, improving product knowledge, reviewing merchandise, and being relaxed, poised, and confident. Appropriate appearance means dressing in a manner appropriate to the business. For example, in recent years both Levi Strauss and the Lee Company have encouraged their employees to wear the products their company sells when representing the company. Consequently, their employees appear at national meetings wearing jeans and chambray shirts while other attendees are wearing suits and ties. Retail employees are also encouraged to wear apparel consistent with the products they are selling, i.e., in sporting goods departments, sellers wear active sportswear; in career wear departments, sellers wear career wear. Employees also must be sensitive to the "audience of the day." If a special presentation will occur involving a person or company known to be conservative or traditional, pulling the navy blue suit out of the closet is probably an appropriate move.

Ongoing improvement of selling practices is essential. Some companies develop sales presentations that sellers memorize in order to present a complete, effective selling process every time. However, an accomplished seller knows that carbon-copy sales presentations are not appropriate for every customer. Many of the components are the same, but the strategy is adapted to the individual needs of each customer. Effective sellers constantly hone their skills and look for new ideas about how to help their customers better understand the benefits of their products and how they match their needs.

Effective sellers continually try to learn more about their products and their competitor's products. Knowledge needs to go beyond a superficial listing of the product features. Understanding alternate designs, manufacturing processes, global sources, performance, and quality provide the seller with an arsenal of information that can be used to satisfy customer needs. Retail sales associates always need time to become acquainted with new merchandise and newly arranged sales floors. Knowing what, how much, and where merchandise is located is essential for good customer service. With this type of preparation, the seller can be relaxed, poised, and confident in his or her ability to do the job.

Categories of Product Knowledge

Well-prepared sellers need to be well informed on a broad variety of topics, such as general market trends in relation to the products for which they are responsible, as well as current assortments and company policies. Being a well-informed seller means making a constant effort to gather, evaluate, and improve product knowledge.

For example, sellers might answer the following questions from the global market:

- What are cutting-edge technologies, new designs, fashions, fads, and best sellers?
- What are the characteristics of competing brands and price lines?
- What is available at competing outlets?
- What are their assortments and their prices?

Sellers need answers to the following questions to understand the current selling period:

- What styles, sizes, and colors are available in house?
- Where is the merchandise located or how can it be acquired?
- How do prices and pricing policies compare with competitors?
- What is the desirability and availability of coordinating or companion products?
- What are the features and benefits of the products?
- What are the options in relation to stockouts?
- What are the firm's return and exchange policies?

Sellers gather information by regularly reading the trade press and daily newspapers. Attending trade shows where products are shown at wholesale provides a broad perspective on the totality of what is available in the market. Since many sellers do not have the opportunity to attend trade shows, buyers, designers, and merchandisers often provide training related to fashion trends, assortment strategies, and product performance attributes. Catalogs and detailed product information provided by vendors may contain the most detailed product descriptions available. Since it is time consuming to study all of this information, it requires extra effort on the part of sellers to make time to absorb this information.

Evaluating Potential Customers

Sellers in the wholesale area are challenged to perpetuate the loyalty of current customers and, at the same time, find new customers. Sellers in the retail area, for the most part, are challenged to sell merchandise to the customers that come in the door. But the information they need to gather is quite similar:

- Is there a want or need that can be satisfied?
- Is there an ability to pay?
- Who has the authority to buy?
- Are the needs consistent with the merchandise?

Characteristics of past customers are often used as a guide for determining potential future customers. Sellers at wholesale often look for centers of influence that can be drawn upon by networking. Sellers at retail in full- and premier-service organizations also may use networking to identify new customers.

Greeting and Approaching Customers

Effective sellers have the ability to make and maintain customer contact. Making customer contact may take the form of a phone call or e-mail for an appointment, a personal visit to an office, or greeting a customer on a retail sales floor. Maintaining customer contact may require another phone call or e-mail to deliver a sales pitch, a personal visit to present a product, or engaging in conversation with the customer. In the world of selling, usually many more customer contacts are made than sales. Maintaining the contact so product benefits can be discussed is a key to selling.

In a retail setting, it is common courtesy to contact a customer immediately upon entering the store. Some firms set a standard for making a greeting less than 30 seconds after a customer enters. **Greeting customers** is commonly regarded as a welcome to the store and as a shoplifting deterrent. The friendliness and sincerity of the greeting establishes the shopping atmosphere for the customer. The greeting is particularly important if the seller is already engaged with another customer. "Hi, I'll be with you in a minute. If you are looking for holiday dresses, they are to the right in the back." The greeting should be natural and appropriate to the personality of the seller.

Making contact is as easy as greeting the customer by saying "Hello," but maintaining contact is an art form. It may be useful to observe the customer to learn as much as possible before approaching him or her. A brief observation might reveal how hurried the customer is and whether he is shopping for himself or someone else. If the customer is part of a group, the seller might be able to determine which person is the shopper, what type of goods they are looking for, and which person is the decision maker.

There are three common techniques for approaching customers for the first time. The **merchandise approach** is used when the shopper seems to be viewing specific merchandise. The greeting usually includes a casual "Hello" and a comment about the merchandise like, "These just came in yesterday. Aren't they terrific?" The **personal, informal, or social approach** is used if the customer approaches the seller or if the customer appears to be browsing. The greeting might be a positive statement such as simply "Hi," or may include a comment on the weather, business, merchandise, customer's clothing, or customer's children. For a **service approach,** avoid the standard "Can I help you?" because of the easy "No thank you, I am just looking" response, unless the customer obviously needs help. Maintaining a pleasant, professional attitude is essential.

Determining Customers' Needs and Wants

It is essential to determine the potential customer's needs and wants in order to know what merchandise to show and how to show it. It may be helpful to distinguish between needs and wants. **Needs** might be described as practical or functional desire; **wants** may be described as emotional desire. Since most consumption is by U.S. citizens above the poverty level, the majority of purchases are motivated by emotional desire although they may be justified by functional need. Strategies to determine customer needs and wants include:

• Determine what type of product/service the customer is seeking.
• Ask questions related to intended use.
• Listen carefully to what the customer says.
• Briefly summarize the customer's needs and wants.
• Ask questions to narrow the selection, if necessary.

Ask questions to determine the customer's needs and wants. To question does not mean to interrogate. Questions should be nonthreatening and should encourage dialogue between the seller and the customer. Phrase questions so they cannot be answered by a simple "yes" or "no." Open-ended questions confirm your interest in the customers well-being and encourage the customer to talk about their needs. **Open-ended questions** begin with "what," "why," "how," or "tell me," and encourage the customer to elaborate when responding. The seller can quickly determine how purposive the customer is and how defined he or she is in identifying the desired product. The seller can also help the customer to define a product available in the current assortment that will suit his or her needs. Examples of open- and **closed-ended questions** related to customer's needs and wants include:

closed—Is this the product you are looking for?
open—What type of product are you looking for?

closed—Is this within your price range?
open—What is the price range that you would consider?

closed—Do you like this color?
open—What colors might you consider?

closed—Do you have anything in your wardrobe that will go with this?
open—What will you be wearing this with?

closed—Will you need more than a dozen?
open—What are your volume requirements?

Questioning moves the seller toward a sale. Careful listening keeps the seller on track. Listening is the key to determining customer needs and wants. Most people do not listen effectively. Distractions are many. It takes concentrated effort to keep the seller's mind tuned to what the customer is saying. Listening improves if eye contact is maintained. Sellers must also be alert to a customer's body language for signals related to product priorities.

After questioning and listening, the seller then must decide on the appropriate action. The preferred option is taking the customer to the merchandise of primary interest and providing selection assistance. Options also include pursuing additional conversation or backing off and letting the customer browse or self-select merchandise. The seller maintains contact with the customer by checking in regularly to see if assistance is needed. The appropriate strategy is determined by the method most likely to meet the needs and wants expressed by the customer.

Presenting the Merchandise/Providing Selection Assistance

Providing **merchandise selection assistance** requires showing the merchandise and discussing its benefits and features. If possible, show more than one item that would seem to satisfy the customer. This might include similar items in different colors or at different prices. Be careful not to prejudge how much the customer will spend or to assume the customer will want to buy the lowest-priced item. Point out features at different price points. Be sure to discuss why one costs more than another.

Show the merchandise that will appeal to the customer based on the customer needs analysis. Be sure that the merchandise selected meets the needs of the customer. Have the customer examine the merchandise. Explain the benefits of the merchandise and the price of the product in relation to its benefits. Discuss the features of the product that provide those benefits.

A seller might also include compatible or coordinating items in the presentation. This provides an opportunity for comparing attributes and possibly a multiple sale. However, presenting too many choices may be confusing. Enhance decision making by helping the customer state preferences and remove items from view that the customer rejects or are not compatible with the customers' preferences.

Always handle the merchandise in a way that shows the merchandise is special. Treat items with pride. Involve the customer with the merchandise. Encourage him or her to examine the product, hold it, try it out, or, if appropriate, try it on. This promotes ownership for the customer. Talk about the merchandise. Tell about its features and benefits. To present merchandise effectively the seller must relate his or her knowledge of the products/services to the needs and wants of the customer.

Merchandise Features and Benefits

Customers buy merchandise for the benefits it provides, not the features related to the product. **Product features** are characteristics of the product. **Product benefits** are statements of what the product will do to or for the customer. Benefits relate directly to customer needs and wants, while product features are the sources of the benefits. See Table 11.2 for examples of product features and benefits. Features and benefits are usually described on hang tags, labels, or packaging materials or in catalog copy. By showing merchandise to the customer, customer needs can be better defined.

Handling Objections

Sellers should anticipate **customer's objections;** they may occur at any time during the sale. From a seller's perspective, objections are indications of interest by the customer, a way of learning more about customer's needs and wants, something blocking the way of closing the sale, and should not be taken personally. Objections may be caused by:

- The seller showing merchandise that is not well matched to the customer's needs and wants.
- The customer not recognizing benefits of the merchandise.
- The seller showing merchandise not within the customer's price range.

Table 11.2

Applying product knowledge by distinguishing between features and benefits.

Examples of Product Features	*Corresponding Product Benefits*
1. The appearance, style, or design of the product	1. Good taste, beauty, fashion
2. Brand name of product or manufacturer	2. Quality, reputation, snob appeal, dependability
3. Materials from which the product is made	3. Easy care, durability, superiority
4. How product is made	4. Beauty, workmanship, durability, safety
5. What can be expected of the product in use	5. Economical, convenient, enjoyable, efficient
6. How the product is used	6. Versatility, reliability, cost effectiveness
7. How to take care of the product	7. Easy care, economical
8. History and background of the product	8. Intrigue, uniqueness
9. How the product compares with competing brands	9. Advantages, disadvantages, similarities, differences

Sellers can use objections to better understand the customer's viewpoint. Careful listening is as important when dealing with objections as when trying to determine a customer's needs and wants. Acknowledge the customer's objections without agreeing or disagreeing. "I see." "I understand." "I appreciate what you are saying." The seller must try to identify core issues related to the objections. Restating the objections to test the core issues can provide an opportunity to better understand the customer's perspective and to determine what else the customer needs to know. When dealing with price objections, emphasize value by reviewing benefits and how they relate to the customer's needs and wants. Compare features of lower-priced products and talk about investment.

It is important to respond to the customer's objections honestly and sincerely by relating objections to the merchandise benefits. Be attuned to nonverbal signals. It may be necessary to suggest different merchandise than was originally shown. Restating benefits and features related to core issues helps to reassure the customer that the product is suitable.

Closing the Sale

The purpose of **closing the sale** is to get the customer to agree to buy the product. It is the seller's responsibility to help the customer make a buying decision. There are definite signals, signs of interest by the customer indicating it is time to close:

- Closely inspecting merchandise
- Asking questions about details
- Asking questions about delivery
- Smiling
- Nodding
- A big sigh

When the customer provides the signals, it is the seller's job to ask for the sale. A number of different closing strategies may be appropriate given the specific situation:

- Direct close—"Does this product serve your needs?" "Are you ready to make this purchase?"
- Take it for granted close—"I'll ring this up."
- Method of payment close—"Would you like this on your JCPenney charge?"
- Companion merchandise close—"We have shoes and a belt that are perfect with this suit."
- Delivery/service close—"We can deliver this tomorrow. Shall I call the tailor?"
- Summing up close—"This sleeping bag is good for 30 below zero, it is waterproof, and it is 20 percent off the regular price." "Your ad will explain your products and be seen by 1,000 people who attend the trade show."
- Last-chance close—"This is the last day of the sale." "This model is being discontinued."
- Choice close—"Would you prefer the green or the blue? Or perhaps both?" "Would you prefer a full-page or a half-page ad?"
- Gentle persuasion close—"Why don't you take it with you. It will save you the time of returning to buy it. If you decide it doesn't meet your needs, with our return policy, you can always return it."
- Come back close—used when it is obvious that customer is not going to buy on this visit; if possible, set a specific time to return.

It is important for the seller not to be afraid to ask for the sale. Not every customer will buy, but more will if they are asked for the sale.

Alternate Selling

If it is not possible to close the sale, the seller's first priority is to show interest and concern that it is not possible to meet the customer's needs. **Alternate selling** involves discussing options of how the customer might be able to receive the merchandise he or she desires. Try to determine if other merchandise might meet the customer's needs or wants. Suggesting competing sources where the seller knows the desired merchandise is likely to be in stock is the sincerest form of customer service. It proves the seller has the customer's best interest at heart and might generate customer loyalty based on giving up a sale.

Enlarging the Sale

The ability to expand a sale with companion products or other merchandise can result in greater satisfaction for the customer and a substantial increase in sales overall. Customers may be also willing to buy a larger quantity of the original product. This process is sometimes called suggestion, suggestive, or add-on selling and may occur in any part of the selling process. **Suggestion selling** can save the customer time in shopping for coordinating or related items in the future and/or help the customer to select related accessories.

A seller should suggest additional merchandise to every customer. Even a customer in a great hurry may listen to suggestions for future merchandise while the sale is being processed. Effective suggestion selling should add to the customer's enjoyment of the original purchase, add to the functionality or use of the first purchase, add another product that meets the customer's needs, or plant an idea for a future purchase.

Suggestion selling should fit the person, the time, and the situation. Avoid closed-ended questions just as in the approach and greeting phase, e.g., "Would you like to look at a scarf to go with this blouse?" "No." Use positive statements about the merchandise. "Look at these scarves; they are the perfect accent for this blouse." When the customer agrees to buy the scarf, continue. "The other item to complete this look is these earrings. . ." Don't stop with one item; keep playing the percentages. Continue suggesting merchandise until the customer is satisfied with the total purchase.

There are eight categories of multiple sale merchandise:

1. More of the same item
2. Compatible merchandise (see previous discussion)

3. Merchandise the customer needs

4. Fashion, fad, trend merchandise

5. Best sellers

6. New merchandise

7. Price promotional, clearance, or special purchase merchandise

8. Selected "surprise" merchandise that the seller wants everyone to see no matter what.

The seller should be creatively prepared to use the method or methods most suited to a particular customer and situation.

Follow-Up

The purpose of the **follow-up** is to solve any problems related to the sale and to develop and maintain good customer relations. Follow-up begins during the processing of the current sale. Collecting personal information about the customer and his or her family to develop a listing for a personal sales book might be part of the process. Ask the customer if he or she would like to be called when new or special merchandise arrives.

It is common to use the customer's name whenever possible to personalize the process. Throughout the sale, be friendly, courteous, efficient, and show genuine interest in the customer. Knowing and using correct procedures makes processing the sale comfortable for the customer. State pleasure in having the opportunity to serve the customer. Offer to add the customer to a mailing list so he or she will receive notices of special events. It might be appropriate to ask for suggestions of other prospects the seller might contact at the customer's recommendation. Thank the customer for shopping and invite a return to the store. The first contact outside the current sale might be a hand-written note thanking the customer for their patronage.

Handling Merchandise Returns

Merchandise return policies are important factors in determining a customer's choice of vendors. When retail buyers/merchandisers negotiate purchase contracts, terms related to refunds or discounts for markdowns of unsold merchandise need to be a part of the discussion. When retail customers experience bad service related to merchandise returns, they often do not complain to the retailer, they simply do not come back. They are also much more likely to tell their friends about their frustrating experience than about a satisfactory one. Each happy customer will tell five people about their experience; each unhappy customer will tell nine. More than 90 percent of unhappy customers won't be back (Anton, 1996). JCPenney says it costs six times as much to get a new customer as it does to keep an existing customer. It is common for more than two-thirds of a company's business to come from existing customers.

It is the seller's job to handle merchandise returns according to the company policy. Remember that great majority of customers are honest, fair, and reasonable and their returns of merchandise are legitimate and justifiable. It is not the seller's job to judge the customer, but to process the return. A smile and a good attitude are essential. Use the process to chat with the customer about the merchandise, their needs, and to do suggestion selling.

Dealing with Difficult/Unhappy Customers

Regardless of the quality of the selling process, sometimes customers are difficult or unreasonable and sometimes they are justifiably unhappy. Keeping in mind that most customers are satisfied helps put difficult customers in the proper perspective. The unhappy customer tends to direct his or her anger and frustration at the person who is available, even though this person is unlikely to be the cause of the problem. Therefore the representative of the seller must not take the customer's dissatisfaction personally. It is essential for the individual dealing with the complaint to remain calm and objective. The following sequence will facilitate processing a complaint:

- Listen. Let the customer unload.
- Empathize, show concern, and let the customer know you care.
- Ask open-ended questions.
- Restate the facts.
- Avoid offering excuses or placing blame on someone else.
- Offer options.
- Agree on a solution.
- Take action.
- Follow up.

In this simple list form, it looks like dealing with a frustrated customer should be very straightforward. It seldom is, but if the person handling the complaint is well informed about company procedures and can remain calm, they stand a good chance of successfully resolving the situation.

Learning Activity 11.2

Practicing effective selling

Form the class into groups. Identify a retailer each group will represent. Use coats or books or other things in the room as merchandise to mock up a display. Each person in each group will play one of three roles: customer, seller, and critic. Customers will exit then return to be greeted by the seller. The customer and seller will engage in conversation related to the selling process. The critic will stand by, observe, and take notes on the interaction. When the selling process is completed, the three people will sit down and discuss the interaction. The critic will report observations and the group will discuss how to improve the process. Then the three people will rotate roles and repeat the process.

        Case 11.2   *The art of haggling* *

Items with variable pricing such as jewelry, furniture, clothing, hotel rooms, and long taxi rides are prime candidates for price-cutting demands, negotiation experts say. Haggling is practiced at every stage of ownership exchange in the textile and apparel complex including sale of goods to the ultimate consumer. Haggling is also an essential component of the hiring and firing of merchandising professionals. For some, haggling on a price is instinctive, while for others it's a game.

The consumerism that swept the United States in the 1990s turned haggling from the sign of a cheapskate to the hallmark of an enterprising shopper. As Americans shed their reluctance to haggle, the price threshold at which we'll ask for a break dropped. A survey of 1,000 consumers by America's Research Group found the point at which most were comfortable asking for a discount is $200—down from $500 in 1990. More consumers are applying negotiating skills to everyday purchases.

"You can haggle for virtually anything," said C. Britt Beemer, and research firm's founder. Goods such as gasoline and products on Wal-Mart's shelves offer little room for negotiation, said Leonard Greenhalgh, a management professor at Dartmouth College in Hanover, New Hampshire. "But anything that has a list price and a lot of margin, you ought to be able to haggle for."

Still, most people aren't eager to make a case for a better deal, and younger consumers are especially reticent. Only 28 percent of those ages 18 to 25 said they feel comfortable haggling all the time, compared with 44 percent of consumers 50 and older, Beemer said.

There's good reason to get over a haggling aversion these days, Beemer said. "If someone spends more than $200 or $300 at a store, oftentimes they can negotiate something—it may not be a better price, but it may be added savings or the store waving some other charge." Fixed prices are often a haggler's enemy because bar codes hold clerks accountable to a set cost, Greenhalgh said. At the same time, it never hurts to ask for a manager with the authority to negotiate a price break, especially for services such as lodging, he said.

Items on the Table for Negotiation by the Ultimate Consumer

- Major household appliances. Even if you don't get a lower price, a worthy trade-off may be a waived delivery charge, installation fee, or a free extended warranty.
- Electronics. If you buy a computer, see if you can get a free printer or upgraded memory at no charge, Beemer said. Consumers also can use the delivery charge as leverage of last resort when bargaining for a big-screen TV.
- Clothes. Some chain stores won't drop below a certain price or markdown any-

thing that's already discounted below costs, but some smaller stores may be more receptive to bargaining. A store that won't budge on price may be willing to drop the alteration charge.
- Taxi and limousine services. The driver may be open to negotiating a fee instead of letting the meter run blindly, Greenhalgh said. That's especially true on long rides from drivers who lease their vehicles.
- Furniture. Most people can haggle prices down, but newlyweds setting up a new house are in a particularly strong position to negotiate a bulk discount if they plan to stick with one supplier, Greenhalgh said, noting that he negotiated 25 percent off his own total tab. "I was kicking myself later because the guy would've probably taken 40 percent."

Strategies for Negotiation by Anybody for Anything

- *Prepare before you begin.* Getting the right attitude, gather information on the other party's best interest, and decide what your best interests are. The right attitude includes being objective, confident, detached, and engaged in critical thinking. Ask questions of the other party to understand their issues. Be prepared to negotiate based on your priorities. Be open-minded about possi-

(continued)

Case 11.2 *(continued)*

ble solutions that you had not previously considered.

- *Getting started.* Walk in, shake hands, sit down, and smile. Encourage the other party to do the same. Talk about the issues involved in the negotiation. Try to get the other party to do the same. Then ask the other party to set some parameters for consideration.
- *Moving the process along.* Ask more questions. Reiterate your position on the issues. Use silence to get the other party to talk. If there is little possibility of a so-

lution, suggest a mediator or, if necessary, suggest establishing ground rules for fair negotiation.

- *Getting to the finish.* Narrow down the issues on the table. Propose a possible resolution. Don't hurry the other party or yourself. Listen to alternatives. Consult your priorities. If it is satisfactory, ask the final question. "Have we got a deal?" If it is not satisfactory, walk away.

*Based on Gerencher (2003) and The only four-page guide… (1996).

 Learning Activity 11.3

Negotiating just about anything

1. What are the fundamental principles of successful negotiation?
2. What aspects of customer/vendor relationships at the retail level are shaping the retail sector?
3. To be satisfied with the outcome, why is it essential to be prepared to walk away?

Improving Customer/Vendor Relationships

Most manufacturers and retailers are striving to improve customer service. Some are continually striving to improve customer service. Even Nordstrom, which is recognized as one of the most outstanding customer service companies in the world, has improving customer service as its primary goal (Spector & McCarthy, 1995). For some firms, improving customer service means changing corporate structures, organizational priorities, and management strategies. For many firms, it means a major cultural change. Corporate culture change often means changing the way people think and act—no small task. "The single most visible factor that distinguishes major cultural changes that succeed from those that fail is competent leadership at the top" (Kotter & Heskett, 1992, p. 84).

There are distinct differences between leadership and management. **Management** embodies budgeting, organizing, and controlling. **Leadership** embodies empowerment: directing, motivating, and inspiring (Adair-Heeley, 1991; Kotter & Heskett, 1992). How an organization's leaders believe things should be done drives a firm's culture (Schneider, 1994). Table 11.3 compares aspects of management and leadership. Management results in

Table 11.3

The difference between management and leadership. *

Management	Leadership
Planning and Budgeting—establishing detailed steps and timetables for achieving needed results then allocating the resources necessary to make that happen.	*Establishing Direction*—developing a vision for the future, often the distant future, and strategies for producing the changes needed to achieve that vision.
Organizing and Staffing—establishing some structure for accomplishing plan requirements, staffing that structure, delegating responsibility and authority for carrying out the plan, providing policies and procedures to help guide people, and creating methods or systems to monitor implementation.	*Aligning People*—communicating the direction by words and deeds to all those whose cooperation may be needed; influencing the creation of teams and a coalition that understand the vision and strategies and accept their validity.
Controlling and Problem Solving—monitoring results vs. planning in some detail, identifying deviations, and then planning and organizing to solve these problems.	*Motivating and Inspiring*—energizing people to overcome major political, bureaucratic, and resource barriers to change by satisfying very basic, but often unfulfilled, human needs.
Outcome—Produces a degree of predictability and order, and has the potential of consistently producing key results expected by various stakeholders (e.g., for the customer, always being on time; for stockholders, being on budget).	*Outcome*—Produces change, often to a dramatic degree, and has the potential of producing extremely useful change (e.g., new products that customers want, new approaches to labor relations that help make a firm more competitive).

*Kotter & Heskett (1992, p. 99).

predictable outcomes; leadership results in adaptability to current conditions and progress to the future.

Implementation of quick response (QR) business systems embodies improvements in customer service because QR permeates the customer/vendor relationship. Implementation of QR, in most cases, requires a change in corporate culture. Firms operating in a leadership environment are more adaptable to change than those operating in a management environment (see Table 11.4). **Adaptive corporate cultures** are able to be **agile,** i.e., "capable of operating profitably in a competitive environment of continually, and unpredictably, changing customer opportunities" (Goldman, Nagel, & Preiss, 1995, p. 3). Agile companies must go beyond being customer-centered to being centered on the customer-perceived value of products (Goldman, Nagel, & Preiss, 1995).

The behaviors itemized by Kotter and Heskett (1992) in Tables 11.3 and 11.4 epitomize the leadership/management behaviors that support the **Behavioral Theory of the Apparel Firm** with quick response business systems (BTAF) discussed in Chapters 1 and 2. Merchandising as a constituency is dependent on teamwork and successful interactions within and among constituencies to support planning, developing, and presenting product lines. The assumption of a **marketing concept** means the ability of a firm to meet its goals is partially dependent on satisfying the needs and wants of external coalitions that are exchange

Table 11.4

*Adaptive vs. unadaptive corporate cultures**

	Adaptive Corporate Culture	*Unadaptive Corporate Culture*
Core Values	Most managers care deeply about customers, stockholders, and employees. They also strongly value people and processes that can create useful change (e.g., leadership up and down the management hierarchy).	Most managers care mainly about themselves, their immediate work group, or some product (or technology) associated with that work group. They value the orderly and risk-reducing management process much more than leadership initiatives.
Common Behavior	Managers pay close attention to all their constituencies, especially customers, and initiate change when needed to serve their legitimate interests, even if that entails taking some risks.	Managers tend to behave in a somewhat insular, political, and bureaucratic manner. As a result, they do not change their strategies quickly to adjust to or take advantage of changes in their business environments.

*Kotter & Heskett (1992, p. 143)

partners, particularly their customers (Houston, 1986). The marketing concept, as a philosophy of the firm, is implicit to the firm with leadership structures and adaptive cultures. The marketing concept reflects a mode of operation for the firm that directs the agendas and activities of individual constituencies. Seeing the marketing concept as a standard mode of operation is essential for firms that wish to improve customer/vendor relationships. Merchandisers cannot plan, develop, and present product lines without the support of all of a firm's constituencies.

Case 11.4   *Partnering, finally more than a buzzword**

"Partnership" is beginning to have real meaning in retailer-vendor relationships. Back in the late 1980s, Wal-Mart pioneered what it called "partnership," or a new relationship between retailers and their suppliers. The theory was that the two camps would start working together to better serve the consumer, and thus, both sides would start working together to better serve the consumer, and thus, both sides would prosper. Many other large retailers leaped to join the partnership frenzy, but the results, while favorable to retailers, were decidedly less so for many manufacturers.

Suddenly, suppliers were required to perform or subsidize many of the retailer's traditional functions, such as warehousing, merchandising, planogramming, advertising, market research, and a host of other things. But at the same time, merchandisers continued to hammer suppliers in negotiations, driving prices and profits down for their "partners." A joke making the rounds at the time was that if you looked up the word partner in the Wal-Mart dictionary, it said see love-slave.

In the past few years, however, the robust economy and increasing sophistication of both retailers and vendors seems to have generated a truer sense of equality and shared interest between the two communities. Vendors are now being rewarded more often and more richly for their increased assumption of merchandising, store-level inventory, and other duties.

Category management was perhaps the genesis of this new detente. Whereas previously, retailers had been loath to share information, but demanded extensive data from suppliers, category management finally opened up the retailer's books to its partners and allowed those suppliers to gain a better understanding of each individual customer's needs. It also allowed vendors the freedom to alter the mix on a store-by-store basis, thus concentrating on the more profitable areas of their business,

(continued)

Case 11.4 (continued)

cutting down on returns and markdowns, and reacting far more quickly to changing regional tastes.

For example, one vendor notes that after working closely with a leading retail chain, editing the assortment, and realigning promotional and advertising strategies, sales increased more than 500 percent through that customer alone. "We're all working together to take cost out of the system and to better serve the customer." One major shift has been to "deconfuse" the customer. That means fewer, but better-known, brands as well as clearer signage and packaging. Where at one point, retailers carried as many as eight brands at a variety of price points for a particular merchandise class, today most carry two or three major brands plus a promotional brand. There's been a lot of consolidation to get brands and SKUs down to a reasonable level. "We've worked with a lot of major retailers to prune the assortments and we're seeing a lot more open communication and cooperation as we become more important to their business."

*Based on Hisey (2001).

Summary

Merchandisers play a primary role in customer/vendor relationships throughout the textiles and apparel trade matrix. Merchandisers are frequently responsible for buying and/or sourcing materials for apparel manufacturers, training sales representatives on how to present product lines, buying and/or sourcing finished goods for retailers, and training retail sellers in product knowledge and presentation strategies. Merchandisers negotiate merchandise contracts and follow-up based on satisfactory or unsatisfactory results. Merchandisers are both sold to and sell.

Without appropriate customer service, planning, developing, and presenting product lines can be a frustrating exercise. In the manufacturing sector, sales representatives are commonly part of the marketing constituency. In the retail sector, sales associates are commonly part of the operations constituency. Cooperative interaction, flexibility, and teamwork are essential for successfully executing the merchandising strategy.

Firms are increasingly recognizing opportunities for customizing product lines and services to customers needs. Today's technology makes it possible to operate very large firms in ways that will serve hundreds, thousands, maybe even millions of unique markets. The evolution of QR business systems into time-based competition, partnerships, and agility has just begun.

Key Concepts

adaptive corporate culture	full service	personal, informal, social
agile	greeting a customer	approach
alternate selling	leadership	personal selling service
Behavioral Theory of the	limited service	premier customer service
Apparel Firm (BTAF)	management	product benefits
closed-ended question	marketing concept	product features
closing the sale	merchandise approach	self service
customer needs	merchandise selection	service approach
customer service	assistance	suggestion selling
customer's objections	needs	wants
follow-up	open-ended question	

◎ Integrated Learning Activity 11.4.1

Improving customer service with secret shoppers

1. Purposes of the project:
   - Gain knowledge of the selling process as it impacts personal service.
   - Experience the selling process from the customer's viewpoint by secretly shopping at local retail establishments.
   - Evaluate the selling concepts in the retail environment through retailer and educational interaction.
   - Experience retail management functions by making suggestions for improving the effectiveness of personal service.
2. Develop a personal selling service evaluation instrument to be used by secret shoppers. Topics to be addressed include:
   - Store appearance (stock, display, cleanliness).
   - Staff (grooming, friendliness, knowledge).

- Selling process (approach and greeting, identification of customer wants and needs, merchandise demonstration and handling, objection handling, suggestion selling, closing the sale, and follow-up).
- Overall service (efficiency, interest, product knowledge, availability, and responsiveness)
- Overall impression of the store.
- Activity level at the time of shopping.

3.   Each student will secretly shop three different stores acting as a customer. Immediately following the shopping experience, the student will record his or her observations on the secret shopper instrument before shopping another store.

4.   Discuss each student's secret shopping experience in class. Identify similarities and differences and things that are most consistently problems.

5.   Identify management actions that might improve customer service in each store.

Recommended Resources

Anton, J. (1996). *Customer relationship management.* Upper Saddle River, NJ: Prentice Hall.

Customer Service training manuals for major retailers, for example, The Limited and The Gap.

Gaskill, L. R., & Kunz, G. I. (1991, Summer). Commitment to customer service: An interactive learning strategy. *Journal of Home Economics,* 83(2):29–32.

Goldman, S. L., Nagel, R. N., & Preiss, K. (1995). *Agile competitors and virtual organizations: Strategies for enriching the customer.* New York: Van Nostrand Reinhold.

Spector, R., & McCarthy, P. D. (1995). *The Nordstrom way.* New York: Wiley.

References

Adair-Heeley, C. B. (1991). *The human side of just-in-time.* New York: American Management Association.

Anton, J. (1996). *Customer relationship management.* Upper Saddle River, NJ: Prentice Hall.

Berman, B. B., & Evans, J. R. (1995). *Retail management.* Englewood Cliffs, NJ: Prentice Hall.

Cathcart, J. (1988). Winning customer service. *Management Solutions,* 33.

D'Innocenzio, A. (2003, January 11). Stores tighten return policies. *Des Moines Register,* 6D.

Davidow, W. H., & Uttal, B. (1989). Coming: The customer service decade. *Across the Board,* 26: 33–37

Fleischer, J. (2001, May 2). Online apparel buyers wearing down the return key. *Daily News Record,* 12.

Gaskill, L. R., & Kunz, G. I. (1991, Summer). Commitment to customer service: An interactive learning strategy. *Journal of Home Economics,* 83(2):29–32.

Gerencher, K. (2003, May 25). The art of haggling. *Des Moines Sunday Register*, 3D.

Goldfarb, M. (1989). Developing a customer focus. *Business Quarterly,* 54.

Goldman, S. L., Nagel, R. N., & Preiss, K. (1995). *Agile competitors and virtual organizations: Strategies for enriching the customer.* New York: Van Nostrand Reinhold.

Ghosh, A. (1990). *Retail management.* Chicago: Dryden Press.

Hisey, P. (2001, May). Finally more than a buzzword. *Retail Merchandiser,* 24–25.

Houston, F. S. (1986, April). The marketing concept: What it is and what it is not. *Journal of Marketing,* 50:80–87.

Kotter, J. P., & Heskett, J. L. (1992). *Corporate culture and performance.* New York: The Free Press.

Lele, M. M. (1987). *The customer is key.* New York: Wiley.

Lewison, D. M. (1994). *Retailing* (5th ed.). New York: Macmillan.

Schneider, W. E. (1994). *The reengineering alternative.* New York: Irwin.

Spector, R., & McCarthy, P. D. (1995). *The Nordstrom way.* New York: Wiley.

The only four-page guide to negotiating you'll ever need. (1996). *Harvard Management Update,* Article Reprint No. U9609A.

Zemke, R. (1986). Contract! Training employees to meet the public. *Training,* 23(8):41–45.

Career Opportunities

12

Merchandising-

Related Career

Development

Learning Objectives

- Explore career development theory.

- Examine job titles, career development levels, and areas of specialization via a taxonomy of merchandising careers.

- Discuss methods of career advancement.

- Examine means for selecting an employer.

areers have been an important subject of inquiry from sociological, psychological, and organizational perspectives since the 1920s, with a concentration of publications in the 1970s. Several researchers have summarized and evaluated research related to careers including Glaser (1968), *Organizational Careers: A Sourcebook for Theory;* Minor (1992), *Career Development: Theories and Models;* Hall (1976), *Careers in Organizations;* Stevens-Long (1979), *Adult Life: Developmental Processes;* and Van Maanen (1977), *Organizational Careers: Some New Perspectives.* More academic attention has been paid to apparel merchandising careers related to the retail sector than the manufacturing sector, although the strong trends toward vertical integration have blended the two in many firms over the last 15 years.

The Concept of Career Development

For purposes of this discussion, **career** is defined as the individually perceived sequence of attitudes and behaviors associated with work-related experiences and activities over the span of the person's life (Hall, 1976). Research regarding careers has had two dominant themes: career choice and career development. **Career choice** is the process of selecting an area of specialization as a focus of one's work. Holland's *Making Vocational Choices: A Theory of Careers* (1973) is a prime example of the culmination of vocational research focusing on career choice. Holland developed a classification for personality interest styles that includes realistic, investigative, artistic, social, enterprising, and conventional. He then identified occupations that correspond to the interest styles and developed a "self-directed search" to determine appropriate occupations according to one's personality. Career-choice research tends to focus attention on the young adult. This approach seems to assume that career choice is made only once during early adulthood — not a very realistic expectation in today's job market.

Futurists see today's college students making at least three major specialization changes during their total working career. The rapid increase in the use of information technology is expected to make some jobs and career paths completely disappear, while new, currently unknown career opportunities will emerge. Thus, in today's job market, making a career choice during young adulthood is merely a place to begin; that choice will not necessarily fulfill one's entire work life.

Career development is the lifelong process of examining the possibilities for work-related experiences and activities and deciding, with awareness, what one wishes to do with one's life (*"Born free,"* 1978). It is part of the development of the adult as an evolving, growing human being. Career-development research has identified stages of development and associated those stages with the age range at which each occurs. The concepts for the stages, age classification, and terminology differ with each researcher. For example, Erikson's (1959) stages of development are childhood (0–15), identity (15–25), intimacy (25–35), generativity (35–65), and ego integrity (65+). Super (1957) identified stages of development that are more career specific: growth (0–15), exploration (15–25), establishment (25–45), maintenance (45–65), and decline (65+). More recently, Super and Ginzberg have contributed the idea that career development and even career choices, are the result of a process rather than a point-in-time event (Minor, 1992).

"A significant limitation of all developmental career theories, as well as almost all other career theories, is that the supporting research has been done [almost] exclusively on men" (Minor, 1992, p. 13). Some of the findings have been generalized to women, however, but sometimes inappropriately. In fact, some research related to women's careers suggests that career development for women is considerably different than for men.

Three interrelated **realms** tend to dominate adult life in the western world: relationships/marriage, family, and employment. Men are often stereotypically regarded as being more "serious" about their employment, meaning they are more likely to give their career priority over their other life roles. Karelius (1982) found that men tend to be **"life-structure modifiers,"** while women regard changes in their lives as "rebirth of individual potential." For example, a change in a man's career, such as a geographic job transfer, has traditionally been accompanied by the movement of his family to the new location. This provides modification of his job environment, but continuity in his family life. His wife, if employed, would probably resign from her job and find another in the new location. This frequently involves starting over at entry level and retraining for new responsibilities. Karelius found this **"rebirth of potential"** to be a common occurrence in the lives of females, thus slowing career development.

Because traditional western family-structure places males in the role of the bread-winners and females as homemakers, men have not often had to choose among spouse, parent, and career. Many women, however, do have to make that choice. Women continue to experience more role conflict than men. A recent survey revealed that men in top management tend to have wives who are full-time homemakers; women in top management tend to be single. Numerous other studies have demonstrated that women in two income households are still responsible for the vast majority of home and childcare. Consequently, in order to give adequate attention to their careers, many women give up or postpone marriage and/or childbearing until their careers are well-established.

It is well-documented that women are paid less 10 to 30 percent less than men with similar job responsibilities and hold fewer executive positions. These phenomena have had many explanations including the following:

- Women spend less time at work than men.
- Women are less dedicated to work than men.
- Women take time off for child bearing and then must restart their careers.
- Women do not want "executive" responsibility.

A recent news report focused on a study by the women's advocacy group Catalyst related to the number of women who hold seats on boards of directors of Fortune 500 companies. "Women held 13.6 percent of corporate director seats in 2003, up from 12.4 percent in 2001 and 9.5 percent in 1995." The study reports that if the rate of increase continues, women will hold 25 percent of director seats by 2025. The rate of increase was credited to the need for corporate boards to become more "independent" because of the wave of corporate scandals that have been in the news. It was predicted that the search for more qualified candidates with fewer ties to the chief executives and other directors will give more women a chance to serve on boards (More women hold..., 2003).

📖 *Learning Activity 12.1*

Career development perspectives of males and females

1. What might it mean to say that men are "life-structure modifiers"? Think of some examples from your experience of how men's life structures have been modified in the process of career development?
2. What might it mean to say that women regard career changes as "rebirth of individual potential"? Think of some examples.
3. The research on which the concepts of "life-structure modifiers" and "rebirth of individual potential" were based was completed in 1982. Are these concepts still appropriately applied to career development of men and women? Are there changes that have occurred that might moderate the application of these concepts?

Career Development in Relation to the Firm

Dalton, Thompson, and Price (1977), recognizing the importance of organizational constraints, combined career stage/life cycle theory with **organizational theory.** In their model, career growth is a dynamic process that is the result of the interaction of three primary forces: the job(s) assigned the individual in the organization; the interaction of the individual with others inside and outside the organization; and the personal development of the individual in this setting(s). This approach to career development recognizes the importance of the environment in which one works and its relationship to career growth and success. A research study involving 2,500 engineers found a "negative correlation after age 35 between age and performance rating" (p. 20). The researchers found poor performance was often blamed on obsolescence, and so recommended continuing education or additional coursework. However, data analysis revealed that high performers were no more likely to have taken continuing education courses than low performers (Dalton, Thompson, & Price, 1977).

Thus, Dalton et al. embarked on another study to try to identify how high performers differ from low performers. This time they interviewed 550 professionally trained employees, including 155 scientists, 268 engineers, 52 accountants, and 75 university professors. When they looked at the time employed relative to performance rating, they found that high performers who were early in their careers were performing different functions than high performers who were in the middle of their careers. Both these groups had different responsibilities from high performers whose careers were near completion.

The Dalton et al. model identifies four distinct **stages of career development** of professionally trained persons based on the dynamic interaction of three primary forces: primary relationship with fellow workers, central activities of a job, and psychological orientation to the firm (see Table 12.1). The four stages might be best identified by the primary relationships to fellow workers (apprentice, colleague, mentor, and sponsor) with corresponding developments of central activities and psychological orientation. Dalton et al. found that, "it was the individuals who were moving successfully through these stages who had high performance ratings. Conversely, individuals who remained in the early stages were likely to be low-rated" (p. 22). Their research also pointed out there may be some faulty assumptions on the part of firms and educators about the relationship between career growth and education; continuing education courses are not a "quick fix" to make an individual more productive. An individual's productivity is much more complex than that.

Apparel manufacturing and retailing firms provide environments for career development for more than two million employees in the United States. Apparel-related businesses have unique characteristics because of the intense focus on product change (Kunz, 1987). It is in the firm's environment that each employee takes advantage of opportunities, experiences frustrations, and makes career decisions. Examining the career development available to apparel firm managers and executives helps one understand career opportunities and operation of apparel businesses.

Table 12.1

Stages of successful career development. *

Career Stage	Performance Functions		
	Primary Relationship with Fellow Workers	*Central Activities of a Job*	*Psychological Orientation to the Firm*
Stage 1: entry level	apprentice	helping, learning, and following directions	dependence
Stage 2: middle management	colleague	being an independent contributor	independence
Stage 3: senior management	mentor	training	assuming responsibility for others
Stage 4: executive leadership	sponsor	shaping the direction of the organization	exercising power

*Based on Dalton, Thompson, & Price (1977).

Learning Activity 12.2

Career growth and success

1. Examine Table 12.1. Paraphrase the words in each cell of the table. Do your interpretations of each concept make sense together?
2. Look up the words *apprentice, colleague, mentor,* and *sponsor* in several dictionaries. Do these words mean what you thought they did? What dictionary definitions are appropriate to this model?
3. As a college graduate, would you expect to enter a merchandising career in Stage 1 of the Dalton et al. model? How long do you think it would take to move on to Stage 2?
4. How might you use the Dalton model to establish goals for a merchandising internship?

Merchandising-Related Careers

Merchandising—especially retail merchandising—has long been the career focus of textiles and clothing academic programs. The first college-level merchandising program was offered by the Home Economics program at the University of Washington in 1917. The program included a combination of nutrition, home management, textile and nontextile merchandising, salesmanship, and an internship. Merchandising programs were designed to provide opportunities for women to move into business careers (Paoletti, 1985). "Collegiate education in retailing began in 1919 with the founding of The Training School for Teachers of Retail Selling (now the Institute of Retail Management) at New York University. Other universities soon followed suit" (Hollander, 1978, p. 3).

In the retail sector, as with most businesses, women are still clustered in lower-level sales and clerical positions, while upper management remains well over 70 percent male. Annual managerial turnover in retailing has been estimated at between 24 percent and 54 percent. This means that up to half of total management level employees leave every year, denoting a rapidly changing work environment that provides much opportunity for young people. Retailers regularly recruit on college campuses and often have well-established executive training programs for merchandising positions.

The recruiting process for merchandising positions in the manufacturing sector is much less structured. Manufacturers hire fewer new college graduates, and thus are less likely to recruit on college campuses. They are more likely to advertise positions in the trade press or network to hire people with merchandising experience from retail executive training programs. New merchandising graduates can get positions with manufacturers, but the path requires more initiative on the part of the student.

In many people's minds, merchandising as a process and as a career is still associated only with retailing. Consequently, merchandising career-related research has focused primarily on the retail sector, in particular on the job of buyer. Only in the last 20 years have many textiles and clothing programs expanded their scope to include manufacturing, distribution, and now e-commerce in the discussion of merchandising-related career opportunities. This opens up career development opportunities throughout the business sector and throughout the world.

Nevertheless, the retail sector remains a primary on-the-job training ground for merchandising-related positions. Retail based part-time jobs, summer work, field experiences, and internships are valued by both manufacturers and retailer recruiters because potential executive/managerial trainees have been exposed to the nature of the merchandising process, the intensity of product change, the challenges associated with working with a variety of opinionated people, and the difficulty of satisfying customers. Research has shown that retail executive and managerial recruits who have merchandising coursework and work experience are more likely to be retained and promoted by their initial employer. Primary factors contributing to retention are realistic expectations of the graduate related to the job and improved ability of the graduate to select an employer that can offer the opportunities desired. See Case 12.1.

     Case 12.1   E-talent: A tangled search process*

A good cybermerchant is hard to find, and harder still to keep. As traditional retailers evolve into brick-and-click retailers, they're shifting their search engines into high gear to deal with severe recruiting challenges. The challenge is largely a scarcity of talent, according to headhunters and retail consultants, who are having a field day. Over the last year, 30 percent of retail search practice has been for e-commerce. Job search professionals say staffing Internet retail operations is more complicated than recruiting for traditional retail posts, especially for stores making their first foray into cyberspace. The issues range from determining salaries and benefits to deciding what career backgrounds, educational backgrounds, and personalities are best suited for leading the on-line store.

Wannabe Internet merchants face formidable challenges. There's mounting competition, and new sites continue to pro-

(continued)

Case 12.1 (continued)

liferate. Recruiting experts assembled a model for the ideal candidate to lead the e-business: part pragmatic merchant and part cyberspace visionary. Because e-tail base salaries typically aren't competitive with those in the general market — because of startup costs and funding issues — new e-tailers have to dangle stock options or some sort of equity to get the best employees. Arnold Aronson, managing partner and director of retail strategies at Kurt Salmon Associates, said retailers recruiting for the Web should require strong merchandising skills. "One thing that gets lost in Internet hysteria is that a product is still a product, regardless of where it's sold."

Aronson said the ideal brick-and-click recruits have a dual background in merchandising and the Internet. A lot of companies are moving personnel internally, from brick-and-mortar or from mail-order operations, over to run e-commerce businesses. Having a merchant lead the business by and large has been a successful strategy. It is a natural segue — taking merchants from retail and catalog companies and putting them into the Internet operation.

*Based on Moin & Williamson (2000).

Taxonomy of Merchandising Careers

The taxonomy of merchandising careers represents the system of career development in merchandising related to the retail sector. It was developed as part of a larger project, my Ph.D. dissertation, entitled Career Development of College Graduates Employed in Retailing (Kunz, 1986), as well as a follow-up study I conducted in 1990 (See Table 12.2). The taxonomy identifies: 1) areas of specialization of apparel-related retail firms as associated with career development; 2) levels of career development within these areas of specialization; 3) job titles within levels; and 4) the relationships in career opportunities among areas of specialization. Job titles in the merchandising area of specialization have been updated to include retail product development and quick response based on Gaskill (1992), Hare (1993), Parr (1993), and Wickett (1995). Interestingly, many of the job titles related to merchandising are the same in both the manufacturing and retail sectors. The actual job description associated with the title varies firm by firm in both sectors.

The taxonomy emerged as a result of the process of constantly comparing data reflecting the diverse experiences of 42 retail executives. Since about two-thirds of the informants for this research spent most of their careers in stores or merchandising divisions, the depth of comparison in these parts of the taxonomy is greater than that of the other areas of specialization. In depth interviews with 42 retail executives allowed them to describe their career development experiences in their own language, thus revealing the "insider" perspective of career development. Table 12.3 provides profiles of the retail executive participants. Notice the range of education levels, diversity of majors, and salary ranges in relation to years in retailing. Salaries for many retail executives are now proportionally higher than those reflected in the table but are still indicative of the range of differences. Retailers have traditionally recruited candidates with a variety of backgrounds into their executive training programs.

Relationship of the Taxonomy to BTAF

The taxonomy can be regarded as a description of retail merchandising career development within the context of Behavioral Theory of the Apparel Firm (Kunz, 1995). The taxonomy of merchandising careers was derived using qualitative, inductive research methods and insider perspectives similar to those used for development of BTAF. The areas of specialization in the model of the behavioral theory are intended to represent a generic apparel firm, whereas the taxonomy of merchandising careers as it now stands is based only on the retail sector. Unfortunately, comparable career development research has not been conducted within the manufacturing sector.

Using the Taxonomy

I developed a coding system to simplify the use of the taxonomy to describe career development. A two-digit **career code** represents both the **area of specialization** and the **career level** within that specialization. The first digit in the career code represents the area of specialization: merchandising = 1, stores = 2, personnel = 3, advertising and sales promotion = 4, management information systems = 5, and operations/finance = 6.

The areas of specialization used in the taxonomy are not necessarily consistent with the organization of any particular retail firm, but rather represent generic classifications according to specialization that relate to career development in retail organizations.

The second digit in the career code, a number from 0 to 9, represents a career level with the possible job titles at that level. For example, career code "25" means the responsibility

Table 12.2

Taxonomy of merchandising careers.

Career Code	Merchandising Specialization
10	merchandise clerical; merchandise detail; merchandise technician; advertising coordinator
11	intern; buying trainee, merchandising trainee; allocator
12	assistant buyer; supervisor of stores, assistant designer
13	associate buyer; planner-distributor; branch store coordinator; product development coordinator, technical designer
14	buyer, product manager, product development manager; designer; brand development manager; purchasing manager, quick response liaison
15	senior buyer; planning-distribution manager; merchandise counselor
16	divisional merchandise manager; merchandise administrator
17	senior merchandise manager; product development manager
18	vice-president of merchandising; general merchandise manager; vice-president of product development; vice-president of design
19	senior vice-president; design director; fashion director; quick response director, executive vice-president

Career Code	Stores Specialization
20	sales associates; display, stock person; commission sales
21	intern; manager in training; assistant sales, department, counter manager; head of stock
22	department, receiving, customer service, sales manager; personnel coordinator; small store assistant manager
23	branch personnel, group sales, area manager or leader; customer service supervisor
24	merchandise, display, office, assistant, visual merchandising coordinator; small store manager
25	personnel, group, operation, assistant, branch manager
26	store manager, store general manager, senior store manager
27	district, cluster store, creative display manager; senior district manager
28	vice-president; regional administrator or manager; visual merchandising manager, branch store director
29	senior vice-president, director of stores

Career Code	Personnel Specialization
30	training instructor; employment clerical; employment coordinator; college relations representative
31	regional representative
32	college relations, assistant, training director or manager; personnel administrator
33	employment representative; training coordinator; associate manager staff training
34	executive training manager; senior recruiter
35	corporate training director or counselor; personnel, training, employee standards manager
36	divisional manager executive placement; executive development administrator
37	general manager of personnel
38	vice-president of personnel
39	senior vice-president; director of personnel or human resources

Career Code	Advertising and Sales Promotion Specialization
40	advertising copy writer; color coordinator
41	account executive

42	advertising assistant
43	special events coordinator
44	fashion, advertising, sales, promotions, special events director
45	
46	
47	
48	vice-president of sales promotion; vice-president of trend merchandising; special events director
49	senior vice-president; director of sales promotion

Career Code	Management Information Systems Specialization
50	clerical
51	sales leader
52	supervisor; assistant manager
53	
54	consumer affairs; telemail manager
55	MIS system manager
56	administrator
57	
58	vice-president
59	senior vice-president

Career Code	Operations and Finance Specialization
60	clerk; credit counselor
61	control trainee
62	auditor; credit, department manager, or supervisor
63	accounts payable manager; systems, shortage, financial analyst
64	inventory control manager; shortage auditor
65	shortage, charge, controller, or coordinator
66	divisional cash, shortage control manager, or administrator or controller

67	assistant corporate controller, quick response administrator
68	vice-president of control administration
69	senior vice-president of operations

Career Code	Senior Executives
100	president
101	chief operating officer
102	chief executive officer; chairman
103	co-owner
104	owner
105	owner-manager
106	owner, vice-president
107	owner, president
108	owner, chairman
109	

Career Code	Jobs Outside Retailing
200	not in work force
201	student
202	homemaker
203	secretary, receptionist, clerical
204	sales, showroom representative; social worker
205	merchandiser
206	marketing manager
207	self-employed
208	other
209	other

Table 12.3

Profiles of informants for taxonomy of merchandising careers. *

Informant Number	Job Title	Store Type
4	Owner and Vice-President	Specialty
5	Owner and President	Specialty
7	Store Manager	Specialty
11	Senior District Manager	Specialty
12	Co-owner, President, and Manager	Specialty
14	Buyer	Department
15	Assistant Store Manager	Specialty
17	President, Chief Operating Officer	Department
18	Divisional Merchandise Manager	Department
19	Buyer	Department
22	Customer Service Manager	Discount
24	Operations Manager	Discount
25	Store Manager	Discount
37	Owner, Manager	Specialty
40	Planning, Distribution Manager	Department
41	Buyer	Specialty
42	Vice-President and Retail Consultant	Department
44	Training and Employment Standards Manager	Department
45	Vice-President, Merchandise Information	Department
46	Vice-President and Store Manager	Department
47	Senior Buyer	Department
48	Divisional Merchandise Manager	Department
58	General Store Manager	Department
74	Owner and President	Specialty
90	President and Chief Executive Officer	Department
103	Assistant Buyer	Discount
104	Group Manager	Department
105	Divisional Merchandise Manager	Department
109	Vice-President and Control Administration	Department
130	Divisional Merchandise Manager	Department
132	Senior Buyer	Department
133	Merchandise Administrator	Department
134	Telemail and Consumer Affairs Manager	Department
135	Buyer	Discount
136	Group Department Manager	Specialty
144	Employment Representative	Discount
150	Corporate Training Director	Department
157	Divisional Merchandise Manager	Department
158	Assistant Buyer	Discount
159	College Relations Manager	Department
160	College Relations Representative	Department
161	Acting Store Manager	Department

*Kunz (1986).

Years in Retailing	Age	Sex	Income Range (000)	College Degree	Major
21	44	m	75–100	BS	Agriculture
24	43	m	45–50	AA	Business
16	44	f	15–20	—	—
16	34	f	40–50	AA	Liberal Arts
13	32	f	15–20	—	Merchandising
12	30	f	25–30	BS	Design
11	31	f	10–15	—	—
30	52	m	75–100	BA	Business
24	50	f	50–75	—	—
5	24	f	20–25	BS	Merchandising
11	46	f	20–25	—	—
13	35	m	30–40	BA	Biology
13	30	m	30–40	AA	Retailing
8	31	m	20–25	BS	Business
14	36	f	NA	BS, MA	German
15	38	f	25–30	BA	Merchandising
12	34	m	75–100	BA	Psychology
8	32	m	30–40	BA, MBA	Psychology
9	34	f	75–100	MS1	Political Science
14	36	f	50–75	BS	Merchandising
11	33	m	30–40	BA	Sociology
11	33	m	40–50	BS	Business
25	NA	m	NA	—	—
9	42	f	30–40	BES1	Business
12	36	m	1,001	BS, MBA	Marketing
8	28	f	40–50	BS	Merchandising
19	37	f	40–50	—	—
10	33	f	50–75	BBA	Business
18	40	m	50–75	BS, MBA	Business/Accounting
17	39	m	75–100	BS, MBA	Economics
16	39	f	25–30	BS	Merchandising
9	31	f	40–50	BS	Merchandising
11	33	f	20–25	BS	Merchandising
11	33	f	50–75	BS	Merchandising
5	28	f	20–25	BS	Merchandising
4	25	f	30–40	BBA	Business
6	35	f	25–30	BA1	Sociology
21	43	f	40–50	BS	Home Economics
6	28	f	40–50	BS	Merchandising
3	24	m	20–25	BS	Accounting
2	27	f	15–20	BBA	Business
12	36	f	15–20	—	—

falls within the stores specialization —2— and includes the jobs of personnel, group, operation or assistant manager, and small store manager —5. According to the taxonomy, all of these jobs may be held by people that are on relatively the same career level in the specialization. Note that a "25" is similar to someone with a career code "15" in the merchandising division or "35" in the personnel division. Therefore, it is possible to describe moves from one job to another or one specialization to another in terms of major lateral or vertical changes in career status. In order to complete the career-development picture, job titles of top executive management, such as president or chief executive officer, are identified by a 100 number, while jobs outside of retailing have a 200 number.

As with BTAF, the areas of specialization identified in the taxonomy are generic — they are not necessarily the functions identified in organizational charts of a particular retail firm. Whether a retail organization actually had organizational divisions similar to the areas of specialization identified in this taxonomy was dependent on the size and type of retailer and the type of terminology the retailer used. Smaller stores did not necessarily have the formal areas of specializations, but still performed the functions identified by these areas in the taxonomy. For example, in a small organization, a retail buyer (15) may perform the functions of department manager (23) and fashion director (19). Responsibilities that were a part of a particular job assignment were not necessarily all at the same career level but, according to informants, the primary responsibilities were what determined the career status in the organization.

None of the retail organizations included in the sample had all the career levels indicated by the taxonomy. For example, the career ladder in the merchandising specialization in one department store included trainee (11), associate buyer (13), senior buyer (15), merchandise counselor (16), and general merchandise manager (17). The taxonomy represents the diversity of career levels and job titles in retail organizations and is intended to include the areas of specialization within which any particular retailer's career path could be represented.

The taxonomy is a useful tool for tracing career paths of merchandising managers and executives either for research purposes or for analyzing career development opportunities within or among retail organizations. A **career path** is the sequence of jobs held by an individual. It is possible to see the major area of responsibility and the steps for advancement by simply recording a series of two digit numbers. The career path of each informant was traced using the taxonomy codes. This resulting information is included in Table 12.4.

For example, the career path of informant #133 was 12, 22, 14, 26, 16. This reflects that the individual started in the merchandising specialization as an assistant buyer, went to stores as a sales manager, returned to merchandising as a buyer, went to stores as a store manager, and returned to merchandising as a merchandise administrator. She made two

Table 12.4

Number of retail employers and career paths of informants.

Participant Number	Sex	Years in Retailing	Number of Employers	Career Path Using Career Codes from the Taxonomy of Merchandising Careers
7	f	16	4	204, 25, 204, 25
11	f	16	3	20, 60, 12, 12, 24, 25, 21, 25, 27, 27, 27
12	f	13	3	24, 25, 103
14	f	12	2	30, 12, 14, 14, 14
15	f	11	6	20, 20, 24, 26, 21, 24
18	f	24	2	20, 22, 13, 14, 16
19	f	5	3	60, 20, 11, 13, 14
22	f	11	1	20, 20, 20, 20, 21, 22, 22, 22, 22, 22, 23
40	f	14	1	11, 22, 12, 14, 15, 15
41	f	15	2	11, 22, 12, 14, 15, 14
45	f	9	3	22, 12, 54, 58
46	f	14	3	12, 22, 12, 14, 25, 25, 16, 26, 17, 26, 28
74	f	9	2	30, 104
103	f	8	2	12, 22, 14, 12, 12
104	f	19	1	20, 21, 12, 22, 22, 12, 14, 25, 25
105	f	10	3	12, 12, 14, 25, 15, 16
132	f	16	2	11, 20, 22, 12, 12, 14, 14, 15
133	f	9	1	12, 22, 14, 26, 16
134	f	11	3	21, 11, 12, 62, 12, 22, 52, 54
135	f	11	4	11, 12, 12, 14, 14, 14
136	f	5	1	22, 22, 22, 23, 23
144	f	4	2	31, 30, 31, 32, 33
150	f	6	5	204, 204, 204, 204, 204, 12, 35
157	f	21	1	20, 12, 13, 14, 14, 16, 16
158	f	6	2	11, 22, 12, 14, 15, 12
160	f	2	1	30
161	f	12	1	20, 21, 23, 24, 25
4	m	21	4	11, 12, 204, 26, 106
5	m	24	5	22, 14, 26, 15, 25, 25, 26, 26, 14, 107
17	m	30	7	14, 16, 16, 19, 100, 100, 100
24	m	13	2	20, 22, 21, 24, 25, 24, 25
25	m	13	2	20, 22, 22, 22, 25, 24, 24, 25, 26
37	m	8	3	204, 25, 14, 105
42	m	12	2	12, 14, 26, 28, 29, 19, 209
44	m	8	2	12, 23, 14, 54, 35
47	m	11	1	11, 12, 14, 14, 14, 15
48	m	11	1	12, 14, 14, 14, 16
58	m	25	5	20, 14, 16, 17, 26
90	m	12	3	204, 16, 18, 19, 100
109	m	18	4	63, 64, 66, 64, 67, 68
130	m	17	4	11, 2 2, 12, 14, 26, 26, 16
159	m	3	1	60, 20, 12, 22, 32

changes between specializations at approximately the same career level as indicated by 12 to 22, and 26 to 16. The career path of another informant was 11, 12, 12, 14, 14, 14. This individual started as a trainee, became an assistant buyer and held two different assistant buyer positions, and then was promoted and held three different buying positions. It is immediately evident by the numbers that the experiences of the first informant interchange between the stores and merchandising specializations. All of the experiences of the second informant were within the merchandising specialization and career advancement had stopped at the buyer level.

Analysis reveals that women in this sample moved back and forth slightly more frequently between merchandising and stores than men. Women averaged 2.5 **lateral and backward moves** in their retail careers; men averaged 2.2. The backward moves often occurred with a change in specialization, and the next step was frequently advancement for both men and women. These career paths suggest that the stereotypical perspective of successful career development as upward vertical movement in the organizational structure is inappropriate. Perhaps teachers as well as retail recruiters should discuss the importance of lateral as well as possible backward movement in the career path to gain diversity of experience upon which career advancement might be based.

Career path analysis of this sample supports Minor's (1992) suggestion that career development patterns differ between men and women and helps explain why it is not appropriate to use the same career development model for both genders. The increased career movement that women exhibited in this sample may be explained by Karelius' (1982) "rebirth of potential" concept where women make more frequent job changes due to a relocated spouse. This may necessitate women to start new jobs at lower levels than previously held, slowing career development, and taking longer to reach senior executive positions and salary equity.

Because this was a selected sample, one must use care in generalizing the findings. However, numerous issues for additional research were raised by the study:

1. How do lateral and backward movements in retail career paths vary by gender? Do women tend to accept these types of moves more frequently than men? If so, why? How do these differences affect promotability, earning power, and final career level attained?

2. How does the length of time in each area of specialization affect career path and final career level attained? How does length of time in each position affect career path and final career level attained? Does this vary with gender? Is it perceived to be more desirable to move frequently to gain a wide variety of experiences, or is an employee more valuable if they have significant depth in one specialization?

3. How do merchandising professionals progress to senior executive positions? What areas of specialization are most important in their career paths? Does the path to a senior executive position vary with gender?

The taxonomy of merchandising careers needs further development through additional research related to merchandising responsibilities in the manufacturing sector. Of the areas of specialization now included in the taxonomy, the management information systems (MIS) function has changed greatly because of its relationship to information technology. The development of quick response business systems is closely tied to MIS because of requirements for electronic data interchange and Internet communications.

Learning Activity 12.3

Taxonomy of merchandising careers

1. Examine the sequence of job titles included in the merchandising area of specialization. What is the meaning of a lateral career move? Give an example based on the taxonomy. What are the advantages and disadvantages of a lateral career move?
2. What is the meaning of a vertical career move? Give an example based on the taxonomy. What are the advantages and disadvantages of a vertical career move?
3. How do you see yourself in terms of career goals? Can you see yourself with senior management responsibilities or as CEO (chief executive officer)? Why?
4. In the merchandising area of specialization, a buyer is usually viewed as middle management while a divisional merchandise manager, the buyer's boss, is often seen as the bridge position between middle and senior management. According to the Dalton, et al., model, what types of experiences does the divisional merchandise manager need to have to prepare to move into senior management?

Career Advancement

In my dissertation research, I found the orientation of individuals within retail organizations to be extremely vertical. For example, when an informant was asked who he or she worked for, the answer was often the immediate superior's name rather than the retail organization's name. When asked who he or she worked with, the interviewee reported a combination of the superior and his or her assistants. Seldom was there very much formal interaction with others at his or her career level either within or outside their division or pyramid. This vertical orientation may be responsible in part for the informants' impatience toward **career advancement**.

Many interviewees reported they had received increases in salary and/or job title every 9 to 18 months during their retail careers. Some retail organizations created job titles to give the illusion of advancement in situations where it was not possible to advance people to the next career level. For example, if the ranks of buyer and divisional merchandise manager were relatively stable with low turnover, it became a problem to sufficiently reward buyers who were doing a good job. In that situation, some stores created a position of "senior buyer," acknowledging the individual had given long and/or superior service to the organization. This title change may also have involved additional responsibility, more dollar volume, and/or more people to supervise. One of the department store organizations had "associate buyers" and "senior buyers" instead of "assistant buyers" and "buyers." When there was a question of titles, "associate buyer" and "senior buyer" had a higher-status sound to them than "assistant buyer" and "buyer." It was not clear whether the distinction was real, in terms of responsibility, or artificial, simply endowing status only. One informant said that the title "senior buyer" gave the buyer more impact in the market when working with vendors (Informant #26).

It is important to note that an individual may not have to move to the next career level in order to gain what is commonly called a promotion. A **promotion** was often identified by an upgraded job title, increased responsibility, or increased pay in the same job. For example, a buyer may be promoted by being assigned an additional department or by being transferred to a different area with larger dollar volume or more difficult merchandise. The individual remained a buyer but had a higher status because of increased buying responsibility. Promotions of this sort were common within career levels. However, the move to the next career level, as indicated by the taxonomy of merchandising careers, was regarded by informants as a major change in career status.

Some organizations used the title "vice-president" as a status reward for people in upper management. One informant, when asked what the title "vice-president" meant in her retail organization said, "It means that you get better football tickets" (Informant #133). In another organization, when describing the conditions under which a woman was made vice-president, one respondent said ". . . now vice-president of trend merchandising and fashion coordination . . . her title increased, job description remained about the same" (Informant #105). Other organizations use the vice-president title much more stringently. The numbers of vice-presidents in the retail firms studied ranged from 0 to 33.

The merchandising division was regarded as the place to be, the place where the decisions were made, where the action was. The merchandiser's job was often regarded as the "best job," the job that was closest to the pulse of the business. One company was described as a "buyer-run" organization (Informant #132). The concept, though, seems a little dated because in recent years several layers of management have been added between buyer and president and buyers have decreasing responsibilities in stores. As firms became larger, buyers had increasingly become selectors of merchandise, while others took on the responsibilities of how much to buy, how it was to be distributed to stores, how it was to be merchandised on the sales floor, and even when it was to be marked down for clearance. The process of buying merchandise had become a team effort.

Management Development

Retailers exhibited at least two **theories of management development:** 1) development of expertise through specialization and 2) development of expertise through broad job experience, or "rounding out" the executive (Kunz, 1986).

> If an individual indicates potential beyond that job (now held), management is forced to make a decision. Do we want to let this person mature for another year and dot the i's and cross the t's or would we benefit better from his taking the 85 percent and then growing into a larger job that would not only benefit him in terms of his growth and development, but also have his knowledge impact a greater area of our business . . . The question is what are you trying to produce? Are you trying to produce managers for larger portions of your business or are you interested in developing a cadre or team or real expert, long-term buyers . . . They are hungry for those people (managers). Retailing is a business that can respond very specifically and very dramatically to an individual's efforts . . . (Informant #42)

The trend seems to be toward the **theory of specialization,** particularly as firms become larger. Each merchandising employee becomes responsible for more dollars, thus creating a need to be very good at what he or she does. For example, in some department stores, the buyer's job has been split to create a parallel position of planner/distributor. The role of the planner/distributor is to analyze the business, plan assortments, and distribute merchandise to stores. The planner/distributor also handles all communication with the stores about the merchandise (Informant #40). One buyer, when told about this organizational plan, agreed with this setup. "That frees you to do your job, buying" (Informant #19). It also means the only time the buyer sees or is involved with the merchandise is at the market or when he or she works with the sales representative. It seems to me the buyer would have an extremely limited view of the organization with such a narrow definition of responsibility.

Some of the retailers interviewed made it a point to move people from one division or area of specialization to another so that young managers/executives could gain broader experience. Other organizations, such as specialty chain stores, had most of their jobs within the stores themselves, with comparatively few in other divisions, thus making exposure to other divisions of the business nearly impossible. For example, one specialty chain had 150 stores and less than half a dozen buyers that supplied the merchandise for all of those stores (Informant #4). Obviously, there were few jobs available in the merchandising division as compared with the stores division. The advancement path was frequently trainee or manager in training, assistant manager, manager, district manager, regional manager, and vice-president of stores. Comparatively few people were able to make the jump from manager to district manager in the stores organization, with only about 10 percent of the number of store-manager jobs at the district-manager level. Promotion at the store-manager level normally involved moving to a store with larger volume. District and regional managers traveled daily, while a promotion to regional manager usually involved a move to the corporate headquarters.

The strategy of specialization may be effective in the short run, but may create problems in the long run. Who will occupy those top management positions that require a broad view of the total operation? Another view of the breadth of career path was provided by a vice-president of control administration:

> . . . having worked in the financial side for a number of years . . . I took the opportunity to go out to the store line. I worked both merchandising and operations. Quite frankly, I probably would be in that line today had it not been for circumstances in '73 when the recession hit . . . They cut back greatly on their staffing. I was in the store line at the time and found myself working a minimum of 65 to 80 hours and 6 days a week. It was really taking a toll on me and my family . . . However, that experience has probably lasted through my career even though I am in the financial world now I am very sympathetic to the needs of the merchants and store line people . . . having been someone who has been on both sides of it has allowed me not to have tunnel vision and to keep in mind what merchants need. I know what the guts of the business is about. It is a merchandising business. We have to respond to their (stores and merchandising) needs. My areas here are purely support function and it's hard sometimes to keep that perspective in our area of the business (Informant #109).

Regardless of store type, a merchandising career required a high level of commitment to the business. Few informants were involved in any kind of community activities, only those at the very top of the executive ladder where such involvement was expected as a part of their job. When executives were asked how many hours they worked in a week, most had to figure it out and many did not include the hours that they worked at home. The job was not viewed from the standpoint of how many hours were worked weekly but rather "whatever it takes to get the job done." "Not enough time" was no excuse. A divisional merchandise manager said she usually stopped at a "branch" on the way home (Informant #18). The president of one department store reported that he often spent Sunday afternoons walking the floors of the competition — with his family. He said he did not regard that as work (Informant #90). One informant reported that the most important thing an executive had to learn to be successful was how to relax, how to leave the job, and not allow the job to dominate her life 24 hours a day (Informant #41). Interestingly, the firm where the executives worked the fewest hours per week expressed the greatest dissatisfaction with their employer, their jobs, and their careers (Kunz, 1986).

Many of today's students aspire to running their own business. A study of 76 female entrepreneurs of apparel manufacturing reported that the primary benefit of running their own business was "being their own boss" (46 percent) followed by "having full responsibility" (27 percent). These entrepreneurs maintained a support network with work and family (Horridge & Craig, 2001).

Computers and the Merchandising Environment

Many informants in the Kunz study regarded computer systems as a burden that slowed down information processing, limited their options, and provided information they didn't need and didn't want. One informant had recently changed jobs, having moved from a firm with one of the most advanced computer systems to a firm with very little computer support. The computer system of the former employer was regarded as "nice," but not essential to the informant's job success (Informant #41). (Remember these interviews were conducted in 1984 and 1985, a time when the microcomputer was just getting established in general use.)

Some vendors believe that retail merchandisers became more sophisticated because of the quantity of information that became available with computer systems (Chanil, 1992). Certainly higher-level analytical skills were required to manage the technology (Kean, 1987). Large-store buyers were found to be more quantitatively oriented and small-store buyers more customer oriented (Fiorito & Fairhurst, 1993). At the same time retail buyers report that negotiating with sales representatives is still one of their most important competencies (Kotsiopulos, Oliver, & Shim, 1993). Some buyers, however, lament being more of an analyst than a buyer due to the huge amount of paperwork (Chanil, 1992).

Other buyers and account managers have indicated that technology has freed up time so they can concentrate on their important jobs of selecting, placing, and evaluating new merchandise. Computer-based inventory management systems encourage merchandisers to make decisions based on information, not instinct (Hartnett, 1993). Some say the advances in technology caused the buyer to be "less of a merchandiser and more of a financial problem-fixer" (Chanil, 1993). Some designers feel merchandisers are overworked and are concerned they are losing touch with the market because of this (Parola, 1988). Other buyers spend more time in the market and stores due to their new merchandise planning system (Hartnett, 1993).

In some firms, traditional retail buying responsibilities have been segmented and are now handled by two or three people. For example, the Macy's merchandising system uses a team of three employees to identify short-term sales opportunities and exploit them. The retail buyer is responsible for doing market research, buying, and developing price; the planner does the assortment planning and the allocation process. Assistant buyers may be involved with expediting — tracking goods, handling questions from the field, executing promotions, and following up on price changes (Hartnett, 1993) — and they are using technology to accomplish these tasks. Of course, the most technology intensive retailing is Internet retailing. See Case 12.2.

  Case 12.2 *Ashford.com names Cheryl Holland*
vice president of merchandising. *

Upscale e-tailer Ashford.com has appointed Cheryl Holland vice-president of merchandising, a newly created post at the firm, which signals the growing importance of melding merchandise expertise with user-friendly technology on the Web.

Holland has joined Ashford.com from Halls Merchandising, a high-end specialty chain, where she was vice-president and merchandising manager, and developed its merchandising plan for couture, ready-to-wear, fine jewelry, accessories, shoes, and cosmetics.

"The chief financial officer was handling the role before but the business has exploded so fast, the company realized it needed someone from the fashion trade with a merchandising background," Holland said. Holland brings more than 30 years of merchant experience to her new position.

Prior to Halls Merchandising, Holland was responsible for the fashion direction for the former BATUS stores group, which included Saks Fifth Avenue and Marshall Field's. Before BAYUS, she established the fashion merchandising department at Federated Department Stores' former Sanger Harris unit, where she drove the chain's private label program. Holland has also served as vice-president of fashion merchandising and product development at Federated's Rich's division in Atlanta.

"Cheryl's knowledge of buying patterns, excellent relationships with leading brands, and immense experience in the retail industry will help us optimize our product selection for our customers," said Kenny Kurtzman, chief executive officer of Ashford.com, in a statement, "She will be instrumental in the companies' drive toward profitability, as she has the talent and the expertise to create merchandising strategies that increase margins across all categories."

Holland said Tuesday that her priorities at Ashford are: "assessing the 13 categories we carry; working with the brands at Ashford.com to build their presence on the site; looking to add brands where need to in jewelry and fine jewelry — and working hard to enhance our diamond business."

Her broader vision for the two-year-old site, she said, is "to keep our merchandise offer focused on the customer. But the challenge," she added, "is not seeing the customer every day, like you do on the sales floor."

"It was not an easy decision," Holland said of her leap into e-tailing after a career in traditional retail. "I realized from my own experience online and what I've seen in the media that luxury e-commerce was gaining momentum. And I was impressed by Ashford's management team and business plan. For those reasons, I wanted to join in."

*Seckler (2000).

Keys to Career Advancement

For those who see themselves in top management, timely career advancement is extremely important. When informants were asked for criteria that provided the basis for promotion, all responded the same way: job performance. Job performance was measured by individual contribution to gross margin and company profits (Kunz, 1986). However, from the complete interviews emerged several other factors that contributed to the speed of career advancement. These included:

- Educational background—Little credit was given to education for career success by my informants, but most informants with advanced degrees were on the fast track, the firms were moving those people very quickly up the career ladder—and most informants with no degrees or two-year degrees were clustered in low paying stores positions.

- Mentoring—People in power who know young people and value their potential can recommend them for special opportunities and provide strategic guidance for their careers.

- Choosing an employer that offers advancement potential—Some firms have more room for young people than others and are structured so they can provide a diverse group of professional experiences in a single setting. This can provide better preparation for advancement either within or outside the firm.

- Networking—Taking advantage of opportunities, projects, and jobs that provide growth experiences, visibility, and chances to meet professionals in and related to your field is essential. "It's who you know." Some say 80 percent of job opportunities are never advertised. People are promoted or invited to apply via internal and external recommendations.

- Recognizing the necessity for self-marketing—Presenting oneself in the best possible light is an on-going challenge. Talking about one's ability and successes in an interesting and convincing manner is difficult, but necessary. It takes practice. If you want a new opportunity, you have to convince others you can do it. If you want more money, you have to ask for it.

- Intent of the organization toward the individual—Department-store retailers have an intense need for career department managers. Specialty chain retailers have an intense need for career store managers. Firms must have employees that fulfill their needs. Employees need to understand their employers' needs and how they can maximize their opportunities within those constraints.

- Intent of the individual toward the organization—Not everyone wants to be in or is suited to top management. Finding an employer who has opportunities to match an individual's career aspirations and can draw out his or her best performance is a real challenge.

📖 *Learning Activity 12.4*

Career advancement

1. Who holds the primary responsibility for an individual's career opportunities and advancement?
2. What career advancement strategies should college students work on during their academic careers?

Selecting an Employer

Firms that are growing and making money are the best employers for young people. Conversely, stagnant and struggling firms tend to have too many middle management employees and little room for career advancement of new recruits. Having the power to be able to decide where to begin the postcollege degree segment of one's career is a challenge. The power is dependent on the efforts of an individual to create a **marketable combination** of educational background, professional experiences, and personal attributes that is attractive to multiple employers. A four-year college degree is often now a minimum requirement for a merchandising-related executive training or management training position. But it is still not a guarantee of a position. Getting a good job, merchandising related or otherwise, is just plain hard work. It requires planning, organizing, practicing, presenting, persisting, accepting criticism, and dealing with rejection. Taking 6 months to a year to select the first full-time employer is common; and it can take 6 months to 2 years thereafter to make job changes. Many people change employers several times before they find the best match between their abilities and available career opportunities in environments offered by different firms.

Environments for Merchandising-Related Careers

Business in general and apparel firms in particular, have experienced a great deal of turmoil in recent years. Mergers, downsizing, information technology, management philosophy, verticalization, and global competition have all been sources of change.

Retail Environments

The six Midwest-based department stores included in my dissertation research provide the examples cited here. One had been on the brink of financial disaster, brought in new management, closed several stores, and restored order. Another had merged with another large department store division, resulting in the consolidation of the merchandising divisions in one city and the development of all new operating systems. Another had been taken over by a large non-retail corporation. The department store that gave the impression of being extremely dynamic and had the highest level of satisfaction and security among its employees merged with another department store division and moved the headquarters to another city. Finally, the long-time president of another department store was asked to step down, a move that was followed by a dramatic shake-up of middle and upper management.

Many informants pointed out the pressures present in the retail environment, including the expectations of superiors:

> We do an annual meeting in November that is really a "state of the union" when various assorted directors of the company talk about their various accomplishments and look to the future. In that meeting every year the chairman gives the ending address. Each year he speaks about the track getting faster. The reaction in the organization is always very stimulating. Good people are very challenged by that. Mediocre and bad people are threatened (Informant #45).

Another source of pressure in today's environments is created by major changes such as mergers and reorganization. This has been a constant source of turmoil over the past 10 years as more and more companies buy or take over other companies to take advantage of economy of scale available because of electronic communications. These changes force executives to deal with larger volume, more stores, and more departments. At the same time, cost cutting moves like the reduction of clericals and assistant buyers and withdrawing salespeople from the selling floors are commonly implemented. This resulted in less assistance for executives during stressful times and less customer service to support badly needed sales. Buyers indicated that it was very frustrating to ". . . put all that energy into selecting, assorting, and distributing the merchandise only to have no one available to sell it." One major retailer reversed the trend of fewer people on the sales floor and ordered dramatic increases in sales staff, heralding the beginning of a trend that continues for some department stores today with a strong focus on customer service.

Specialty stores, particularly specialty chain stores, offer different types of career experiences than department stores. The type of ownership and organization of the specialty stores vary. Some are independent, single-unit, privately owned stores; others were multi-unit privately owned stores; still others were corporately owned chain organizations with hundreds or sometimes thousands of stores. Some of the single-unit stores were very small, others comparatively large. All now have centralized buying organizations. Buying takes place in the headquarters; selling takes place in stores.

Turnover of store management personnel can be the most disruptive influence in the specialty chain stores. Recruiting, training, and motivating store personnel to perform at a necessary level are an on-going challenge. Young people with or without college degrees sometimes become store managers after less than six months on the job. That may seem desirable from a career standpoint, but only if the employee could actually handle the job. Insufficient training and too much responsibility too soon is a major contributor to the turnover problems in some organizations. In specialty chain organizations, district managers who supervised a group of store managers play key roles in the longevity and effectiveness of store managers.

Some specialty chains try to deal with inexperienced managers by centralizing decision making. This leaves some store managers feeling underutilized and ineffective because their responsibilities are to implement instructions that "come down" from corporate. They feel their lack of opportunity for innovation and lack of flexibility to adapt to the local market inhibits the success of the store. At the same time, some specialty stores have the ability to generate a fierce loyalty among their employees. The managers tell "war stories" about long hours and unreasonable demands and then, in the next breath, would swear they do not want to work for anyone else.

In specialty chain organizations it is not unusual for a person who starts in sales to take a cut in pay when they move into store management. In sales, they received hourly pay, frequently with overtime, and sometimes sales commissions; as a manager they are salaried, so there is no additional compensation for overtime. Managers are also responsible for controlling selling costs, so they frequently take additional shifts on the sales floor, increasing their time on the job to 60 to 80 hours a week with no increase in pay.

Mass retailers tend to offer yet another set of priorities. My discount/mass retailer respondents worked for one retailer, three informants in the headquarters and four in stores. They talked of long hours and hard work, as did most respondents, but they were also very enthusiastic about their employer, their work environment, and their career opportunities. As with the specialty chain stores and some of the department stores, there was a clear separation between career paths in stores and merchandising; in fact it was very unusual for someone to make a transfer from stores to the corporate division merchandising organization. This limitation in career opportunities was not seen as a problem by the discount store employees. They not only liked their jobs, but thought they worked for the best retail organization in the country. On a job-for-job basis, they had the highest salaries among the respondents. This is not to imply that all employees of discount retailers are satisfied with their jobs and receive high salaries. However, in today's job markets, mass retailers are a major source of employment in today's retail sector and should not be overlooked.

In my study, it was unusual for employees to move between the major types of store organizations (department, specialty, and discount) when they changed jobs, yet job changing was very common. Of the 42 respondents, 16 had had three or more retail employers; only 14 had been employed by the same organization throughout their retail careers. For the most part, respondents tended to seek or be sought by stores of similar organization and merchandise type when they were changing jobs. Today, it is still more difficult to move from the specialty store ranks into department stores or mass retailers.

The major exception to "staying within the store type" was the discount/mass retailer that hired regularly from the department store ranks for their corporate organization. The people who were able to accept the challenging opportunity in the discount organization needed to disassociate themselves from the strong merchandise orientation they had known in the department and specialty stores. The discount stores' orientation, instead, was "on the numbers" rather than on beauty, fashionability, or quality of the merchandise. They recognized that the purpose of being in business was to make money — and money was made by serving the customer and by having the most effective merchandising and stores organizations. The "best merchandise" was the merchandise that provided the necessary gross margin to cover costs and sufficient turnover to make a profit.

Product Development and Manufacturing Environments

Information technology, verticalization, and global competition have been major sources of change for textile and apparel retailers and manufacturers. It is increasingly difficult to tell the difference between a manufacturer and a retailer. Both manufacturers and retailers are involved in product development and sourcing products in the world-wide market. Product development collaboration has become more common between manufacturers and retailers. It is possible to get a job with a firm that has traditionally been a manufacturer (Liz Claiborne) and have similar responsibilities and opportunities as if the job was with Target. Technology permeates everything. But there is still room for innovation. Read Case 12.3 for a fascinating combination of merchandising and marketing genius resulting in the creation of a new garment classification, performance apparel.

📁   *Case 12.3*   **The making of Under Armour***   📁

America has been spandexed. Once restricted to a select few in biking shorts and running tights, the multitudes are now strutting around in the skintight athletic clothing called Under Armour. At sporting goods stores, dozens of racks of Under Armour and similar apparel from its competitors including Nike and Reebok cover an area half the size of a basketball court. Hats and caps and socks and underwear all wick away sweat like miraculous paper towels that absorb and dry in minutes.

It all began at the University of Maryland, when Kevin Plank, special team's captain on the Terrapin football team, became frustrated with changing his sweat-soaked cotton t-shirt three of four times a game. After graduation, he researched textile materials and developed his first prototype of a microfiber t-shirt designed to keep a player dry and light throughout a game or practice and sold $17,000 of shirts out of the trunk of his car. Under Armour was born.

Under Armour is a line of moisture wicking, microfiber clothing that pulls perspiration away from the skin to keep athletes cool, dry, and light throughout the course of a game, practice of workout. The microfiber blend includes elastin, a new polyester related elastomer, which gives it the tight fit, and an inner fabric that wicks away the moisture. Most styles are compression garments that also help prevent muscle fatigue while working out. The line includes apparel for all seasons and climates: socks, underwear, shirts, leggings, caps, shorts, tanks, and hoods. According to a study at North Carolina State University, a sweaty Under Armour shirt is more than 2 pounds lighter than a sweat-soaked cotton t-shirt. The study also showed that the core body temperature of athletes after 20 minutes on a treadmill was lowered when wearing Under Armour, allowing for less fatigue.

Football powerhouses Georgia Tech and Arizona State were the first college teams to purchase the gear, followed by the NFL's Atlanta Falcons. The number of teams on both levels has increased every year since. By 1997, 12 NCAA Division I-A teams and 10 NFL teams were wearing it, and Under Armour® made its first appearance in the Super Bowl when the Green Bay Packers defeated the New England Patriots. Under Armour's popularity has never been limited to football, however, and with different applications of the gear came the need for an expanded product line. ColdGear™ (long-sleeve shirts for winter) was introduced, followed by the versatile AllseasonGear™, then TurfGear™ (worn under football pads), a version of the original HeatGear™

(continued)

(short sleeves for basketball and biking) with long sleeves for protection on artificial surfaces.

In 1998, Under Armour signed a licensing deal with the NFL Europe League to become its official supplier of performance apparel. The relationship is heading into its fifth season. Also, a new gear was added to the line-up: LooseGear, a version of the original HeatGear with a generous fit.

In 1999, Under Armour, signed on with Eastbay catalog (circulation 7 million) and became the fastest selling softgood product in Eastbay history. Later that year, Under Armour struck a deal with Warner Bros. to supply gear for its football movies *Any Given Sunday* and *The Replacements*. More movies should follow.

The new millennium kicked off with both teams in the NCAA Championship Football game (Virginia Tech and Florida State) wearing Under Armour. Later that year, after placing its first national print advertisements, Under Armour helped launch the XFL football league with a product contribution to all of its players. Some 12 million who tuned in to the inaugural game saw Under Armour and its distinctive interlocked double half-circle logo up close during the game and in the locker room through execusive half-time coverage. The league was short-lived, but by the end of the year, Under Armour could be found in more than 1,500 retail outlets raising sales to $115 million.

*Based on Under Armour (2002) and Klein (2003).

 ## Learning Activity 12.5

Environments for merchandising careers

1. What aspects of Under Armour's growth are merchandising related?
2. What aspects are marketing related?
3. The name of Nike's competing product line is Dry-Fit. How does a name like Under Armour contribute to the product's success?
4. Make a list of the factors related to the growth and development that have contributed to Under Armour's success.
5. Refer back to Table 12.2, Merchandising Taxonomy. What jobs has Kevin Plank probably held to grow his company to over $115 million in sales over a 10-year period?

Recruiting for Merchandising Positions

Three major components are usually part of the screening criteria for recruiting merchandising personnel: formal education, work experience, and personal attributes. Table 12.5 provides lists of possible standards related to the first two of these criteria. The standards a particular firm/recruiter uses depend on their perception of the value of formal education and previous work experience relative to job requirements.

Recruiting standards related to **educational background** range from no requirement for a degree to preference for advanced degrees from selected schools. Some firms also have preferences for a particular major as well as grade-point requirements. Grade-point average (GPA) is sometimes used as a measure of work ethic, rather than valued as a measure of academic achievement. Interviewees should be prepared to talk about their GPA in a positive manner regardless of whether the firm has this requirement. A recruiter may use the

Table 12.5

Possible standards related to formal education and work experience that might be criteria for recruiting merchandising personnel. *

Formal Education	Work Experience
• no degree • AA degree, one- or two-year degree • any BA, BS, or BBA four-year degree • any BA, BS, or BBA from selected schools • any BA, BS, or BBA in business or textiles and clothing • BA, BS, or BBA in business or textiles and clothing from selected schools • any MA, MS, or MBA in business or textiles and clothing • MA, MS, or MBA in business or textiles and clothing from selected schools	• none • any paid activity that develops transferable skills • customer service related work experience • retail or manufacture merchandising related work experience • informal internship/field experience • formal internship/field experience • retailer or manufacturer related management level experience • retailer or manufacturer management level merchandising related experience from firms with nationally respected training programs

*Developed by G. I. Kunz.

grade point discussion as a measure of how able an individual is to take responsibility for his or her own actions.

As indicated by Table 12.5, **standards for work experience** may range from no requirements to managerial level on-the-job training. Some firms may have their own training programs where a new employee is regarded as a trainee for six months to a year. New recruits are moved systematically around the company to observe and experience all facets of the operation before they are assigned to their first job in the career-development system. Other firms have only a few hours or a few days of orientation before the first job assignment begin. These firms may be more dependent on training and transferable skills gained in previous work experience.

Personal attributes are the primary selection criteria in some interview situations. Recruiters look for enthusiasm, intensity, articulateness, purposefulness, listening skills, and a sense of humor. Some use "pressure tactics" during interviews to test poise. They view interviewees' nonverbal communication as evidence of self-worth and confidence. For the most part, recruiting is treated as more of an art instead of a science, although increasing numbers of companies are using tests of various kinds to provide some substantive evaluation of potential employees' worth to the company. Interviews require practice in talking about yourself and what you have to offer.

Recognizing Transferable Skills

Obvious key components when preparing to select an employer include academic background and career-related work experience. Creating the ability to choose an employer requires effort beyond the obvious. Individuals must recognize transferable skills and be able to articulate those skills in resumes, cover letters, portfolios, and interviews. **Transferable skills** are abilities gleaned from life's experiences that can be applied in multiple settings. For example, recognizing and articulating that waiter/waitress jobs provide experience in time management, judging priorities, accepting praise and criticism, managing stress, and problem solving helps recruiters see value in this previous work experience. Because of the variety of transferable skills acquired, diversity of work experience can often be presented as an advantage.

Resumes, cover letters, portfolios, and interviews are tools for communicating with potential employers. All require thorough preparation. Effective cover letters reflect knowledge of the company and communicate what the applicant can bring to the business. Recruiters may receive hundreds of resumes for one open position. One criterion for evaluating a resume is to make note of what you see if you look at it for 10 seconds. Make sure a recruiter or employer sees active verbs describing experiences resulting in transferable skills. Describe your leadership and management skills, training, creativity, and initiative. Present information in such a way that exemplifies how education and work experience can be applied to new settings.

Portfolios have long been part of the job hunt for designers, architects, and graphic artists. Today, merchandisers can also use a portfolio effectively. The portfolio might include projects from coursework, including merchandise plans, product development projects, concept boards, etc. The portfolio might also use photographs or videotapes of work-related or internship activities and projects, such as visual merchandising, fashion shows, departmental layout, etc.

Summary

Merchandising-related career development is a process that evolves through a series of vertical and lateral moves throughout the organization and industry. Kunz developed the taxonomy of merchandising careers to provide a framework for tracing this movement by examining the levels and areas of specialization chosen by retailing executives. The taxonomy evolved by using the constant comparative method of data analysis to create areas of specialization, job titles, career levels, and the relationships among areas of specialization. It is now possible to trace the career paths of merchandising executives, which will be helpful to the career development of industry employees. The taxonomy is also a useful tool in organizational analysis, can serve as a framework for career development research, or assist students in better understanding merchandising-related career opportunities.

Merchandising careers are characterized by high pressure, fast pace, long hours, frequent travel in some jobs, and total involvement with the business. Present market conditions, management and organizational changes, and developing technology have created additional dimensions of stress as well as opportunities for people in merchandising careers. The vertical orientation within the career path has been moderated in those organizations creating product teams that include a merchandiser, a marketer, a production liaison, and a product manager. The product teams are responsible for the product from conception to delivery to the stores. The use of teams improves the breadth in career experience necessary for advancement into top management. In spite of the pressures and degree of commitment that is required in merchandising, many people are thriving in the environment and would seek merchandising careers if they were to begin all over again.

Key Concepts

area of specialization	career path	promotion
backward career move	educational background	rebirth of potential
career	lateral career move	stages of career development
career advancement	life-structure modifiers	standards for work experience
career choice	marketable combination	theories of management devel-
career code	organizational theory	opment
career development	personal attributes	theory of specialization
career level	portfolio	transferable skills

Integrated Learning Activity 12.6.1

Examining the electronic hiring process

Electronic searches are the name of the game for identifying potential candidates for open positions. Case 12.4 describes the process L.L.Bean has implemented to facilitate their selection process.

1. What services are provided by the software?
2. What are the advantages and disadvantages of using the software for the hiring manager?
3. What are the advantages and disadvantages for the applicants?
4. What are the implications for how resumes are presented? For example, size of font, amount of white space, organization of ideas, type of paper, etc.
5. What are the implications for an outsider who wants to work for L.L.Bean?

     Case 12.4   L.L.Bean streamlines hiring process. *

Jobs at L.L.Bean are being filled more efficiently since the apparel retailer implemented a recruiting application that systematically scans resumes for qualification and posts employment opportunities internally. Bob Schmidt, employment manager at L.L.Bean, said that the solution has cut the time needed to fill a position by nearly one-third, from an average of 60 to 90 days to between 45 and 60 days. The Freeport, Maine-based company is using the solution for all areas of recruitment, from store-level positions to corporate posts.

Because the solution improves the company's ability to match candidates' skills and experience to available jobs, costs per hire have also dropped, said Schmidt, though he declined to specify by how much. "Traditionally, we'd advertise in the newspaper or go to a search agency and have the job filled," Schmidt said. Currently, the retailer has about 10,000 resumes in its database. "As that number grows, there's more of an opportunity to search for candidates without having to do traditional advertising.

Because the solution posts current job openings internally, L.L.Bean can draw more talent from its own labor pool and spend less on recruiting externally. Schmidt said that the company can run reports comparing how many people are hired, internal versus external, to gain a broad perspective on hiring trends.

Implemented more than a year ago, the solution is being used to fill positions at all levels of L.L.Bean's corporate structure. In total including the catalog operation, flagship stores, children's stores and outlets, the company employs about 4,000 people.

The e-recruiting software, from Personic of Brisbane, Calif., works like an advanced search engine, scanning for the key words that point to an applicant's credentials. The solution flags only those resumes that satisfy specific job skills and experience established for a particular position. Schmidt said that the system can search for relevant information, such as previous employment and experience, education, and residence. The solution is applied to both electronic and paper-based resumes, the later of which are scanned into the system.

Any department can search for applicants using the same centralized database of resumes. Hiring managers can pull up names onto their computers "rather than having to go to another department to find a resume of keep copies of a resume in case an opening comes up," said Schmidt. Resumes are less likely to be lost in the shuffle this way.

Even if an applicant sends a resume to a single department, the system will determine what other departments may recruit that individual. "We've found folks who applied for one job but had skills that applied to a different job, and we called them and made some hires," said Schmidt. Moreover, L.L.Bean is more likely to retain employees because they can peruse the system for internal advancement opportunities.

*Based on L.L.Bean streamlines hiring process (2000).

Integrated Learning Activity 12.6.2

Develop a resume suitable for applying for a merchandising-related internship.

Be sure to include educational background, career-related work experience, and personal attributes, with an emphasis on transferable skills related to merchandising responsibilities. Make the presentation as concise as possible while using active verbs to present your transferable skills. Don't neglect service jobs like retail sales and food service. They provide opportunities for leadership, multitasking, and problem solving.

Find reasons to use words like organized, created, initiated, led, and managed. Be sure to include a key word list related to qualifications for the type of jobs you are interested in to facilitate resume selection by electronic means.

Recommended Resources

Avery, C. E. (1989). Profiling the career development of women fashion merchandising graduates: A beginning. *Clothing and Textiles Research Journal,* 7(3):33–39.

Bluestone, B., Hanna, P., Kuhn, S., & Moore, L. (1981). *The retail revolution: Market transformation, investment, and labor in the modern department store.* Boston: Auburn House.

Fiorito, S. S., & Fairhurst, A. E. (1993). Comparison of buyers' job content in large and small retail firms. *Clothing and Textiles Research Journal,* 11(3):8–15.

Gaskill, L. R., & Sibley, L. R. (1990). Mentoring relationships for women in retailing: Prevalence, perceived importance, and characteristics. *Clothing and Textiles Research Journal,* 9(1):1–10.

Hare, D. (1993). The role of the quick response director. Proceedings of the Quick Response '92 Conference, 243–248.

Hartnett, M. (1993, September). Buyers: Endangered species? *Stores,* 75:53–55.

Horridge, P. E., & Craig, J. S. (2001). Female business owners in apparel manufacturing: An integrative perspective. *Clothing and Textiles Research Journal,* 19(3):89–102.

Parr, M. (1993). The role of a quick response director. Proceedings of the Quick Response '93 Conference, 15–32.

Proceedings of the Quick Response '93 Conference. (1993). Pittsburgh, PA: Automatic Identification Manufacturers, Inc.

References

"Born free": A world of options. (1978). Department of Psychoeducational Studies, College of Education, University of Minnesota.

Chanil, D. (1992, July). Partnerships: Illusion or reality? *Discount Merchandiser,* 32:20–26 & 58.

Chanil, D. (1993, July). Grappling with changes in retail. *Discount Merchandiser,* 33:28–32, 37 & 71.

Dalton, G. W., Thompson, P. H., & Price, R. L. (1977). Research: The four stages of professional careers—A new look at performance by professionals. *Organizational Dynamics,* 6(3):19–42.

Fiorito, S. S., & Fairhurst, A. E. (1993). Comparison of buyers' job content in large and small retail firms. *Clothing and Textiles Research Journal,* 11(3):8–15.

Gaskill, L. R. (1992). Toward a model of retail product development: A case study analysis. *Clothing and Textiles Research Journal,* 10(4):17–24.

Glaser, B. (1968). *Organizational careers.* Chicago: Aldine.

Hall, D. T. (1976). *Careers in organizations.* Glenview, IL: Scott Foresman.

Hare, D. (1993). The role of the quick response director. Proceedings of the Quick Response '92 Conference, 243–248.

Hartnett, M. (1993, September). Buyers: Endangered species? *Stores,* 75:53–55.

Holland, J. L. (1973). *Making vocational choices: A theory of careers.* Englewood Cliffs, NJ: Prentice Hall.

Hollander, S. C. (Ed.). (1978). Retail education (special issue). *Journal of Retailing,* 54(3).

Horridge, P. E., & Craig, J. S. (2001). Female business owners in apparel manufacturing: An integrative perspective. *Clothing and Textiles Research Journal,* 19(3):89–102.

Karelius, K. L. (1982). A study of early adult development and motivation for enrollment of women and men who enrolled in graduate school during the age thirty transition (ages 28–32). Unpublished doctoral dissertation, Michigan State University.

Kean, R. C. (1987). Definition of merchandising: Is it time for a change? In R. C. Kean (Ed.), *Theory building in apparel merchandising,* pp. 8–11. Lincoln: University of Nebraska–Lincoln.

Kotsiopulos, A., Oliver, B., & Shim, S. (1993). Buying competencies: A comparison of perceptions among retail buyers, managers, and students. *Clothing and Textile Research Journal,* 11(2):38–44.

Kunz, G. I. (1986). Career development of college graduates employed in retailing. Dissertation Abstracts International, 46, 3619-A. University Microfilm No. DA604886.

Kunz, G. I. (1987). Apparel merchandising: A model for product change. In R. C. Kean (Ed.), *Theory building in apparel merchandising,* pp. 15–21. Lincoln: University of Nebraska–Lincoln.

Kunz, G. I. (1995). Behavioral theory of the apparel: A beginning. *Clothing and Textiles Research Journal,* 13(4):252–261.

L.L.Bean streamlines hiring process. (2000, July 5). *Women's Wear Daily,* 140.

Minor, C. W. (1992). Career development: Theories and models. In D. H. Montross & C. J. Shinkman (eds.), *Career development: Theory and practice,* pp. 7–34. Springfield, IL: Charles C Thomas.

Moin, D., & Williamson, R. (2000, May 22). E-talent: A tangled search process. *Women's Wear Daily,* 18 & 20.

More women hold Fortune 500 board seats, study finds. (2003, December 6). *The Tribune,* C8.

Paoletti, J. B. (1985, May). The origins of fashion merchandising programs in home economics. *ACPTC Newsletter,* No. 8.

Parola, R. (1988, October 17). The anatomy of design. *Daily News Record,* 41–45.

Parr, M. (1993). The role of a quick response director. Proceedings of the Quick Response '93 Conference, 15–32.

Seckler, V. (2000, July 12). Ashford.com names Cherly Holland vice-president of merchandising, *Women's Wear Daily*, 4.

Stevens-Long, J. (1979). *Adult life developmental processes.* Palo Alto, CA: Mayfield.

Super, D. E. (1957). *The psychology of careers: An introduction to vocational development.* New York: Harper.

Under Armour. (2002). Company history (www.underarmour.com). Accessed December 26, 2003.

Van Maanen, J. (Ed.). (1977). *Organizational careers: Some new perspectives.* New York: Wiley.

Wickett, J. L. (1995). Apparel retail product development: Model testing and expansion. Master's thesis, Iowa State University.

above-market price   Price set in the upper range of prices for a particular product type; includes additional markup on first price or higher than average initial markup.

accurate response   Determining what forecasters can and cannot predict well and redesigning merchandise planning processes to minimize the impact of inaccurate forecasts (Fisher, Hammond, Obermeyer, & Raman, p. 84).

adaptive corporate culture   Organization capable of operating profitably in a competitive environment of continually changing customer opportunities (Goldman, Nagel, & Preiss, 1995).

adjusted gross margin   The revenue available after merchandise procurement costs are paid (gross margin minus merchandise procurement costs).

additional markup   Difference between first price and above-market/premium price.

additional markup cancellation   Reduction in above-market/premium price to first price.

advanced dating   Merchandise purchase contract term; making the invoice due date set for a date in the future.

aesthetic benefits   Includes sensual pleasure, beauty, aroused emotion, creative expression, and identity; result in pleasure or satisfaction (Fiore & Kimle, 1997).

African Growth and Opportunity Act   Trade agreement enacted in 2000 to promote trade between the Unite States and Africa.

agility   Dynamic, context-specific, change-embracing, and growth-oriented (Goldman, Nagel, & Preiss, 1995); requires information based decision-making along with flexible supply and distribution systems.

alternate selling   Showing concern about not meeting customers' needs and suggesting different kinds of merchandise the customer might like.

Americas trading bloc   The combination of North America (Canada and the United Staes) and Latin America (Mexico, Central and South America, and West Indies).

anticipation dating   Merchandise purchase contract term; providing a discount for paying the invoice early.

Asian/Pacific Rim trading bloc   Countries in the East, Southeast, and South Asia.

Association of Southeast Asian Nations (ASEAN)   Trade group formed in 1977, made up of countries in Asia including Brunei, Cambodia, Indonesia, Laos, Malaysia, Myanmar, Philippines, Singapore, Thailand, and Vietnam.

assortment   Range of choices offered at a particular time; usually determined by style, size, and color (Glock & Kunz, 1995).

assortment dimensions   Traditional terms are assortment depth and breadth; measurable assortment dimensions include assortment factors, stock-keeping units (SKU), volume, and assortment variety.

assortment distribution   The allocation of volume across assortment factors at the classification level.

assortment diversity   The range of relationships that can exist between assortment volume and assortment variety; a combination of the total number of units in the assortment (assortment volume) and the number of SKUs in the same assortment (assortment variety).

assortment diversity index (ADI)   A predictor of the impact of volume per SKU for the assortment on financial productivity.

assortment error   Difference in distribution of assortment factors (usually style, size, and color for apparel) between planned and actual demand.

assortment factors   Dimensions defining the characteristics of a product for purposes of identifying and describing it; usually style, size, and color.

assortment planning　The process of determining the range of merchandise choices to be made available at a given time.

assortment plans　Documents that may include model stocks, basic stocks, and automated replenishment.

assortment variety　The total number of SKUs in an assortment.

assortment volume　The total number of units in an assortment.

assumption　Something believed to be true but not necessarily proven to be true; the foundation from which theory departs.

at-market price　Similar to competitors offering the same products.

back-end systems　Related to the inventory management phase; takes place after resources are committed.

backward career movement　A move to a lower career level than the previous one.

balanced assortments　A well-planned variety of styles, sizes, and colors for special appeal to a specific market; must result in satisfied customers and meet merchandising goals.

basic goods　Classifications that experience little demand for change in styling from one merchandising cycle to the next.

basic income statement　Documents that include fourteen basic elements that provide information about income measurements and income modifications.

behavioral theories of the firm　Emphasizes the role of human behavior in explaining the activities of the firm; addresses issues like how organizational objectives are formed, how strategies evolve, and how decisions are reached within those strategies.

Behavioral Theory of the Apparel Firm (BTAF)　Views the apparel firm as a coalition of employees that share some common goals; the apparel firm is divided into six areas of specialization known as internal constituencies.

below-market price　Less than competitors offering the same products; may be based on lower than normal markup.

benchmarks　Points of comparison; indicators of levels of success.

better price range　Above average pricing for product class implying higher quality but not exclusive design; widely used in upscale department and specialty stores.

bill of lading (B/L)　A written receipt given by a carrier for goods accepted for transportation.

billed cost　List price less quantity, trade, and other discounts as stated on an invoice.

bottom-up planning　Merchandise planning beginning with people at the lowest levels of the organization in closest contact with customers.

bridge price range　The price line between better and designer; some features of couture goods; featured in designer boutiques in department stores and in designer named specialty stores.

budget price　Below average price for the product class; widely used by mass and discount retailers.

buyer　Employee of a manufacturing or retailing firm who commonly purchases designer name, brand name, and/or private-label goods to fill out their line plans.

career　The individually perceived sequence of attitudes and behaviors associated with work-related experiences and activities over the span of the person's life (Hall, 1976).

career advancement　A move to a career level higher than the previous one.

career choice　The process of selecting an area of specialization as a focus of one's work.

career code　A two-digit number representing both the area of specialization within which a job responsibility is held and the career level within that specialization according to the Taxonomy of Merchandising Careers.

career development　The lifelong process of examining the possibilities for work-related experiences and activities and deciding with awareness what one wishes to do with one's life ("Born Free." A world of options, 1978).

career level A stage in career advancement.

career path The sequence of jobs held by an individual.

Caribbean Basin Initiative (CBI) Formed in 1987, before NAFTA, to provide incentives for the United Staes to do business with other countries in Central America and the West Indies.

Caribbean Basin Trade Partnership Act (CBTPA) Trade agreement enacted in 2000 to promote trade between the Unite States and the Caribbean.

cash discount Reduction in billed cost as incentive to pay the invoice on time.

cash on delivery (COD) Payment term; no discounts are allowed and merchandise must be paid for in cash or by certified check when delivered.

certificate of origin A document that certifies the goods referred to were manufactured in a specific country.

change-intensive products Products that change very frequently due to fashion and seasonal influences.

close-ended questions Questions that can be answered by "yes" or "no" and do not encourage the customer to elaborate when responding.

closing the sale Getting the customer to agree to buy the product.

codes of conduct Rules that promote fair and responsible business practices that protect the rights of production employees.

commercial systems Computer programs available for sale from computer software and consulting firms.

comparison price Price offered in advertising or on price tickets as representative of "regular price" or the value of the product.

constructs The fundamental variables of a theory.

contract dating Determines when a cash discount can be taken and when an invoice is due to be paid.

cost The value given up in order to receive goods or services; the amount invested in order to have a product.

cost, insurance, freight (CIF) Shipping term; ownership is transferred as soon as merchandise is shipped; billed costs includes merchandise cost, insurance, and freight.

cost of goods sold the amount the firm has paid to acquire or produce the merchandise sold (cost of merchandise available for sale minus cost value of remaining inventory).

cost-plus pricing Pricing process that realizes a specified level of markup from each product offered for sale.

counter sample A copy of the prototype garment made by the production contractor.

cover letter A tool for communicating with potential employers; reflects knowledge of the company and communicates what the applicant can bring to the business.

creative design The phase in product development that focuses on analysis, creativity, and the formation of product groups that are unique while reflecting the line concept.

current sales When a customer makes a purchase and the store records the sale during a time frame defined as current, could be a day, week, month, or year.

customer-driven business systems Firms that focus on their customers and satisfying their customer's needs within the business definition of the firm.

customer needs Something necessary to the customer, including merchandise type, style, and price; customer service, including responsiveness, promptness, knowledgeable people, accuracy, and accessibility.

customer response system (CRS) Merchandise assortments that are truly customer driven by determining what customers want in advance and planning assortments so the merchandise the customer wants is available when he or she wants it.

customer returns and allowances Cancellation of sales because of merchandise returns and refunds or price adjustments because of customer dissatisfaction.

customer service Any interaction between a customer and a firm's personnel.

customer wants Something the customer desires.

customer's objections Negative comments coming from the customer about the merchandise, the store, the service and/or willingness to buy.

Customs House broker An agent in a port who facilitates Customs clearing on behalf of a company; a person or a firm licensed by the Treasury Department to prepare and file Customs entries, arrange payment of duties due, take steps to release goods from Customs, and represent clients in Customs matters.

cut, make, pack, and quota (CMPQ) sourcing Defines basis of contract costs when sourcing production; the sourcing company is responsible for product development including development of designs, patterns and product specifications, and sourcing materials; the contractor provides labor and equipment to cut, sew, and pack products and includes quota rent in total costs.

data integrity Information that accurately represents reality.

date on invoice dating (DOI) Merchandise purchase contract term; regarded as normal or ordinary dating for invoice payment.

delivery and allocation plans Plans that determine when, what, and how much merchandise will be received where.

development package The final result of the creative design and line adoption processes.

differentiated products Products that can be identified from similar products produced or distributed by competing firms.

displaying The process of making merchandise accessible for a customer to buy.

distressed goods Merchandise not salable at the intended first price; seconds, overruns, samples, last season's goods, and retailer returns.

distributing The process of receiving, sorting, storing, allocating, picking, and shipping merchandise.

diverse assortments Assortments with few units allocated per SKU, five or less on the average.

dollar open-to-buy The difference between planned merchandise to receive and merchandise on order at retail.

dollar open-to-buy at cost The amount of dollars planned for spending at wholesale in the market.

dollar plans Traditional form of merchandise budget; the dollar allocation to departments or merchandise categories; determines the amount of merchandise that can be made available for sale, but does not outline strategies to support other improvements in performance.

dynamic merchandising process Planning, developing, and presenting of product lines that is continuously integrating new information.

economic theories of the firm Theories of the firm based on micro-economic assumptions; emphasizes profit maximization.

educational background Degrees or other formal educational experiences in an educational institution.

electronic data interchange (EDI) The computer-to-computer exchange of business documents, such as sales information, purchase orders, or invoices in a standard format.

end of month (EOM) dating Merchandise purchase contract term; discounts and due dates are calculated from the end of the month when the invoice is dated rather than the invoice date itself.

even-dollar pricing A pricing system that uses even dollars for prices; in apparel, this pricing system is typically used for better, bridge, and designer goods.

Euro currency The common unit of money used by countries in the European Union.

European Trading Bloc Countries in Eastern and Western Euorpe.

European Union (EU) Formed in 1993, now includes including Austria, Belgium, Denmark, England, Finland, France, Germany, Greece, Ireland, Italy, Luxembourg, Netherlands, Portugal, Spain, Sweden, the United Kingdom, and 10 new members from Eastern Europe.

everyday-low pricing (EDLP) Pricing strategy that focuses the attention of customers on fair value at their convenience.

executive constituency Management of an apparel firm, generally consists of heads of functional areas of specialization/constituencies and the owner/manager or chief executive officer/president.

external coalitions According to Behavioral Theory of the Apparel Firm (Kunz, 1995), outside groups with which the firm interacts; competitors, customers, families of employees, shareholders, and suppliers.

external partnering Merchandising tactics that include timely sharing of sales and inventory information.

fabric forward rule Part of the U.S./Canadian Free Trade Agreement that requires apparel to be made from fabric manufactured in the United States or Canada in order to qualify for free trade.

fashion goods Merchandise classifications that experience demand for change in styling from one merchandising cycle to the next.

finance constituency One of the six internal constituencies of the firm, according to the Behavioral Theory of the Apparel Firm; evaluates the profitability of past business and helps set goals for future business.

first price Original retail price; may or may not be the same as list price or the price the customer first sees on a price ticket; first price is the base price for retail price structures.

flexible materials "soft" materials used in clothing manufacturing that easily accommodate the shape and movement of the human body comfortably.

focused assortments Assortments with many units allocated per SKU, usually ten or more.

follow-up Developing the customer relationship after a sale is made by collecting contact information and using this to let customers know about special sales or new merchandise.

forecasting Predicting the future based on several factors from the past integrated with current trends and environmental factors.

free alongside the ship (FAS) Merchandise purchase contract term; the vendor will pay for transportation of goods to the dock where the ownership is transferred to sourcing firm; all shipping costs are borne by the sourcing firm.

free on board (FOB) Shipping term used in merchandise purchase contracts; FOB origin or FOB factory means ownership is transferred when goods are loaded on a transporting vehicle and the buyer bears the shipping costs; FOB distribution center or FOB store means ownership is transferred when the goods are delivered at their destination and the vendor bears the freight costs.

front-end systems Related to the planning phase of merchandising and takes place before resources are committed.

full package sourcing (FPS) Merchandise purchase contract term; the contractor provides everything required to make the garment (purchases materials, develops samples, makes garments, and ships first quality goods to the sourcing company); no fabric or findings are owned by the sourcing company.

full service Sales persons incorporate a personal selling service into the customer service environment including amenities such as free gift wrap, alterations, delivery, and convenient parking.

fundamental merchandise budget foundation of expanded merchandise budget; last years sales, percent increase or decrease, planned sales, planned reductions, merchandise to receive, first price, and number of units.

guaranteed access levels (GALS)   Import quantity not limited by quotas.

garment purchase agreement (GPA)   Legal contract to purchase a stated quantity of goods at a certain price, within specified dates, and on stated terms and conditions.

General Agreement on Tariffs and Trade (GATT)   A worldwide trade agreement whose fundamental purpose was to promote free trade by reducing trade barriers; replaced by World Trade Organization (WTO).

globalization   From a business standpoint, the term globalization is associated with viewing multiple sites in the world as markets and/or sources for producing or acquiring merchandise.

gross margin (GM)   The revenue available for covering operating expenses and generating profit; sometimes called gross profit (net sales minus cost of goods sold).

gross margin return on inventory (GMROI)   The financial ratio that shows the relationship between the gross margin in dollars and the average inventory investment.

gross profit   *See* "gross margin."

gross sales   The total revenue received by a firm from sale of goods and services in a period of time including both cash and credit sales.

Harmonized System of Tariffs   A globalized international trade taxation system.

high-low pricing   Pricing strategy that involves periodic and sometimes very frequent temporary markdowns to stimulate customer traffic; also known as promotional pricing.

implementation of technology   One of the two phases of the diffusion of innovations, according to Rogers (1983); occurs as the technology is put to use.

in-stock   The particular stock-keeping unit (defined by style, size, and color) is immediately available to buy.

in-store shopping behavior   A behavioral model looking at how situational factors, shopping intentions, and stock situations affect in-store purchase decisions (Kunz & Song, 1996).

income measurements   Different expressions of revenue gained while running a business for a defined period; gross sales, net sales, gross margin, operating profit, and net profit.

income modifications   The reasons for the differences in income measurements in an income statement; customer returns and allowances, cost of goods sold, procurement costs, operating expense, and other income and/or expenses.

income statement   A summary of a firm's revenue and expenses for a defined period of time; usually prepared on a monthly, quarterly, and/or annual basis.

initial delivery   Part or all of the initial order that is shipped at the beginning of the selling period.

initial markup   Difference between wholesale price and first price.

Initial markup based on retail   calculation method preferred by retailers.

initiation of technology   One of the two phases of the diffusion of innovations, according to Rogers (1983); represents the decision to adopt the technology.

interactive planning   A teamwork activity with input from all of the firm's constituencies; a combination of top-down and bottom-up planning.

internal constituencies of the firm   Areas of specialization within a firm according to Behavioral Theory of the Apparel Firm (Kunz, 1995).

internal line-adoption   Presenting the line inside the firm in order to develop consensus and support for the proposed applications of specific products to the line plan.

internal partnering   The coordination of merchandising activities within a company to ensure greatest efficiency, typically through the use of cross-functional teams made up of members of different departments in a company.

Internet An electronic communication network that connects computer networks around the world.

inventory The stock of merchandise available at any given time.

inventory-to-sales ratio method of planning inventory A method of inventory planning that a merchant should maintain a certain ratio of goods on hand to monthly sales; commonly used for fashion/seasonal goods that vary in sales.

invoice payment terms Guidelines that determine how much of the billed cost will be paid by the retailer and when it is due.

Item 807/Chapter 9802 A special provision in the U.S. tariff schedules that allows products to be designed and cut in the United States exported, sewn in a foreign country, and then imported with tariffs assessed only on value added.

job-off price Price for selling distressed goods to a jobber or diverter; may be sold by the piece or by weight.

joint product development Key component of merchandising in a quick response environment; retailer merchandisers work with manufacturer merchandisers and designers to develop the line concept, establish line direction, and plan and develop products.

just-in-time (JIT) A business philosophy that focuses on removing waste from all the organizations' internal activities and from external exchange activities (O'Neal & Bertrand, 1991).

knockoff Adaptation or modification of a style from another firm's line; usually offered for sale at a lower price than the original (Glock & Kunz, 1995).

labor exploitation Making profit from the labor of others without giving just return.

landed cost The cost of goods up to the time they are delivered to the distribution center of the buyer.

late-selling-period discount A price reduction offered from a manufacturer to a retailer that can be used to extend production and the sale of items or clear finished goods still in stock.

lateral career move A move between specializations or job titles maintaining the same career level.

learning The result of educating for long-term outcomes (Barr & Tagg, 1995).

learning organization An organization that continuously improves; employees determine the next logical step and initiate on-going improvements.

letter of credit Written document issued by a bank at the request of a buyer authorizing a seller to claim payment in accordance with certain terms and conditions; may or may not be irrevocable or transferable.

life structure modifiers Event(s) that change the way someone lives but, at the some time, allow continuity.

limited service Combines some aspects of self service and full service environments; requires customers to self select merchandise.

line adoption Determines what merchandise groups will be applied to the line plan; what designs will become styles in the line, model stocks, gross margins, prices, and expected volume for each merchandise group.

line concept Includes the look and appeal that contributes to the identity and salability of the line.

line development The process of determining the styles, fabrications, colors, and sizes to be offered for sale; applying real merchandise to the line plan.

line preview Time when a season's line is presented to the sales staff by the merchandising and marketing constituencies (Glock & Kunz, 1995).

liquidation price See job off price.

list price Suggested retail price used in manufacturer's/wholesaler's catalogs and price sheets; an estimate of the value of the product to the ultimate consumer; the base for wholesale price structures.

loading Merchandise purchase contract term; adjusting billed cost so the same discount rate is applied to all invoices

lost sales Result when a customer goes to a different source or quits shopping.

low-end price range The lowest relative price for the product category; used by flea markets, outlets, street vendors, one-price discount stores; high risk of poor quality merchandise.

make plan When merchandisers achieve the sales increase and planned sales so that the income statement shows a successful year.

make to order Producing products after receiving the purchase orders.

management Embodies budgeting, organizing, and controlling.

manufacturer A person or company in the business of designing and producing something by hand or by machines usually in large quantities and with division of labor.

manufacturer's wholesale price List price less quantity, seasonal, and trade discounts.

markdown Difference between first price and promotional or clearance price.

markdown cancellation Elimination of a markdown to restore first price; may be accompanied by another markdown or an additional markup to establish the next price a customer will see.

markdown money A discount included in some purchase contracts that compensates retailers for price markdowns and discounts needed to clear inventory.

market-driven A company that identifies and evaluates unmet needs of the customers in relation to the firm's capabilities, and then merchandises, produces, and markets accordingly.

marketable combination A mixture of educational background, professional experiences, and personal attributes of a certain individual that is attractive to multiple employers.

marketing concept A philosophy of the firm that directs the agendas and activities to satisfy the needs and wants of external coalitions that are exchange partners, particularly their customers (Houston, 1986).

marketing constituency One of the six internal constituencies of the firm according to the Behavioral Theory of the Apparel Firm; responsible for broadly defining a company's market, shaping and strengthening the image of the company and its products through promotion, optimizing sales opportunities, and developing alternate strategies for corporate growth.

matrix buying Tool used by large retailers for improving the effectiveness of their line development processes; the merchandising group identifies its best and/or most dominant suppliers and creates a list of preferred vendors for each merchandise classification.

measures of success Those benchmarks that determine the level of success of an individual in a company.

merchandise approach One of the three techniques of retail customer approach used when the shopper seems to be viewing specific merchandise; the greeting usually includes a casual "Hello" and a comment about the merchandise.

merchandise assortment The relative number of styles, colors, and sizes in a merchandise offering.

merchandise budget Planned sales, dollar investment, and open-to-buy by merchandise category or classification; the financial framework of a merchandise plan.

merchandise categories Major components of the total merchandise mix.

merchandise classification Group of products within a merchandise category.

merchandise cost The value given up to receive goods or services or the amount invested to have a product.

merchandise group Products that are reasonable substitutes for each other from the perspective of customers; products that are similar in function, selling period, and price.

merchandise/line development The process of determining the styles, fabrications, colors, and sizes to be offered for sale; applying real merchandise to the line plan.

merchandise/line plan Combination of budgets and assortment plans; based on sales history, goals, and forecasts; framework for line development.

merchandise/line planning Process of developing budgeting and assortment plans based on sales history, goals, and forecasts.

merchandise/line presentation Process required to evaluate the line and make it visible and salable.

merchandise mix The complete offering of products by a particular manufacturer or retailer.

merchandise/product line Consists of a combination of styles that satisfy similar or related customer needs, can be sold within the targeted price range and marketed with similar strategies.

merchandise selection assistance Showing the merchandise and discussing its benefits and features.

merchandise subclasses Groups of merchandise within classes.

merchandise to receive Products expected to be received at the retail level in order to achieve planned sales; could be measured in dollars, units, or SKUs.

merchandising Planning, developing, and presenting product lines for identified target markets with regard to pricing, assorting, styling, and timing (Glock & Kunz, 1995).

merchandising and operating ratios Ratios that are stated as a percent of net sales that appear on an income statement.

merchandising calendar A schedule that shows the merchandising cycle that shows the months of the year, the weeks in the merchandising cycle, and accounts for seasonal events, selling and transition periods, and the pricing and delivery plans.

merchandising constituency One of the five internal constituencies of the firm according to the Behavioral Theory of the Apparel Firm; responsible for interpreting customers' apparel preferences for the rest of the firm.

merchandising cycle One-year period from the first week of February to the last week of January.

merchandising technology The systematic application of information technology and telecommunications to planning, developing, and presenting product lines in ways that reflect social and cultural value.

model stock A plan for a merchandise assortment according to assortment factors; identifies how many of each assortment factor should be included in the assortment.

moderate price range Goods sold at average price for the product class; also described as upper moderate and lower moderate; widely used in department and specialty chain stores.

Multi-Fiber Arrangement (M-FA) Trade regulation operating as a system of quotas for textiles and apparel based on bilateral agreements among over 60 member countries; designed to protect the textile and apparel industries in developed countries from excessive imports from low-wage developing countries.

multiple delivery strategy Using more than one shipment of a given merchandise assortment based on an initial order and reorder(s).

needs Practical or functional desires.

net profit before taxes The figure on which a firm pays income tax.

net sales Actual revenue from sale of goods and services (gross sales — customer returns and allowances).

North American Free Trade Agreement (NAFTA) Trade agreement enacted in 1994 between U.S., Canada and Mexico; purpose is to promote economic growth through expanded trade and investment.

open-ended questions Questions that begin with what, why, how, or tell me and encourage elaboration when responding.

open-to-buy A means of controlling merchandise investment before and during a selling period; planned merchandise to receive minus merchandise on order

operating profit   What remains after all financial obligations related to running the business are met (adjusted gross margin minus operating expense).

operations constituency   One of the five internal constituencies of the firm, according to the Behavioral Theory of the Apparel Firm; manages the organization's resources of people and physical property.

organizational pyramid   A visual model that shows the various organizational tiers that make up a firm.

other income and expenses   Additional revenue or costs related to operating the firm other than from selling goods and services.

overhead/operating expense   All costs associated with running a business other than the cost of merchandise sold and procurement costs.

pattern check run (PCR)   Production of samples to ensure all aspects of construction and sizing have been clearly communicated and can be properly executed by the contractor.

penetration pricing   Pricing strategy designed to establish a value image in the mind of the customer while increasing market share.

percent markdown   Markdown dollars as a percent of net sales

percentage variation method of planning inventory   Adjusting stock levels in relation to actual variations in sales; appropriate for basic/seasonal and fashion/staple goods.

percent increase of decrease method of planning sales   Last years sales plus some percent increase or decrease.

perceptual map   Two-dimensional diagram of relationships among concepts.

periodic replenishment method of planning inventory   Automated replenishment with computer— generated orders managed either by the vendor or the retailer; appropriate for basic/staple goods.

permanent markdown   Reduction in price reflecting decline in merchandise value based on salability.

personal/informal/social customer approach   Used if the retail customer approaches the seller or if the customer appears to be browsing; the greeting might be a positive statement such as simply "Hi," or include a comment on the weather, business, merchandise, customer's clothing, or customer's children.

personal selling service   Close interaction of the seller and customer to assist with the selection and purchase of merchandise.

planned cost   Price determined by the wholesale price offered by the manufacturer or the cost estimates provided by product developers.

planned sales   An estimate of sales based on previous sales that is part of a merchandise budget.

planograms   The output of retail space management technology originally developed for grocery stores.

port of entry   A place with Customs authorities designated for the entry and clearance of vessels and goods; major ports include Oakland, Los Angeles, New York City, and Miami.

point-of-sale (POS)   as recorded by a cash register.

portfolio   A tool used in presenting oneself to a potential employer; might include photographs, drawings, videotapes, projects from coursework, etc.

postadoption product development   Includes a group of processes required to perfect a design into a style and make the style producible; part of the line development process also called technical design.

potential sales   Exist if the customer postpones purchases or browses.

preadoption product development   Focuses on analysis, creativity, and the formation of product groups that are unique but reflect the line concept; part of the line development process also called creative design.

predatory pricing   Illegally selling items at very low markup or below merchandise cost to eliminate competition.

preliminary inspection certificate (PIC)   Authorizes shipment of goods when they have passed a final audit at the offshore contractor; required by the bank to release funds to pay the contractor.

premier service   Provides intensive interaction with customers where few limits are placed on what sellers can do to satisfy customers; first priority of the company is to satisfy customers.

premium price   *See* above-market price.

pre-selling-period discount   A discount offered to retail merchandisers by manufacturers when the merchandiser agrees to purchase merchandise early, ahead of the traditional buying period.

prestige pricing   Pricing strategy intended to reflect a quality/value/service image for people willing to pay "regular price"; also known as status, psychological or above-market pricing.

price   The amount asked for or received in exchange for a product.

price endings   How a price is stated, using either even dollar amounts or odd price endings.

price lining   Offering merchandise at a limited number of price points that reflect differences in merchandise quality (Mason, Mayer, & Ezell, 1984); selling items of varying costs for the same price.

price points   Specific prices representing a price line.

pricing plan   A tool that includes planned merchandise cost, dollar and percent initial markup, first price, price promotions include percent temporary markdowns, promotional prices, permanent markdowns, and clearance prices to help determine sales.

pricing policy   A framework provided by a company that gives guidelines for how items should be priced for sale.

pricing strategy   A particular combination of pricing components designed to appeal to a firm's target customers and contribute to achieving a firm's goals.

private label   Private label is "merchandise that bears a retailer's own name brand rather than that of a designer or manufacturer " (Jernigan & Easterling, 1990, p. 565).

procurement costs   Ordering and shipping costs associated with acquiring merchandise.

product benefits   What the product will do for a customer.

product development   The design and engineering of products to be serviceable, producible, salable, and profitable (Glock & Kunz, 1995).

product features   Characteristics of the product such as color, style, fabric, etc.

product velocity   The speed with which a product passes through the industry matrix; average inventory during a selling period.

production driven   Making goods that can be produced conveniently and efficiently with little consideration of market demand.

promotion   An upgraded job title, increased responsibility or increased pay in the same job.

promotional discount   Special arrangements in price made by the manufacturer to promote sales.

promotional price   Price intended to increase total revenue by generating additional customer traffic.

propositions   Something that describes the next level of complexity in theory development; they predict outcomes related to interactions of constructs.

proprietary software systems   Computer programs and technology developed by individual firms for their own use.

purchase of finished goods   Acquiring goods ready for use by the ultimate consumer.

quantity discount   Reduction from list price related to efficiencies of volume of purchase; incentive to make larger or multiple purchases.

quick markdown pricing   Pricing strategy designed to provide high value for the bargain shopper; used for fashion and seasonal goods that have several selling periods per year.

quick response (QR)   A comprehensive business strategy incorporating time-based competition, agility, and partnering to optimize the supply system, the distribution system, and service to customers.

quick response constituency   Area of specialization according to Behavioral Theory of the Apparel firms.

quick response merchandise replenishment   A customer-driven process of planning and placing reorders, as well as handling, shipping, receiving, distributing, if necessary, and displaying merchandise with the shortest possible lead time.

quota rent   Purchase of quota from a firm that has excess quota for export of a specific classification of goods from a specific country; cost depends on market demand at a particular time and place.

Radio Frequency Identification tags   *See* smart labels.

real time   Something that is happening in the present time, or "right now."

rebirth of potential   An event that causes a radical change in one's life; starting all over again.

reduced list price   List price less seasonal and quantity discounts.

reductions   Anything other than sales that reduces the value of inventory; markdowns, theft, inventory damage, etc.

regular price   Price perceived to be the "usual" or "normal" price for a product.

reorder   A request to replenish merchandise previously stocked.

resale price maintenance   Also known as vertical price fixing, occurs when manufacturers control the retail prices of their product; it is an illegal practice.

retail line presentation   The process of selling a product line to the ultimate consumers through a variety of avenues including retail stores, Internet shops, and/or television home shopping programs.

retail merchandise cost   Wholesale price less discounts and allowances; may include transportation costs.

retail method of inventory   The value of inventory as determined by retail prices.

retailer   A firm that sells goods and services to the ultimate consumer.

retailing   Selling goods and services to the ultimate consumer.

returns and allowances   A cancellation of sales because of merchandise returns and refunds or price adjustments related to customer dissatisfaction.

safety stock   Amount of merchandise required on hand to prevent stockouts until the reorder can be received.

sales   Dollars generated by transfer of ownership of goods.

sales goals   Expected sales of goods or services to a target market for an identified period of time.

sales per square foot   Dollars generated for each square foot of a particular store, showroom, or other space.

sales promotion   A marketing strategy intended to increase total revenue.

sales representatives   Individuals representing a company or product line to retailers and ultimate consumers.

sales volume   Total sales for the classification during the selling period being evaluated.

scanning   Electronic interpretation of information via bar-codes, pictures, or other documents.

seasonal discount   Reduction from list price relating to time of purchase in a selling period; a manufacturer may offer pre-selling period, late-selling period, and end-of-the-selling period discounts.

seasonal goods   Classifications that experience changes in market demand during a merchandising cycle related to ethnic and cultural events, holidays, and weather changes.

self service   Customers provide their own selling service.

selling   The process of changing ownership of goods or services.

selling period   Time period during which a particular product line or merchandise assortment is salable.

selling price Price a customer pays for a product; wholesale price in the manufacturing sector; may be higher or lower than first price in the retail sector.

service approach The standard "Can I help you?" greeting used in sales.

shipping terms Determines who bears the transportation costs and when the buyer takes title/ownership of the merchandise; free on board (FOB); cost, insurance, freight (CIF); free along side the ship (FAS).

shopper's intentions Relate to the purpose of the shopping trip; relate to product type and have three forms: specific item in mind, general item in mind, and no item in mind (Song & Kunz, 1996).

six-month plan Traditional merchandise dollar plan; establishes the levels of investment to be available for merchandise lines and product classifications for each selling period and each month of the year.

SKU Stock keeping unit.

smart labels Special tracking labels that may eventually replace bar codes by allowing retailers and manufacturers to keep track of an item; also known as Radio Frequency Identification tags.

sourcing Determining the most cost efficient vendor of services, materials, production and/or finished goods at the specified quality and service level with delivery within an identified time frame.

Special Regime Agreement formed in 1988 to provide incentives for the United States to trade and do business within the Americas.

square meter equivalents (SME) The amount of fabric required to make a garment or a group of garments.

standard deviation Twice the square root of the variance; useful statistic for forecasting.

staple goods Classifications that are in continuous demand throughout a merchandising cycle; demand is not greatly affected by the time of the year.

stock on hand Current inventory.

stock-keeping unit (SKU) Designation of a product at the unit level for merchandise planning or inventory purposes; usually represents a combination of style, size, and color (Glock & Kunz, 1995).

stock-to-sales ratio method of planning inventory Is done by dividing the total inventory for the period by the sales for the same period; appropriate for fashion/seasonal goods.

stocking or introductory allowances Discounts or promotions provided by manufacturers to persuade retail buyers to stock certain merchandise for the first time.

stockout The particular stock-keeping unit desired by the customer is not immediately available.

strategic partnering Establishment of collaborative and cooperative relationships among business partners; an informal form of vertical integration.

strategic pricing software Computer applications that help companies establish a pricing system to maximize profits.

style sheet Describes products to Customs for establishment of duty rates and quota classifications; requires merchandiser input to describe garment's construction and fabric.

styling Characteristic or distinctive appearance of a product; the combination of features that make it different from other products of the same type.

suggested retail price List price.

suggestion selling Expanding a sale with companion products or other merchandise.

tariff Taxes on goods that are imported or exported.

taxonomy A classification system describing some phenomena.

Taxonomy of Apparel Merchandising Systems (TAMS) A comprehensive system that describes the elements of merchandising.

technical package Product specifications supplementing the Garment Purchase Agreement detailing construction, measurement, patterns, and markers.

technology   The application of scientific and other knowledge to practical tasks by ordered systems that involve people and organizations, living things and machines (Pacey, 1983, p. 6).

temporary markdown   Reduction in price for sales promotion; markdown will be canceled at end of special price period.

theories of management development   Ways in which managers develop inside the organization; development of expertise through specialization and/or development of expertise through broad job experience.

theory   An idea or statement that helps describe, organize, and predict happenings in relation to something.

theory of diffusion of innovation   A process model for adoption of innovations within the organization that divides the innovation process into two sequential stages called initiation and implementation (Rogers, 1983).

theory of specialization   The employee's responsibilities are increased and his/her area of specialization gets more focused allowing the employee to become very knowledgeable in that specific area.

Theory-x management style   Managing a firm based on top-down communication; based on the assumptions that employees really don't want to work and that the primary motivation for work is money.

Theory-y management style   Incorporates multidimensional communication, problem solving, and empowerment in all parts of the organization.

third party merchandising   Services provided by consulting company.

tiers in organizational pyramid   Hierarchical levels in the organizational structure influencing the manner in which merchandise might be planned.

time-based competition   Time is recognized as the firm's most fundamental resource.

top-down planning   The executive constituency develops the business plan; usually based on growth plans and prescribes sales goals and dollar investment in merchandise usually for a six month period or a year; focus is on sales goals.

trade discount   Reduction from list price granted to a firm that performs some marketing or distribution function.

trade universe   All firms, collectively, that are subjects of consideration at once.

training   A relatively short-term activity involving teaching how to produce specific, predetermined results as quickly as possible.

transferable skills   Abilities gleaned from life's experiences that can be applied in multiple settings.

transition assortments   Assortments with a moderate number of units allocated per SKU, between six and ten on the average according to Assortment Diversity Index.

two plus two pricing   A form of price markup used by some retailers.

transition periods   Time periods between selling periods in the merchandising calendar.

U.S. Customs Service   Agency responsible for application of duty rates and quota classifications.

U.S./Canadian Free Trade Agreement   Free trade agreement between the United States and Canada enacted in 1988 with the purpose of promoting free trade between the two member countries.

unit   A single piece of merchandise.

unit plans   Traditional assortment plan; the quantity (units) of goods that could be made available during the selling period; dollar allocated divided by average merchandise price.

universal product code (UPC)   A 12-digit code representing a unique product item.

utilitarian benefits   Relates to aesthetic theory; comfort, protection, quality, social acceptance, status, efficiency, and value and provide social or economic gain (Fiore & Kimle, 1997).

value added   Labor, administration, selling costs, and operating profit.

variety   Number of stock-keeping units in an assort`

wholesale market   A site where manufacturers show lines to retail buyers.

wholesale price   List price less quantity, seasonal, and trade discounts.

wholesale price structures   Based on list prices and determines the price of the styles in the line at wholesale.

World Trade Organization (WTO)   Worldwide trade regulation organization replaced GATT, whose fundamental purpose is to increase international trade by reducing trade barriers.

Worldwide Responsible Apparel Production (WRAP)   Created by the American Apparel Manufacturers Association (now called American Apparel and Footwear Association) to established a code of conduct as well as a system of certification of production facilities.

yarn forward rule   A rule of origin stating that all yarn manufacturing, fabric manufacturing, and garment manufacturing processes must take place in a particular country or countries.

zero-based budgeting   No previous levels of sales or productivity are assumed.

zero to zero inventory   Merchandise is purchased and stocked specifically for a particular selling period and anything not sold during the selling period is marked down for clearance; goods not sold on clearance are liquidated.

INDEX